SECOND EDITION

INTRODUCTION TO INVESTIGATIONS

John S. Dempsey
Suffolk County Community College

THOMSON

WADSWORTH

Australia · Canada · Mexico · Singapore · Spain · United Kingdom · United States

THOMSON

WADSWORTH

Senior Acquisitions Editor, Criminal Justice: Jay Whitney
Development Editor: Shelley Murphy
Assistant Editor: Dawn Mesa
Editorial Assistant: Paul Massicotte
Technology Project Manager: Susan DeVanna
Marketing Manager: Dory Schaeffer
Marketing Assistant: Neena Chandra
Advertising Project Manager: Stacey Purviance
Project Manager, Editorial Production: Jennie Redwitz
Print/Media Buyer: Becky Cross

Permissions Editor: Charles Hodgkins
Production Service: Linda Jupiter, Jupiter Productions
Text Designer: Adriene Bosworth
Photo Researcher: Roberta Spieckerman
Copy Editor: Sandra Beris
Proofreader: Henrietta Bensussen
Cover Designer: Yvo Riezebos
Cover Image: Patrick Doherty/Getty Images
Compositor: Bookcomp, Inc.
Text and Cover Printer: Transcontinental Printing (Louisville)

Printed in Canada
4 5 6 7 06

For more information about our products, contact us at:
Thomson Learning Academic Resource Center
1–800-423–0563
For permission to use material from this text, contact us by:
Phone: 1-800-730-2214
Fax: 1-800-730-2215
Web: http://www.thomsonrights.com

Library of Congress Control Number: 2002110749

ISBN 13 : 978-0-534-57646-2
ISBN 10 : 0-534-57646-X

Wadsworth/Thomson Learning
10 Davis Drive
Belmont, CA 94002–3098
USA

Asia
Thomson Learning
5 Shenton Way #01–01
UIC Building
Singapore 068808

Australia
Nelson Thomson Learning
102 Dodds Street
South Melbourne, Victoria 3205
Australia

Canada
Nelson Thomson Learning
1120 Birchmount Road
Toronto, Ontario M1K 5G4
Canada

Europe/Middle East/Africa
Thomson Learning
High Holborn House
50/51 Bedford Row
London WC1R 4LR
United Kingdom

Latin America
Thomson Learning
Seneca, 53
Colonia Polanco
11560 Mexico D.F.
Mexico

Spain
Paraninfo Thomson Learning
Calle/Magallanes, 25
28015 Madrid, Spain

ABOUT THE AUTHOR

John S. Dempsey was a member of the New York City Police Department (NYPD) from 1964 to 1988. He served in the ranks of police officer, detective, sergeant, lieutenant, and captain. His primary assignments were patrol and investigations. He received seven citations from the department for meritorious and excellent police duty. Since retiring from the NYPD, Dempsey has been Professor of Criminal Justice at Suffolk County Community College on Eastern Long Island. He has won the college's prestigious "Made A Difference" award for his teaching and work with students. He is the author of *Policing: An Introduction to Law Enforcement* (published by West in 1994), *An Introduction to Public and Private Investigations* (West, 1996), and *An Introduction to Policing,* 2nd ed. (Wadsworth/West, 1999).

Dempsey holds associate and bachelor's degrees in behavioral sciences from the City University of New York, John Jay College of Criminal Justice; a master's degree in criminal justice from Long Island University; and a master's degree in public administration from the John F. Kennedy School of Government, Harvard University.

In addition to teaching, Dempsey is a mentor at the State University of New York, Empire State College, and lectures frequently around the country on criminal justice issues. He is a member of the American Society of Criminology, the Academy of Criminal Justice Sciences, the Northeast Academy of Criminal Justice Sciences, the Criminal Justice Educators Association of New York State, the International Association of Chiefs of Police, and the American Society for Industrial Security. He is married and has four children and three grandchildren.

This book is dedicated to my special guardian angel, my daughter, the toughest and bravest person I have ever known, Anne Marie Dempsey, 1970–2002.

BRIEF CONTENTS

CONTENTS

CHAPTER 6

Criminalistics and Technology   119

PREFACE

TO THE STUDENT

Introduction to Investigations, Second Edition, is a basic introductory text for college students who are interested in learning who investigators are, what they do, and how they do it. The investigations profession is a noble one. I sincerely hope that this text teaches you something about how to continue the great tradition of investigating.

Introduction to Investigations, Second Edition, is designed to give you a general overview of investigations so that you can understand why and how investigations are conducted. It will show you the jobs available in the investigating industry and how you can go about getting them, what skills you will need, and what you will do if and when you get these jobs. In addition, I try to give you an idea, a sense, and a flavor of investigating. I want you to get a clear look at investigating, not only for your academic interest but, more importantly, to help you determine if investigating is what you want to do with the rest of your life. After all, is that not what much of college should be about— making an intelligent, well-informed career choice, as well as learning about life?

This text combines coverage of both public (police) and private investigations. The purposes, methods, and tools of both are similar. Furthermore, police are deemphasizing traditional retroactive investigations in favor of proactive investigative techniques and community and problem-solving policing, and this is opening new doors to job opportunities in private investigations.

TO THE INSTRUCTOR

Introduction to Investigations, Second Edition, has undergone extensive revision since its first publication. In response to student and reviewer feedback, this edition provides the latest in academic and practitioner research as well as the latest statistical information and information on court cases, the Internet, careers, and criminalistic and technological advances.

Here are some highlights of the most important changes to this edition:

- All previous chapters have been revised and updated and some have been consolidated.
- Six new chapters have been added on violent crimes, property crimes, narcotics and drug offenses, computer crime, terrorist activities, and private sector investigations.
- A unique focus on the ability of the Internet to aid in investigations has been added.
- A text-specific Web site is available with tutorial quizzing, online glossary, flashcards, games, Internet links, InfoTrac College Edition activities, Internet activities, and course resources and updates.

PEDAGOGICAL FEATURES

Each chapter includes the following pedagogical elements:

- *Chapter Goals* serve as chapter "road maps" to orient students to the main learning objectives of each chapter.
- *Chapter Introduction* previews the material to be covered in the chapter.
- *Chapter Summary* reinforces the major topics discussed in the chapter and helps students check their learning.
- *Learning Checks* are questions that test the student's knowledge of the material presented in the chapter.
- *Application Exercises* are projects that require students to apply their knowledge to hypothetical situations much like those they might encounter in actual investigations work. They can be assigned as final written or oral exercises or serve as the basis of lively class debates.

- *Internet Exercises* ask the student to research investigating topics on the Internet.

BOXED FEATURES

In an effort to increase student interest, several types of boxed features have been incorporated into each chapter to supplement the text.

- *You Are There!* These take the student back to the past in order to review the fact pattern in a particular court case or present details about a significant event or series of events. They are intended to give students a sense of actually being at the scene of an investigation or other event.
- *Dempsey's Law.* These recount personal experiences from my own police career, or dialogues between students and myself in class. They are intended to provide a reality-based perspective on investigating and policing, including the human side of each.
- *Investigations on the Net.* These provide specific information for students about sources on the Internet they can use for their academic and professional growth, as well as their own interest.
- *Career Focus.* These provide examples of the many jobs available in investigations.
- *Guest Lectures.* These are perspectives written by professionals in the field of investigations.

SUPPLEMENTS

A fully updated version of the *Instructor's Manual* is available for this new edition. For each chapter of the text it includes learning objectives, detailed chapter outlines, key terms, classroom exercises, discussion questions, tips, media resources, and a test bank. Each test bank contains twenty multiple-choice questions, fifteen fill-in-the-blank questions, fifteen true-false questions, and three essay questions.

The book's Web site, which contains the many great tools to enhance learning described earlier, is easily accessible from Wadsworth's full-service Criminal Justice Resource Center at http://www.cj.wadsworth.com. This site provides instructors and stu-dents alike with a wealth of free information and resources, such as the Criminal Justice Timeline, What Americans Think, BookFinder, Terrorism: An Interdisciplinary Perspective, National Criminal Justice Reference Service Calendar of Events, and much more.

The Criminal Justice Resource Center also includes Web sites with chapter-specific resources for instructors and students. For instructors, the sites offer password-protected instructor's manuals, Microsoft PowerPoint presentation slides, and other material.

Available to qualified adopters. Please consult your local sales representative for details.

ACKNOWLEDGMENTS

So many people helped me make a successful transition from the world of street cop to the academic world, and so many more helped in the production of this book. I hope I have not forgotten anyone.

First, I have to thank Bob Arrigon, Pat Ungarino, and Al Cofone at Suffolk County Community College for hiring this kid from the Bronx who had never taught college; also, my academic chair at Suffolk, Mike Higginson, and Joe Vollaro, also at Suffolk, for all their help and kindnesses over the years. Thank you too to Toni Kania, Amy Ruth Tobol, and Ed Saueracker at State University of New York, Empire State College, for all their kindnesses to me. Thank you also to those invaluable college administrative assistants—Fran Basile, Annette Guerrera, Kathy Stasky, Lisa Braglia, and Kim Jordan—for all you have done for me.

I would also like to thank all the professors across the country, particularly those former women and men in blue who have made that transition from the streets to the classroom, for their adoption of my other books and for their kind words and sage advice. They have always and will always inspire me.

To my editors Shelley Murphy and Sabra Horne: thanks for all your support and assistance and particularly your patience and gracious understanding during this especially stressful period. For the intelligent and excellent copyediting of Sandra Beris and the super production efforts of Jennie Redwitz, Linda Jupiter, and Roberta Spieckerman—my sincere admiration and thanks. A special thank you to my able manuscript assistant John D. Dempsey for his help in word processing.

A note of appreciation to Professor Steve Gilbert of SUNY–Canton for his gracious assistance in the final stages of manuscript review and his hard work and intelligent creation of the excellent Web site that accompanies this text. Also, thank you to Professor Karel Kurst-Swanger of SUNY–Oswego for the preparation of the instructor's guide and test bank.

To the following reviewers of the Second Edition, my profound thanks for your advice, guidance, and particularly your respect for scholarship and our discipline: Dean van Bibber, Fairmont State College; Michael Grimes, Miami Dade Community College; and Robert Peetz, Midland College.

I also wish to gratefully acknowledge the invaluable help provided by the reviewers of the previous edition of this text: Larry D. Andrews, Missouri Western State College; David A. Armstrong, McNeese State University; John O. Ballard, Rochester Institute of Technology; Patrick J. Hopkins, Harrisburg Area Community College; Gary N. Keveles, University of Wisconsin–Superior; Julius O. Koefoed, Jr., Kirkwood Community College; Walter B. Lewis, St. Louis Community College at Meramac; Kenneth L. Mullen, Appalachian State University; Chester L. Quarles, University of Mississippi; Jayne T. Rich, Atlantic Community College; John Sargent, Jr., Kent State University; William A. Sposa, Bergen Community College; and Gary W. Tucker, Sinclair Community College.

The many students who came to my office or class wanting to know about the material I have put into this text were the inspiration for this work. This book is for you. To all the great men and women I worked with in the NYPD, the heart of this book comes from you.

A special thank you to the following friends who continually serve as my academic and intellectual stimulation. To my former NYPD partners, the scholars Jim Fyfe, Bill Walsh, and Pat Ryan—you inspired me to follow in your path; to Dave Owens—thanks for your great friendship and your leadership in our professional associations; to the members of the Great Uncaught, my speaking partners around the country, Lorenzo Boyd, Jim Burnett, Pat Faiella, Jim Ruiz, Donna Stuccio, and Ed Thibault; to all my other wonderful colleagues who hang with me and trade war stories with me whenever we meet throughout the country, I hope I don't forget anyone—Professors Elaine Bartgis, Jack Claffey, Lynton Clark, Bob Fernandez, Irene Fiala, Linda Forst, Denise Gosselin, Rich Hegney, Rob Hoff, Marty Hurrah, Dave Kramer, Ed LeClair, Tom Lenahan, Sharon RedHawk Love, John Linn, Dale McCleary, Jeff Magers, Tony Markert, Kathy Pierino, Bob Riedl, Rick Steinmann, Dave Streater, Ralph Rojas, Liz Wiinamaki, Gay Young, and all the others I have probably forgotten to include—anything I have achieved in scholarship I owe to you all. It is always an honor and privilege to be in your gracious company.

A special tribute to all the heroes of 9/11/01 who rushed in so that others could get out; you are truly symbols of the great public servants who work in emergency services in our nation.

To my family—Marianne, my love and best friend; my children, John, Anne Marie, Donna, and Cathy; and my daughter-in-law Diane and my son-in-law John—you all are my inspiration. To Mae and Danny: you can never know how important you were to us. To my friend and great physician Doctor Dov Statfeld, thanks for all you have done for my family. Finally, to Daniel Joseph, Nicolette Ashley, and Erin Anne Marie, my grandchildren: Who loves you more than the Grand Dude?

John S. Dempsey
Long Beach, New York

THE HISTORY OF INVESTIGATIONS AND THE INVESTIGATIONS INDUSTRY

CHAPTER GOALS

1. To acquaint you with the rich, colorful history of investigating, both public and private, including the French and British roots of investigating, and the U.S. nineteenth- and twentieth-century experience

2. To show you how academic studies of investigating and the twentieth-century due process revolution changed investigating

3. To acquaint you with the current investigating industry in the United States, including public and private investigating, and show you where the jobs are and how one can obtain them

4. To show you what public investigators do

5. To show you what private investigators do

INTRODUCTION

Would you ever think that there was a time when there were no official police agencies to investigate crimes? Do you ever wonder how the current public and private investigating industry came about? Did you ever watch movie or TV detective shows and wonder if the detectives in them were like their real-life counterparts? Do you know anything about the jobs available in public and private investigations and how you might obtain them? This chapter will answer these questions.

This chapter discusses the rich, colorful history of investigating, beginning in Europe with the early thief-takers of France and England and going on to London's Bow Street Runners. We discuss the first public investigators in France and England in the nineteenth century. We then cross the ocean to look at nineteenth-century investigating in the United States, starting in our early eastern cities and then going on to the frontier to look at private and federal investigating there. The chapter continues with a discussion of the twentieth-century investigating experience in the United States, including local investigating, federal investigating, scientific assistance in investigating, and the research and due process revolution and investigating. It should be noted that the most intense investigation in U.S. history—the investigation of the disasters of September 11, 2001, the terrorist attacks on the World Trade Center and the U.S. Pentagon, and the activities that led to these attacks—owes a great debt to the pioneering investigators and academics mentioned in this chapter.

The chapter also discusses the current investigating industry in this country, including public and private investigators. It discusses what they do and how they do it and will show you where the jobs are in this industry and how you can go about obtaining one.

BEFORE PUBLIC INVESTIGATING

We do not know much about the very early history of policing or investigating. Policing—maintaining order and dealing with lawbreakers—had always been a private matter. Citizens were responsible for protecting themselves and investigating crimes committed against themselves. In fact, modern-style police departments didn't appear until the fourteenth century in France and the early nineteenth century in England. Despite this, research has shown that around the fifth century B.C., Rome created the first specialized investigative unit, consisting of **questors,** or *trackers of murder.*[1] However, most of our knowledge of the roots of policing and investigating comes from France and England.

There was no official police or law enforcement investigative process in Europe until well into the nineteenth century. Neither were there any official investigative agencies. Even with the advent of formal police departments, the police were primarily concerned with the prevention of crime by conspicuous uniformed police patrol. If a crime was reported or discovered, the police merely took a report. It was a group of private individuals—thief-takers and the Bow Street Runners—who served as the earliest investigators of crimes.

Thief-Takers

Before formal police departments there were individuals who served as a form of private police in sixteenth-, seventeenth-, and eighteenth-century France and England. They were called **thief-takers.** Thief-takers were private citizens, with no official status, who were paid by the king for every criminal they arrested, similar to the bounty hunters of the American West.

The main role of the thief-takers was to combat robbery committed by *highwaymen*, whose heroes were the likes of such legendary outlaws as Robin Hood and Little John. By the seventeenth century, highwaymen such as Jack Sheppard and Dick Turpin made traveling through the English countryside so dangerous that no coach or traveler was safe. In 1693, an act of Parliament established a monetary reward for the capture of any highwayman or road agent. The thief-taker was paid upon the conviction of the highwayman and also received the highwayman's horse, arms, money, and property.

The thief-taker system was later extended to cover offenses other than highway robbery, and soon a sliding scale of rewards was established. Arresting a burglar or a *footpad* (street robber), for example, was worth the same as catching a highwayman, but catching a sheep stealer or a deserter from the army brought a much smaller reward. In some areas, homeowners joined together and offered supplementary rewards for the apprehension of a highwayman or footpad in their area. In addition, whenever there was a serious crime wave Parliament offered special rewards for thief-takers to arrest particular felons.

Often a criminal would agree to become a thief-taker and catch another criminal in order to receive a pardon from the king for his own crime. Thus, many thief-takers were themselves criminals. Thief-taking was not always rewarding because the thief-taker was not paid if the criminal was not convicted. It also could be dangerous, because the thief-taker had to fear the revenge of the criminal and his relatives and associates. Often, a thief-taker would seduce a young person into committing a crime, then have another thief-taker arrest the youth during the offense. The two thief-takers would then split the fee. Others framed innocent parties by planting stolen goods on their persons or in their homes. Although some real criminals were apprehended by the professional thief-takers, the system generally created more crime than it suppressed.

One of the most notorious thief-takers of the early 1700s in England was Jonathan Wild. Wild was well known among the criminal element in London as a brothel operator and the first great criminal mastermind in England. He conceived the idea of charging a fee for locating and returning stolen property to its lawful owners. As his private thief-taker business prospered he also began to apprehend criminals wanted by the government. Wild was totally unscrupulous. Upon learning of a theft, he would attempt to persuade the thieves to give him the stolen goods in return for a portion of the money paid by the victim for the return of the property. Wild was very successful at criminal detection and was responsible for the arrest and execution of hundreds of felons. Eventually he was found guilty of stealing the very property he returned to grateful owners, which brought about his own execution. On May 24, 1725, as he was being taken to the execution site, thousands of people jeered, showering him with stones and dirt. He was hanged before a cheering throng of spectators estimated at more than five thousand. However, after his death, Wild became a folk hero. His body was disinterred and his skull and skeleton exhibited publicly as late as 1860.

The Bow Street Runners

Henry Fielding, the eighteenth-century novelist best known for writing *Tom Jones*, can also be credited with laying the foundation for the first modern police force.

In 1748, during the heyday of the English highwayman, Fielding was appointed magistrate in Westminster, a city near London. He moved into a house on Bow Street, which also became his office. In an attempt to decrease the high number of burglaries, street and highway robberies, and other thefts, Fielding established relationships with local pawnbrokers. He would provide them with lists and descriptions of recently stolen property and ask them to notify him should such property be brought into their pawnshops. He then placed the following ad in the London and Westminster newspapers:

> All persons who shall for the future suffer by robber, burglars, etc., are desired immediately to bring or send the best description they can of such robbers, etc., with the time and place and circumstances of the fact, to Henry Fielding Esq., at his house in Bow Street.[2]

Fielding's actions brought about what we can call the first official crime reports. He was able to gain the cooperation of the High Constable of Holborn and several other public-spirited constables. Together they formed a small investigative unit, which they called the Bow Street Runners. These were private citizens who were not paid by public funds but were permitted to accept thief-taker rewards.

NINETEENTH-CENTURY INVESTIGATING

The nineteenth century saw the emergence of official, publicly funded governmental police investigating units. Such units first appeared in Europe, particularly France and England. Investigation units then began to develop in the United States, both in urban centers and on the frontier.

France

On the European continent, police originally were in charge of all civil administration that was not church-related. The French police in the eighteenth century, for example, not only investigated crime, made arrests, and maintained public order but also regulated markets and manufacturing, ensured food supplies, licensed newspapers, and were responsible for street cleaning, lighting, and paving. Gradually, other departments were set up, allowing the police to specialize in the maintenance of law and order.

The French led the way in developing specialized detectives when the king's chief minister, Cardinal Mazari, hired one hundred *exempts* (investigators) in 1645. The leaders of the French Revolution felt a repugnance for this old-regime system and abolished the detective branch, but a new one was created by Napoléon Bonaparte in 1817.

The *Police de Sûreté* (Security Police), France's new police detective bureau, was created in Paris in 1817 under the leadership of the notorious French criminal and police informant Eugène François Vidocq. The first Paris police detective bureau consisted of four detectives and increased over several years to twenty-eight members. Between January and December 1817, when it had only twelve members, the squad made 772 arrests. Those arrested included 15 murderers, 108 burglars, 5 armed robbers, and more than 250 thieves of various descriptions.

In 1809, while serving a prison sentence, Vidocq offered his services as an informer to the Paris police. The prefecture of the Paris police assigned him to inform on fellow prison inmates. In return for his information he was allowed to escape custody. In 1817, under police authorization, Vidocq formed the first Paris police detective bureau. Eugène François Vidocq (1775–1857) served as chief of the Sûreté from 1817 to 1827.

Vidocq—whose maxim was "It takes a thief to catch a thief"[3]—was responsible for what has become known as the **French method of detective work.** The French Sûreté's detectives routinely employed clandestine methods against both political and criminal suspects and retained a large number of spies and informers. Because it was Vidocq's contention that major crimes and criminals were best handled by criminals themselves, he quickly hired about twenty ex-convicts he had known in prison. These men formed the basis of the newly expanded Sûreté. Vidocq would then arrest his own men on bogus charges and send them to prison, where they served as spies, gathering information on crimes and criminals inside and outside of prison. When they had collected enough useful information, Vidocq arranged for his men to escape prison, or he had them feign their own deaths. They were carted from prison in coffins, only to rise again to serve the Sûreté once more.

Vidocq's undercover men, though former convicts and felons themselves, were loyal to Vidocq unto death. They were also grateful to this greatest of detectives because he had old charges and prison sentences pending against many of them dismissed. Vidocq later wrote,

> During the ten years I spent at the head of the Sûreté, I hardly employed any but ex-convicts, often even escaped prisoners. I preferred to choose men whose bad record had given them a certain celebrity status. I often gave these men the most delicate missions. They had considerable sums to deliver to the police or prison offices. They took part in operations in which they could easily have laid hands on large amounts. But not one of them, not a single one, betrayed my trust.[4]

In response to charges by police officials that his men were actually thieves and pickpockets, Vidocq ordered his detectives to wear gloves at all times, stating that a pocket can be picked only by a bare hand. Vidocq became famous throughout Europe. It is reported that he wore various disguises and changed these disguises as often as ten times a day to infiltrate criminal groups.

After ten years as head of the detective bureau, Vidocq resigned. He then began his own private investigations business. He was asked by thousands of crime victims to help obtain the return of stolen property. He also formed a "trade protection society"—a forerunner of today's credit check. For a fee, any shopkeeper or business establishment could obtain the particulars regarding the financial solvency of new customers. At one time, more than eight thousand shopkeepers subscribed to this service.

In his role as a **private investigator,** Vidocq was arrested more than two hundred times. He was never convicted of a crime, but the legal expenses of these repeated arrests and the rumors of his dishonesty brought about his bankruptcy. Vidocq died in 1857.

England

London's first large-scale organized police department, the London Metropolitan Police, was created through the efforts of Sir Robert Peel, who successfully managed to have the Metropolitan Police Act of 1829 passed by Parliament. The first officers were nicknamed "bobbies" after Sir Robert Peel. They were housed in a building that had formerly been occupied

DEMPSEY'S LAW
Legendary Detectives: Eugéne François Vidocq

Professor Dempsey, that French guy you told us about, Vidocq, sounds pretty cool. Do you have other stories about him?

Sure. It is reported that Vidocq was a master of disguise. In one case he appeared as a white-haired, misshapen old man, hobbling around on a cane, looking for his young wife who, he said, had run away with a younger man. He described the scoundrel who had stolen his wife to one shopkeeper after another. Finally, a woman working in a tailor shop told Vidocq she knew who the man was and gave him the address. Vidocq next appeared at the address as a much younger man in the disguise of a coal deliverer, his arms and face blackened with soot. He worked outside the house until nightfall, when the man he was looking for, a notorious jewel thief named Fossard who had stolen a fortune in gems, appeared and went into the house. A short time later, accompanied by a squad of heavily armed gendarmes, Vidocq burst through the door of the house and arrested the culprit, recovering eighteen hundred francs, along with the stolen jewels.

Here is another story. There was a woman named Madame Noël, who seemed to be a respectable music teacher. She gave piano lessons to upper-class children and claimed to be the widow of a man who had been guillotined during the French Revolution, thus implying that her deceased husband had been nobility. In truth, she was the mother of one of the most notorious criminals in Paris, Noël of the Spectacles, who was in prison. Madame Noël had a large house and a network of hideouts where she hid fugitives and escaped prisoners. Vidocq thought long and hard to create a disguise that would convince the clever Noël that he was a friend of her imprisoned son. He remembered a man named Captain Germain, who was friendly with Noël's son. Germain was about the same height and weight as Vidocq, but his hair was black, he wore a beard, and he had a long, narrow nose. Vidocq blacked his hair with dye, grew a beard, and used gum arabic to lengthen his nose. He rubbed his wrists and ankles with abrasive materials to create the kind of blisters convicts acquired when wearing shackles. He obtained a sack of lice and slept near it until he was covered with the vermin, as were most escaped convicts. He then obtained prison clothing and appeared at Noël's house claiming to be Germain and begging to be taken in and hidden from the police he said were searching for him.

Madame Noël examined Vidocq carefully, noting the marked prison clothes, the marks and blisters on his hands and feet, even the lice he had supposedly carried from his prison cell. She pronounced him a genuine escaped convict and sent him into her system of hideouts. After learning the addresses of the places that housed scores of escaped convicts, Vidocq summoned his police squads and arrested Noël and several hundred wanted felons.

SOURCE: Jay Robert Nash, *Encyclopedia of World Crime* (Wilmette, IL: Crime Books, 1990).

by Scottish royalty, thus all police officers and the public referred to the London Metropolitan Police as *Scotland Yard*. The early London police were reluctant to engage in criminal investigations because this would involve working in plainclothes, dealing with criminal informants, and engaging in covert operations. The police felt the public would turn against them if they operated like "spies"—the contemporary image of detectives originating in France. In their early years, however, Metropolitan constables were temporarily relieved from patrol to investigate crimes on their beats.

Thomas Repetto, talking about the philosophy behind detective work, gives us an idea why England, with its emphases on community-based policing, tried to avoid a French-type approach to investigating.

> Whereas the detective's clientele were mostly criminal and his contacts necessarily furtive, detective and thief were, in fact, fellow craftsmen who shared a great many of the same perceptions and values. Both recognized that criminal behavior was normal in some milieus and viewed arrest and punishment as part of the game. Given the intimacy and shared values, it was inevitable that deals would be struck, ranging from outright corruption to the exchange of information for

favors. Indeed, most policemen and some judges believed without such deals the detectives could not function. The public, however, could not be told that the detectives worked through informers and deals, since in many cases these skirted the law and public morality.[5]

Despite their fears of detective operations, high crime rates forced the London police to open up a detective branch at Scotland Yard in 1842. Under the administration of London police commissioner Richard Mayne, the detective force numbered no more than sixteen men, and its operations were restricted by Mayne's distrust of clandestine detective methods. In 1867, Irish rebels blew up a wall of Clerkenwell Prison, killing four people and injuring forty. The detective branch was criticized for its failure to act in response to prior warnings of the event. Mayne himself escaped dismissal only because of his long service, but he died shortly afterward.

In 1868, as a result of the Clerkenwell incident, the number of headquarters detectives was increased to approximately 40, and an additional 180 detectives of all ranks were assigned to the various local division headquarters. In 1877, three of the four chief inspectors of the headquarters were convicted of accepting bribes. A formal investigation was undertaken by a government commission, and the following year the Criminal Investigation Division (CID) was created and put in charge of both headquarters and division detectives. The CID was placed under the civilian leadership of Howard Vincent, a London lawyer. Vincent had no police experience but was eager to achieve. When he heard of the government investigation of the detectives he rushed to Paris to study the French Sûreté, where the detectives routinely employed clandestine methods against both political and criminal suspects and retained a large number of spies. Vincent then made a report of his findings to the Home Secretary and talked himself into appointment to the well-paid directorship. Under his regime, the CID was severely criticized for employing "French" methods.

The early years of the CID were a time of great activity by Irish nationalists. Because revolution in Ireland was blocked by the Royal Irish Constabulary and the army, the rebels turned to a terror campaign in England. During the years from 1883 to 1885 they bombed railroads, subways, the Tower of London, and even Scotland Yard itself. A special squad of CID detectives was formed to deal with these terrorists and came to

be known as the Special Branch of the CID. In 1887, detectives managed to intercept an Irish American terrorist and break up a plot to plant a bomb in Westminster Abbey during Queen Victoria's jubilee ceremony. After that incident, the movement receded. But the Special Branch remained in existence, turning from investigations of Irish revolutionaries to other foreigners.

In 1884, Vincent retired as head of the CID and was replaced by Patrick Quinn, a member of the Special Branch. In 1918, Quinn retired and was knighted, becoming the first police officer from the ranks to be so honored.

Among the most infamous of England's crimes were the Jack the Ripper murders; this case is still the subject of enormous controversy. The generally agreed-upon facts are that between August and November 1888, five London prostitutes were murdered and mutilated by a single individual. The cases caused immense fear in London and a loss of public confidence in the police. The crime also exposed the helplessness of the detectives when faced with a real mystery. Methods and sources of information successful against local offenders or professional thieves were useless against the Ripper. The murders took place within a quarter-square-mile area, and the killer was able to disappear quickly, suggesting that he might have had a refuge in the neighborhood. In the aftermath of the case, the CID was raised to a strength of seven hundred. The CID still remains a force in British policing.

United States

The American criminal justice system, particularly the police, owes its heritage to the English experience. When discussing the history of nineteenth-century investigating in the United States, we must distinguish between public investigating in the East, private investigating on the American frontier, and federal investigating in general.

Public Investigating: The East America's early police departments formed in the mid-1800s on the East Coast, then quickly spread to cities in the Midwest. Like London's police department, these departments concentrated mostly on uniformed patrol to deter crime. Many of America's early public detectives, such as Francis Tukey, in Boston, and Allan Pinkerton, in Chicago, were appointed to their positions by mayors in response to public pressure to halt an increase in crime. Tukey, appointed as Boston's new marshal in 1846, hired three officers to serve as Boston's first detective bureau. These first Boston detectives recovered $16,000 worth of stolen property in 1850 and $62,000 in 1860. Chicago appointed Allan Pinkerton as its first detective in 1849. Philadelphia started its first detective bureau in 1859 under Chief of Detectives Wood. During its first year, the eight-man unit arrested 481 suspects and recovered $25,000 in stolen property.

The history of public investigating in the nineteenth century in New York City tells us a great deal about those times. In 1836, the Common Council—the forerunner of the City Council—decided that the meager number of so-called watchmen employed to protect a city numbering two hundred thousand inhabitants was inadequate. Also realizing that these early police officers would be far more effective if they were less conspicuous, the council granted permission for the hiring of an additional 192 men who, unlike their peers, would not be required to wear the distinctive watchman's hat, and would have the new title of roundsmen. Equivalent to the rank of sergeant, roundsmen were, in short order, more accurately referred to by members of the public as shadows.

This dramatic increase in personnel, although significant, was still not enough, according to High Constable Jacob Hayes, predecessor to today's police chief. Under his direction since 1803, the police department—or Night Watch, as it was still called—was greatly expanded by 1838 to include an additional 132 roundsmen, along with 784 watchmen, 12 captains, 24 assistant captains, and of course, a superintendent of the watch.

Then, with the passing of the Municipal Police Act in 1844, the watch was reorganized as the Municipal Police. In 1857, the New York City Police Department under the supervision of then Captain George Walling designated twenty police officers as detectives. Walling, in charge until 1860, divided the detective force into squads responsible for specific crimes. Each squad maintained records of complaints and arrests. Each detective was required to submit daily reports on the progress and disposition of cases. Walling also created, for the first time, specialized squads to handle specific offenses. The Detective Bureau of New York was formally established by an act of the New York State legislature in 1882.

Due to allegations of corruption, the board of police commissioners decided to reorganize the detective force in January 1875. It was split, with twenty-five headquarters detectives assigned to the more serious crimes as delegated by the superintendent of police, and two ward detectives or wardsmen sent to each of the thirty-one patrol precincts to handle the less serious crimes.

Even though police officers and detectives received the same yearly salary of $2,700, rivalry and general discontent between the two groups quickly sabotaged any efforts to reform the system. By 1880, yet another reorganization was needed. The man chosen this time to head the central detective office was Captain Thomas J. Byrnes, until then commanding officer of the Fifteenth Precinct.

Destined to become a legend in his own time, Byrnes had been selected because of his thorough understanding and knowledge of street criminals and their environment. He had also been responsible for arresting most of the culprits involved in a $3 million bank robbery in 1879. Having recovered much of the money, Byrnes was highly recommended for the position.

The methods Byrnes used as commanding officer of the central detective office were unconventional, but the results, in his mind, justified the means. In his effort to protect Wall Street brokers from pickpockets, thieves, and swindlers, Byrnes created a frozen zone in the financial district, the perimeter of which was marked by a "death line." With orders to arrest any known criminal who was foolish enough to cross this line, crime in this area was virtually eliminated.

The day before President Grant's funeral in 1885, Byrnes had every known pickpocket rounded up, including those from the suburbs who had just stepped off the train expecting a good day's take. With these criminals detained at headquarters until the event was over, the day of the funeral was probably the safest in the city's history. Not one member of the public reported a single incident of that most common of all nineteenth-century offenses—pickpocketing.

Later, the board of police commissioners centralized all detectives by transferring the precinct wardsmen back to headquarters. A fund separate from the patrol force payroll was created to pay detectives, and the new rank of detective sergeant was created.

By 1885, the detective bureau numbered 128 men and was growing. Appointed superintendent of police in 1892, Byrnes left the post that had made him famous, only to retire in 1895—the year when

Theodore Roosevelt was appointed to the board of police commissioners.

American detectives were originally recruited directly from civilian life, often from the criminal underworld. However, they frequently became involved in scandals. Therefore, it soon became necessary to select detectives from the uniformed patrol force.

Private Investigating: The American Frontier On the American frontier there was no real law enforcement except for the local town marshal, appointed by the town's mayor, and the elected county sheriff. Private police were much more effective than public law enforcement agencies on the frontier. Although they often acted in the same manner as the English thief-taker—taking a percentage of the stolen property they recovered—America's private police were much more professional and honest than early England's.

Many say that Allan Pinkerton could be called America's Founder of Criminal Investigation. Pinkerton was born August 25, 1819, in Glasgow, Scotland, and emigrated to the United States. He worked for a short time as a deputy sheriff in Cook County, Illinois, and was then appointed the first detective of the Chicago Police Department in 1849. In 1850 he was appointed as a special U.S. mail agent in Chicago investigating mail thefts. In the early 1850s he opened his own private detective agency in partnership with Chicago attorney Edward Rucker. Their agency, the North-Western Police Agency, was an immediate success.

Pinkerton pioneered numerous investigative techniques, such as shadowing or suspect surveillance and undercover operations. His agency was the first to hire a female detective, Kate Warne, in 1856. Pinkerton established a code of ethics for his employees and made sure they kept it. He prohibited his employees from accepting gratuities or rewards and removed politics from his operations.

At the outbreak of the Civil War in 1861, Pinkerton offered his services to the federal government and was assigned the task of protecting President Lincoln. He is credited with detecting and preventing at least one assassination plot. In addition to protecting Lincoln, he operated an espionage unit that gathered military

YOU ARE THERE!
Legendary Detectives: Thomas Byrnes

One of America's foremost early detectives was Thomas Byrnes. Byrnes, born in Ireland in 1842, came to America as a boy. He served in the Union Army and joined the police department in 1863. By 1870 he became a captain, and in 1879 he solved a $3 million bank robbery in his precinct. This led to his appointment as commanding officer of the Detective Bureau of New York. Byrnes trained his detectives in recognizing individual criminal techniques (*modus operandi*, or method of operation). He wrote *Professional Criminals of America* (1886), in which he included pictures, descriptions, and the working traits of hundreds of active criminals.

Byrnes began the practice of assembling a rogues' gallery containing pictures of known offenders from throughout Europe and America and established a daily lineup of arrested thieves, called the Mulberry Street Morning Parade, for masked detectives and victimized citizens to look at. Repetto tells us:

He also established working regulations for criminals. For example, he drew a deadline at Fulton Street, north of the Wall Street district, and forbade any criminal to enter the district on pain of physical punishment, and he required crooks new in town to check in at headquarters. As a result of his contacts, detectives were able to recover stolen goods with remarkable speed—a feat which won admiration from prominent citizens.

Unfortunately, Byrnes also used torture and the third degree to enforce the law, along with physical beatings and psychological torture. One psychological torture was the sweat box, a small room in which a prisoner would be kept for days with no human contact. The prisoner was fed by an unseen hand.

SOURCE: Thomas Repetto, *The Blue Parade* (New York: Free Press, 1978).

intelligence. He personally made several undercover missions under the alias of Major E. J. Allen. On one occasion he posed as a Confederate supporter and was given a personal tour of enemy lines by a top-ranking officer.

By the 1880s, the Pinkerton National Detective Agency had offices in nearly two dozen cities. In the West, Pinkerton's customers included the United States Department of Justice, various railroad companies, and major land speculators. The agents arrested train robbers and notorious gangsters, like members of the James Gang in the 1880s, and Robert Leroy Parker (Butch Cassidy) and Harry Longbaugh (the Sundance Kid) in the early 1900s. They also arrested John and Simeon Reno, who organized the nation's first band of professional bank robbers. They were hired in the East by mining and manufacturing companies to suppress labor organizations such as the Molly Maguires in 1874 and 1875, and to suppress the Homestead Riots in Pittsburgh in 1892. Wealthy eastern bankers were also among their clients. The "Pinkertons," as they were called, employed informants throughout the United States and its territories, and offered cash rewards for information.

Among Allan Pinkerton's other major accomplishments were establishing the practice of handwriting examination in U.S. courts and proposing a plan to centralize criminal identification records. He also advanced the cause of international police cooperation by sharing information with Scotland Yard and the French Sûreté. Pinkerton died on July 1, 1884.

In competition with the Pinkerton agency during the latter part of the nineteenth century was the Rocky Mountain Detective Association, which pursued and apprehended bank and train robbers, cattle thieves, murderers, and the road agents who plundered highways and mining communities throughout the Southwest and Rocky Mountain areas.

Another competitor was Wells, Fargo & Co., started in 1852 by Henry Wells and William G. Fargo as a banking and stock association designed to capitalize on the emerging shipping and banking opportunities in California. The company operated as a mail-carrying service and stagecoach line out of more than one hundred offices in the western mining districts. Because they carried millions of dollars in gold and other valuable cargo, they found it necessary to create their own guard company to protect their shipments. The Wells-Fargo private security employees were effective in preventing robberies and thefts. Moreover, criminals who were able to hold up their banks and carriers were relentlessly hunted down by specially trained and equipped agents.

Federal Investigating   Since its earliest days, our federal government has employed investigators to detect revenue violations. However, their number was limited and their responsibilities narrow. In 1789, the U.S. government appointed investigators, known collectively as the Revenue Cutter Service, to prevent smuggling. In 1829, the U.S. Postal Service appointed investigators to investigate mail fraud. In 1865, Congress created the United States Secret Service to combat the counterfeiting of U.S. obligations such as currency, bonds, and stamps. In 1903, two years after the assassination of President McKinley, the Secret Service assumed the responsibility of guarding the president.

TWENTIETH-CENTURY INVESTIGATING

The twentieth century saw the advancement of the public investigating concept to most local police departments in the United States. It also saw the further development of investigating units at the federal level, particularly the Federal Bureau of Investigation (FBI) and the Treasury Department's Narcotics Bureau, now known as the Drug Enforcement Administration (DEA). The twentieth century also saw the increased use of science in investigating crime, the use of academic research to study police investigations and establish new methods to investigate crimes, and the due process revolution that changed investigating practices.

Local Investigating

By the twentieth century most major police departments had detective squads that were assigned to investigate all crimes. In his history of the Chicago Police Department from 1890 to 1925, Mark H. Haller gives us an idea of the way twentieth-century detectives worked:

> In order to understand the interrelationships of police and professional thieves, it is necessary to keep in

YOU ARE THERE!

Pinkerton and President Abraham Lincoln

Allan Pinkerton, the founder of the Pinkerton National Detective Agency, is credited with saving the life of Abraham Lincoln, president-elect of the United States.

As Pinkerton was investigating threats against a railroad, he uncovered information regarding a conspiracy to kill Lincoln as he traveled through Maryland during his procession to Washington to take his presidential oath. Pinkerton foiled the plot by arranging for Lincoln to travel through Baltimore in disguise—as an invalid in a shawl. Pinkerton's operatives cut telegraph wires on the route and detained reporters until Lincoln reached Washington. Lincoln arrived safely in Washington, D.C., and took the oath of office, becoming president of the United States.

Pinkerton had an earlier relationship with Lincoln. When he founded his detective agency, he provided security services to the Illinois Central Railroad. Together with the railroad's vice president, George McClellan, he consulted with the railroad's lawyer, Abraham Lincoln. Later, McClellan, one of Lincoln's Union generals and eventually chief of all Union forces, hired Pinkerton to head his intelligence branch. Operating under the pseudonym E. J. Allen, Pinkerton's operatives provided valuable information from behind enemy lines. Pinkerton himself conducted intelligence missions behind enemy lines.

SOURCES: Edwin C. Fishel, *The Secret War for the Union: The Untold Story of Military Intelligence in the Civil War* (New York: Houghton Mifflin, 1996), and J. Anthony Lukas, *Big Trouble: A Murder in a Small Western Town Sets Off a Struggle for the Soul of America* (New York: Simon & Schuster, 1997).

YOU ARE THERE!

The History of the Secret Service

Many of us today think the only duty of the Secret Service is executive protection, however this is not so and was not the reason for the unit's creation.

The Secret Service was created by Congress in 1865 as a bureau of the Department of the Treasury to preclude the counterfeiting and forgery of products of the government's monetary system. Because it was the federal government's only general law enforcement agency, its responsibilities were expanded to include smuggling, piracy, mail robbery, and land fraud. The Secret Service also conducted post-Civil War investigations of the Ku Klux Klan and served as intelligence and anti-espionage agents during the Spanish-American War and World War I.

In 1901, after the assassination of President William McKinley, the Secret Service was given the responsibility of protecting the president. Today, the Secret Service also protects the vice president; the immediate families of the president and vice president; the president-elect and the vice president-elect and their immediate families; former presidents and their wives, along with their children; major presidential and vice presidential candidates; and visiting heads of foreign governments.

The Secret Service remains in charge of preventing the counterfeiting and forgery of the government's monetary system.

mind a number of factors. To begin with, the main expertise of a detective was his knowledge of the underworld—his ability to recognize criminals and to keep informed concerning when and how they operated. For these purposes, detectives developed informers and maintained extensive informal relationships with the underworld. Often they exchanged freedom from arrest for information. Even conscientious detectives were so involved with the underworld that there was only a thin line between guardians against crime and partners with criminals. In addition, relationships between detectives and thieves were often influenced by the fact that some thieves had ties with politicians made by performing services on election day or by hanging out in saloons operated by persons with political influence. As a result, there was often an uneasy alliance of professional thieves, police, and politicians.[6]

Haller also tells us that close relationships between detectives and criminals were a basis for harassment. One of the standard crime control measures used by detectives was to "vag" known criminals until they left town. That is, known criminals were arrested for the crime of vagrancy (having no money or other visible means of support) and taken to court to be fined. Faced with repeated arrests, thieves often sought a more congenial city in which to practice their profession.

Another common tactic, used when a particularly notorious crime occurred or when newspapers complained of a crime wave, was for police officials to order dragnet or sweep arrests. The purpose of these sweeps was to drive the "lawless elements" underground and, no doubt, to present the appearance of police vigor. Those arrested in dragnet raids were searched and interrogated. In August 1905, Chicago chief John M. Collins told a special squad of fifty-four detectives, "You are the men who are to catch thieves and hold-up men. I am going to send you into each quarter of the city after suspicious characters. There must be no partiality. Arrest every man you see loafing around with the look of a criminal. The streets will be safer with those fellows at Harrison Street Station. Pickpockets and confidence men are included in my orders."[7]

The chief also told the press, "We can't do away with the dragnet. The detectives and patrolmen get their orders to bring them all in. . . . And the chances are that nine times out of ten the persons picked up are not guilty of the crime. But if the tenth time we should get the guilty man we are well repaid, as is society."[8]

Haller also points to the corruption that was endemic to policing as well as to detectives:

> In the coordination of con games in 1914, the bunco squad insisted that a con man newly arrived in the city would be subject to arrest unless he sought out a member of the squad and made a payment of $20.00. This gave the con man the privilege of operating; but, if a victim made a complaint to the police, then the con man involved was expected to share 10 percent of the take with the police—apparently as a penalty for operating so ineffectively that a complaint resulted. The system even allowed for credit arrangements. A down-

and-out con man could request permission to work until he had earned his $20.00 fee.[9]

Many police departments began to establish specialized detective units to address particular crimes. The New York City Police Department, for example, established the Pickpocket Squad in 1924. The Pickpocket Squad was composed of twenty-two men and handled six types of pickpockets: "Patch-pocket workers (any flat pocket applied to the outside of a garment), fob-pocket workers (small vest pocket used for a watch on a chain), lush worker (theft from an intoxicated individual), toilet worker (theft from public bathroom stalls), bag opener (men and women), and the pants-pocket worker."[10]

The New York police also established a Gunmen's Squad in 1929, consisting of fifty-five plainclothes men and eight supervisors. According to the NYPD's annual report of 1929, the Gunmen's Squad was "composed of a number of men in each borough, in plainclothes, under the supervision of a superior officer and was organized for the purpose of driving loafers, criminals, gangsters, and disorderly characters from the street, speakeasies, pool parlors, dance halls, and other breeding places of immorality and crime."[11] The Gunmen's Squad had at its disposal six heavily armored motorcycles complete with sidecars, which, it was reported, "kept 198 known gangsters on the run."[12] They also "axed" every illegal still they found.

Federal Investigating

In the twentieth century the federal government greatly expanded its investigatory forces. The Bureau of Investigation, the forerunner of the Federal Bureau of Investigation, was created in 1908. However, it was an inept, inefficient organization.

In 1921, J. Edgar Hoover, an attorney working for the United States Department of Justice, was appointed assistant director of the Bureau of Investigation by President Warren G. Harding. In 1924, President Calvin Coolidge, upon the retirement of the director, appointed Hoover to fill the vacancy. Over the next forty-eight years Hoover was reappointed as director of the FBI by every United States president and remained director until his death in 1972. Under Hoover's leadership the FBI changed from an inefficient organization into what many consider the world's primary law enforcement agency. Among his major contributions were these: hiring accountants and lawyers as special agents; introducing the FBI Uniform Crime Reports, which have since 1930 been the leading source of crime and arrest statistics in America; developing the National Crime Information Center (NCIC); developing the FBI's Ten Most Wanted Criminals program, otherwise known as Public Enemies; developing the FBI Academy at Quantico, Virginia; and popularizing the FBI through the media as incorruptible, crime-fighting G-men. The FBI created a crime laboratory and made its services available free to state and local police.

Hoover wrote several books, including *Persons in Hiding*, published in 1938, which related thrilling accounts of criminal cases; *Masters of Deceit: The Story of Communism in America and How to Fight It*, which sold two and a half million copies; and numerous other essays on communism and crime. After his death, Hoover's reputation diminished with revelations about his use of the media to build a myth about the FBI, his single-mindedness about communism, and his domestic surveillance of prominent Americans.

In 1914 the U.S. Congress passed the Harrison Act, making the distribution of nonmedicinal drugs a federal crime. At first, enforcement of that law was placed in the hands of the Internal Revenue Service. In 1920 it was moved to the Prohibition Bureau, and in 1930 a separate Narcotics Bureau was established in the Treasury Department. The first director of the Narcotics Bureau was Harry Anslinger, who through the 1930s campaigned vigorously to alert the nation to the dangers of even one puff of a marijuana cigarette. Soon the bureau, now the Drug Enforcement Administration, took its place as a premier law enforcement agency.

Scientific Assistance in Investigating

The twentieth century saw the development of the use of *criminalistics* in investigating crime. The major contributors to our current knowledge of criminalistics and their primary contributions were these: Alphonse Bertillon (criminal identification and police photography), Edward Richard Henry (fingerprints), Karl Landsteiner (blood evidence), Calvin H. Goddard (ballistics), Rudolph Reiss (forensic photography), and Alec Jeffreys (DNA profiling or genetic fingerprinting). These famous scientists and their contributions to the field of criminalistics are covered in detail in chapter 6 of this text.

Another important contributor to the use of scientific methods in investigating crime was August Vollmer. Vollmer was chief of police in Berkeley, California, from 1905 to 1932 and is generally known as the Father of American Policing. He instituted many practices that helped professionalize U.S. police and investigators. Among those practices was incorporating university training as a part of police training. Also, Vollmer introduced the use of intelligence, psychiatric, and neurological tests to aid in the selection of police recruits and initiated scientific crime detection and crime-solving techniques, including the use of the polygraph with criminal suspects. Vollmer's contributions are also covered in chapter 6 of this text.

The Research Revolution and Investigating

In the wake of the urban riots of the 1960s a great deal of researcher interest shifted to the police. The creation of the Law Enforcement Assistance Administration generated much research into the workings of our criminal justice system, particularly police organizations and policing. This kind of research pointed out shortcomings in police practices and policies. For example, researcher Lawrence W. Sherman reported: "Lack of analysis plagues police efforts at catching criminals as well as preventing crime. The most wasteful police activity aimed at apprehending criminals—detective investigations—was guided by almost no analysis until very recently. Most cases received roughly equal levels of effort, regardless of the likelihood of their leading to an arrest."[13]

The academic studies of investigating revealed that the reality of detective work usually had little in common with its media representations. Benefiting from the many studies, police administrators made the following generalizations about detective operations:

- The single most important determinant of whether or not a crime is solved is not the quality of the work performed by the detectives but rather the information the victim supplies to the first patrol officer who reports to the scene of the crime.[14]

- Detectives are not very effective in solving crimes: Nationally, police are only able to clear (solve) about 21 percent of all serious crimes reported to them.[15] Because only about one-third of all crimes are ever reported to the police, their real clearance rates are much lower than 21 percent because police can't clear crimes not reported to them.[16] Patrol officers, not detectives, are responsible for the vast majority of all arrests; in fact, in one study patrol officers made 87 percent of all arrests.[17]

Prior to the Rand study of the criminal investigation process (see next paragraph), the investigation of almost all felonies, and some misdemeanors, was the sole responsibility of the detective division.[18] The patrol officer merely obtained information for a complaint or incident report and referred the case to the detectives for follow-up investigation. Theoretically, detectives would reinterview each complainant and witness, respond to the scene of the crime, and search for clues and leads that could solve the crime.

In 1975, the Rand Corporation think tank found that much of a detective's time was spent in nonproductive work (93 percent of the time was spent on activities that did not lead directly to solving previously reported crimes) and that investigative expertise did little to solve cases. The Rand report said half of all detectives could be eliminated without negatively influencing crime clearance rates.[19] The report also stated,

> The single most important determinant of whether or not a case will be solved is the information the victim supplies to the immediate responding patrol officer. If information that uniquely identifies the perpetrator is not present at the time the crime is reported, the perpetrator, by and large, will not be subsequently identified. Of those cases that are ultimately cleared but in which the perpetrator is not identifiable at the time of the initial police incident report, almost all are cleared as a result of routine police procedures.
>
> Our data consistently reveal that an investigator's time is largely consumed in reviewing reports, documenting files, and attempting to locate and interview victims on cases that experience shows will not be solved. For cases that are solved (i.e., a suspect is identified), an investigator spends more time in post-clearance processing than he does in identifying the perpetrator.[20]

The effectiveness of detectives was also called into question by a study conducted by the Police Executive Research Forum (PERF) in 1981. Data from the study disclosed that if a crime is reported while in progress, police have about a 33 percent chance of making an arrest; however, the probability of arrest declines to about 10 percent if the crime is reported one minute later and to 5 percent if more than fifteen minutes elapse before the crime is reported. In addition, as time elapses between the crime and the arrest, the chances of a conviction are reduced, probably because the ability to recover evidence is lost. Once a crime has been completed and the investigation is put into the hands of detectives, the chances of identifying and arresting the perpetrator diminish rapidly.[21]

The Rand and PERF findings were duplicated in a study of detective work by Mark Willman and John Snortum in 1984. They analyzed 5,336 cases reported to a suburban police department and found that in the majority of solved cases the perpetrator was identified at the scene of the crime and usually no scientific detective work was called for.[22]

Police departments across the United States responded to the academic studies of investigating in a number of ways. First, they shifted the focus and management of their investigations. Next, they implemented a new focus on the real crime problem by establishing innovative programs such as **repeat offender programs (ROPS),** decoy programs, and stakeout and sting programs.

In 1983, the National Advisory Commission on Criminal Justice Standards and Goals recommended the increased use of patrol officers in the criminal investigation process. They recommended that every police agency should immediately direct patrol officers to conduct thorough preliminary investigations and that agencies should establish written priorities to ensure that investigative efforts be spent in a manner that would best achieve organizational goals. They further recommended that investigative specialists (detectives) should only be assigned to very serious or complex preliminary investigations.[23]

As a consequence of the Rand study of the criminal investigation process and other studies, the Law Enforcement Assistance Administration (LEAA) funded research that ultimately led to the publication and wide dissemination of a new proposal on methods that should be used to investigate past crimes, *Managing Criminal Investigations* (MCI).[24] MCI offers a series of guidelines that recommend expanding the role of patrol officers to include investigative responsibilities, and designing a new method to manage criminal investigations by including solvability factors, case screening, case enhancement, and police and prosecutor coordination.[25]

Under an MCI program the responding patrol officer is responsible for a great deal of the follow-up activity that used to be assigned to detectives, including: locating and interviewing the victim and witnesses, detecting physical evidence, and preparing an initial investigative report that will serve as a guide for investigators. This report must contain proper documentation to indicate if the case should be assigned for continued investigation or immediately suspended for lack of evidence.[26]

The other important innovation under the MCI is the use of a managerial system that grades cases according to their solvability, with the intent that detectives work only on cases that have a chance of being solved. Some solvability factors are these: Is there a witness? Is a suspect named or known? Can a suspect be identified? Will the complainant cooperate in the investigation?

Each solvability factor is given a numerical weight, then the total weight of all solvability factors—the total score—determines if the case will be investigated or not (case screening).[27] The MCI method of managing investigations is designed to put most of an investigator's time and effort into very important cases only and cases that actually can be solved.

The **research revolution** also benefited greatly from the studies of criminals by American criminologist Marvin Wolfgang, who discovered that only a few criminals are responsible for most of the predatory street crime in the United States. Nevertheless, this small group of people commit a tremendous amount of crime each year.

As already noted, repeat offender programs were among the most significant innovations. Borrowing from Wolfgang's research, police started to direct their investigative resources to the career criminal. There are two main ways to conduct an ROP program.

The first is to target certain people for investigation. Once a criminal is identified, the police can use surveillance techniques, following the individual and waiting to catch him or her in the act of committing a crime or immediately after a crime occurs.

The second way is through case enhancement. The concept of case enhancement involves the use of extra efforts and resources to investigate cases regarding suspects with extensive prior criminal records. Specialized career criminal detectives can be notified of the arrest of a robbery suspect by other officers and then determine from the suspect's conviction or arrest rate whether the arrest merits enhancement. If it is decided to enhance the case, an experienced detective assists the officer in preparing the case for court and debriefs the suspect to obtain further information. An important police tactic in case enhancement is to establish a liaison with the district attorney's office. By doing so, the police can alert the prosecuting attorney to the importance of the case and the suspect's past record in order to ensure more zealous efforts by the prosecutor.

The establishment of proactive police initiatives in the areas of decoy, blending, and stakeout operations also came in response to the academic studies. These operations are discussed in detail in chapter 10, which covers the investigation of violent crimes. Stings—another major proactive type of investigation—are discussed in chapter 11, which examines the investigation of property crimes.

Other major developments of the 1990s were the drastic reduction in crime rates throughout the United States and the establishment of cold case squads to conduct renewed investigations of old cases that had remained unsolved and largely unworked due to the sheer volume of violent crimes before the 1990s. Cold case squads are discussed at length in chapter 10.

The Third Degree and the Due Process Revolution and Investigating

Unfortunately, we cannot discuss the history of investigating in the United States without discussing the use of what has come to be known as the third degree. The term ***third degree*** refers to the use of torture to obtain confessions.

There are two theories concerning the origins of this term. The first theory traces it back to the highest order of Freemasonry, the "Third Degree." "Its use to refer to relentless grilling of a suspect by police officers is thought to come from the rigorous tests that, formerly at least, the candidate for the Master Mason rank had to pass."[28]

The second theory was proposed in 1910 by Richard Sylvester, president of the International Association of Chiefs of Police, who claimed it has origins in the criminal justice system. He suggested that the "first degree" is presumably the arrest, the "second degree" is the transport to a place of confinement, and the "third degree" signifies the interrogation.[29]

Jerome H. Skolnick and James J. Fyfe devote an entire chapter of their 1993 book *Above the Law: Police and the Excessive Use of Force* to the subject of the third degree and provide many examples of its use.

Captain Cornelius Willemse of the New York police in a book titled *Behind the Green Lights* contrasted the public and the police idea of the third degree. "To the public," he wrote, "the third degree suggests only one thing—a terrifying picture of secret merciless beatings of helpless men in dark cells of the stations." The detective, Willemse said, saw it differently. To him, it was strategic, purposeful pressure, not the imposition of punishment for the sake of retribution. "To him it means any trick, idea and stunt, risk of action he may use to get the truth from a prisoner." Although Willemse acknowledged a repertoire of coercive and deceptive police tactics, he took care to point out that these were not necessarily violent. Detectives might roll up their sleeves and carry a rubber hose but would not actually beat the suspect. They might arrange for shrieks or groans accompanied by slapping sounds to come from an adjoining room; they might construct lies about the evidence in their possession; they might insert police officers in cells to masquerade as prisoners; they might play on the suspect's jealousy or keep drugs from addicts. But Willemse acknowledges that there were no limits on how far police might go to break down a suspect: "The 'third degree,' too, means rough stuff when required . . . against a hardened criminal," he boasted. "I never hesitated. I've forced confessions with fist, blackjack, and hose—from men who would have continued to rob and kill if I had not made them talk."[30]

Emanuel H. Lavine described the subject of the third degree he had witnessed. A Polish immigrant was thought to have murdered a man who had succeeded him in the affections of his betrothed. The man was about twenty-five years old with a powerful neck and seeming immunity to pain. The detectives beat him repeatedly with a rubber hose, but it was no use. The man wore out their arms and their patience, but would not talk.[31]

The detectives were friendly with a dentist who solved their problem. The police took the prisoner to the dentist's, where the dentist proceeded to grind into the man's molars with a rough burr until a "voluntary" confession was obtained. Then the dentist filled the holes, assuring the detectives that it was impossible to determine the age of a filling because, after several hours, the acids of the mouth quickly discolor the area. They were assured that they could lie confidently about how the confession was obtained.

The use of the third degree by the police was common knowledge and commonly accepted practice in the United States. By the 1930s, however, the third degree came under attack, first by the American Bar Association's Committee on the Lawless Enforcement of the Law in 1930 and then by the National Commission on Law Observance and Enforcement, more commonly known as the Wickersham Commission, in 1931.

In 1929, President Herbert Hoover had created the National Commission on Law Observance and Enforcement with George W. Wickersham as its chair. This was the first national study of the U.S. criminal justice system. The commission issued a report in 1931, popularly known as the Wickersham Report. Two volumes of the report, *Lawlessness in Law Enforcement* (Volume 2) and *The Police* (Volume 14), concerned themselves solely with the police. *Lawlessness in Law Enforcement* portrayed the police as inept, inefficient, racist, and brutal and accused them of committing illegal acts. The volume concluded that "the third degree—the inflicting of pain, physical or mental, to extract confessions or statements—is extensively practiced."[32] In the 1930s the United States Supreme Court began to address the problem of the third degree. In *Brown v. Mississippi* (1936), the Supreme Court finally put an end to the almost official pattern of brutality and violence used by the police to obtain confessions from suspects.[33] The case involved the coerced confessions, through beatings, of three men. Speaking for the Court, Chief Justice Charles E. Hughes wrote the following:

> Because a State may dispense with a jury trial, it does not follow that it may substitute trial by ordeal. The rack and torture chamber may not be substituted for the witness stand. The State may not permit an accused to be hurried to conviction under mob domination—where the whole proceeding is but a mask—without supplying corrective process. . . . The **due process** clause requires "that state action, whether

through one agency or another, shall be consistent with the fundamental principles of liberty and justice which lie at the base of all our civil and political institutions". . . . It was difficult to conceive of methods more revolting to the sense of justice than those taken to procure the confessions of these petitioners, and the use of the confessions thus obtained as the basis for conviction and sentence was a clear denial of due process.

Although *Brown v. Mississippi* officially ended the use of torture by the police, for nearly two decades the Court continued to address in cases the problems inherent in police interrogations, leading up to the landmark case of *Miranda v. Arizona*.[34] (The history of these cases will be discussed fully in chapter 7, "Interviews and Interrogations.")

PUBLIC INVESTIGATING TODAY

Although public investigators can work for local, state, or federal government agencies, they often use similar methods (such as working with bomb- or drug-sniffing canines) to perform their jobs. Here, members of the Los Angeles Bomb Squad patrol Los Angeles International Airport with their dog, Brenda.

The investigating industry is a major one in the United States and a source of many jobs. The industry includes a public sector and a private sector. Both public and private investigating are covered in this chapter.

Public investigators today work for local, state, and federal government agencies. This section will cover local and state investigators, federal investigators, and international aid to investigating. It will then answer the question: "What do detectives do and how do they do it?"

Local and State Investigators

Most local and state police departments have their own investigating units, which are generally called *detective squads* or *detective divisions*. The persons conducting their investigations are usually members of the department who have been designated detectives or investigators. Some departments call their investigators inspectors. Detectives are usually not considered ranking or supervisory officers in a department's chain of command but are generally in charge of all operations and decisions at a crime scene.

There are two distinct models of state-level law enforcement agencies. One is a centralized model, which combines the duties of major criminal investigations with the patrol of state highways. The centralized state police agencies generally assist local police departments in criminal investigations when requested and provide identification, laboratory, and training assistance for local departments.

The second state model is the decentralized model. In this model there is a clear distinction between traffic enforcement on state highways and other state-level law enforcement functions. The states that use this model, usually in the South and the Midwest, as well as some in the West, generally have two separate agencies, one a highway patrol and the other a state bureau of investigation.

Although the duties of the various state-level police departments vary considerably, their most common duties are highway patrol, traffic law enforcement, and the patrol of small towns, rather than investigations.

Many counties, towns, and cities around the nation have investigators in their regulatory agencies, such as the health department, code enforcement department, and building department.

INVESTIGATIONS ON THE NET

----

911 hotjobs.com
http://www.lawenforcementjob.com

For an up-to-date list of Web links, go to
http://info.wadsworth.com/dempsey

Federal Investigators

Two U.S. government departments administer federal law enforcement agencies: the Department of Justice and the Treasury Department. Numerous other federal agencies have law enforcement functions. Each of the agencies discussed in this section have a presence on the Web and students are urged to access these sites to obtain information about these agencies, their duties, and the many jobs they have available.

| **EXHIBIT 1.1** | **Major Federal Investigating Agencies** |

Department of Justice
Federal Bureau of Investigation
Drug Enforcement Administration
Immigration and Naturalization Service
U.S. Marshals Service
Treasury Department
Bureau of Alcohol, Tobacco and Firearms
Internal Revenue Service
U.S. Customs
Secret Service

Department of Justice The United States Department of Justice is the primary legal and prosecutorial arm of the United States government. The Department of Justice is under the control of the U.S. Attorney General and is responsible for enforcing all federal laws, representing the government when it is involved in a court action, and conducting independent investigations through its law enforcement services. The department's Civil Rights Division prosecutes violators of federal civil rights laws, which are designed to protect citizens from discrimination on the basis of their race, creed, ethnic background, or gender. These laws apply to discrimination in education, housing, and job opportunity. The Justice Department's Tax Division prosecutes violators of the tax laws. Its Criminal Division prosecutes violators of the federal criminal code for such criminal acts as bank robbery, kidnapping, mail fraud, interstate transportation of stolen vehicles, and narcotics and drug trafficking.

Finally, the Justice Department maintains administrative control over the Federal Bureau of Investigation, the Drug Enforcement Administration, the U.S. Marshals Service, and the Immigration and Naturalization Service.

FEDERAL BUREAU OF INVESTIGATION The Federal Bureau of Investigation (FBI) is the largest federal law enforcement agency (with the exception of the military) and the best known. The FBI has approximately ten thousand special agents and is the primary agency charged with the enforcement of all federal laws not falling under the purview of other federal agencies. The main headquarters of the FBI is in Washington, D.C., but it has field offices in major American cities and in San Juan, Puerto Rico. The head of the FBI is known as the director and is appointed by the president of the United States, subject to confirmation by the Senate.

In addition to the ten thousand special agents, the FBI employs approximately eleven thousand nonenforcement personnel who perform such duties as fingerprint examinations, computer programming, forensic or crime laboratory analysis, and administrative and clerical duties.

All special agents must attend the FBI Academy in Quantico, Virginia. In addition to the special agents, other law enforcement officers and officers from some foreign governments attend the academy.

Contrary to popular opinion, the FBI is not a national police force. It is an investigative agency that may investigate acts that are in violation of federal law. The FBI may also assist state and local law enforcement agencies and investigate state and local crimes when asked to do so by those agencies.

Today, the FBI focuses its investigations on organized crime activities, including racketeering, corruption, and pornography; bank robbery; white-collar crime, including embezzlement; and stock and other business fraud. The FBI is also at the forefront of our government's efforts against domestic terrorist activity and trains special anti-terrorist teams to prevent and respond to terrorist attacks. It maintains surveillance on foreign intelligence agents and investigates their activities in this country. The role and actions of the FBI regarding terrorism have expanded greatly since September 11, 2001. This will be discussed in chapter 13, "The Investigation of Terrorist Activities."

DRUG ENFORCEMENT ADMINISTRATION The Drug Enforcement Administration (DEA) was previously part of the Treasury Department and was called the Bureau of Narcotics. It was renamed and shifted to the Justice Department in 1973. The DEA is at the vanguard of the nation's war on drugs by engaging in drug interdiction, conducting surveillance operations, and infiltrating drug rings. The agency also tracks illicit drug traffic, registers manufacturers and distributors of pharmaceutical drugs, tracks the movement of chemicals used in the manufacture of illegal drugs, and leads the nation's marijuana eradication program.

U.S. MARSHALS SERVICE There are ninety-four U.S. marshals, one for each federal judicial district. They are appointed by the president of the United States, subject to confirmation by the Senate. The marshals, who are assisted by approximately eighteen thousand deputy marshals, perform many functions. Their primary functions are the transportation of federal prisoners between prisons and courts and the security of federal court facilities. The marshals also protect witnesses at federal trials, apprehend federal fugitives, execute federal warrants, operate the Federal Witness Security Program, and are in charge of handling the seizure and disposal of property resulting from criminal activity.

The Federal Witness Security Program, or Federal Witness Protection Program, is responsible not only for the protection of federal witnesses but also for the relocation and creation of new identities for witnesses who turn, or flip, against former associates and testify against them in court. (To *turn* or *flip* means to cooperate with authorities and obtain or give evidence regarding former partners in crime.) Two notable criminals who have participated in the Federal Witness Protection Program are Henry Hill (the protagonist in Nicholas Pillegi's *Wiseguy*, which served as the source of the 1991 movie hit *Goodfellas*) and Salvatore "Sammy the Bull" Gravano (the underboss of the Gam-

bino crime family and a self-admitted participant in nineteen murders, whose testimony led to the conviction in 1992 of his boss, John Gotti).

IMMIGRATION AND NATURALIZATION SERVICE The Immigration and Naturalization Service (INS) polices the thousands of miles of land and sea borders of the United States to prevent the entrance of illegal aliens. It also conducts investigations of smuggling rings that brings thousands of illegal immigrants into the country each year. The INS also is in charge of admitting foreigners who qualify for United States citizenship. The branch of the INS that guards our borders is called the Border Patrol.

 INVESTIGATIONS ON THE NET

U.S. Department of Justice
http://www.usdoj.gov

Federal Bureau of Investigation (FBI)
http://www.fbi.gov

Drug Enforcement Administration (DEA)
http://www.usdoj.gov/dea

U.S. Marshals Service
http://www.usdoj.gov/marshals

Immigration and Naturalization Service
http://www.ins.usdoj.gov

For an up-to-date list of Web links, go to
http://info.wadsworth.com/dempsey

 CAREER FOCUS
Jobs at the FBI

Most federal law enforcement agencies, like most employers throughout society today, advertise their job openings on the Internet. For example, the FBI has a special section on its Web site called *FBI Employment*, which advertises its special agent, support employment, and internship opportunities. Access this site at http://www.fbijobs.com

CAREER FOCUS
Internships at the FBI

Many federal agencies offer intern programs for students. The Honors Internship Program is one of the programs the FBI offers. The agency describes the qualifications as follows:

> Each summer, a special group of outstanding undergraduate and graduate students are selected to participate in the FBI Honors Internship Program in Washington, D.C. The program offers students an exciting insider's view of FBI operations and provides a chance to explore the many career opportunities within the Bureau. At the same time, the program is designed to enhance the FBI's visibility and recruitment efforts at colleges and universities throughout the United States.
>
> Due to the very selective and highly competitive nature of the Honors Internship Program, a limited number of internships are awarded each summer. Only individuals possessing strong academic credentials, outstanding character, a high degree of motivation, and the willingness to represent the FBI upon returning to their respective campus will be selected. In order to be considered, individuals must meet the following qualifications:

- Undergraduate students should be enrolled in their junior year at the time they apply to the program.
- Graduate-level students must be enrolled in a college or university and attending full time.
- Students must have a cumulative grade point average of 3.0 or above.
- All candidates must be United States citizens.
- Candidates must supply a copy of a college term paper written by the applicant.
- Candidates must prepare a completed SF-86, *Questionnaire for National Security Position*.

Applicants must travel at their own expense for an interview at the FBI Academy. Final selection will be contingent upon background investigation by the FBI, who will coordinate all internships with appropriate school officials.

SOURCE: Federal Bureau of Investigation, *Honors Internship Program;* http://www.fbi.gov/employment/honors.htm.

Treasury Department The U.S. Treasury Department has administrative control over four very important federal law enforcement agencies: the Bureau of Alcohol, Tobacco and Firearms; the Internal Revenue Service; the Customs Service; and the Secret Service.

BUREAU OF ALCOHOL, TOBACCO, AND FIREARMS The Bureau of Alcohol, Tobacco, and Firearms (ATF) is the nation's primary agency for enforcing federal laws relating to alcohol, tobacco, and firearms violations. It enforces laws pertaining to the manufacture, sale, and possession of firearms and explosives; attempts to suppress illegal traffic in tobacco and alcohol products; collects taxes; and regulates industry trade practices regarding these items.

The ATF assists other domestic and international law enforcement agencies as the nation's primary agency for tracing of weapons and explosives. The ATF traces these weapons through its records of manufacturers and dealers in firearms.

Other duties are the investigation of arson-for-profit schemes and arson and bombings at federal buildings or other institutions that receive federal funds.

INTERNAL REVENUE SERVICE The Internal Revenue Service (IRS), the nation's primary revenue-collection agency, is charged with the enforcement of laws regulating federal income tax and its collection. The investigative arm of the IRS is its Criminal Investigation Division (CID). CID agents investigate tax fraud, unreported income, and hidden assets. In its efforts against organized crime figures and major drug dealers, the federal government often uses the CID to target these individuals with the goal of prosecuting them for tax evasion. Also, many other law enforcement agencies solicit the help of the CID in an attempt to prosecute major drug dealers and other criminals who are in possession of large amounts of undeclared income.

CUSTOMS SERVICE The Customs Service conducts inspections and collects import duties and import taxes at more than three hundred ports of entry into the United States. The Customs Service also detects and intercepts illegal drugs, counterfeit consumer goods, and other contraband entering the country. In addition, customs is charged with preventing strategic high technology from being smuggled outside the United States.

The Customs Service, the second-largest federal law enforcement agency, also plays a big role in the war on drugs. The agency seizes and holds for civil forfeiture boats, planes, and other vehicles used to transport illegal drugs into the country. Civil forfeiture results in the owner's loss of legal ownership of his or her confiscated property, and the individual must sue the government for its return.

SECRET SERVICE The Secret Service is responsible for protecting the president, vice president, and other government officials and their families, along with former presidents. The Secret Service coordinates all security arrangements for official presidential visits, motorcades, and ceremonies with other federal government agencies and state and local law enforcement agencies. The Secret Service has uniformed and nonuniformed divisions.

The Secret Service is responsible for protecting the president, vice president, and other government officials and their families. Here, Secret Service agents protect President George W. Bush as he leaves a conference in Washington, D.C., in 2002.

INVESTIGATIONS ON THE NET

U.S. Treasury
http://www.ustreas.gov

Bureau of Alcohol, Tobacco, and Firearms
http://www.atf.treas.gov

Internal Revenue Service, Criminal Investigation Division
http://www.ustreas.gov/irs/ci

U.S. Customs
http://www.customs.ustreas.gov

U.S. Secret Service
http://www.ustreas.gov/usss

For an up-to-date list of Web links, go to http://info.wadsworth.com/dempsey

The Secret Service is also responsible for the integrity of the federal government's money supply, including currency, checks, bonds, securities, and stamps, and it investigates forgeries and counterfeiting of these items. In addition, the Secret Service is actively involved in investigating the growing tide of computer fraud in the United States.

Other Federal Investigative Agencies The Postal Inspection Division of the U.S. Postal Service is the third largest federal law enforcement agency. It is also one of the oldest, having been created in 1836. Postal inspectors investigate illegal acts committed against the postal service and its property and personnel, such as cases of fraud involving the use of the mails; use of the mails to transport drugs, bombs, and firearms; and assaults on postal employees while they are exercising their official duties.

Criminal law enforcement divisions are also found in the Securities and Exchange Commission (SEC), the Interstate Commerce Commission (ICC), the Federal Trade Commission (FTC), the Department of Labor, the Department of Health and Welfare, and the Department of State. The Department of State's Bureau of Diplomatic Security was created in 1986 to investigate matters involving passport and visa fraud. The United States Supreme Court has its own police depart-

INVESTIGATIONS ON THE NET

U.S. Postal Inspection Service
http://www.usps.gov

For an up-to-date list of Web links, go to
http://info.wadsworth.com/dempsey

ment employing approximately two hundred officers. Even the National Gallery of Art has its own law enforcement unit.

International Aid to Investigating

Criminal investigations sometimes extend beyond the borders of the United States. Interpol (the International Criminal Police Organization) is a worldwide organization established to enhance cooperation among nations regarding common police problems.

Interpol was founded in 1923, and the United States became a member in 1938. The mission of Interpol is to track and provide information that may help other law enforcement agencies apprehend criminal fugitives, thwart criminal schemes, exchange experience and technology, and analyze major trends of international criminal activity. It attempts to achieve its mission by serving as a clearinghouse and depository of intelligence information on wanted criminals. Its main function is informational, and it is not an investigative or an enforcement agency. A police official of any member country may initiate a request for assistance on a case that extends beyond that country's jurisdiction. One hundred and forty-six nations belong to Interpol, which is headquartered in France. The United States representative to Interpol is the U.S. Treasury Department.

INVESTIGATIONS ON THE NET

Interpol
http://www.interpol.com

For an up-to-date list of Web links, go to
http://info.wadsworth.com/dempsey

What Do Public Investigators Do and How Do They Do It?

The detective division of a police department is the unit charged with solving, or clearing, reported crimes. (*Clearing* is police terminology for solving crimes.) In traditional detective operations, the detectives conduct a follow-up investigation after a member of the patrol force takes the initial report of the crime and conducts some sort of preliminary investigation.

According to police tradition, a detective or investigator reinterviews the victim of the crime and any witnesses; collects evidence and processes the crime scene; conducts a canvass (a search of the area for witnesses); interrogates possible suspects; arrests the alleged suspect; and prepares the case, with the assistance of the district attorney's or prosecutor's office, for presentation in court.

The detective generally begins his or her investigation upon receipt of an incident report or a complaint report prepared by the officer who conducted the initial interview with the victim. The incident report contains identifying information on the victim, details of the crime, identifying information on the suspect or suspects or a description, and identifying information on any property taken.

Each incident report is given a chronological, serial number that serves as the official record of the crime as reported to the police. When the crime involves insured property, a victim may obtain this number from the police in order to give it to his or her insurance company.

As the detective begins the investigation, he or she maintains a file on the case, using follow-up reports for each stage of the investigation. The incident report and the follow-up reports are generally placed in a case folder and serve as the official history of the crime and its investigation. This folder is then used by the prosecutor to prosecute the case in court. The complaint report and the follow-up reports may also be subpoenaed by a defendant's attorney under the legal process known as *discovery*, which allows a defendant to have access, prior to a trial, to the information the police and prosecutor will use at the trial.

Record keeping in investigations is very important for several reasons. First, criminal trials often occur a year or more after the investigation is concluded, and investigators must be able to refresh their memories

The fictional NYPD detective Andy Sipowicz, portrayed by actor Dennis Franz, is a media example of the detective mystique.

Detectives work out of uniform, perform no patrol duties, and are generally paid at a higher rate than regular uniformed officers. Detectives generally enjoy much greater status and prestige than patrol officers, and have historically been seen as the heroes and heroines of police work in novels, television, and the movies—consider Sherlock Holmes, Andy Sipowicz, Inspector Clouseau, Cagney and Lacey, Crockett and Tubbs, Dirty Harry Callahan, and other fictional detectives. Are real live detectives as heroic, smart, individualistic, tough, hardworking, and mysterious as their fictional counterparts? Or is there a mystique attached to the detective position?

Commenting on the detective mystique, Herman Goldstein has written:

> Part of the mystique of detective operations is the impression that a detective has difficult-to-come-by qualifications and skills, that investigating crime is a real science, that a detective does much more important work than other police officers, that all detective work is exciting, and that a good detective can solve any crime. It borders on heresy to point out that, in fact, much of what detectives do consists of very routine and rather elementary chores, including much paper processing; that a good deal of their work is not only not exciting, it is downright boring; that the situations they confront are often less challenging and less demanding than those handled by patrolling police officers; that it is arguable whether special skills and knowledge are required for detective work; that a considerable amount of detective work is actually undertaken on a hit-or-miss basis; and that the capacity of detectives to solve crimes is greatly exaggerated.
>
> This is not meant to imply that what detectives do has no value. In a large number of cases, good detective work identifies the perpetrator and results in an apprehension. The dogged determination and resourcefulness of some detectives in solving cases are extremely impressive. But, in the context of the totality of police operations, the cases detectives solve account for a much smaller part of police business than is commonly realized. This is so because in case after case, there is literally nothing to go on: no physical evidence, no description of the offender, no witness and often no cooperation, even from the victim.*

Prior to the academic studies of investigating conducted in the 1970s, the detective mystique was considered real. It was believed that each crime was completely investigated, that all leads and tips were followed to their logical conclusion, and that the case was successfully solved. This was not the reality.

*Herman Goldstein, *Policing a Free Society* (Cambridge, MA: Ballinger, 1977), pp. 55–56.

© Michael Gerber/CORBIS

before testifying. Second, if an investigator charged with a particular case retires, is transferred, or otherwise cannot complete the investigation, the case must be transferred to another investigator. The presence of a well-organized, well-documented case folder makes it unnecessary for the new investigator to retrace all prior investigatory actions such as canvasses, interviews, and interrogations. (Nevertheless, it is a good practice for the investigator to go over old ground; something that was overlooked may turn up.)

Detective units may be organized on a decentralized or a centralized basis. In a decentralized system, each precinct in a city will have its own local detective squad that investigates all crimes occurring in the precinct. Detectives or investigators in a decentralized squad are considered generalists.

In a centralized system, on the other hand, all detectives operate out of one central office or headquarters and each is responsible for particular types of crime in the entire city. These detectives are considered specialists. Some departments separate centralized or local squads into those dealing with crimes against persons and those dealing with crimes against property. Some departments operate specialized squads for the most serious crimes. Such specialized units may include a homicide squad, sex crime squad, robbery squad, burglary squad, forgery squad, pickpocket and confidence squad, and bias crimes squad, for example.

Some cities use both decentralized and centralized investigatory units. The decentralized squads operate out of a local precinct and refer some of their cases to the specialized centralized squads, such as sex crimes, homicide, or arson squads, while investigating less serious cases themselves.

PRIVATE INVESTIGATING TODAY

The private investigating industry is generally considered part of private security. The *Hallcrest Report: Private Security and Police in America* (Hallcrest I) released in 1985, estimated that 1.1 million people were employed in private security and that almost $22 billion was spent for private security.[35] The *Hallcrest Report II* (Hallcrest II), released in 1990, revealed that spending for private security had risen to $52 billion by 1990. In addition, 1.5 million people were employed annually by private security agencies. Researchers esti-

DEMPSEY'S LAW

Becoming a Police Detective or Investigator

Professor Dempsey, I want to become a detective with the city police, but I want to skip the uniform stuff. I want to just become a detective right away.

It doesn't work that way, Frank. Most police departments do not put new people in their detective units. Becoming a detective is a promotion from the uniformed patrol police officer, trooper, or deputy sheriff rank. It takes many years of experience and an outstanding record of achievement to be considered for promotion to detective or investigator.

INVESTIGATIONS ON THE NET

Burns
http://burnsinternational.com

Kroll's Associates
http://www.krollworldwide.com

National Association of Investigative Specialists (NAIS)
http://www.pimall.com/nais/home.html

Associated Detectives of Illinois, Inc.
http://www.the-adi.com

Association of Certified Fraud Examiners (ACFE)
http://www.cfenet.org

National Association of Legal Investigators
http://www.nalionline.org

For an up-to-date list of Web links, go to http://info.wadsworth.com/dempsey

mate that private security expenditures rose to over $100 billion by the year 2000. Private policing is growing at a much faster rate than public policing.[36] This section will answer the questions: Why do we need private investigators? What do private investigators do and

CAREER FOCUS
Pinkerton and Wackenhut

Pinkerton and Wackenhut, two of the largest employers of private security employees and private investigators in the United States, like most modern corporations today, advertise and recruit on the Internet. They have special sections on their Web sites for this purpose. For Pinkerton, go to http://www.pinkertons.com/employment. For Wackenhut, go to http://www.wackenhut.com/jobs.

how do they do it? It will also cover the scope of the private investigating industry, and the image of the private investigator.

Many of the major private investigating firms, as well as many small ones, have a presence on the Web. Students are urged to access these sites to find the many jobs and career opportunities in this area. Several professional organizations in this industry also have a presence on the Web.

Why Do We Need Private Investigators?

In the wake of the academic studies of detective operations that revealed that much of the work detectives do is unproductive and does not lead to solving crimes, many police departments drastically cut the number of persons they had assigned to detective units. Today, generally only 10 percent of a department's personnel are assigned to detective duties. Furthermore, with the MCI program most cases do not get an investigation. If you are the victim of a crime that does not merit an investigation, your only recourse may be to hire a private investigator if you want the crime solved.

We also need private investigators because police power and resources are limited. There are areas of criminal and noncriminal activity where conventional law enforcement is either ill equipped or otherwise prohibited from getting involved. In cases of suspected insurance fraud, for example, most public police agencies have neither the personnel nor the financial resources to undertake intensive investigations. The search for runaway children too is far too large a problem for public agencies, and the surveillance of unfaithful spouses is beyond the authority and jurisdiction of any public service agent.

What Do Private Investigators Do and How Do They Do It?

Hallcrest II reports that many law firms and insurance companies use investigative services and personnel on a continuous basis. In addition, it reports that private investigative services and personnel are commonly retained for: background investigations, including credit checks on personnel applicants; internal theft or other employee crimes; undercover drug investigations; the location or recovery of stolen property; and the securing of evidence to be used before investigating committees, boards, or in civil or criminal trials.[37]

A review of popular magazines and newspapers reveals that private investigators are involved in the following broad areas: investigating art thefts,[38] investigating terrorism cases,[39] investigating kidnapping cases,[40] following lovers and spouses,[41] helping Hollywood stars clear their names of damaging gossip,[42] conducting financial investigations for corporations and foreign governments,[43] checking prospective mates (with the threat of AIDS this could be very important),[44] attempting to free wrongly convicted convicts,[45] exposing defense fraud,[46] investigating business fraud,[47] working for corporate clients, investigating corporate drug rings, tracing stolen goods, tracking lost assets,[48] finding lost pets,[49] and investigating insurance fraud and serving subpoenas.[50]

The following is a comprehensive list of duties that may be performed by the private investigator:

- Assist attorneys in case preparation
- Perform accident reconstruction for insurance companies and attorneys
- Review police reports for attorneys (many private investigators are former members of police departments and thus able to interpret police terminology and jargon)
- Conduct surveillance and observations for insurance companies and attorneys
- Do background investigations of possible spouses
- Do background investigations of possible employees

- Investigate criminal cases that police do not investigate due to lack of resources or ability to solve
- Run credit checks
- Run financial resources checks
- Investigate missing persons cases that the police cannot investigate due to a lack of resources
- Investigate missing persons cases that are not police cases because no crime was involved
- Check into conduct of spouses or lovers
- Conduct suicide investigations
- Provide personal protection
- Provide executive protection
- Provide premise or meeting protection
- Prepare travel itineraries for business executives and others to ensure they will have safe traveling connections
- Conduct honesty or "shopper" testing
- Investigate insurance or workers' compensation frauds
- Work undercover for private firms to uncover criminal activity, drug use, or work rule violations

- Investigate product liability claims
- Serve subpoenas

The fundamental difference between the private investigator and the public investigator is the investigative objective. Whereas police and public investigators are primarily concerned with the interests of society, the private detective serves organizational and individual interests.

As noted, many private investigators are former police detectives or federal agents. Similar to the public investigation, the private investigation may overlap into a criminal area. However, the private investigator has no authority by state law to investigate a legally proscribed crime and should in all cases involving criminal violations inform the appropriate law enforcement agency.

Scope of the Industry

Private investigators' businesses may be structured as individuals doing business as private contractors, as sole proprietorships, as partnerships, or as corporations. In addition, many businesses and industries have their own internal (proprietary) investigators. Both

---

DEMPSEY'S LAW
Jobs for College Students in Investigating

Professor Dempsey, are there jobs for college students in the private investigations business?

Sure, there are many jobs for college students in the private investigations business—both part-time jobs while you are in college and full-time jobs when you finish college. Let me give you a few examples.

Eric, Vanessa, Nancy, and Nick all worked for local private investigators while attending our college. They served subpoenas, made observations, and did surveillances. Many local private investigators call me at my office and ask me to recommend students for them to interview.

What type of students do you recommend, Professor?

I only recommend students who have high grades, a good class attendance record, and effective writing

ability. My reputation depends on the type of students I recommend.

What about full-time jobs after graduation, Professor?

I'll give you some examples here also. Rich became a police officer with the county five years ago. He had such an outstanding record that he was recently promoted to detective/investigator and is now working in a robbery squad. Cindy was hired as an investigator with U.S. Customs. She had a 4.0 grade point average here and at her four-year school. I have also had students hired by large national companies as investigators in their proprietary security departments and other students hired by the largest private investigating firms, such as Pinkerton and Wackenhut.

private and proprietary investigators serve similar functions. There are also numerous large nationwide private investigating firms in the United States.

Law firms frequently hire private investigators to assist in case preparation for civil and criminal trials. Insurance companies use private investigators to investigate arsons, life insurance fraud, large theft claims, workers' compensation fraud, automobile accidents, and product liability. Utility companies hire private investigators for a variety of reasons—for example, to look into obscene or threatening phone calls, thefts from pay phones, illegal use of telephone equipment, or long-distance billing fraud.

Most investigations conducted by security personnel concentrate on such areas as background checks for employment, insurance, and credit applications; civil litigation matters on assignment from private attorneys; and investigation of insurance or workers' compensation claims. Frequently investigators are brought in to work undercover to detect employee dishonesty, pilferage, or shoplifting.

The U.S. Department of Labor, Bureau of Labor Statistics, in its yearly *Occupational Outlook Handbook* reports that private detectives and investigators held about sixty-one thousand jobs in 1998. About one out of four was self-employed. Approximately a third of salaried private detectives and investigators worked for detective agencies, while another third were employed as store detectives in department or clothing and accessories stores. The remainder worked for hotels and other lodging places, legal services firms, and in other industries.[51]

According to the Department of Labor, the employment of private detectives and investigators is expected to grow faster than the average for all occupations through 2008. In addition to growth, replacement of those who retire or leave the occupation for other reasons should create many new job openings, particularly among salaried workers. Increased demand for private detectives and investigators will result from fear of crime, increased litigation, and the need to protect confidential information and property of all kinds. More private investigators also will be needed to assist attorneys working on criminal defense and civil litigation. Growing financial activity worldwide will increase the demand for investigators to control internal and external financial losses, and to monitor competitors and prevent industrial spying.[52]

The Image of the Private Investigator

The image of the private investigator has always been a rather poor one. As depicted in movies, television shows, and novels, and perhaps in real life, private investigators are rather sleazy individuals who either operate illegally or on the fringes of the law. This image has changed recently, according to Sam Brown and Gini Graham Scott in their 1991 book *Private Eyes: The Role of the Private Investigator in American Marriage, Business, and Industry*:

> The stigma through the last half-dozen decades of the P.I. image has been that of an aloof, alcoholic, uneducated ex-cop who followed errant wives and husbands. Today's private investigation business is a whole other ballgame. State regulatory agencies plus continuing education plus professional associations have made the P.I. a respected member of the community. New steps are constantly taken in the industry to increase ethical standards and commitment to excellence.[53]

SUMMARY   This chapter discussed the rich, colorful history of investigating. It covered the early thief-takers of France and England and the Bow Street Runners. It then discussed the first public investigators in France and England in the nineteenth century, as well as U.S. public investigators in the East, private investigators on the frontier, and federal investigating in general. The chapter then discussed the twentieth-century investigating experience in the United States, including local investigating, federal investigating, scientific assistance in investigating, and the research and due process revolution and investigating.

This chapter also covered the investigating industry, both public and private. As for public investigating, this chapter covered local and state investigators, federal investigators, and international aid to investigating. It answered the questions: What do detectives or investigators do and how do they do it? As for private investigating, the chapter answered the questions: Why do we need private investigators and what do private investigators do and how do they do it? Finally, it covered the scope of the industry and the image of the private investigator.

LEARNING CHECK

1. Discuss the history of investigating in Europe during the seventeenth, eighteenth, and nineteenth centuries.
2. Compare and contrast the French and English systems of investigation.
3. Describe some of the changes to investigations caused by the academic studies of investigations in the twentieth century.
4. Describe what a police investigator does after a citizen reports a crime to the police.
5. Select three federal investigative units and describe the types of investigations they conduct.

APPLICATION EXERCISES

1. Ever since you can remember, you have always wanted to be an investigator, public or private. Early this year, your university developed the first time machine. Because of your 4.0 grade point average and participation in extracurricular activities at the university, you have been asked if you want to be part of the first time machine trip. Of course, you say yes. Begin as follows: Pick a time period of history to which to travel. Then, choose your occupation, public or private investigator. Finally, select a case from that time period and prepare an investigatory report on that case.
2. Arrange for an interview with the detective squad that covers the area of town in which your home is located. Sit with a local detective, ask a few questions, and observe what is happening around you. Next, arrange for an interview with a private investigator. Sit for a few hours, ask a few questions, and observe what is going on around you. Then prepare a report comparing and contrasting the observations you made in both offices.

WEB EXERCISES

1. Select a public investigating agency and access its Web site. Use the Web site to obtain the necessary information to apply for a position with that agency.
2. Select a private investigating agency and access its Web site. Use the Web site to obtain the necessary information to apply for a position with that agency.

KEY TERMS

due process	questors
French method of detective work	repeat offender programs (ROPs)
Managing Criminal Investigations (MCI)	research revolution
private investigator	thief-takers
public investigator	third degree

2

THE INVESTIGATIONS PROCESS

CHAPTER GOALS

1. To define and illustrate the purposes of investigating

2. To outline the qualities and skills necessary to be an effective investigator, and the selection and training of investigators

3. To detail the major types of investigations: criminal and noncriminal, reactive and proactive, and overt and covert

4. To provide an overview of investigating by discussing the investigative questions; patterns, leads, tips, and theories; commencement of the investigation; and verification of the crime

5. To show the importance of ethics in investigating

INTRODUCTION

This chapter will define an investigation and illustrate its purposes. It will discuss the qualities and skills necessary to be an effective investigator and the selection and training of investigators. It will then discuss the primary types of investigations: criminal and noncriminal, reactive and proactive, and overt and covert.

This chapter will then outline the structure and pattern of an investigation by discussing the investigative questions and the investigating concepts of patterns, leads, tips, theories, commencement of the investigation, and verification of the crime. It will also include a discussion of the very important subject of ethics in investigations.

AN OVERVIEW OF INVESTIGATING

Investigations are a major part of life in the United States. All of us conduct investigations on a daily basis, sometimes in our jobs and sometimes in our private lives. An investigation can be very simply defined as a process used to examine and inquire into something systematically and thoroughly. We investigate what we will buy while shopping (we look at prices and quality), we investigate what we will select as a meal, we investigate the colleges we might attend. We collect facts all the time and then we make decisions based on those facts. That, very simply, is an investigation.

Defining an Investigation

Ferdico's *Criminal Law and Justice Dictionary* defines the word *investigate* as follows: "to examine and inquire into something systematically and thoroughly."[1] The word investigate can be traced back to the Latin word ***investigare,*** meaning "to search into." *Investigare* is based on another Latin word, ***vestigare,*** meaning "to track or to trace."[2] An **investigation,** thus, is the systematic and thorough examination and inquiry into something or someone. The definition of an investigation, however, is not complete without a reference to its end result or product—the report. Thus, the most complete definition of an investigation is that it is the systematic and thorough examination or inquiry into something or someone (the collection of facts or information) and the recording of this examination or inquiry in a report.

When a woman asks a private investigator to conduct an investigation of her husband because she believes he is having a sexual relationship with another person, the investigator conducts the investigation primarily by conducting surveillances and reporting the results to the woman. In the report, the investigator reports on the activities of the husband during the times of the surveillances. The investigator reports the facts—only the facts—making no inferences from these facts. For example, if the man is observed walking into a motel with another woman, that is what the investigator should report. The investigator cannot infer from these facts that the man had sex with the woman.

When a public investigator responds to the scene of a double murder, he or she reports on the facts of the case: the bodies, the physical evidence, the identity of the suspect, the answers to the questions asked, and the results of all the other activities engaged in by the investigator that will be discussed throughout this book. That information is put in a report. The report does not tell a story through speculation; it systematically and chronologically reports the facts of the case. Just the facts.

Purposes of an Investigation

As already stated, the investigation consists of the collection of information and the recording of it in a report. In criminal cases, the report serves as the basis of the prosecution; in private investigator cases, the report serves as the product for which the client pays.

Investigators frequently work with attorneys—prosecutors, defense attorneys, and civil attorneys. The role of the investigator is distinctly and significantly different from the role of the attorney. In the U.S. adversarial system of law, the attorney is an advocate for the client. The attorney's role is to present the facts and arguments that most favor his or her client. The attorney has an obligation to win the case for the client. The investigator, on the other hand, has the obligation to present all the facts, not just the facts that favor a client's case. The attorney is an advocate; the investigator is a truth seeker.

The investigative process serves many purposes in both public and private cases, including these:

determining if there is sufficient factual evidence to support or defeat each element of a cause of action; accumulating the necessary factual evidence to prove or defeat a case at trial or to form the basis for a settlement; locating leads to additional evidence; locating persons or property; and finding evidence that might be used to discredit (impeach) a witness or the opponent.[3]

The Association of Trial Lawyers of America offers this list of practices that should be performed in all investigations:

- A logical sequence must be followed.
- Real, physical evidence must be legally obtained.
- Real, physical evidence must be properly stored and preserved.
- Witnesses must be identified, interviewed, and prepared for any potential or actual litigation.
- Leads must be developed.
- Reports and documentation must be collected.
- Information must be accurately and completely recorded.
- Evidence collected must correlate to the claim, cause of action, or offense charged.[4]

Judging the Effectiveness of an Investigation

How does one judge the effectiveness of an investigation? In the private investigator case described previously, is the investigation a success only if the investigator finds evidence that the subject is, indeed, having an affair? In the double murder described previously, is the investigation a success only if the investigator identifies the murderer of the two people and apprehends that person? The answer to both questions is no. Often, a crime cannot be solved—there are no witnesses, there is no physical evidence, the investigator can find no motive. An investigator can spend hours conducting surveillances and yet be unable to confirm the client's suspicions.

The success of an investigation can only be judged by its quality, not by the end result. Were all the proper investigatory steps followed, all the right questions asked? Generally, the quality of the investigation is judged by the quality of the written report of the investigation. The report tells the story.

Art or Science?

When we attempt to place investigating into an academic or occupational framework, we must ask the question: Is investigating an art or a science? The word *art* connotes human skill as opposed to the laws of nature or science. When we think of art, we generally think of writing, music, painting, poetry, or other crafts or professions. Although there are certain rules in most of the arts, there is significant freedom of expression and personal conduct. When we think of the word *science*, we generally mean the systematic knowledge and study of natural or physical phenomena. Science generally connotes finding the truth based on observation, experimentation, and the rules of logic. When we think of science, we generally think of the pure sciences, such as biology, chemistry, or physics, and the applied sciences of medicine, dentistry, and engineering. These fields have strict rules and definitions that must be followed to obtain knowledge or to practice the science.

Is investigating art or science? In fact, investigating is a mixture of both. Investigating is a science because there are certain rules that should be followed to conduct a successful investigation and because the pure sciences and applied sciences play an increasingly important role in the investigating process. Investigating is an art because it depends on the human skills of the investigator, including interpersonal communication and creativity. The science and art of investigating will be covered extensively throughout this book.

QUALITIES AND SKILLS NEEDED IN INVESTIGATING

Investigating is a complex undertaking, and persons desiring to enter this profession need a variety of personal qualities and skills. Among the personal qualities required are intelligence and reasoning ability, curiosity and imagination, experience with people and life, perseverance, energy, sensitivity and empathy, discretion, integrity, and character. Among the skills required are good observation and memory abilities, report writing capability, proficiency in crime scene techniques, and the ability to communicate with all types of people.

Peter R. DeForest, F. E. Gaenssien, and Henry C. Lee write that investigators must possess five personal attributes that enhance their ability to detect crime: an unusual capability for observation and recall; the power of deliberation and deduction, including rational thinking; extensive knowledge of the law, rules of evidence, scientific aids, and laboratory services; the power of imagination; and a working knowledge of social psychology.[5]

Investigative units also need investigators with a variety of investigative skills. Jerry Thomas, a retired veteran of the Los Angeles Police Department with twenty years as an investigator, writes that officers who can undertake a variety of tasks are invaluable, particularly in departments that cannot afford specialized units. He states that a mix of personalities is another requirement of investigative units:

> If the guy who runs the art museum is murdered, there are some very good, qualified, smart investigators that you wouldn't send out because of their personalities. At the same time, if I had a group of investigators who were educated at St. John's or graduated from Princeton, I would not send them to investigate a case on the waterfront. Not because they don't have the experience or the expertise or the intelligence, but because they don't have the innate ability to go out there and not get mad when some longshoreman says something about the type of pants they're wearing. They don't need to get involved in some other issue other than the reason why they're there.[6]

Investigators also need clerical skills and unending patience for the ever-present piles of paperwork, which take up much investigatory time. In this regard, Detective Steve Finkelberg, an investigator with the Washington, D.C., Metropolitan Police Department says: "You have special equipment for the crime scene, special equipment for search warrants and other jobs. But in the office, you have to have lots of typewriters, computers, and files. Seventy percent of the job is typing, so you have to have the ability to use a typewriter or a computer."[7]

SELECTION AND TRAINING OF INVESTIGATORS

Investigating is a complex undertaking and requires the proper mix of personnel selection and training. This section will discuss the selection and training process in investigating.

Selecting Investigators

In most state and local law enforcement agencies, investigators are promoted from the ranks of the uniformed officers. Generally, investigators are selected on the basis of their performance; however, some agencies require prospective investigators to pass a battery of examinations before being assigned as an investigator.

The Pennsylvania State Police's Criminal Investigation Assessment Unit (CIA Unit) is one example of a state investigative agency that requires experience and extensive testing for prospective investigators. To qualify for assignment in the CIA Unit, troopers must have served a minimum of three years with the state police. The selection process includes a formal interview and a written test. In addition, a certified psychologist evaluates each candidate's psychological and emotional stability, maturity level, and ability to cope with the stress of dealing with violent crimes. The candidates' levels of formal education, investigative experience, and ability to write and speak clearly also factor into the selection process.[8]

Federal investigators are selected on the basis of several criteria. Candidates must first complete federal form "Application for Federal Employment" (SF 171). This form is reviewed by federal officials, and if an application seems suitable, appointments are scheduled for written examinations, oral interviews, and physical and medical tests. A candidate must successfully pass all of the examinations in order to be considered for a federal investigative career. The major hiring agency for the U.S. government is the United States Office of Personnel Management.

In order to become a private investigator in most jurisdictions a person has to be licensed by an appropriate state agency. Most jurisdictions require a combination of experience and successful completion of written tests in order for an investigator to be licensed. However, many private investigators hire assistants who work under the licensed investigator's license.

Training Investigators

The investigative function is somewhat different from the normal police function and requires specific training in numerous areas, including crime scene processing, interviewing and interrogating, locating sources of information, surveillance, undercover

CAREER FOCUS
Federal Investigators

The U.S. government has numerous jobs for investigators. An interested applicant can obtain job position information directly from any federal agency or through the United States Office of Personnel Management. The Office of Personnel Management can be accessed over the Internet at http://www.usajobs.opm.gov.

investigating, case management, and report writing. Some departments have formal training programs for newly assigned investigators, whereas others rely primarily on on-the-job training provided by experienced fellow investigators.

One large municipal police agency has a four-week formal course of training for newly designated investigators. The curriculum is as follows: Forensic Evidence, Crime Scene Investigation, Homicide Investigation, Burglary Investigation, Robbery Investigation, Special Victim Crime Investigation, Report Writing, Interviewing and Interrogation Techniques, Drugs of Abuse, Domestic Terrorism, Tracing and Sources of Information, Surveillance, Art Theft Investigation, Police Media Relations, Special Frauds and Pickpockets, Loan Sharking, Registering Confidential Informants, Constitutional Law, Courtroom Testimony, Credit Card Fraud, Fingerprints/Latent Prints, and Auto Crime.

Some departments that do not have their own training programs for investigators send their investigators to some of the various training programs across the nation. Some large private investigating agencies operate their own training schools; Wackenhut Corporation is an example. Wackenhut Training Institute is accredited by the University of Maryland, which

INVESTIGATIONS ON THE NET

Federal Law Enforcement Training Center (FLETC)
http://www.fletc.gov

For an up-to-date list of Web links, go to http://info.wadsworth.com/dempsey
----

awards continuing education units (CEUs) or continuing professional education units (CPEs) for successful completion of specified course work.[9]

Investigators for the federal government are trained at the Federal Law Enforcement Training Center (FLETC), with the exception of the FBI and DEA, which have their own training academies.

TYPES OF INVESTIGATIONS

Investigations can be categorized into a few main types: **criminal** or **noncriminal investigations,**

YOU ARE THERE!
Law Enforcement Training at the FLETC

The Federal Law Enforcement Training Center (FLETC), established by Congress in 1970, is located at the Glynco Naval Air Station near Brunswick, Georgia. This training center provides training for officers and investigators from fifty-nine federal agencies. Since 1983, the FLETC has provided advanced or specialized training for state and local police through its National Center for State and Local Law Enforcement Training, also located on the FLETC campus. Each year, more than twenty thousand students graduate from the FLETC, including nearly four thousand state and local officers. The average training curriculum consists of legal studies, enforcement techniques, behavioral science, enforcement operations, computer-economic crime, firearms, and physical techniques. For more information on these programs, see the summary of operations and programs (available from the Federal Law Enforcement Training Center, Glynco, Georgia).

One of the greatest benefits of the FLETC concept is that each agency does not have to operate its own training unit and thus can save significant funds through consolidated training. Such facilities would be too costly for a single agency to staff and maintain.

SOURCES: Charles F. Rinkevich, "The FLETC Concept," *FBI Law Enforcement Bulletin*, Jan. 1993; Federal Law Enforcement Training Center, "About Us," http://www.fletc.gov.

EXHIBIT 2.1   **Sample of Investigative Training Courses, 2001**

- Criminal Investigative Techniques 1: International Association of Chiefs of Police (IACP)
- Investigation of Sex Crimes: Southern Police Institute
- Crime Scene Processing Workshop: Institute of Police Technology and Management
- Interviewing and Interrogation: John E. Reid and Associates
- Executive Protection: American Society for Industrial Security (ASIS)

SOURCES: *Police Chief*, July 2001; *Law and Order*, June 2001; *Security Management*, June 2001.

reactive or **proactive investigations,** and **overt** or **covert investigations.** These categories are not mutually exclusive. For example, a criminal investigation may be reactive as well as overt, whereas another criminal investigation may be proactive and covert.

Criminal-Noncriminal

A crime is any act that the government has declared to be contrary to the public good, that is declared by statute to be a crime, and that is prosecuted in a criminal proceeding. In some jurisdictions, crimes only include felonies and/or misdemeanors. Generally, a felony is a crime for which a person may be imprisoned for at least a year and a day, whereas a misdemeanor is a class of criminal deviance punished by a maximum $1,000 fine and/or up to one year in a county or city jail. A misdemeanor is less serious than a felony.[10]

In the United States, crimes are usually investigated by the public police with the goal of prosecuting the person responsible for the crime through the U.S. criminal justice system. Criminal investigations, however, can also be conducted by private investigators.

Noncriminal investigations involve the investigation of noncriminal incidents or events. Noncriminal investigations may be conducted by the public police or private investigators. The main difference between noncriminal investigations by the public police and by private investigators is that police investigations are funded by the government, whereas private investigations are paid for by individual clients or businesses.

Reactive-Proactive

A reactive investigation is one that is instigated on the basis of a complaint registered by a victim or client. For example, a person is the victim of a robbery and reports this robbery to the police—the police then conduct a reactive investigation.

There are two types of reactive investigations: the *preliminary investigation* and the *follow-up* or *latent investigation.* The preliminary investigation is the initial inquiry into a reported crime and is generally conducted by a uniformed patrol officer. The first arriving uniformed patrol officer establishes control of the crime scene, determines if additional assistance will be necessary, and notifies supervisors and investigators, if appropriate, for further investigation. This patrol officer also conducts a preliminary search of the area of the crime to determine if the suspect is still present; renders first aid to any injured parties; detains, separates, and interviews any possible suspects or witnesses; and restricts access to the area where the crime was committed to prevent the destruction of evidence. He or she also prepares the first written report of the crime, which is generally called an *incident* or *complaint report.*

The follow-up or latent investigation is conducted by police investigators or detectives and involves all the activities that will be discussed in this text, including processing physical evidence, interviewing witnesses,

Law enforcement officers carry out reactive investigations of incidents. Here, a New York State Trooper interviews some teens who witnessed an incident that led to a man's death.

© Syracuse Newspapers/Gary Walts/The Image Works

interrogating suspects, conducting record searches, conducting surveillances, and following other investigatory practices.

Jack Kuykendall described three categories of reactive investigations: *walk-throughs*, or those cases in which the suspect is easily determined and located and detectives must only observe legal guidelines to reach a solution; *where-are-theys*, or those cases in which the suspect has been tentatively identified but has not been located; and *whodunits*, or those cases in which there are initially no suspects.[11] Kuykendall further wrote that the majority of all solved cases are walk-throughs. Where-are-theys may have simple solutions or be complex mysteries. But a substantial majority of crimes reported to police fall into the whodunits category and are rarely solved.

Proactive investigations are investigations conducted by the police based on their own initiative. The proactive investigation is designed to catch a criminal in the act of committing a crime, rather than waiting until a citizen reports a crime. The main types of proactive investigations are decoy operations, repeat offender programs, and undercover drug operations.

Decoy operations take several forms, among them *blending* and *decoy*. In blending, officers dressed in civilian clothes try to "blend" into an area and patrol it on foot or in unmarked police cars in an attempt to catch a criminal in the act of committing a crime. Officers may target areas where a significant amount of crime occurs, or they may follow particular people who appear to be potential victims or potential offenders. In order to blend, officers assume the roles and dress of ordinary citizens—construction workers, shoppers, joggers, bicyclists, physically disabled persons, and so on—so that the officers, without being observed as officers, can be close enough to observe and intervene should a crime occur.

In decoy, officers dress as, and play the role of, potential victims—drunks, nurses, businesspeople, tourists, prostitutes, blind people, isolated subway riders, or defenseless elderly people. The officers wait to be the subject of a crime while a team of backup officers are ready to apprehend the violator in the act of committing the crime. Decoy operations are most effective in combating the crimes of robbery, purse snatching, and other larcenies from the person; burglaries; and thefts of and from automobiles.

In undercover drug operations, officers pose as purchasers of illegal drugs and arrest the dealers at some point after the purchase. In low-level, "buy-and-bust" undercover drug operations, a police backup team usually arrests the dealer shortly after the purchase. In higher-level undercover drug operations, the police will make a series of buys, usually trying to purchase larger amounts of drugs from higher levels of the drug dealing operation.

Some people believe that proactive investigations involve entrapment by the police. This belief is wrong because these proactive actions by the police do not force people to violate the law, they merely provide an opportunity for people to do so. Providing a person an opportunity to violate the law is not entrapment. (*Entrapment*, which can be defined as inducing an individual to commit a crime he or she did not contemplate for the sole purpose of instituting a criminal prosecution against the offender, will be covered in detail in chapter 9.)

Overt-Covert

An overt investigation is one that is conducted openly—investigators do not try to hide their true identity or hide the fact that they are conducting the investigation. Most reactive investigations are overt.

A covert investigation, on the other hand, is conducted in secret—the investigator tries to hide his

Proactive investigations are usually covert. Here, an undercover officer arrests a suspect.

© A. RAMEY/Photo Edit

DEMPSEY'S LAW

But She Was Six Feet Tall and Looked Like She Was Twenty-Three!

A Proactive, Covert Investigation

Professor Dempsey, you're talking about proactive and covert investigations. Are they, like, stings?

Yes, Daniel. Stings are generally proactive and covert investigations, meaning that they are initiated by the police and are secret or undercover.

My father was the victim of a sting last night. He owns a deli, and this young woman came in about 6 P.M. She took a six-pack of Bud from the box, paid my father for it, and immediately left the deli. Five minutes later the police came in and told my father that he had just sold beer to a minor and issued him a summons.

Dan, business owners have to be very careful when selling beer, alcohol, or cigarettes to youthful-looking people. The police in your father's area are very aggressive in enforcing the laws regarding beer, alcohol, and cigarette sales. Many of the students in our criminal justice program volunteer to work with the police in these sting operations.

Yeah, professor, but my father said she looked like she was about twenty-three years old, not nineteen, like the police told him. He said she was about six feet tall, real foxy, and dressed to the nines. Doesn't the fact that my father thought she looked older relieve him of criminal responsibility?

Not in this state, Dan. We have a legal concept called *strict liability* regarding certain laws. Sale of alcohol is one of those laws. Strict liability means that the

prosecutor does not have to prove criminal intent on the part of the person committing a crime. Just the mere fact that he sold her the alcohol and the fact that she was less than twenty-one is enough to charge him with the crime.

Professor Dempsey, I probably shouldn't admit it, but I think I'm the one Dan is talking about. Sorry about that, Dan. I didn't know that was your father's store.

Kimberly, you were volunteering with the Sixth Precinct again yesterday evening?

Yeah, we hit eight delis and two liquor stores on Route 25. I was only carded in one place and I couldn't make a buy because I didn't have proof and the guy refused to sell me the beer. The police gave summonses in the other nine places because they sold to me without carding me.

NOTE: My real student Kimberly volunteered many hours with her local police department doing proactive, covert, sting operations related to the illegal sale of alcohol. Regarding her work with police, Kimberly says, "It definitely makes store owners aware to who they are selling alcohol to. Fifteen-year-olds can go in and get beer sometimes; it's pathetic." Kimberly's parents are proud of their daughter's involvement with the police and say, "Kimberly is certainly aware of the important issues in our community and we couldn't be more proud of her." Kimberly is attending college and is considering law enforcement as a career choice.

---

identity and the fact that he is conducting an investigation. Generally, proactive investigations are covert. Covert investigations are more commonly called *undercover investigations*.

THE INVESTIGATING QUESTIONS

An investigation may be looked upon as the answering of a series of questions to obtain information or facts. There are six series of questions that the investigator may ask, known as the who, what, where, when, how,

and why questions. They are designed to uncover as many facts as possible regarding a crime or incident.

I use an acronym to ensure that students do not forget any of these six questions. The acronym is the obviously silly-sounding word **NEOTWY** (people tend to remember silly-sounding words). NEOTWY is formed by using the last letter of each of the questions: when, where, who, what, how, and why.

The following list illustrates the many types of questions that might be asked to obtain all the necessary facts in an investigation.

- *When questions* When did the crime or incident occur? When was it discovered? When was it reported? When were the police and other appropriate persons notified? When did the police arrive at the scene? When was the victim or subject last seen? When was the victim or subject last heard from? When was the subject apprehended?

- *Where questions* Where was the crime or incident discovered? Where was it committed? Where was the suspect seen? Where were the witnesses? Where was the victim found? Where were the weapons or other instruments found? Where does the suspect live? Where does the victim live? Where is the suspect now? Where does the suspect frequent? Where was the suspect found?

- *Who questions* Who is the victim? Who discovered the crime or incident? Who reported it? Who saw or heard anything relating to it? Who had a motive or other reason for it? Who did it? Who aided or assisted the person who did it? Who witnessed it? Who are associates of the person who did it?

- *What questions* What happened? What did the witnesses see or hear? What evidence has been found? What was done with the evidence? What weapons or other instruments were used? What was the MO (modus operandi, or method of operation)?

- *How questions* How did the crime or incident take place? How did the suspect get to the scene? How did the suspect leave the scene? How much damage was done? How much property was taken? How much skill, knowledge, and expertise was necessary to commit it?

- *Why questions* Why did the crime or incident take place? Why were these particular weapons or instruments used? Why was a particular MO used? Why did the witness talk? Why did someone report it? Why did the witnesses show reluctance to talk?

Exhibit 2.2 shows some NEOTWY questions posed in the O. J. Simpson case—the 1994 murders of Nicole Brown Simpson and Ronald Goldman. These questions may have been instrumental in the adjudication of the case.

EXHIBIT 2.2   **NEOTWY Questions and the O. J. Simpson Case**

When
- When did it happen?
- When were the bodies discovered?
- When was the last time O. J. saw Nicole?

Where
- Where did it happen?
- Where was O. J. when it happened?
- Where was evidence found?

Who
- Who was murdered first?
- Who witnessed the murders?
- Who had a motive to commit the murders?

What
- What happened?
- What weapon(s) was/were used?
- What was the MO?
- What was O. J. doing during the time of the murders?

How
- How were the murders committed?
- How did the suspect(s) get to the crime scene?
- How did the suspect(s) leave the crime scene?

Why
- Why did the suspect(s) commit the murders?

PATTERNS, LEADS, TIPS, AND THEORIES

Patterns, leads, tips, and *theories* are components of the investigative process that enable investigators to learn and understand the facts of the occurrence with which they are dealing.

Patterns

A **pattern** is a series of similarities that may link particular cases or indicate that the same person is committing a series of crimes. Patterns could include time of day, day of the week, description of the suspect, MO, type of weapon being used, type of victim, location, and other variables.

A noteworthy case involving a specific pattern was the Son of Sam, or .44 caliber killer, case in New York

City in 1976 and 1977. During a period of just over a year a series of eight assaults on young persons occurred, all of them involving the use of a .44 caliber Charter Arms "Bulldog" revolver. Seven people were killed and six people injured. David Berkowitz was eventually arrested and charged with all eight assaults.

All of the assaults, except the fifth one, involved striking similarities in time of day, time of month, type of victim, location, modus operandi, and type of weapon.

Leads

Leads are clues or pieces of information that aid in the progress of an investigation. Leads can be physical evidence or information received by witnesses or other persons or through surveillances, undercover investigations, and record searches. A lead is anything that can assist an investigator in resolving an investigation.

In the aforementioned Son of Sam case there were numerous leads, including two letters reportedly written by the suspect, and the key lead—a traffic ticket placed on Berkowitz's automobile.

Tips

Tips are leads provided by citizens that aid in the progress of an investigation. Generally, tips involve the identity of the suspect. In the Son of Sam case, there were thousands of tips, including the names of seven thousand persons believed to be the killer.

Theories

Theories are beliefs regarding the case based on evidence, patterns, leads, tips, and other information developed or uncovered in a case. Theories are important because they direct the investigation. Investigators have to be very careful in building theories about a case, because if the theory is wrong, it may lead them in the wrong direction.

There were numerous theories in the Son of Sam case. But the primary theory was that the killer was a lone, demented shooter who had trouble with relationships with women. David Berkowitz fit that theory. However, later revelations in the case suggest the possibility that Berkowitz was not the only killer but rather a member of a cult of killers who were committing the crimes.[12]

COMMENCING THE INVESTIGATION

Generally, the criminal investigation commences when the police became aware of a criminal incident, either from the report of the victim or the discovery of the crime by the police. The police assign a case number, or complaint number, to the case. The case is then evaluated to determine if a full investigation will be committed—the more serious the case, the greater the likelihood that it will be investigated. Sometimes the criminal case will be investigated by the patrol section of the police department; however, in more serious or noteworthy cases, the case will be assigned to investigators or the detective unit of the police department.

Generally, the noncriminal investigation commences when a client solicits the assistance of a private investigator to perform investigatory services. Usually the private investigator interviews the client and requests her to sign a contract and pay a retainer for investigatory services. The private investigator usually charges an hourly fee for all investigatory services performed.

VERIFYING THE CRIME REPORT: FALSE REPORTS

Sometimes a person will falsely report a crime or incident for personal reasons. Investigators must carefully verify the crime or incident report before charging an innocent person with a crime.

A noteworthy false accusation of a crime was the Susan Smith case in South Carolina. On October 25, 1994, Mrs. Susan Smith, female, white, twenty-three, told the police that an unidentified gunman commandeered her car at a traffic stop in Union, South Carolina, and drove off with her two sons, Michael, age three, and Alexander, fourteen months. She described the carjacker as a black male between twenty and thirty years of age. She assisted the police in preparing a sketch of the suspect. The sketch was released to the press.[13]

Prior to the alleged carjacking, Mrs. Smith, a secretary at a textile mill, had filed for a divorce,

© Reuters NewMedia/CORBIS

Susan Smith, in court in South Carolina in November 1994, provides a perfect example of the need to verify all crime reports. Smith claimed that an armed gunman had stolen her car and kidnapped her two children inside it. In fact, Smith herself had pushed the car into John D. Long Lake, causing their deaths by drowning.

contending that her husband, the assistant manager at the Union Winn-Dixie grocery store, had committed adultery. Mrs. Smith had full custody of the children, which Mr. Smith did not challenge.

For more than a week police searched for the children, using volunteers, helicopters, and bloodhounds. By October 31, 1994, the police admitted to having no clues to the boys' whereabouts. At this point the case gained national and international attention, leading to a nationwide manhunt for the carjacker. Yellow ribbons appeared, and people packed churches in Union and elsewhere to pray for the safe return of the two boys. Mrs. Smith appeared on national television with her estranged husband pleading for assistance in finding the carjacker and her children.

Then, on November 2, after having failed a lie detector test, Susan Smith admitted that she had strapped the two boys into car seats in the rear of the car and then pushed the car into John D. Long Lake, causing their deaths. She reported that she was despondent over a failed relationship with another man and was planning to commit suicide but at the last moment changed her mind and killed only the boys. When the lake was dragged, the bodies of the two boys were found.

ETHICS IN INVESTIGATING

Ethics can be defined as the practical normative study of the rightness and wrongness of human conduct. All human conduct can be viewed in the context of basic and applied ethical considerations. Basic ethics are the rather broad moral principles that govern all conduct, whereas applied ethics focus these broad principles on specific applications. For example, a basic ethical tenet assumes that lying is wrong. Applied ethics would examine and govern under what conditions such a wrong would indeed take place and deal with constructing resultant personal conduct, for the subject matter of ethics is human conduct.[14] There has been a growing interest in ethics in the law enforcement and investigative literature in recent years.[15]

In a chapter titled "Investigative Ethics" in *Critical Issues in Criminal Investigation*, James N. Gilbert addresses ethical problems in the investigatory areas of entrapment, interrogations, courtroom deception, and narcotics. Gilbert concludes:

> The ethical dilemmas which face our police will not disappear as the world becomes more sophisticated and technological. On the contrary, such developments only widen the gap between professional behavior and possible unethical actions. As judicial guidelines become more complex [and] criminal operation more skilled, the temptation toward unethical conduct increases. Accordingly, education and training which address the poignant issue of ethical decision making will truly aid the investigator.[16]

 INVESTIGATIONS ON THE NET

- -

Institute for Criminal Justice Ethics
http://www.lib.jjay.cuny.edu/cje/html/institute.html

Criminal Justice Ethics **(journal)**
http://www.lib.jjay.cuny.edu/cje/html/cje.html

For an up-to-date list of Web links, go to http://info.wadsworth.com/dempsey

- -

EXHIBIT 2.3   **American Society for Industrial Security (ASIS) Code of Ethics and Ethical Considerations, June 27, 1980**

Preamble

Aware that the quality of professional security activity ultimately depends upon the willingness of practitioners to observe special standards of conduct and to manifest good faith in professional relationships, the American Society for Industrial Security adopts the following Code of Ethics and mandates its conscientious observance as a binding condition of membership in or affiliation with the society.

Code of Ethics

Article I.   A member shall perform professional duties in accordance with the law and the highest moral principles.

Article II.   A member shall observe the precepts of truthfulness, honesty, and integrity.

Article III.   A member shall be faithful and diligent in discharging professional responsibilities.

Article IV.   A member shall safeguard confidential information and exercise due care to prevent its improper disclosure.

Article V.   A member shall not maliciously injure the professional reputation or practice of colleagues, clients, or employers.

Ethical Considerations on Article I

I-1.   A member shall abide by the law of the land in which the services are rendered and perform all duties in an honorable manner.

I-2.   A member shall not knowingly become associated in responsibility for work with colleagues who do not conform to the law and these ethical standards.

I-3.   A member shall be just and respect the rights of others in performing professional responsibilities.

Ethical Considerations on Article II

II-1.   A member shall disclose all relevant information to those having a right to know.

II-2.   A right to know is a legally enforceable claim or demand by a person for disclosure of information by a member. Such a right does not depend upon prior knowledge by the person of the existence of the information to be disclosed.

II-3.   A member shall not knowingly release misleading information, nor encourage or otherwise participate in the release of such information.

Ethical Considerations on Article III

III-1.   A member is faithful when fair and steadfast in adherence to promises and commitments.

III-2.   A member is diligent when employing best efforts in an assignment.

III-3.   A member shall not act in matters involving conflicts of interest without appropriate disclosure and approval.

III-4.   A member shall represent services or products fairly and truthfully.

Ethical Considerations on Article IV

IV-1.   A member is competent who possesses and applies the skills and knowledge required for the task.

IV-2.   A member shall not accept a task beyond the member's competence nor shall competence be claimed when not possessed.

Ethical Considerations on Article V

V-1.   Confidential information is nonpublic information the disclosure of which is restricted.

V-2.   Due care requires that the professional must not knowingly reveal confidential information or use a confidence to the disadvantage of the principal or to the advantage of the member or a third person unless the principal consents after full disclosure of all the facts. The confidentiality continues after the business relationship between the member and his principal has terminated.

V-3.   A member who receives information and has not agreed to be bound by confidentiality is not bound from disclosing it. A member is not bound by confidential disclosures made of acts or omissions that constitute a violation of the law.

V-4.   Confidential disclosures made by a principal to a member are not recognized by law as privileged in a legal proceeding.

Exhibit 2.3 continued

The member may be required to testify in a legal proceeding to information received in confidence from his principal over the objection of his principal's counsel.

V-5.   A member shall not disclose confidential information for personal gain without appropriate authorization.

Ethical Considerations on Article VI

VI-1.   A member shall not comment falsely and with malice concerning a colleague's competence, performance, or professional capabilities.

VI-2.   A member who knows, or has reasonable grounds to believe, that another member has failed to conform to the Society's Code of Ethics shall present such information to the Ethical Standards Committee in accordance with Article XIV of the Society's Bylaws.

SOURCE: Reprinted with permission of American Society for Industrial Security.

EXHIBIT 2.4   **Pinkerton's Rules of Conduct**

The Company and its employees shall not:

1. Engage in any unlawful activity or use unethical or reprehensible practices to obtain information, or engage in any controversial or scandalous case which might damage the Company's reputation.

2. Accept business from persons with disreputable reputations, or from those engaged in an illegitimate, disreputable, or questionable enterprise.

3. Induce a person to commit a crime (entrapment).

4. Knowingly engage in work for one client against the interest of another client.

5. Guarantee success, or accept business for a fee contingent upon success.

6. Accept rewards or gratuities or permit its employees to do so.

7. Engage in work in behalf of a defendant in a criminal action.

8. Compromise with felons, or negotiate for the return of stolen property.

9. Seize (repossess) property without due process of law.

10. Obtain secret formulas, processes, designs, records, the names of customers, or other private business information.

11. Represent claimants against insurance companies and self-insures (self-insured individuals).

12. Shadow jurors.

13. Engage in wiretapping.

14. Collect amounts.

15. Investigate the morals of women, except in criminal cases or on behalf of their employers.

16. Obtain information or evidence for use in divorce actions.

17. Investigate public officers in the performance of their official duties.

18. Investigate a political party for another.

19. Investigate the lawful activities of a labor union.

20. Report the union affiliations of employees or prospective employees.

21. Report the events transpiring at labor union meetings or conventions, except those open to the public without restrictions.

22. Shadow officers, organizers, or members of a labor union for the purpose of reporting their lawful union organizing, or other lawful activities.

23. Supply the names of union members, officers, organizers, or sympathizers.

24. Report to employers the reaction and attitude of employees and union officers and representatives expressed or implied, with respect to union organizing or bargaining processes.

25. Arrange to report on the lawful organizational activities of employees and their collective bargaining processes, irrespective of whether the report be made to an employee of the Company or indirectly to the client.

Exhibit 2.4 continued

26. Supply persons to take the place of those on strike.

27. Furnish armed guards upon the highways for persons involved in labor disputes.

28. Interfere with or prevent lawful picketing during labor controversies.

29. Transport in interstate commerce any person with the intent of employing such person to obstruct or interfere with lawful picketing.

30. Furnish to employers any arms or ammunition, etc.

It is unlawful to:

1. Interfere with, restrain, or coerce employees to join or assist any labor union.

2. Interfere with or hinder the lawful collective bargaining between employees and employers.

3. Pay, offer, or give any money, gratuity, favor, consideration, or anything of value, directly or indirectly, to any person for any oral or written report of the membership meetings, or lawful activities of any labor union, or for any written or oral report of the lawful activities of employees in their collective bargaining.

4. Advise orally or in writing anyone of the membership of an individual in a labor organization.

5. Supply persons to take the place of those on strike.

6. Furnish armed guards upon the highways for persons involved in labor disputes.

7. Interfere with or prevent lawful picketing during labor disputes.

8. Transport in interstate commerce any person with the intent to employ such person to obstruct or interfere with peaceful picketing.

9. Furnish to employers arms or munitions, etc.

10. Attempt to influence anyone to disclose records or information made secret by law and not available to the public.

11. Obtain business secrets.

12. Obtain names of customers.

13. Tap wires.

14. Eavesdrop.

15. Possess or carry a weapon without being licensed to do so (in some states).

16. Impersonate a law enforcement officer.

17. Shadow jurors.

18. Compound a felony.

19. Collect accounts (in some states).

20. Report on the race, color, religion, and place of origin of any person (in some states).

21. Wear a military uniform without authority.

SOURCE: Reprinted with permission of Pinkerton.

EXHIBIT 2.5   **Law Enforcement Code of Ethics**

As a law enforcement officer, my fundamental duty is to service the community; to safeguard lives and property; to protect the innocent against deception, the weak against oppression or intimidation, and the peaceful against violence or disorder; and to respect the constitutional rights of all to liberty, equality and justice.

I will keep my private life unsullied as an example to all and will behave in a manner that does not bring discredit to me or to my agency. I will maintain courageous calm in the face of danger, scorn, or ridicule; develop self-restraint; and be constantly mindful of the welfare of others. Honest in thought and deed both in my personal and official life, I will be exemplary in obeying the law and the regulations of my department. Whatever I see or hear of a confidential nature or that

is confided to me in my official capacity will be kept ever secret unless revelation is necessary in the performance of my duty.

I will never act officiously or permit personal feelings, prejudices, political beliefs, aspirations, animosities, or friendships to influence my decisions. With no compromise for crime and with relentless prosecution of criminals, I will enforce the law courteously and appropriately without fear or favor, malice or ill will, never employing unnecessary force or violence and never accepting gratuities.

I recognize the badge of my office as a symbol of public faith, and I accept it as a public trust to be held so long as I am true to the ethics of police service. I will never engage in acts of corruption or bribery, nor

Exhibit 2.5 continued

will I condone such acts by other police officers. I will cooperate with all legally authorized agencies and their representatives in the pursuit of justice.

I know that I alone am responsible for my own standard of professional performance and will take every reasonable opportunity to enhance and improve my level of knowledge and competence.

I will constantly strive to achieve these objectives and ideals, dedicating myself before God to my chosen profession . . . law enforcement.

SOURCE: *Police Chief,* Jan. 1992, p. 15. Reprinted by permission. Copyright held by the International Association of Chiefs of Police. Further reproduction without express written permission from IACP is strictly prohibited.

EXHIBIT 2.6 The Police Code of Conduct

All law enforcement officers must be fully aware of the ethical responsibilities of their position and must strive constantly to live up to the highest possible standards of professional policing.

The International Association of Chiefs of Police believes it important that police officers have clear advice and counsel available to assist them in performing their duties consistent with these standards, and has adopted the following ethical mandates as guidelines to meet these ends.

Primary Responsibilities of a Police Officer

A police officer acts as an official representative of government who is required and trusted to work with the law. The officer's powers and duties are conferred by statute. The fundamental duties of a police officer include serving the community, safeguarding lives and property, protecting the innocent, keeping the peace, and ensuring the rights of all to liberty, equality, and justice.

Performance of the Duties of a Police Officer

A police officer shall perform all duties impartially, without favor or affection or will and without regard to status, sex, race, religion, political belief, or aspiration. All citizens will be treated equally with courtesy, consideration, and dignity.

Officers will never allow personal feelings, animosities, or friendships to influence official conduct. Laws will be enforced appropriately and courteously, and in carrying out their responsibilities, officers will strive to obtain maximum cooperation from the public. They will conduct themselves in appearance and deportment in such a manner as to inspire confidence and respect for the position of public trust they hold.

Discretion

A police officer will use responsibly the discretion vested in his position and exercise it within the law.

The principle of reasonableness will guide the officer's determinations, and the officer will consider all surrounding circumstances in determining whether any legal action shall be taken.

Consistent and wise use of discretion, based on professional policing competence, will do much to preserve good relationships and retain the confidence of the public. There can be difficulty in choosing between conflicting courses of action. It is important to remember that a timely word of advice rather than arrest—which may be correct in appropriate circumstances—can be a more effective means of achieving a desired end.

Use of Force

A police officer will never employ unnecessary force or violence and will use only such force in the discharge of duty as is reasonable in all circumstances.

The use of force should be used only with the greatest restraint and only after discussion, negotiation and persuasion have been found to be inappropriate or ineffective. While the use of force is occasionally unavoidable, every police officer will refrain from unnecessary infliction of pain or suffering and will never engage in cruel, degrading, or inhuman treatment of any person.

Confidentiality

Whatever a police officer sees, hears, or learns of that is of a confidential nature will be kept secret unless the performance of duty or legal provision requires otherwise.

Members of the public have a right to security and privacy, and information obtained about them must not be improperly divulged.

Integrity

A police officer will not engage in acts of corruption or bribery, nor will an officer condone such acts by other police officers.

Exhibit 2.6 continued

The public demands that the integrity of police officers be above reproach. Police officers must, therefore, avoid any conduct that might compromise integrity and thus undercut the public confidence in a law enforcement agency. Officers will refuse to accept any gifts, presents, subscriptions, favors, gratuities, or promises that could be interpreted as seeming to cause the officer to refrain from performing official responsibilities honestly and within the law. Police officers must not receive private or special advantage from their official status. Respect from the public cannot be bought; it can only be earned and cultivated.

Cooperation with Other Police Officers and Agencies

Police officers will cooperate with all legally authorized agencies and their representatives in the pursuit of justice.

An officer or agency may be one among many organizations that may provide law enforcement services to a jurisdiction. It is imperative that a police officer assist colleagues fully and completely with respect and consideration at all times.

Personal-Professional Capabilities

Police officers will be responsible for their own standard of professional performance and will take every reason-able opportunity to enhance and improve their level of knowledge and competence.

Through study and experience, a police officer can acquire the high level of knowledge and competence that is essential for the efficient and effective performance of duty. The acquisition of knowledge is a never-ending process of personal and professional development that should be pursued constantly.

Private Life

Police officers will behave in a manner that does not bring discredit to their agencies or themselves.

A police officer's character and conduct while off duty must always be exemplary, thus maintaining a position of respect in the community in which he or she lives and serves. The officer's personal behavior must be beyond reproach.

SOURCE: *Police Chief,* Jan. 1992, pp. 16–17. Reprinted by permission. Copyright held by the International Association of Chiefs of Police. Further reproduction without express written permission from IACP is strictly prohibited.

For students and readers interested in ethics, the *Institute for Criminal Justice Ethics* exists to foster greater concern for ethical issues among practitioners and scholars in the criminal justice field.

Exhibits 2.3 through 2.6 (pp. 39–43) provide statements on ethical standards from the American Society for Industrial Security (ASIS), Pinkerton, and the International Association of Chiefs of Police (IACP). Two essays on the importance of ethics in investigating can be found at http://www.info.com/ dempsey.

 INVESTIGATIONS ON THE NET

American Society for Industrial Security (ASIS)
http://www.asisonline.org

International Association of Chiefs of Police (IACP)
http://www.theiacp.org

For an up-to-date list of Web links, go to
http://info.wadsworth.com/dempsey

SUMMARY

As this text went into production in October 2001, the investigating agencies of the United States of America, including local, state, federal and private, were in the beginning stages of the largest and most important investigation in the nation's history—the terrorist bombings of the World Trade Center and the U.S. Pentagon on September 11, 2001. The processes used in this investigation are essentially the same as those discussed in this chapter.

An investigation can be very simply defined as a process used to examine and inquire into something systematically and thoroughly. This chapter defined an investigation and showed the purposes of an investigation. It then discussed the skills and qualities necessary to be an effective investigator, as well as the selection and training of investigators to develop and improve their investigatory skills. It discussed the three main types of investigations: criminal and noncriminal, reactive and proactive, and overt and covert investigations.

The chapter then showed the structure and pattern of an investigation by discussing the investigative questions and the investigating concepts of patterns, leads, tips, theories, commencement of the investigation, and verification of the crime. Finally, it discussed the importance of ethics in investigations.

LEARNING CHECK

1. Define an investigation.
2. What are the major skills and qualities necessary to be an effective investigator?
3. Discuss the difference between a reactive investigation and a proactive investigation. Give an example of each.
4. Discuss the basic components of an investigation and show the importance of each in the investigating process.
5. Why are ethics important to investigating?

APPLICATION EXERCISES

You have been a police officer in the City of Big Problems for the past five years. You have an outstanding arrest record and a reputation as a hardworking, ethical, community-minded officer. The rumor mill in the department has it that there are going to be two openings for promotion to the department's detective division this year. You hear that you are one of a few candidates for these promotions. This is what you have always wanted. You can almost taste the promotion.

There have been a series of commercial burglaries on your beat. You have investigated them without results. Some residents on your beat have informed you that Bigman Doper, a crack addict, has been boasting among his friends that he committed the burglaries. You interview Bigman. He denies any involvement in the burglaries and tells you to "blow off and stop dissing me."

One day after work, in the locker room, you are complaining to a fellow officer, Hotshot Cassidy, a twenty-year veteran, that you really believe that Bigman was involved in the burglaries, but you have no proof. Cassidy responds, "Hey, kid, just flake the dude, plant some evidence on him." He tells you to break a window of a store on your beat, take some property, and then say you saw Bigman do it, and then pick him up and use the property and your false accusation against him.

As you are leaving the locker room, he concludes, "Hey, kid, he's a junkie dirt bag anyway. Your beat would be better off without him. And don't forget, with that collar, you're sure to get that detective promotion."

What are you going to do? Why?

WEB EXERCISES

1. Use the Internet to find the homepages of several police departments in your area. Search their sites to obtain their policies on ethics or professional conduct.

2. Use the Internet to research a major criminal investigation in your area. (You may want to access the sites of local or national newspapers or news services.) Assume that you are investigating this case and prepare a list of the major investigating questions you would ask persons involved in this investigation.

KEY TERMS

covert investigation	noncriminal investigation
criminal investigation	overt investigation
ethics	patterns
follow-up investigation	preliminary investigation
investigare	proactive investigation
investigation	reactive investigation
latent investigation	theories
leads	tips
NEOTWY	*vestigare*

CHAPTER GOALS

1. To show you the importance of police personnel at the crime scene, including the first responding patrol officer, the investigator, and the criminalist or crime scene unit

2. To alert you to the importance of protecting the crime scene and show you how it is done

3. To give you a general idea of the steps involved in the processing of a crime scene, including photographing, searching, collecting physical evidence, recording, and reconstructing the crime

4. To emphasize the important physical evidence that may be present at a crime scene and the methods used by crime scene personnel to process that evidence

5. To alert you to the role of the private investigator in crime scene investigations

INTRODUCTION

One of the most crucial stages of a criminal investigation is the response to and processing of the crime scene, the location where the crime was committed. Anyone watching the many criminal trials covered in the media sees how defense attorneys criticize the police handling of crime scene evidence. The methods used by the police at the crime scene can be crucial to the identification of the suspect and the successful litigation of the case in court.

In the American criminal justice system, the criminal investigation generally falls under the purview of the public police, who respond to the crime scene, attempt to arrest the suspect or suspects of the crime, and conduct the actual investigation of the crime. They conduct the crime scene investigation by processing the crime scene for physical evidence, interviewing possible witnesses, interrogating possible suspects, and arresting the suspect.

Students interested in investigating should have a basic knowledge of the mechanics of crime scene investigation. This chapter defines the crime scene and discusses the duties of all police personnel who are there, including the first responding patrol officer, the investigator, and the criminalist or crime scene unit. It emphasizes, however, that at many crime scenes across much of our nation the uniformed police officer performs the bulk of the crime scene investigation work. It discusses the warrant requirement at the crime scene and the preservation of the crime scene evidence by protecting it and establishing a temporary headquarters or command post. It then discusses processing the crime scene, including the tasks of photographing, sketching, searching for evidence, recording, and reconstructing the crime. The chapter goes on to talk about processing crime scene evidence, including the concept of chain of custody and marking and packaging evidence. It describes different types of physical evidence—fingerprints, blood, hair, soil, bite marks, tool fragments, and tool marks. The chapter concludes with a discussion of the role of the private investigator in crime scene cases.

THE CRIME SCENE

The **crime scene** may be defined as the area where a crime has been committed (the inner perimeter), the immediate area surrounding the scene, including any entrances and exits to and from the scene (the outer perimeter), and anywhere that evidence of the crime can be found (the extended perimeter). A crime scene can be extended from the actual area in which the crime occurred to any area where the suspect flees to or leaves evidence. For example, if a murder occurs in Mississippi and the suspect flees the scene and travels to Florida, the crime scene can extend to the entire area of travel, because it might contain evidence of the crime. In order to determine how the crime occurred and who committed it, the processing of a crime scene involves numerous persons and duties. It involves the initial response of the first law enforcement patrol officer to the scene and the response of the investigator and **criminalist** or **crime scene unit.** It also involves their efforts to preserve the integrity of the crime scene evidence, photograph and sketch the scene, and attempt to reconstruct the events that transpired at the scene.

Although millions of crimes are reported in the United States every year, limited law enforcement resources prevent the police from establishing a crime scene at every crime. The painstaking, deliberate, and sophisticated procedures described in this chapter are usually reserved only for the most serious crimes, such as homicides, rapes, serious robberies with significant injuries, bombings and other explosions, and serious burglaries.

The processing of the crime scene is generally the first step in the investigation of a serious crime. Later steps include the canvassing and questioning of witnesses, the interrogating of possible suspects, and all the other investigative functions and duties that are discussed in this text.

Because our definition of a crime scene extends to anywhere that evidence of the crime took place, the extended crime scene can include a distant clandestine gravesite in which a body was buried. The process of searching for a clandestine grave often includes law enforcement agents, geophysicist and chemist technicians, academics, and private volunteers. It also involves defining and refining areas of high potential. The role of technology in the search for a clandestine grave is to target potential subsurface disturbances. The decay of human remains can be detected using dogs and gas detectors and by testing soil pH. Other nonintrusive ways include satellite photography, botany and geophysics techniques, infrared surveillance systems, ground-penetrating radar, and metal detectors.[1]

The Warrant Requirement at the Crime Scene

Investigators have to give serious consideration to the need to obtain a search warrant prior to processing and searching a crime scene. The basic rationale for obtaining a search warrant since the Supreme Court case *Katz v. United States* (1967) is that whenever government agents intrude into an area where there is a reasonable expectation of privacy, a Fourth Amendment search has occurred that must be justified either by a warrant or by one of the exceptions to the warrant requirement.[2] In *Mincey v. Arizona* (1978), the Court refused to recognize a crime scene search as one of the well-delineated exceptions to the search warrant requirement. As a result, crime scenes are given no special consideration under the Fourth Amendment. If a crime occurs in an area where there is a reasonable expectation of privacy, then law enforcement officers are compelled to obtain a search warrant before the crime scene search.[3]

To obtain a valid search warrant, officers must fulfill two critical requirements of the Fourth Amendment. First, they must establish probable cause for their belief that the location contains evidence of a crime, and second, they must describe that evidence. It is very simple to justify the granting of a search warrant for a crime scene, because by its very nature a crime scene establishes the probable cause for obtaining the warrant. Descriptions of the evidence believed to be present at the scene are generally relatively generic—for example, blood, a weapon, and the like.[4]

Yet despite the general requirement to obtain a search warrant, most crime scenes do not permit the police sufficient time to do so before making initial entries onto the scene. Consequently, they are forced to rely on exceptions to the warrant requirement to justify these searches. The most common justifications are *consent, emergency* (exigent circumstances), *public place,* and *plain view.*

The consent exception can apply to many crime scenes because often the person who has summoned the police to the scene can consent to the search. However, in order for the crime scene search to be constitutional, consent must be given voluntarily by a person reasonably believed by law enforcement officers to have lawful access to and control over the premises.[5]

The emergency exception also applies to many crime scenes. Traditionally, courts have recognized three different types of emergencies: threats to life or safety, destruction or removal of evidence, and escape. It is indeed difficult to imagine a crime scene that would not automatically present officers with the necessary belief that at least one of these exigent circumstances exists. However, once they are inside the premises and have done whatever is necessary to resolve the emergency, the emergency is over. The officers must have a warrant or one of the other exceptions to the warrant requirement to remain on the premises or to continue their search.

Although officers cannot conduct a full-scale search of a crime scene under the emergency exception, certain investigative steps that may lead to the discovery of evidence fall well within its scope. For instance, officers arriving on the scene of a violent crime unquestionably can sweep the premises in an effort to locate other victims, or the suspect, if they reasonably consider that either is present. If a body is found at the scene, taking the medical examiner to view and collect the body is deemed a reasonable step. If officers have probable cause to believe a crime scene contains evidence that will be destroyed if not quickly recovered, that evidence may be retrieved as part of the emergency. Officers may also secure doors and control people on the premises to guarantee that the scene is not **contaminated**—that is, evidence is destroyed. Finally, if the crime scene is in a public place or evidence is in plain view a warrant is not required.

Kimberly A. Crawford, writing in the *FBI Law Enforcement Bulletin,* states that law enforcement agencies should have a well-crafted policy on search warrants that guides officers who respond to crime scenes so that the admissibility of evidence will be ensured. This policy should explain how officers can make a warrantless entry of the crime scene to do an initial assessment of the danger to life or safety and the destructibility of evidence; provide steps they can take to resolve a particular emergency, such as protective sweeps, searches for destructible evidence, diagramming, photographing, and videotaping; detail how to

YOU ARE THERE!
Do You Need a Search Warrant at a Crime Scene?

THOMPSON V. LOUISIANA

A woman shot her husband to death, wrote a suicide note, took an overdose of sleeping pills, and lay down on a bed to await death. After some reflection, however, the woman decided to call her daughter and ask for help. The daughter quickly notified the sheriff's officer and rushed to her parents' home.

When sheriff's deputies responded to the call, the daughter admitted them to the scene of the attempted suicide and homicide. The unconscious woman was immediately transported to the hospital, and after completing a search for other victims or suspects, the deputies secured the house. Thirty-five minutes later, homicide investigators arrived on the scene and began what was described as a "general exploratory search for evidence of a crime" that lasted approximately two hours. During the search, they examined every room of the house and recovered three important items of evidence: a pistol found in a dresser, a torn note found in a bathroom wastepaper basket, and a suicide note tucked inside a Christmas card on top of a dresser.

The woman eventually survived her suicide attempt and was prosecuted for the murder of her husband. Before the trial, the defense moved to suppress the three items of evidence found by the homicide investigators during the search of the home. After considerable disagreement in the state courts, the case was ultimately referred to the Supreme Court of the United States. The Court ruled in *Thompson v. Louisiana* that the exploratory search was a violation of the Fourth Amendment and ordered that the critical evidence be suppressed.

UNITED STATES V. JOHNSON

Detroit police responded to a report that a fourteen-year old kidnapping victim was being held in the defendant's apartment. The officers' knock on the door was answered by the victim, who confirmed the report and advised the officers that she could not open the door, because the defendant, who was not in the apartment at the time, had locked her behind an armored gate. The officers made a forced entry into the apartment and freed the victim.

Once freed, the victim told officers that the defendant had raped her at gunpoint several times and threatened to kill her and her entire family if she attempted to escape. The victim showed the officers the closet where the defendant kept his weapons. The officers searched the closet and found three guns and a quantity of ammunition, all of which was seized. The remainder of the apartment was not searched at that time.

The defendant, who had a prior felony conviction, was subsequently indicted and prosecuted in federal court on charges of being a convicted felon in possession of weapons and ammunition. However, the U.S. Court of Appeals for the Sixth Circuit in *United States v. Johnson* found that the victim did not have sufficient access and control over the area to validate a consent search of the closet. Although the Court ruled the entry of the premises was lawful, it concluded that the emergency ended once the officers had released the victim and were assured that neither the defendant nor anyone else who needed their assistance was in the apartment. Thus, entering the closet to retrieve the defendant's weapons exceeded the scope of the emergency search, and the evidence was suppressed.

SOURCES: *Thompson v. Louisiana*, 105 S.Ct. 409 (1984); *United States v. Johnson*, 22 F.2d. 674 (6th Cir. 1994); Kimberly A. Crawford, "Crime Scene Searches: The Need for Fourth Amendment Compliance," *FBI Law Enforcement Bulletin*, Jan. 1999, pp. 26–31.

obtain written consent to conduct a thorough search from a person who has clear authority over the area; and detail how to obtain a search warrant when consent is denied or there is no one who can provide lawful consent.[6]

DUTIES OF POLICE PERSONNEL AT THE CRIME SCENE

Three distinct categories of police personnel are often involved in a crime scene investigation: the first responding patrol officer, investigators, and the criminalist or the crime scene unit. Most larger police agencies assign separate and distinct duties to each of these categories of personnel. But the majority of police agencies in the United States are very small, with only five to ten officers. In many agencies the patrol officer performs all of the duties generally assigned to investigators or criminalists. Some departments request the assistance of neighboring larger departments or county or state criminal investigation units.

The First Responding Patrol Officer

Generally, a uniformed police officer, deputy sheriff, or state trooper is the first law enforcement officer on the scene. It is the duty of this officer to arrest the suspect—if he or she is still present and if probable cause exists—and to give first aid to the victim if there is an injury. The **first responding patrol officer** must also question any possible witnesses at the scene. He must safeguard the scene in order to prevent unauthorized persons from entering it and preserve the integrity of any physical evidence. Generally, after quickly assessing the situation, the patrol officer notifies his supervisors and requests that investigators and criminalists respond to the scene.

The first responding officer must appreciate the importance of preventing or controlling any changes in the crime scene. The officer must ensure that he does not introduce change into the crime scene. The patrol car should be parked away from the crime scene, both to prevent affecting evidence left by the suspect and to prevent any suspect still on the scene from observing the officer.[7]

The officer should obtain the names of possible witnesses but avoid interviewing a witness or suspect at length. This should be left to follow-up investigators. First-responding officers should document in writing every action and movement they take, keeping in mind that this is likely to be the subject of examination and cross-examination if there is a trial.

The Investigator

Upon notification that a serious crime has been committed, the investigator is expected to respond immediately to the crime scene. Once on the scene, the first step the investigator should take is to interview the first-responding patrol officer who is already there, keeping in mind that person's duties. The investigator should question the patrol officer about possible suspects or witnesses who may still be present and the exact conditions that were present when he arrived. The patrol officer should be reminded to document all of the actions that were taken at the scene, because these actions may be crucial in an eventual criminal prosecution of the case.

Once the investigator has interviewed the first patrol officer, he must take charge of the crime scene by clearing it of all unauthorized persons. In most law enforcement agencies in the United States, the investigator or detective is the highest-ranking member of the police department at the crime scene and so makes the key decisions about processing the scene and investigating the crime. The investigator must ensure that all complainants, witnesses, and suspects are removed from the scene to the station house or other police facility for interviewing or processing by designated police personnel.

© Reuters NewMedia/CORBIS

Safeguarding the crime scene is among the most important duties of the first police personnel who arrive there. Here, officers string crime scene tape around the perimeter of a building in Boca Raton, Florida, in October 2001, after Anthrax was found at the location.

The investigator is the highest-ranking member of a police department at a crime scene. Here, an investigator coordinates activities at the scene of a triple homicide in the parking lot of the Isabella County Courthouse in Mount Pleasant, Michigan, in March 2002.

In many larger police agencies, several investigators may respond and engage in investigatory duties. In these cases, one of them should be designated **the primary, lead,** or **case investigator.** Any other police personnel, including other investigators, report to and comply with the directions of this investigator. It is this investigator's obligation to control all investigative activities and eventually present the case to the appropriate prosecutor if an arrest is made or a prosecution commenced.

The Criminalist or Crime Scene Unit

Many police departments employ the services of criminalists, sometimes referred to as *forensic technicians* or *crime scene technicians*. These individuals generally work in a police department's crime lab and respond to crime scenes, where they collect and process physical evidence as requested by the primary investigator. Later, they process the evidence at the crime lab. Criminalistics, also called forensic science, is discussed in chapter 6.

Some police departments employ the services of a separate crime scene unit, which responds to crime scenes to collect and process physical evidence. The evidence is then brought to the crime lab, where it is further processed by criminalists. Often, crime scene units consist of specially trained police officers or a combination of police officers and criminalists.

PRESERVING CRIME SCENE EVIDENCE

Preserving the crime scene evidence is often the key to the proper processing of the scene and the eventual admission of evidence into court for the successful prosecution of a case.

The goal of a crime scene investigation is to preserve the scene in as **pristine**—pure and unchanged—a condition as possible for as long a time as possible. In other words, conditions at the scene should remain as close as possible to the conditions that existed when the crime occurred. Unnecessary handling of evidence destroys its pristine nature, resulting in contaminated evidence. In addition, evidence goes through physical changes and its evidentiary value diminishes over time, so it must be processed at the crime lab as soon as possible. Finally, the processing of the crime scene investigation cannot go on forever. There will be pressure on the police to close down the scene and return the area to normal. For example, consider a murder committed at the entrance to the cafeteria on your campus. How long would it be before the college administration puts pressure on the police to reopen the cafeteria for normal use?

Protecting the Crime Scene

The public and other unauthorized persons (persons not involved in the actual investigation) must be kept away from the crime scene. The best way to do this is to establish a police line—an area where the public or other unauthorized persons are not permitted to enter. The police line is generally established by roping off the outside perimeter of the crime scene with police barriers and brightly colored crime scene tape. "Crime Scene—Do Not Enter" signs are placed on the barriers and the tape. The physical presence of uniformed officers on the perimeter of the line also assists in the protection of the crime scene.

INVESTIGATIONS ON THE NET

APBnews.com
Try this site to obtain media stories on the latest crimes, crimes of the century, unsolved crimes, serial murders, and similar material: http://www.apbnews.com

For an up-to-date list of Web links, go to http://info.wadsworth.com/dempsey

One particular problem for the police in protecting the crime scene is the arrival and activities of the press. The print and electronic media quickly gather at newsworthy crime scenes to obtain information and take photos, both still and video, of police activities. The media cannot be allowed to cross the police line because they may interfere with the investigation or even destroy evidence.

Another problem for the police is the response of other officers who are not connected with the immediate investigation, including media relations personnel, police administrators, and other officers who are merely curious and basically just want to see what's going on. They can be very disruptive to the investigation by getting in the way.[8] Worse, they too can destroy evidence.

Generally, when a crime scene is contaminated, the offender turns out to be a curious officer, detective, or supervisor. Widespread trampling over the crime scene by too many people can prove very damaging to investigations. Often, the result is that several of the more sensitive forensic techniques—such as trace analysis, bloodspatter interpretation, and DNA comparison—cannot be used to their fullest potential. Crime scene technicians have noted the futility of collecting hair or fiber samples after a roomful of officers have shed all over the scene. Footwear and tire track evidence may be rendered worthless when officers wander unimpeded through the crime scene.[9]

Not long ago, a sheriff's department was forced to conduct a mass fingerprinting of its detective unit after a particularly sensational homicide crime scene became overrun with curious personnel. Considerable time and effort went into eliminating officers' fingerprints from the pool of legitimate prints. In another case involving a different agency, a set of crime scene photographs showed supervisory personnel standing on a blood-soaked carpet.[10]

Experts assert that when the integrity of fingerprints and shoeprints is jeopardized, it is time for agencies to rethink their approach to crime scene work. Although departments have tried artificial means of scene protection—such as having visitors sign release forms agreeing to provide elimination fingerprints, hair samples, and semen specimens, or establishing two-perimeter crime scenes (with the inner perimeter reserved for real forensic work)—these responses have been called "mere salves" for a problem that demands more meaningful attention.[11]

D. H. Garrison, Jr., a criminalist in the Forensic Services Unit of the Grand Rapids, Michigan, police department believes that the role of detectives and supervisors in protecting crime scenes cannot be stressed enough. These individuals are responsible for the investigation. Investigators who conscientiously limit the number of visitors to a crime scene ultimately may save themselves a great deal of difficulty.[12]

Garrison maintains that the simplest and most productive way for supervisors and detectives to discourage crime scene contamination is to set a good example by their own behavior. And to enhance the protection of evidence, he too suggests that police administrators should draft and enforce a written policy on crime scene protection and preservation, a policy that is clear and carries the same weight as any other departmental rule. Garrison's written policy on protecting the crime scene contains the following elements:

- The officer assigned to the crime scene's main entry must log in all visitors, including name, rank, stated purpose, and arrival and departure times. Absolutely no undocumented visitors should be allowed in the crime scene area.

- All officers at the scene must complete a standard report describing their involvement and their specific actions while at the scene.

- All visitors must make available any requested exemplar (hair, blood, shoeprints, fingerprints, and so on) for elimination purposes.

- The highest-ranking officer entering a crime scene must assume responsibility for all subsequent visitors to the scene.

Garrison believes that this final point of the policy would ensure that any supervisory officer who visits the scene to "have a look around" stays at the site until either the crime scene technicians finish their work or a higher-ranking officer arrives. This should discourage pointless "tourism."

Establishing a Temporary Headquarters or Command Post

Consistent with the concept that no unnecessary personnel should be present at the crime scene, no activity should occur that may contaminate or destroy its pristine nature.

Thus, at any crime scene that may be in operation for a lengthy period of time, a **temporary headquarters** or command post must be established for investigators, criminalists, and other necessary personnel. This temporary headquarters should be located at a point near the outer perimeter of the scene but sufficiently removed from the inner perimeter. Of course, the crime scene itself must *never* be used as a temporary headquarters. The temporary headquarters is the working and meeting site for all personnel involved in the investigation—a sort of nerve center. It is the location where all necessary personnel report and are logged in before entering the crime scene. It can be used for holding meetings, making telephone calls, and conducting other communications with appropriate agencies or investigators. It can also be used for processing and storing all evidence before its removal to the crime lab.

Many locations can be used as temporary headquarters—a nearby house at the scene of an inside murder in a residential area, or a nearby store or business at a crime scene in a commercial or industrial area. Perhaps the best temporary headquarters, if a department can provide it, is a vehicle that can be driven to and parked near the crime scene.

Crime scene teams in police departments across the country benefit from the availability of new forensic tools that allow them to process crime scenes more quickly and thoroughly. However, when officers transport these tools to major crime scenes, serious problems may arise because the tools can get damaged if they are stuffed into overcrowded storage compartments of vehicles.

To avoid such breakage, officers often leave some tools behind, and this means making extra trips between the crime scene and their offices to retrieve them. In fact, often officers spend more time searching for equipment than using it. Teams must also cope with limited work space at crime scenes, resulting in a lag time between the collection of evidence and its processing. The length of that delay often determines whether a crime is solved at all. To deal with this problem, many police departments purchase and equip **crime scene vehicles.**

For example, the Anchorage, Alaska, police department's crime scene team evaluated the problems

DEMPSEY'S LAW

Professor, How Do You Handle the Press?

Professor Dempsey, when I watch the TV news of major crime scene searches I notice reporters and cameras all over the place. How do you keep these media people away? It seems like they can really mess up an investigation.

They sure can, if you're not able to control them. I had a technique that I used to use that worked pretty well for me at crime scenes. It can be a very touchy situation because the crime scene has to be protected, yet the public has the right to know what is going on in an investigation. Freedom of the press is a very important right to U.S. citizens.

When I was establishing the police line around the crime scene, I would direct one of the officers to establish a particular area for the press as near as possible to the scene. I would set the area off by using wooden police barriers. I would ensure that it was close enough to the scene that they could get photos of the police activity so they could impress their editors.

Also, I would assign a liaison officer to this press area, and at regular intervals, have one of the investigators feed the liaison officer general details of the investigation as they unfolded. Of course, we were very careful with what we gave the press— anything that could have jeopardized the investigation was never given out.

© AP Photos/Joe Marquette

Evidence found at a crime scene must be processed immediately. Here, the Washington, D.C., police bring a mobile crime scene vehicle onto the site in Rock Creek Park, where the skeletal remains of missing intern Chandra Levy were found in May 2002.

mentioned here and decided to purchase a major crime scene response vehicle that allows the department not only to store and transport the necessary equipment but also to process more evidence at crime scenes. In the past, the department used a converted passenger van as their crime scene vehicle. When it became clear that the van no longer served their needs, members of the crime scene team sought other options. They examined large truck frames with specially designed boxes, large vans with trailers, and custom-built campers with trailers, but finally settled on a customized motor home. With a list of desired options in hand, the team met with representatives of the manufacturer to map out design specifications. The vehicle had to accommodate their current equipment needs and also provide room for growth. Starting with a base model vehicle and drawing on the experience of the motor home manufacturer, the team adapted already-proven designs to their law enforcement needs. The result was a new crime scene vehicle that would satisfy their needs for years.[13]

Today, the Anchorage crime scene team uses the vehicle for more than just storing and carrying equipment. It accommodates eight people for holding meetings, viewing crime scene videos on a VCR unit, and performing other tasks. It has a work area equipped with two computers that can connect to the network at the police station. With the computer system, officers can search criminal histories immediately and construct and print crime scene diagrams, property and evidence forms, and property tags and they can complete property inventories for search warrant returns.

The vehicle has two telephones—one land-line unit with scrambling and coding capability and one cellular phone carried by the team leader for instant communication with detectives, district attorneys, or other critical personnel. Faxes can be sent and received to facilitate the processing of search warrant applications. A bathroom and shower area doubles as a wet-storage compartment for evidence.

The rear half of the vehicle is the evidence work area. A latent fingerprint processing chamber that measures two feet by two feet by five feet can be divided into several smaller chambers or opened to its full height. Access panels above and below allow for repair or replacement of fans and heating units. Next to the fuming tank sits a large washtub for dye staining. Items are dried directly above the sink, which has a work counter next to it. A specially designed comparison photo stand can be placed over the sink. This area contains ample storage space for equipment, with an additional storage area for evidence near an outside door. Access to the rear work area is strictly limited to technicians.

The vehicle provides ample storage for portable lights and lengths of plastic pipe, which are used at outdoor crime scenes to construct tents or to fabricate blackout areas in order to search for fiber evidence with an alternate light source.

A sixty-five-hundred-kilowatt generator with several hundred feet of extension cords powers the portable lights and even the entire vehicle when the engine is turned off. Electrical outlets are located at each corner of the vehicle on the outside near ground level, with two more mounted at the top near the center.

PROCESSING THE CRIME SCENE

The National Institute of Justice has published a set of helpful guidelines for private and public law enforcement, the *Crime Scene Search and Physical Evidence Handbook*. This manual emphasizes the importance of proper crime scene processing:

DEMPSEY'S LAW
He Became the Neighborhood Hero

Professor Dempsey, where do you establish a temporary headquarters in a densely populated residential neighborhood?

Well, sometimes you may have access to a crime scene vehicle or a community room in a housing development, but often you have to rely on the cooperation and courtesy of a business or homeowner to allow you to set up temporary headquarters in their business or home.

Professor, you mean someone would let the police take over their home and turn it into a temporary police station?

Yes, they do it all the time. But their cooperation usually depends on how you treat them. Remember the advice I always give you about getting people to cooperate with the police.

Sure, Professor. People usually come at you the way you go at them—meaning treat people with respect and they'll generally return that respect.

Good. Now, to give you an example, I recall a triple murder on Jefferson Street in the Bedford Stuyvesant neighborhood in Brooklyn, New York. It was a quiet residential block consisting of three-story brownstones. It was a pretty gruesome murder. All three victims had had their hands bound behind their backs, plastic bags were tied around their heads, and also they had been stabbed multiple times. One victim was found on the first floor in the living room; the other two were found in an upper bedroom. I knew it was going to be a lengthy investigation and I would have to establish a temporary headquarters. There was no crime scene vehicle available, and obviously I would not use the crime scene as the temporary headquarters.

As I was standing outside the brownstone, I noticed an elderly man standing on the steps of a brownstone across the street. He was obviously interested in our comings and goings. I walked across the street and identified myself to the man. I asked the man if he had witnessed anything. He replied that he had not noticed anything and did not know the residents of the brownstone where the murders occurred. He said he was surprised to see so many police cars and detectives on the block as it was such a quiet block. He said that even a passing patrol car on routine patrol was exciting to him. He appeared quite excited by our presence. He told me he had retired more than twenty years earlier from his job as a city subway conductor and now did little except watch television, read, and eat and sleep. He complained to me about being bored in his retirement years. I decided to act on his obvious enthusiasm over the police presence and his boredom.

I told him we were investigating a serious crime and asked if we could use a room or two of his residence as a temporary headquarters. I explained to him that we needed a place to log all investigators in and out of the crime scene; a place where we could use a phone to make appropriate notifications and inquiries; and a place to process necessary paperwork. I told him our investigators and criminalists needed the use of bathroom facilities and joked that we needed a place to drink our coffee. He invited us in and gave us the use of his kitchen and dining room. He even asked his wife to make coffee for us and went to the store and bought several boxes of donuts for us. I guess he knows cops.

He never got in our way, but he seemed very interested in our activities and was always within earshot. A couple of days later, after the crime scene was over, I was driving down Jefferson Street and observed the old man holding court on his front stoop. He seemed to have his neighbors mesmerized by his retelling of the details of the murder investigation on his block.

Aside from any other consideration, the investigator should consider the crime scene as highly dynamic— that is, undergoing change—and fragile in the sense that the evidence value of items it contains can be easily downgraded. Usually, there is only one opportunity to search the scene properly. Making a good preliminary survey of the layout helps to use that opportunity to best advantage.[14]

Processing the crime scene involves general preliminary duties, photographing, sketching and preparing scale models, searching and recording the crime scene, and reconstructing the crime.

The International Crime Scene Investigators Association is a professional organization for those interested in processing crime scenes.

INVESTIGATIONS ON THE NET

International Crime Scene Investigators Association
http://www.icsia.com

For an up-to-date list of Web links, go to http://info.wadsworth.com/dempsey

Preliminary Duties

First, the primary investigator must designate personnel to assist him at the crime scene and make sure that the necessary equipment is available at the scene. Next, the primary investigator can proceed with a preliminary survey or scan of the scene so that it can be properly identified and protected. No evidence should be touched or moved until this preliminary scan is completed. During the preliminary scan the investigator should start to prepare his narrative description of the crime scene by taking notes. Notes should be written in a notebook, although a tape recorder or video camera may also be used, especially for interviews. Still, the information should be transferred to a notebook as quickly as possible. The investigator should also make a preliminary crime scene sketch in the notebook. The eventual report that will be created from the notes will have to be an authentic, factual, and unbiased representation, with no hearsay evidence contained in it.

After the preliminary scan, the primary investigator should assign specific duties to all members of the investigative team and brief them on exactly what is expected of them.

Before we examine each of the specific crime scene duties, it may be helpful to review an overall description of the crime scene investigation. Exhibit 3.1 offers a summary of crime scene rules. Exhibit 3.2

summarizes the steps in the primary processing of the crime scene.

Just before beginning the primary search of the overall crime scene, photos of the scene—long-range, midrange, and close-up photographs—should be taken. After these initial photos have been taken, the primary search should be conducted as carefully and completely as possible. All areas of the scene must be inspected. The primary investigator conducts the search with the help of team members. Whenever a piece of evidence is discovered, the primary investigator views it and records it in the narrative description of the scene. At this point, photographs of the evidence should include a measuring device next to the item photographed to indicate the precise size of the item. Any item at the scene that may have been touched by the suspect should be processed. This should be done as carefully as possible in order not to destroy any other evidence at the scene.

The proper powder, chemicals, or laser should be used to locate latent print evidence that may be present. Certain items, such as paper, glass, and metal, can be packaged at the scene and taken to the crime lab for processing. All latent evidence should be lifted and

---

EXHIBIT 3.1 **Crime Scene Rules**

- Do not use the crime scene as a temporary headquarters.
- Do not unnecessarily touch anything. This prevents the destruction of evidence and avoids the embarrassment of having your fingerprints on the evidence.
- Get names of all persons present at scene, including police officers, coroner, and so on, and forward the list to the police identification unit for elimination fingerprint comparison.
- Keep all unnecessary persons out of the crime scene.
- Do not wrap any evidence that might contain fingerprints in any type of cloth. Use paper envelopes or paper bags.
- If outdoors, rope off area and protect evidence from the elements, if possible without moving it.
- Try to determine points of entry and exit.
- Examine for presence of latent prints.
- Locate any objects that might have been handled by the suspect or suspects and process them.
- Maintain a copy of the case history for your files.

EXHIBIT 3.2   **Steps in Primary Processing of Crime Scene**

- Safeguard and secure the scene.
- Visually inspect or scan the crime scene—don't touch.
- Take notes.
- Photograph the scene.
- Sketch the scene.
- Conduct the crime scene search.
- Process physical evidence found at the scene.

marked with the identity of the person who located, processed, photographed, and lifted it. (The section on fingerprints describes the process of lifting.) Once this is done, all other evidence should be collected, packaged, marked, and where necessary, forwarded to the crime lab for analysis. Each packaged item of evidence should be marked with the time, date, and exact location where it was found. The location where the evidence was found should be as precise as possible.

Last, the primary investigator should make a final survey of the scene to be sure that no evidence has been overlooked. When this step is completed, he should check all the packaged evidence to ensure that each piece is properly marked with the date, time, location, type of evidence, and name of the officer who located, recovered, and processed it. The primary investigator should then verify that documentation of all the tasks assigned to members of the team is complete and that each task has been properly performed.

Photographing

With its improved technology—as in better cameras and high-speed color film—photography remains the foundation and starting point for most of the visual recreation of the crime scene. Photographs are often used to show a jury where items of evidence were located at the scene.

At their best, photographs can present a logical story in visual form. In order to do this the scene must be as undisturbed as possible before the photographs are taken. This helps establish that the conditions as portrayed in the pictures truly illustrate the original and uncontaminated features of the scene.

Certain procedures must be followed for photographs to be acceptable in court. These procedures

ensure their validity. Both the number of photographs and the manner in which they are taken are important. Each roll must have an identifier photograph to indicate the case report number and other pertinent information.

A crime scene investigator usually has only one chance to document the crime scene as it was found, therefore it is never possible to take too many photographs. The initial photographs showing the overall scene should be taken using a technique called *overlapping.*

Overlapping involves photographing the entire scene in a clockwise manner. The photograph is composed so that a specific object is pictured on the right side of the first photograph. The second photograph then has that same object in view on the left side. This right-to-left pattern continues with each subsequent photograph until the entire scene is recorded.

Furthermore, in order to exhibit the crime scene adequately, the sequence of photographs showing all pertinent locations should be represented by a progression of general-to-specific photos. In order to accomplish this, as the clockwise sequence of overlapping photos are taken the photos should be taken from three vantage points: long range, midrange, and close-up. As each photograph is taken, a **photographic log** should record what it depicts.[15]

The photographic log is necessary because of the number and types of photos that are normally taken at the crime scene. It records the chronology of the photos taken and the pertinent technical and practical data to explain the photos and place them into the perspective of the crime scene. Circumstances and location determine the specific information to appear in the log, but several pieces of information are always imperative. Exhibit 3.3 presents a sample photo log including the essential points. Exhibit 3.4 presents crime photography rules.

When the photographs are printed, they should be marked like any other piece of evidence from the scene. This procedure, called *backing,* is accomplished by placing the investigator's initials, the date the photograph was taken, a brief description of what the photograph represents, and an indication of direction. The direction indicator can simply be letters such as *C/F/S*—camera facing south. This procedure is helpful in correlating the photographs with the crime scene sketch during testimony in court, which may occur long after the photographs were taken. A felt-tip

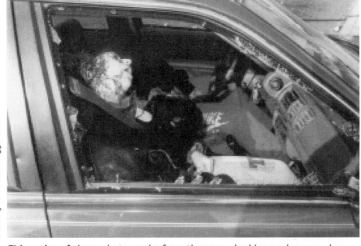

Courtesy of Michael Higginson

This series of three photographs from the same double murder case shows the different vantage points from which crime scene photos should be taken: long range, midrange, and close-up.

pen may be used to back the photographs, or the information can be written on a label that is affixed to the back of each photograph.

Often it is difficult to locate a small piece of evidence in outdoor photographs. *Circling* is a helpful procedure here. You hold the photograph backwards, with the print side toward the light, allowing the evidence on the front of the photograph to be seen. Then, you draw a circle on the back side to allow someone to testify to the location of the evidence. The jury can use the same technique during their deliberations.[16]

Often investigators respond to fatal auto accidents or other crimes involving autos. Photographs play an important role in investigating these incidents. The National Institute of Justice recommends that auto accident investigators take photographs of the following:

- The overall scene of the accident from both approaches to the point of impact.
- The exact positions of the vehicles, injured persons, and objects directly connected to the accident.
- All points of impact, marks of impact, and damage to real property.
- All pavement obstructions and defects in the roadway.
- Close-ups of damage to vehicles; one photograph should show the front and one side of the vehicle, and another should show the rear and other side of the vehicle.
- Skid marks; if possible, photographs should be taken before the vehicle has been moved and again after it has been moved.
- Tire tracks, glass, and other associated debris.[17]

Recent innovations in **forensic photogrammetry**—the making of 3-D measurements of the real world directly from photographs for use in courts of law—and close-range photogrammetry make it possible for investigators

EXHIBIT 3.3   Sample Photographic Log

Photo number:	1	2	3	4	5	6	7
1. Identity of photographer							
2. Date and time							
3. Location of crime							
4. Description of photograph							
5. Type of camera used							
6. Type of film used							
7. Light source							
8. Distance from camera to subject							
9. Environmental conditions							
10. Focal length of lens							
11. Shutter speed							
12. Lens aperture							

to make unlimited, high-accuracy measurements at crime and accident scenes directly from standard photographs taken at the scene. The photogrammetric measurements are made in the office or lab after the scene is photographed, so there is little impact on the investigator processing the scene. Because anything in the pictures can be measured, the scene is effectively preserved and can be "revisited" at any time. With accurate measurements generated easily, the scene can be re-created as a computer model, with all spatial relationships intact and available for presentation in court.[18]

Here is an example of poor crime scene photography work. The failure of investigators to comply with proper photographing procedures during the investigation of the death of former White House counsel Vincent Foster, in Fort Marcy Park in Arlington, Virginia, in 1993, led to considerable controversy over whether his death was a suicide or a murder. Investigators failed to take photographs of the body before moving it. They also failed to take photographs of Foster's car and the relative positions of the body and the car. The mistakes made by the investigators shocked crime scene experts. Vernon Geberth, author of *Practical Homicide Investigation*,[19] which has been called the authoritative text on death investigations, commented on this event:

> Crime scene photographs are permanent and comprehensive pieces of evidence. It's imperative. It's a basic requirement. It's extremely important in an investigation because it shows the body's position and other patterns which can never be re-created. . . . Who's to say this was a suicide? If this is true [that proper photographs were not taken], this is the most sloppy death investigation I have ever heard of.[20]

EXHIBIT 3.4   Crime Photography Rules

- Take numerous photographs of the general crime scene and all entrances to and exits from the scene.
- Take two photos of objects less than six inches in length: one close-up, to obtain a large image, and one at a distance of at least six feet to indicate background and perspective.
- Photograph fingerprints before they are lifted.
- Use markers or pointers to clarify important aspects of a photograph, such as bloodstains, bullet holes, or tire marks. However, photos should be taken of this evidence prior to the marking procedure.
- Photographs of homicide scenes should show the significant aspects of the body in relationship to the scene.
- Identification photographs taken at the morgue should show the head, in profile and full face, and the wounds, depicting size and shape.
- Any photograph to be used as evidence should be carefully examined to ensure there are no misleading aspects.

Robert Ressler, a former special agent with the FBI and the author of several books and many articles on homicide investigations, also seemed shocked by the failure of investigators to take proper photographs in the Foster case. "It's unspeakable. I can't imagine [that] any competent investigator would not take crime-scene photographs."[21]

Sketching

Even when photographs have been taken at the crime scene it is essential that a handmade **crime scene sketch** be made as well while processing it. Sketches supplement photographs taken at the crime scene, just as photographs supplement sketches.

In fact, although photographs are essential to the recording of the crime scene they may actually distort reality because they do not show exact distance relationships between key items of evidence and surrounding items. A crime scene sketch should depict the overall area, allowing coordination of the photographs with the locations of the evidence. The sketches are not intended to be engineering or artistic masterpieces, just line drawings or diagrams that accurately depict the scene and are proportionally correct.

Crime scene sketches can, however, go beyond a simple line drawing. They can indicate the sequence of events, location of evidence, and distances in a large area. Plastic overlays are a useful tool for sketches and can add perspective to the scene.

There are two basic kinds of sketches: the *rough sketch,* prepared by the investigator at the crime scene, and the *finished sketch,* which may be prepared later

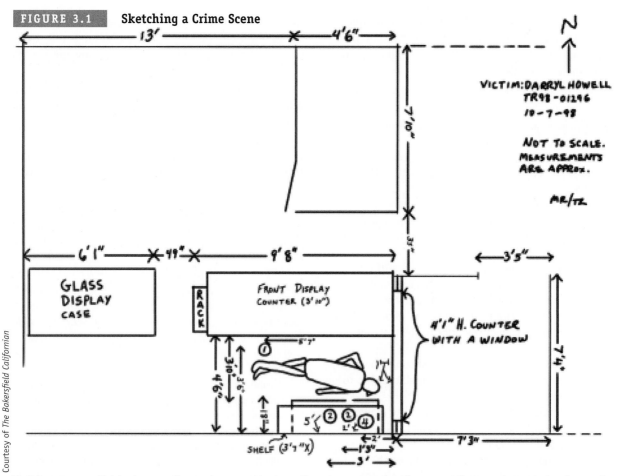

FIGURE 3.1   **Sketching a Crime Scene**

Courtesy of The Bakersfield Californian

Sketches are essential in documenting a crime scene because they show proportionally correct distances between key items of evidence and surrounding items. This sketch reflects a 1998 crime scene in Taft, California.

by a professional for presentation in court. Exhibit 3.5 summarizes the purposes of crime scene sketches.

EXHIBIT 3.5 **Purposes for Crime Scene Sketches**

- Records the exact location and relationship of pieces of evidence to other pieces of evidence and surroundings
- Refreshes the memory of the investigators and witnesses
- Provides a permanent record of conditions otherwise not easily recorded, such as distances involved in large areas; topography; paths of vehicles in accidents; movements of the victim and suspect; skid marks
- Assists prosecutor, judge, and jury to understand the conditions at the crime scene
- Helps in questioning suspects and witnesses
- Eliminates unnecessary and confusing details

Constructing Scale Models

How crime scene evidence is presented in the courtroom can have a dramatic impact on the outcome of a trial. For more complex crime scenes, a scale model may be necessary. Although photographs and sketches have been investigation standards for years, there has been a move lately for investigators to be more creative. Scale models are one way to simulate a crime scene. Scale models assist the prosecutor in several ways: they re-create the scene in a three-dimensional manner and enable the jury to view it as it appeared at the time of the incident; they allow witnesses to "walk through the scene" and visually relate to incidents as they are being explained; they limit the ability of the defense to confuse the jury because the scene is in front of them; and they can easily be moved to the deliberation room for use as an aid by the jury.

A recent article by Robert H. Lloyd, a retired Detroit police crime scene investigator who is currently a criminalist with the Thornton Police Department in Thornton, Colorado, offers practical guidelines for investigators considering using scale models in court presentations.[22] Lloyd states that the ultimate success and value of scale models is proportionate to the amount of planning done prior to the courtroom presentation. Planning should begin

the moment an investigator enters the boundaries of the crime scene. While processing the scene, from the first photograph to the final sketch, the investigator must pay attention to details necessary for later re-creation.

Before a model is constructed, the prosecutor should be consulted to determine the scope of the model she wishes to use in court. In most cases a complete model is necessary. Essential components are videotapes, a complete set of photographs, and a set of blueprints. When using blueprints, care must be taken to ensure that they accurately reflect the scene at the time of the incident.

Accuracy is the key to using models; thus, models must be to scale. A scale of one inch to one foot is a good ratio for most. If more than one floor is involved in the crime scene, they should be constructed one at a time. Each measurement must be double-checked before cutting or gluing. As each room develops, furniture and evidence must be checked to ensure proper placement and scale. If a wall or furniture is omitted, it should be noted symbolically by lines or markings. When using lines to indicate bullet trajectory, fluorescent markers can transform a plain white line into a piece of evidence that will stand out.

Lloyd concludes: "A careful . . . crime scene model is impressive. When supplemented with quality photographs, diagrams, and videotapes, the jury can accept the accuracy of the exhibits presented during the trial."[23]

The Forensic Diagramming and Animation Section of the Illinois State Police (ISP) has developed another type of model that consists of three-dimensional (3-D) body charts that show the victim's wounds from a knife, gun, or other object. These can replace extremely graphic crime scene photos that a judge might refuse to allow in court. Crime scene animation is another kind of model that is made on a computer and presented in court on video and allows for a virtual walk-through of the crime scene.[24]

Searching for Evidence

Once general photographs and diagrams of the crime scene have been completed, the actual search for physical evidence can begin. As already mentioned, in large police departments, many investigators and criminalists may be involved in the search or the specialized crime scene unit. In small departments a single investigator may carry out all of the duties in processing the scene or the first patrol officer at the scene may be the only one available.

When several people are involved, the primary investigator should give each one a specific responsibility: one designated as the photographer; one the master note taker who records the time, location, and description of each item of evidence; another the evidence collector who collects, marks, and packages the evidence; another the master sketch artist who makes the various sketches necessary. By this time the temporary headquarters should have been set up.

A specific plan or method should be used to start the search. Crime scene experts describe particular types of searches, such as the *strip search,* in which searchers look for possible evidence by walking side by side; the *spiral search,* where searchers follow each other in a concentric circle from the outside to the center of the crime scene; the *zone search,* where the scene is divided into quadrants, with each quadrant searched by one searcher; and the *wheel search,* where the searchers start at the center of the crime scene and "spoke out" in different directions to the outer limits of the scene. The particular type of search chosen is not vital and is usually determined by the number of searchers present and the size and particulars of the crime scene. The most essential point is that some logical plan be used so that searchers do not wander about in a random fashion.

The search should be conducted as a team effort with all members of the team working together. When an item of evidence is uncovered the entire team should stop, and each member should perform his or her particular job: photographing, measuring, recording, collecting, or packaging the evidence. The selection of the evidence to be collected and later processed at the crime lab should center on evidence that could identify the suspect and indicate the modus operandi of the crime.

Recording

The basic foundation of a good investigation is recording and processing notes. Accurate, comprehensive, and chronological notes not only serve to coordinate the investigation but also allow the investigator to present the strongest case possible during trial. So it is important to record any details that might be of value later on. Daily review of investigative notes is essential to maintain the correct order and eliminate items that are no longer pertinent. This is especially important during a lengthy investigation.

Notes may be defined as any type of information relevant to a specific incident, situation, or investigation. Notes help to compensate for loss of memory between the time of the investigation and the preparation of reports for court testimony. The facts and circumstances surrounding an incident will be more clearly and accurately remembered when referring to notes.

The main reasons for recording notes at the crime scene are that they support and complement the sketches and photographs taken at the crime scene; together with sketches and photographs, they preserve the crime scene; and they allow for a crime scene to be analyzed and evaluated without revisiting it.

Notes serve as an aid during interviews and interrogations because they eliminate duplication; resolve points of conflict; enhance formation of logical and pertinent questions; assist in the evaluation of new information based on previous knowledge; serve as an outline for preparing a complete report; and can refresh the memory of witnesses prior to courtroom testimony. Finally, their review may result in new leads.

The notes taken should contain only information relevant to the investigator's current case and no extraneous information or personal opinions. They should answer the questions: When? Where? Who? What? How? Why? The following information about the crime scene should be included in the notes:

- Time, date, location, and weather conditions
- Case number
- Identities of persons interviewed
- Names of all persons at the scene at the time of occurrence
- A complete list of activities performed at the crime scene, including the search, observations, photographs, sketches, casts, and evidence found
- Statements from involved parties, recorded on separate pages, with quotes listed verbatim, together with time, date, and location of questioning, as well as the identity of all persons present during the interview

CAREER FOCUS
Crime Scene Personnel

CRIME SCENE TECHNICIAN, CITY OF CORAL GABLES, FLORIDA: ANNUAL SALARY $31,369–$42,038

Performs specialized, technical work gathering evidence at crime scenes. Detects, collects, preserves, packages, and transports evidence. Processes for latent fingerprints. Performs forensic photography and produces crime scene drawings. Prepares comprehensive written reports. Testifies as expert witness in court. Operates vans, trucks, hand and power tools, laboratory and camera equipment. Duties involve strenuous physical activity under severe working conditions. Minimum qualifications include graduation from high school or GED, completion of specialized training programs related to forensic science and criminal investigations, and one year of experience in crime scene processing, forensic work, or related field. A comparable amount of training, education, or experience may be substituted for minimum qualifications. Must possess valid Florida driver's license. Must pass written test for Crime Scene Technician and obtain certification by the International Association for Identification within eighteen months of employment.

IDENTIFICATION SPECIALIST III, CITY OF CHANDLER, ARIZONA: ANNUAL SALARY $43,423–$60,789

Incumbents to this position will perform and oversee detailed technical evidence collection and crime scene documentation work. This is a skilled, journey-level identification laboratory position that performs technical evidence work with demonstrated expertise in at least two forensic disciplines from one of the following areas: evidence collection, chemical processing, photography, or latent print processing.

Some examples of duties are to serve as supervisor of the lab in the absence of the Identification Supervisor; process and investigate major crime scenes to record, document, and collect physical evidence, including fingerprint evidence; using cameras, measurement techniques, and special physical evidence collection and packaging procedures; and to recover and search for latent fingerprint evidence in order to identify persons leaving prints. The position will also process print/impression evidence.

Four years general identification experience with a law enforcement agency, or at least the last two years experience as an Identification Specialist II with the City of Chandler. Experience must include coursework in photographic sciences and fingerprinting classification, AFIS latent print operator certification, and AFIS 10-print certification.

SOURCE: International Crime Scene Investigators Association; http://www.icsia.com/jobposts.htm.

The notebook used to record the crime scene investigation should be small enough to be carried in a pocket. A bound notebook is preferable so that the notes remain intact and the pages cannot be removed or lost.

Separate notebooks should be used for each major investigation, including homicides, serious assaults, bombings, rapes, kidnappings, and robberies with a serious injury. With less serious crimes, several cases may be recorded in a single notebook, but pages must be numbered for each new investigation and a new page initiated for each new investigation. A pen should be used because it is permanent and generally more legible. Any errors made should not be erased but should be lined out and initialed. Shorthand and abbreviations should not be used because they may result in errors in transcription.

Because notes are an integral part of the investigation, extreme care has to be exercised to ensure their veracity. Comprehensive, accurate records of all phases of an investigation should result in competent testimony in court that is not embarrassing. Investigators must be aware that their notes may be subpoenaed into court during the discovery process.

Reconstructing the Crime Scene

During the crime scene investigation the investigators and criminalists attempt to determine how the crime happened. Once the crime scene is closed down, investigators attempt to reconstruct the crime scene to study it and review and test theories. A definition of **crime scene reconstruction** is this: "The use of scientific methods, physical evidence, deductive and inductive reasoning, and their interrelationships to gain explicit knowledge of the series of events that surround the commission of a crime."[25] In order to reconstruct the crime scene, the investigators use all the information and documentation they collected while processing the crime scene, including the photographs, sketches, scale models, and notes.

A recent article in the *Journal of Forensic Identification* explains crime scene reconstruction and recommends that the scientific method become the standard methodology for this process. Investigators conduct informal crime scene reconstruction while processing, documenting, and collecting evidence; this process is often subconscious. In contrast, the formal, second phase of crime scene reconstruction is a conscious process. It takes place after the processing of the scene, analysis of the evidence, and completion of all investigative procedures. The methodology for crime scene reconstruction needs standardization for it to mature.

The scientific method is a proven systematic process of problem solving that follows six steps: stating the problem; developing a hypothesis for the explanation or solution of the problem; testing the hypothesis by experimentation; formulating a theory; using theories to predict events; and considering as a scientific law a theory that holds up under testing as an accurate predictor.[26]

The hypothesis in crime scene reconstruction needs to be narrow in scope and precise. The investigator must give equal emphasis to all feasible and reasonable possibilities when considering answers to questions. Opinions must rest on an analysis of the physical evidence and known facts. Results must be reviewable, testable, and repeatable. In addition, opinions must always be open to new knowledge. The use of the scientific method can overcome obstacles to the admission of testimony.

The Association for Crime Scene Reconstruction (ACSR) is a professional organization of law enforcement investigators, forensic experts, and professionals interested in crime scene reconstruction.

INVESTIGATIONS ON THE NET

Association for Crime Scene Reconstruction
http://www.acsr.com

For an up-to-date list of Web links, go to
http://info.wadsworth.com/dempsey

PROCESSING CRIME SCENE EVIDENCE

The American Society for Industrial Security, a professional association for members of the private security industry, reported the following in its *Basic Guidelines for Security Investigations:* "Collection and preservation of evidence are only a part of any professional investigation, but they frequently prove to be the most important part in solving a crime and prosecuting a suspect. An otherwise efficient investigation can be ruined by careless evidence or inadequate knowledge of this vital aspect of the work."[27]

This section discusses the processing of items of evidence collected at the crime scene, including the principle of chain of custody, marking evidence, and packaging evidence, and types of evidence found at the crime scene, including fingerprints, blood, bite marks and bruises, soil, hair, shoe or tire impressions, tool fragments and tool marks, glass, and paint. Specific information on the marking and packaging of many types of physical evidence can be found at http://www.info.wadsworth.com/dempsey.

Processing Items of Evidence

To conform to legal requirements related to its introduction in a judicial proceeding, the investigator must be able to identify each piece of evidence, sometimes even years after it was collected; describe the location and condition of the item at the time it was collected;

assist in establishing that from the time of its collection until presentation in court, the evidence was continuously in proper custody (chain of custody); and assist in describing any changes that may have occurred in the evidence between the time of collection and its subsequent introduction as evidence in court.[28]

Chain of Custody

Chain of custody is the term used to describe the identification and control of evidence from the time it is collected at the scene until it is entered into evidence in court. The legal chain of custody must be maintained at all times. The chain of custody involves receipting for any movements of the evidence. For example, when the investigator brings an item of evidence to the crime lab, it is noted and receipted for by the evidence storage clerk; when the evidence storage clerk gives the evidence to a criminalist, this is noted and the criminalist must sign for the evidence; and so on with every contact with the evidence.

Chain of custody is one of the most crucial issues in crime scenes. If officers fail to follow chain of custody procedures critical evidence may be suppressed. In addition, if chain of custody issues are raised in a trial, the jury may suspect the prosecution's case. An example of chain of custody problems occurred in the O. J. Simpson case when admissibility and weight of evidence became a significant problem because of delays by the police in immediately booking evidence.

The computer has made the process of maintaining complete and efficient chain of custody and property management inventory easier. A full line of inventory systems, including bar code equipment and software, reduces the labor involved in booking evidence and issuing it out and back in again.[29]

Marking Evidence

Evidence must be marked to ensure that its identity can be legally established in court. When the evidence is presented in court, the investigator will be asked to prove it is the same as that found at the scene. Normal descriptions of the items of evidence are not sufficient; distinctive symbols, marks, or initials should be used. These can be written, scratched, or carved on the evidence but should be as small as possible and appear in a manner and location that does not damage the item or alter its value. For evidence that is placed in an evidence container (plastic, paper, or box), the container must be marked for identification even if the item inside is also marked. When property or evidence tags are placed on large items, the tag must be securely attached and marked as well. All items of evidence, their serial numbers and distinctive characteristics, identification markings by investigators, and so on must be recorded in the investigator's notes and all reports about the case.

Packaging Evidence

Evidence must be preserved in its natural state. Each item must be preserved and packaged separately. For example, a bloody knife found at a crime scene cannot be packaged in the same envelope as a bloody shirt found at the same crime scene. If this was done, the blood from the knife could contaminate the blood on the shirt and vice versa.

Various types of packages or containers can be used. The following are some of the ones recommended for specific types of evidence:

- Plastic or cellophane envelopes are suitable for small dry objects.
- Paper envelopes are suitable for folded paper bundles containing very small items or powdery material. It is important that the envelopes and all corners be properly sealed. Paper envelopes should not be used for fiber evidence; a vial or pillbox should be used instead.
- Vials, pillboxes, capsules, and similar containers are suitable for certain types of evidence.
- Garments and large exhibits may be placed in bags or rolled in paper.
- Paper or plastic envelopes may be sealed around the ends of large exhibits, such as tools or automobile bumpers, with plastic tape to prevent the loss of any evidence that is adhering to the exhibit.
- Plastic bags should never be used for damp or biological evidence because of bacterial or fungal actions.
- Clean and new containers should always be used to prevent contamination.

There are many different ways to collect and process evidence. A recent article in *Law Enforcement Technology* mentions the use of "super glue" to process and develop latent fingerprints; using evidence tape to collect trace evidence such as hairs, fibers, and tiny pieces of debris because it has an aggressive adhesive; and other innovative, simple procedures.[30]

Evidence should be stored in a safe, evidence vault, locker, or some other location where unauthorized persons do not have access.

Fingerprints

Fingerprints are the most useful evidence for suspect identification at a crime scene and the subsequent conviction of the offender. The need for improved detection of fingerprint evidence has been a driving force in the development and deployment of advanced crime scene technology.

A fingerprint consists of skin oils, perspiration, and sometimes contamination left on a surface. The traditional method of "lifting" fingerprints involves dusting the surface, usually with a black powder that preferentially sticks to the print details. After the print is developed onto the powder, the print is photographed and then lifted from the surface with adhesive tape, then placed on a white card for maximum contrast and classified by a fingerprint technician.

There are certain problems with the traditional lifting of latent prints. Generally, the prints must be fairly fresh. Also, they cannot be lifted from textured, sticky, or oily surfaces, or even certain plastics, because the powder sticks to the background as well as to the print. Finally, the print can only be lifted once, leaving no margin for error.

A new technique called *photonics* is addressing this problem. This technology is essentially the manipulation of light to allow a criminalist to see what was not previously visible. Photonics can be used directly at the crime scene to find critical pieces of evidence that can't be tested and identified by other means. Photonics can enhance the contrast between the evidence and background, so that microscopic or otherwise hidden evidence becomes much more visible. This is accomplished by using differences in fluorescence, reflection, or absorption between the evidence and background surfaces.[31]

Several fluorescence-enhancing chemicals have been developed to process potential fingerprint evidence at crime scenes using photonics technology. The most popular of these is Redwop (*powder* spelled backwards). Redwop is specifically made for fingerprint detection. Like black powder, it sticks to a fingerprint, but its fluorescence makes it very easy to differentiate from background scatter, particularly on textured or otherwise difficult surfaces. Another fluorescent technique uses super glue (actually, *cyanoacrylate*). In this application, the surface under

---

TECHNOLOGY IN INVESTIGATIONS

The Power of Fluorescent Print Detection: The Polly Klass Case

The power of fluorescent print detection was demonstrated in the Polly Klaas kidnap-murder case in Petaluma, California. The young victim was abducted from her bedroom by an unknown intruder. Police used black powder methods to discover several prints, none of which matched the subsequently identified suspect.

In an effort to locate more evidence, the FBI's Evidence Response Team (ERT) was called upon. ERTs are trained and equipped with the latest forensic technology. Agents from the San Francisco ERT processed the scene using an Omniprint 1000. After the victim's wooden bed frame was dusted with

Redwop, illumination at 450nm revealed a clear palmprint.

A suspect was subsequently arrested, but he denied any knowledge of the crime. However, when learning of the palmprint evidence, he admitted to the crime and directed investigators to the location of the victim's body. The palmprint was the only print that matched the suspect and could not have been found by traditional fingerprint techniques.

SOURCE: Mary C. Nolte, "The Role of the Photon in Modern Forensics," *Law and Order*, Nov. 1994, pp. 51–54.

examination is first exposed to super glue fumes. A fluorescent dye such as Rhodamine 6G is then rinsed over the surface. The dye adheres to the super glue detail and not the background, allowing imaging of the print using blue or green illumination. Fingerprint analysis and comparison is discussed more fully in chapter 6, "Criminalistics and Technology."

Blood

Blood can be classified as having come from humans or animals. Human bloodstains can be classified into one of the four international blood groups: A, B, AB, or O. Bloodstains may be valuable evidence in many crimes. Although conventional blood typing cannot identify blood as having come from a particular individual, race, or gender, it can be helpful in eliminating suspects. The development of DNA technology (genetic fingerprinting) has begun to change the role of blood evidence. DNA will be discussed in depth in chapter 6.

The physical appearance of the blood can sometimes be useful. Whether it is in the form of a pool, drops, stains, or splashes can give investigators important information about the crime. Sometimes the appearance can also help to establish the approximate time the crime occurred.

Bloodstain pattern analysis is the study of the bloodstains and bloodstain patterns resulting when liquid blood is acted on by physical forces and deposited on various surfaces, including the clothing of the individuals present at the crime scene. When examined by a qualified analyst these bloodstain patterns can yield valuable information about the events that led to their creation. The information gained can then be used for the reconstruction of the incident and the evaluation of the statements of the witnesses and the crime participants.[32]

Richard Saferstein, former chief forensic scientist at the New Jersey State Police Laboratory, states that the location, distribution, and appearance of bloodstains and spatters may be useful for interpreting and reconstructing the events that must have occurred to have produced the bleeding. He states also that a thorough analysis of the significance of the position and shape of blood patterns with respect to their origin and trajectory is exceedingly complex and requires the services of an expert examiner.[33] An in-depth study of this subject has been published.[34]

A professional association of forensic experts specializing in the field of bloodstain pattern analysis is the International Association of Bloodstain Pattern Analysts (IABPA).

 INVESTIGATIONS ON THE NET

International Association of Bloodstain Pattern Analysts
http://www.iabpa.org

For an up-to-date list of Web links, go to
http://info.wadsworth.com/dempsey

Bite Marks and Bruises

Bite marks on a victim's body can be instrumental in murder cases because the bite pattern on the body can be matched to a suspect's dental pattern. Bruises on a body can also be important in these cases, as well as in child abuse cases. The use of the photonics technology described earlier can detect bite patterns and subdermal bruising, even many days after the original body trauma.[35]

Soil

The forensic examination of soil can be instrumental in solving a case. Because of the nature of soil, it is imperative that investigators properly document the exact location from which they collect samples. Hand-drawn or detailed commercial maps best illustrate specimen collection sites and their spatial relation-

---

EXHIBIT 3.6   **Types of Bloodstain Patterns**

- *Smear (swipe)* An object such as a bloody hand or bloody clothing is moved across a surface.
- *Wipe* When blood is already on the object or surface and the pattern is disturbed by an otherwise bloodless object moving through it.
- *Smudge* Activity has obliterated what could have been fine detail such as a bloody or latent fingerprint.

SOURCE: Larry Ragle, *Crime Scene: From Fingerprints to Autopsies to DNA Testing: A Fascinating, In-Depth Introduction to the World of Forensic Investigation* (New York: Avon, 1995).

YOU ARE THERE!

Bite Marks on Victim Lead to Murderer

Carla Terry was found murdered in January 1991. Alfred Swinton was suspected of being the murderer, but it took seven years and the development of new forensic techniques and software to confirm it.

When paramedics found Terry, they tried to revive her, took her to the hospital, and cleaned her up, unwittingly destroying forensic evidence. For seven years, prosecutors suspected Swinton, but felt there was not sufficient evidence to indict. The case went cold until 1998 when the district attorney brought the case to Dr. Gus Karazulas, chief forensic odontologist at the Connecticut State Police Forensic Science Lab. Karazulas used new, previously unavailable image-processing software to make the features of bite marks on Terry's body more visible. He then laid an image of Swinton's bite pattern, using newly created software, on top of the enhanced image of the bite marks. Swinton's bite pattern matched the bite mark at fifteen points of comparison, and prosecutors had the evidence they needed to bring him to trial.

In March 2000, a jury found Alfred Swinton guilty of murdering Carla Terry and sentenced him to sixty years in prison. Swinton is also a suspect in the deaths of seventeen other women.

SOURCE: "Police Forensic Science Lab Uses Image-Enhancing Software to Identify Killer," *Police Chief*, June 2001, p. 78.

ships. Questioned samples taken from the ground surface, such as those taken from the tread pattern of a shoe, should be compared to known specimens collected from like places. In addition, because time governs the factors that affect soil formation, timeliness in evidence collection is important.[36]

To be sure that examiners get an adequate representation of soil variability, investigators should collect a sufficient number of known soil specimens at crime scenes and from surrounding areas. Establishing the uniqueness of the soil at a particular location to the exclusion of others greatly strengthens the association between specimens. In most cases, a 35-millimeter film canister of soil from each location is sufficient for comparison.

All samples should be packaged dry, sealed, and properly labeled. Investigators must allow moist soil samples to air-dry overnight at room temperature before packaging. And they should not overlook the collection of alibi soil samples. They should collect these alibi samples from areas that suspects could claim as the source of the questioned soil. A suspect may contend, for example, that soil recovered from the shovel used to dig a victim's grave actually came from a garden.

Scent Evidence

Scent is defined as the bacterial, cellular, and vaporous debris enshrouding the individual. This debris is the result of dead or dying skin cells, which the body sheds at a rate of approximately forty-thousand each minute. Air currents project the scent away from the body. The debris becomes deposited in the environment as a scent trail. The uniqueness of human scent permits law enforcement to use scent evidence for several purposes, including following a suspect directly from a crime scene; determining a suspect's direction of travel from a crime scene, or even locating additional evidence the suspect leaves behind; and locating and recovering missing persons, whether dead or alive.[37]

Dogs, particularly bloodhounds, because of their extraordinary sense of smell, are very useful for investigators in following scent evidence. A properly trained dog can successfully follow trails that are up to ten days old, but they work best in the first twenty-four hours after the scent was deposited. Anything a suspect has touched, worn, or eliminated (for example, bodily fluids, including blood and urine) can serve as scent evidence, but articles of clothing worn close to the skin are most useful. Investigators or evidence technicians should collect the scent evidence and place it in clean paper bags.

Hair

Hair can be classified as having come from humans or animals, but technology has not yet progressed to the point where it can be stated that a hair definitely came from a specific person. Currently, hair found at a crime

INVESTIGATIONS ON THE NET

National Police Bloodhound Association
http://www.icubed.com/~npba

Law Enforcement Bloodhound Association
http://www.leba98.com

For an up-to-date list of Web links, go to
http://info.wadsworth.com/dempsey

YOU ARE THERE!

Scent-Discriminating Canines Find the Evidence

In July 1998, a migrant worker in Northern California lured two men, a woman, and the woman's son and daughter into a cow pasture, where he had prepared a gravesite two weeks earlier. First, the suspect shot the men and placed them in the grave. Then, he restrained the woman and sexually assaulted her in front of her two small children. While the suspect bludgeoned the boy and buried him, the woman managed to escape. After burying the young girl alive, the suspect fled.

Within twenty-four hours of this quadruple murder, scent-discriminating dogs found the material used to restrain the woman, located the grave site, and provided investigators with leads indicating the suspect's whereabouts. By following the suspect's scent trail and using eyewitnesses' accounts, investigators identified a pay telephone the suspect had used. From information obtained from subpoenaed telephone records, they apprehended the suspect in Southern California.

SOURCE: Robert Hunt, "The Benefits of Scent Evidence," *FBI Law Enforcement Bulletin*, Nov. 1999, pp. 15–18.

scene can be examined with one of three results: *inconclusive* (it is neither similar or dissimilar to the suspect's hair); *exclusionary* (it cannot be considered similar to the suspect's hair); *similar* (it is possible that the hair left at the scene came from the suspect). This last result is corroborative only, never conclusive by itself.

The part of the body that the hair came from can be determined based on the hair's length, size, stiffness, and general appearance. The examination of hair can determine the person's race, but not gender or age. It can be established whether or not the hair was pulled out forcibly if the root end is present. Hair evidence is commonly found in many crimes, particularly homicide and sexual assault cases. Human hair falls naturally from the head at a constant rate, so a suspect may unwittingly leave a hair sample at a crime scene. Or hair may be pulled from a suspect's head during a violent offense. In addition, in cases where victims are struck with weapons or blunt objects, hair may stick to the surface of the weapon.

Sometimes hair contains debris, such as grease globules, cosmetics, oily bodily secretions, and dust. Examination can indicate that hair has been treated chemically—that is, dyed, bleached, or straightened. At a crime scene, investigators search for hair samples on furniture, the floor, and other objects. Hair collected from different locations should be packaged separately.

Shoe or Tire Impressions

Shoe or tire impressions can be very important in locating a suspect and placing that person at the scene of a crime. Impressions from shoes or tires are often found where the suspect of the crime hastily entered or left the scene and overlooked the impressions. After photographing, measuring, and sketching the impression, investigators preserve the evidence by making a plaster cast of it.

Shoeprints and tire prints are of two types: *contamination prints* and *impressions*. Contamination prints result when the shoe or tire has substance on it, such as dirt or blood, that leaves a print on a hard surface. Impressions, in contrast, are left on a soft surface such as sand or mud.

A new computer software program developed by the police in Scottsdale, Arizona, the Shoeware Linking and Identification Program (SLIP), simplifies the process of identifying this kind of evidence from a crime scene. The software includes all areas of the sole of a piece of footwear, as well as all logos or text on it.[38]

Tool Fragments and Tool Marks

Pieces of tools (tool fragments) that might have been damaged during a crime may later be matched to a broken tool in the possession of a suspect.

Tool marks may be left if windows or doors have been forced with screwdrivers or pry bars, locks have been snipped with bolt cutters, or safes have been hit with hammers, chisels, or punches. All of these tools leave marks that, under favorable conditions, can be identified just as definitively as fingerprints. Tool marks are most commonly found in burglaries. They may be found on windowsills and window frames, doors and door frames, cash register drawers, file cabinets, or cash boxes or safes.

Tool marks are of two types: *impressions* and *sliding* or *cutting marks*. For example, a hammer that has been pounded on a surface does not hit directly, so it leaves both some sliding marks and an impression.

Glass

Glass is an excellent source of positive identification because two pieces of glass rarely contain the same proportions of sand, metal, oxides, or carbonates.

When a criminal breaks a window, minute pieces of glass can usually be found in his clothing or footwear, or on the surface of his clothing. The area of the actual break in glass is also critical in the examination. Investigators can determine whether the glass was broken from the inside or outside of a building. Pieces of glass can also be processed for fingerprint evidence.

In hit-and-run accidents (cases where the driver flees the scene of the accident), pieces of glass can be used to show common origin by means of a jigsaw match with the glass from a suspect's vehicle.

Paint

Paint is frequently transferred from one object to another during the commission of a crime. Paint may be smeared on tools during unlawful entry or chipped off surfaces. It may flake off automobiles during hasty getaways after an impact.

Evidence Checklist

It's a good idea for investigators to maintain a checklist for physical evidence that can be referred to during the search for, collecting, and processing of physical evidence at the crime scene to ensure that no necessary steps or procedures are omitted. The investigator can use the FBI guidelines shown in Exhibit 3.7 to construct such a checklist.

THE ROLE OF THE PRIVATE INVESTIGATOR IN CRIME SCENE CASES

Often, a defense attorney will hire a private investigator to reinvestigate the police investigation that resulted in the arrest of the attorney's client. In these situations, the private investigator canvasses the area where the crime took place in an attempt to find new witnesses. He or she also reinterviews police witnesses and victims, as well as the defendant.

Private investigators seek access to all of the police reports in a case through the discovery or disclosure process. They review the reports and look for inconsistencies and mistakes. Often, they attempt to re-create the crime scene to test certain theories or hypotheses.

In the O. J. Simpson murder case, the defense attorneys hired numerous private investigators, including John McNally, a former New York City detective, to reinvestigate the murders of Nicole Brown Simpson and Ronald Goldman.[39]

In another example, Richie Haeg, a private investigator from Coram, New York, was hired by Amy Fisher's attorney to reinvestigate the shooting of Mary Jo Buttafuocco in the notorious Amy Fisher—Lethal Lolita case. Based on Haeg's investigation, the Nassau County district attorney allowed Fisher to plead guilty to a much lesser crime than the one for which she had originally been charged. By examining the medical and evidence reports, Haeg was able to convince authorities that the girl's account of her actions were credible. Fisher had stated that she had hit Mary Jo Buttafuocco on the side of the head with the gun and the gun accidentally discharged. The medical evidence—a grazing wound to the side of the head—and the presence of broken pieces of the gun on the Buttafuocco porch, backed up her story.

Haeg's investigation also was instrumental in having Joey Buttafuocco, Fisher's paramour, imprisoned for statutory rape. His investigators visited numerous motels on Long Island and obtained copies of the registration slips that Buttafuocco signed when he checked into these motels with Fisher.

EXHIBIT 3.7   FBI Guidelines for the Crime Scene Search

A crime scene search is a planned, coordinated, and legal search by law enforcement officials to locate physical evidence.

Basic Premises

- The best search options are typically the most difficult and time-consuming.
- Physical evidence cannot be overdocumented.
- There is only one chance to search the scene properly.
- There are two search approaches: conduct a cautious search of visible areas, avoiding evidence loss or contamination; after the cautious search, conduct a vigorous search of concealed areas.

Preparation

- Obtain a search warrant, if necessary.
- Discuss the search with involved personnel before arrival at the scene, if possible.
- Establish a command headquarters for communication and decision making in major or complicated crime scene searches.
- Ensure that personnel are aware of the types of evidence usually encountered and the proper handling of the evidence.
- Make preliminary personnel assignments before arrival at the scene, if possible.
- Ensure that assignments are in keeping with the attitude, aptitude, training, and experience of personnel. Personnel may be assigned two or more responsibilities: person in charge (scene security, administrative log, preliminary survey; narrative description; problem resolution; final decision making); photographer (photography and log); sketch preparer (sketch and log); evidence recorder (evidence custodian and log).
- Establish communication between medical examiners, laboratory personnel, and prosecuting attorneys so that questions during the crime scene search can be resolved.
- Coordinate agreements with all agencies in multi-jurisdictional crime scene searches.
- Accumulate evidence collection and packaging materials and equipment.
- Prepare the paperwork to document the search.

- Provide protective clothing, communication, lighting, shelter, transportation, equipment, food, water, medical assistance, and security for personnel.
- In prolonged searches, use shifts of two or more teams. Transfer paperwork and responsibility in a preplanned manner from one team to the next.

Approach

- Be alert for evidence.
- Take extensive notes.
- Consider the safety of all personnel.

Secure and Protect

- Take control of the scene immediately.
- Determine the extent to which the scene has been protected. Obtain information from personnel who have knowledge of the original condition.
- Designate one person to be in charge of final decision making and problem resolution.
- Continue to take extensive notes.
- Keep out unauthorized personnel.
- Record who enters and leaves.

Preliminary Survey

The survey is an organizational stage to plan for the search.

- Cautiously walk through the scene.
- Maintain administrative and emotional control.
- Select a narrative technique, such as written, audio, or video.
- Take preliminary photographs.
- Delineate the extent of the search area. Usually, expand the initial perimeter.
- Organize methods and procedures.
- Recognize special problem areas.
- Identify and protect transient physical evidence.
- Determine personnel and equipment needs. Make specific assignments.
- Develop a general theory of the crime.
- Take extensive notes to document the scene, physical and environmental conditions, and personnel movements.

Exhibit 3.7 continued

Evaluate Physical Evidence Possibilities

This evaluation begins upon arrival at the scene and becomes detailed in the preliminary survey stage.

- Ensure that the collection and packaging materials and equipment are sufficient.
- Focus first on evidence that could be lost. Leave the least transient evidence last.
- Ensure that all personnel consider the variety of possible evidence, not only evidence within their specialties.
- Search the easily accessible areas and progress to out-of-view locations. Look for hidden items.
- Evaluate whether evidence appears to have been moved inadvertently.
- Evaluate whether the scene appears contrived.

Narrative

The narrative is a running description of the crime scene.

- Use a systematic approach in the narrative.
- Nothing is insignificant to record if it catches one's attention.
- Under most circumstances, do not collect evidence during the narrative.
- Use photographs and sketches to supplement, not substitute for, the narrative.
- The narrative should include: case identifier; date, time, and location; weather and lighting conditions; identity and assignments of personnel; and condition and position of evidence.

Photography

- Photograph the crime scene as soon as possible.
- Prepare a photographic log that records all photographs and a description and location of evidence.
- Establish a progression of overall, medium, and close-up views of the crime scene.
- Photograph from eye level to represent the normal view.
- Photograph the most fragile areas of the crime scene first.
- Photograph all stages of the crime scene investigation, including discoveries.
- Photograph the condition of evidence before recovery.

- Photograph the evidence in detail and include a scale, the photographer's initials, and the date.
- When a scale is used, first take a photograph without the scale.
- Photograph the interior crime scene in an overall and overlapping series using a wide-angle lens.
- Photograph the exterior crime scene, establishing the location of the scene by a series of overall photographs including a landmark.
- Photographs should have 360 degrees of coverage. Consider using aerial photography.
- Photograph entrances and exits.
- Photograph important evidence twice: a medium-distance photograph that shows the evidence and its position to other evidence; a close-up photograph that includes a scale and fills the frame.
- Acquire prior photographs, blueprints, or maps of the scene.

Sketch

The sketch establishes a permanent record of items, conditions, and distance and size relationships.

- Sketches supplement photographs.
- Sketch number designations should coordinate with the evidence log number designations.
- Sketches are normally not drawn to scale. However, the sketch should have measurements and details for a drawn-to-scale diagram, if necessary.
- The sketch should include: case identifier; date, time, and location; weather and lighting conditions; identity and assignments of personnel; dimensions of rooms, furniture, doors, and windows; distances between objects, persons, bodies, entrances, and exits; measurements showing the location of evidence (each object should be located by two measurements from nonmovable items such as doors or walls); and key, legend, compass orientation, scale, scale disclaimer, or a combination of these features.

Crime Scene Search, Record, and Physical Evidence Collection

- Use a search pattern such as a grid, strip or lane, or spiral.
- Search from the general to the specific for evidence.

Exhibit 3.7 continued

- Be alert for all evidence.
- Search entrances and exits.
- Photograph all items before collection and notate the photographic log.
- Mark evidence locations on the sketch.
- Complete the evidence log with notations for each item of evidence. If feasible, have one person serve as evidence custodian.
- Two persons should observe evidence in place, during recovery, and being marked for identification. If feasible, mark directly on the evidence.
- Wear gloves to avoid leaving fingerprints.
- Do not excessively handle the evidence after recovery.
- Seal all evidence packages at the crime scene.
- Obtain known standards such as fiber samples from a known carpet.
- Make a complete evaluation of the crime scene.
- Constantly check paperwork, packaging, and other information for errors.

Final Survey

The final survey is a review of all aspects of the search.
- Discuss the search with all personnel.
- Ensure that all documentation is correct and complete.
- Photograph the scene showing the final condition.

- Ensure that all evidence is secured.
- Ensure that all equipment is retrieved.
- Ensure that hiding places or difficult access areas have not been overlooked.

Release

- Release the crime scene after the final survey.
- Crime scene release documentation should include the time and date of release, to whom released, and by whom released.
- Ensure that the evidence is collected according to legal requirements, documented, and marked for identification.
- Consider the need for specialists such as a blood-pattern analyst or a medical examiner to observe the scene before it is released.
- Once the scene has been released, reentry may require a warrant.
- The scene should be released only when all personnel are satisfied that the scene was searched correctly and completely.
- Only the person in charge should release the scene.

SOURCE: Federal Bureau of Investigation, "Crime Scene Search," *Handbook of Forensic Sciences* (Washington, DC: Federal Bureau of Investigation, 2001); see http://www.fbi.gov/hq/lab/handbook/scene1.htm.

SUMMARY

The most horrific crime scene investigation ever to be conducted in U.S. history commenced on September 11, 2001. The inner perimeter of the crime scene was dispersed throughout the eastern coast of our nation, from New York City to Virginia. The entire crime scene encompassed the whole world. This crime scene involved the joint efforts of all of the investigating agencies in this nation and essentially followed the patterns depicted in this chapter.

This chapter has shown that one of the most crucial stages of a criminal investigation is the response to and processing of the crime scene, which is the location where the crime was committed. In the American criminal justice system, the criminal investigation generally falls under the purview of the public police who respond to the crime scene, attempt to arrest the suspect or suspects of the crime, and conduct the actual investigation of the crime by processing the crime scene for physical evidence, interviewing possible witnesses, interrogating possible suspects, and arresting the suspect.

This chapter defined the crime scene and discussed the duties of all police personnel there, including the first responding patrol officer, the investigator, and the criminalist or crime scene unit. It discussed the preservation of the crime scene evidence by protecting it and establishing a temporary headquarters or command post. It looked at processing the crime scene, including the tasks of photographing, sketching, and searching for physical evidence at the crime scene, recording all these activities, and reconstructing the crime. The chapter discussed processing physical evidence at the crime scene, particularly fingerprints, blood, hair, fibers, soil, bite marks, tool fragments, and tool marks.

LEARNING CHECK

1. What are the primary duties of the first patrol officer at the crime scene?
2. What are the primary duties of the investigator at the crime scene?
3. Discuss the methods police agencies can take to protect the crime scene and maintain its pristine nature.
4. Name the tasks that must be performed at the crime scene and briefly explain each one.
5. Name several types of evidence that may be present at a crime scene and explain the value of each in the successful investigation of the crime.

APPLICATION EXERCISE

At approximately 11 p.m. on Sunday, June 12, 1994, thirty-four-year-old Nicole Brown Simpson, whom the media described as a stunning blonde, and a male acquaintance, Ronald Goldman, age twenty-six, were found savagely murdered outside Simpson's $500,000 condo in Brentwood, California. The Los Angeles Police Department responded to the crime scene, processed it, and found key evidence.

Research this case through local or national newspapers and prepare a report on the crime scene procedures conducted by the police and the importance of the evidence they collected and preserved.

Note: When researching a case through the media it is important to realize that early accounts may have significant errors of fact because reporters need to meet deadlines in submitting their stories. Therefore, it is necessary to follow the case through the media for several weeks.

WEB EXERCISE

Use the Internet to find and research the 1932 murder of the child of the famous U.S. aviator Charles A. Lindbergh. Obtain the facts of the crime and details about the crime scene. Analyze the crime scene work done by the police and make specific criticisms of their work based on the knowledge you gained from this chapter.

KEY TERMS

bloodstain pattern analysis	criminalist
chain of custody	first responding patrol officer
contaminated	forensic photogrammetry
crime scene	photographic log
crime scene reconstruction	primary, lead, or case investigator
crime scene sketch	pristine
crime scene unit	temporary headquarters
crime scene vehicle	

CASE MANAGEMENT AND REPORT WRITING

4

CHAPTER GOALS

1. To define and show you the importance of case management systems in investigations and the U.S. legal system

2. To emphasize the importance of proper note-taking procedures in investigating

3. To explain and give you samples of the various official reports used in investigations

4. To show you the importance of maintaining a well-documented case folder in investigations

5. To show you the basics of report writing and, we hope, make you a better report writer

INTRODUCTION

In May 2001 Timothy McVeigh was scheduled to be executed for the murder of 168 people in the 1995 bombing of the Alfred P. Murrah Federal Building in Oklahoma City. Just days before the scheduled execution, the FBI admitted that it had inadvertently withheld information from McVeigh's defense attorneys. Specifically, it had withheld thousands of case reports made during the investigation of the bombing trial. The execution was postponed, and there was tremendous criticism of the FBI.

Essentially, the FBI had admitted a *Brady* violation to the discovery requirements of the U.S. legal system based on the landmark U.S. Supreme Court case *Brady v. Maryland*.[1] *Brady* requires that all evidence favorable to an accused person must be turned over to his or her defense attorneys at trial.

Subsequently, the courts ruled that the information that the FBI had withheld was not exculpatory or impeaching toward the evidence that had led to McVeigh's guilty verdict; the withholding of it did not change the facts in the case.

The investigator's job is to collect information to solve or clear a case. It involves among other functions searching for and collecting physical evidence, interviewing victims and witnesses, and interrogating suspects. However, without appropriate and effective case management and report writing procedures, the investigator's efforts would be futile. Case management is the procedure for collecting, recording, organizing, and preserving all the various information gathered in an investigation. It involves officially documenting all incidents and investigatory actions in a case. This chapter defines case management and explains its importance, purpose, and procedures associated with it.

The chapter covers note taking and writing official investigative reports, both preformatted reports, including incident or complaint reports and follow-up reports, and reports to supervisors or clients, including preliminary, progress, and final reports. It also discusses the preparation of observations by investigators and the basics of describing persons and property. It covers the case folder and its contents and organization. The chapter also discusses the legal requirements for case management under *Brady*.

It should be noted that most police and private investigating agencies have their own case management procedures that they have developed and that work best for them. The case management procedures discussed in this chapter—including specific forms and reports—are generic in nature and have worked well for this author.

CASE MANAGEMENT

Case management is defined as the procedure for collecting, recording, organizing, and preserving all the various information gathered in an investigation. In effect, it is an official history of the case.

Case management is necessary in all types of investigations. No one, no matter how intelligent, can remember all the details in a case. Successful case management begins at the beginning of an investigation and continues until the conclusion of the case. It involves note taking, report writing, and maintaining an up-to-date, accurate case file or **case folder** that contains the incident report and all follow-up reports on the investigation including the interview and interrogation reports. It also contains all official records, photos, sketches, and management reports, including the case index sheet, the investigative plan, and the assignment sheet.

The ultimate goal of the case management system is to allow the presentation of the information collected to a jury in a criminal case or to a client in a private case. The case management system involves all the facts related to the incident under investigation and all investigatory steps and facts uncovered in investigating the case.

Case management includes the following activities:

- *Taking notes* on the facts observed at the scene of a crime or incident and taking notes on canvasses and interviews of victims, witnesses, or other persons involved in the investigation and the interrogation of suspects

- *Preparing official reports* that document the activities performed by the investigator

- *Maintaining a separate case folder* that contains all the reports, documents, tapes, and other information documenting the investigation

Purposes of Case Management

Case management serves several purposes.

First, it keeps track of what has been done and what remains to be done on a case. The investigator working the case can review the case management folder to refresh his or her memory or to reflect on facts that have been uncovered. Trials and hearings often occur a year or more after an investigation is concluded, and investigators must be able to refresh their memories before testifying; the case folder is critical here. In addition, other investigators and investigative supervisors or managers can use the case management folder to review the facts and progress of the case.

Second, if an investigator charged with a particular case retires, is transferred, or cannot complete an investigation for another reason, the case will be turned over to another investigator. In the event that a new investigator is assigned to the case, he or she need only read the case management folder to get a handle on it. Without a case management system and effective report writing systems, all the information already gathered would be lost. The newly assigned investigator would have to start the investigation all over again, including reinterviewing all persons connected to the case.

Third, the case management system serves as the basis for the adjudication of the case for the prosecutor or other appropriate attorney. It also serves as the basis of the report to the client in a private investigation case.

Finally, the case management system can be subject to the discovery process in the U.S. legal system.

Since the information in the case management system is subject to discovery, it is important now to spend a few minutes discussing what discovery is. **_Discovery_** can be defined as a pretrial procedure whereby the opposing litigants supply information to each other that is necessary to their positions at trial.

In a criminal case, the prosecution is obligated to share information with the defense attorneys and defendants during discovery. Specific types of information are made available before trial, including results of any tests conducted, psychiatric reports, and transcripts or tape-recorded statements made by the defendant, and any evidence favorable to the accused either because it is exculpatory (tending to exonerate a person of allegations of wrongdoing) or because it is

impeaching. Discovery is commonly known in U.S. criminal procedure as **_Brady_ material** after the landmark U.S. Supreme Court case described in the introduction to this chapter. Under the rules of _Brady,_ the accused is entitled to know what evidence of guilt the prosecutor has so that his attorney can prepare an adequate defense. In other words, the rules of criminal procedure are tilted in favor of the defendant. The rationale behind this is that presumably the prosecutor has more resources to investigate the case than the defendant does.

Discovery in a civil process can take a number of forms. One of the more common forms is a _deposition,_ also known as an examination before trial (EBT), which can be taken in two ways. One way to accomplish a deposition is to have a witness appear at the office of one of the attorneys in the case and answer questions put to him or her by the attorney. The witness is under oath, and a stenographer records the questions and responses verbatim. Another way is to question a witness in the presence of both attorneys; the witness is subjected to direct questioning by one and cross-examination by the other. As in the first instance, everything said is recorded. Like all forms of discovery, a witness's testimony may be so devastating to one party's case that the attorney may urge her client to reach a settlement with the other party rather than go to trial.

A second form of discovery is an _interrogatory_. An interrogatory is a series of written questions directed to one of the parties in the case by the other party. Unless the questions are answered, the person may be cited for contempt. Truthful answers must be given because the same questions may be asked at trial while the individual is under oath.

A third form of discovery in a civil case involves the production of physical evidence by one of the parties. The judge may issue a subpoena _duces tecum,_ which is a court order requiring a person to appear in court and produce specified documents pertinent to the case.

In civil litigation discovery is designed to expedite the legal process. If certain facts can be agreed upon by both parties before the trial, these facts will only need to be recorded as having been stipulated (agreed to) as true by both sides. In a personal injury case, for example, the extent of the plaintiff's injury might be

YOU ARE THERE!
Two Landmark Cases on Discovery

BRADY V. MARYLAND

A man named Brady was charged with murder. He took the stand in his own defense and admitted to participating in the crime, but declared that his confederate, Boblit, was the one who actually killed the victim. Various statements had been made to police and prosecutors by Boblit. The prosecutor denied Brady access to these statements, alleging confidentiality. Following Brady's conviction, some of this evidence came to light and proved favorable and exculpatory to Brady. He sought an appeal, claiming that he had been denied due process because these important statements had been withheld during his trial. The Supreme Court agreed with Brady and overturned his murder conviction, stating that: "suppression by prosecution of evidence favorable to an accused upon request violates due process where evidence is material either to guilt or to punishment, irrespective of good faith or bad faith of prosecution."

Based on this case, there are three components of a *Brady* violation: the evidence at issue must be favorable to the accused, either because it is exculpatory or because it is impeaching; the evidence must have been suppressed by the state, either willfully or inadvertently; and prejudice must have ensued.

STRICKLER V. GREEN

A man named Strickler was convicted of capital murder in Virginia and sentenced to death. During the trial, Strickler's attorney was permitted to examine the prosecutor's files for exculpatory evidence. However, the prosecutor did not advise the defense counsel that police files might have contained exculpatory information favorable to Strickler that may have impeached the veracity of one of the witnesses against him. Strickler filed a habeas corpus petition, alleging that the prosecutor had a duty to reveal police documents that may have impeached witnesses against him.

The Supreme Court ruled that although the *Brady* rule had been violated in part, the materiality of the evidence would not have affected the trial outcome. The Court held that undisclosed documents impeaching eyewitness testimony as to circumstances of abduction of victim were favorable to Strickler for purposes of *Brady*; Strickler reasonably relied on the prosecution's open-file policy and established cause for procedural default in raising a *Brady* claim; but Strickler could not show either materiality under *Brady* or prejudice that would excuse this procedural default.

SOURCES: *Brady v. Maryland*, 373 U.S. 83 (1963); *Strickler v. Greene,* 119 S.Ct. 1936 (1999).

---

agreed upon by both sides because the real issue is not whether the plaintiff was injured but whether the defendant was liable for the injury. Such an agreement simplifies the case for the jury, enabling it to concentrate solely on the issue of liability.

Formalized Case Management Procedures

Most investigative agencies, whether public or private, have formalized case management procedures that assign particular duties and time frames for conducting investigating procedures and completing reports.

One large U.S. police department requires its investigators to prepare the first written investigative report within three working days of the receipt of the case. It requires the first-line supervisor to review each case with each investigator within seven working days to determine if an investigation should be terminated or continued. It requires the establishment of a folder for each case that is to be continued and mandates all the particular reports and enclosures that must be included in the folder.[2]

This police department further requires the supervisor to review all active cases between the eighth and twenty-first day of their receipt to ensure that all

EXHIBIT 4.1 Case Management Procedures for a Major Police Department

DETECTIVE GUIDE

PROCEDURE No.   204-11

CASE MANAGEMENT			
DATE ISSUED **10-2-93**	DATE EFFECTIVE **10-9-93**	REVISION NUMBER **93-1**	PAGE **1** of **2**

Misc. 1953-I (Rev. 6-93)-h2

PURPOSE

To insure increased supervisory direction and control of investigations.

PROCEDURE

Upon being assigned to investigate a case, in addition to Detective Guide procedure 204-01, "Investigation General - Procedure:

**DETECTIVE/
INVESTIGATOR**

1. Submit COMPLAINT FOLLOW-UP (PD313-081) within three (3) working days of receipt of case, <u>except</u> in missing persons cases, (see Detective Guide procedure 204-13, "Investigation - Missing/Unidentified Persons").

SUPERVISOR

2. Review each case with investigator within seven (7) working days.
    a. Determine whether investigation should be terminated or continued
    b. When investigation is terminated COMPLAINT FOLLOW-UP must indicate that the complainant was interviewed and reason for recommending closing
    c. Include statement that case was reviewed and supervisor authorized closing
    d. If evidence property involved, PROPERTY CLERK'S INVOICE (PD521-141) part 5, will be forwarded with description of circumstances under "Remarks" and date closed.
3. Establish Case Folder when case is to be further investigated beyond initial investigation and include:
    a. COMPLAINT FOLLOW-UP, photographs, lab reports, rap sheets, etc.
    b. Index Sheet (Misc. 965).
        (1) ALL COMPLAINT FOLLOW-UP's will be numbered consecutively on INDEX SHEET and in appropriate caption of FOLLOW-UP
        (2) All other items will be listed on INDEX SHEET with brief description without numbering
    c. Investigative Plan (Misc. 966, 967)
    d. ON LINE BOOKING SYSTEM ARREST WORKSHEET (PD244-159)
    e. PROPERTY CLERK'S INVOICE
    f. Court complaint forms
    g. Any individual unit "work sheets," etc.

4. Review all active cases between the eighth (8th) and twenty-first (21) day following receipt.
    a. Enter on latest COMPLAINT FOLLOW-UP:
        (1) Statement that case reviewed
        (2) Date of review
        (3) Signature
        (4) Set new review date if further investigative effort required.
5. Maintain an Individual Detective Case Log (Misc. 963) for each investigator assigned.
    a. Log will be kept in appropriate binder at supervisor's desk.

Exhibit 4.1 continued

	CASE MANAGEMENT		
DATE ISSUED **10-2-93**	DATE EFFECTIVE **10-9-93**	REVISION NUMBER **93-1**	PAGE **2 of 2**

Misc. 1953-I (Rev. 6-93)-h2

NOTE   Detective Assignment Sheet (Misc. 494) will continue to be maintained.

6. Establish Pattern Investigation Folder when crime pattern uncovered and assign investigator.

DETECTIVE/
INVESTIGATOR
7. Maintain Pattern Investigation folder containing;
   a. Index Sheet
   b. Copies of COMPLAINT REPORTS (PD313-152), COMPLAINT FOLLOW-UPS and any other material that might be of value to pattern investigation.
   c. Investigative Plan.
8. Prepare duplicate COMPLAINT FOLLOW-UP in pertinent cases for inclusion in Pattern Investigation Folder.

NOTE   Pattern Investigation Folder will be assigned Pattern Investigation number beginning with "001" each year; they will not receive a case number.

SUPERVISOR
9. Review these investigations within thirty (30) days.
   a. Indicate review on INVESTIGATIVE PLAN part 2 (worksheet).
   b. Investigations will not be terminated without review nor will they extend beyond thirty (30) days without supervisor's approval.

ADDITIONAL
DATA
Priority Case Status will be given only to certain cases handled by precinct squads as determined by squad supervisor. These are cases which may, for example, foster unusual concern for persons involved, involve large amounts of property or money, may create unusual community interest or have relationship to organized crime. Supervisor will advise squad commander of these cases and keep him apprised of significant changes by typed report as they occur.

SOURCE: NYPD.

investigative steps have been taken. Exhibit 4.1 spells out case management procedures used by that department.

NOTE TAKING

Case management begins with the note taking done by the investigator at the scene of the crime or incident. The practice of recording information on pieces of paper or the proverbial "back of a matchbook" is extremely unprofessional and investigators should never resort to it. Any important information recorded in the investigator's notebook should be duplicated in official investigatory reports as soon as possible, preferably when the investigator returns to the office.

Each investigator should maintain an individual personal notebook to record all essential facts or information collected at all stages of an investigation as contemporaneously as possible. (Exhibit 4.2 provides a sample of notes taken after a witness interview.) Ideally, the investigator's notebooks should be bound and numbered in sequence; each notebook should be

FIGURE 4.2 **Entries in an Investigator's Notebook Related to a Witness Interview**

August 18, 1994, 1600 hours, Victoria's Secret, Gulf View Mall, New Port Richie, Fl., Case # 465, stabbing of

John Smith at entrance to Victoria's Secret store on August 17, 1900 hours. Re-interview of clerk, AnneMarie

Jones, F-W-18, home 2521 Seaport Drive, Tarpon Springs, Fl., home # 803–694–1742, business #

803–929–1000. Present: Inv. Sally Green.

—Re-interview Ms. Jones re: stabbing of John Smith. Ms. Jones stated that she had no further information to

add regarding the descriptions of the attackers given on 8/17.

compact so that it can be easily carried and accessible whenever necessary during the course of an investigation. Each page of the notebook should be numbered in order to counter subsequent claims that an investigator removed certain pages of the book to hide or alter information. If it is not feasible for an investigative unit to have bound, sequentially numbered notebooks with consecutive preprinted page numbers, it is strongly recommended that the investigator consecutively number each page of the notebook in his own handwriting.

The investigator should enter his name, agency or firm, and the dates the notebook was opened and closed on the front cover of the book or on the first page. The name of the case and the case number should also be entered on the front cover or first page. A separate notebook should be maintained for each major case an investigator is working on if the case will involve many investigative steps. However, when investigators are handling many cases, it is impractical to keep a separate notebook for each case. Instead, they might keep all notes on each case on as many pages of the notebook as necessary, preceding each entry with the name of the case and the case number. When going on to a new case, they would use a fresh page of the notebook, again preceding any information with the name of the case and the case number.

Notes should be taken of all observations and discoveries made at the beginning of the investigation, including names, addresses, phone numbers, and descriptive information on all persons present at the crime scene or scene of the incident, and similar information on other persons involved in the investigation. The investigator should note and describe any physi-

cal evidence or possible evidence at the scene. The preliminary crime scene sketch, as described in chapter 3, should be made in the notebook too.

Because many investigations involve interviewing many people, including victims, witnesses, informants, possible subjects, and record keepers, sufficient information about these interviews needs to be entered in the notebook. The most important information is the time, date, location, and the identity of all persons present at the interview, including other investigators or police personnel. Although it may not be possible to write a verbatim account of all of the information obtained in an interview, the investigator should attempt to record all important facts gathered and provide a summary of the information given by the interviewee.

Many people might hesitate to participate in an interview when they see the investigator pull out a notebook and begin taking notes. It is best to ask the interviewee for permission to take notes before actually doing so. If the interviewee objects to the note taking, the investigator should accede to such an objection and then record the information gathered in the interview as soon as possible after it is over.

Some investigators use handheld tape recorders to document information provided in an investigation, particularly interviews. A tape recorder can be advantageous because it produces a verbatim record of the interview with no danger of misinterpreting, slanting, or misquoting. However, the investigator should never rely solely on the tape recorder because it can malfunction, and background noises can distort the recording. The investigator should transfer essential information from the tape to the notebook as soon as possible. If a tape recorder is used, proper headings (time, date, location, persons present, case name, and case number) should be recorded on the tape prior to the interview. The tape must also be identified on its exterior with the same information, and it should be stored in the case folder.

Just as some people might not wish to participate in an interview if notes are being taken, some may also object to talking into a tape recorder. It is best to ask for permission to tape the interview before actually doing so.

When a notebook is completely filled, it should be kept for future reference and filed in consecutive order in a secure location in the investigator's office. As we already discussed, the investigator's notebook, like all reports and documents in a case, can be subpoenaed for examination by the court and by the opposing attorneys during the discovery process. When called to testify in a court case, investigators should bring their notebooks, along with all other pertinent documents and reports, to the courtroom; they will be allowed to refer to these notes and reports while testifying to refresh their memory. Nevertheless, they should request permission from the judge prior to referring to their notes.

REPORT WRITING

Ferdico's Criminal Law and Justice Dictionary defines the word *report* in its verb and noun forms. As a verb it is "to give a detailed account of what has been learned from observation or investigation." As a noun it is "an official or formal account of facts or proceedings that is written or announced."[3] *The Dictionary of Criminal Justice* defines *report* as "the accurate recording of facts, usually transcribed in written form."[4] Thus, a report, by definition, is the very basis of the police investigation—it tells the story of what has occurred. Because of the importance of reports and report writing in investigating and policing, numerous textbooks have been published on the subject.[5]

Investigators maintain several important official reports while investigating cases. These may generally be categorized as *preformatted reports* and *written reports*.

Reports are essential in case management because they tell the story of what has occurred in the investigation. Here, investigators at a Los Angeles precinct review homicide reports.

© Joe Rodriguez/Stockphoto.com

Preformatted Reports

Preformatted reports are prepared on forms made available by the investigator's agency. Generally, the investigator fills in boxes or spaces with information on the incident under investigation. The main types of preformatted reports are *incident reports, follow-up* or *investigatory action reports, property reports, lab reports,* and *supervisory review reports.*

Incident reports sometimes referred to as complaint or field reports, are preformatted reports that serve as the first official report prepared in a criminal investigation. They are generally prepared by the first responding uniformed police officer to the scene of a crime or incident. The incident report contains identifying information on the victim or person making the report; details of the crime or incident; identifying information on the perpetrator or perpetrators, or a description of them; details of the case or incident; and identifying information on any property taken. The incident report could be seen as the birth certificate of a case—it begins the investigation. Exhibit 4.3 presents a sample incident report.

In a private investigating agency, the initial interview report detailing the services being requested by a client serves the same purpose as the incident report—it too may be seen as a kind of birth certificate.

Each incident report serves as the official record of the incident and is assigned a chronological serial

EXHIBIT 4.3 **Sample Police Department Incident Report**

Complete All Applicable Captions

SOURCE: NYPD.

number (case number) for reference purposes. If the crime involves insured property, the victim may request this number from the police in order to give it to an insurance company when filing a claim. Generally, case or serial numbers are assigned in chronological order at the start of a calendar year. A private investigative agency, for example, might number the first case it logs in 2002 as 2002–1, with the next case 2002–2, and so on. A police investigating unit might give prefixes to the case number, indicating the unit doing the investigation, such as IA# or 60P#. The case number should be entered on all forms, reports, and enclosures (record checks, photos, sketches, and so on) pertinent to each case.

Finally, a master index or tracking sheet should be maintained for all cases accepted during the year (that is, of all the incident reports), indicating the case number, date of receipt, complainant or client, subject or type of investigation, investigator assigned, date closed, and remarks detailing if and when a case is reassigned to another investigator and the identity of that investigator.

Follow-Up Reports Follow-up, or investigatory action, **reports** are generally preformatted reports on each investigatory action performed in the follow-up investigation of the incident. The follow-up reports create the history of the investigation. Each action taken by an investigator, including the response to and processing of the crime scene, interviews, interrogations, record searches, and other actions should be entered on a follow-up or investigatory action report and filed in the case folder. Each follow-up report should be consecutively numbered and cross-referenced to the case number. For example, if a particular case had been given the case number 2002–617 on the incident report, the follow-up report would be numbered in consecutive order: 2002–617-1, 2002–617-2, 2002–617-3, and so on).

The information in the follow-up report generally comes from the notes the investigator took in the field. The follow-up report should be prepared as soon as possible when the investigator returns to the office. See Exhibit 4.4 for a sample follow-up report.

Property Reports Property reports are preformatted reports containing information on any property seized or collected by the investigator. They contain the de-

scription of the property and information on where and how it was found.

Property reports should be given their own consecutive serial numbers and cross-referenced to the incident and follow-up reports.

Lab Reports Lab reports are preformatted reports that contain information on property seized or collected by the investigator that requires a laboratory examination. Generally, there are two types of lab reports: *requests for laboratory analysis* and *results of laboratory analysis.* The request for laboratory analysis is prepared by the investigator and submitted to the laboratory conducting the analysis. The result of laboratory analysis is prepared by the criminalist conducting the analysis and submitted to the investigator and the court.

Supervisory Review Reports   All cases should be reviewed on a periodic basis by investigative supervisors or managers to ensure they are being investigated in a timely and effective manner. Generally, the best method of reviewing the progress of an investigation is to review the case folder and its contents. Are all necessary documents present? Have all interviews, interrogations, observations, record searches, and similar investigative actions been entered on appropriate follow-up reports? Is the case index sheet current? Have all reports been properly numbered and cross-referenced? The supervisor or manager should enter the results of the review, the date of the review, and his or her signature on a supervisor review report and enclose it in the case folder.

Official Written Reports

Official written reports are narrative reports prepared from scratch by the investigator using a typewriter, word processor, or computer. The most frequent written reports are *observations* and *reports to supervisors or clients.*

Observations An observation is the detailed written report of any actions witnessed by an investigator while conducting an investigative surveillance. An example of an observation in a police investigation would be the record of events witnessed by the investigator while conducting a surveillance on a suspected

EXHIBIT 4.4   **Sample Police Department Follow-Up Report**

DO NOT USE THIS FORM TO REPORT: CRIME CLASSIFICATION CHANGES, CASE CLEARANCES, INITIAL ARREST ON THE COMPLAINT, RECOVERED PROPERTY, ADDITIONAL STOLEN PROPERTY SERIAL NUMBERS OBTAINED FOR PROPERTY PREVIOUSLY REPORTED, CRIME INCIDENT DATA, USE COMPLAINT FOLLOW-UP (PD 313-081) TO REPORT THE PRECEDING.

COMPLAINT - FOLLOW UP INFORMATIONAL PD 313-081A (Rev. 4-89)-31			PAGE ____ OF ____ PAGE						14 PERP 1

Form fields (left section):

- Crime | Pct. | OCCB No. | Complaint No. | Date of This Report
- Date of Orig. Report | Date Assigned | Case No. | Unit Reporting | Follow-Up No.
- Complainant's Name - Last, First, M.I. | Victim's Name - If Different
- **Witness No. 1:** Last Name, First, M.I. | Address, Include City, State, Zip | Apt. No.
- Home Telephone | Business Telephone | Position / Relationship | Sex | Race | Date of Birth | Age

Perpetrators:

- Total No. of Perpetrators | Wanted | Arrested | Weapon — ☐ Used ☐ Possessed | Describe Weapon (If firearm, give color, make, calibre, type, model, etc.)
- **Perp. No. 1:** Wanted ☐ | Arrested ☐ | Last Name, First, M.I. | Address, Include City, State, Zip | Apt. No | Res. Pct.
  - Sex | Race | Date of Birth | Age | Height Ft. in. | Weight | Eye Color | Hair Color | Hair Length | Facial Hair | NYSID No.
  - ☐ Eyeglasses ☐ Sunglasses | Clothing Description,
  - Nickname, First Name, Alias | Scars, Marks, M.O., Etc. _____
  - *(Continue in "Details"):*
- **Perp. No. 2:** Wanted ☐ | Arrested ☐ | Last Name, First, M.I. | Address, Include City, State, Zip | Apt. No | Res. Pct.
  - Sex | Race | Date of Birth | Age | Height Ft. in. | Weight | Eye Color | Hair Color | Hair Length | Facial Hair | NYSID No.
  - ☐ Eyeglasses ☐ Sunglasses | Clothing Description,
  - Nickname, First Name, Alias | Scars, Marks, M.O., Etc.
  - *(Continue in "Details"):*

AREA WITHIN BOX FOR DETECTIVE / LATENT FINGERPRINT OFFICER ONLY. THIS BOX WILL BE UTILIZED BY INVESTIGATOR WHENEVER POSSIBLE AND MUST BE FULLY COMPLETED WHEN USING THIS FORM TO CLOSE A CASE "NO RESULTS."

- Comp. Interviewed ☐ Yes ☐ No | In Person ☐ | By Phone ☐ | Date | Time | Results: Same as Comp. Report ☐ - Different (Explain in Details) ☐
- Witness Interviewed ☐ Yes ☐ No | In Person ☐ | By Phone ☐ | Date | Time | Results: Same as Comp. Report ☐ - Different (Explain in Details) ☐
- Canvass Conducted ☐ Yes ☐ No | If Yes - Make Entry in Body Re: Time, Date, Names, Addresses, Results | Crime Scene Visited ☐ Yes ☐ No | If Yes - Make Entry in Details Re: Time, Date, Evidence Obtained
- Complainant Viewed Photos ☐ Yes ☐ Refused ☐ Future | Results:
- Witness Viewed Photos ☐ Yes ☐ Refused ☐ Future | Results:
- Crime Scene Dusted ☐ Yes ☐ No | By (Enter Results in Details) | Crime Scene Photos ☐ Yes ☐ No | By (Enter Results in Details)
- If Closing Case "No Results," Check Appropriate Box and State Justification in Details:
  - ☐C-1 Improper Referral   ☐C-2 Inaccurate Facts   ☐C-3 No Evidence / Can't ID   ☐C-4 Uncooperative Complainant   ☐C-5 "Leads" Exhausted

DETAILS:

Right margin reference numbers: 14 PERP 1, PERP 2, 15 PERP 1, PERP 2, 16 CHOICE 1, CHOICE 2, 17 CHOICE 1, CHOICE 2, 18 CHOICE 1, CHOICE 2, 19 CHOICE 1, CHOICE 2, 20 PERP 1, PERP 2, 21 PERP 1, PERP 2, 22 PERP 1, PERP 2, 23 PERP 1, PERP 2, 24 PERP 1, PERP 2

Left margin reference numbers: 1, Witness No. 1, 2, Perpetrators, 3, 4 PERP 1, PERP 2, 5 PERP 1, PERP 2, 6 PERP 1, PERP 2, 7 PERP 1, PERP 2, 8 PERP 1, PERP 2, 9 PERP 1, PERP 2, 10 CHOICE 1, CHOICE 2

Bottom section:

- CASE ☐ACTIVE ☐CLOSED | DATE REVIEWED / CLOSED | IF ACTIVE, DATE OF NEXT REVIEW
- REPORTING OFFICER: | RANK | SIGNATURE | NAME PRINTED | TAX REG. NO. | COMMAND
- REVIEWING / CLOSING SUPERVISOR: | CASE CLOSED: C _____ OR B _____ | ENTER DESIGNATION | SIGNATURE | C.O.'s INITIALS

SOURCE: NYPD.

drug location. It would include the mention of an unusual pattern of vehicular or pedestrian traffic around the location, such as the entry of many persons into a premises. This particular observation may be one of several that might lead to the issuance of a search warrant by a magistrate. An example of an observation in a private investigation would be the report of a subject's actions while being followed and observed by an investigator in a domestic or spousal case. This observation might be one of several that would form the basis of the final report to the client.

The details of any observations made are usually entered in the investigator's notebook. They are then entered on an observation form and placed into the case folder as soon as possible after the investigator returns to the office. Exhibit 4.5 shows a sample observation.

EXHIBIT 4.5   Sample Observation

Case #2002–102

Client: Mrs. Mary Smith

Subject: Mr. John Smith

Date: October 16, 2002

On October 16, 2002, at 0900 hours I observed Mr. John Smith leave his residence at 1640 NW 8th Street, Miami, and enter his 1994 Lexus, Florida registration 29DT456. He drove to a private residence, 1408 SW 16th Street, Miami, where he parked in front. At approximately 0945 hours a white female, in her mid-thirties, wearing jeans and an orange blouse, left the residence and entered Smith's auto. They then drove to the Hyatt Regency Hotel at 941 NW 1st Street, where Smith parked in the hotel parking lot at 1015 hours. Smith and the female left the auto, entered the hotel, and proceeded to the hotel registration desk. They then entered the elevator and proceeded to the fifth floor, where they entered room 502.

At 1410 hours Smith and the female were seen leaving the elevator and returning a key to the clerk at the registration desk. Smith and the female then returned to his car. Smith returned to the 1408 SW 16th Street residence, where the female left the car and reentered the residence after a few minutes of conversation with Smith in the auto. Smith then returned to his residence.

Property and utility records checks reveal that 1408 SW 16th Street is owned and occupied by Mr. Steven Green and his wife Mrs. Jennifer Green.

Reports to Supervisors or Clients There are three general types of reports that investigators prepare for their supervisor or client: the *preliminary report,* the *progress or interim report,* and the *final report.* These reports should also be included in the case folder.

- The preliminary report to the investigator's immediate supervisor or client is usually forwarded through the chain of command to the agency head. This report is generally reserved for very serious cases and is based on the need for a manager or client to know the facts of the occurrence. The preliminary report identifies and gives the facts of the case and the status of the investigation. In police cases, the preliminary report is generally the basis of the information given to the news media. In private cases, it may summarize to the client the details of the case as reported to the investigator by the client and then explain how the investigator is going to proceed with the case. Of course, often it is not a good idea to send the client this or any case report to a home or business (most obviously in a domestic case). Alternative means of reporting should be developed between the investigator and the client.

- In lengthy investigations, the progress or interim report serves to keep managers or clients apprised of the progress of the investigation. These reports may be required either at fixed intervals or when key developments call for immediate notification.

- When an investigation is terminated, a closing report should be prepared by the investigator for the supervisor or client. Investigations are generally terminated on the successful solving or clearing of the case, or when all leads are exhausted and there appear to be no further investigatory actions that may be taken. The preparation of a final report does not preclude the reopening of the case at a later time if additional information should emerge. The final report should include a summary of the results of the entire investigation.

Purpose and Quality of Reports

Reports serve three main purposes. First, they create the permanent official record of the relevant information obtained during the investigation. Second, they provide other investigators with leads and information so they can understand and advance the investigation. Third, they serve as the basis for the prosecution of a criminal case and possible adjudication of a noncriminal case.

Reports should be objective, accurate, complete, and concise. They should be based on the facts uncovered in the investigation and not on the investigator's opinion. They should provide a true representation of the facts, including information both favorable and unfavorable to the person being investigated. Persons should be completely identified, and statements and opinions of subjects and witnesses should be clearly presented as such. Information developed in the investigation should be verified by statements of other witnesses and by reference to official records or other reliable sources.

Reports should provide answers to the when, where, who, what, how, and why questions. Recall the discussion of the acronym NEOTWY from chapter 2. This silly-sounding word is formed from the last letters of each of the six questions that need to be asked in each investigation.

Points of Information to Include

Most investigative agencies have their own rules and formats for the preparation of reports—and in particular the written narrative reports, which require more writing skills than preformatted reports. However, the following guidelines cover the majority of these rules. Every written report should contain *administrative data, synopsis, details,* and *conclusions and recommendations.*

- Generally, administrative data go at the very beginning of the report. They provide the date the report was prepared, the case number, identity of the complainants and subjects and investigator, classification of the case (robbery, missing person, surveillance, and so on), and the status of the investigation (pending or closed).

- The synopsis is a brief narrative describing the investigation in general and what is to follow in the report. It is a one-paragraph summary of the contents.

- The details section of the report is the complete, objective narrative account of the investigation.

DEMPSEY'S LAW
NEOTWY

Professor Dempsey, I hear that you use a special word to determine the most basic questions to ask in an investigation. I learned in my journalism class to ask six questions when writing an article—the professor called them "the five Ws and H." The five Ws are when, where, who, what, and why. The H is for how.

Sure, Jennifer, I know that, but I think my way is easier. The word is NEOTWY.

NEOTWY?

Yes. When you take the last letter of each of the following words and put them into one word it comes out as *NEOTWY.* These words form the basic questions you need to ask in any investigation. Also, they are the basic facts given in any news story or report of a crime. When: *N.* Where: *E.* Who: *O.* What: *T.* How: *W.* Why: *Y.*

Obviously NEOTWY is a very silly word, but once you hear it or see it, you will never forget it. Do you think you could remember the six basic questions you need to ask in any interview with the help of this word, Jennifer?

Yes, Professor. NEOTWY.

The details section can be several paragraphs long, with each paragraph containing a separate investigative step in chronological order.

- The conclusions and recommendations section of the report is the report's summary. It condenses the key information and makes recommendations for the continuance of the investigation.

Exhibit 4.6 depicts a sample final written report. Exhibit 4.7 depicts a sample format for a written report.

Description in Reports

The ability to describe persons accurately is one of an investigator's most important skills. An investigator must be able to describe a suspect or other person as

EXHIBIT 4.6   **Sample Final Report**

From: Commanding Officer, 60th Precinct
To: Department Firearms Discharge Review Board
Subject: INVESTIGATION RELATIVE TO DISCHARGE OF FIREARM BY MEMBER OF THE SERVICE

1. At approximately 2312 hours, Thursday, May 20, 1976, Police Officer James Roloph, shield 27927, 60th Precinct Anti-Crime Unit, while on duty, fired one shot at Charles Bayard, Male, Black, 36 years of age, of 2828 West 28th Street, Brooklyn, which struck him in the left buttocks and leg as he attempted to stab Officer Roloph with a knife while on the sidewalk in front of 2828 West 28th Street. At the same time Sergeant John Dempsey, shield 1654, 60th Precinct Anti-Crime Unit Supervisor, fired one shot in the air to terminate the assault being made on Officer Roloph by Troy Bayard, male, Black, 17 years of age of 2828 West 28th Street, son of Charles Bayard, as he repeatedly struck Officer Roloph from behind with a tire iron. There were no injuries or damage resulting from this shot.

2. Investigation discloses that Sergeant Dempsey, Officer Roloph and Police Officer Dominick Fumando, shield 2948, all assigned 60th Precinct Anti-Crime Unit were performing tour of duty 1740 hours, May 20 to 0210 hours May 21, 1976 and were patrolling westbound on Mermaid Avenue in department auto 885 in the vicinity of West 29th Street when approximately fifteen to twenty male Hispanics pointed to group of ten blacks, both male and female, who were walking north on West 29th Street and stated that they were the perpetrators of a "cutting." The officers drove into West 29th Street whereupon the group of blacks began to run into a parking lot which runs from West 28th to West 29th Streets, adjacent to 2828 West 28th Street At the entrance to the parking lot Sergeant Dempsey and Officer Roloph got out of the auto and shouting that they were police officers and displaying their shields began to pursue the group on foot. Officer Fumando then drove the car further into the lot passing Sergeant Dempsey as he did so. As Officer Fumando exited the auto, he observed Charles Bayard brandishing a knife at Officer Roloph, attempting several times to slash him. A smaller male, Troy Bayard, was behind Officer Roloph striking at him with a tire iron as several others armed with sticks in the area began to converge on Roloph from all directions. Officer Fumando approached to assist Roloph, and upon seeing the knife, drew his gun and then struck Troy over the head with his weapon, knocking him to the ground. The man with the knife then turned sideways and slashed several times at Fumando. It was at this time that Roloph, who had drawn his revolver when first confronted with the knife, fired one shot which struck Charles Bayard. After being shot, Charles Bayard fled approximately forty feet where he was tackled, subdued and handcuffed.

3. At the same time, Sergeant Dempsey, who was approximately ten feet behind Officer Roloph, observed the man striking at Roloph's back repeatedly with the tire iron and feared for Roloph's life should the tire iron strike his head. Dempsey was unable to reach Roloph quickly because of the distance and the persons between them and fired one shot to terminate the assault on the officer. This shot caused all to stop in their tracks and enabled Fumando to temporarily disable Troy Bayard and terminate his assault on Roloph. As Charles Bayard ran across the street after being shot, Troy again got up with the tire iron and ran across the street after his father, but was persuaded to drop the tire iron at that point.

4. Both Charles and Troy Bayard were removed to Coney Island Hospital and treated by Dr. Estilo. Charles Bayard was treated for gunshot wound of the left buttock and leg and admitted. Troy was treated for mastoid lacerations and minor contusions and released. Assistant District Attorney Robinson was present and took statements. Both Bayards were arrested and charged as follows:

      a. Charles Bayard: Attempted Murder
                                Possession of Dangerous Weapon
                                Resisting Arrest
                                Criminal Possession of a Controlled Substance (Marijuana)
      b. Troy Bayard: Assault 2nd Degree
                                Possession Dangerous Weapon (tire iron)
                                Resisting Arrest

5. Further investigation reveals that Troy Bayard alleged to have witnessed a parked auto being struck by another vehicle which left the scene. As he attempted to write down the plate number he was assaulted by two male Hispanics who told him to mind his own business and punched and kicked him. His mother, Venetta, who attempted to come to his aid, was slapped and knocked down by one of these males. Charles Bayard, upon hearing of this, left his apartment

Exhibit 4.6 continued

to confront these males and was interrupted by the arrival of the police. Armando Torres, male, Hispanic, 19 years-of-age of 2891 Mermaid Avenue was identified by Troy Bayard and arrested and charged with Assault 3rd degree on his complaint.

    6. A canvass of the area disclosed only one witness who admitted to seeing any portion of the incident. This was Juanita Rose of 2828 West 28th Street, apartment 6 E, who stated that she heard a noise and went to her sixth floor balcony from which she observed a lot of pushing and fighting. She saw Charles Bayard run across the street pursued by two males who knocked him down, and hit him over the head. Apparently, she did observe some of the last portion of the incident, but she insists that she heard a large car crash closely followed by what looked to her like a gang fight followed by at least four shots. Her statement appears to be contradictory in many aspects to that made by others including the defendants, although she did observe one member in an unmarked car pick up something from the ground which she assumed was a knife.

    7. The scene was searched by Emergency Service number eight, truck number 5550, Police Officer Baker, shield 10272 and Detective Bauer, shield 1018, under the supervision of Lieutenant George Chakedis, Internal Affairs Division (temporarily assigned to this command), and no other injury to persons or damage to property was found. The tire iron and knife were recovered at the scene and vouchered. Inspection of the wound indicated that the bullet entered the left buttocks and exited the left hip. A search of the scene failed to locate the spent bullet.

    8. Officer Roloph's revolver a .38 calibre Smith & Wesson Chief, serial number 8J6996 and the revolver of Sergeant Dempsey a .38 calibre Smith & Wesson Chief, serial number 487017 were checked and each disclosed one fired and four live rounds. Officer Fumando's .38 calibre Smith & Wesson Chief, serial number 485956 contained five live rounds. All revolvers are five shot weapons and listed on Force Record Cards. Weapons examined by Police Officer Egger, shield 3282, Ballistics Section. Ballistics Case number 6624 assigned. None of these members have previously been involved in shooting incidents.

    9. Officer Roloph was treated at Coney Island Hospital by Dr. Makauju for contusions of his neck muscles and released. He reported sick at 0730 hours, May 21, 1976. Firearms Discharge Assault Report prepared.

    10. The personnel records of the members involved in this incident are as follows:
        a. Sergeant Dempsey is the recipient of seven departmental awards and no disciplinary action.
        b. Officer Fumando is the recipient of 4 departmental awards and no disciplinary action.
        c. Officer Roloph is the recipient of ten departmental awards and no disciplinary action.

    11. The following were notified:
    Deputy Inspector Valle, Brooklyn South Area, Zone 2
    Sergeant Kulaaka, Current Situations Desk
    Attorney Bill Robinson, Brooklyn District Attorney's Office
    Police Officer O'Connell, Emergency Service
    Police Officer Lovitch, Ballistics
    Detective Luongo, 60 Precinct Detective Unit

    12. The following forms were prepared:
    Complaint Report #s: 4765, 4766
    Aided #: 1267—Police Officer Roloph
    Line of Duty Injury Report—Police Officer Roloph
    Witness to Injury of Police Officer Report
    Arrest #s: 24676—Troy Bayard
    24677-Charles Bayard
    24683—Armando Torres
    Voucher #s: 963643—knife
            963644—tire iron
            963645—controlled substance

    13. This investigation disclosed that when Officer Roloph fired his shot at Charles Bayard both he and Officer Fumando were under attack by Mr. Bayard and feared for both his and Officer Fumando's life. In light of this, this shot was justified both under the penal law and the guidelines as set forth in Interim Order 118, series 73. Although the shot

Exhibit 4.6 continued

fired by Sergeant Dempsey can be called a warning shot [warning shots are prohibited by the NYPD shooting policy], it can only be considered one in a technical sense. Sergeant Dempsey saw that Officer Roloph was under attack by a man wielding a tire iron who had already struck the officer several times and feared that the next blow would strike him on the head with possible fatal consequences. Since he was unable to immediately reach him and could not fire at the assailant (Troy Bayard) since persons were in the line of fire he selected the only alternative which was to fire one shot into the air. This shot was intended to force the assailant to cease his assault. This was successful since it gave Officer Fumando the opportunity to strike Troy Bayard thus ending the assault. Recommend no disciplinary action be taken against Sergeant Dempsey since this can be deemed to be only a technical violation of the guidelines as set forth in Interim Order 118, series 73, without which there could have been disastrous consequences.

Nathan Markowitz
Captain
Commanding Officer, 60th Precinct

NM:art
Distribution
Police Commissioner
Chief of Field Services
C.0. Patrol Borough Brooklyn South
C.0. Patrol Borough Brooklyn South, Zone 1
File
Enclosures
Sketch of Scene
Photos

SOURCE: NYPD.

EXHIBIT 4.7   **Sample Format for a Written Report**

Administrative Data
Date:
Case #:
From:
To:
Subject:

Synopsis

1. NEOTWY

Details

2.
3.
4.
5.
6.

Conclusions and Recommendations

7.
Signature:
Title/Office:

---

accurately and completely as possible. An investigator must also be able to identify a subject correctly from a physical description.

Exhibit 4.8 offers a sample of the key information that should be included in a physical description. Obviously, a witness or other person may not be able to give all the information included here. The most important pieces of information for the investigator to obtain are gender, race, age, height, weight, hair color, facial hair, and distinctive marks, such as scars, tattoos, and moles, on the body. In cases in which a witness is reporting a crime that just occurred, the investigator should attempt to obtain a good description of the clothes and accessories (rings, chains, and so on) worn by the suspect.

Often an investigator must give a complete description of a suspect—for example, in a missing person or fugitive case. Exhibit 4.9 shows the information that would be most helpful in finding a person. When describing a person it is best to use a formal method of description starting with the person's "pedigree"— that is, gender, race, and age. After the pedigree, the

EXHIBIT 4.8   **Describing a Person**

Physical Description

Gender	Male / Female
Race	White / Black / Hispanic / Asian / Native American / Pacific Islander / Other
Height	___ ft. ___ in. to ___ ft. ___ in. (always put height in ranges)
Weight	____ lbs. to ____ lbs. (always put weight in ranges such as 180–200 pounds)
Build	slim / medium / heavy / obese / muscular / athletic
Posture	erect / stooped / slumped
Complexion	fair / dark / red / tanned / pale / freckles / acne / acne scarred / rough / smooth
Hair	color / obviously dyed
Hair	bald / partially bald / receding hairline / thick / thin / coarse / straight / wavy / kinky / permed / processed / bushy
Hair	length
Eyes	color brown / blue / hazel / gray (be aware that eye color can change with contact lenses)
	bloodshot / large / small / deep-set / protruding / slanted / cross-eyed / narrow / squinting / close-set / wide apart
Eyelashes	long / short
Eyeglasses	worn / not worn / type / color of lens / color of frames
Eyebrows	color / thin / bushy / penciled / arched / horizontal
Nose	long / medium / short / thin / thick / straight / broken / pointed / flat / turned up / turned down / pointed to right / pointed to left / nostrils (large, small, high, low, flared)
Mustache	type / color / length or size
Beard	type / color / length (always compare eyebrows, mustache, beard, and sideburns color to hair color)
Sideburns	color / length
Cheeks	full / fleshy / sunken
Cheekbones	high / low / prominent
Mouth	turned up or down at corners
Lips	thin / thick / puffy / overhanging / protruding / cracked / scarred / red / pale / blue
Teeth	white / yellow / stained / broken / missing / loose / braced / capped / false / bridgework

Chin	small / large / normal / square / pointed / flat / double / dimpled / cleft
Jaw	long / short / wide / narrow / thin / fleshy / square / heavy
Ears	small / medium / large / close to head / projecting from head / oval / round / rectangular / triangular / pierced / cauliflowered / hairy
Neck	small / medium / long / straight / Adam's apple
Shoulders	small / heavy / narrow / broad / square / round / stopped
Hands	long / short / broad / narrow / thin / rough / bony / soft / smooth / hairy
Fingers	short / long / thick / stained / mutilated
Fingernails	length / polished (color) / dirty / stained
Distinctive Marks	scars / marks / pockmarks / tattoos / moles / birthmarks
Voice	accent (foreign / regional) / pleasant / well modulated / pitch (low / high) / speech impediment (lisp / stutter / slurring) / gruff / polite
Walk	stride (long / short) / limp / energetic / slow / fast / drags one foot

Clothing

Hat or cap
Overcoat
Coat
Jacket
Slacks or trousers
Suit
Dress
Shirt
Tie
Belt
Shoes
Socks
(Note color, type, material, condition, how worn)

Jewelry

Rings
Watches
Chains
Earrings
Pins
Bracelets
Necklaces
Cuff links
(Note color, type, material, condition, how worn)

EXHIBIT 4.9 **Complete Description of a Suspect**

Name:
Physical description:
Address (past and present):
Social security number:
Alias, A/K/A (Also Known As):
Nicknames:
Associates: names / addresses (past and present)
Relatives: names / addresses (past and present)
Habits (jogger / dancer / weight lifter / ladies' man / etc.):
Frequents (health clubs / bars / racetracks / etc.):
Criminal record:
Military record:
Employment history:

investigator should complete as many of the categories shown in Exhibit 4.8 as possible, in the same order as given.

HOW TO WRITE A REPORT

Some say that report writing is one of the most tedious duties required of an investigator. Yet it is also one of the most important. An investigator's ability is often judged on the basis of his or her written reports.

Experienced investigators may conduct an extensive investigation only to negate their efforts by failing to document their findings properly. Some investigators may justify their inability to prepare detailed reports by believing they can keep all the information "in their head" or that the original information they collected in their notebook is sufficient. But professional investigators realize that written reports are their agency's official record of an investigation and must contain the information required to support any arrest, prosecution, or court action.

Investigation report writing is simply telling someone about something that happened or what was done—a factual narrative. The best way to describe a thing or event is to tell it quickly. Writing a report can be almost as easy as telling a story. An investigator's written report is not much more than that—telling a story. We all tell stories easily and well, to each other

and often to a hushed courtroom. However, writing is a more formal way of telling a story—we must spell out the words, create sentences, organize them in paragraphs, punctuate. Thus, writing is more complex.

For many of us, writing can also be difficult. The reasons probably go back to our earlier schooling. We were taught spelling, outlining, vocabulary, rules of grammar, English composition, punctuation, and sentence structure. We were taught to have a clear idea of what we wanted to say and to picture our audience, then outline ideas in the order of their importance, and then.... In other words, we were taught that we had to prepare to write. Many of us believed that we had to postpone the writing itself until we had it all worked out in our heads or on paper. Then we would start to write and become preoccupied with the spelling, the sentence structure, the punctuation. Nothing would happen, no words would pour out, the page would stay blank, and we would panic. The harder we would try to make it happen, the less we would accomplish until, absolutely frustrated, we would take the first reasonable opportunity to abandon the writing. (Think about your last term paper or written class project!)

But the typical investigatory report should not be a hard project to complete. Usually, the report seeks only to document what has happened. In other words, the work has been done, the evidence has been examined and evaluated, the interviews have been conducted, the observations have been made. Now the investigator just needs to report it.

When we tell a story, the words almost tumble out by their own weight. We have an audience that isn't going to hang around for long and we get caught up in our stories too. That's why people want to hear them. We care about our stories and the people or characters in them and that comes across to our audience.

Just Write It: Free Writing

So what's the best way to write an investigatory report? *Just write it.* It can be written in longhand on a scratch pad, on one side of the page, and skipping lines, because a lot of what will be written will later be thrown away—as all good writers do. Or, a typewriter or a word processor can be used. (Personally, I prefer a computer with word processing software.) The next step is to write the first thing that comes to mind, and everything that comes after, because that is the best way to determine what to say and how to say it. In other words, it is best to start with an idea of what must be written—a follow-up report on an interview, a progress or interim report on an existing case, and so on—and then simply start writing. And not stop for anything! It is important not to think about spelling, where the commas go, what is the right word—one should never cross out words or go back—but just keep putting it on paper as quickly as possible. If we get stuck, the thought may pop into our heads: I can't do this, I can't think what to write. If that happens, it's a good idea to write, "I can't do this, I can't think what to write"—and then just keep on writing. The point of this first draft is to write for ten to fifteen minutes without stopping. At the end of that period, it is time to stop, put the writing aside, leave the typewriter or computer, and take a short break. A soda, a glass of water, or a cup of coffee is in order, or just a look out the window—anything to think about something other than the writing. After the break, ten minutes or so should be spent in reading over what was written. Now it's important to find the main idea—a kind of center of gravity—in what was written, and summarize that in one sentence. Even if it's not entirely clear, it's a good idea just to guess; the point will surface soon enough.

Just Write It Again

In the next ten to fifteen minutes, a second draft should be written in the same way, trying to keep in mind the main idea. If that's not possible, or even if what gets written now seems to have nothing to do with what was written earlier, it's important not to worry. The truth is that most writers know more than they think they know about their subject. There are facts and observations in everyone's subconscious (not in their notebooks) that will surface and pop onto the blank page if they are allowed to—through writing freely, without judgment, without editing.

It is important to "free-write" in this way at least three separate drafts before even thinking about crossing out a word or spelling it right. The result is a very satisfying pile of words, phrases, and sentences—the raw material for a final draft.

The next step in the process is to revise what was written. Here, the writer decides what is the main point or idea or fact, the next in importance, and so on down the line. (It helps to write these down and number

them.) For those using a pen and paper or a typewriter, scissors come in handy to cut up the paragraphs; they can be shifted around so that the information that has to do with the same idea is all together. (This is known as the "cut-and-paste" technique.) With a word processor or a computer, it's even easier to cut and paste. Any writing that doesn't fit or make sense or feel right should be deleted. It is important to trust your instincts. Enough words have already been produced; the irrelevant may be discarded. Now is the time to write the final draft.

Find Your Voice

The final draft is easy; the bulk of the work was already done in the free writing and the revision stages. Some writers can just paste or join the sections together, writing new connecting passages, working on whatever new occurs to them. In the last step—editing—the spelling, sentence structure, and grammar are tidied up. Most word processing programs and even some typewriters have spellcheck and grammar features that make the editing processing easier.

The important thing to keep in mind when writing an investigative report is that anyone can do it. If you can tell a story, you can write it. People soon learn that the faster they put the words down on paper, the easier the writing will be. And the voice producing the words will naturally fit the thoughts and ideas they want to express: words flowing into other words, a storm of words.

Technology: Use It, Don't Fight It!

Although reports may be handwritten and given to a secretary to prepare, it is preferable for an investigator to have basic clerical and computer skills, as discussed in chapter 2. If you are contemplating a career as an investigator, you should take courses in writing, basic word processing, and keyboarding. These skills will give you the edge in getting hired because employers will be spared the cost of hiring clerical or secretarial employees to prepare your basic investigatory reports.

Computerized Report Writing

Many investigative agencies and police departments use computerized digital dictation systems for report writing. With a digital dictation system, officers simply

EXHIBIT 4.10   **How to Write More Concisely: One Word Is Always Better Than More**

Bad Phrasing	Good Phrasing
made a note of the fact	noted
square in shape	square
despite the fact that	although
at a high rate of speed	rapidly
in the State of California	in California
with reference to	about
in the amount of	for
subsequent to	after
is of the opinion	believes
in spite of	despite
month of February	February
red in color	red
in the event that	if
the perpetrator of the crime	the suspect
at that point in time	then

SOURCE: Wayne W. Bennett and Karen M. Hess, *Criminal Investigation*, 4th ed. (St. Paul, MN: West, 1994), p. 89. Reprinted with permission of the publisher.

pick up a touch-tone telephone and dictate their report. The digital processor handles the voice much like data, storing it in binary code on a hard disk on the compact microprocessor. Digital systems are superior to conventional tape recorders or dictating systems in their random-access feature—that is, they can locate and play back any item almost instantly.

Wesley Blanchard of the Warwick Police Department in Rhode Island, which has adopted digital dictation, says, "Input is simple: just pick up any touch-tone telephone, dial in, punch in your ID, work type, and case number, and begin talking. . . . The gain in productivity over the first six months of the system's operation was dramatic—perhaps even sensational."[6]

Another advance in **computerized report writing** is the Computer-Assisted Report Entry (CARE) system, which was developed by the St. Louis County Police Department in Missouri. This computerized system is based on a CARE operator who leads officers through preformatted screens and questions, allowing them to complete reports in a matter of minutes. The CARE system has reported the following accomplishments:

- It frees officers to spend more time on patrol by reducing report writing and notification times.

DEMPSEY'S LAW

The Most Important College Course for a Prospective Investigator

Professor Dempsey, I really want to be a private investigator when I complete college. Is this course, Criminal Investigations, the best course to provide me with the tools to meet my goal?

I get this question often. I generally reply with a story about a former student, Vanessa, who paid her way through college by working for a local licensed private investigator. She did the normal things that people who work for P.I.s do. She made discreet observations, conducted surveillances, served subpoenas, took photographs, conducted interviews, and took statements. And, of course, she prepared written reports on each investigatory action she engaged in.

One day in class, with Vanessa's permission, I asked her which of the college classes she had taken had best prepared her to become a successful investigator. I thought I knew what her answer would be, and I did.

She replied, "Professor Dempsey, of course your criminal investigation course was extremely helpful. You covered interview techniques that I will never forget, and sources of information and ways to obtain information, and surveillance techniques and all the other essentials to investigating. But to tell you the truth, I think the most important courses I took, the ones that gave me the skills my boss was most appreciative of, were my English composition course, my keyboarding course, and my word processing course. My boss constantly complimented me on the quality of my reports—he even intimated that because I wrote such good reports I saved him the cost of hiring an extra secretary for the office."

So my answer to my students is that any courses that force you to think logically and to write will prepare you for an investigatory career. You are what you write.

- It improves the quality, accuracy, and timeliness of police reports and management reports by standardizing the collection of information and creating a centralized, legible online database.

DEMPSEY'S LAW
Writing Assistance Online

Professor: Are there any computer sites that can help me with my report writing, specifically my spelling, grammar and vocabulary?

Yes. There is a terrific site called Refdesk.com that can give you all kinds of assistance. Refdesk.com can give you access to numerous dictionaries, including *Merriam-Webster's Collegiate Dictionary* and *Collegiate Thesaurus*, and to sites that will help you with your grammar and writing style. Go to that site at http://www.refdesk.com and then enter the site map. To get to Merriam-Webster directly, go to http://www.m-w.com.

EXHIBIT 4.11   Contents of the Case Folder

Index sheet
Incident report
All follow-up or investigatory action reports
Interview and interrogation reports
Record checks
Photographs
Sketches
Evidence reports
Evidence analysis reports
Computer printouts
Audiotapes
Videotapes
Medical examiner's reports

- It provides citizens and county police officers with a convenient, efficient, round-the-clock police reporting service.

- It improves the availability and timeliness of police report information by electronically processing, aggregating, distributing, and filing these documents.

- It improves follow-up investigation procedures by providing the officer with complete information in a shorter period of time.[7]

THE CASE FOLDER

The case folder is the repository of all the investigatory actions that have occurred during an investigation. It is the folder or book that forms the history of the investigation. It contains the incident or complaint report, all the follow-up or investigatory action reports, and reports to supervisors, as well as all other documents such as evidence analysis reports, criminal record checks, requests to examine records, computer printouts, records obtained, receipts, copies of interview and interrogation reports, photos, tapes, and anything else that may pertain to the investigation, including news media accounts.

Exhibit 4.11 details the contents of a typical case folder and Exhibit 4.12 shows an index sheet that can be used to keep track of all the contents of the case folder.

COMPUTERIZED CASE MANAGEMENT

In addition to their use in report writing, computers are being used extensively in investigating and law enforcement for many purposes, including crime analysis, dispatching, and automated investigations. (Chapter 6, "Criminalistics and Technology," covers the extensive use of computers, automation, and technology in investigating.) In this section, we focus on **computerized case management.**

The advantage of using computers in case management is their automated database capability. An automated database is an enormous electronic filing cabinet that can store information and retrieve it in any desired format. The possible list formats available in a database are only limited by the data that are entered.

HOLMES

HOLMES (an acronym for Home Office Large Major Enquiry System and a reference to the legendary fictional detective Sherlock Holmes) is a sophisticated computer program developed for British investigators to aid them in managing complex investigations. (In

EXHIBIT 4.12   **Sample Case Index Sheet**

INDEX SHEET

Complaint #_____   Case #_____

ITEM NO.	DATE	ITEM (Include brief description of item/subject matter)

ALL COMPLAINT FOLLOW-UPS (PD313-081) will be consecutively
numbered on this sheet. All other items submitted (photographs,
Laboratory Reports, Property Vouchers, etc.) will also be included
on the sheet, but will not be numbered.

Misc. 965 Revised 12/75

SOURCE: NYPD.

Great Britain, an investigation is called an *enquiry*.) HOLMES is a complete case management system that can process, organize, recognize, interrelate, and retrieve all aspects of information on a case. It also keeps track of ongoing progress—or the lack of it—in investigations. The system was created in response to the infamous Yorkshire Ripper case, in which thirteen women were killed between 1974 and 1981. When the perpetrator was finally apprehended in 1981, it was discovered that he had been detained and questioned by at least six different police forces in connection with the attacks. Because sharing of information on related cases was so cumbersome for the neighboring forces at that time, none of them ever made the connection.[8]

Sergeant Glenn Moore of the St. Petersburg Police Department in Florida, traveled to England to study HOLMES for his department. Moore pointed out that every person involved in an investigation could be up

to date on its status in minutes: "All they have to do is ask HOLMES."[9]

Since then, the St. Petersburg Police Department has adopted HOLMES and uses ten computer terminals tied into it. Information on criminal cases is constantly being entered, evaluated, reviewed, processed, and analyzed on the various screens. Thousands of pages of information are readily available to any investigator working on the case at any time.

Every piece of paper in a case is first evaluated by a "receiver and indexer," who decides how it is to be entered into the system so it can be retrieved quickly. Inputters then enter the material into any of the six indexes or data classifications in the system. A document may suggest that certain follow-up actions are required, such as interviewing a new lead. These actions will be brought up by the "statement reader" and sent to the "action allocator." Thus, all potential leads are noted and immediately assigned to follow-up action. The follow-up actions are entered into the computer and HOLMES enters them into a master progress report. Every time the case manager checks on the progress of a case, he or she can see immediately what has and has not been done by all those connected with it. Even news releases issued are entered into the computer. If a suspect is questioned later on about facts in the case, the investigators know whether or not any pertinent details were leaked to the press.

Information in the system can be recalled or combined in any desired format. For example, the investigator might ask to see information on anyone whose name has come up more than two or three times during the investigation. If this program had been used in the Yorkshire Ripper case, the suspect's name would have appeared regularly early in the investigation.

HOLMES can locate multiple uses of one name in the records of any one case at the lightning speed of more than one million words a minute. It can also scan all descriptions of people connected in any way to a case and advise if any of them comes close to the description of the main suspect. This description can include such items as the make or color of the car or boat driven or owned.

As marvelous as HOLMES is, it does not take the place of a good investigator; it just gives him or her more brainpower to work with. It still takes a well-trained staff to gather the data that are fed into the system and then determine how to use them. Still, the system helps investigators follow up on leads, generate new leads, and then piece together seemingly unrelated information by organizing evidence in new ways and by linking scattered leads. Access to all information is so streamlined that it is estimated that thousands of hours are saved on each case.

Other Computerized Systems

Computerized case management is still in its infancy. However, computer software companies are constantly developing new systems to aid investigators. Here are some examples:[10]

- Microset, a Canadian company, has developed a program whose focus is on managing the volumes of paperwork needed before a case can be brought before the crown attorney (the Canadian counterpart of the U.S. prosecutor). Based on the philosophy that a police force is made up of work groups that need specific tools to do their jobs, Microset created a case tracking program for the Toronto Metropolitan Police Department designed to run on laptop computers. The program helps investigators prepare the paperwork they need for court and track the evidence and supplementary reports involved in each case.

- D. M. Data has introduced C-PIMS (Police Information Management System), featuring integrated modules that provide for onetime data entry from a variety of locations and the automatic sharing of information among users. The system is capable of performing an online name search by alpha name, "soundalike" name, or alias; by case number; by address; and by physical description, as well as by a number of other criteria. The system has modules to create files for names, warrants, property, and citations. It also performs case management and crime analysis.

- Ameritech has developed RIMS (Records Information Management System), which contains a records management module designed to tie all information together automatically without requiring explicit operator actions. Included is an automated solvability function, criminal profiling, crime analysis, case management, and the ability to interface with the separate ACE (Automated Control of Evidence) component. ACE features an interactive query that lets the user cross-reference the database in several ways at the same time, as well as a tool that lets investigators identify relationships between cases, property, and people.

SUMMARY

The investigator's job is to collect information. Among other functions, that involves searching for and collecting physical evidence, interviewing victims and witnesses, and interrogating suspects. But without an appropriate and effective case management system and report writing procedures, all these efforts would be futile. Case management is the system for collecting, recording, organizing, and preserving all the various pieces of information gathered in an investigation. It is the process of officially documenting all incidents and investigatory actions in a case.

Many people—including students—detest paperwork. Some prospective investigators think their future jobs will consist of going out and investigating crimes, solving the crimes, and then arresting the perpetrator. They don't realize how much paperwork is involved in investigating. In reality, more time is spent in documenting the investigation than in doing the investigation.

To bring home to you the importance and seriousness of case management procedures, consider the following scenario. One of your loved ones is murdered. Investigators quickly arrest a suspect. You think the investigators did a great job. But then, at trial, the suspect's defense attorneys punch holes in the prosecution's case, continually pointing out tremendous inconsistencies and deficiencies in the various written reports and forms prepared in the case. As a result, the jury determines that the sloppy and conflicting processing of the case gave them reasonable doubt as to the defendant's guilt. The defendant walks out of court acquitted. How do you feel about the investigators now?

LEARNING CHECK

1. Discuss the main reasons for properly recording an investigation using a case management system.
2. Discuss the most important information about interviews that should be entered in an investigator's notebook.
3. Identify the main investigatory reports and explain the use of each one.
4. Discuss the basics of writing a good report.
5. Discuss the concept of computerized case management systems and explain some benefits of these systems.

APPLICATION EXERCISE

Interview a family member, friend, or fellow student about a criminal incident (if you know no one who was involved in such an incident use a report from the newspaper) and write a preliminary report about it. Use the techniques indicated in the report writing section of this chapter. Remember that the preliminary report identifies and give the facts of the case. See Exhibit 4.7 for a sample format of a written report. And, remember NEOTWY.

WEB EXERCISE

Research the Internet site of a large police agency or a federal law enforcement agency and locate a description of a major case or crime the agency has just cleared. After reviewing the details of the case, prepare a list of the types of reports that had to be prepared for the case (for example, incident, follow-up, property, lab, and so on). Give a brief description of the specific details that would have been included in each report.

KEY TERMS

Brady material

case folder

case management

computerized case management

computerized report writing

discovery

follow-up report

incident report

official written reports

preformatted reports

5

LAW, EVIDENCE, AND INVESTIGATING

CHAPTER GOALS

1. To introduce you to the role of law and the U.S. legal system in investigating

2. To introduce you to the rules of evidence and their importance in investigating

3. To acquaint you with the types of evidence that are used in investigations, including direct evidence, circumstantial evidence, and prima facie evidence

4. To explain the forms of evidence that are used in investigations, including testimony of witnesses, documentary evidence, and real evidence

5. To acquaint you with the methods that should be used by the investigator when testifying in court

INTRODUCTION

Imagine that you are an investigator assigned to a double murder case. You respond to the crime scene, perform all the responsibilities and duties of the investigator, and use the techniques described in this text. You believe you know who the suspect is. In your haste to apprehend him, you bend some rules to get your evidence. After all, you know this person is guilty.

Based on your investigation you arrest the suspect, book him, and he goes before the courts. You feel you have done a good job and that by arresting him you have achieved justice for the two victims and their families. About a year later the case goes to trial and you testify about your actions and investigation. You expect justice to be done, that the suspect will be found guilty and held responsible for his actions. But much of the evidence that you collected is not admitted into the trial because you violated the rules of evidence. The evidence that is admitted is not believed by the jury and the suspect is found not guilty. He walks. You question the state of justice in our nation. Something must be wrong!

What is wrong? *You.* Our legal system has survived since the very beginning of our nation and it is a system of rules that must be obeyed and followed. If the investigator breaks the rules, the evidence cannot be admitted. If the evidence is not admitted, the suspect will go free.

Several years ago, the American public was fascinated by a high-profile, spectacular criminal trial: the O. J. Simpson murder trial. In that trial, former football great Orenthal James (O. J.) Simpson was charged with the brutal murder of his former wife, Nicole Brown, and her friend Ronald Goldman, in 1994 in Los Angeles. Simpson was represented in court by numerous high-profile attorneys. This case, which received enormous coverage from the media, caused many to question the U.S. legal system. They questioned the innumerable delays, the actions of the attorneys, and the media. This trial highlighted many of the problems in our legal system. As the trial came to a close, Simpson was acquitted of all charges and released. Essentially, in this case, the jury did not believe the evidence collected by the investigators.

We must remember that the U.S. legal system is not perfect and requires the fullest competence and integrity of those who work within it, but it still is the best and fairest legal system developed by humankind. Evidence is an essential tool of this system, and the investigator must know the rules of evidence in the context of the system in which it plays such a major role.

In order to see evidence in its proper manner, an investigator should have knowledge of law, the U.S. legal system, the rules of evidence, and courtroom testimony. This chapter discusses law in general and the U.S. system of law in particular, including criminal and civil law. It also discusses evidence: types of evidence; forms of evidence; and the rules of evidence, including materiality, relevance, competency, presumptions, judicial notice, opinion evidence, and the hearsay rule and its exceptions. The chapter also discusses the role of the investigator in courtroom testimony.

LAW

Law can generally be defined as a system of standards and rules of human conduct that impose obligations and grant corresponding rights, as well as a system of institutional rules on the creation, modification, and enforcement of these standards. Law, in brief, governs our relationships with each other: our marriages and divorces, the running of our businesses and the relationships with our local merchants, the purchase or lease of property, and all the obligations we have to each other as fellow human beings.

Law defines for society behavior that is *proscribed* (forbidden) and *prescribed* (mandated). In this section we present a brief history of the development of law and some of the major types of law in our society.

Today, the Internet provides numerous ways for the student to research laws and legal cases, and several sites are provided in this text.

History of Law

Most societies throughout history have developed methods of governing relationships among their members and resolving conflicts. Some of these methods have been extremely complex, and some have been extremely primitive. The concept of **evidence** has been essential in all these systems.

One of the earliest known systems of law was the Code of Hammurabi, which was established by King Hammurabi of ancient Babylon in about 2000 B.C.

YOU ARE THERE!
The O. J. Simpson Murder Case

On Sunday, June 12, 1994, somewhere between the hours of 10 and 11 P.M., Nicole Brown Simpson, the ex-wife of former football star O. J. Simpson, and a male acquaintance, Ronald Goldman, were brutally murdered in front of Nicole's expensive townhouse in Brentwood, California.

Investigation by the Los Angeles Police Department revealed that earlier that evening Nicole and O. J. had attended separately a dance recital in West L.A., both leaving at approximately 6 p.m. At approximately 6:30 p.m., Nicole, her two children, and other family members and friends dined at the trendy Mezzaluna Italian restaurant in Brentwood. O. J. was not invited to the dinner. At approximately 8:30 P.M. Nicole and her party left the restaurant, and she returned home with her children. Later, she received a call from her mother stating that she might have left her eyeglasses at the restaurant. Nicole called the restaurant and was told the eyeglasses had been found. Her friend Ronald Goldman, a waiter at the restaurant, offered to bring them to Nicole's home after he got off work. At approximately 9:45 P.M. Goldman left the restaurant. At approximately midnight the dead bodies of Nicole Simpson and Ronald Goldman were found by neighbors.

Detectives investigating the murder left the murder scene and traveled to O. J. Simpson's $5 million mansion several miles away, also in Brentwood, to attempt to notify him of the murder of his ex-wife. There, the detectives received no answer at his gate and then observed blood on the left door of Simpson's white Ford Bronco, which was parked outside the house. The detectives, fearing that there could be injured or dead persons inside the Simpson property, entered the property without a search warrant and began to interview people residing there. While inside the property the detectives found evidence, including bloodstains and a bloody glove that matched a bloody glove found at the murder scene.

At approximately 11:00 P.M. on the night of the murder, O. J. Simpson traveled from his residence to Los Angeles International Airport, where he boarded a flight to Chicago. At approximately 5:34 A.M. on June 13, 1994, he arrived in Chicago and checked into a room at the O'Hare Plaza Hotel, where he had made reservations days earlier. That morning the police telephoned Simpson at his hotel to notify him of his ex-wife's murder, and he flew back to Los Angeles. At approximately noon on Monday Simpson was taken to L.A. police headquarters for several hours of questioning and then released.

During the week that followed there was intense media coverage of the case, including reports of a 1988 arrest of Simpson for spousal abuse and a 911 tape recording of a frantic call Nicole Brown Simpson had made to the police in 1993, with the angry voice of O. J. Simpson raging in the background.

On Friday, June 17, 1994, at 8:30 A.M., the LAPD called Simpson's attorney, Robert Shapiro, saying they were ready to arrest Simpson for the double murder. Shapiro reported that he would bring Simpson to police headquarters. At approximately 2 P.M., police reported that Simpson had not surrendered and was being considered a fugitive. At approximately 5 P.M., the police, responding to a citizen's tip, pinpointed Simpson as the passenger in his friend Al (A. C.) Cowlings' Ford Bronco, which was being driven on L.A. freeways. The police then proceeded on a nearly fifty-mile "low-speed pursuit" of that car. During the pursuit, Simpson called 911 from the car cellular phone to state that he was armed, threatened to kill himself, and wanted to talk to his mother. At approximately 8 P.M., the car entered Simpson's property. After about forty-five minutes of negotiations, police persuaded Simpson to leave the car and enter his house. After being searched, Simpson was allowed to call his mother, use the bathroom, and drink a glass of orange juice. The low-speed pursuit and negotiations were watched by approximately ninety million Americans on live television.

A six-day preliminary hearing held in late June and early July resulted in O. J. Simpson being bound over for murder.

His criminal trial began in November 1994. Two-hundred fifty days and 126 witnesses later, the jury voted to acquit Simpson of all charges. The jury deliberation lasted less than four hours. The police have not reopened the investigation.

SOURCE: *People v. Simpson* (1995).

DEMPSEY'S LAW
Researching Law on the Net

Professor, what are the best Web sites to access legal information, Supreme Court cases, laws, and the like?

There are several that I use and recommend to my students.

The first is my favorite general reference site on the Net, which is Refdesk.com (http://www.refdesk.com). If you go onto this site and then go to "Subject Categories" and click on "Legal Resources," you will get to the Refdesk.com Law/Legal Information Resources. Or you can get there directly by going to http://www.refdesk.com/factlaw.html. From this site you can access any of Refdesk.com's 190 legal information resources links.

There is also an excellent site established by Cornell Law School. This site, the Legal Information Institute, at http://www.law.cornell.edu/lii.html, receives over seven million hits a week. From this site you can get a tremendous amount of information.

Another excellent site is law.com at http://www.law.com, and you can also access sites for each particular state at law.com/regionals. For example, if you are interested in California law, you can access www.law.com/regionals/ or go directly to www.law.com/regionals/ca/

There were also early law systems among the ancient Egyptians, Hebrews, Greeks, and Romans. Roman law had a major influence on modern law as the Roman Empire spread throughout Europe. Roman law was highly developed, containing some of the elements of modern law: legislation, administrative edicts, and judicial reasoning on the basis of legal tradition.

After the fall of Rome, the Roman legal tradition was carried on by the emperor of Constantinople. In 528 A.D., Emperor Justinian consolidated all the vast array of laws in his empire and established the Justinian Code. The Justinian Code is the cornerstone of today's civil law system. Civil law (not to be confused with the U.S. system of civil law, which will be explained later in this chapter) is a system of law in which all laws are extensively codified, and decisions are based on the legal code as designed by the legislature, rather than on binding judicial precedent. Today, the civil-law tradition is the dominant legal system on the European continent, in South America, and in Scotland, Quebec, and the American state of Louisiana. The Napoleonic Code, a civil law system developed in 1804, spread to the many former French colonies of Northern Africa. Another civil law system, the Germanic Code, developed in 1896, was later adopted by Japan and pre-communist China. Other significant legal systems, particularly the Islamic law of the Middle East and the Soviet legal system, gained prominence throughout many parts of the world.

The primary heritage of the United States legal system is England's common law. Unlike other parts of the world, England did not embrace the civil law system, instead developing its own legal tradition that we now know as common law. **Common law** refers to a traditional body of unwritten legal precedents created through everyday practice and supported by court decisions during the Middle Ages in English society. As new situations or problems developed in English society, they were addressed by English judges. The decisions of these judges became the law of the land. These decisions generally incorporated the customs of society as it operated at the time. Common law is frequently referred to as *judge-made law.* Because of the paucity of written legal statutes in England, the English judges formalized the customs and mores of the times into court decisions and applied the same rules throughout the entire country. These decisions were facilitated by written reports of the judicial rulings, which were kept by the courts and served as authority or precedent for subsequent judges. Common law became the basis for the legal systems of most of the English-speaking nations of the world.

English common law was strengthened by the Magna Carta of 1215 A.D. This *great charter*, signed by King John of England, guaranteed basic liberties for English citizens and ruled that any acts of Parliament, England's legislature, that contradicted common law would be void. Our U.S. tradition of due process of law and many of the rights guaranteed to criminal defendants in the Fifth and Sixth Amendments to the U.S. Constitution owe their origins to the Magna Carta.

Types of Law

Very simply, law has been traditionally divided into *public law* and *private law*. Public and private laws that establish the rules of behavior that govern our relationships with each other (proscribed and prescribed rights and obligations) are generally called *substantive law*. The criminal codes, often called *penal laws*, of the various U.S. states and the federal government are an example of substantive law—these laws define crimes, acts we cannot commit against each other.

Public and private laws that specify the methods to be followed in adjudicating substantive law cases to ensure they are conducted in a way that protects the rights and duties of the participants are called *procedural law*. The various state and federal criminal procedure laws, often called *codes of criminal procedure*, are examples of procedural law—these laws define the rules and methods that must be applied when adjudicating legal cases. Evidence plays a major role in both public and private law.

Public Law Public law concerns the structures, powers, and operations of a government, the rights and duties of citizens in relation to the government, and the relationships of nations. Public law can be divided into *constitutional law, administrative law, criminal law,* and *international law*. For our purposes we will limit our discussion of public law to criminal law.

Criminal law consists of laws that impose obligations to do or forbear from doing certain things, the infraction of which is considered to be an offense not merely against the immediate victim but also against society. Most such laws are backed up by sanctions or punishments, which are applied in the event of conviction. Major breaches of the criminal law, usually defined as those punishable by imprisonment for more than one year, are termed *felonies*. Less serious crimes, called *misdemeanors*, are punishable by imprisonment for a shorter period or by fines or both.

Private Law Unlike public law, private law does not involve government directly but rather indirectly as an adjudicator between disputing parties. Private law provides rules to be applied when one person claims that another has injured his or her person, property, or reputation or has failed to carry out a valid legal obligation. In this chapter we will refer to private law as *civil law*. Civil law governs the relationships between individuals in the course of their private affairs. It deals with such matters as contracts, property, wills, and torts. When two or more persons have a dispute, it is in the best interest of society as a whole to ensure that the dispute is resolved peacefully in a court of law. Unlike criminal law, the government is not an active participant in the case. The government's main interest in civil cases is to provide a forum—a court of law—in which to resolve the dispute. The government's main role in civil cases is to ensure that the case is resolved peacefully according to law.

Based on the types of legal rights and obligations involved, civil law is conventionally subdivided into six major categories: *tort law* (a tort is a legal injury one person has caused another—for example, when a traffic accident involves personal injury or property damage), *property law, contract and business law, corporation law, inheritance law,* and *family law*.

It should be noted that both a criminal law action and a civil law action can arise out of the same set of facts or the same incident. For example, if one person assaults another and causes an injury, the injured person can call the police and cause the assaulter to be arrested. That person may then be processed in the criminal court. But in addition, the injured person may instigate a civil action and sue the assaulter in civil court in order to make the assaulter pay for medical bills.

THE U.S. LEGAL SYSTEM

The system of law used in the United States is known as the **adversarial system** or adversarial procedure. This is the form of trial procedure that is also used in England and other common law countries. The defense and prosecution both offer evidence, examine witnesses, and present their respective sides of the case as persuasively as possible. The judge or jury must then rule in favor of or against the defendant in the case.

The adversarial system is different from the *inquisitorial system*, which is used in countries with civil law systems. In the inquisitorial system, the court, together with the prosecution and the defense, investigate the case before it. The court staff and the judge gather evidence and conduct investigations, and the judge's decision of guilt or innocence is based on the investigation.

The adversarial system is clearly distinguishable by its sharply defined roles for litigants and judges. Our system of judicial decision making involves two contestants (generally, attorneys representing their clients) arguing their case before a neutral and mostly passive judge.

The underlying assumption of the adversarial process is that truth is most likely to emerge as a by-product of the vigorous conflict between intensely partisan advocates, generally attorneys, each of whose goal is to win. The duty of advocates or attorneys in the adversarial system is to present their side's position in the very best possible light and to challenge the other side's position as vigorously as possible. The adversarial system is similar to a sporting event with two teams competing against each other.

The major components of the U.S. adversarial system are the criminal-civil law process, the trial, the jury, and the discovery process. (This chapter covers the first three; the discovery process was discussed in detail in chapter 4.)

Anyone interested in the U.S. legal system would probably want to view the U.S. Supreme Court's own Web site, which contains its current calendar; a gallery of the current justices with their pictures, biographies, and decisions; a gallery of former justices; the Supreme Court's rules; and information about the Court's organization, authority, and jurisdiction. As of April 2000, the Court began making its decisions available on its site.

The Criminal-Civil Law Process

The *criminal law process* refers to criminal laws and crimes, whereas the *civil law process* refers to the civil law and concepts such as torts (personal wrongs) rather than crimes (public wrongs).

A criminal law process generally begins when a person notifies the police that a crime has been committed against him or her, or when the police observe a person committing a crime. Generally, the police make a *summary arrest* (without a warrant) or secure an arrest warrant from a criminal court and arrest the person—the *defendant*—believed to have committed the crime on the authority of the warrant. The case is then processed in a criminal court. The *complainant,* or the person against whom the crime was committed, is represented by a public prosecutor, generally

INVESTIGATIONS ON THE NET

Supreme Court of the United States
http://www.supremecourtus.gov

Supreme Court Cases
http://supct.law.cornell.edu/supct/

American Bar Association
http://www.abanet.org

The Constitution of the United States
http://www.law.cornell.edu/constitution/constitution.overview.html

For an up-to-date list of Web links, go to http://info.wadsworth.com/dempsey

termed a *district attorney.* The defendant has a constitutional right to an attorney in the criminal trial. If the defendant is indigent—that is, has no money to hire an attorney—the court is required to provide him or her with an attorney in felony cases or other cases that may result in a prison term, according to the U.S. Supreme Court cases of *Gideon v. Wainwright* (1963) and *Argersinger v. Hamlin* (1972).[1]

A civil law process generally begins when a person (the *plaintiff*) files a complaint or lawsuit (*sues*) against another person (the defendant) for an alleged wrong committed against him or her in order to obtain legal redress. The case is then processed in a civil court. Generally, both parties are represented by attorneys.

Criminal and civil law processes are very similar. The main difference between the two procedures is that defendants who lose a civil suit may be forced to pay damages to the plaintiff and perhaps have their property confiscated in the process, whereas in the criminal law process defendants may be deprived of their liberty by being sent to prison or jail.

In the criminal and civil law processes, the burden of proof, or standard of proof, is also different. *Burden of proof* can be defined as the requirement of a litigant to persuade the trier of the facts (the jury or judge) that the allegations made against the other party to an action are true.

The burden of proof in civil law is the preponderance of the evidence standard; in other words, a preponderance, or majority, of the evidence must support the plaintiff's allegations against the defendant. If the plaintiff fails to meet this standard, the defendant will win the case.

The standard of proof in criminal law is *beyond a reasonable doubt*. Note that there is a difference between factual guilt—that the person really committed the crime for which he or she is accused—and legal guilt. Unless the determination of legal guilt is accompanied by strict adherence to the rules of criminal procedure, there is denial of due process of law. No matter how firmly we may be convinced that the accused actually committed the crime, the full coercive power of the state cannot be imposed until legal guilt has been proven beyond a reasonable doubt. Our belief that a person is innocent until proven guilty reflects the difference between factual and legal guilt.

The Trial

A trial is a formal legal examination before a court of civil or criminal issues between two parties: the plaintiff and the defendant. Most cases, civil and criminal, never reach the trial stage. In most civil cases, after the lawsuit has been filed, the attorneys for both parties meet and discuss the facts of the case, take statements for each party, and attempt to reach an out-of-court settlement. After conferring and engaging in pretrial negotiations, the attorneys come to an informal agreement, eliminating the need for a jury trial.

Most criminal cases are also settled without a trial. In these cases the accused is brought before a judge for arraignment—the first appearance before the judge in the criminal process. At the arraignment, the accused is formally notified of the charges and asked to enter a plea. The accused may plead *not guilty, guilty,* or *nolo contendere*, which literally means "no contest." A nolo contendere plea is generally a face-saving device—the defendant does not admit to guilt but admits a reluctance to fight the charges. If a guilty plea or nolo contendere plea has been entered, the judge is free to impose any sentence allowable for such a crime as if the defendant had been convicted at trial. If a not guilty plea is entered, the defendant is scheduled for trial. Generally, however, the defendant's attorney and the prosecutor work out a plea bargain in which the defendant agrees to plead guilty in exchange for leniency or some other consideration on the part of the judge.

The Sixth Amendment to the U.S. Constitution guarantees a criminal defendant the right to a jury trial in criminal cases. The Sixth Amendment also guarantees, among other things, the right to a "speedy and public trial," an "impartial jury," and the "assistance of counsel." The Seventh Amendment to the U.S. Constitution requires the federal government to guarantee a jury trial in certain kinds of civil cases.

If a trial does occur, a judge—the presiding officer of the trial court—usually rules on matters of legal procedure and sentences and a jury determines guilt or innocence. However, in a criminal case, a defendant may request a *bench trial,* where the judge serves as the jury or decider of guilt or innocence.

The Jury

A jury is a body of laypersons randomly selected to determine facts and to decide guilt or innocence in a legal proceeding. It is generally believed that a jury must consist of twelve persons and that the jury's verdict must be unanimous. However, this is not so. Although twelve jurors have generally deliberated as

---

EXHIBIT 5.1   **The Steps of a Jury Trial (Simplified)**

Voir dire

Prosecutor's opening statement to the jury

Defense attorney's opening statement to the jury

Prosecutor's presentation of evidence and direct examination

Defense attorney's cross-examination

Defense attorney's presentation of evidence and direct examination

Prosecutor's cross-examination

Defense attorney's closing statements to the jury

Prosecutor's closing statements to the jury (summation)

Judge's instructions to the jury on the law, evidence, and standards of proof

Jury deliberation and voting

Pronouncement of the verdict

Judicial sentencing

SOURCE: Marvin Zalman and Larry Siegel, *Criminal Procedure: Constitution and Society* (St. Paul, MN: West, 1991), p. 655. Reprinted with permission.

the triers of fact in criminal cases, the U.S. Supreme Court in *Williams v. Florida* (1970) ruled that a six-person jury in a criminal trial does not deprive a defendant of the constitutional right to a jury trial. The Court upheld a Florida law permitting the use of a six-person jury in a robbery trial. In this case the Court wrote, "We conclude, in short, as we began; the fact that a jury at common law was composed of precisely twelve is a historical accident, unnecessary to effect the purposes of the jury system and wholly without significance 'except to mystics.'"[2]

In addition, the U.S. Supreme Court ruled that trial verdicts in criminal cases do not have to be unanimous. In *Apodaca v. Oregon* (1972), the Court held that the Sixth and Fourteenth Amendments to the U.S. Constitution do not prohibit criminal convictions by less than unanimous jury verdicts in noncapital cases. In this case, the Court upheld an Oregon statute requiring only ten of twelve jurors to convict a defendant of assault with a deadly weapon, burglary, and grand larceny.[3] Similar provisions regarding the number of jurors and the unanimous juror verdict exist in civil court procedures among the various states.

The mechanics of the U.S. jury system vary with each state, but the function does not. Once selected and sworn in, the juror is questioned by the attorneys, the judge, or both about background or possible bias. This is known as *voir dire* examination. If an attorney believes there is reason a juror should not sit on the jury, that juror can be challenged "for cause" and replaced by another juror. The attorneys also have a limited number of additional challenges, called *peremptory challenges,* for which no reason need be given in order to dismiss a juror from a case.

The jury always deliberates in private and is never compelled to reveal its reasons for a decision. After the verdict is announced, usually by the jury foreperson— the person speaking for the jury—a jury may be polled. Here, each juror is asked in open court whether the verdict delivered by the foreperson is his or her own. Occasionally a jury will be *sequestered,* or separated from society, so that its members are protected from an onslaught of media attention or public opinion concerning the case on which they were assigned. At the end of a trial, if a jury cannot agree on a decision, the result is a *hung jury.* The case may then be re-tried before a different jury.

In a civil case, such as a personal injury action, the jury determines liability and the amount of the award as well. In most criminal cases, the jury renders a verdict of innocence or guilt, but the judge sentences the defendant.

EVIDENCE

The word *evidence* includes all the means by which an alleged fact, the truth of which is submitted to scrutiny,

---

EXHIBIT 5.2   Fourth, Fifth, and Sixth Amendments to the U.S. Constitution

The Fourth Amendment

The right of the people to be secure in their persons, houses, papers, and effects, against unreasonable searches and seizures, shall not be violated, and no warrants shall issue, but upon probable cause, supported by oath or affirmation, and particularly describing the place to be searched, and the person or things to be seized.

The Fifth Amendment

No person shall be held to answer for a capital, or otherwise infamous crime, unless on a presentment of a grand jury, except in cases arising in the land or naval forces, or in the militia, when in actual service in time of war or public danger, nor shall any person be subject for the same offense to be twice put in jeopardy of life or limb; nor shall be compelled in any criminal case to be a witness, against himself, nor be deprived of life, liberty, or property, without due process of law; nor shall private property be taken for public use, without just compensation.

The Sixth Amendment

In all criminal prosecutions the accused shall enjoy the right to a speedy and public trial, by an impartial jury of the State and district wherein the crime shall have been committed, which district shall have been previously ascertained by law, and to be informed of the nature and cause of the accusation; to be confronted with the witnesses against him; to have compulsory process for obtaining witnesses in his favor, and to have the assistance of counsel for his defense.

is established or disproved. The purpose of evidence is to lead to the truth of a charge. The laws or rules of evidence are the rules governing its admissibility. These rules have as their primary purpose the screening out or elimination of all evidence that is irrelevant (not applicable to the issue at hand) or that confuses the issues rather than assisting in the discovery of the truth.

The judge in a case determines the admissibility of the evidence and the jury determines its weight, or credibility. Either side in a criminal or civil proceeding may introduce evidence. Evidence is presented through the testimony of witnesses. Generally, one of the first orders of business in a trial is to segregate the witnesses from the courtroom proceedings in order to prevent them from tailoring their testimony to fit the evidence that has already been presented. This procedure is not followed for defendants, who have a right to be present throughout the proceeding.

Information is elicited from the witness through a series of questions and answers. The attorney calling the witness first questions that person in direct examination, and then the opposing attorney cross-examines the same witness. The process continues until one or the other attorney informs the judge that she has no more questions for this witness.

Many chapters of this book, particularly chapter 3, "The Crime Scene," chapter 6, "Criminalistics and Technology," and chapter 7, "Interviews and Interrogations," but also chapters 10 through 15, which deal with individual types of crimes, contain a lot of information about specific forms and types of evidence (see Exhibit 5.3 on page 110).

TYPES OF EVIDENCE

There are three general types of evidence: *direct evidence, circumstantial evidence,* and *prima facie evidence.*

Direct Evidence

Direct evidence directly establishes the main facts at issue in a case (the elements of the crime in criminal cases, the elements of the tort or other wrong in civil cases).

Direct evidence has been described as the testimony of witnesses who looked on while an act was being committed. It is evidence that proves the facts in dispute directly, without an inference or a presumption being drawn from any other set of facts. Evidence is direct when the facts in dispute are communicated by persons who have actual knowledge of the facts by means of their five senses—taste, touch, smell, sight, and hearing.

For example, in a murder case, if a person saw the accused actually shoot the victim, that person's testimony would be direct evidence of the shooting. In a civil case, the testimony of a person who witnessed a traffic accident would be considered direct evidence.

Circumstantial Evidence

Circumstantial evidence establishes a fact or circumstance from which a court may infer another fact at issue. A witness's report that she heard a gunshot, then observed a certain person with a gun in his hand, and then saw a person lying on the ground injured by a gunshot, is an example of circumstantial evidence. Although the person testifying did not see the shooting, the facts are so closely associated that it may reasonably be inferred that the person with the gun is the one who shot the person on the ground.

Circumstantial evidence often requires the jury to fit pieces of evidence together to complete the picture, just as one might fit the pieces of a jigsaw puzzle. The attorney presenting circumstantial evidence attempts to provide the necessary pieces of evidence to construct a credible and viable case.

Circumstantial evidence also includes physical evidence found at the crime scene, such as fingerprints, blood, bloodstains, fibers, and the like.

Prima Facie Evidence

Prima facie evidence is evidence that, standing alone, unexplained or uncontradicted, is sufficient to establish a given fact. Literally, from the Latin, *prima facie* means "at first sight." Prima facie evidence is sufficient on its face to prove a fact unless or until it is overcome by other evidence. An example of prima facie evidence of a homicide is one person testifying that he or she saw someone shoot another person to death. This evidence standing alone, uncontradicted or unexplained, would be sufficient to convict the offender of

DEMPSEY'S LAW
It's Just a Circumstantial Case

Professor Dempsey, you talk about the importance of circumstantial evidence in cases, yet I always hear attorneys on television say, "It's just a circumstantial case" or "All they have on my client is circumstantial evidence." I don't understand it. Isn't circumstantial evidence just a house of cards that will fall of its own weight, as one attorney put it?

I can understand your confusion. First, we have to remember that our American system of law is adversarial—one side against another side. The strongest case wins. It's like a boxing match. It's not uncommon for attorneys to attack their opponent's position. Some even like to try their cases in the public arena. Let me give you some examples of circumstantial evidence in order to impress upon you its importance. Let's talk about the O. J. Simpson case.

As you know, the evidence in the murder of O. J. Simpson's ex-wife Nicole Brown Simpson and her friend Ronald Goldman was all circumstantial. There was no direct evidence, meaning there were no

eyewitnesses to the crime. But there was plenty of circumstantial evidence. The man who heard the dog barking and the husband and wife who found the dead bodies were not witnesses to the crime. Their testimony was circumstantial evidence, but it was important evidence because it helped put pieces of the puzzle together. It helped establish time of death, which was very important in the case. Remember, also, the testimony of the limousine driver and the houseguest, Kato Kaelin. Their testimony was also circumstantial but helped to establish O. J.'s presence at a particular time. Also, all the physical evidence in the case—the bloodstains, the hairs in the knit hat, the bloody gloves—were all pieces of circumstantial evidence. Circumstantial evidence is very important evidence. A person can be convicted or acquitted solely on circumstantial evidence.

However, remember too that in the Simpson case the jury didn't believe the evidence.

the homicide. However, the offender may attempt to overcome the prima facie evidence by presenting evidence that the shooting occurred in self-defense. Prima facie evidence may be direct or circumstantial.

FORMS OF EVIDENCE

Evidence is presented in court in three basic forms: *testimony of witnesses, writings or documentary evidence,* and *real* or *physical evidence.* All three forms of evidence may be direct or circumstantial.

Testimony of Witnesses

A witness is generally any person who is able to observe, recall, and relate the details of some past event. A witness must take an oath or affirmation or otherwise demonstrate the trustworthiness of his or her testimony. Any witness and the **testimony** presented

must pass the *rule of competence* (discussed later in this chapter).

Documentary Evidence

Documentary evidence includes not only those tangible writings or pictures visible to the eye but also those sounds audible to the ear. Documentary evidence may include written documents, motion pictures, photographs, tape recordings, and other similar means of recording information.

Real Evidence

Real evidence (material objects) consist of tangible objects introduced at a trial in order to prove or disprove a fact at issue. Real evidence speaks for itself; it requires no explanation, just identification. Guns, fingerprints, bloodstains, and fiber evidence are all examples of real evidence.

© Larry Kolvoord/The Image Works

There are many different types of real or tangible evidence; examples include guns, fingerprints, bloodstains, and fiber evidence. Here, an Austin, Texas, Police Department evidence supervisor checks an evidence number on an item being stored in its evidence storage locker.

RULES OF EVIDENCE

The **rules of evidence,** or the laws of evidence, are a set of regulations that act as guidelines for judges, attorneys, and law enforcement personnel who are involved in the trials of cases. These rules, laws, or guidelines assist in determining how the trial is to be conducted; which persons may be witnesses; the matters about which they can testify; the method by which articles at a crime scene can be introduced into a trial; and what is admissible and what is not. Each U.S. state has its own set of rules of evidence that govern its criminal and civil law systems. This section discusses the following rules of evidence: *materiality, relevance, competency, presumptions, judicial notice, opinion evidence,* and *the hearsay rule* and its exceptions.

EXHIBIT 5.3   **Evidence Covered in This Text**

Evidence	Chapter
Bite marks	3
Blood	3, 6
Blood spatter	3
Bruises	3
Confessions	7
Computer evidence	14
Crime scene evidence	3
DNA	6
Fibers	3
Fingerprints	3, 6
Footwear impressions	3
Glass	3
Hair	3
Interviews	7
Interrogations	7
Paint	3
Photographs	3, 6
Scale models	3
Scent	3
Sketches	3
Skid marks	3
Soil	3
Statements	7
Tire tracks	3
Tool fragments and tool marks	3

Materiality

Materiality refers to whether or not the evidence presented is significant and important to the outcome of the case. Material evidence has great significance to the facts of the case. It is evidence upon which the jury members place much weight or that they think is important in proving the facts in dispute. The judge and the jury determine the materiality of evidence presented.

Relevance

Relevance refers to whether or not the evidence has a bearing on the issues in the case—that is, whether or not the evidence will assist in proving or disproving a particular point that the jury should consider in determining the defendant's guilt or innocence. Relevant evidence tends to prove or disprove a fact in dispute. It explains or sheds some light on the issues involved in the case. It is evidence that logically, naturally, and by reasonable inference tends to establish some fact. The judge determines what evidence is relevant.

Not all relevant evidence may be admitted into a trial. Evidence that has a tendency to prejudice the jury unduly may be excluded. For example, the prior convictions of an accused may be relevant in establishing guilt, but because of the prejudicial effect of such convictions, they are generally not admissible.

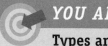

YOU ARE THERE!

Types and Forms of Evidence in the O. J. Simpson Case

Testimony by the police officers and detectives who responded to the crime scene:

- *Type:* Circumstantial
- *Form:* Testimony of witness

Hairs found in a knit hat found at the murder scene:

- *Type:* Circumstantial
- *Form:* Real evidence

Bloodstains found in O. J. Simpson's driveway:

- *Type:* Circumstantial
- *Form:* Real evidence

Competency

Competent evidence is admissible, in contrast with evidence that is not. For example, a confession may shed light on the facts of a case, yet because of some irregularity in obtaining it, the judge may rule that it is not admissible—it has no **competency.**

Our legal system places a premium on due process and the fairness of the procedures used for conviction in criminal cases. The courts have outlined procedures to be followed in the course of gathering evidence and preparing for trial. These rules apply to the court process and to the police in the gathering of evidence. When the police violate the rules established by the courts through the process of judicial review, the courts decline to allow the improperly collected evidence in a trial. The refusal to allow such "tainted evidence" is called the *exclusionary rule.*

The exclusionary rule was first established in the case of *Weeks v. United States* (1914), in which the Supreme Court stated that if there were no exclusionary rule, "the protection of the Fourth Amendment . . . might as well be stricken from the Constitution."[4] Although the *Weeks* ruling initially applied only to cases in federal courts, the Supreme Court extended the rule to state cases in *Mapp v. Ohio* (1961).[5]

Presumptions

Presumptions are deductions in law that may be made from certain sets of facts. Presumptions are recognized because they follow the normal course of events. Experience has proven that each time a given set of facts arise, the end results are almost always the same. Under these circumstances, it is logical to presume that the same results will continue to take place. Most presumptions are *rebuttable,* which means the presumption must stand unless overcome by evidence to the contrary. The jury is bound by a presumption unless it is overcome by evidence to the contrary. The following are some common presumptions in law:

- *Presumption of innocence.* This presumption is one of the basic foundations of our legal system. A defendant is presumed innocent until pronounced guilty by a court.

- *Presumption of sanity.* All people are presumed sane unless they can prove to the court that they are legally insane.

- *Children under a certain age are not capable of committing a crime.* In most jurisdictions children under age seven cannot be charged with a crime. Similarly, in most jurisdictions children under age sixteen who are alleged to have committed a crime are not charged for that crime but rather for a status offense titled juvenile delinquency; there are, however, exceptions.

Here are some other rebuttable presumptions:

- People intend the ordinary consequences of their voluntary acts.
- People take ordinary care of their own concerns.
- Evidence willfully suppressed by a defendant would be adverse if produced.
- Official duty has been regularly performed.
- The ordinary course of business has been followed.
- A writing is dated truly.
- A man and a woman deporting themselves as husband and wife have entered into a lawful contract of marriage.
- The law has been obeyed.
- A ceremonial marriage is valid.

YOU ARE THERE!

The Exclusionary Rule: Judge Kennedy-Powell's Ruling on the Admissability of Evidence in the O. J. Simpson Case

This decision concerns the court's determination whether the warrantless entry into the property of O. J. Simpson and the recovery of certain important items of physical evidence (bloodstains and a bloody glove which matched a bloody glove found at the murder scene) on the morning of Monday, June 13, 1994, were justified in the light of exigent circumstances.

Judge Kathleen Kennedy-Powell

The detectives testified that they were concerned about those children [the Simpson children had been taken to a Los Angeles police station after their mother's dead body was found] and wanted to make arrangements with regard to those children. They get to the gate and here, again, it seems to me they really do extraordinary things to try to make contact with the persons inside. I mean the testimony was that they rang the bell for some fifteen minutes to try to rouse somebody from within the house. They could hear that phone ringing from out at the gate. There's no response. But what do they see? And this, apparently, also is uncontroverted in light of the testimony that was presented. There's a light on upstairs; there's a light on downstairs. There's several vehicles in the driveway, a suggestion that there are persons inside.

They see what they believe to be blood on the door handle or near the door handle of this white Bronco. A white Bronco that is parked on a public street where the officers have a right to be, and the court sees no problem with the observing or recovery of the blood samples from the door of the Bronco.

So, seeing what they believe to be blood and having seen droplets of blood leading away from the location, the officers even now are doing more to get in touch with the people inside by calling the Westec Security, who apparently dispatches at least one, if not two, vehicles to the location and eventually gives the police the telephone number. What they get at that point is an answering machine.

Defense lawyers in this case did an excellent job on cross-examination. But when one looks at the result of that cross-examination, basically there were really no holes put in any of those detective's testimonies that they felt that they were acting in an emergency situation at the time. This would be a very easy decision for me if, in fact, these officers went in

there like storm troopers, fanning out over the property, examining every leaf, every car, every closet, every nook and cranny of this location, but the testimony as elicited by the officers and as supported by the witnesses that testified on behalf of the defense, show that this was not what happened.

What the testimony was, is that the officers went in search of persons on the property. They went into the guest quarters of Mr. Kaelin, woke him up.

We have to judge the officers' conduct and the exigency if there was one, not based upon what all of us know today but based upon what the officers knew at the time. And the information that they had been provided by Westec Security was that there was a live-in maid at the location. Additionally, Westec Security advised them that they had not been informed that there was going to be a vacation and absence of the residents from that location.

We know now, obviously, that there was no dying person or injured person on the property at the Simpson estate at that time. We know that all the persons who were supposed to be there were accounted for. Mr. Simpson was in Chicago, Mr. Kaelin was in his quarters, Ms. Arnelle Simpson had been out and returned about one o'clock in the morning. And GiGi, the maid, was on her night off. But the officers didn't know that at the time.

And we know from Mr. Kaelin's testimony that there was a loud, jarring, banging on the wall of his guest quarters, one that scared him, that he didn't know the origin of, that he had mentioned to several other persons but had never really investigated himself. So the officers have that information from Mr. Kaelin and Detective Fuhrman walks down that path.

He doesn't go anywhere else on the property. Officers make no attempt to go upstairs; they don't start opening cupboards, lifting up carpets, opening vehicles. He goes down that path to the area approximately adjacent to the air conditioner where that noise was seen and the picture jarred from the wall and finds a glove. A glove that appears to be the apparent mate to the glove found at the crime scene.

Contrary to the suggestions in the defense argument that a ruling allowing the officers' conduct—finding that it was reasonable and that there were exigent circumstances—would mean the

You Are There! continued

end of the Fourth Amendment and the Constitution and anarchy, I disagree.

The court finds that they [the detectives] were, in fact, acting for a benevolent purpose in light of the brutal attack and that they reasonably believed that a further delay could have resulted in the unnecessary loss of life. And, therefore, the court denies the defense motion to suppress and will allow the

introduction into evidence of the glove that was recovered and of the spattered blood spots that were located on the driveway once the sun came up, as well as the bloodstains from the Bronco, which was in plain view on the public street.

SOURCE: Preliminary hearing in *People v. Orenthal James Simpson*, July 8, 1994.

- The identity of a person can be made by the identity of the name.
- An unlawful intent is presumed from doing an unlawful act.
- Things have happened according to the ordinary course of nature and the ordinary habits of life.
- Flight from the police indicates guilt.

Judicial Notice

Judicial notice refers to the concept that certain kinds of facts do not need to be proved by formal presentation of evidence because the court is authorized to recognize their existence without proof. This rule applies to matters of general or common knowledge— for example, historical and geographical facts, a state's own laws, weights and measures, and the like.

Opinion Evidence

The general rule of evidence is that **opinion evidence** is not admissible in a trial. Witnesses may testify only to facts, not to their effect or result, or to their conclusions or opinions based on the facts. Witnesses can only testify to what they have observed, directly through the medium of their senses—sight, hearing, touch, taste, or smell.

There are two major exceptions to the opinion rule. The first involves the *lay* (ordinary, nonexpert) *witness* and the second applies to the *expert* (specialist) *witness*.

The Lay Witness The lay witness may express an opinion on matters of common observation where an opinion is the only logical way to convey the information. These opinions are permitted only concerning subjects of which the average person has considerable

experience and knowledge. Some examples of matters of common observation in which an opinion may be expressed by a lay witness are physical properties such as color, weight, size; approximations of a person's age; race, nationality, and language; emotional states; apparent physical condition of a person; intoxication; and approximate speed of vehicles.

The Expert Witness Expert witnesses may testify as to their opinion on evidence. An expert is a person skilled by means of education, training, or experience in some art, trade, or science to the extent that he or she possesses information not considered common knowledge among ordinary people. The opinion of an expert can be admitted when it concerns matters of a technical nature that require interpretation for the purpose of assisting the judge and jury in arriving at a correct conclusion. Expert testimony is not proof but rather evidence that can be accorded its own credibility and weight by the judge and jury.

Experts cannot testify as expert witnesses until they have satisfied the court that they have the proper skill, knowledge, and professional or educational background. There are numerous examples of subjects on which expert opinion may be given in court, including medical, scientific, and criminalistic matters.

The Hearsay Rule and Exceptions

Hearsay can be considered rumor, or secondhand information. It is information that has been told to a witness by someone else. Hearsay evidence is generally not admissible in court. Hearsay evidence proceeds not from the personal knowledge of the witness but from mere repetition of what the witness has heard another person say, meaning it relies on the veracity or competency of the other person. Hearsay applies to verbal statements and also to written material. Hearsay is anything that is not within the personal knowledge of the witness.

The following are the primary reasons for the exclusion of hearsay testimony:

- The author of the statement is not present in court and under oath.
- There is no opportunity for cross-examination of the author of the statement.
- There is no opportunity for the court to observe the author's demeanor.
- There is a possibility of error in the passage of information from one person to another.

An example of hearsay evidence would be the testimony of a witness that a neighbor told her that a certain person—the defendant—robbed a bank. This would not be admissible evidence because the witness has no personal knowledge about the acts of the defendant, knowing only what the neighbor said. Under the Sixth Amendment right of confrontation with witnesses, this witness's statement cannot be admitted because the neighbor's statement cannot be cross-examined.

Although hearsay is not usually admissible in a judicial proceeding, certain exceptions to this rule have been established through necessity. This necessity usually results because the original *declarant*—the person who made a statement—is unavailable to testify for some reason, and the information is such that in the best interest of justice it should be introduced so that the facts of the case may be determined. In order to introduce hearsay into evidence as one of the exceptions to the rule, three basic requirements must be met: generally, the original declarant must be unavailable to testify; the testimony must shed some light on the establishment of the facts of the case and the information cannot be presented through any other source; and there must be some test of the trustworthiness of the statement in lieu of the oath and the right of cross-examination.

Many exceptions to the hearsay rule have developed over the years, primarily because the circumstances surrounding them tend to minimize greatly the possibility of error or fraud. The major exceptions are *dying declarations, spontaneous declarations (res gestae), former testimony, past recollection recorded, business records,* and *confessions and admissions.*

Dying Declarations A dying declaration can be defined as that evidence resulting from the act or declaration of people made under a sense of impending death that relates to the cause of their death. The dying declaration of a victim concerning the circumstances of the act that induced the dying condition, including the identity of the person who caused the injury, is admissible in court. In order for the dying declaration to be admissible, the victim must have believed that he or she was dying, must in fact have subsequently died, and must have been competent at the time the statement was made.

This exception to the hearsay rule is generally limited to murder cases in which the out-of-court declarant named the killer and described specific details of the homicide. Dying declarations were developed as an exception to the hearsay rule because of the extreme necessity of getting the facts before the jury. A good example of the need to override the hearsay rule in certain murder cases is that the perpetrator and the victim may have been the only ones present at the murder scene, and thus are the only ones with knowledge of what actually happened.

The rationale for the dying declaration exception to hearsay is that dying declarations have intrinsic assurances of trustworthiness, making cross-examination unnecessary, because it is presumed that a person in the process of dying will not lie.

Spontaneous Declarations (Res Gestae) Spontaneous declarations—also known as res gestae, spontaneous utterances, spontaneous exclamations, and excited utterances—are statements made in response to some sudden and shocking event such as an accident or crime. The primary requirement for these statements to be admissible under an exception to the hearsay rule is that there must have been some event startling enough to produce such nervous excitement and that the utterance was a natural and involuntary reaction to the occurrence. These statements may be admitted through the testimony of a witness present at the time the utterances were made.

An example of a spontaneous declaration admissible in a trial for a traffic accident would be the statement of someone who heard a person yell, "My God, that man just drove right through a red light." An example of a spontaneous declaration in a criminal assault case might be someone who heard a person at the crime scene say, "I just saw the man in the red shirt stab the other man!"

Former Testimony The testimony given by a witness at a prior proceeding is admissible in a subsequent trial in certain circumstances as an exception to the hearsay rule. The essential requirement for the admissibility of the former testimony is the current unavailability of the witness who gave the former testimony.

Past Recollection Recorded Past recollection recorded is a memorandum or record concerning a matter about which a witness once had knowledge but now has insufficient recollection to allow her to testify fully and accurately. The past recollection record must be shown to have been made when the matter was fresh in the witness's memory.

Investigators referring to their notes is a good example of past recollection recorded.

Business Records The admissibility of business records, or business entries, is one of the older exceptions to the hearsay rule. Admission into court of the records of telephone calls made from a particular telephone, or the registries of persons checking in or out of hotels or motels, are examples of the business records exception to the hearsay rule. Normally, these records are admitted into evidence by people who have knowledge that these records are maintained in the general course of business although they might not have made the record themselves.

Confessions and Admissions An investigator can testify about a person's confession or any admissions made by a person. Because confessions and admissions are acknowledgments of guilt, the presumption exists that it is not likely that a person would voluntarily confess unless guilty. (Confessions, admissions, and police interviews and interrogations are covered in chapter 7.)

COURTROOM TESTIMONY

Investigators are often called into court or before other official bodies to present testimony, and juries are often influenced by their appearance and demeanor on the witness stand. It is imperative that investigators have a working knowledge of courtroom procedures

© AP Photos/Don Halasy

Investigators frequently testify in court. Here, a bomb squad detective points to a photograph of evidence from a fire-bombed subway car during the trial of a man charged with forty-five counts of attempted murder in New York City.

and the proper way to appear and testify in court. This section discusses the preparation, appearance, and demeanor necessary for court, as well as the testimony itself.

Preparation

Upon being notified of an impending court appearance the investigator must ensure that the case is complete and a final report prepared. The investigator then must arrange for a pretrial conference with the attorney who is calling him into court. At this conference, the investigator must organize the facts and evidence and prepare a summary of the investigation for the attorney. He must provide the attorney all reports and other relevant documents or exhibits, including photos, lab reports, and summaries of interviews and interrogations. At the pretrial conference, the investigator will review the evidence, discuss the strengths and weaknesses of the case, and discuss the probable line of questioning to be used by both attorneys in the case.

Just before the trial the investigator should review the case, his notes, the evidence, and the final report. The investigator should also ensure that all evidence is available for presentation to the court.

Appearance and Demeanor

The investigator's appearance in court is extremely important. How the jury will perceive the investigator's credibility will in part be determined by his appearance, demeanor, and professionalism. The investigator should be well groomed and dressed in professional business attire. For a man, professional business attire is a conservative suit; for a woman, it is a conservative suit or dress.

Christopher Vail, a retired investigator for the Inspector General of the U.S. Department of Health and Human Services, offers the following advice to investigators on preparation, appearance, and demeanor in court:

- Know which courtroom you'll be testifying in. If you are unfamiliar with the particular courthouse or courtroom, check it out before the trial so you will know your way around.

- Do not discuss anything about the case in public or where your conversation may be overheard. Anyone could turn out to be a juror or defense witness!

- Treat people with respect, as if they were the judge or a juror going to trial. Your professionalism, politeness, and courtesy will be noted and remembered—especially by those who do see you in court in an official capacity.

- Do not discuss your personal life, official business, biases, prejudices, likes and dislikes, or controversial subjects in public, for the same reasons. You might impress a judge, juror, defense counsel, or witness the wrong way.

- Judges and attorneys have little patience with officers appearing in court late, so be on time. Know when you will be expected to be called to testify.

- Dress appropriately. Look businesslike and official. If in uniform, it should be clean, neat, and complete. If not in uniform, a sports coat and slacks are as appropriate as a business suit (male and female officers alike).

- Avoid contact with the defense counsel and any defense witnesses before the trial. Assume that they will try to get you to say something about the case that is to their advantage.[6]

Testimony

At trial, investigators are subject to direct examination by the attorney presenting the evidence and normally to cross-examination by the opposing attorney as well. Direct examination is the initial questioning of a witness or defendant by the attorney who is using the person's testimony to further her case. Cross-examination is questioning by the opposing attorney for the purpose of assessing the validity of the testimony. After direct examination and cross-examination, each attorney may "re-direct" or "re-cross" the witness.

Before testifying, investigators are called to the witness stand and asked to take an oath to tell the truth. They should answer "here" when their name is called and move directly to the front of the witness stand, walking behind the tables occupied by the attorneys. They should bring any notes or reports to the witness stand in a clean manila file folder. When asked to take the oath, they should face the court clerk, hold up the palm of their right hand, and answer in a firm, clear voice, "I do," to the question, "Do you promise to tell the truth, the whole truth, and nothing but the truth, so help you God?" They should then proceed to the witness stand and be seated.

The attorney presenting an investigator as a witness in direct examination will ask the individual to state his or her name and profession. Investigators should reply slowly, deliberately, and loudly enough to be heard by everyone in the courtroom. Attorneys use the question-and-answer technique for examining witnesses. Generally, they ask a single, pointed question requiring the witness to respond. The answer should be "yes" or "no" unless the attorney asks for elaboration. The investigator should hesitate momentarily before answering in order to fully digest the question and also to allow an attorney to raise an objection if appropriate. If the investigator does not understand the question, he should ask the attorney to repeat it. Investigators should realize that certain types of statements are inadmissible in court, including opinions, hearsay, privileged communications, and statements about the defendant's character and reputation. They should answer questions directly and not volunteer information. They should refer to their notes to recall exact details but not rely exclusively on the notes. They should admit calmly when they do not know an answer to a question; should admit any mistakes made in testifying; and should avoid jargon, sarcasm, and humor.

They should state only facts and not try to color or exaggerate their significance. They must realize that even the slightest fabrication of testimony is perjury and likely to be discovered during the course of the trial. Perjury, which is a criminal offense, occurs when a person makes a false statement while under oath or affirmation.

The questioning by the opposing attorney in the case—the cross-examination—is usually the most difficult part of testifying. The opposing attorney will attempt to cast doubt on the witness's direct testimony in an effort to make her case more credible. This practice is known as *impeachment*—the process of discrediting or contradicting the testimony of a witness to show that the witness is unworthy of belief and to destroy the credibility of the witness in the eyes of the jury or judge.

Several methods are used to impeach or attack the testimony and credibility of a witness:

- Showing that the witness's previous statements, personal conduct, or the conduct of the investigation are inconsistent with the witness's testimony in court

- Showing that the witness is biased or prejudiced for or against the defendant because of a close relationship, personal interest in the outcome of the case, hostility toward the opposing party, or similar biases

- Attacking the character of the witness by revealing prior criminal convictions or other irrefutable characteristics that would render testimony unworthy of belief

- Showing the witness's incapacity to observe, recollect, or recount due to mental weakness, a physical defect, influence of drugs or alcohol, or the like

- Showing that the witness is in error, that the facts are other than as testified[7]

If the opposing attorney asks the investigator whether he has refreshed his memory before testifying, the investigator should admit to this fact. To do otherwise would be inconsistent with the proper preparation for court testimony. Similarly, discussions with attorneys, other investigators, and witnesses about a case are proper because they assist in the proper preparation for court testimony; the investigator should answer in the affirmative if asked about these prior discussions.

Regardless of how an investigator's testimony is attacked or challenged by the opposing attorney, the investigator should treat the opposing attorney with respect. Investigators should not regard the opposing attorney as an enemy but as a necessary player in the legal process. They should convey no personal prejudice or animosity through their testimony and should not allow themselves to become provoked or excited. The best testimony is accurate, truthful, and in accordance with the facts. Once again, it is a good idea to pause briefly before answering questions. This short pause will allow the prosecutor or other attorney to raise an objection to the question, if appropriate.

When both attorneys have concluded their questioning, investigators should remain seated until instructed to leave. They should then immediately leave the courtroom or return to their seat if appropriate.

EXHIBIT 5.4   The Ten Commandments of Courtroom Testimony

    I. Relax and be yourself.
   II. Answer only questions that are before you.
  III. Refer to your report only when allowed.
  IV. Paint the crime scene just as it was.
   V. Be ready to explain why you are remembering details in court if they are not in your report.
  VI. Avoid jargon or unduly difficult language.
 VII. Avoid sarcasm.
VIII. Maintain your detachment.
  IX. You don't need to explain the law.
   X. Explanation of what you said is possible on rebuttal.

SOURCE: George Hope, "Ten Commandments of Courtroom Testimony," *Minnesota Police Journal*, Apr. 1992, pp. 55–60.

SUMMARY

Go back and re-read the introduction to this chapter. Now that you have finished this chapter, do you understand why the investigator in the introduction lost his case? Do you understand why this should be so?

This chapter discussed law in general; the U.S. legal system; the definition of evidence; types of evidence, including direct, circumstantial, and prima facie evidence; and forms of evidence, including testimony of witnesses, documentary evidence, and real evidence. The chapter also examined the rules of evidence, including materiality, relevance, competency, presumptions, judicial notice, opinion evidence, and the hearsay rule and its exceptions. Finally, the chapter discussed courtroom testimony by the investigator.

LEARNING CHECK

1. Discuss the U.S. adversarial system of law.
2. Discuss the difference between direct evidence and circumstantial evidence and give an example of each.
3. Define *evidence* and name and discuss the three general types and the three general forms of evidence.
4. Discuss the differences between testimony that may be offered by the lay witness as opposed to testimony that may be offered by the expert witness.
5. Name and discuss three exceptions to the hearsay rule.

APPLICATION EXERCISE

Attend a criminal or civil trial at a courthouse in your area and prepare a report showing the effect of the rules of evidence on the court procedure. Note the objections raised by the attorneys and the ruling on these objections made by the judge. Explain the judge's decisions through your knowledge of the contents of this chapter. If you cannot attend a trial, research an actual case through the national media and prepare a similar report.

WEB EXERCISE

Use the Internet to access the federal rules of evidence, as well as your state's criminal procedure laws regarding evidence. Prepare a report comparing and contrasting both laws as they relate to three of the following topics: materiality, relevancy, competency, opinion evidence, and the hearsay rule.

KEY TERMS

adversarial system	materiality
circumstantial evidence	opinion evidence
common law	presumptions
competency	prima facie evidence
direct evidence	real evidence
documentary evidence	relevance
evidence	rules of evidence
hearsay	testimony
judicial notice	

CRIMINALISTICS AND TECHNOLOGY

6

CHAPTER GOALS

1. To introduce you to the importance of criminalistic evidence in investigating and give you a brief history of it

2. To show you how a modern crime laboratory is organized and what it does and to introduce you to the most modern criminalistic techniques, including DNA profiling or genetic fingerprinting

3. To introduce you to the role of the expert witness in presenting criminalistic evidence in court

4. To acquaint you with the latest technological advances in investigating involving computers, fingerprints, and photographic and surveillance techniques

5. To alert you to the threat to civil liberties caused by rapidly advancing technology

INTRODUCTION

DNA, AFIS, advanced criminalistic and forensic techniques, video cameras, VCRs, microcomputers, personal computers, cash machines, cell phones, and satellites: these technologies are all very familiar to us today. But little was known about them on the day these innovations were born. The past several decades have seen advances in technology that most people alive at the time would never have dreamed possible. Science and the computer chip have revolutionized society, and investigators have benefited.

The technology has also changed the face of law enforcement and our justice system, and investigators must be well versed in it. The controversy over the collection and analysis of physical evidence at many crime scenes—most notoriously in the 1994 O. J. Simpson case—clearly indicates the importance of science and criminalistics in today's investigations.

This chapter discusses the role of science and technology in investigating and solving crimes. It highlights the importance of forensic science or criminalistic evidence in criminal investigations and the court process and relates the history of forensic science or criminalistics. It discusses the modern crime lab, and in general, scientific techniques used in the lab to examine specific evidence. It explores the most recent advances in criminalistics that are revolutionizing investigating, including DNA profiling, or genetic fingerprinting, and discusses the role of criminalistic evidence and expert testimony in the courtroom.

The chapter also discusses the latest technology in investigating, including computers; advanced fingerprint technology, including automated fingerprint identification systems; advanced photographic techniques, including age-progression photos and automated composite sketching; and advanced technology in investigative surveillance. The chapter concludes with a discussion of the possible threat to civil liberties posed by modern technology.

THE IMPORTANCE OF CRIMINALISTICS IN INVESTIGATING

The terms **forensic science** and **criminalistics** are often used interchangeably. Forensic science, the more general of the two terms, is that part of science applied to answering legal questions. It is the examination, evaluation, and explanation of physical evidence related to crime.[1]

Criminalistics is actually just one of several branches of forensic science. Others include pathology, toxicology, physical anthropology, odontology, psychiatry, questioned documents, ballistics, tool work comparison, and serology. In order to simplify the information in this chapter for the nonscience student, however, the word *criminalistics* will be used interchangeably with forensic science.

The California Association of Criminalists defines criminalistics as "that profession and scientific discipline directed to the recognition, identification, individualization, and evaluation of physical evidence by the application of the natural sciences to law-science matters."[2]

According to the National Institute of Justice (NIJ), criminalistic evidence includes fingerprints, blood and bloodstains, semen stains, drugs and alcohol, hairs and fibers, and firearms and tool marks.[3] Forensic technicians, forensic scientists, and forensic chemists—all of whom are also known by the more generic term *criminalist*—generally specialize in one or more of the following areas: analysis of trace evidence, serology, drug chemistry, firearms and tool marks, and questioned documents.

In court, criminalistic evidence is presented through laboratory analysis by an expert prepared to interpret and testify to the scientific results, thus distinguishing forensic evidence from other forms of physical or tangible evidence such as stolen goods, articles of clothing, and other personal property.

The NIJ states that criminalistic evidence plays three important roles in the judicial process. First, it establishes the elements of a crime. For example, testing suspected controlled substances proves they are drugs and thus may help to prove that a crime has been committed. Second, it associates or disassociates defendants with crimes. Certain criminalistic evidence—particularly fingerprint and firearms evidence—can conclusively link a defendant to a crime; evidence such as blood, semen, hair, and fibers can tentatively link a defendant to a crime; and criminalistic evidence also can help exonerate a defendant when laboratory results are inconclusive or when they definitely disassociate the defendant from the crime. Third, it helps reconstruct the crime or the crime scene.[4]

In a study of criminalistic evidence and the criminal justice system the NIJ discovered that the police are on average about three times more likely to clear (that is, solve) cases when scientific evidence is gathered and analyzed; prosecutors are less likely to agree to enter into plea negotiations if criminalistic evidence strongly associates the defendant with the crime; and judges issue more severe sentences when criminalistic evidence is presented at trials.

As a result of their research into criminalistics and the criminal justice system the NIJ has made the following policy recommendations:

- Courts and prosecutors must press for greater funding of crime laboratories.

- Increased funding should be used primarily to broaden and intensify the caseloads of crime labs beyond predominant analysis of drug and alcohol evidence.

- There must be greater pressure for prosecutors to use forensic science.

- Prosecutors need to become more comfortable using scientific evidence—for example, by having more face-to-face contact with scientists and more experience in the direct examination of experts and the presentation of results to judges and juries.

- Justice officials should devote greater attention to the contents of laboratory findings and their proper interpretation.

- Prosecutors need to take a more aggressive approach in the use of scientific evidence by considering the potential utility of such information in all cases where it is available.[5]

 INVESTIGATIONS ON THE NET

American Academy of Forensic Sciences
http://www.aafs.org

For an up-to-date list of Web links, go to
http://info.wadsworth.com/dempsey

A society for the professionals dedicated to the application of science to the law is the American Academy of Forensic Sciences (AAFS) whose membership includes physicians, criminalists, toxicologists, attorneys, dentists, physical anthropologists, document examiners, engineers, psychiatrists, educators, and others who practice and perform research in the many diverse fields relating to forensic science.

Despite the truly amazing advances made in the field, the 1990s and early 2000s brought significant attention to the problems of crimes labs and scientific evidence. In 1994, the criminal trial of O. J. Simpson for the murder of his former wife and her friend was covered on national television and captured the attention of the world. Two hundred and fifty days and 126 witnesses later, despite overwhelming scientific evidence to the contrary, the jury voted to acquit Simpson of all charges. The LAPD was accused of gross incompetence in its handling of both the crime scene and the forensic evidence.

In 1997 the Justice Department's inspector general reported that the FBI's renowned crime laboratory was riddled with flawed scientific practices that had potentially tainted dozens of criminal cases, including the bombings of the federal building in Oklahoma City in 1994 and the World Trade Center in New York in 1993. The inspector general's findings resulted from an eighteen-month investigation that uncovered extremely serious problems at the laboratory that had been a symbol of the FBI's cutting-edge scientific sleuthing.[6] The dramatic series of problems and its alleged bungling of scientific evidence and criminal investigations led the national magazine *Time* to produce a cover article entitled, "What's Wrong at the FBI: The Fiasco at the Crime Lab."[7]

Most recently, in 2001 Joyce Gilchrist, an Oklahoma City Police Department forensic scientist, was accused of a series of mishaps involving at least five cases in which she either made significant errors or overstepped the acceptable limits of forensic science. When the governor of Oklahoma launched a review of every one of the thousands of cases that she had handled during her career, it was found that in twelve of them the defendants were awaiting the death penalty, and in another eleven the defendants had already been put to death.[8]

YOU ARE THERE!

Problems with Police Chemist Cast Doubt on Suspects' Guilt

Jeffrey Pierce was convicted of rape in 1986 on the basis of forensic evidence, including scalp hairs, pubic hairs, and semen samples, collected and analyzed by an Oklahoma City Police Department forensic chemist. In 2001, under a new state law, the Oklahoma Indigent Defense System won approval to submit the evidence used in the case for independent DNA testing. In April 2001, the preliminary results showed that the DNA taken from the rapist's hair did not match Pierce's. In addition, an FBI analysis of the hair samples contradicted the chemist's original hair testimony. As a result of the new tests, Pierce was released from prison, and the chemist, Joyce Gilchrist, was placed on administrative leave.

Gilchrist had analyzed such evidence as blood, hair, semen, and fibers from 1980 until 1994, when she was promoted to a supervisory position. After the Pierce case revelations, the Oklahoma governor ordered a review into every felony conviction linked to analyses done by her to make certain that no one else had been wrongly convicted. Among those hundreds of cases of convictions were eleven in

which the defendant had already been executed and twelve in which the defendant was on death row.

The state then gave the Oklahoma Indigent Defense System $725,000 to hire two attorneys and conduct DNA testing of any evidence analyzed by Gilchrist that had led to a conviction. A preliminary study of eight cases found that in at least five, she had made outright errors or overstepped the acceptable limits of forensic science. There were also allegations that she had withheld evidence from the defense and failed to perform tests that could have cleared defendants.

Why had this happened? Over the years, Gilchrist's work had come under criticism from her peers, defense lawyers, and judges. She was reprimanded by one professional organization and expelled from another. But despite all the criticism, local police and prosecutors had never scrutinized her work.

SOURCE: Jim Yardley, "Flaws in Chemist's Findings Free Man at Center of Inquiry," *The New York Times*, May 9, 2001, p. A1; Wendy Cole, Maggie Sieger, and Amanda Bower, "When the Evidence Lies," *Time*, May 21, 2001, pp. 37–40.

A BRIEF HISTORY OF CRIMINALISTICS AND FINGERPRINTING

The study of the history of criminalistics is the study of great pioneers in policing and science. This section explores the origins of the techniques, most of which are still in use today, and the contributions of pioneering scientists and technicians in the fields of anthropometry (criminal identification by means of body measurements), photography, fingerprinting, blood analysis, ballistics, criminalistics training and the development of crime labs, and the revolutionary DNA profiling or genetic fingerprinting.[9]

Anthropometry

Before the development of the science of **anthropometry,** all criminal records in France and England

were based on name. So, career criminals could simply give a different name every time they were arrested. A career criminal with six prior arrests, for example, could go before a judge as a first offender and receive more lenient treatment. Then, Alphonse Bertillon and the science of anthropometry changed all that.

Anthropometry is the use of body measurements to record the identity of arrested criminals. It was one of the first scientific methods not based on name to be used for the identification of criminals. In 1879, Bertillon held a minor clerical position with the Paris police. His main duty was to enter the physical descriptions of arrested and wanted suspects onto record cards. Bertillon realized that the mere recording of basic facts—such as name, height, weight, and hair color—did not ensure identification of habitual criminals because they often would change their physical appearance, as well as their names.

Bertillon reasoned that a foolproof method of identification could be based on physical characteristics that were unchanging and unalterable. His system, known as the **Bertillon measurements,** involved measuring the human body in eleven key locations, such as the distance from the bottom of the feet to the top of the head (height), the trunk, the person's reach, and the left foot. The eleven measurements of a criminal were recorded, along with eye, hair, and skin color. Bertillon calculated that the chances of two different suspects having the same measurements would be 4,194,304 to 1.

Bertillon's system of anthropometry was formally recognized in 1888, and spread to most countries of the world. That year, Bertillon was promoted to chief of the Department of Judicial Identity, the identification bureau of the French police.

Photography

Alphonse Bertillon also did pioneering work in the field of police photography. He is credited with developing the modern police ***mug shot***—the standard method of photographing arrested suspects. His mug shot method included photographing suspects in both full face and side profile, with each one sitting exactly the same distance from the camera. Suspects are still photographed in this way today.

Another of Bertillon's innovations was the *metric photograph*, which incorporated a metric scale along the photo's border to show the true size of the item in the picture. He was also responsible for the ***portrait parlé*** (which may be translated as *speaking picture*), a method of describing the human head in an extremely detailed manner that emphasized the uniqueness of each part of it. The portrait parlé was the predecessor of today's composite drawing. Bertillon also experimented in ultraviolet photography and developed methods of using this technique to examine questioned documents.

And Bertillon's interests were not limited to body measurements and photographs. In 1902, he became the first identification expert in Europe to solve a murder case by means of fingerprint evidence only. He also invented a method of preserving plaster casts by using a metallic replica.

Fingerprinting

Fingerprinting is the identification method that replaced anthropometry. Today it remains the primary method used to identify criminals positively. Fingerprints result from the series of friction ridge outlines that exist at the end joint of each finger on the fleshy side. The ridge characteristics (or patterns) on a person's fingers are different from each other and from those of all other persons. No two persons can have an identical fingerprint. Furthermore, these friction ridges and patterns form before birth and do not change during a person's lifetime.

Although fingerprinting became the primary method of criminal identification at the start of the twentieth century, the use of fingerprinting can actually be traced back to the first century, when a Roman lawyer introduced a bloody fingerprint at a trial and successfully defended a child accused of murdering his father. Fingerprints were also used as identifying marks on legal contracts during the T'ang Dynasty in eighth-century China.

Although examples have been found of the use of fingerprints throughout history, the science of fingerprints as we know it today did not evolve until the end of the nineteenth century with the pioneering work of Juan Vucetich, Francis Galton, and Edward Richard Henry. Juan Vucetich joined the Buenos Aires police department and was appointed the chief of its anthropometric bureau in 1889 to establish the Bertillon method of identification there. However, Vucetich became frustrated by identification problems associated with the method and began research into fingerprints to overcome that frustration. By 1891, he had devised a system of fingerprint classification based on ten fingers. Shortly thereafter, he became the first individual in South America to obtain a criminal conviction based on fingerprints as the only item of evidence.

In 1919, he submitted a proposal to fingerprint the entire population of Argentina. This proposal became law. However, the Argentineans rebelled against it, and various protests, riots, and attacks on Vucetich's office forced the law's rapid repeal. But Vucetich's fingerprinting system was the first complete system of fingerprinting classification. It gained widespread use, especially in Latin American countries, and is still used in its original or modified form in many South American police departments. Vucetich died in 1926.

Francis Galton, an English physician and a cousin of Charles Darwin, was the first person to write a definitive study of *dactylography,* or fingerprint identification, entitled *Finger Prints,* published in 1892. Galton, whose major fields of study were statistical research and anthropology, compiled much scientific data to prove that fingerprints are both unchanging and unique for each individual. He showed mathematically that there are approximately sixty-four billion chances to one of two fingerprints being identical.

A British official, Edward Richard Henry, developed an interest in criminal identification while serving as inspector general of the Bengal police, in India. Like Vucetich,, Henry found anthropometry unsatisfactory. He studied under Galton, basing much of his subsequent work on Galton's principles. After also studying Vucetich's system, Henry developed his own fingerprint classification system based on patterns and shapes. He described his new system in his book *Classification and Uses of Finger-Prints*, published in 1901. Henry's work was the primary factor in the adoption of fingerprinting as a means of criminal identification by England's Scotland Yard. Henry was appointed commissioner of the London Metropolitan Police in 1903. Modifications of his system are used today by nearly all English-speaking countries.

Blood Analysis

The knowledge of blood and its properties has been very important in the development of criminalistics.

Ballistics technology plays a major role in modern criminalistics. Here, a Syracuse, New York, investigator is using a comparison microscope to examine markings on bullets and casings. Two bullets can be seen together with this equipment.

Karl Landsteiner, an Austrian medical doctor and pathologist, discovered certain characteristics of blood in 1901. He separated blood into the blood groupings A, B, AB, and O that we still use today. He was also the pioneer in forensic serology—the scientific study of bodily fluids, particularly blood. His blood grouping discovery enabled other criminalists to assist criminal investigators in developing methods used to blood-type dried bloodstains.

Ballistics

The science of **ballistics** is crucial to the study of criminalistics. There were at least five early developers of the science of ballistics, but among the earliest was Calvin H. Goddard.

Goddard was a United States Army physician and hospital administrator. He developed a system to trace bullets to the weapons from which they were fired. Then, in 1926, he founded the Bureau of Forensic Ballistics in New York. This group perfected the ballistics comparison microscope and assembled the first complete collection of handguns, powders, and bullets for comparison purposes.

Criminalistics Training and Crime Labs

Many people were responsible for the development of forensic training and crime laboratories.

- Edmond Locard, one of the most famous criminalists in history, founded the internationally known Institute of Criminalistics in Lyons, France, and authored an encyclopedia of criminalistics, *Traité de Criminalistique*. Locard was known for his famous quote, "Every contact leaves a trace."

- Rudolph Reiss, an early student of Bertillon, was a university professor of police science and a director of several crime laboratories. He specialized in forensic photography and was one of the first to teach a university course on forensic photography. He was also a pioneer in his work on ink discharge, forged fingerprints, and preservation of footprints.

- Harry Soderman, a Swedish student of Locard's, was a private criminalist in Stockholm, where he became the head of the Institute of Police Science at the University of Stockholm in 1931. As an expert on crime laboratories he assisted the New York City Police Department in establishing its crime lab in 1934. In 1935 he coauthored with John O'Connell, a New York City police inspector, the classic text *Modern Criminal Investigation*. This text was used to teach forensic science techniques to a generation of detectives.

- August Vollmer, the police chief of Berkeley, California, organized and headed the Institute for Criminology and Criminalistics at the University of California at Berkeley. This institute was the first of its kind in the United States and paved the way for many criminalistics laboratories in the United States. Under his supervision, John A. Larson, one of his officers, developed the first practical polygraph (lie detector) in 1921. Vollmer was the first police administrator to institute formalized in-service detective training.

- The oldest forensic laboratory in the United States was established in 1923 by the Los Angeles Police Department. The Chicago Police Department established a scientific crime detection laboratory at Northwestern University after they were unable to solve the infamous 1929 St. Valentine's Day murders: seven men were killed in a warehouse, execution-style. It is generally believed that the murders were ordered by gangster Al Capone against the rival Bugs Moran gang, but the killers in this case were never caught. More widespread interest and developments in criminalistics followed the 1935 trial of Bruno Hauptmann, who was convicted of the kidnapping and murder of the infant son of Charles Lindbergh, the national hero who had completed the first solo nonstop flight across the Atlantic Ocean. Hauptmann was sentenced to the death penalty for this crime and executed. Many today question his guilt.

DNA-Genetic Fingerprinting

In 1984 professor Alec Jeffreys discovered the concept of **DNA profiling,** or **genetic fingerprinting,** at the University of Leicester, England. DNA, actually, deoxyribonucleic acid, is a genetic compound found in every cell of the human body. Jeffrey's discovery has led to major new studies in criminalistics. (DNA profiling is discussed at length later in this chapter.)

THE MODERN CRIME LAB

There are more than three hundred crime laboratories in the United States today. Eighty percent of them are located in police agencies.[10] Most large police departments operate their own crime laboratories. Smaller departments may contract out the use of large county crime labs or state police crime labs. Some departments use the services of the FBI lab.[11]

Private (that is, nongovernmental) labs are taking on greater importance in the U.S. legal system. Their analyses are increasingly being introduced into criminal and civil trials, often not only as evidence but also to contradict evidence presented by a prosecutor that was analyzed in a police lab.

This section presents an overview of the major criminalistics and specialty forensic sections of the modern crime lab.

Major Criminalistic Sections

As indicated in Exhibit 6.1 on p. 128, most crime labs have the following sections, which concentrate on different criminalistic evidence: ballistics, serology, criminalistics, chemistry, and document analysis. Each is covered in the following paragraphs.

Ballistics The ballistics section of the crime lab conducts scientific analysis of guns and bullets. (*Ballistics* is the science of the study of objects in motion and at rest.) Examination of firearms evidence involves the identification, testing, and classification of firearms submitted to the lab. Technicians examine microscopically a bullet, cartridge case, or shotgun shell in order to determine if it was fired from a specific firearm to the exclusion of any other firearm.

The ballistics examination provides the investigator with such information related to shooting cases as

A Hall of Fame of Criminalistics

Criminalist	Primary Innovation
Alphonse Bertillon (1853–1914)	Criminal identification
Juan Vucetich (1858–1926)	Fingerprints
Francis Galton (1822–1911)	Dactylography
Edward Richard Henry (1850–1931)	Fingerprint classification system
Karl Landsteiner (1868–1943)	Blood types
Calvin H. Goddard (1891–1955)	Ballistics
Edmond Locard (1877–1966)	*Encyclopedia of Criminalistics*
Rudolph Reiss (1876–1929)	Forensic photography
Harry Soderman (1902–1956)	Coauthor, *Modern Criminal Investigation*
August Vollmer (1876–1955)	Father of modern U.S. criminalistics
Alec Jeffreys (1950–)	DNA profiling or genetic fingerprinting

YOU ARE THERE!

The Will West Case

The **Will West case** was instrumental in the demise of anthropometry as the primary means of criminal identification. In 1903, a man by the name of Will West was committed to the U.S. penitentiary at Leavenworth, Kansas. Upon arrival he was measured using the Bertillon system and photographed. West denied having been in the penitentiary before. After taking his photo and measurements the measuring clerk checked the penitentiary's records and found a previous file with nearly identical measurements and a photograph of a man who appeared to be the prisoner. But Will West still denied that he had ever been in the prison. The record clerk, upon further examination, found that the file card actually belonged to inmate William West, who was already a prisoner in Leavenworth, having been committed to a life sentence on September 9, 1901 for murder.

The Will West case led to the belief that anthropometry could lead to mistaken identifications and that another more positive method was necessary to ensure proper identification.

SOURCE: Federal Bureau of Identification, *Fingerprint Identification* (Washington, DC: Federal Bureau of Identification, 1975).

comparison of a spent (that is, fired) bullet to a suspect weapon; the type and model of weapon that may have been used in a shooting; the description and operating condition of a suspect weapon; the bullet trajectory of a bullet wound (the line of fire and firing position of the shooter); the possibility of an accidental discharge of a weapon as opposed to a purposeful discharge; the trigger pull (amount of force required to fire a particular weapon); the shooting distance in possible suicide cases; and restored serial numbers from a weapon in which the original serial numbers were altered or obliterated.

To determine whether a suspect firearm was used in a particular shooting, ballistics experts test-fire a bullet from it into a tank of water known as a *ballistics recovery tank*. The spent bullet is then compared to the bullet taken from a victim or the crime scene using a *ballistics comparison microscope*. The rationale behind this testing is that bullets fired from a gun receive a mark on them from the lands and grooves of the barrel of the gun. These small individualistic markings are called *striae*. Bullets fired from the same gun should have similar markings.

In 1994, a computerized ballistics identification system that stores bullet "signatures" in a database was established to allow ballistics examiners to determine quickly whether a spent bullet may be linked to a crime. The new technology was hailed as a revolutionary

DEMPSEY'S LAW
So You Want to Be a Criminalist

Professor Dempsey, I love studying science and I love police work. I think I want to become a criminalist and work in a crime lab some day. What should I major in when I go on to my four-year school next year— criminal justice or science?

There have been several studies conducted to determine what crime laboratory managers look at when considering hiring new personnel.

In a study of 156 laboratory managers, the managers stated that chemical knowledge was the most important attribute they sought when hiring new employees. The majority of them preferred graduates from a traditional chemistry background.

In a survey of members of the American Society of Crime Laboratory Directors, researchers discovered that these members expressed the strongest entry-level hiring preference for applicants with undergraduate science training plus a master's degree in criminalistics and the least preference for applicants with a baccalaureate in criminalistics. The same researcher also surveyed 125 forensic scientists employed by the Michigan State Police Forensic Science Division and found the majority stated that the best preparation for the job was a master's degree in criminalistics or in one of the physical or biological sciences.

Also, in a later survey of 351 members of the American Society of Crime Laboratory Directors, the majority of the respondents reported that when hiring people for their crime labs they preferred people with master's degrees in criminalistics or in physical or biological science.

Well, Professor Dempsey, it looks like it's going to be graduate school for me when I finish my four-year degree!

SOURCES: K. Higgins and C. Selavka, "Do Forensic Science Graduate Programs Fulfill the Needs of the Forensic Science Community?" *Journal of Forensic Sciences, 33*(4), 1988, pp. 1015–1021; J. Siegel, "Appropriate Educational Background for Entry Level Forensic Scientists: A Survey of Practitioners," *Journal of Forensic Sciences, 33*(4) 1988, pp. 1065–1068; C. A. Lindquist, "Criminalistics in the Curriculum: Some Views from the Forensic Science Community," *Journal of Criminal Justice Education, 5*(1), 1994, pp. 59–68.

---

advance in the painstaking, time-consuming science of ballistics. This new technique, called Bulletproof, a trademarked name, was used on a pilot basis by the Bureau of Alcohol, Tobacco and Firearms (ATF) and the Washington, D.C., Metropolitan Police Department. "It's an amazing system," said Jack Killorin, the ATF's chief spokesperson. "We're literally at a point where the technology is going to allow us to do the same kinds of things for the unique marks left on expended projectiles that's now being done for fingerprints."[12]

The software-driven Bulletproof system includes a customized microscope, video camera, specimen manipulator, image digitizer, and a series of computers. The video camera and microscope record the unique telltale markings and grooves made as a soft lead bullet is fired through a gun barrel, then digitally translate the information for computer storage and future analysis. The system alerts the operator if a possible match has already been entered into the database by providing the examiner with a list ranked numerically. The examiner can then retrieve the stored image for a side-by-side visual comparison, eliminating the need to track down the original specimen. It also allows examiners to magnify any portion of the stored images.

Ballistics experts with the Metro Dade, Florida, Police Department tested the system with 230 fired bullets, including five "unknowns." It searched more than fifteen hundred comparisons before homing in on the two matches for each unknown entered into the database—"hits" the system made during its first search. The same task—a manual search and comparison that usually involves rifling through drawers containing thousands of samples collected over time by police— would have taken years.

In addition to examining guns and bullets, firearms examiners can help investigators determine if a suspect recently fired a weapon. Investigators can

YOU ARE THERE!

Future Forensic Scientists Take a Crack at Arlington's Cold Cases

As part of a joint arrangement between George Washington University and the Arlington County, Virginia, police department, students working toward a master's degree in forensic science will get invaluable experience working on "cold" homicide cases, some going back as far as fifteen years.

This joint program, which began in September 2000, uses students to reexamine unresolved cases. The seven interns who were accepted into the program reorganize cold case files into a death investigation file format and prepare physical evidence, if available, for submission to the forensic lab for reexamination, placing particular emphasis on DNA.

SOURCE: "Future Forensic Scientists Take a Crack at Arlington's Cold Cases," *Law Enforcement News*, Jan. 31, 2001, p. 5.

EXHIBIT 6.1	Major Sections of the Crime Laboratory

Section	Function
Ballistics	Examination of guns and bullets
Serology	Examination of blood, semen, and other body fluids
Criminalistics	Examination of hairs, fibers, paints, clothing, glass, and other trace evidence
Chemistry	Examination of drugs and alcohol
Document analysis	Examination of handwriting and written documents

SOURCE: Professor Paschal L. Ungarino, Suffolk County Community College, New York.

INVESTIGATIONS ON THE NET

FBI Crime Lab
http://www.fbi.gov/hq/lab/labhome.htm

For an up-to-date list of Web links, go to http://info.wadsworth.com/dempsey

use the dermal nitrate or paraffin test to determine if there is any gunpowder residue on a suspect's hands or clothing.

Another new computerized ballistics system, DRUGFIRE, has also come online. This system, which deals with the comparison of shell casings and bullets, is a national database giving firearms examiners the ability to link firearms and projectiles used in drive-by, serial, gang, and drug-related shootings across the nation.[13] DRUGFIRE is maintained by the FBI. The ATF maintains the Integrated Ballistics Information System (IBIS). Another of the ATF's weapons against illicit gun sales is ONLINE LEAD, a computerized database of the

records the ATF keeps on more than a million guns seized in crimes. The system allows investigators to tell almost instantly whether the same person or store keeps showing up repeatedly as the source of a gun used in the commission of a crime. The data can then be sorted in ways that could lead to the identification of organized gun distribution rings. By 2000, the various national law enforcement ammunition-tracing databases created since 1993 held more than eight hundred thousand images of bullets and shell casings. More than eight thousand matches have been made in over sixteen thousand cases. Law enforcement officials say that computer ballistic imaging technology is the most important forensic advancement since the development of the comparison microscope over seventy years ago.[14]

A professional organization for persons interested in firearms and ballistics examinations is the Association of Firearms and Tool Mark Examiners (AFTE). For persons interested in ballistics, there is also a nonprofit Web site established to introduce viewers to forensic firearms identification as an educational and investigative aid.

Serology The crime lab's serology section analyzes blood, semen, and other body fluids found at a crime scene—obviously important evidence in homicide and sexual assault cases. If blood on a suspect's shirt can be matched to the victim's blood, it can place the suspect at the crime scene. If semen found in a rape victim or on her clothing can be matched to a suspect's, it can link the perpetrator to the crime. Certain tests are useful in this process. The *hemin crystal test* will determine if a particular stain is actually blood. The *precipitin test* will determine if the blood is human, animal, or a mixture of both. Other tests can determine the specific blood type of the stain. Tests can also detect the existence of semen in stains and match the semen to a particular blood type. Laboratory tests can reveal if a stain is semen, if sperm is present, and if a person was a secretor. If so, it can establish blood groups.

The use of the chemical luminol can produce evidence that blood was at a scene even if the area was meticulously cleaned. When luminol is sprayed on an area, a luminescence or glow is produced if blood has been present. The development of DNA profiling or genetic fingerprinting has revolutionized the serology capacity of the crime lab.

Criminalistics The criminalistics section of the crime lab studies myriad pieces of physical evidence that may connect a suspect to a crime or a crime scene. Often this evidence is crucial to the understanding of the crime scene and the identification of perpetrators. A perpetrator may unknowingly take something from a crime scene (for example, fibers from the victim's carpet may be found on the suspect's clothing) or may leave something at the crime scene (a shoeprint in the mud outside the victim's window or marks from a tool used to pry open the victim's window).

The matching of samples of evidence found at the crime scene to a particular subject can be instrumental in the identification and successful prosecution of a suspect. (See also the discussion of evidence in chapter 3.) The following are some examples of crime scene evidence that can be of value in an investigation.

GLASS Fragments of glass found at a crime scene can give an investigator a great deal of useful information. Traces of blood, clothing, hair, or fingerprints can be found on glass fragments. When a suspect is arrested, these same fragments can conclusively establish the individual's presence at the scene if they are also found on his or her clothing.

Glass can also indicate how a crime was committed. Investigators can study conchoidal fractures, radial fractures, and concentric breaks to determine how the glass was broken, the angle at which a bullet was fired, and even which bullet was fired first through a window with multiple bullet holes.

EXHIBIT 6.2   **Services Provided by the FBI Crime Laboratory**

Chemistry

Computer analysis and response

DNA analysis

Evidence response

Explosives

Firearms and tool marks

Forensic audio, video, and image analysis

Forensic science research

Forensic science training

Hazardous materials response

Investigative and prosecutory graphics

Latent prints

Materials analysis

Questioned documents

Racketeering records

Special photographic analysis

Structural design

Trace evidence

SOURCE: *FBI Laboratory Services;* www.fbi.gov/hq/lab/org/labchart.htm.

 INVESTIGATIONS ON THE NET

Bureau of Alcohol, Tobacco and Firearms
http://www.atf.treas.gov

Association of Firearms and Tool Mark Examiners
http://www.afte.org

Firearms forensic identification information
http://www.firearmsID.com

For an up-to-date list of Web links, go to
http://info.wadsworth.com/dempsey

YOU ARE THERE!
How Luminol Solved a Murder

In a rural community, the dismembered body of a dead woman—a waitress at a local restaurant—was found at the side of a road. The woman had been sexually assaulted and her body mutilated. Neither the victim's clothing nor a murder weapon could be found. There were no witnesses. Examination of the body revealed that the woman's arms and legs had been severed with either a saw or a large knife with a serrated edge.

Investigators were able to find out that a certain man who frequented the restaurant where the woman worked had been unsuccessfully attempting to date the woman. Witnesses told the police that on the night she disappeared, the man appeared to be agitated when she refused to wait on his table.

Several years later, investigators were able to gain further evidence against the man that gave them the necessary facts to obtain a search warrant. While executing the warrant, they found a large table saw in a workshop behind the suspect's house. A close examination of the saw led to the discovery of several hairs that appeared to be human. There was no blood visible on the saw or in the workshop.

The area was sprayed with luminol, which produces a luminescence if blood has been present. Luminol is used in cases where the police believe an attempt was made to hide or alter bloodstains. Based on the luminol testing it was determined that a wall in the workshop, the saw, and other items in the workshop contained enough traces of the victim's blood for identification.

The suspect was arrested and tried for the murder. He was found not guilty by reason of insanity. He remains confined to a state hospital.

SOURCE: Dusty Hesskew, *Law and Order*, Nov. 1991, pp. 31–33.

Glass offers a wealth of information because of differences in the way it is made. It varies widely in physical and chemical composition, and has numerous impurities. Through the use of refractive index analysis, dispersion analysis, densities analysis, and spectrographic analysis, a crime lab can link glass from a suspect's clothing to that collected at a crime scene, or specify the type of vehicle from fragments collected at a hit-and-run accident.

HAIRS AND FIBERS Hairs and fibers can be vital pieces of evidence. They can be found on a victim's clothing and in objects at the crime scene, such as bed linen, carpets, and furniture. Hair can indicate the perpetrator's race and gender. Investigators can tell which part of the body hair came from. They can see whether it was pulled out forcibly or fell out naturally, or if it was smashed with a blunt object or sheared with a sharp instrument.

Fibers are also very specific in the information they reveal. Because they vary dramatically in color, source, shape, and composition, they actually have more identifying characteristics than hair. The case of the Atlanta child murders in 1980 and 1981, in which approximately thirty African-American boys were murdered, was an important case involving fibers as criminalistic evidence.

FINGERNAIL SCRAPINGS Two types of evidence can be taken from fingernail scrapings and fingernails at a crime scene. First, when fingernails are trimmed and collected from a victim, scrapings of hairs, fibers, skin, or blood from under the nails can reveal a variety of information about the crime and the perpetrator, especially in cases in which the victim struggled with the perpetrator. Second, when a broken fingernail is left at the scene and later compared to the nails of a suspect, it can include or exclude that person from the list of suspects. Much like fingerprints, nails are unique to each individual and rarely change through life. Fingernails can be examined in much the same way as tool marks, bullets, and casings. Because the striae on nails is on the same scale as that found on fired bullets, the same type of comparison microscope is used.

IMPRESSIONS AND CASTS Impressions and casts taken of footprints at a crime scene can be very important to the investigator because no two people wear shoes in precisely the same way or show damage in the same places. Footprints can include or exclude a suspect, as well as tell investigators whether he was walking or running, was carrying a heavy object, or seemed unfamiliar with the area or unsure of the terrain.

Chemistry The chemistry section studies alcohol and possible drugs or controlled substances gathered in investigations and arrests. This section analyzes most of the cases handled by the crime lab.

The most commonly used standard for the degree of intoxication in criminal cases such as driving while intoxicated (DWI) or driving while under the influence (DUI) is the measure of alcohol concentration in the suspect's blood. The alcohol concentration level determined by the lab is instrumental in the eventual prosecution of these alcohol-related crimes.

The chemistry section also tests substances believed to be in violation of the drug laws. Using chemical and other tests, chemists can identify the type of drug in a substance, as well as the percentage of a drug in a particular mixture.

Testing employees for the use of drugs and controlled substances is very common in private industries today. An expert in corporate drug testing offers businesses that wish to test their employees for drug use with the following advice:

> It is critical that the company selects a laboratory carefully. It should pick the highest-quality lab and make sure it is certified by the National Institute of Drug Awareness (NIDA). NIDA only certifies labs that are specialists in forensic drug testing. Personnel of a non-NIDA lab may not be trained in, or consistently follow procedures that will stand up in court. The lab should test a sample twice, first with a screening test, usually enzyme multiplied immunoassay testing (EMIT) and second, if the first test is positive, a confirmation test using gas chromatography—mass spectrometry testing. The lab should be required to keep all positive samples for one year. Employees will appreciate knowing that if they ever test positive for substance abuse, the sample will be available for them to test independently at another lab.[15]

DOCUMENT ANALYSIS The document analysis section studies handwriting, printing, typewriting, and the paper and ink used in the preparation of a document in order to provide investigators with leads on the identity of the writer. The document technician can compare requested handwriting exemplars (samples of the suspect's handwriting requested by the police) with the questioned document. This is a very important type

---

 YOU ARE THERE!

Criminalistics and Good Old Detective Work Find Suspect in Hit-and-Run That Killed Jockey's Wife

In January 2001, Marjorie Cordero, wife of famed jockey Angel Cordero, was struck and killed by an auto as she crossed a road near her home in Greenvale, New York. Among the evidence left at the scene by the hit-and-run driver was a headlight and a two-inch by three-inch plate of fiberglass from a header panel of the car. Eventually this evidence enabled police to make an arrest in May 2001.

Criminalists from the Nassau County Police Department's Scientific Investigation Bureau analyzed the headlight and the fiberglass and determined that these pieces of evidence came from a 1987 or 1988 black Mercury Cougar. They ran that description through the state Department of Motor Vehicles database and found there were hundreds of cars of that model in the Nassau County and eastern Queens area. During the weeks that followed, investigators looked at more than three hundred Mercury Cougars—staking out driveways, glancing at header panels—before zeroing in on the suspect's car. They obtained a warrant to search it, and the piece of black fiberglass recovered at the scene fit into the header panel of the suspect's car like a missing piece from a jigsaw puzzle.

SOURCE: Oscar Corral, "Hit-Run Arrest: Cops Find Suspect in Incident That Killed Marjorie Cordero," *Newsday*, May 2, 2001, p. A3.

YOU ARE THERE!
How Criminalistic Evidence and Fibers Led to a Serial Murderer

For twenty-two months in 1980 and 1981, the residents of Atlanta, Georgia, lived in fear and outrage as a serial killer methodically hunted down their children. The body count reached thirty before the killer was apprehended. The victims ranged in age from seven to twenty-eight, and most were young males. Some were shot or strangled; others were stabbed, bludgeoned, or suffocated. All the victims were African American. The deaths of so many young black people gave rise to a variety of theories and accusations, including belief in a plot by white supremacists to systematically kill all African American children. Atlanta became a city under siege and inevitably attracted the attention of the entire country, including the federal government.

It appeared the murders would never stop until one night, as police staked out a bridge over the Chattahoochee River, they heard a car on the bridge come to a stop, followed by a distinct splash caused by something being dropped into the river. They pulled Wayne B. Williams, twenty-three, over for questioning and finally arrested him as a suspect in the child murder cases. Williams was found to be a bright young African American who lived with his retired parents and was involved in photography. A media and police "groupie," Williams would often listen on his short-wave radio and respond to ambulance, fire, and police emergency calls. He would then sell his exclusive pictures to the local newspapers. At age eighteen he was arrested for impersonating a police officer. He spent one year at Georgia State University but dropped out when he felt his "rising star" was moving too slowly.

Wayne's freelance work as a cameraman was never steady, and he began to focus his energies on music. As a self-employed talent scout, he eventually lured his victims into his control. He was known to distribute leaflets offering "private and free" interviews to African Americans between the ages of eleven and twenty-one who sought a career in music. At his trial, Williams was depicted as a man who hated his own race and wanted to eliminate future generations. He was described as a homosexual, or bisexual, who paid young boys to have sex with him. A fifteen-year-old boy claimed he had been molested by Williams, and several witnesses testified they had seen him with some of the victims.

Williams denied guilt. The prosecution had only elaborate forensic evidence—consisting of fibers in his car that matched fibers on the furniture in the homes of some of the victims—on which to base their case against him. The forensic fiber evidence suggested a distinct link between Williams and at least ten of the homicides and indicated a pattern in the murders. The judge ruled the evidence admissible, and Williams was found guilty of murdering two of his older victims, Nathaniel Cater, twenty-seven, and Ray Payne, twenty-one. Due to the strength of the fiber evidence, the judge sentenced Williams to two consecutive life sentences. He was eventually named as being responsible for twenty-four of the Atlanta slayings.

SOURCE: Eric W. Hickey, *Serial Murderers and Their Victims* (Belmont, CA: Wadsworth, 1991).

---

of analysis in investigating ransom notes, anonymous letters, and possible forgeries.

Document analysis can also determine if there were any additions, changes, or deletions made. The paper on which a document is written can provide a number of clues to the investigator, such as the manufacturer, date of production, the pH and fiber composition, trace elements, and chemical elements, including fibers, waxes, dyes, fluorescent brighteners, and fillers.

A private lab specializing in document analysis describes its services this way: "Scientific examination of anonymous letters; printed, written and typewritten documents to determine authenticity, alterations, and indented writing. Court-qualified, expert witness and lecturer."[16]

The U.S. Secret Service has developed a new computer tool: the Forensic Information System for Handwriting (FISH). The innovative automated handwriting technology allows examiners to treat writing data with

INVESTIGATIONS ON THE NET

American Society of Questioned Document Examiners
http://www.asqde.org

U.S. Secret Service
http://www.ustreas.gov/usss/home.htm

For an up-to-date list of Web links, go to http://info.wadsworth.com/dempsey

---

EXHIBIT 6.3 Forensic Specialties

Section	Examination Type
Forensic pathology	Dead bodies
Forensic physical anthropology	Skeletal remains
Forensic odontology	Teeth formation
Forensic toxicology	Poisons
Forensic entomology	Insects at death scenes

SOURCE: Professor Paschal L. Ungarino, Suffolk County Community College, New York.

special mathematical programs and search them against previously entered writings. According to Richard A. Dusak, a document analyst for the U.S. Secret Service in Washington, D.C., "The Secret Service has been able to effect case solutions, consolidate investigative information and identify previously unknown individuals with the aid of the Forensic Information System for Handwriting."[17]

The American Society of Questioned Document Examiners (ASQDE) is a professional organization for forensic document examiners.

Specialty Forensic Sections

Some laboratories also have other extremely specific, sophisticated forensic specialties. Exhibit 6.3 lists and explains the most common ones. These sections are generally operated by a pathologist, coroner, or medical examiner rather than a law enforcement agency.

Forensic pathologists can determine the manner and cause of death (natural, suicide, accident, homicide), the time of death, the type of instrument used to commit homicide, and whether injuries to the body were antemortem or postmortem (before death or after death). Forensic pathology also attempts to establish the identity of the victim as well as age, gender, height, and weight, and the age of mutilated or decomposed bodies and skeletons.

The forensic toxicologist can establish the existence, type, and amount of poison used. The forensic toxicologist can also determine whether or not a lethal amount of poison was present in a dead body so as to exclude other causes of death. The American Board of Forensic Toxicology is a professional organization for forensic toxicologists that maintains standards for those who practice in the field.

Forensic physical anthropologists study human remains (such as skeletons, bones, skull fragments) to identify a corpse and to determine the cause of death. The American Board of Forensic Anthropology (ABFA) is a professional organization for forensic physical anthropologists.

Forensic entomologists use insect evidence to uncover circumstances of interest to the law. For example, the time of death can usually be determined using insect evidence gathered from and around a corpse. The American Board of Forensic Entomology is a professional society of interest to forensic entomologists.

Forensic odontologists study teeth and related evidence. Teeth can indicate the deceased's identity or age. Forensic odontologists also study bite marks on victims and can match them to a suspect's bite mark exemplar. The American Board of Forensic Odontology is a professional organization of interest to persons interested in this field.

Crime Lab Accreditation

Crime lab accreditation is designed to ameliorate some of the problems raised earlier in this chapter: mistakes made by our nation's crime labs.

The American Society of Crime Laboratory Directors (ASCLD) is a nonprofit professional society of crime laboratory directors devoted to the improvement of crime laboratory operations through sound management practices. Its purpose is to foster the common professional interests of its members and to promote and foster the development of laboratory management principles and techniques. Its Crime Laboratory Accreditation Program is a voluntary program in which any crime laboratory may participate to

INVESTIGATIONS ON THE NET

American Board of Forensic Toxicology
http://www.abft.org

American Board of Forensic Anthropology
http://www.csuchico.edu/anth/ABFA/

For an up-to-date list of Web links, go to
http://info.wadsworth.com/dempsey

---

demonstrate that its management, operations, personnel, procedures, equipment, physical plant, security, and personnel safety procedures meet established standards. The accreditation process is part of a laboratory's quality assurance program, which should also include proficiency testing, continuing education, and other programs to help the laboratory give better overall service to the criminal justice system. The ASCLD maintains that the process of self-evaluation that leads to accreditation is in itself a valuable management tool for the crime laboratory director.

The American Board of Criminalists (ABC) certifies lab employees. Because it ensures that lab personnel are all held to the same standard, certification

YOU ARE THERE!

The Body Farm: The Forensic Anthropology Center

The Forensic Anthropology Center, also known as *the body farm*, is an outdoor laboratory for studying the sequence of decomposition in human remains at the University of Tennessee's Institute for Public Service in Knoxville. It was established more than twenty years ago by Dr. William Bass, an emeritus professor of anthropology at the university. This three-acre site provides students and researchers with the opportunity to study twenty-five to thirty corpses as they decompose. In March 2001, the FBI sent thirty-six employees to the body farm to broaden their knowledge of the subject.

SOURCE: "Is Your Crime-Scene Work a Crime? Help Will Soon Be on the Way," *Law Enforcement News*, Mar. 15, 2001, p. 1.

INVESTIGATIONS ON THE NET

American Board of Forensic Entomology
http://web.missouri.edu/cafnr/entomology/index.html

American Board of Forensic Odontology
http://www.abfo.org

For an up-to-date list of Web links, go to
http://info.wadsworth.com/dempsey

---

helps analysts fend off courtroom salvos about their experience, background, and training.

Clearly, accreditation and certification are needed in our nation's labs.

MODERN CRIMINALISTIC TECHNIQUES

Over the past decade science has revolutionized investigating and the process of criminalistics. Among the major modern techniques discussed in this section are DNA profiling, ultraviolet forensic imaging, and other new technologies involving neutron activation, scanning electron microscopes, and gas chromatograph-mass spectrometer technology.

DNA Profiling

Deoxyribonucleic acid (DNA) is the basic building code for all of the human body's chromosomes and it is the same in each cell of an individual's body, including skin, organs, and all body fluids. Because

INVESTIGATIONS ON THE NET

American Society of Crime Laboratory Directors
http://www.ascld.org

American Board of Criminalistics
http://www.criminalistics.com

For an up-to-date list of Web links, go to
http://info.wadsworth.com/dempsey

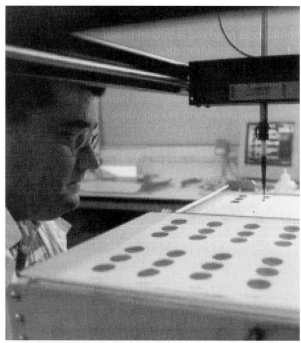

© AP Photos/Mark Foley

DNA databases can help investigators solve crimes and ensure that those who are guilty are convicted in court. Here, a Florida Department of Law Enforcement crime lab technician views robotic blood staining, called *aliquoting*, as part of Florida's DNA databasing system.

the characteristics of certain segments of DNA vary from person to person it is possible to analyze certain substances such as blood, hair, semen, or body tissue and compare them to a sample from a suspect.

Forensic science consultant Richard Saferstein, former chief forensic scientist of the New Jersey State Police Laboratory and author of the text *Criminalistics: An Introduction to Forensic Science*, tells us that portions of the DNA structure are as unique to each individual as fingerprints. He writes that inside each of the sixty trillion cells in the human body are strands of genetic material called *chromosomes*. Arranged along the chromosomes, like beads on a thread, are nearly one hundred thousand genes. Genes are the fundamental unit of heredity. They instruct the body cells to make proteins that determine everything from hair color to susceptibility to diseases. Each gene is actually composed of DNA specifically designed to carry out a single body function. Scientists have determined that DNA is the substance by which genetic instructions are passed from one generation to the next.[18]

DNA profiling, also called genetic fingerprinting or DNA typing, has shown much promise in helping investigators solve crimes and ensuring that those guilty of crimes are convicted in court. It is the examination of DNA samples from a body fluid to determine whether they came from a particular subject. For example, semen on a rape victim's jeans can be positively or negatively compared with a suspect's semen.

DNA is powerful evidence. Howard Safir, former police commissioner of New York City, described DNA typing as the primary tool for law enforcement in reducing crime in the twenty-first century. Elizabeth Devine, former supervising criminalist in the Scientific Services Bureau of the Los Angeles County Sheriff's Department says, "The power of what we can look for and analyze now is incredible. It's like magic. Every day we discover evidence where we never thought it would be. You almost can't do anything without leaving some DNA around. DNA takes longer than fingerprints to analyze but you get a really big bang for your buck."[19]

DNA profiling has been used in criminal investigations since 1987.[20] The FBI has made great progress in improving the technology since opening its first DNA typing laboratory in October 1988.

To show the further utility of DNA profiling, the U.S. Defense Department has established a repository of genetic information for the more than two million members of the U.S. armed forces as a way of identifying future casualties of war. DNA is collected and stored by the Armed Forces Institute of Pathology. Formerly, unidentified dead were identified, if possible, by fingerprints and medical records. However, DNA can now be used to identify people from body parts, like a single leg.[21]

DNA technology in law enforcement has changed rapidly. The latest procedure—**PCR-STR** (polymerase chain reaction–short tandem repeat)—has several distinct advantages for law enforcement over **RFLP** (restricted fragment length polymorphism), an earlier procedure. The newer PCR-STR requires only pin-size samples rather than the dime-size samples needed for RFLP. Also with this process, samples degraded or broken down by exposure to heat, light, or humidity can be analyzed; only two days are needed for laboratory analysis compared to eight weeks for RFLP; and the entire DNA process can be automated, greatly reducing the possibility of human error.[22]

The DNA Analysis Unit of the FBI laboratory analyzes body fluids and body fluid stains recovered as evidence in violent crimes. Examinations include the identification and characterization of blood, semen, saliva, and other body fluids using traditional serological techniques and related biochemical analysis. Once the stain is identified, it is characterized by DNA analysis using RFLP or PCR techniques. The results of the analyses are compared to results obtained from known blood or saliva samples submitted from the victims or suspects.[23]

This unit also uses mitochondrial DNA **(MtDNA)** analysis, which is applied to evidence containing very small or degraded quantities of DNA from hair, bones, teeth, and body fluids. The results of MtDNA analysis are then also compared to blood and saliva submitted from victims and suspects.

Another current DNA innovation is **CODIS** (Combined DNA Index System). CODIS contains DNA profiles obtained from subjects convicted of homicide, sexual assault, and other serious felonies. Investigators are able to search evidence from their individual cases against the system's extensive national file of DNA genetic markers.[24]

CODIS provides software and support services so that state and local laboratories can establish databases of convicted offenders, unsolved crime scenes, and missing persons. It allows these forensic laboratories to exchange and compare DNA profiles electronically, thereby linking serial violent crimes, especially sexual assaults, to each other, and to identify suspects by matching DNA from crime scenes to convicted offenders. As of 2001, CODIS was installed in 104 laboratories in forty-three states and the District of Columbia. (All fifty states have enacted DNA database laws requiring the collection of a DNA sample from specified categories of convicted offenders. Most currently take samples from convicted felons, but they vary on which types of felons. Some states are trying to pass legislation to take samples from all persons charged with a felony; some are even considering collecting them from people convicted of misdemeanors.) More than five hundred federal, state, and local DNA analysts have received CODIS training. The FBI laboratory has even provided CODIS software and training to criminal justice agencies in other countries. The National DNA Index System (NDIS) is the final level of CODIS and supports the sharing of DNA profiles from convicted offenders and crime scene evidence submitted by state and local forensic laboratories across the United States.[25]

The current version of CODIS contains two indexes: a Convicted Offender Index and a Forensic Index. The former index contains DNA profiles from those convicted of violent crimes, and the latter contains DNA profiles acquired from crime scene evidence. The CODIS system is also separated into different segments, from the local to the national level. The system stores the information necessary for determining a match (a specimen identifier, the sponsoring laboratory's identifier, the names of laboratory personnel who produced the profile, and the DNA profile). To ensure privacy, it does not include such things as social security numbers, criminal history, or case-related information.[26]

The FBI maintains a national database, whereas each state has one designated database location, and each participating locality maintains its own local database. Thus, it is possible for each locality to cross-reference a DNA profile against other DNA profiles around the country. Furthermore, it is likely that an international DNA database may be implemented, allowing law enforcement officials to identify suspects both nationally and internationally.

In March 2000, the FBI reported that the CODIS program had assisted in more than eleven hundred investigations in twenty-four states. As of 2001, CODIS contained DNA profiles from approximately three hundred thousand convicted offenders. DNA evidence has also been used to clear suspects. By 1999, more than sixty-one people had been exonerated as a result of DNA typing.[27]

History of DNA in U.S. Courts The use of DNA in U.S. courts has an interesting history. The process has gained popularity at an exponential rate since its introduction in the United States in 1987. It was initially hailed as "foolproof" and 99 percent positive. Most of the positive claims about DNA profiling were based on the testimony of interested parties, such as prosecutors and scientists from companies involved in DNA testing. Defense attorneys were often unable to combat DNA evidence in court or find experts to testify against it. Generally, defendants, when confronted with a DNA match, pleaded guilty in a plea bargain—until the Castro case.

YOU ARE THERE!
The First Use of DNA Typing in a Criminal Case

DNA profiling was the subject of *The Blooding* by Joseph Wambaugh. This book describes the brutal beating and murder of two young girls in the English county of Leicestershire. Although the police have no clues to the identity of the killer, eventually a young man whom Wambaugh called only the "kitchen porter," confesses to the murder of the first girl and is also charged by the police with the second murder. Hoping to get physical evidence to corroborate this confession, the police ask Alec Jeffreys, a young geneticist at nearby Leicestershire University and the man who discovered genetic fingerprinting, to compare DNA samples from the victims with the DNA of the defendant.

After performing his testing, Jeffreys tells the police that their suspect definitely did not commit the murders. He also tells them that the same one man—not their suspect, however—is responsible for the murders of both girls.

The police decide to embark on a campaign of "blooding" to find the killer. They "request" that all men within a certain age group who live, work, or have business in the area appear at the police station and submit to a venipuncture (the drawing of a vial of blood). The blood is then analyzed using Jeffrey's technique. But even after more than forty-five hundred men give a sample of their blood, the police have no suspects. Eventually it is discovered, over a few beers in a local pub, that a young man, Colin Pitchfork, had paid another young man, Ian Kelly, to appear and be "bloodied" for him. When the police approach Pitchfork, he willingly confesses to both murders. His blood samples are then tested, and the DNA reveals that he is, indeed, the murderer of both girls.

It must be emphasized that the DNA analysis did not solve the case, although it did eliminate a suspect and it did confirm guilt. Even if DNA profiling is fully accepted by the scientific community, it will never replace regular detective work.

SOURCE: Joseph Wambaugh, *The Blooding* (New York: William Morrow, 1989).

On February 5, 1987, twenty-three-year-old Vilma Ponce and her two-year-old daughter were stabbed to death in their apartment in the Bronx, New York. There were few leads until police arrested the building's superintendent, Joseph Castro, and found some dried blood in the grooves of his watch. When questioned, he said the blood was his own. Prosecutors sent the blood from the watch, samples of the victim' blood, and a sample of Castro's blood to a firm called Lifecodes for testing.

Lifecodes declared a match between the DNA from the blood on the watch and the DNA from Vilma Ponce's blood. Defense attorneys Barry Scheck and Peter Neufeld located experts who agreed to testify against the admission of the DNA typing evidence. For twelve weeks the evidence was argued before New York Supreme Court Acting Justice Gerald Sheindlin, who listened to experts from both sides. The experts for the defense were able to uncover such serious blunders committed by Lifecodes in its performance of the tests that the prosecution's expert witnesses recanted

their position. In an unprecedented move, two expert witnesses for the defense and two for the prosecution issued a joint statement: "The DNA data in this case are not scientifically reliable enough to support the assertion that the samples . . . do or do not match. If these data were submitted to a peer-reviewed journal in support of a conclusion, they would not be accepted. Further experimentation would be required."[28]

Ultimately, Justice Sheindlin ruled the evidence of the match inadmissible, and the case against Castro was dismissed. (You may remember the names of the two attorneys in this case: Scheck and Neufeld. They later played pivotal roles in the acquittal of O. J. Simpson.)

The main problem with DNA profiling at the Castro stage was that it could not pass the *Frye test*. This test was based on the court case *Frye v. United States*, in which the court ruled that novel scientific evidence will not be accepted into evidence until it has gained general acceptance in the particular scientific discipline in which it belongs.[29] Although DNA was accepted by some courts and rejected by others, its reliability had to be held in question until it gained general acceptance by the scientific community.[30]

In 1992, a unanimous decision by the U.S. Court of Appeals for the Second Circuit Court, one of the most influential federal appeals courts, began to change court rulings nationwide on DNA evidence. The court approved the use of DNA evidence and affirmed the conviction of Randolph Jakobetz for kidnapping and rape. The evidence on which he was convicted involved an FBI analysis of the DNA from semen recovered from the victim and matched to Jakobetz through a blood test.

Legal experts have said that this decision was the first clear-cut guidance from the federal appellate bench on the use of DNA fingerprinting. Previously, many courts would not allow DNA evidence to be used at a trial unless it was presented first at a pretrial hearing. Under the new ruling, courts could allow DNA evidence without such hearings and let the jury determine the worth of the evidence. In this case, the court seemed to have overruled the *Frye* test by ruling that scientific evidence was like any other and could be admitted if its "probativeness, materiality, and reliability" outweighed any tendency to mislead, prejudice, and confuse the jury."[31]

The Jakobetz case was followed by two other important U.S. Supreme Court cases, *Daubert v. Merrell Dow Pharmaceuticals* (1993) and *General Electric Co. v. Joiner* (1997), which further undermined the restrictive *Frye* test by ruling that federal courts should generally allow admission of all relevant evidence. This ruling applied to all evidence in civil and criminal cases, including DNA evidence and other forensic science issues.[32]

In 1992, after a two-year study, a twelve-member panel consisting of forensic, legal, and molecular biology experts endorsed DNA profiling in the identification of suspects in criminal cases. Conducted under the auspices of the National Academy of Sciences, the study concluded that DNA fingerprinting is a reliable method of identification for use as evidence in criminal trials, but it found problems with current methods of sampling, labeling, and general quality assurance. The panel of experts recommended that accreditation be required of forensic laboratories performing this work.[33]

The panel also advised the courts to consider the reliability of new DNA typing techniques on a case-by-case basis when determining the admissibility of DNA evidence. The panel's report, *DNA Technology in Forensic Science*, called for the creation of a national DNA profile data bank that would contain DNA samples and document information on the genetic makeup of felons convicted of violent crimes. This report led to the creation of CODIS, described earlier.

The National Commission on the Future of DNA Evidence was created in 1998 at the request of the U.S. Attorney General. Its mission is to examine the future of DNA evidence and how the Justice Department can encourage its most effective use. One of the duties of the commission is to submit recommendations to the Attorney General that will ensure more effective use of DNA as a crime-fighting tool and foster its use through the entire criminal justice system. Other focal areas include crime scene investigation and evidence collection, laboratory funding, legal issues, and research and development.[34]

Current Technology In 2000, the National Commission on the Future of DNA Evidence reported:

> The great variability of DNA polymorphisms has made it possible to offer strong support for concluding that DNA from a suspect and from the crime scene are from the same person. Prior to this . . . , it was possible to exclude a suspect, but evidence for inclusion was weaker than it is now because the probability of a coincidental match was larger. DNA polymorphisms brought an enormous change. Evidence that two DNA samples are from the same person is still probabilistic rather than certain. But with today's battery of genetic markers, the likelihood that two matching profiles came from the same person approaches certainty.
>
> Although the evidence that two samples came from the same person is statistical, the conclusion that they came from different persons is certain (assuming no human or technical errors). As a result of DNA testing, more than seventy persons previously convicted of capital crimes and frequently having served long prison terms have been exonerated. And there are everyday exculpations, since about a quarter of analyses lead to exclusions.[35]

The commission made the following conclusions and projections for the near future:[36]

- We emphasize that current state-of-the-art DNA typing is such that the technology and statistical methods are accurate and reproducible.

- Methods of automation, increasing the speed and output and reliability of STR methods, will continue. In particular we expect that portable, miniature chips will make possible the analysis of DNA directly at the crime scene. This can be telemetered to databases, offering the possibility of immediate identification.

- By 2005, the CODIS database should be well established, with more than one million convicted felon profiles on file. Interstate comparisons will be commonplace and international comparisons increasingly feasible. . . . Greater automation and higher throughput approaches will help reduce the backlog. . . . We also expect integration of computers and Internet with analytical techniques to permit direct transmission of test data between laboratories.

- By 2010, we expect portable, miniaturized instrumentation that will provide analysis at the crime scene with computer-linked remote analysis. This should permit rapid identification and, in particular, quick elimination of innocent suspects.

- In the future, it is likely that an increasing number of suspects will be identified by database searches.

DNA Databases and Current Issues Initially, DNA fingerprinting or profiling was used to confirm the identity of an individual already suspected of committing a specific crime; now the use of offender DNA databases has altered the way a criminal investigation can proceed. Very small amounts of DNA recovered from a crime scene can be used to link an otherwise unknown suspect to the crime. The existing offender DNA databases have been upheld over Fourth Amendment challenges, because of the minimal privacy expectations offenders have as a result of their status as offenders.

Some believe that the growing practice of using voluntary DNA samples to link the donor to other unsolved crimes should be curbed. However, police and prosecutors defend the strategy, claiming that it allows them to take full advantage of the technology to solve crimes. Darrell Sanders, chief of police in Frankfort, Illinois, says, "If we get someone's DNA legally, how can we justify giving him a free pass on something else he once did?" Defense attorneys, such as Barry Scheck, foresee the potential for abuse, "As it is, there's

nothing to stop police from setting up a DNA base of 'the usual subjects.'"[37]

Another issue is the implementation of a universal DNA database containing DNA fingerprints from every member of society. Some believe this would not withstand constitutional scrutiny, because free persons have no diminished expectations of privacy as prisoners do. In addition, some feel that a universal DNA database would allow the government to intrude without suspicion on an individual's privacy.[38]

DNA Training The National Commission on the Future of DNA Evidence has produced a CD-ROM entitled *What Every Law Enforcement Officer Should Know About DNA Evidence*. It is designed to teach law enforcement officers about the best practices for the identification, preservation, and collection of DNA evidence at various types of crime scenes. The training CD-ROM details collection and packaging procedures for DNA evidence and offers an overview of the history of the use of DNA evidence in criminal trials. Lessons teach how a crime scene is processed for DNA evidence; how to collect, package, and transport DNA evidence; the sources, locations, and limitations of DNA evidence; the importance of elimination and reference samples; and how to use CODIS to solve crimes. The CD also covers applications of DNA evidence at specific types of crime scenes, including a homicide, a sexual assault, a burglary, and a violent crime. Students enter each crime scene as an evidence technician and are given choices about how to handle DNA evidence. After completing the CD, students take a test.[39]

In 2001, the National Institute of Justice released a bulletin titled *Understanding DNA Evidence: A Guide for Victim Service Providers*. This discussed the important role forensic DNA evidence plays in solving criminal cases, particularly brutal sexual assaults and homicides, and advised victim service providers that they need to know the significance of DNA evidence in the cases they are dealing with. The bulletin explained how to identify DNA evidence and counsel victims on its value in apprehending and convicting offenders. The bulletin included three case studies that reflect the power of a DNA match and reveal the complexities involved in the criminal justice system.[40]

DNA Warrants In October 1999, the Milwaukee, Wisconsin, county prosecutor made an innovative

EXHIBIT 6.4   **Milestones in the Development of DNA**

Date	Development
1900	A,B,O blood groups discovered
1923	*Frye v. United States*
1983	PCR first conceived by Kerry Mullis
1984	First DNA profiling test developed by Alec Jeffreys
1986	First use of DNA to solve a crime and to exonerate an innocent subject (Colin Pitchfork case)
1986	First acceptance of DNA testing in a U.S. civil court
1987	First use of DNA profiling in a U.S. criminal court
1987	Castro case
1992	Publication of *DNA Technology in Forensic Science*
1992	Jakobetz case
1993	*Daubert v. Merrell Dow Pharmaceuticals*
1997	*General Electric Co. v. Joiner*
1998	Creation of the National Commission on the Future of DNA Evidence
2000	Publication of *The Future of Forensic DNA Testing*

SOURCES: National Institute of Justice, *The Future of Forensic DNA Testing: Predictions of the Research and Development Working Group* (Washington, DC: National Institute of Justice, 2000); John S. Dempsey, *An Introduction to Policing*, 2d ed. (Belmont, CA: Wadsworth, 1999); Norah Rudin, "Forensic Science Timeline," http://www.forensicdna.com/Timeline.htm.

legal move regarding DNA in an effort to prevent the statute of limitations from expiring in a case against an unknown person suspected in a series of kidnappings and rapes. The prosecutor filed a John Doe warrant, not uncommon in cases where a suspect's identity is unknown. What made this case different was the means used to identify the suspect. The warrant identifies the assailant as "John Doe, unknown male with matching deoxyribonucleic acid (DNA) at five locations."[41] Since this happened, DNA warrants have been used a great deal.

Ultraviolet Forensic Imaging

Ultraviolet forensic imaging, or invisible light technology, is in increasing use in forensics and has been helpful in solving crimes. One application of ultraviolet light is in the photographing of bite marks on human skin, because the ultraviolet light provides more detail and contrast in an injured area than standard lighting techniques. The photographs show wounds in greater detail than would be possible with conventional photography.

Ultraviolet lighting techniques have also been used to scan entire crime scenes after the areas have been searched by technicians and investigators. Using this technology, evidence missed during the initial search, including footprints, fingerprints, and trace metal fragments, has been found. Medical and dental experts report that this application of ultraviolet light promises to be an indispensable tool for law enforcement agencies in the investigation of crime scenes.[42]

Other Techniques

The FBI's Forensic Science Research and Training Center is leading the way in the development of the most advanced forensic techniques. The lab provides information and services to more than three hundred crime labs throughout the nation. The following are among the latest techniques: *Neutron activation* can be used to test evidence at a crime scene. With neutron

YOU ARE THERE!
New State DNA Data Bank Leads to Arrest in Three-Year-Old Rape

In the early morning hours of December 21, 1999, a female television producer was attacked by a man who forced her down a stairwell in a building on a busy street in midtown Manhattan. He then raped her and tried to force her to withdraw money from a nearby automated teller machine before fleeing with her watch and umbrella.

In May 2001, a suspect, Lashange LeGrand, thirty-four, a convicted robber who had been released from prison three years earlier, was arrested by the NYPD and arraigned on rape, robbery, and sodomy charges. The arrest resulted from information provided to the police from the state police laboratory, which matched DNA from a semen sample on the victim's blouse to a DNA sample taken from LeGrand the previous year under a state law that requires certain felons, particularly violent ones, to submit DNA samples even after their release.

The law took effect in December 1999 and in less than two years the state collected eighty-two thousand samples from convicted offenders and registered fifty-three matches for previously unsolved crimes.

At the time of the attack LeGrand, who had eight aliases and an arrest record stretching back more than a decade on charges including grand larceny, burglary, and drug possession, was still on parole from a 1991 robbery conviction for which he had served seven years. Apparently aware of the increasing collection of DNA evidence, the suspect used tissues in an effort to wipe up after the attack, but the police were still able to retrieve the semen sample.

SOURCE: Kevin Flynn, "Felon's DNA Evidence Leads to His Arrest in a 1999 Rape," *The New York Times*, May 15, 2001, p. B3.

YOU ARE THERE!
Royal Canadian Mounted Police Extends DNA Technology to Trees

The Royal Canadian Mounted Police (RCMP) Forest Crime Investigation Unit is working with researchers in British Columbia to develop DNA identification systems that would allow them to source stolen trees back to the stumps left in the ground.

The British Columbia government estimates that lost taxes from foresters' stolen, downed tree are in excess of Can$20 million a year; the value of the stolen timber is much higher. The forest sector and its related activity is the leading industry in British Columbia, and many towns and cities rely directly on the sector. But here is the problem: if the RCMP gets a call that somebody's cutting, they can do surveillance and try

to catch the person in the act. But if they don't actually observe the cutting, they have to physically match the stolen wood to the site—that is, unload a truck and try to fit the tree back together. If they can't determine where the wood came from, they can't charge anyone with theft.

Using DNA to identify lumber could make life much tougher for lumber thieves, but the technology is in its infancy. DNA evidence pertaining to wood has not yet been entered into a court of law in Canada.

SOURCE: Alan Harman, "RCMP Extends Technology to Trees," *Law and Order*, Nov. 2000, pp. 58–61.

activation, an element is bombarded with neutrons and made radioactive, then analyzed. The *scanning electron microscope* can magnify material up to a hundred thousand times. It can uncover and identify extremely minute particles of trace evidence, such as gunpowder residue. The *gas chromatograph-mass spectrometer* can separate and identify the components of extremely minute mixtures.[43]

EXPERT CRIMINALISTIC TESTIMONY IN THE COURTROOM

Criminalistic evidence is introduced into the criminal trial in most cases by the prosecutor. It may also be introduced by the defense attorney in order to support claims of the defendant or to rebut evidence presented by the prosecution.

The person in the crime lab—either the criminalist or the forensic technician—who analyzed particular evidence is called to the witness stand to present analysis techniques and findings to the court. Before testifying, the person must first qualify as an expert in the field. During the process of qualifying, the attorney presenting the evidence questions the individual about education, experience, and specialized, relevant knowledge ordinarily not possessed by the average layperson. In addition to formal education, experience, and specialized knowledge, an expert witness should publish in specialized journals, conduct research, and maintain active membership in pertinent professional organizations in order to be considered current in the field. Once qualified, experts may testify on their opinion about the evidence.

After the first attorney concludes the initial questioning, the opposing attorney may also ask questions about credentials. The witness is then either designated as an expert witness by the court or stipulated as such by the other attorney. Expert witnesses must be able to describe their work and its significance to the jury in plain, everyday language that they can understand.

Often both sides in a criminal proceeding will present their own expert witnesses to testify to different findings on the same evidence. In cases such as this, judges and juries must decide between two different interpretations.

This kind of courtroom testimony gained increased importance after the prosecution in the O. J. Simpson case failed to prove its case in court. As Ron Urbanovsky, director of the Texas Department of Public Safety's statewide system of crime labs, said, "Part of the Simpson case fallout was that we've seen much longer and stiffer cross-examinations in court. Testimony that used to take two to three hours now takes eight to twelve hours, and it's grueling. We are asked to be perfect in an unperfect world."[44]

COMPUTERS IN INVESTIGATING

Today, most law enforcement agencies have computer systems to help them in their duties. In addition, many private security firms and private investigators rely on computer systems to assist them in the investigating process. This section concentrates on two applications of computers in investigations: automated information systems and computer-aided investigations. Other sections in this chapter discuss the role of computer technology in other aspects of investigating.

Automated Information Systems

The availability of **automated information systems** has revolutionized police work and investigations. An automated information system, or automated database, is an enormous electronic filing cabinet that can store information and retrieve it in any desired format. For example, if an investigative agency has a database of all persons convicted of a particular crime, an investigator can search the database to retrieve information regarding all or any one person in the database, all males, all females, all whites, all African Americans, all persons arrested on a particular date, and so on.

The FBI's National Crime Information Center (NCIC) is the premier automated database for the criminal justice system. (See chapter 8 for a complete description of NCIC.) The FBI also maintains the Violent Criminal Apprehension Program (VICAP) database, which contains information on unsolved murders. VICAP has been used increasingly to track down serial murderers. (VICAP is covered in detail in chapter 10.)

In addition to these national databases, local law enforcement agencies maintain their own databases. Also, private investigators and private investigating and security firms have a tremendous number of automated databases available for their use. (See chapter 8.)

Computer-Aided Investigations

Computer-aided investigation is revolutionizing the criminal investigation process. Today, computers are widely used for criminal and private investigations. The rationale is that by using computers investigators can feed incident data of a particular crime into the computer, which can then interface with criminal record data and incident data to search for and find possible matches. (Chapter 4 offers examples of computer-aided investigation systems.)

FINGERPRINT TECHNOLOGY

Fingerprints offer an infallible means of personal identification.

Criminal identification by means of fingerprints is one of the most potent factors in apprehending fugitives who might otherwise escape arrest and continue their criminal activities. This type of identification also makes possible an accurate determination of the number of previous arrests and convictions, which results in the imposition of more equitable sentences by the judiciary. In addition, this system of identification enables prosecutors to present their case in the light of the offender's previous record. It also provides probation officers and the parole board with definite information on which to base their judgments in dealing with criminals in their jurisdiction.

Fingerprints may be recorded on standard fingerprint cards or they may be recorded digitally and transmitted electronically to the FBI for comparison. By

---

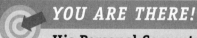

YOU ARE THERE!

His Personal Computer Solved the Crime

A burglar was identified and picked up just a few hours after committing a crime. Released from prison only two weeks earlier, he was identified by fingerprints recovered at the scene. The Danbury, Connecticut, police officer who processed the scene of the 8 P.M. burglary was in his lab by 9:45 P.M. and was able to identify the man through his fingerprints by 10 P.M. Detectives spotted him strolling on the avenue forty-five minutes later.

How did the police officer break the case? Using his personal computer, he ran a software program called Felon/Find'r and entered the classification of the listed latent print. The computer displayed a list of suspects; the suspect that he sought was among them.

SOURCE: Bill Clede, "Computer Chatter," *Law and Order*, Jan. 1994, p. 45.

Some Fingerprint Facts

Three Classifications

Three fingerprint classifications form the basis for all ten-print classification systems presently in use.

- *Loops.* Fingerprints that are characterized by ridge lines that enter from one side of the pattern and curve around to exit from the same side of the pattern. Some 60 percent of fingerprints are loops.
- *Whorls.* Fingerprints that include ridge patterns that are generally rounded or circular in shape and have two deltas. Some 30 percent of fingerprints are whorls.
- *Arches.* Fingerprints characterized by ridge lines that enter the print from one side and flow out of the other side. Some 5 percent of fingerprints are arches.

Three Types

Most people refer to any fingerprint discovered at a crime scene as a latent print. But there are really three basic types of prints:

- *Visible prints* are made by fingers touching a surface after the ridges have been in contact with a colored material such as blood, paint, grease, or ink.
- *Plastic prints* are ridge impressions left on a soft material such as putty, wax, soap, or dust.
- *Latent (invisible) prints* are impressions caused when body perspiration or oils present on fingerprint ridges are transferred to the surface of an object.

SOURCE: Richard Saferstein, *Criminalistics: An Introduction to Forensic Science*, 7th ed. (Englewood Cliffs, NJ: Prentice-Hall 2001).

comparing fingerprints at the scene of a crime with the fingerprint record of suspect persons, officials can establish absolute proof of the presence or identity of a person.[45]

Basic Categories of Fingerprints

There are two basic categories of fingerprints: *inked prints,* or ten-prints, and *latent prints.*

- Inked prints or ten-prints are the result of the process of rolling each finger onto a ten-print card (each finger is rolled onto a separate box on the card) using fingerprinting ink. Inked prints are kept on file at local police departments, state criminal justice information agencies, and the FBI. An arrested person is fingerprinted and those inked prints are compared with fingerprints on file of known criminals. Inked prints or ten-prints are also taken for numerous other types of investigations, such as employment background and license applications.

- *Latent prints* are impressions left at a crime scene. These prints may be lifted and then compared with inked prints on file in order to establish the identity of the perpetrator. Like inked prints, latent prints are produced by the

ridged skin on human fingers. They may also be left by palms and soles of the feet. (See the later section on palmprints.) Latent print examiners analyze and compare latent prints to known prints of individuals in an effort to make identifications or exclusions. The uniqueness, permanence, and arrangement of the friction ridges allow examiners to positively match two prints and determine whether an area of a friction ridge impression originated from one source to the exclusion of others.

A variety of techniques, including use of chemicals, powders, lasers, alternate light sources, and other physical means, are employed in the detection and development of latent prints. If a latent print has limited quality and quantity of detail, examiners may perform microscopic examinations in order to make conclusive comparisons.

Sometimes a latent fingerprint found in dust may be the only clue in an investigation in which there are no other leads. Even though this kind of print actually was caused by some of the dust being removed—because it adhered to the ridges of the skin that touched there—methods of lifting these prints are now available.[46]

Lasers can be used to lift prints from surfaces that often defy traditional powder or chemical techniques, including glass, paper, cardboard, rubber, wood, plastic, leather, and even human skin.[47] The use of lasers in fingerprint lifting allowed the FBI to detect a forty-year-old fingerprint of a Nazi war criminal on a postcard.[48] In a recent article, the special agent in charge of the Forensic Services Division of the U.S. Secret Service cited numerous cases of the successful use of sophisticated fingerprint technology. He mentioned such high-profile cases as the original bombing of the World Trade Center and the killing of two CIA employees in Langley, Virginia.[49]

Latent prints found at a crime scene can assist in the identification of possible suspects. Here, an Onondaga, New York, Sheriff's Department deputy dusts a container for prints at the crime lab.

© Syracuse Newspapers/The Image Works

Automated Fingerprint Identification Systems

By the 1980s **automated fingerprint identification systems (AFIS)** began to be developed. An AFIS enables a print technician to enter

TECHNOLOGY IN INVESTIGATIONS
How to Find and Develop Latent Fingerprints

- *Carbon dusting powders.* When finely ground carbon powder is applied lightly to a surface with a camel's-hair or fiberglass brush, it will adhere to perspiration residues left on the surface and can render an invisible impression visible. Print technicians apply powder of a contrasting color to the color of the surface being dusted. The "raised" print is then photographed, lifted off the surface with transparent tape, and then transferred to a card that has a contrasting color to the color of the powder used on the tape.

- *Iodine fuming.* Crystals of iodine are placed in a glass container called a fumer along with the article suspected of containing latent prints. When the crystals are heated, iodine vapors will fill the chamber and make the latent print visible. Iodine prints are not permanent and begin to fade once the fuming process stops. The resultant fingerprint must be immediately photographed. This method is particularly useful for obtaining prints from paper or cardboard.

- *Silver nitrate.* A solution of silver nitrate in distilled water is sprayed or saturated on paper believed to have latent prints. When the paper is exposed to light the print becomes visible.

- *Ninhydrin.* The chemical ninhydrin is sprayed over large cardboard or paper containers; if a latent print is present it will become visible.

- *Super glue fuming.* Cyanoacrylate treated with sodium hydroxide is placed in a chamber with an object believed to contain latent prints. The resultant fumes from the glue adhere to the latent print, making it visible.

- *Ultraviolet light.* A UV lamp (black light) can be effective in a darkened environment to expose latent prints.

- *Laser:* A laser when directed at a surface can cause the perspiration forming a latent fingerprint to fluoresce, thus making the print visible.

- *Alternative light source.* An ALS operates under the same principle as a laser and can make latent fingerprints fluoresce and become visible. It is much more portable than the laser.

SOURCES: Larry Ragle, *Crime Scene* (New York: Avon, 1995); Richard Saferstein, *Criminalistics: An Introduction to Forensic Science*, 7th ed. (Englewood Cliffs, NJ: Prentice-Hall, 2001).

---

unidentified latent prints into the computer. The computer then automatically searches its files and presents a list of likely matches, which can then be visually examined by a fingerprint technician in order to find the perfect match. In addition, using AFIS technology, a person's prints can be taken and stored into memory without the use of traditional inking and rolling techniques.[50]

The first locally funded, regional automated fingerprint identification system in the United States was NOVARIS (Northern Virginia Regional Identification System). NOVARIS can look for prints having similar characteristics at the rate of 297 prints per second. It then prints out a listing of individuals whose fingerprint patterns match 75 percent or more of the fingerprint detail pattern submitted.[51] The Los Angeles Police Department estimates that fingerprint comparisons that in the past would have taken as long as sixty years can now be performed in a day.[52] Washington, D.C., police report that computerized print systems enable them to make more than one hundred identifications a month from latent prints taken at a crime scene. Other departments reporting successful results using automated fingerprint identification systems are San Jose, California; Houston, Texas; and Minneapolis, Minnesota.[53]

Here are more examples of the success of automated fingerprint identification systems:

- Since the Milwaukee, Wisconsin, police department implemented its AFIS, 232,000 ten-print cards have been entered into the system with a 37 percent identification rate on unknown latent

YOU ARE THERE!

Fingerprints and the FBI Disaster Squad

The FBI's Latent Print Unit forms the nucleus of its disaster squad, which renders assistance in identifying victims at disaster scenes. Since 1940, the squad has responded to over two hundred disasters worldwide and identified over half the victims by fingerprints or footprints. Members of the squad use special techniques to examine fingers and hands of unknown deceased to obtain identifiable prints. Automated searches of identifiable prints can be conducted in the IAFIS database. If classifiable prints are obtained from all ten fingers, manual searches can also be conducted in the CJIS civil fingerprint file.

SOURCE: Federal Bureau of Identification, "Latent Print Unit"; http://www.fbi.gov/hq/lab/org/lpu.htm.

DEMPSEY'S LAW

Can a Person Change Fingerprints?

Professor Dempsey, can a person change his or her fingerprints?

Many students ask this question. It is impossible to change one's fingerprints, although many criminals have tried to obscure them. Perhaps the most celebrated attempt to obliterate fingerprints was that of the notorious 1930s gangster John Dillinger, who tried to destroy his own prints by applying a corrosive acid to his fingers. Ironically, prints taken at the morgue after he was shot to death compared with fingerprints taken at the time of a previous arrest proved that his efforts had failed.

Noted criminalist Richard Saferstein writes that efforts to intentionally scar the skin on one's fingers can only be self-defeating, for it would be totally impossible to obliterate all the ridge characteristics on the hand and the presence of permanent scars merely provides new characteristics for identification.

prints. A Milwaukee police official reports that many serious crimes in the area are now solved with "no suspect information at all—just a fingerprint."[54]

- The Royal Canadian Mounted Police (RCMP) operate a national AFIS system that takes prints from all Canadian law enforcement agencies and holds 2.6 million ten-print cards. A networking system has been in place since early 1990 that allows seven remote sites with compatible equipment to access the central site's system in Ottawa. At its central AFIS site, alone, the RCMP made seventeen hundred latent hits in one year.

- An example of the way in which AFIS technology can help in criminal investigation was its use in Nevada by the Washoe County Sheriff's Office. Nevada—along with Alaska, California, Idaho, Oregon, Utah, Washington, and Wyoming—uses the services of Western Identification Network (WIN), a regional AFIS. The Washoe County Sheriff's Office arrested an unknown person on charges of using stolen credit cards to obtain money from automatic teller machines. A WIN AFIS search identified the suspect as a repeat offender with a prior criminal record in Oregon, which led in turn to an FBI record check indicating that he was wanted by the U.S. Secret Service, the State of North Carolina, and the District of Columbia for fraud and weapons violations. The suspect had also been arrested in seven states, using multiple aliases.

- In the late 1990s, the Providence, Rhode Island, police department, purchased an AFIS system and in a short time entered more than five hundred thousand latent fingerprints into the system and solved numerous crimes that would not have been solved using previous systems.[55]

- As of 1998, the Maryland automated fingerprint system had linked 435 offenders to unsolved crimes, including four homicides, sixty-five rapes, and fifty-nine robberies.[56]

- The Hennepin County (Minnesota) Sheriff's Department, along with the police departments of Redlands and Ontario, California, is experimenting with the latest AFIS technology, IBIS (Identification Based Information System), which captures fingerprint and photo images at a crime

YOU ARE THERE!

Fingerprints Are Infallible Evidence—Aren't They?

Fingerprint evidence rests on the idea that no two people have the same print. First admitted into court in 1911, fingerprint evidence has generally been accepted by the relevant scientific community and very easily passed the *Frye* test on acceptability of scientific evidence. Since then courts have accepted fingerprint evidence without much scrutiny. However, some legal experts say that this may be changing, based on the landmark 1993 *Daubert v. Merrell Dow Pharmaceutical* case.

In *Daubert*, the U.S. Supreme Court asserted that "general acceptance" or the *Frye* standard is not an absolute prerequisite to the admissibility of scientific evidence and relegated to the trial judge the task of ensuring that an expert's testimony rests on a reliable foundation and is relevant to the subject of the trial. Thus, the Court ruled that trial judges must serve as "gatekeeper" in judging the admissibility and reliability of scientific evidence presented in their courts. The Court suggested the following guidelines: the scientific technique or theory can be and has been tested; the technique or theory has been subject to peer review and publication; the technique's potential rate of error has been judged; standards controlling the technique's operation exist and are maintained; and the scientific theory or method has attracted widespread acceptance in a relevant scientific community.

Some experts now question our confidence in the accuracy of a match between prints carefully taken in a police station and less-than-perfect prints recovered at a crime scene. They also question whether fingerprint identification could be challenged on the grounds that it has not been adequately tested, that the error rate has not been calculated, and that there are no standards for what constitutes a match. The first recent challenge to fingerprint identification was in *United States v. Byron C. Mitchell* in 1999.

The admissibility of fingerprint evidence was challenged in this case in the Eastern District of Pennsylvania, involving the trial of a man accused of driving a getaway car in a robbery. The prosecution said the man's prints were on the gearshift and door of the car. The defense argued that fingerprints could not be proven to be unique. Government experts vigorously disputed this claim. After a hearing, the judge upheld the admissibility of fingerprints as scientific evidence and ruled that human friction ridges are unique and permanent, and human friction ridge skin arrangements are unique and permanent.

Since Mitchell, other case challenges have been filed in courts, but none has yet kept fingerprints out of a trial. The debate continues.

SOURCES: Malcolm Ritter, "Fingerprint Evidence Faces Hurdles," http://www.aafs.org/leadstory1.htm; Richard Saferstein, *Criminalistics: An Introduction to Forensic Science*, 7th ed. (Englewood Cliffs, NJ: Prentice-Hall, 2001).

---

scene on a handheld remote data terminal (RDT). The images are then transmitted across the law enforcement communications network to an AFIS database and to the FBI's NCIC 2000 database. If a match is found, the system returns the individual's name and date of birth directly to the RDT. The system also can query existing criminal history and warrants files and provide information in minutes.[57]

Newer, Less Costly Systems Until very recently, AFIS technology has been extraordinarily expensive and therefore used only by the largest agencies. The technology provided excellent high-speed fingerprint matching once fingerprint databases became large enough. Still, a drawback was that each system has been stand-alone—that is, systems could not exchange information rapidly. But there are now software-based systems using open-system architecture. In other words, any brand of computer based on the UNIX operating system will work with them.[58] These systems are also designed to exchange fingerprint and other data over the wire with other criminal justice information systems, using the widely accepted Henry system of fingerprint classification (described earlier in this chapter).

CAREER FOCUS

Forensic Print Analyst

Forensic Print Analyst, Hillsborough County, Florida: annual salary: $36,536–$54,826.

Duties may include, but are not limited to, comparing latent prints to known impressions, preparing reports of findings, and performing limited print processing and related duties as required. Applicants should be skilled in all areas of fingerprint identification with an ability to compare and identify difficult latent prints to known prints, as well as an ability to communicate effectively both orally and in writing. Minimum qualifications are six years of experience in inked fingerprints, three years experience as a latent print examiner, or certification as a latent print examiner with the IAI.

SOURCE: International Association for Identification; http://www.theiai.org/jobs/hillsborough.html.

These systems, designed for use in a booking facility, can use ink and paper fingerprints or can employ Live-Scan, an optical fingerprint scanning system, to read the suspect's prints. The scanner uses electronic capture of the suspect's fingerprint pattern, using five hundred DPI resolution, electronic quality analysis, and automatic image centering. The booking officer begins with a single-finger or dual-digit search, placing the suspect's finger on the scanner for reading. If the computer finds a possible match, the officer gets news of a hit within minutes. The computer selects the most likely matches, which then must be verified by a human operator. If there is no hit, the computer adds the fingerprint to its database automatically. Only one hour's training is necessary for a booking officer to operate the system.

These systems also have electronic quality checking, image enhancement, and ten-print system capability. They can scan fingerprint cards, reducing them to electronic records, and store them for future reference. They can also print fingerprint cards from electronically scanned Live-Scan fingerprints. Training for a latent fingerprint examiner takes several days because of the numerous features in this system. A latent fingerprint examiner can link separate crime scenes using single latent prints, which can point to a common perpetrator or a pattern.

Live-Scan The use of Live-Scan stations allows fingerprints and demographic information to be electronically captured, stored, and transmitted in minutes. Greater use of applicant fingerprints is among the many reasons why ten-print live-scan stations are increasing nationwide. Built-in quality-control software helps reduce human errors. Because there is no ink, there is no smearing. If a mistake is made, a print can be retaken until one high-quality record is obtained. There is no need to print a person again for local, state, and federal agencies, because the Live-Scan can make copies. Also, higher-quality fingerprints mean a greater likelihood of the AFIS finding a match in its database without human verification.[59]

Nationwide, smaller law enforcement agencies have found that they receive much faster response times from these systems when they use Live-Scan equipment that is connected to the AFIS. California uses such a system to fingerprint applicants for school employment in background checks, as required under state law.

IAFIS In 1999, the FBI laboratory began using the FBI Criminal Justice Information Services (CJIS) division's Integrated Automated Fingerprint Identification System **(IAFIS)**. This system provides the capability to search latent fingerprints against the largest criminal fingerprint repository in the world, which contains the fingerprints of more than thirty-six million individuals. This allows the FBI to make identifications without benefit of a named suspect to help solve a variety of crimes.[60]

IAFIS is primarily a ten-print system for searching an individual's fingerprints to determine whether a prior arrest record exists and then maintaining a criminal arrest record history for each individual. The system also offers significant latent print capabilities. Using IAFIS, a specialist can digitally capture latent print and ten-print images and perform several functions with each, including enhancing to improve image quality; comparing latent fingerprints against suspect ten-print records retrieved from the criminal fingerprint repository; searching latent fingerprints against the ten-print fingerprint repository when no suspects have been developed; doing automatic searches of new arrest ten-print records against an unsolved latent fingerprint repository; and creating special files of ten-print records to support major criminal investigations.[61]

The IAFIS project has its roots in the 1960s and 1970s, when the FBI began investigating the feasibility of automating the fingerprint identification process. During that time, the Identification Division, predecessor to CJIS, began working with the National Institute for Standards and Technology to develop algorithms for searching and matching fingerprints using computer technology.

In the year 2000, the fingerprint databases of the FBI, the FBI's IAFIS, and the Immigration and Naturalization Service (INS), Ident, were merged. Formerly, federal, state and local law enforcement officials did not have access to all fingerprint information captured by border patrol agents, and INS did not have access to the FBI's records when its agents apprehended suspects at the border. The merging of the two systems was prompted by the inadvertent release by the INS in 1999 of Angel Maturino-Resendez, the suspected serial killer—known as the "railroad killer"—who was alleged to have stowed away on trains and murdered eight people near rail lines during a three-state killing spree. Border patrol agents had picked up Maturino-Resendez for illegal entry into the United States and sent him back to Mexico. The agents were unaware that he was wanted by the Houston police and the FBI for questioning in the murders. Within days of his release, Maturino-Resendez killed four of his victims. Eventually he surrendered to Texas Rangers in July 1999.[62]

Innovations in Other Countries Other countries have also made innovations in fingerprinting technology. The New Zealand police have combined several advanced techniques to put their fingerprint experts at the forefront of world technology. They combine high-intensity forensic light, video cameras, computer enhancement technology, and AFIS technology to obtain information at a crime scene. In one case, a section of clear tape had been used to tie up a victim during an armed robbery. When the tape was brought in for fingerprint processing, it was discovered that fingerprints were superimposed on both sides of the tape. Technicians used sophisticated lighting and computerized technology to uncover a workable print in thirty-five minutes despite problems with background detail and complexity. A search through AFIS revealed matching prints on record, and the perpetrator was arrested.[63]

The United Kingdom is using its National Automated Fingerprint Identification System (NAFIS) in most of the police forces in England and Wales. NAFIS integrates automated fingerprint technology and criminal justice records at a national level, linking a database of about five million ten-print fingerprints sets and two million crime scene marks. NAFIS is capable of making one million comparisons per second for the most urgent cases, enabling fingerprints taken from the scene of a crime to be searched against local or national databases in a matter of minutes.[64]

The International Association for Identification (IAI) is a professional organization for those interested in fingerprint identification, latent prints, and AFIS.

Automated Palmprint Technology

Recent advances in biometrics have made it possible for automated palmprint systems to complement standard AFIS technology. The technology works in the same manner as its AFIS counterpart, but instead of fingerprints it captures the four core areas of the palm and converts them into data for storage in a palmprint repository. On arrest, suspects have their palms scanned along with the fingerprints. After a palmprint is lifted from a crime scene, it too is scanned and entered into the database for matching. The palmprint matching processor will then return a rank-ordered notification of match candidates to the workstation. Before palmprint technology, if police didn't have a suspect to compare prints to, the only way they could make a palmprint match was to manually compare latent palmprints with hundreds of thousands of individual prints sitting in repositories. In most cases, for obvious reasons, this simply was not possible.[65]

Automated palmprint technology has been in development for some time, but it has only recently come onto the market. One reason for this is the complicated nature of a palmprint itself. The palm area contains up to a thousand minutiae (small characteristics), compared to the approximate one hundred minutiae found in the average fingerprint. This difference in size means that an automated palmprint system must actively scan and match a larger area, requiring complex refining of the technology to ensure the highest accuracy rate possible.

YOU ARE THERE!
DNA Couldn't Find the Suspect, But IAFIS Did

The Georgia Bureau of Identification (GBI) and the Pleasant Prairie, Wisconsin, police department (PPPD) were both looking for the same rape suspect in crimes committed in their jurisdictions. The PPPD contacted the GBI because they noted common characteristics in the rapes: victims all worked as clerks at retail strip malls near interstate highways. The PPPD sent fingerprint and DNA samples for examination. Through DNA testing, the GBI tied those two rapes to one in Florence, Kentucky, but could not identify the suspect.

After exhaustive investigation efforts with the PPPD, including a requested subject analysis by the FBI's Violent Crime Apprehension Program, had yielded no viable leads, the GBI submitted the Wisconsin print for examination by the FBI's IAFIS database. Within minutes, the search produced the name of a suspect.

The man was located in jail in Lawrenceville, Georgia, where he was being held on an unrelated crime. GBI was granted a search warrant to obtain a blood sample. Although he denied any involvement in the crimes, his blood was matched to DNA samples from the serial rapes. A few days after the sample was taken, he used a bedsheet to hang himself in his jail cell. He implicated himself in other rapes before his death.

The lesson from this investigation is the value of the IAFIS latent search technique. In spite of exhaustive investigative efforts, none of the other organizations' efforts were able to identify a suspect for these serial crimes. IAFIS did.

SOURCE: "Unsolved Case Fingerprint Matching," *FBI Law Enforcement Bulletin*, Dec. 2000, pp. 12–13.

YOU ARE THERE!
Solve This Crime

A man meets a woman in a singles bar. She invites him to her apartment. He has a drink with her in the apartment and then shoots and kills her. The detectives investigating the case can find no one who saw the man and woman together. They have no suspects. While processing the crime scene, they find the two glasses from which the man and woman drank. Using forensic techniques, they dust the glasses and come up with a partial latent print, caused by the contact of the man's finger against the glass.

Comparing an unknown latent print or partial latent print to a known print used to be an extremely difficult undertaking because there are millions of fingerprint files in police departments around the country as well as in the FBI's records. In order to match the unknown print to a known print—assuming that our murderer had been fingerprinted—a latent print examiner would have to search through countless numbers of fingerprints hoping to find a match. This is similar to looking for the proverbial needle in the haystack.

Fortunately, automated fingerprint identification system (AFIS) technology is available today. Using it, investigators may be able to solve this case.

INVESTIGATIONS ON THE NET

FBI Latent Print Examinations
http://www.fbi.gov/hq/lab/handbook/
examlatp.htm

**Fingerprint Identification Technology in
Civil Applications**
http://www.morpho.com/news_room/library/
whitepapers/civil_afis.htm

International Association for Identification
http://www.theiai.org

For an up-to-date list of Web links, go to
http://info.wadsworth.com/dempsey

BIOMETRIC IDENTIFICATION

Fingerprints and palmprints are only two forms of **biometric identification.** Biometric systems use a physical characteristic to distinguish one person from another. Other systems involve the face, the eyes, the hands, and the voice. A 1998 study of the accuracy, applications, costs, legal issues, and privacy issues associated with potential uses concluded that biometric systems have enormous potential for public and private organizations alike.

Biometric systems serve two purposes: identification and authentication. They can help identify criminals, prevent welfare fraud, aid security in corrections, support border control, conduct criminal background checks, and establish identities on driver's licenses.[66]

Biometric systems already on the market can identify and authenticate people with a high degree of accuracy. Fingerprints remain the best choice for applications involving large numbers of users. Iris-based systems (which scan the human eye) may equal or exceed fingerprints in accuracy, but the limited number of vendors and lack of precedent for iris recognition make them less attractive. Hand-geometry systems have proven themselves in physical control, particularly in prisons, which require high levels of accuracy and security. Voice recognition proves least accurate but might be the best alternative to verify someone's identity over the phone. Facial recognition

systems create opportunities to identify people unobtrusively and without their cooperation, as in video surveillance, and they can be added to digital photo systems used for mug shots or driver's licenses.

Facial identification technology and its potential impact on crime control were examined in a futures study that focused on the history of identification systems, the nature and status of the technology, and privacy issues. The study noted that facial recognition technology compares a real-time picture from a video camera to digital pictures in a computerized database to identify a person. It has potential for both access security and the identification and apprehension of criminals.[67]

A project funded by the National Institute of Justice developed a surveillance system using real-time facial recognition technology to increase the usefulness of currently existing closed circuit TV-compatible surveillance software. The system is a state-of-the-art, automated facial recognition surveillance system that could be extremely useful to law enforcement, intelligence personnel, and CCTV control room officers.[68]

British police plan to monitor closed-circuit surveillance video cameras with facial recognition software. In Britain, more than two hundred thousand video cameras are used for surveillance, many watching streets and shopping areas. In Newham, a borough of London, the local police use a system that includes 140 street cameras and 11 mobile units. A computer will monitor video cameras set to watch for known criminals. When the system recognizes someone, it will alert the police.[69]

In July 2001, Tampa, Florida, police started using security cameras to scan the city's streets for people wanted for crimes. The computer software program used, called *FaceIt,* was linked to thirty-six cameras scanning crowds in Tampa's nightlife district, matching results against a database of mug shots of people with outstanding arrest warrants. Tampa is the first city in the country to use this technology on such a wide basis. A city spokesperson said, "It's a public safety tool, no different than having a cop walking around with a mug shot." He added that on a local street of restaurants, nightclubs, and stores crowded with twenty thousand people, "Your expectation of privacy is somewhat diminished, anyway." But the legal director for the

American Civil Liberties Union of Florida disagreed, saying it amounted to subjecting the public to a digital lineup. "This is yet another example of technology outpacing the protection of people's civil liberties. It has a very Big Brother feel to it."[70]

Using the FaceIt software, police officers in a nondescript command center in a neighborhood building monitor a bank of television screens filled with faces in the crowd, zooming in on individuals and programming the equipment to scan them. The computer breaks down each facial image into something similar to a map, checking eighty reference points. If the system matches more than a dozen of those points against an image in its database, it indicates a match. The system operator then determines if the images are similar enough to radio a uniformed officer who investigates and makes an arrest if appropriate. The system doesn't catalogue anything; if a face is not in the database the system does not keep it.

A similar system was used at the Super Bowl in January 2001 at Raymond James Stadium in Tampa. During the game, the computer spotted nineteen people in the crowded stadium who had outstanding warrants. In the intense security efforts following the September 11, 2001 terrorist attacks, FaceIt technology has been used extensively to screen visitors to federal facilities. A recent example was its use to screen visitors to Liberty Island in New York, the site of the Statue of Liberty. The technology attempted to match the faces of visitors waiting to board the ferry to the island with its terrorist database.

 INVESTIGATIONS ON THE NET

Biometric Resource Center
http://www.biomet.org

For an up-to-date list of Web links, go to
http://info.wadsworth.com/dempsey

ADVANCED PHOTOGRAPHIC TECHNIQUES

Photography has always played an important role in investigating. Innovations and advanced techniques have increased its utility. This section discusses *mug shot imaging, age-progression photography,* and *composite sketching.*

Mug Shot Imaging

Mug shot imaging is a system of digitizing a picture and storing its image on a computer so that it can be retrieved at a later time. The picture is taken with a video camera and then transferred to a color video monitor, where it appears as an electronic image. When the image is filed, the operator enters the identifying data such as race, gender, date of birth, and subject's case number. Using this system, victims of crimes can quickly view possible mug shots on a computer screen. The Orange County, Florida, sheriff's office is using a mug shot imaging system with a laser printer to produce wanted flyers for those sought on warrants. The pictures on these flyers are very clear, with excellent resolution.[71]

Major John J. Pavlis, who commands the Court Services Bureau of this sheriff's office, writes that this system could also be used as follows:

- Photos of missing children or other missing people, once digitized, could be sent to all locations that have imagery workstations. Quality pictures could then be sent quickly to officers in the field.

- Photos of all department employees could be digitized and kept in files for use in internal affairs investigations.

- Photos of wanted individuals, once digitized, could be sent to other agencies via computer.[72]

A good example of mug shot imaging is the ALERT (Advanced Law Enforcement Response Technology) system, which allows a photo of a subject to be transmitted from one police vehicle to others, giving officers an immediate view of a wanted suspect or a missing person.[73] In the first demonstration of this system in 1997, digital photographs were transmitted between two specially equipped police vehicles—one parked in College Station, Texas, the other sitting in an Alexandria, Virginia, hotel parking lot. The Alexandria Police Department spokesperson said it took about twenty seconds.[74]

Automated systems that capture and digitize mug shots can incorporate biometric facial recognition technology. The Los Angeles County Sheriff's Department installed a system than can take the composite drawing of a suspect or a video image of someone committing a crime and search it against its database of digitized mug shots. The department also intends to search for suspects on a "Megan's Law CD," which is a photo database of registered sex offenders.[75]

Age-Progression Photographs

One of the newest innovations in investigative photography is the **age-progression** or age-enhanced **photo**. The ability to recognize a face may be thwarted by the changes that naturally occur to the face with age. So, in the early 1980s, two medical illustrators, Scott Barrows and Lewis Sadler, developed techniques for producing age-progression drawings. Today, thanks to a computer algorithm, the process that used to take hours using calipers, ruler, and pen can be completed in seconds. Developed by a colleague of Barrows and Sadler, the age-progression program systematizes the

YOU ARE THERE!
Finding Missing Children Through Age-Progressed Photos

An Oakland, California, investigator reached out across the United States and Canada with age-progressed images of two missing brothers. After exhausting every lead, the investigator turned to the television program "Unsolved Mysteries."

On the evening of the broadcast, hundreds of calls poured in from the Albuquerque, New Mexico, area. Authorities located the two children in a trailer on the outskirts of town, where they were living with their mother and her new husband—a known drug dealer. The boys were returned to their father, who had not seen them in several years.

Although the aged images of the boys were very accurate, the relentless determination of the investigator and the assistance of the public are what ultimately solved this case.

SOURCE: Gene O'Donnell, "Forensic Imaging Comes of Age," *FBI Law Enforcement Bulletin*, Jan. 1994, p. 9.

YOU ARE THERE!
The Capture of John List Through Age-Progression Photos

In 1987, the FBI's Newark, New Jersey, field office forwarded a request for forensic assistance to the Special Projects Section of the FBI laboratory for age-enhanced photos of J. E. List, who had eluded detection since murdering his entire family seventeen years earlier.

The FBI produced age-enhanced photographs of List and forwarded them to the field office. The office then publicized an age-enhanced photograph in various national publications. A woman recognized the man from the photograph in a supermarket tabloid. He was her neighbor, living under the assumed name Robert P. Clark. The neighbor dared Clark's wife to confront her husband with the photo, but the woman never did.

Two years later, in 1989, the television show "America's Most Wanted" featured a plaster bust, prepared by a forensic artist, based on the photograph of List. By this time List had moved to Midlothian, Virginia, a suburb of Richmond. Convinced that Clark was in fact John List, his former neighbor asked her son-in-law to call the FBI and provide investigators with his new address. When agents confronted the man, he denied that he was List. But fingerprints from a gun permit application filed a month before the slayings revealed the truth. He was arrested and returned to New Jersey, where he was convicted of murder and sentenced to life in prison.

SOURCE: Gene O'Donnell, "Forensic Imaging Comes of Age," *FBI Law Enforcement Bulletin*, Jan. 1994, pp. 5–10.

knowledge of the anatomy of fourteen major bones and more than one hundred muscles and how they grow. It also shows the change in relationship, over time, of forty-eight facial landmarks, such as the corners of the eyes and the nose. Computers have enabled the National Center for Missing and Exploited Children to arrange to have thousands of age-progressed pictures printed onto milk cartons and flyers. The FBI uses its own age-progression program for adult faces. It allows artists to do such things as thin hair, add jowls, or increase wrinkles while maintaining the basic facial proportions. The FBI's software for aging children's faces allows pictures of parents and older siblings to be fused into photos of missing children to obtain a more accurate image.[76]

Composite Sketches

Investigators have for many years sought the assistance of forensic artists in preparing composite sketches. The FBI began to use composite sketching in 1920; other agencies had been using it even before that. These portrait-style drawings generally require hours of interview, drawing, and revision. Today the FBI has converted its book of photographs, used for interviewing witnesses for composites, into hand-drawn images using forensic imaging. These images are entered into a computer where they form the basis of a database that will automatically generate similar images. Once the witness selects features from the catalogue, the composite image appears on the computer screen in just a few minutes.[77]

Computer software can also allow officers to produce a digitized composite photo of a suspect based on the recollections of victims and witnesses. The resulting photo can then be compared with thousands of digital mug shots stored in the growing number of databases in jurisdictions all over the nation, including those states that now issue digitized photos on driver's licenses. Included in this software is a data bank of thousands of facial features from which witnesses select the ones that best fit their description of suspects. Software users, who need no formal artistic training, can adjust the composite by using a scanner to adjust the facial features chosen by the witness.[78]

Often, an artist is not even necessary. With practice, investigators can place the features on the screen and modify the image as the witness instructs. The system

Facial recognition systems, based on one of the latest forms of biometrics technology, create opportunities to identify people unobtrusively, as in video sureveillance. Here, Dr. Joseph Atick, President and CEO of Visionics Corporation, displays his high-tech face scanner to members of the Florida House and Senate Select Committee of Public Security in Demember 2001.

can be loaded into a laptop computer to further speed up the process by taking it directly to a crime scene. It can also be accessed through a modem hookup or put online, with an artist in another city available to prepare the composite while a witness views and suggests changes.

A new CD-ROM program called "Faces, the Ultimate Composite Picture," has been developed that provides nearly four thousand facial features that can be selected to create billions of faces. The designers used photos taken of approximately fifteen thousand volunteers, ages seventeen to sixty, to acquire images of hair, eyes, chins, and more. Instead of a police artist trying to coax the memory of an offender's face from a frightened victim, artists and even victims themselves can create photo-quality composites in about thirty minutes.[79]

TECHNOLOGY AND INVESTIGATIVE SURVEILLANCE

Police agencies and investigators use surveillance for a variety of reasons, including to provide cover for an undercover officer and an arrest team in a buy-and-bust narcotics operation or to gather intelligence or establish probable cause for arrest. Today's advances in

INVESTIGATIONS ON THE NET

Forensic Art

http://www.forensicartist.com

For an up-to-date list of Web links, go to
http://info.wadsworth.com/dempsey

----

technology provide us with more surveillance devices than ever before.[80] Formerly, surveillance equipment might have consisted of a broken-down van used to store a camera and a pair of binoculars. Today's investigators have high-tech state-of-the-art listening, recording, and viewing devices, high-tech surveillance vans, night vision devices, and surveillance aircraft, among other innovations.

Aspect Technology and Equipment Inc. offers an interesting and informative Web site for anyone interested in technology equipment for law enforcement. It discusses light intensification systems (such as night vision goggles, night vision scopes, night vision pocket scopes, and infrared illuminators), thermal imaging systems, surveillance systems (such as wireless video

YOU ARE THERE!

Carjacker Identified by Computerized Composite Photo System in Twenty Minutes

Los Angeles County Sheriff's Sergeant William Conley used the latest technology to apprehend a carjacker who had stolen a 1997 Honda and beaten the vehicle's owner. Based on the victim's recollection of the suspect's appearance, Conley entered those features into a computerized composite photo system to form a mug shot that was compared to thousands on file in the county's database of digitized photos. In just twenty minutes, Conley was able to pull up a likeness of the suspect as well as his address. Deputies arrested the man at his home; he subsequently confessed to the crime and is now serving a five-year sentence.

SOURCE: "No More Pencils, No More Books," *Law Enforcement News*, Jan. 31, 1998, p. 5.

and audio systems, miniature pinhole board cameras, miniature microphones, miniature video and audio recorders, miniature video and audio transmitters and receivers, covert body video and audio systems, and long-range cameras and lenses), and vehicle tracking systems.

Listening, Recording, and Viewing Devices

In today's technically advanced world there is no limit to the number of affordable devices that allow people to listen electronically to, record, or view incidents in real time. Generally, devices that can record conversations are called *recorders*. Some are as small as a matchbook and can be concealed in an area or worn by a person. Other devices, called *transmitters*, are designed specifically to be worn on a subject's body. They transmit conversations to a "listening post" where other investigators are stationed. The investigators can follow the conversation and perhaps intervene if the investigator wearing the transmitter is in danger. The investigators manning the listening post can also record the conversation on a recorder.

Electronic surveillance generally uses three basic components: transmitter, receiver, and recorder. Additional requirements are an antenna and a power supply. In many cases, all these components are built into a kit. Factors that affect the system's quality and versatility are the sensitivity of the receiver, the quality of the transmitter, the versatility of the recorder, and the number of internal and external power supplies and accessories. Audio Intelligence Devices (AID), a subsidiary of Westinghouse Electric, is one of the largest suppliers of electronic surveillance equipment. It supplies intelligence kits, body transmitters, tracking systems for vehicle and cargo, "bug" detectors, telephone intercept devices, miniature cameras, video transmitters and receivers, and pinhole lens cameras, as well as an

INVESTIGATIONS ON THE NET

Aspect Technology and Equipment
http://www.aspecttechnology.com

For an up-to-date list of Web links, go to
http://info.wadsworth.com/dempsey

----

entire line of night vision equipment, surveillance vans, and training equipment. AID also operates the National Intelligence Academy, which trains officers in surveillance technology and operations.[81]

"Bugs" are miniature devices that can be placed at a location to transmit conversations held at that location to a listener who can be quite a distance away. Very often these bugs are used in corporate espionage and are illegal. There are also available parabolic and shotgun microphones or bionic ears, which can monitor conversations from outside a premise. The use of such bugs has led to the birth of a new industry, often referred to as *sweeping*, where technicians check or sweep rooms, residences, or telephones for these illegal devices.

Investigators also have at their disposal a tremendous amount of miniature still and moving cameras and camcorders that can be used to record any selected event. These devices are advertised in investigative and security trade magazines and at trade shows or conventions nationwide.

Surveillance Vans

A vehicle specialist describes today's state-of-the-art surveillance van. "When talking about surveillance vehicles today, . . . we tend to think of a van whose interior looks slightly less complex than the bridge of Star Trek's *USS Enterprise*."[82]

This specialist describes the ideal surveillance van's equipment: power periscopes operated by a joystick; six cameras to cover 360 degrees of a van's exterior, plus a periscope-mounted observer's camera; videotape decks to record everything happening on the street; quick-change periscope camera mounts; portable toilets; video printers; motion detection cameras; night vision cameras; cellular telephones; AM/FM cassette entertainment systems; CB radio, police radio, police scanners; and other personalized equipment.

Vehicle Tracking Systems

Vehicle tracking systems, also sometimes referred to as transponders, bumper beepers, or homing devices, enable investigators to track a vehicle during a surveillance. These systems are actually transmitters that can be placed on a subject's vehicle. The tracking system consists of the transmitter on the subject's vehicle and

a receiver, which picks up the signal from the transmitter. There are three basic systems on the market:

- *RF (radio frequency) tracking systems* are usually short-range systems that operate on a signal from a transmitter placed on the target vehicle. The receiver receives the signal using three or four antennas and determines the direction of the target vehicle.
- *Cellular tracking systems* work similarly to RF tracking systems but make use of transmitters that link to cellular telephone towers to track the target vehicle. Often a cellular telephone serves as the transmitter signal that the tracking system employs. Tracking range is limited to the range of towers in the area.
- *Global positioning system (GPS) tracking systems* make use of GPS satellites to pinpoint the location of a target vehicle. (See the following section for more on these.)

Night Vision Devices

Among the most sophisticated surveillance devices in use today are enhanced **night vision devices,** including monocular devices small enough to hold in one hand, which can be adapted to a camera, video camera, or countersniper rifle. An expert describes the potential of such devices:

> Perhaps an automobile slowly approaches you in the dark with its lights out. With a normal night vision scope you can see it clearly—but you can't see through the windshield to see who's driving the car. Switch on the infrared (IR) laser, and it illuminates a spot through the windshield so you can identify the operator. In another case, at night a man lurks on the porch of a mountain cabin. In normal mode only the cabin and porch are clearly visible. The IR laser illuminates a spot to show the person waiting in the shadows.[83]

As far back as 1800, Sir William Herschel discovered the fact that every object emits thermal energy in the infrared (IR) wavelengths. His son, Sir John Herschel, took the first IR photographs of the sun approximately forty years later. Infrared surveillance systems appeared toward the end of World War II as a covert way to observe the enemy at night. The Germans were the first to use IR systems as impressive nighttime tank killers. The Soviets developed IR systems in the 1960s and 1970s. Since then these systems have been used by the United States during the Korean, Vietnam, and Gulf Wars.[84]

A more sophisticated form of infrared technology is thermal imaging (TI), which does not require any light at all. Traditional night vision equipment requires minimal light, such as from the moon. Thermal imaging can not only see through darkness but also through fog, mist, and smoke. It is especially useful in penetrating many types of camouflaging. Thermal imaging takes advantage of the infrared emission but does it passively, so only the user knows when it is in operation, not the subject.[85]

IR and TI systems can be mounted on police vehicles and pan possible subjects in all directions. Display screens can be mounted in patrol cars or investigators' cars, and joysticks can be used to direct the panning of the cameras.[86]

Law enforcement agents from U.S. Customs and the border patrol make extensive use of thermal imagers. These heat-sensing cameras detect the presence and location of a human; then an image intensifier makes the image clearer so that identification is possible. They are used for myriad law enforcement and investigatory purposes, such as search-and-rescue missions, fugitive searches, perimeter surveillance, vehicle pursuits, flight safety, marine and ground surveillance, structure profiles, disturbed surfaces, hidden compartments, environmental hazards, and officer safety. Other emerging uses of thermal imaging are the obtaining of more accurate skid-mark measures at a crash scene and the obtaining of evidence at a crime scene that cannot be observed with the human eye.[87] The U.S. Border Patrol also uses many other different night vision technologies in their duties, including infrared cameras, night vision goggles, handheld searchlights with a band that reaches more than a mile, seismic and infrared sensors, and fiberscopes.[88]

INVESTIGATIONS ON THE NET

Law Enforcement Thermographers' Association
http://www.leta.org

For an up-to-date list of Web links, go to
http://info.wadsworth.com/dempsey

The Law Enforcement Thermographers' Association (LETA) is a professional association dedicated to promoting the ethical use of thermal imaging in support of law enforcement operations.

Surveillance Aircraft

Airplanes are being added to law enforcement's arsenal of surveillance devices. Two STOL (short take-off and landing) aircraft were showcased at the International Association of Chiefs of Police (IACP) conference in 1991. These aircraft do not require extensive landing fields and have proved to be very successful in surveillance operations.

Fixed-wing aircraft and rotorcraft complement ground-based vehicles in hundreds of police agencies worldwide and aid search-and-rescue operations, surveillance, and investigative missions. Advanced electronic and computer systems for aircraft now include real-time video downlinks and low-light surveillance.[89]

INVESTIGATIONS ON THE NET

Law Enforcement Technology (journal)
http://www.letonline.com

For an up-to-date list of Web links, go to
http://info.wadsworth.com/dempsey

Global Positioning Systems

Global positioning systems (GPS) are the most recent technology available to help law enforcement and investigators. The GPS is a network of twenty-four satellites used by the U.S. Department of Defense to pinpoint targets and guide bombs. They are equipped with atomic clocks and equally accurate position measuring telemetry gear. GPS has been used for everything from helping hikers find their way through the woods to guiding law enforcement officers to stolen vehicles.[90] When GPS is combined with geographic information systems (GIS) and automatic vehicle locations (AVL), officers can tell where they are on a map and the dispatch center can continuously monitor the officers' location. Police departments can determine the location of each patrol vehicle without any communication from the officer who is driving. In a car wreck, such a system could automatically notify the dispatcher of a possibly injured officer at a specific location. Also, if an officer engages in a high-speed chase, such a system would provide the vehicle's location automatically, or if an officer is injured in an encounter with a suspect, it can suggest that help be sent immediately.

GPS is also used by fleet operators in the private sector to track fleets for routing purposes and for rolling emergencies. It can be used to track the route over time and to monitor the vehicle's speed. GPS is also used for crime mapping, tracking, and monitoring the location of probationers and parolees around the clock.[91]

Fear of Technology by Civil Libertarians

It should be noted that not everyone is happy with the new surveillance technology. Civil libertarians fear that such developments as improved computer-based files and long-range electronic surveillance devices will give the police and investigators more power to intrude into the private lives of citizens.[92] Even *Popular Mechanics* magazine worries about the civil liberties issues of enhanced investigative technology:

Along with the advantages, however, has come new potential for abuse. For example, the same computer databases that make AFIS possible could also be used for random searches that might focus suspicion on people because they have stayed in a homeless shelter, or because they fall into certain categories based on age, race, or other discriminatory criteria. Thus, the task of ensuring that upholding the law does not interfere with the privacy and freedom of those it is meant to protect grows simultaneously more difficult and more important.[93]

In his book *Taking Liberties: A Decade of Hard Cases, Bad Laws, and Bum Raps*, noted civil liberties lawyer Alan M. Dershowitz of Harvard University Law School comments on the 1986 Supreme Court case *California v. Ciraolo*.[94] In this case the court ruled that evidence obtained by the police in the course of flying over and photographing a person's property was not a violation of the person's Fourth Amendment rights. Dershowitz says: "You can be sure that our constitution's Founding Fathers would have been appalled at this breach of privacy. A person's home—whether a walled estate, a plantation, or a small cottage—was regarded as his castle, free from the intruding eye of government, without a warrant based on probable cause."[95]

SUMMARY   In the introduction to this chapter we stated that technology has revolutionized much of our society, including criminalistics. The advances of science, especially DNA, can help law enforcement solve many crimes and ensure that the guilty are brought to justice. These advances can also show us past mistakes—such as those committed by forensic chemist Joyce Gilchrist. Following up on this story, we can now report that in late August 2001, DNA reanalysis of evidence originally developed by Gilchrist in the case of Malcolm Rent Johnson, which led to his conviction in 1982 of rape and murder and eventually to his execution on January 6, 2000, revealed that Gilchrist's original analyis was in error.[96] DNA analysis was not available at the time she made her original erroneous analysis. Would Johnson have been executed if DNA analysis was available at that time?

This chapter discussed the role of the physical sciences and technology in investigating. It discussed the importance of forensic science or criminalistic evidence in investigations and the U.S. legal system, and the modern crime laboratory and the areas of expertise covered, including ballistics, serology, chemistry, criminalistics, and document analysis. It also discussed certain specialty sections, including forensic pathology, forensic toxicology, forensic physical anthropology, forensic ento-mology, and forensic odontology. The chapter then examined the latest criminalistic technology, including DNA profiling or genetic fingerprinting, discussing the con-cepts behind this revolutionary technology and its current status in the U.S. court system. The chapter also reviewed the introduction of criminalistic evidence in the courtroom and the role of the expert witness.

This chapter looked at technology in investigating, including computers, and advanced fingerprint technology. It examined advanced photographic techniques, including mug shot imaging, age-progression photos, and automated composite sketching. The chapter discussed advances in technology for investigative surveil-lance, vehicle tracking systems, night vision devices, and global positioning systems. It concluded with a discussion of the threat to civil liberties posed by modern technology.

LEARNING CHECK

1. Name three pioneers of criminalistics and discuss their contributions to our cur-rent knowledge in this area.

2. Name the main sections of the modern crime lab and briefly discuss the type of evidence each one analyzes.

3. What is DNA profiling or genetic fingerprinting? What is its status in the U.S. court system today?

4. Explain the latest advances in fingerprint processing.

5. List and discuss some of the advanced photographic techniques being used in investigating today.

APPLICATION EXERCISES

1. Arrange to tour a public or private crime laboratory and prepare a report on what you observe.

2. Conduct research on a recent criminal case and show how forensic evidence resulted in a conviction or acquittal in court.

3. Assume that, in a private investigation, you have been hired to investigate the fol-lowing case.

John and Diane Wilson, the son and daughter of Marianne and Jack Wilson, both prominent surgeons in your town, were kidnapped as they played on their front lawn nearly twenty years ago. The twins were three years old at the time. The police conducted a massive nationwide investigation, with negative results. The case received extensive media attention for several years. Last week the Wilsons got a telephone call from a woman, Donna Anne, who told the following story, "I am a twenty-three-year-old woman whose parents have just died. Our parents told my twin brother and me that they adopted us when we were very young, but they were always secretive about who our real parents were. Last week, while research-ing a report for my criminal investigations course, I came upon the story of the kidnapping of the Wilson twins, your children. I talked to my Aunt Cathy about the case and she became agitated and refused to discuss it with me any further. My brother and I believe that we could be your children."

The Wilsons ask you to investigate the possibility of this story's truth before they agree to meet with the twins. They are distraught over the phone call and could not tolerate a meeting if there wasn't a chance that these might be their long-lost children. They tell you they are afraid this call could be a scam. They provide you with photographs of the children taken before they were kidnapped. They tell you that their children were never officially fingerprinted by the police before their disappearance, but they give you several toys that were handled by the twins when they were young. They tell you that the police reported to them, at the time of the disappearance, that the toys and photographs could not help in this case. Based on your reading of this chapter, list the primary steps you can take to investigate.

WEB EXERCISES

1. You are working as an intern with a small local police department that does not have a crime lab and sends their evidence to the state lab. The chief, knowing of your interest in forensic science and computers, asks you to help her understand DNA. She says she uses the Internet and would like to look at a few sites that will increase her understanding as a layperson. Select at least three sites that may help the chief and provide her with the names and Internet addresses and a few sample pages of each site's coverage of DNA.

2. The honors program of your school is sponsoring a symposium entitled "The Challenge to Privacy Faced by Increased Law Enforcement Technology." You have been selected by your professor to research this subject and present some background information to your class before the symposium. She asks you to search the Web and find several sites on this topic and prepare a brief report on some major issues that might arise at the symposium.

KEY TERMS

age-progression photos	forensic science
anthropometry	genetic fingerprinting
automated fingerprint identification systems (AFIS)	global positioning systems (GPS)
	IAFIS
automated information systems	MtDNA
ballistics	mug shot
Bertillon measurements	night vision devices
biometric identification	PCR-STR
CODIS	portrait parlé
computer-aided investigation	RFLP
criminalistics	ultraviolet forensic imaging
DNA profiling	Will West case

INTERVIEWS AND INTERROGATIONS

7

CHAPTER GOALS

1. To show you the importance of interviews in the investigating process and methods used by successful interviewers to obtain information

2. To acquaint you with innovations in interviewing techniques, such as the cognitive interview, and special techniques in interviewing special populations, such as children and victims of sexual abuse

3. To acquaint you with technical aids that are available for use in the interview-interrogation process: hypnosis, the polygraph, the psychological stress evaluator, narcoanalysis, and the study of body language

4. To show you the importance of the interrogation process in investigating, methods used by successful interrogators in conducting one, and the guidelines set forth by the United States Supreme Court over the years for conducting interrogations

5. To show you the techniques used by interviewers and interrogators in recording interviews and interrogations for later use and for presentation in court

INTRODUCTION

> In order to obtain the confession the defendants were
> made to strip and were laid over chairs and their
> backs were cut to pieces with a leather strap with
> buckles on it and they were likewise made by the
> said deputy definitely to understand that the whipping
> would be continued unless and until they confessed,
> and not only confessed, but confessed to every matter
> of the detail as demanded by those present. The
> defendants made their confession on April 1, 1934,
> were indicted on April 4, went on trial on April 5,
> and were convicted and sentenced to death on
> April 6, 1934.[1]

The U.S. criminal justice system and the actions of U.S. investigators have changed significantly since this sordid account of a coerced confession in the landmark United States Supreme Court case, *Brown v. Mississippi* (1936). Obtaining statements from suspects is still an important part of investigations, but today legal restrictions apply.

Much of an investigator's time is spent in conducting interviews or interrogations, and most of the information an investigator obtains is from these interviews and interrogations. Most of the case clearances in public and private investigations result from information received in interviews and interrogations.

Investigators use interviews and interrogations to obtain information in both public and private investigating. Generally, interviews are used when talking to victims or witnesses and interrogations are used when talking to suspects. However, the interview and the interrogation are very similar. They are both attempts to obtain information and determine the truth.

In this chapter we examine the traits and qualities of a successful interviewer-interrogator; the types of interviews that may be conducted; the setting in which they should be conducted; and the preparation necessary for a successful interview or interrogation. We discuss the interview itself, including the necessary approach, warm-up, start, and actual questioning involved. We then discuss techniques and approaches involved in interviewing certain special populations, such as children, victims of sexual abuse, and those reluctant to talk to interviewers. We also cover certain techniques or technology that can aid the investigation-interrogation process, such as the cognitive interview, hypnosis, the polygraph, the psychological stress evaluator, narcoanalysis, and the observation and interpretation of body language.

The chapter also discusses the interrogation, including its purpose, ideal setting, and successful techniques for conducting it. It traces the development of current legal rules on interrogation by reviewing relevant decisions of the U.S. Supreme Court in landmark cases from 1936 to the present. The chapter also looks at methods used to record the interview or interrogation, including written statements and videotaping.

It should be noted that the information in this chapter regarding the interviewer is not limited to investigators but can be used by people in many different occupations. Physicians, for example, require interviewing skills to diagnose a patient's illness properly. Attorneys require interviewing skills, both in and out of the courtroom.

THE INTERVIEWER

The success of the interview depends on the interviewer's abilities and skills. Successful interviewers must exude self-confidence and professionalism in appearance and demeanor. They should be adaptable, objective, patient, persuasive, insightful, and sensitive to individual rights. Also, interviewers must be able to develop rapport with the person being interviewed in order to obtain a complete interview. Exhibit 7.1 lists desirable and undesirable interviewer traits.

THE INTERVIEW

Obtaining information is the essential goal of any investigation. Therefore, **interviews** are the most critical stage of an investigation because, generally, they are the primary source of information. Author Richard D. Morrison reports, "The most critical aspect of any criminal investigation are the interviews. Communication between the investigator and witness must be exceptional if a competent statement is to be obtained."[2]

Purpose

The interview is often the key to closing the investigation or to obtaining sufficient information to continue it. The investigator must remember that even in crimi-

EXHIBIT 7.1   Traits of the Interviewer

Desirable	Undesirable
Professional	Rigid
Objective	Win-at-all-cost attitude
Adaptable	Prejudiced
Patient	Aloof
Persuasive	Timid
Self-confident	Judgmental
Tactful	Condescending
Friendly	
Respectful of individual rights	
Courteous	

nal cases a subject is under no obligation to answer any questions. Selecting the proper place, time, and method of interviewing is predicated on the fact that the subject is not required to participate in the interview. The utmost attention should be paid to making the interview as acceptable and painless as possible. In that way, a subject may be more inclined to participate.

Types of Interviews

Several types of interviews can be used, depending on whether the interviewee is a witness, a suspect, the victim of a crime, an informant, or an ordinary citizen.

The Witness Witnesses to a crime or incident should be interviewed as soon as possible after the event. All witnesses should also be separated as soon as possible and interviewed separately with as much privacy as possible. Failure to interview witnesses quickly may result in their forgetting information or becoming reluctant to cooperate with investigators.

CAREER FOCUS
Linguist

Contract Linguist, Monitor, Tester, Federal Bureau of Investigation

The Federal Bureau of Investigation has unique and challenging career opportunities for contract linguists in many major U.S. metropolitan areas. These opportunities include various types of language-related services, such as interpreting, testing, monitoring, and translating. Consideration is currently being afforded English-speaking candidates with a professional-level language fluency in Farsi, Pashto, Arabic, Chinese (all dialects), Hebrew, Hindi, Punjabi, Russian, Turkish, Urdu, Vietnamese, and Yiddish.

FBI contract linguists primarily perform document-to-document or audio-to-document translation services on any subject matter for which the FBI has jurisdiction. They translate into English from the target language the speech and/or writings of non-English speaking individuals, and on occasion, render translations from English into the target language.

FBI contract monitors perform summary translations of voice recordings. The subject matter may be in any area for which the FBI has jurisdiction.

FBI contract testers provide oral and written testing services for the purposes of determining the language ability of potential FBI employees, contractors, and on-board employees in English and the target language.

Minimum qualifications for the FBI's contract linguist program are: U.S. citizenship; residence in the U.S. for at least three out of the last five years; ability to pass a battery of language proficiency tests, polygraph examination, and a ten-year scope background investigation.

Interested applicants should contact their local FBI field office or Legal Attaché for specific information or log onto www.fbijobs.com for more information.

SOURCE: Federal Bureau of Investigation; http://www.fbijobs.com/ FBIJobDesc.asp?r=568428294&JC=001401, and http://www.fbi.gov/ page2/linguist.htm.

Richard D. Morrison stresses the importance of the first police patrol units at the scene of a crime in identifying, questioning, and separating witnesses. Under ideal circumstances, the first responding officers should obtain the name, address, phone number, and exact knowledge of the crime from each witness. In addition, they should urge each witness to await the arrival of the investigators. Morrison states that it cannot be emphasized enough how critical this early stage of an investigation is to the overall success of a case; a poor job here can cause many unnecessary hours of work for the investigator and may cause the suspect to remain unidentified and at large.[3]

The **canvass** is one of the most important techniques used in criminal investigations. It is the search of the geographical area of a crime for all possible witnesses. In addition to questioning persons present in the area after the commission of a crime, efforts should also be made immediately to contact all persons who might have knowledge of the crime. After a serious crime, investigators should conduct a door-to-door canvass of all homes or businesses where the occupants might have seen or heard anything. Then, a canvass report should be prepared, noting the addresses that were visited along with the names of people interviewed and what each observed. (See Exhibit 7.2 for a sample canvass report.) Anyone not available for the original canvass should be interviewed at a later time.

In criminal investigations a recanvass should always be conducted on the assumption that the investigator can locate people who were not available initially but might subsequently be found to have been in the area when the crime occurred.

In serious criminal cases numerous recanvasses should be made. The philosophy is that people are creatures of habit, and a person who is shopping, doing business, or traveling in a certain area might also have been engaged in the same activity on the day of the crime.

Even if people say they have no knowledge of the crime they should still be interviewed to see if they observed anything unusual or inconsistent with normal activity in the neighborhood. The neighborhood canvass is extremely important because even if people being interviewed claim no knowledge of the particular crime, they might be able give the interviewer valuable information about the neighborhood itself, the victim, or possible suspects.

The Suspect The interview of a suspect is generally called an **interrogation** rather than an interview. The same rules of interviewing generally apply to the interrogation. However, because the person is suspected of guilt or involvement in the crime, special techniques and often legal restrictions may apply. Interrogations are discussed in greater detail later in this chapter.

The Victim Often the victim of a crime may be suffering from physical injuries or emotional or psychological trauma. Therefore, the investigator's first concern must be to get the victim any necessary medical assistance. However, because the victim may be the only witness or the witness with the best recollection of the event, the investigator must also make every attempt to interview the victim as soon as medical attention is obtained.

When interviewing victims it is imperative that the interviewer display concern, empathy, and understanding in addition to stressing the importance of the victim's statements. Later in this chapter we discuss interviews involving special classes of victims, including children and victims of sexual abuse.

The Informant The word *informant* generally connotes someone who has special knowledge of a crime or incident or an ongoing criminal enterprise. The confidential informant is a person who provides an investigator with confidential information on a past or future crime and does not wish to be known as the

---

EXHIBIT 7.2   **Canvass Report**

Date and Time of Incident: _____

Crime: _____

Area Canvassed: _____

Investigator: _____

Address Apt. #	Person Interviewed	Results of Canvass
_____	_____	_____
_____	_____	_____
_____	_____	_____

"I saw the guy approach the car and fire shots into it. He was about six feet tall, thin build, and had on a green military-like fatigue jacket."

"I didn't see the crime, but Donna had been dating a lot of different guys lately. Maybe you should look into some of those guys."

"I was sleeping, but earlier I had looked out the window and saw this guy in a green coat standing on the corner by himself. I thought it was weird, but . . ."

"I wasn't home, but the past few nights I have seen this weird-looking guy hanging around the neighborhood. I know he wasn't from here 'cause I know everyone around here."

"Last week Donna got dropped off by this dude and they got into this big fight about her dissing him. I got scared. I thought he was gonna kill her. I took down his license plate number just in case. Do you want it?"

source of the information. Chapter 8, "Sources of Information," discusses informants and precautions to be used when dealing with them.

The Ordinary Citizen Investigators interview citizens from all walks of life in their daily routines. These interviews may be done in person or by telephone. The subjects may be public or private officials having information the investigator needs or friends or associates of victims, witnesses, or suspects. Generally these interviews are conducted at the subject's place of business. Therefore, courtesy and measures to ensure voluntary compliance with the investigator's requests are essential.

The Setting

The investigator usually allows the subject to select the location for the interview. It is best to interview the subject at a place that would cause him the least inconvenience. An exception to this is the interview of a possible suspect in a crime, which should be conducted at the investigator's office.

Although an interview should take place as soon as possible after an incident, in cases where a crime victim is emotionally disturbed, it is best to delay it until the victim receives medical assistance or emotional

DEMPSEY'S LAW
What My Grandmother Taught Me

Professor, why do we have to do all these door-to-door canvasses? If anyone saw the crime, they would tell the cops, right?

Tom, you have to understand that not all people go to the police to report incidents they saw. I'll never forget something that happened on my block one day when I was a kid. I was walking home from school and I saw a lot of police officers and detectives on the block. I ran up to my apartment, knowing that my grandmother would have seen what had happened because she spent most of her day leaning over the windowsill and watching everything that happened on the block. We didn't have a television back then.

"Nannie, what happened?" I asked. She described the fight that had occurred on the street and that she

yelled out to them to stop fighting and then told me that one kid had stabbed the other kid and ran away. The police arrived immediately and put the injured boy into an ambulance. She said the police began asking passersby if they had seen anything. She was able to describe both kids perfectly. I said to her, "Did you tell the police?" She replied, "The police never asked me."

I learned a lot from her. I learned that some people don't go to the police; they wait for the police to come to them. There are still a lot of people like my grandmother. Canvasses are very important, Tom. Also, there are many people who might see something happening and not get involved at all. Did you ever hear of Kitty Genovese?

YOU ARE THERE!
The Kitty Genovese Case

Catherine (Kitty) Genovese finished work as a night manager of a bar and drove home in her red Fiat at 3:20 A.M. on a chilly March 13, 1964. As she pulled into a parking space at the Long Island Railroad station adjacent to her home on Austin Street in Kew Gardens, Queens, New York, she observed a man standing under a street lamp near the entrance to her apartment building. She decided to avoid him by walking up Austin Street toward Lefferts Boulevard instead of passing him. The stranger stalked her, attacking her as she reached a darkened bookstore on Austin Street. He stabbed her in the stomach and she screamed. Her screams alerted people in the ten-story apartment house nearby, as lights went on and windows opened—but no one called the police. Genovese staggered bleeding toward her own apartment building, but her attacker returned and stabbed her again. Her screams met again with lights and opened windows, but again no one called the police. The killer stabbed her yet again as she attempted to enter her building. Kitty Genovese died.

Over the next few weeks, detectives conducted door-to-door canvasses and learned that thirty-eight neighbors had witnessed the assault but no one had called the police until 3:50 A.M., thirty minutes after Kitty's first screams for help.

New Yorkers have a reputation for rarely getting involved with their neighbors, but this lack of involvement was beyond the norm. This case was one of the most shameful moments in New York's history, a graphic testament to the chilly alienation of big-city living.

---

support from friends and loved ones. Also, interviews are best conducted during normal business hours and with advance notice.

Each subject of an investigation, witness, or other person should be interviewed separately and with as much privacy as possible. If a subject appears to be nervous to be alone with an investigator, the investigator might suggest that the subject bring a friend to observe the interview.

Preparation

Preparation for an interview is essential. The interviewer should review previous reports on the case, the subject, and any previous statements made by the subject or others relating to the incident. The interviewer should also review the subject's background. It is a good idea to request a criminal records check on a subject in a criminal investigation.

In effect, investigators must do their homework before the interview. This preparation will not only aid the investigation but will convey to the subject the investigator's interest in the case and thoroughness. Furthermore, knowledge of the subject's past can be used to test his credibility during the interview.

The Interview Itself

There are several important points to keep in mind during the interview itself.

The Approach Interviewers should greet the subject in a friendly manner while showing their credentials. A firm handshake and a "Good morning, [name of person], thank you for seeing me" is an effective prelude to the interview. It is best to call adults by their surname preceded by Mr., Mrs., or Ms. If a subject asks to be called by a first name or a nickname, the interviewer should comply with this request and, in turn, offer the subject the option of using his or her own first name. This helps to relax the interviewee and establishes a feeling of trust. It is best to address children and teenagers by their first name. A nickname may be used as a means of putting a juvenile at ease.

The Warm-Up The interviewer should begin the interview by establishing a rapport with the subject. This may be accomplished by finding some common interest with the subject, then spending a few minutes talking about that interest. Some neutral warm-up lines could be, "Have you been following the NBA playoffs?" or "I like your suit, where did you buy it?" or "What do you think of this weather?"

The interviewer should be friendly and personable. People are more likely to talk to someone who appears friendly and interested in them than to someone who appears cold and uninterested. Also, it will facilitate information gathering to let interviewees know how important their cooperation and information are to the successful conclusion of the case.

The Start When the actual interview begins, the interviewer should ask the subject to state all he knows about the incident.

It is very important at this time that the investigator not take notes and not interrupt the subject to ask questions. Interviewers should show a sincere interest in the story being told but avoid any verbal or nonverbal expressions that indicate that they are judging the person's statements, character, or behavior.

Direct Questioning Once the subject finishes telling the story, then the investigator can begin to ask direct questions. Direct questioning may be necessary to clarify certain statements made by the subject, to challenge inconsistencies, or to obtain additional information. If they intend to take notes or want to make a recording of this part of the interview, investigators should first ask the subject's permission. The following techniques will be helpful:

- *Ask one question at a time.* Asking a series of questions without pause or shooting rapid-fire questions at a subject can confuse and distract the person. Investigators should always wait a few moments between the subject's answer and the next question in the event the subject wants to add something to the answer.

- *Avoid yes or no questions.* Most questions cannot be adequately answered with a simple yes or no, but rather require some explanation. Generally, it is best to ask the subject just to talk about all he knows about the incident or person. A question requiring an open-ended response is preferable to a question merely asking for a yes or no answer because it elicits further information in the interviewee's own words. In order to get the most open-ended answer, the interviewer should phrase each question in this manner: "What happened then?" or "Tell me what you saw next."

- *Avoid leading questions.* Investigators should not suggest any answers to a subject but rather should ask a direct question, such as "What happened then?"

- *Keep questions simple.* The investigator should not attempt to confuse the subject. If so, the subject could make mistakes or decide to end the interview.

- *Keep the subject talking.* The investigator can use certain techniques to keep the subject talking. An intense listening posture can show the subject that the interviewer is attentive and interested in hearing what is being said. Interviewers also can keep their own talking to a minimum and at times make use of the long pause. Sometimes it is beneficial to allow a long pause in order to give the subject time to think and organize his thoughts.

- *Use the subject's language.* Investigators should not talk down to a subject or use language the person cannot understand. They should use language that the subject understands, and as the interview goes on, they should ensure that the subject does understand the exact meaning of the words they are using. They should avoid using legal terms, such as *battery* or *assault*, using instead words like *injury* or *hit*, because the interviewee may not know the exact meaning of legal terms.

Ending the Interview

At the end of the interview interviewers should sum up the subject's statements, note any corrections, and offer sincere thanks. They should give their business card to the subject, asking him to contact them if he has additional information on the case. Interviewers should also offer assistance, such as asking if the subject needs a ride home, for example.

INTERVIEWING SPECIAL POPULATIONS

Interviewing special populations, including children, victims of sexual abuse, and recalcitrant witnesses, presents certain problems that may be overcome with the use of specific techniques.

Children

The National Institute of Justice has reported that the testimony of a child victim is often crucial for the successful prosecution of individuals who commit crimes against children. But it also reports that when such crimes are disclosed, the young victims are thrust into a bewildering series of events that can seriously impair their ability to perform as witnesses.[4]

In an article in the *FBI Law Enforcement Bulletin*, David Gullo describes a number of problems that may arise when interviewing children, particularly victims of abuse.[5] He states that investigators who conduct such interviews must possess special skills, such as ability to ask nonleading questions; a good working knowledge of how to structure an interview; and most important, a fundamental knowledge of child development. He states, "Adults may remember what it was like to be a child, but childhood memories are not enough to understand child behavior."[6] Gullo then goes on to explain the five stages of child development to aid interviewers in structuring proper interviews with children:

- *Infancy (birth to two years).* These children are unable to form concepts, are self-centered, and are just learning to trust others.

- *Early childhood (two to four years).* These children are developing basic language skills. They also engage in imaginative behavior, gather information from sense and environment, and are learning independence.

- *Preschool age (four to six years).* These children now use language as their primary mode of communication. However, they still do not understand abstract concepts; therefore, their verbal skills may imply more comprehension than they actually possess. They memorize without comprehension, and their memories are spotty. They can distinguish some fact from fantasy and are capable of lying to get out of a problem situation.

- *School age (six to eleven).* These children continue to master language. They develop group loyalty, usually with members of their own gender, and seldom lie about major issues.

- *Adolescence (twelve to eighteen).* Adolescents undergo profound physical and emotional changes. They may have little rapport with adults and often question the values and beliefs they have been taught. They may be extremely shy in some settings, and very responsive and outgoing in others. They are capable of deception and manipulation, and can cover feelings of shyness and inferiority with an outward show of bravado or hostility.

Victims of Sexual Abuse

In recent years, police have instituted numerous programs to deal with crime victims, particularly victims of rape and sexual abuse. Many police departments have created special investigatory units to deal specifically with sexual abuse victims. Many of these units use female investigators to ease the interview process with both adult and juvenile victims.

Many police departments use **anatomically correct dolls**—dolls made to resemble actual people and their body parts, including sexual organs—in an effort to facilitate interviews of child victims of sexual abuse. These dolls can be useful in reducing stress, establishing rapport, determining competency, and learning the child's sexual vocabulary. Great care is needed, however, in the use of anatomically correct dolls; experts warn that the improper use of dolls can block communication and cause problems for prosecutors in trying the case.[7]

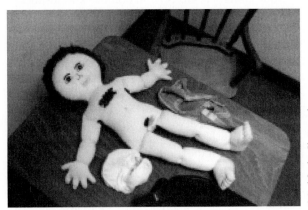

Investigators often use anatomically correct dolls to help obtain information during interviews of child victims of sexual abuse.

© Joel Gordon Photography

GUEST LECTURE

Professor Linda Forst, Captain, Retired, Boca Raton Police Department, on Interviewing Victims of Sex Crimes

The ability to interview people is one of the crucial talents a good investigator possesses. Many cases are made by the information provided by victims, witnesses, and suspects. If an investigator does not have the ability to obtain the needed information there may in fact be no case.

It is preferable to begin developing and fine-tuning this talent while still a patrol officer. Once officers are assigned to the investigative function they should receive training in interview and interrogation, which will further enhance their abilities.

I was fortunate in that I had a mentor. Bernie Collins was a detective in Crimes Against Persons while I was a patrol officer. He was known as one of the best interviewers and interrogators in the county. It was probably due to his unassuming, nonthreatening demeanor. He was able to talk to anyone and establish a rapport and eventually obtain the information he needed. He obtained confessions in cases that other detectives thought would be impossible. When Bernie got a sex crime case while I was working, he got permission from my supervisor to allow me help him work it. As this was the late seventies, police departments weren't as technologically advanced as they are now. I obtained most of my training by standing with my ear to the interview room door and listening to Bernie question suspects. I was able to sit in on the victim and witness interviews, but with suspects a third person could interfere with the dynamics. Watching Bernie make people feel at ease and begin to trust him was watching best practice in action. When I was assigned to the detective bureau several years later, I was able to hit the ground running armed with the knowledge Bernie had given me.

He taught me that intimidation rarely works, especially in sex cases. Sensitive cases are difficult to work and all people involved—victims, witnesses, and suspects—are reluctant to talk about what happened and provide details. The investigator must be sensitive to all the psychological issues at work in these cases and tailor the interviews accordingly. I remember that

after obtaining my first confession from a rapist, I left the room wondering, "Why in the world would that guy admit that to me?" But Bernie's training coupled with my own personal style allowed the man to trust me and share his burden with me. My confidence grew with every case I worked and each confession I obtained.

Since my assignment was in Crimes Against Persons, many of the cases were emotional. I worked a lot of sex cases, some very violent and some that had children as victims. I had to separate myself from the cases and maintain objectivity and professionalism. If I allowed myself to take my emotions and anger out on the suspect, any hope of obtaining a confession was lost.

I remember a case that occurred not too long after I started in the detective bureau. A thirteen-year-old girl was raped in the middle school rest room during school. A male was hiding in a stall and came out and grabbed her. He told her he had a razor blade and would cut her. He dragged her into a stall where he taped her mouth and hands and then sexually assaulted her vaginally and anally. He then fled the school. As he left the building, a teacher asked him what he was doing there but he took off. The teacher recognized him as a former student at the middle school. We were able to determine he was a seventeen-year-old student at the high school, located about half a mile away.

This was an emotional case for everyone concerned. As you would expect, the victim was traumatized by the incident, her parents were very upset and angry, the boy was uncooperative and belligerent, and his parents were unbelieving and angry. Thrown into this mixture was the politics of the school district and anger and embarrassment that this could happen when children were entrusted to their care. There was the usual concern for media attention and public outrage. I had to disconnect myself from these political concerns and concentrate on building the best case possible.

Interviewing Victims of Sex Crimes continued

My first step was to question the victim. I wanted to question her alone and had to carefully persuade her parents to trust me and allow me to take care of their daughter. Her parents' priority was her safety and her emotional health and they did not want to let her out of their sight. I convinced them that those were also my priorities, and I explained my reasons for wanting to question their daughter alone. I was afraid she would not be totally honest with me if her parents were in the room, due to embarrassment or a desire to protect them. Her parents understood this and agreed.

In questioning the victim, I had to go slowly and build her confidence and trust in me. I had to reassure her that anything she had to tell me would not be a shock, that it has happened before to other women. I stressed the importance of telling me everything that happened and assured her we would go slowly and she could stop and take a break whenever she wanted to. I also explained the criminal justice process to her so that she would know what to expect and why her statement and various details were important. I also explained the various community services that were available and how we would also do our best to help her parents. She was very concerned for her parents as her father had some health problems. We spent several hours together but I obtained a good quality statement full of details that would make the case stronger as we corroborated them with the various pieces of physical evidence we gathered.

I also spent time with the parents trying to assist them and helping them to understand what their daughter had gone through and would go through. I had to get my point across that prosecution would be beneficial and that we would make it as easy as we could for their daughter. This was a substantial investment of time but a necessary one. I also truly wanted to help them—and their daughter—through this. It's why I went into law enforcement, to help people.

Interrogating the suspect was another challenge I faced. After spending so much time with the victim and her parents I had a lot of anger toward the rapist. I had to put that aside and work with him to build the strongest case possible.

I also spent time with the suspect's parents. I wanted to find out about his past. I wanted to try and ascertain if there may have been any previous crimes involving him that we should be concerned about.

Out of professional curiosity I also wanted to know if there were any signs that he would commit this type of crime—any behavior that may be significant that we could look for in other children. I also needed to help his parents understand the case and what was going to happen.

As with many cases today, there was a long delay between the time of arrest and the trial. There was a grand jury appearance, depositions, and evidentiary hearings before we went to trial. During that time, I stayed in contact with the victim and her family. I did not want them to get scared or frustrated and decide not to cooperate. I kept them updated on what was happening with their case. It was important that they knew that "we" didn't forget about them. I also tried to help the victim with psychological issues she was facing by making sure she was taking advantage of the rape crisis counseling available. It was an emotionally draining time for all of us and there was a major setback when her father died of a heart attack. The victim blamed herself for her father dying, feeling that the stress of the case and prosecution contributed to his death. It was a difficult time. Eventually we did go to trial and the offender received the maximum penalty for the crime.

I had another case that has always stuck with me. I felt personally rewarded after working it, but I hesitated to mention it due to the risk of perpetuating the rape myth. However, every investigator will encounter false reports of all types of crimes for all types of reasons. This happens in sex crimes as in other crimes, though it is a very minor percentage of the cases.

I was called in one evening around 9 P.M. to investigate a case that involved a young woman who claimed to have been assaulted outside her apartment. The suspect wielded a knife and during the attack the woman received several cuts on her arms. She had gone to a Bible study session at her church and told the other members of her group and they called the police.

From the moment I met the young woman, something just didn't seem right. She was extremely reluctant to talk to me and vague on the details. She had just moved to Florida from the Midwest and was trying to get established. As I listened to her story and her reasons for not wanting to report it to the police, I

Interviewing Victims of Sex Crimes continued

glanced at her arms. I could see evidence of many superficial slash marks on each forearm. When I examined them more closely, I saw that they were indeed very superficial. There were about ten per forearm and they were pretty evenly spaced and seemed to run almost parallel to each other. They were not consistent with defense wounds.

I had to move carefully and slowly. Indicators of a false report are also common for a victim experiencing shock or posttraumatic stress syndrome. To approach this possibility incorrectly could jeopardize any legitimate case.

I moved very slowly in broaching the subject with this young woman. I talked about how sometimes people get involved over their heads and pushed into doing something they don't want to do. I watched her body language and eyes and continued. I questioned her as to whether that could have happened to her, that she didn't intend to call the police or report a rape, but her Bible group backed her into a corner and before she knew it to save face she had to go along. She started crying and said that she just wanted some attention, she wanted someone to care about her, and so she had made up the story. She was surprised when her friends called the police and then "stuck" when we showed up to take the report. I told her that she needed to tell me the truth so we could clear the matter up, but then it was up to her what she

told her friends. I gave her a way to save face with her friends as well as made her feel that I understood how the situation had unfolded. I also suggested she get some counseling and gave her some information on counseling services available. About a year later, I received a thank you card from her saying that she was doing really well. She thanked me for my understanding and compassion and the referral. She had gotten counseling and was doing much better and moving on with her life. It could have been a very negative outcome—wasted investigative hours, an improper arrest, increased stress for the woman as the case moved on, and confrontational encounters as we tried to "unfound" the crime. I was happy with the way the situation turned out.

A lot of these skills of talking to people, reading their body language and correctly mapping your strategy come with time and experience. They can, however, be fortified with education, training, and observation. There is one trait every investigator (and every police officer) must have and that is the ability to talk to people and an adequate comfort level in that arena. Then you can build on those skills and make a difference in case outcomes and consequently peoples' lives and the community. It will be a very rewarding time in your law enforcement career.

Recalcitrant Witnesses

Very often witnesses are **recalcitrant** or reluctant to talk to investigators. The investigator must first realize that no one is obligated to participate in an interview. However, certain techniques may be helpful in getting recalcitrant witnesses to cooperate, such as appeals to the person's logic and reason, civic pride, sense of urgency, the well-being of the community, and the like.

SPECIAL AIDS IN INTERVIEWING AND INTERROGATING

In addition to those techniques useful in the interview itself, other special techniques have been devised over

the years to help investigators obtain interviews and determine the veracity of statements. These techniques include the *cognitive interview, hypnosis, the polygraph, the psychological stress evaluator, narco-analysis* (truth serum), and the *observation and analysis of body language.*

The Cognitive Interview

The **cognitive interview** is an attempt to enhance the completeness and accuracy of eyewitness reports of crimes or other incidents based on a series of special and specific techniques. Research into what is known as cognitive interviewing suggests that the interview style used by a questioner has important implications for how much information that person obtains from subjects. The cognitive interview method stresses choosing a secluded, quiet place, free of distractions, for the interview and encouraging subjects to speak slowly. Among the drawbacks of this method are the amount of time it takes and the need for a more controlled environment than is sometimes possible.[8]

Cognitive interviewing is similar to efforts to assist victims and witnesses to relive an incident, but without the use of hypnosis and without physically returning to the crime scene. Geiselman and Fisher, who have conducted several successful experiments using the cognitive method, explain that it comprises four general and five specific techniques. The four general techniques attempt to get witnesses to:

- *Reconstruct the circumstances.* The investigator instructs the witness to reconstruct the incident in general, including the surroundings, vehicles, weather, lighting, any nearby people or objects, and the person's feelings at the time.

- *Report everything.* The investigator explains that some people hold back information because they are not sure if that information is important. The witness is asked not to omit anything, even things that he may not consider to be important.

- *Recall the events in different order.* The investigator advises the witness to view the event in any order he wishes so that it can be visualized backwards, from the middle toward the beginning or end, or chronologically. This allows the subject to begin with the information that is most clear, no matter where it is placed within the event, and to tie it to other information.

- *Change perspectives.* The witness is asked to remember the incident by viewing it through the eyes of someone else.[9]

The five specific techniques help investigators elicit specific items of information after the narrative phase of the interview:

- *Physical appearance.* Did the suspect remind you of anyone? If you were reminded of someone, try to think why. Was there anything unusual about the suspect's physical appearance or clothing?

- *Names.* Do you think that a name was spoken but you cannot remember what it was? If so, try to think of the first letter of the name by going through the alphabet. Then try to think of the number of syllables.

- *Numbers.* Was a number involved? Was it high or low? How many digits were in the number? Were there any letters in the sequence?

- *Speech characteristics.* Did the voice remind you of someone else's voice? If you were reminded of someone, try to think why. Was there anything unusual about the voice?

- *Conversation.* Think about your reactions to what was said and the reactions of others. Were there any unusual words or phrases used?

Geiselman and Fisher conducted an experiment in which eighty-nine UCLA students were shown filmed simulations of emotionally arousing violent crimes used for training by the LAPD. Three types of interviews were then used to interview the students about their perception of the filmed simulations: traditional police interviews, hypnosis, and cognitive interviewing. The results revealed that more facts were recalled in the cognitive method than under hypnosis or traditional police interviewing methods. In rank order, the most successful interviewing methods were, first, cognitive method, then hypnosis, and then traditional methods last. They also found that cognitive interviewing produced no increase in incorrect or partially constructed information. Further, it reduced susceptibility by interviewees to changing information as a result of leading questions.[10]

Similarly, the National Institute of Justice reported that in five experiments the cognitive interview was found to increase the amount of correct information elicited from eyewitnesses without increasing the proportion of incorrect information. It concluded that it appears that these techniques could be incorporated into the interview skills of law enforcement investigators with a minimum of additional training. Eyewitnesses can adapt to and understand the methods quickly, thus saving valuable time for investigators, who often have demanding caseloads. Police investigators who participated in the experiments and others who have learned of this method already have begun to incorporate the memory-jogging techniques into their interview procedures. The NIJ also reported that cognitive interviewing could avoid the legal concerns that surround the use of another interviewing technique, which we will discuss next: hypnosis.

In addition, recent incidents of DNA evidence revealing that numerous persons had been wrongfully convicted of crimes, as discussed in chapter 6, show there is a need to reexamine the traditional witness interview process.[11]

Hypnosis

Hypnosis was in use as far back as five thousand years ago. Hypnosis places an individual in a state between wakefulness and light sleep, allowing the body to be completely relaxed and capable of intense concentration. It produces "heightened suggestibility" and creates posthypnotic amnesia, in which the events that occurred during the hypnosis are forgotten on the instruction of the hypnotist. This is called the *hypnotic trance.*

The Los Angeles Police Department's staff psychologist and director of the department's behavioral science services unit, Dr. Martin Reiser, has estimated that in 60 percent of felony investigations the use of hypnosis can produce additional information.[12]

Hypnosis has two primary purposes in interviewing. First, it can serve as a key to unlocking a witness's subconscious memory. Often someone who has observed a highly emotional, shocking crime or other traumatic incident represses such information unconsciously. Second, it can allow witnesses to remember particular details that may aid in an investigation, such as letters or numbers in a license plate, color of clothing, or a facial description. While in the hypnotic state the subject is free of stress and anxiety and thus can concentrate on details.

The use of hypnosis as an information-gathering aid is rapidly gaining support throughout the American criminal justice system. Hundreds of criminal investigators from agencies throughout the nation currently use the technique in interviewing certain victims, witnesses, and to a lesser extent suspects. Certain police agencies routinely use hypnosis as an in-service training aid. Many officers have found hypnosis helpful in recalling stolen auto descriptions and suspect descriptions.[13]

Hypnosis also has its critics. The California Attorneys for Criminal Justice, an association of approximately fifteen hundred defense attorneys, argues that the effectiveness of hypnosis has been overrated. As a result of the association's petition, the California

Supreme Court in 1982 banned the testimony of witnesses who had been hypnotized.[14]

Three court cases from the state of Maryland suggest various opinions about the credibility of hypnosis as a means of refreshing memory. In *Harding v. State*, the Maryland Court of Special Appeals accepted the use of hypnosis as a means of refreshing memory, holding that it was no different than referring to notes.[15] In *State v. Mack*, however, the court ruled against the use of a witness's testimony where his memory had been hypnotically refreshed.[16] In 1983, the Maryland Court of Special Appeals, in *State v. Collins*, ruled that the use of hypnosis to restore or refresh the memory of a witness is not accepted as reliable by the relevant scientific community and thus not admissible in court.[17]

The legal admission of hypnotic retrieval of memories is mixed throughout the United States. As of 2001, approximately one-third of the states follow a "totality of the circumstances" test that permits these memories to be introduced into evidence if there is no undue suggestion. A majority of the states follow a "per se exclusion rule" that prohibits any memories retrieved during or after hypnosis from being introduced into evidence.[18] Some states have legislation regulating the use of hypnosis, others regulate hypnosis by case law.[19]

Nevada has allowed hypnotically refreshed testimony to be admissible in both civil and criminal cases since October 1997. It specifies that this evidence is admissible for a witness who has undergone hypnosis to recall events that are the subject matter of the testimony if the witness—or parent or guardian if the witness is a minor—gave informed consent to the hypnosis and the person who induced the hypnosis is a health care provider, a clinical social worker licensed by the state, or an officer, employee, or former officer or employee of a law enforcement agency trained in forensic hypnosis who is not otherwise currently involved in the investigation of the case in which the witness is involved.[20] Today, experts still debate the empirical credibility and thus the admissibility of hypnosis.[21]

The Federal Bureau of Investigation has established a complete set of guidelines for the use of hypnosis as an investigative tool. The following are key components of the FBI's guidelines:

- It should be used only in extremely serious cases.
- No one who has the potential of becoming a suspect is to be hypnotized.

- The U.S. attorney must be consulted and his or her permission obtained.

- The hypnotic interview must be recorded in its entirety, either by video or audio, with video preferred.

- Only medical professionals such as psychiatrists, psychologists, physicians, or dentists who are qualified as hypnotists can conduct the hypnosis.[22]

The Polygraph

The **polygraph**—or its more generic term, the *lie detector*—is a mechanical device designed to ascertain whether a person is telling the truth. First used by the Berkeley, California, police department in 1921, the polygraph records any changes in certain body measurements such as pulse, blood pressure, breathing rate, and galvanic skin response. The effectiveness of the polygraph is based on the belief that a person is under stress when telling a lie, so if a person lies, the machine will record that stress in the body measurements. This area has also recently been called **forensic psychophysiology** or **psychophysiological veracity**.[23]

The word *polygraph* actually means "many writings." During a polygraph test several measurements of the body's activity are recorded on a graph. The three major sections of the polygraph are the *pneumograph*, which measures respiration and depth of breathing; the *galvanograph*, which measures changes in the skin's electrical resistance; and the *cardiograph*, which measures blood pressure and pulse rate. It is interesting to note that the subject does not actually have to answer a question for the machine to measure the person's mental and emotional response to the question.

Some state that the polygraph, although not infallible, can detect physiological changes indicating deception anywhere from 75 percent to 96 percent of the time. Its accuracy depends on the subject, the equipment, and the operator's training and experience. In some cases, the polygraph may fail to detect lies because the subject may be on drugs, is a psychopathic personality, or makes deliberate muscular contractions.[24]

Several early court cases addressed the admissibility of polygraph results: *Frye v. United States* (1923) upheld a trial court's ruling that testimony from polygraph results could not be used in a trial.[25] *State v. Bohner* (1933) recognized the polygraph's value in investigations but would not allow the results to be entered into evidence.[26] *People v. Forts* (1933) ruled that polygraph evidence was inadmissible at trial because of doubts about the machine's efficiency.[27]

However, after the 1993 legal case of *Daubert v. Merrell Dow Pharmaceuticals* (see chapter 6), which overruled the *Frye* decision and gave judges the ability to admit novel scientific evidence on its own merits, the legal trend appears to be moving toward admissibility of polygraph evidence. Individual district courts will likely be left on their own to address these issues on a case-by-case basis within the framework established by higher courts.[28]

The cost of a polygraph to an agency or organization has been estimated at $12,000, including the cost of the machine, furniture, and the examiner's training and certification. The estimated time necessary to conduct the typical polygraph examination is two hours.[29]

Polygraphs can only be administered with the permission of the subject. They can fine-tune the focus of an investigation, confirm witness and victim statements, and even produce a confession from a suspect if used properly. Often, people will confess to a crime after they are notified that they failed a polygraph test, or they may confess before the test. Properly incorporating the polygraph into a law enforcement setting depends on selecting the right person to become a polygraphist, sending that officer to an accredited school, and using the polygraph as a tool to enhance an investigation rather than take the place of one.[30]

Before administering the test the polygraphist should review the case folder and all facts relative to the case in order to decide on the proper tests and the questions to be asked of the subject.

Formerly, the polygraph was used extensively in private industry for screening job applicants and preventing employee theft. The use of the polygraph in preemployment screening was severely limited by the Employee Polygraph Protection Act (EPPA), signed into law in June 1988. The EPPA is covered extensively in chapter 15.[31]

The Psychological Stress Evaluator

A more recent truth detection technique developed in the early 1970s is the psychological stress evaluator

(PSE), which detects inaudible "microtremors" in the human voice. A later version of the PSE is the computer voice stress analyzer (CVSA), which records and measures voices on a computer. Experts report that this technology relies on the skill, technique, and experience of the operator. The psychological stress evaluator has not been admitted as evidence in court and has been forbidden for use in employee testing by the EPPA.[32]

The initial cost of the psychological stress evaluator is $7,000, including the machine and examiner certification. The machine is portable and can be used in field operations. Vendors claim the machine is 98 percent accurate, but the shortage of acceptable studies based on empirical data makes this claim questionable. The suggested examination time is two hours, like the polygraph.

Although the results of the psychological stress evaluator are not admissible in a criminal trial, they can be useful to investigators in developing leads, verifying statements, and checking information. They can reduce investigative costs by focusing on specific suspects. However, once again, such tests can only be administered with the permission of the suspect.

Narcoanalysis

Narcoanalysis or the use of a truth serum is generally not considered an acceptable interviewing technique. Certain drug compounds, such as sodium pentothal or phenobarbital solution, are injected into the subject's bloodstream in order to produce a sleeplike state—a narcosis—wherein the subject is relieved of inhibitions. Other drugs used as truth serums are scopolamine, hyoscine, and sodium amytol.

Narcoanalysis is frequently used by psychiatrists and other mental health professionals to obtain information not available through conscious questioning, but it is rarely used by investigators.

Two writers have indicated that a subject's recall can be aided through the use of truth serum, but they also indicate that this method can be fallible and that any information obtained in this process should be weighed very carefully.[33]

In addition to the unreliability of information received during narcoanalysis, it can be physically dangerous to the subject. Truth serum can cause respiratory failure and impaired brain function. Obviously, if narcoanalysis is conducted, the subject must

voluntarily choose to do it, and it should always be administered by a physician. The results of this procedure are generally not admissible in a criminal case unless both the prosecution and defense witness agree to its acceptance.

Body Language

The existence of **body language** or nonverbal communication has been recognized and studied throughout history. As long ago as 900 B.C. one observer, writing on a piece of papyrus, offered the following description of a liar: "He does not answer questions, or gives evasive answers; he speaks nonsense, rubs the great toe along the ground, and shivers; he rubs the roots of his hair with his fingers."[34]

Charles G. Brougham, a member of the Special Functions Division of the Chicago Police Department, describes certain constant, spontaneous, and involuntary behaviors that people may exhibit when interviewed under stressful conditions and suggests that the following might lead an investigator to be suspicious:

- *Body movements (kinetics).* A calm, emotionless face, along with active arms, hands, legs, and feet, is a distinctive feature of deception.

- *Body positions (proxemics).* Generally Americans have an intimate zone of approximately six to eighteen inches from the body and a personal zone of about eighteen inches to four feet. When an interviewer invades this personal space, he or she creates a high level of anxiety, making it more difficult for the subject to lie.

- *Facial expressions.* When an individual is being deceptive, internal stress will cause the eye-blink rate to increase significantly from one blink every few seconds to one or two blinks per second. Internal stress may also cause the eyes to open wider than normal. Avoiding direct eye contact or looking away can provide additional clues to deception.

- *Physiological symptoms.* When most people lie, myriad physiological changes take place, including perspiration, flushing or paleness of skin, an increase in pulse rate, and the appearance of veins in the head, neck, and throat.

- *Paralanguage.* When suspects are deceptive they may be less fluent and will stutter more. Their

EXHIBIT 7.3   **Body Language and Truth**

Head
- *Tilted.* Cooperative, interested, probably truthful
- *Jutting forward, no tilt, jaw up.* Angry, aggressive, stubborn
- *Chin on chest, no tilt.* Depressed, bored, probably lying

Eyebrows
- *Both raised with mouth partly open.* Surprised, truthful
- *One raised.* Confused, skeptical, probably truthful
- *Squeezed together and lowered.* Angry, worried, confused

Eyes
- *Breaks eye contact (one to two seconds is common), suddenly tensed.* Probably lying and may not resume eye contact until new subject is discussed
- *Looks at ceiling and blinks.* Just decided to confess
- *Pupils fully dilated.* Highly emotionally aroused, probably lying

- *Closed eyes.* Trying to mentally escape, probably lying
- *Narrowed eyes.* Looking for trouble, anticipating the worst
- *Rapid blinking.* Nervous, probably lying

Hands
- *Cover both eyes.* Probably lying
- *Over mouth.* Probably lying
- *On chin.* Probably truthful
- *Touches or rubs nose while talking.* Probably lying
- *Clasped together, hold back of head.* Probably truthful

Legs
- *Men with crossed legs.* Probably lying

Feet
- *Move beneath chair.* Probably lying
- *One tucked beneath the other.* Probably truthful

SOURCE: Daniel D. Evans, "Ten Ways to Sharpen Your Interviewing Skills," *Law and Order*, Sept. 1990, pp. 90–95.

answers may include special vocalizations such as crying, laughing, belching, and space fillers—"uh-uh" and "um."[35]

Obviously, if a person exhibits or does not exhibit particular body language it is not positive proof of her truthfulness or lack of it, but the knowledge will nevertheless help the investigator to better structure the interview.

THE INTERROGATION AND THE *MIRANDA* Ruling

In English common law the lack of a confession was often viewed as a serious deficiency in the government's case, enough to cause a judge or jury to acquit an accused person. Although not required to prove guilt, the emphasis on securing a confession from a suspect remains today.[36]

Most investigators believe that the sooner a suspect is interviewed, the more spontaneous and truthful his answers will be, because he will have less time in which to fabricate deceptive answers and explanations. Experience has demonstrated that if an excessive amount of time passes between arrest and questioning, the suspect often elects not to talk with investigators.[37]

Louis DiPietro, a special agent and legal instructor at the FBI Academy, states that a confession is probably the most substantiating and damaging evidence that can be admitted against a defendant. To be admissible, due process mandates that a confession be made voluntarily. In addition, it mandates the investigator's scrupulous compliance with the U.S. Supreme Court's requirements emanating from the landmark *Miranda* case and other constitutional rights of an accused. DiPietro warns that if the government obtains a nonvoluntary confession, it will be excludable on the grounds of denial of due process of law.[38] For this reason we begin our discussion of interrogations with a review of U.S. Supreme Court rulings on the subject. We pay particular attention to cases leading to the *Miranda* ruling, the *Miranda* case and its ruling, and cases that seem to have led to the erosion of the rule. This section also discusses the *Miranda* rule itself and the nonpolice investigator and the compelled interview of public employees by their employers.

The Path to *Miranda*

The police have many crimes to investigate and often not enough resources to accomplish their mission. Also, in many cases there is not enough physical evidence or there are no eyewitnesses to assist the police in their investigation. Thus, police seek to gain a confession from a defendant, particularly in murder cases, in order to gain a conviction.

The history of the methods used by the police to obtain confessions from suspects has been sordid, including the beatings and torture by the police that came to be known as the third degree. From 1936 until 1966, the Supreme Court issued a number of rulings to preclude this misconduct and ensure compliance with due process as guaranteed by the Bill of Rights. The following landmark cases show the development of rules regarding custodial interrogation during those three decades.

| EXHIBIT 7.4 | The Path to *Miranda* |

Brown v. Mississippi, 1936

McNabb-Mallory Rule, 1957

Escobedo v. Illinois, 1964

Miranda v. Arizona, 1966

The *Miranda* Rules, 1966

The End of the Third Degree In *Brown v. Mississippi* (1936), the Supreme Court put an end to the almost "official" practice of brutality and violence used by the police to obtain confessions from suspects. As described earlier, the case involved the coerced confessions, through beatings, of three men. The Supreme Court suppressed the confessions and emphasized that use of confessions obtained through barbaric tactics deprived the defendants of their right to due process under the Fourteenth Amendment. In effect, the Court said that coerced confessions were untrustworthy, unreliable, and unconstitutional. (For more on the third degree, see chapter 1.)

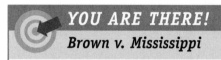

YOU ARE THERE!
Brown v. Mississippi

On March 30, 1934, Raymond Steward was murdered. On that night Deputy Sheriff Dial went to the home of Ellington, one of the defendants, and requested him to accompany him to the house of the deceased, and there a number of white men were gathered, who began to accuse the defendant of the crime. Upon his denial they seized him and hanged him by a rope to the limb of a tree, twice. When they took him down the second time they tied him to a tree and whipped him. The trial record showed that the signs of the rope on his neck were plainly visible during the trial. He was again picked up a day or two later, and again severely beaten until he confessed. The other two defendants, Ed Brown and Henry Shields, were also arrested and taken to jail. In order to obtain the confession the defendants were severely beaten with a leather strap with buckles on it and made to confess to details demanded by the police officers present.

The defendants made their confession on April 1, 1934, were indicted on April 4, went on trial on April 5, and were convicted and sentenced to death on April 6, 1934. The deputy sheriff who administered over the beatings, Deputy Sheriff Dial, testifying in court, responded to an inquiry as to how severely a defendant was whipped by stating, "Not too much for a negro; not as much as I would have done if it were left to me."

On appeal, the Supreme Court ruled that the actions against the three men were violations of their due process rights.

SOURCE: *Brown v. Mississippi*, 297 U.S. 278 (1936).

The Prompt Arraignment Rule *McNabb v. United States* (1943) and *Mallory v. United States* (1957) were cases that involved confessions obtained as a result of delays in the "prompt arraignment" of the defendants before a federal judge.[39] The Court did not address whether or not the confessions were voluntary, the previous standard for admitting them into evidence. Instead, it considered how long it took for law enforcement agents to bring the suspects before a judge

YOU ARE THERE!

McNabb v. United States and Mallory v. United States

The McNabb family consisted of five Tennessee mountain people who operated an illegal moonshine business near Chattanooga. During a raid on their business by federal agents, a police officer was killed. The five were arrested and subjected to continuous interrogation for two days. Two of the McNabbs were convicted based on their confessions, and each was sentenced to forty-five years in prison for murder. In *McNabb v. United States* the Supreme Court ruled that these confessions were in violation of the Constitution because they violated the federal rules of criminal procedure, which required that defendants be taken before a magistrate without unnecessary delay.

In *Mallory v. United States*, the defendant was a nineteen-year-old male of limited intelligence who was arrested for rape in Washington, D.C. He was arrested the day after the crime and taken to the

police station and questioned over a ten-hour period. He confessed under interrogation by the police officer administering the polygraph examination. The Supreme Court again ruled that the delay in bringing the defendant before a magistrate was a violation of the federal rules.

In both of these cases the court did not even consider the question of voluntariness. The new standard that the court adopted was called the *McNabb-Mallory* Rule and considered only the time element between the arrest and the first appearance before a judge. This rule applied only to actions of federal law enforcement officers.

SOURCES: *McNabb v. United States*, 318 U.S. 332 (1943) and *Mallory v. United States*, 354 U.S. 449 (1957).

---

and whether the confessions should be admissible because of this delay.

Entry of Lawyers into the Station House In 1964, the Supreme Court ruled in *Escobedo v. Illinois* that the refusal by the police to honor a suspect's request to consult with his lawyer during the course of an interrogation constituted a denial of his Sixth Amendment right to counsel and his Fifth Amendment right to be free from self-incrimination—rights made obligatory upon the states by the Fourteenth Amendment.[40] The decision rendered any incriminating statement elicited by the police during such an interrogation inadmissible in court. The Court ruled that once a suspect becomes the focus of a police interrogation and is taken into custody and requests the advice of a lawyer, the police must permit access to the lawyer.

Subsequent to his landmark Supreme Court case, Escobedo was arrested for burglary and selling drugs. He was sentenced to prison and paroled in 1975. In 1984 he was again sentenced to prison on sex crime charges involving a thirteen-year-old girl. While free on bond pending an appeal on that conviction he was arrested in Chicago for attempted murder. He pled guilty.[41]

The *Miranda* Ruling

The well-known case of *Miranda v. Arizona* (1966) was the culmination of many Supreme Court decisions focusing on the rights of individuals during police interrogations.[42]

In the *Miranda* case, the Supreme Court ruled that confessions are by their very nature inherently coercive and that custodial interrogation makes any statements obtained from defendants compelled and thus not voluntary. The Court felt that interrogations violate the Fifth Amendment, which guarantees that no one shall be compelled to be a witness against himself or herself in a criminal case, and that this guarantee is violated whenever a person is taken into custody and interrogated.

The Court then established the **Miranda rules,** or *Miranda* warnings, which state that prior to any interrogation of a person in custody the police must do the following:

- Advise the suspect that he has the right to remain silent.

- Advise the suspect that anything he says can and will be used in court against him.

YOU ARE THERE!

Escobedo v. Illinois

On the evening of January 19, 1960, Danny Escobedo's brother-in-law, Manual, was shot to death. The next morning the Chicago police arrested Escobedo and attempted to interrogate him. However, his attorney obtained a writ of habeas corpus, requiring the police to free him.

On January 30, Benedict DiGerlando, who was then in police custody, told the police that Escobedo had fired the fatal shots at his brother-in-law. The police then rearrested Escobedo and brought him to police headquarters. Escobedo told the police he wanted to consult his lawyer. Shortly after the arrest, Escobedo's attorney arrived at headquarters and attempted to see him, but he was denied access to

him. During their stay at headquarters the police caused an encounter between Escobedo and DiGerlando during which Escobedo made admissions to the crime. Later a statement was taken from Escobedo. He was never advised of his rights. He was convicted of the murder of Manual based on his statements.

The Supreme Court reversed Escobedo's conviction based on the fact that the police violated Escobedo's Sixth Amendment rights, rights made obligatory on the states through the Fourteenth Amendment.

SOURCE: *Escobedo v. Illinois* 378 U.S. 478 (1964).

- Advise the suspect that he has the right to consult a lawyer and to have the lawyer present during questioning.

- Advise the suspect that if he cannot afford an attorney, an attorney will be provided, free of charge, for him.

The Court further ruled that if prior to the interrogation or during the interrogation the suspect, in any way, indicates a wish to remain silent or to have an attorney, the interrogation may no longer proceed.[43]

The Erosion of *Miranda*

In the aftermath of the *Miranda* decision, there was tremendous confusion in the legal community over its exact meaning. Consequently a large number of cases were brought to the Court challenging and questioning it. Eventually the Supreme Court of the 1970s and 1980s under Chief Justice Burger began to impose a series of exceptions to the *Miranda* decision. These decisions led noted civil liberties lawyer and Harvard law professor Alan Dershowitz to write an article in 1984 entitled "A Requiem for the Exclusionary Rule," in which he said, "The Burger Court has chipped away at the exclusionary rule—carving out so many exceptions that it is falling of its own weight."[44]

Dershowitz added, after explaining two cases, "Our twenty-five year experiment with the exclusionary rule may well be coming to an end. We have learned precious little from it, because the exclusionary rule was never really given a chance. The public, spurred by politicians' rhetoric, closed its eyes and ears to facts like the following: that only a tiny fraction of defendants (less than half of 1 percent, according to a federal

The landmark Supreme Court case *Miranda v. Arizona,* 1966, required police to notify defendents of their constitutional rights before a custodial interrogation. Here, an officer reads a defendant his *Miranda* rights.

© Michael Newman/Photo Edit

YOU ARE THERE!
Miranda v. Arizona

Ernesto Miranda with his attorney in 1967.

On March 2, 1963, in Phoenix, Arizona, an eighteen-year-old woman walking to a bus stop after work was accosted by a man who shoved her into his car and tied her hands and ankles. He then took her to the edge of the city where he raped her. The rapist drove the victim to a street near her home and let her out of the car. On March 13, the Phoenix police arrested a twenty-three-year-old eighth-grade dropout named

Ernesto Miranda and charged him with the crime. Miranda, who had a police record dating back to the age of fourteen, had been given an undesirable discharge by the army for being a Peeping Tom, and had served time in federal prison for driving a stolen car across a state line.

Miranda was placed in a lineup at the station house and positively identified by the victim. He was then taken to an interrogation room where he was questioned by the police without being informed that he had a right to have an attorney present. Two hours later, police emerged from the interrogation room with a written confession signed by Miranda. At the top of the statement was a typed paragraph stating that the confession was made voluntarily, without threats or promises of immunity, and "with full knowledge of my legal rights, understanding any statement I make may be used against me."

At trial Miranda was found guilty of kidnapping and rape. Upon appeal, the Supreme Court ruled that Miranda's confession was inadmissible.

SOURCE: *Miranda v. Arizona*, 384 U.S. 436 (1966).

---

study) are freed because of the exclusionary rule; and that there has been a marked improvement both in police efficiency and in compliance with the Constitution since the exclusionary rule was established."[45]

Despite Dershowitz's thoughts, the *Miranda* rule still stands. Defendants in custody must still be advised of their constitutional rights prior to any interrogation. However, the Court does recognize certain exceptions to *Miranda*. A sample of post-*Miranda* cases that have led to its weakening follow.

Harris v. New York   In *Harris v. New York* (1971), the Court ruled that statements that are trustworthy, even though they were obtained without giving a defendant *Miranda* warnings, may be used to attack the credibility of a defendant who takes the witness stand.[46] The prosecutor accused Harris of lying on the stand and used statements obtained by the police, without *Miranda* warnings, before the trial to prove it.

Justice Burger, speaking for the Court relative to the *Miranda* rule, wrote: "The shield provided by *Miranda* cannot be perverted into a license to use perjury by way of a defense, free from the risk of confrontation with prior inconsistent utterances. We hold, therefore, that petitioner's credibility was appropriately impeached by use of his earlier conflicting statements."

Michigan v. Mosley   In *Michigan v. Mosley* (1975), the Court ruled that a second interrogation, held after the suspect had initially refused to make a statement, was not a violation of the *Miranda* decision. In the second interrogation, which was for a different crime, the suspect had been read the *Miranda* warnings.[47]

Brewer v. Williams   In *Brewer v. Williams*, decided in 1977, the Supreme Court seemed to extend the meaning of the word *interrogation* by interpreting comments made by a police detective as "subtle coer-

YOU ARE THERE!

Brewer v. Williams

On Christmas Eve, 1968, ten-year-old Pamela Powers was at a Des Moines, Iowa, YMCA with her parents to watch her brother participate in a wrestling match. Pamela told her parents that she was going to use the bathroom. She was never seen alive again. At about the time of Pamela's disappearance, a young boy saw a man, later identified as Robert Williams, walking out of the YMCA carrying a bundle wrapped in a blanket to his car. The boy told police that he thought he saw two legs under the blanket. Robert Williams was a resident of the YMCA, a religious fanatic, and an escaped mental patient. On Christmas Day Williams's car was found abandoned near the city of Davenport, Iowa, 160 miles from Des Moines. On the day after Christmas Williams walked into the Davenport police station house and surrendered. The Davenport police notified the Des Moines police, who arranged to come pick up Williams.

When Detective Leaming arrived at the Davenport police station to pick up Williams, he was advised by Williams's lawyer, Henry McKnight, that he did not want Williams to be the subject of any interrogation during the trip from Davenport to Des Moines. Leaming agreed to the lawyer's request.

In the car on the way back to Des Moines, Detective Leaming, knowing that Williams was a religious fanatic, addressed him as "Reverend" and made what has become known as the "Christian Burial Speech":

> I want to give you something to think about while we're traveling down the road. . . . Number one, I want you to observe the weather conditions. It's raining, it's sleeting, it's freezing, driving is very treacherous, visibility is poor, it's going to be dark early this evening. They are predicting several inches of snow for tonight, and I feel that you yourself are the only person that knows where this little girl's body is, that you yourself have only been there once, and if you get a snow on top of it you yourself may be unable to find it. And, since we will be going right past the area on the way into Des Moines, I feel that we could stop and locate the body, that the parents of this little girl should be entitled to a Christian burial for the little girl who was snatched away from them on Christmas Eve and murdered. And I feel we should stop and locate it on the way in rather than waiting until morning and trying to come back out after a snowstorm and possibly not being able to find it at all.

After this speech, Williams directed the police to the young girl's dead body. Williams was convicted of her murder.

On appeal to the Supreme Court, the Court voted five to four that the detective's Christian Burial Speech constituted custodial interrogation and that the evidence, the body, was illegally obtained and therefore not admissible in court.

But the state of Iowa continued to appeal the *Brewer* decision, and in 1984 the Supreme Court in *Nix v. Williams* promulgated the "inevitability of discovery rule," saying in effect that Pamela Powers's body would have been discovered inevitably and thus should be allowed to be used as evidence in a trial.

SOURCES: *Brewer v. Williams*, 430 U.S. 222 (1977) and *Nix v. Williams*, 467 U.S. 431 (1984).

cion."[48] This case affirmed *Miranda* but is presented here because of a second decision in the case of *Nix v. Williams*.[49] In this case, the state of Iowa continued to appeal the decision reached in *Brewer v. Williams*. In 1984, the Supreme Court, in *Nix v. Williams*, promulgated the "inevitability of discovery rule." Victim Pamela Powers's body would have been discovered inevitably, so it should be allowed to be used as evidence in the trial.

Rhode Island v. Innis In *Rhode Island v. Innis* (1980), the Supreme Court clarified its definition of interrogation by ruling that the "definition of interrogation can extend only to words or actions on the part of police officers that they should have known were reasonably likely to elicit an incriminating response."[50] In this case, a man told the police where he had left a shotgun he had used in a shooting after the police had made remarks about the possibility of a disabled child

YOU ARE THERE!
Rhode Island v. Innis

On the night of January 12, 1975, John Mulvaney, a Providence, Rhode Island, cab driver, disappeared after being dispatched to pick up a fare. His body was discovered four days later buried in a shallow grave in Coventry, Rhode Island. He had died from a shotgun blast to the back of his head.

Five days later, shortly after midnight, the Providence police received a phone call from a cab driver who reported that he had just been robbed by a man with a sawed-off shotgun. While at the police station the robbery victim noticed a picture of his assailant on a bulletin board and informed a detective. The detective prepared a photo array, and the complainant identified the suspect again. The police began a search of the area where the cab driver had brought the suspect. At about 4:30 A.M. an officer spotted the suspect standing in the street. Upon apprehending the suspect, the officer, Patrolman Lovel, advised him of his *Miranda* rights. A sergeant arrived and advised the suspect of his *Miranda* rights. A captain arrived and also advised the suspect of his constitutional rights. The suspect stated that he understood his rights and wanted to speak with an attorney. The captain directed three officers in a caged wagon, a four-door police car with a wire screen mesh between the front and rear seats, to bring the suspect to the police station. While en route to the police station two of the officers engaged in conversation. One, Patrolman Gleckman, testified at the trial: "At this point, I was talking back and forth with Patrolman McKenna stating that I frequent this area while on patrol and (that because a school for handicapped

children is located nearby) there's a lot of handicapped children running around in this area, and God forbid one of them might find a weapon with shells and they might hurt themselves."

Patrolman McKenna testified: "I more or less concurred with him that it was a safety factor and that we should, you know, continue to search for the weapon and try to find it."

The third officer, Patrolman Williams, didn't participate in the conversation but testified as to the conversation between the two officers: "He (Gleckman) said it would be too bad if the little—I believe he said a girl—would pick up the gun, maybe kill herself."

According to police testimony, the suspect then interrupted the conversation, stating that the officers should turn the car around so he could show them where the gun was located. When they reached the crime scene the suspect was again advised of his *Miranda* rights and the suspect said he understood his rights but that he "wanted to get the gun out of the way because of the kids in the area in the school." The suspect then led the police to the area where the shotgun was located.

The defendant Innis was convicted of the murder, but upon appeal, the gun was suppressed. However, in 1980, the United States Supreme Court heard the case and reversed the Rhode Island appeals court, ruling that the officers' statements were not interrogation and the gun was allowed to remain in evidence.

SOURCE: *Rhode Island v. Innis*, 446 U.S. 291 (1980).

finding it (there was a home for disabled children nearby).

New York v. Quarles In *New York v. Quarles* (1984), the Supreme Court created a "public safety" exception to the *Miranda* rule.[51] In this case, a police officer, after arresting and handcuffing a man wanted in connection with a crime, and after feeling an empty shoulder holster on the man's body, asked him where the gun was without giving the man *Miranda* warnings. The

gun was suppressed as evidence because the officer's question was not preceded by the warnings. The Supreme Court, however, overruled the state court and said the officer's failure to read the warnings was justified in the interest of public safety. The Court wrote:

> We conclude that the need for answers to questions in a situation posing a threat to the public safety outweighs the need for the prophylactic rule protecting

YOU ARE THERE!
New York v. Quarles

At 12:30 A.M., police officers Frank Kraft and Sal Scarring were on routine patrol in Queens, New York, when a young woman approached them and told them that she had been raped by a black male, approximately six feet tall, who was wearing a black jacket with the name "Big Ben" printed in yellow letters on the back. She then told them that the man had just entered an A&P supermarket located nearby and that he had a gun. The officers put the woman into the police car and drove to the A&P, where Officer Kraft entered the store while his partner radioed for backup. Kraft observed the suspect, Benjamin Quarles, approaching a checkout counter. On seeing the officer, Quarles turned and ran toward the rear of the store. Kraft took out his revolver and chased Quarles. When Quarles turned the corner at the end of an aisle, Kraft lost sight of him for several seconds. On regaining sight of Quarles, Kraft apprehended him and ordered him to stop and put his hands over his head.

Kraft then frisked Quarles and discovered that he was wearing an empty shoulder holster. After handcuffing him, Kraft asked him where the gun was. Quarles nodded in the direction of some empty cartons and said, "The gun is over there." Kraft then retrieved a loaded .38 caliber revolver from one of the cartons and then formally arrested Quarles and read him his *Miranda* warnings. At trial the judge suppressed Quarles's statement, "The gun is over there," and suppressed the gun because Kraft had not given Quarles his *Miranda* warnings before asking "Where's the gun?"

On appeal from the prosecutor to the United States Supreme Court, the Court reversed the New York ruling and created a public safety exception to the requirement that police give a suspect his *Miranda* warnings before interrogation.

SOURCE: *New York v. Quarles*, 104 S.Ct. 2626 (1984).

---

the Fifth Amendment's privilege against self-incrimination. We decline to place officers such as Officer Kraft in the untenable position of having to consider, often in a matter of seconds, whether it best serves society for them to ask the necessary questions without the *Miranda* warnings and render whatever probative evidence they uncover inadmissible, or for them to give the warnings in order to preserve the admissibility of evidence they might uncover but possibly damage or destroy their ability to obtain that evidence and neutralize the volatile situation confronting them.

Moran v. Burbine In *Moran v. Burbine* (1986), a murder case, the Supreme Court ruled that the police failure to inform a suspect undergoing custodial interrogation of his attorney's attempts to reach him does not constitute a violation of the *Miranda* rule.[52] The Court reasoned that events that are not known by a defendant have no bearing on his capacity to knowingly waive his rights.

Speaking for the Court, Justice O'Connor, commenting on the actions of the police in lying to the lawyer, Munson, wrote:

Focusing primarily on the impropriety of conveying false information to an attorney, he [Burbine] invites us to declare that such behavior should be condemned as violative of canons fundamental to the "traditions and conscience of our people." . . . We do not question that on facts more egregious than those presented here police deception might rise to a level of a due process violation. . . . We hold only that, on these facts, the challenged conduct falls short of the kind of misbehavior that so shocks the sensibilities of civilized society as to warrant a federal intrusion into the criminal processes of the States.

Illinois v. Perkins In *Illinois v. Perkins* (1990), the Supreme Court further clarified its *Miranda* decision.[53] In the Perkins case, police placed an informant and an undercover officer in a cellblock with Lloyd Perkins, a suspected murderer incarcerated on an unrelated charge of aggravated assault. While planning a prison break, the undercover officer asked Perkins whether he had ever "done" anyone. In response, Perkins described at length the details of a murder-for-hire he had committed.

YOU ARE THERE!
Moran v. Burbine

On March 3, 1977, Mary Jo Hickey was found unconscious in a factory parking lot in Providence, Rhode Island. Suffering from injuries to her skull apparently inflicted by a metal pipe found at the scene, she was rushed to a nearby hospital. Three weeks later she died from her wounds.

Several months after her death, the Cranston, Rhode Island, police arrested Brian Burbine and two others for burglary. Shortly before the arrest, Detective Ferranti of the Cranston police had learned from a confidential informant that the man responsible for Hickey's death lived at a certain address and was also known by the nickname Butch. On learning from the arresting officer that Burbine went by the nickname Butch and that he gave his address as the same one previously given by the informant, Ferranti decided to interrogate Burbine about the Hickey murder. Ferranti advised Burbine of his constitutional rights. Burbine refused to speak to the detective. Ferranti spoke to Burbine's two associates and obtained more incriminating information. Ferranti then called the Providence police, who sent three detectives to Cranston to interrogate Burbine.

That evening Burbine's sister called the Providence Public Defender's Office to obtain legal assistance for her brother. A lawyer from the office, Allegra Munson, called the Cranston detective division. The conversation went as follows:

> A male voice responded with the word "Detectives." Ms. Munson identified herself and asked if Brian

Burbine was being held; the person responded affirmatively. Ms. Munson explained to the person that Burbine was represented by attorney and she would act as Burbine's legal counsel in the event that the police intended to place him in a lineup or question him. The unidentified person told Ms. Munson that the police would not be questioning Burbine or putting him in a lineup and that they were through with him for the night. Ms. Munson was not informed that the Providence Police were at the Cranston police station or that Burbine was a suspect in Mary's murder.

Less than an hour after Munson's call, Burbine was brought to an interrogation room and questioned about Mary Jo Hickey's murder. He was informed of his *Miranda* rights on three separate occasions, and he signed three written forms acknowledging that he understood his right to the presence of an attorney and indicating that he did not want an attorney called or appointed for him. Burbine signed three written statements fully admitting to the murder. Based on his written statements Burbine was convicted of murder. Upon appeal the Rhode Island Court of Appeals reversed the conviction.

The United States Supreme Court reversed the court of appeals ruling and ruled that Burbine's constitutional rights were not violated.

SOURCE: *Moran v. Burbine*, 475 U.S. 412 (1986).

When Perkins was subsequently charged with the murder, he argued successfully to have the statements he made in prison suppressed because no *Miranda* warnings had been given before his conversation with the informant and undercover officer. On review, however, the Supreme Court reversed the order of suppression.

Rejecting Perkins's argument, the Supreme Court recognized that there are limitations to the rules announced in *Miranda*. The Court expressly declined to accept the notion that the *Miranda* warnings are required whenever a suspect is in custody in a techni-

cal sense and converses with someone who happens to be a government agent. Rather, the Court concluded that not every custodial interrogation creates the psychologically compelling atmosphere that *Miranda* was designed to protect against. When the compulsion is lacking, the Court found, so is the need for *Miranda* warnings.

The Court in *Perkins* found the facts at issue to be a clear example of a custodial interrogation that created no compulsion. Pointing out that compulsion is determined from the perspective of the suspect, the Court noted that Perkins had no reason to believe that either the informant or the undercover officer had any official power over him, and therefore, he had no reason to feel any compulsion to make self-incriminating statements. On the contrary, Perkins bragged about his role in the murder in an effort to impress those he believed to be his fellow inmates. *Miranda* was not designed to protect individuals from themselves.

Pennsylvania v. Muniz In *Pennsylvania v. Muniz* (1990), the Court ruled that the police use of the defendant's slurred and drunken responses to booking questions (he was arrested for driving under the influence of alcohol) as evidence in his trial was not a violation of *Miranda* rights even though he was never given his *Miranda* warnings.[54]

Arizona v. Fulminante In 1991, in *Arizona v. Fulminante* the Supreme Court further weakened *Miranda* by ruling that a coerced confession might be a harmless trial error.[55] In this case the Court overruled years of precedent to hold that if other evidence introduced at trial is strong enough, the use of a coerced confession could be considered harmless and a conviction upheld. In other words, a coerced confession, by itself, is not sufficient to have a conviction overruled if there is other compelling evidence of guilt.

Minnick v. Mississippi In *Minnick v. Mississippi* (1991), the Court clarified the mechanics of *Miranda* by ruling that once a suspect in custody requests counsel in response to *Miranda* warnings, law enforcement officers may no longer attempt to reinterrogate that suspect unless the suspect's attorney is present or the suspect initiates the contact with the law enforcement agents.[56]

McNeil v. Wisconsin In *McNeil v. Wisconsin* (1991), the Court ruled that an in-custody suspect who requests counsel at a judicial proceeding, such as an arraignment or initial appearance, is only invoking the Sixth Amendment right to counsel as to the charged offense and is not invoking the Fifth Amendment right to have an attorney present during the custodial interrogation.[57]

Withrow v. Williams In *Withrow v. Williams* (1993), the Supreme Court distinguished *Miranda* violations from Fourth Amendment violations with respect to habeas corpus proceedings.[58] The Court held that criminal defendants can continue to raise *Miranda* violations in habeas corpus proceedings, even though it

had previously restricted habeas corpus petitions that raised Fourth Amendment issues.

Davis v. United States In *Davis v. United States* (1994), the Court ruled that after law enforcement officers obtain a valid *Miranda* waiver from an in-custody suspect, they may continue questioning him when he makes an ambiguous or equivocal request for counsel during the questioning.[59] The Court stated that although it may be a good law enforcement practice to attempt to clarify an equivocal request for counsel, that practice is not constitutionally required.

In *Davis*, Naval Investigative Service (NIS) agents investigating a murder obtained both oral and written *Miranda* waivers from the defendant. After being interviewed for approximately ninety minutes, the defendant said: "Maybe I should talk to a lawyer." After asking some clarifying questions, the NIS agents continued to interrogate him. The Court ruled that the defendant's statement was not sufficiently unequivocal to constitute an assertion of his *Miranda* right to counsel.

Stansbury v. California In *Stansbury v. California* (1994), the Court reaffirmed the principle that an officer's uncommunicated suspicions about a suspect's guilt are irrelevant to the question of whether that suspect is in custody for purposes of *Miranda*. Thus, a custody for *Miranda* purposes is a completely objective determination based on facts and circumstances known to the subject. The Court reiterated its earlier holding in *Oregon v. Mathiason* (1977) that *Miranda* warnings are required only when a person is in custody, which can be defined as either a formal arrest or a restraint on freedom of movement to the degree associated with a formal arrest. The Court then stated that this determination of custody depends on objective factors and not on the subjective views of the officers or the subject.[60]

The *Dickerson* Ruling and Beyond

In *Dickerson v. United States* (2000) the Supreme Court ruled that *Miranda* was a constitutional decision that cannot be overruled by an act of Congress.[61]

Charles Thomas Dickerson was charged with conspiracy to commit bank robbery and other offenses. Before trial, he moved to suppress a statement he had made to the FBI on grounds that he had not received *Miranda* warnings before being interrogated. The district court suppressed the statement. The government appealed, saying that two years after *Miranda*, Congress enacted 18 USC 3501, providing that a confession shall be admissible in federal court if it is voluntarily given. The government felt that Congress intended to overrule *Miranda* because the new law required merely voluntariness—not the four warnings as per *Miranda*—as the determining factor in whether a statement will be admissible.

After several appellate decisions the Supreme Court held that *Miranda* was a constitutional decision—that is, a decision that interprets and polices the Constitution—that cannot be overruled by an act of Congress, such as 18 USC 3501. While conceding that Congress may modify or set aside the Court's rules of evidence and procedure that are not required by the Constitution, the Court emphasized that Congress may not overrule the Court's decisions that interpret and apply the Constitution.

The Court cited various other reasons for reaching its conclusion that *Miranda* is a constitutionally based rule. Among them, the Court noted that *Miranda* had become part of our national culture because the warnings were embedded in routine police practice. By holding *Miranda* to be a constitutional decision, the Court reaffirmed that *Miranda* governs the admissibility of statements made during custodial interrogation in both state and federal courts. In light of the *Dickerson* decision, a violation of *Miranda* is now clearly a violation of the Constitution, which can result in suppression of statements in both federal and state courts.[62]

Prior to *Dickerson*, some constitutional scholars expected that the Court might find a way to use the many cases mentioned in the "Erosion of *Miranda*" section to overrule *Miranda*. The Court expressly declined to do so in *Dickerson*. Its decision in this case did not attempt to find and defend an underlying rationale that would reconcile *Miranda* with those previous relevant cases that threatened to undermine or erode *Miranda*.[63]

After *Dickerson* came *Texas v. Cobb* (2001), in which the Supreme Court ruled that the Sixth Amendment right to counsel only applies to the case for which that right was invoked by the suspect and not other cases affecting the suspect.[64]

Raymond Cobb, seventeen, was accused of burglarizing the home of Lindsey Owings. When Owings returned from work he found his house burglarized and his wife and daughter missing. The police conducted an investigation and eventually questioned Cobb about the incident. At the time of the questioning, Cobb was incarcerated on an unrelated offense. After being advised of and waiving his *Miranda* rights, Cobb admitted to the burglary but denied any knowledge of the whereabouts of the woman and child. He was indicted on the burglary and invoked his Sixth Amendment right to counsel. After being freed on bond, Cobb confessed to his father that he had killed the woman and the child. The father reported his son's confession to the police and a warrant was obtained for the boy's arrest on charges of murder.

After the arrest, Cobb was advised of his *Miranda* rights and waived them. He then admitted to the police that he stabbed the wife to death with a knife he had brought with him and then took her body into a wooded area behind the house to bury her. He then returned to the house and found the sixteen-month-old child sleeping on its bed. He took the baby into the woods and laid it near the mother. He then obtained a shovel and dug a grave. Before Cobb had put the mother's body in the grave, the child awoke and began stumbling around, looking for her mother. When the baby fell into the grave, Cobb put the mother's body on top of her and buried them both. Cobb subsequently led police to the grave.

Cobb was convicted of capital murder and sentenced to death. He appealed his conviction on the grounds that the interrogation following his arrest on the murder charges violated his Sixth Amendment right to counsel that had attached and been invoked with respect to the burglary charge. An appellate court agreed, and Cobb's conviction was reversed.

But the Supreme Court reversed the appellate court, ruling that the interrogation did not violate Cobb's Sixth Amendment right to counsel and that the confession was admissible. The Court argued that the right to counsel is "offense-specific," and applied to the burglary charge only and not the murder charge.

The *Miranda* Ruling and the Nonpolice Investigator

Robert J. Fisher and Gion Green state that no law prohibits a private person from engaging in conversation with a willing participant. Should the conversation, however, become an interrogation, the information may not be admissible in a court of law. The standard for admissibility of confessions is that they be made voluntarily. A statement made under duress is not seen as trustworthy and is therefore inadmissible in court. This principle applies equally to police officers and to private citizens. A confession obtained from an employee by threatening the loss of her job or physical harm would be inadmissible and would also make the interrogator liable for civil and criminal prosecution.[65]

Traditionally, most courts have agreed that private persons are not required to use *Miranda* warnings because they are not public law enforcement officers. A few states, however, require citizens to use a modified form of them before questioning, and some states prohibit questioning altogether.

In 1987, however, an appellate court in the case of *State of West Virginia v. William H. Muegge* expanded the *Miranda* concept to include private citizens.[66] William Muegge was detained by a store security guard who saw him place several items of merchandise in his pockets and proceed through the checkout aisle without paying for them. The security guard approached Muegge, identified herself, and asked him to return to the store's office to discuss the problem. The guard ordered Muegge to empty his pockets, which contained several unpaid-for items valued at a total of $10.95. The officer next read Muegge his "constitutional rights" and asked him to sign a waiver of rights. Muegge refused and asked for a lawyer. The officer refused the request and indicated that she would call the state police. At some time, either before or after the arrival of the state trooper, the defendant signed the waiver and completed a questionnaire that contained various incriminating statements. At the trial, the unpaid-for items were admitted and the questionnaire was read aloud over the defendant's objection. Although the appellate court felt that the specific *Miranda* warnings were not necessary, it ruled that whenever a person is in custodial control mandated by state statutes, the safeguards protecting constitutional rights apply and one should not be compelled to be a witness against oneself in a criminal case.

The *Miranda* Ruling and Compelled Interviews of Public Employees

In an article in the *FBI Law Enforcement Bulletin,* special agent Kimberly A. Crawford, a legal instructor at the FBI Academy, discusses compelled interviews of public employees by their employers: "Public employers sometimes find themselves between the proverbial rock and hard place. Like all employers, they want to ensure the honesty and integrity of their employees. However, unlike employers in private industry, public employers are 'government actors' for purposes of the Constitution, and therefore are required to abide by constitutional dictates when dealing with their employees."[67]

Crawford discusses the landmark U.S. Supreme Court case *Garrity v. New Jersey* (1967).[68] In that case, the court held that statements of public employees given the choice by their employers of either answering questions that may be incriminating or being fired cannot be used against them in subsequent criminal proceedings. In this case, the Court also ruled that employees may be compelled to answer questions related to their employment or face dismissal if, by doing so, they are not being compelled to incriminate themselves.

In *Garrity*, a representative of the New Jersey Attorney General's office interviewed several police officers about their roles in a traffic ticket "fixing" scheme. Earlier, the representative advised them that anything they said could be used against them in state criminal proceedings; they had the right to refuse to answer if to do so would incriminate them; and the failure to answer the questions would subject them to removal from office. In effect, the officers were put in the position of either answering the questions and subjecting themselves to possible criminal prosecution, or refusing to answer and facing dismissal from the police force.

The ruling in *Garrity* held that public employers must choose between preserving employees' statements for later use in criminal court by avoiding compulsion during interviews or compelling interviews for disciplinary purposes and thereby immunizing (preventing the use of their statements in court) employees' statements.

In light of the *Garrity* decision and subsequent court rulings, Crawford offers the following suggestions to public employers when they compel interviews with their employees:

- Keep an accurate record of the information provided to employees prior to the interview. Employers should use two separate forms for this purpose. One form, to be used when criminal prosecution is contemplated, should advise employees that they have the right to remain silent and that their cooperation is voluntary. The other form, which would be used when employees are compelled to answer, should advise employees that neither their statements nor evidence gained therefrom can be used against them in a criminal proceeding.

- The form that advises employees of their right to remain silent should make it absolutely clear that the matter under investigation could result in criminal prosecution.

- If employees are subject to multiple interviews, they should be clearly advised prior to each interview whether their cooperation is being compelled.

- Employers should ensure that compelled interviews are incident-specific and that employees are informed of the specific incident under investigation.

- Employers' compelled questions should be specifically, directly, and narrowly related to the performance of employees' official duties.

- Unless conferred by state law or union contract, employees have no legal right to consult with an attorney or to have an attorney present during a noncustodial, compelled interview. The Sixth Amendment right to counsel does not attach until the initiation of an adversarial judicial process with respect to a specific crime. In other words, a compelled interview that takes place prior to the filing of criminal charges does not carry with it the right to counsel.

- Compelled statements can be used to discipline employees, but any other use should be cleared through a legal advisor or prosecutor.[69]

In *LaChance v. Erickson* (1998) the Supreme Court ruled that due process does not give an individual being investigated the right to lie and give false testimony, but rather gives the individual the right to notice and a meaningful opportunity to be heard.[70]

In *LaChance* a U.S. Department of the Treasury supervisory police officer was investigated for his role in a series of "mad laughter" telephone calls to fellow employees. During the investigation, he was interviewed and denied any involvement in the calls. Later, when the allegations proved true, the agency discharged him for falsely denying the allegations. Although he was removed for the falsification charge, he would merely have been suspended for the misconduct charge. The

---

YOU ARE THERE!

Garrity v. New Jersey

A representative of the New Jersey Attorney General's office interviewed several police officers about their roles in a traffic ticket "fixing" scheme. Before being interviewed, the officers were advised that anything they said could be used against them in state criminal proceedings; they had the right to refuse to answer if to do so would incriminate them; and failure to answer the questions would subject them to removal from office. The officers involved in the scheme were thus put in the position of either answering the questions and subjecting themselves to possible criminal prosecution, or refusing to answer the questions and facing dismissal.

Confronted with these warnings, several officers provided the requested information. This information was later used against them in a criminal prosecution that resulted in their conviction for conspiracy to violate the administration of traffic laws. On appeal, the officers argued that in light of the warnings administered prior to each interview, the information provided was "involuntary," and the use of that information in court violated their Fifth Amendment privilege against compelled self-incrimination.

On review, the U.S. Supreme Court agreed with the officers and found that the information they provided was coerced by the threat of losing their jobs. Because police officers, like other members of the public "are not relegated to a watered-down version of constitutional rights," the coercion rendered the officers' statements inadmissible under the Fifth and Fourteenth Amendments to the Constitution.

SOURCE: *Garrity v. New Jersey*, 385 U.S. 493 (1967).

appellate court agreed that the due process requirements of the Constitution permitted him to respond to the charges in a meaningful way, including the right to falsely deny allegations of misconduct.[71]

The Supreme Court rejected this argument, holding that due process does give an individual the right to notice and a meaningful opportunity to be heard but not the right to falsely deny. An employee may not provide a false statement in response to a question; instead, the employee can challenge the employer's right to ask a question by, for example, refusing to answer unless compelled to do so, in which case the law relating to the privilege against self-incrimination would apply.

THE INTERROGATION

As already mentioned, interrogations are similar to interviews except that they usually involve persons believed to have committed a crime or other wrongdoing or who have knowledge about a crime or incident that they are withholding. This section discusses the purpose, setting, and preparation necessary for an interrogation, as well as advice regarding the interrogation and special tactics that may be used in obtaining confessions.

Purpose

The purpose of the interrogation is the same as the purpose of the interview: to obtain information to further the investigation—to find the truth. The primary difference between the two is that the subject of the interrogation is suspected of involvement in a crime. In addition, the interrogation can become much more aggressive and confrontational than the interview. However, as in interviews, a suspect is not required to speak with or cooperate with the investigator.

Setting

The in-custody interrogation should be conducted in a private interview-interrogation room with few or no ornaments and distractions. The furniture should consist of a table and only enough chairs for the suspect and the interrogators. For psychological reasons the interrogators' chairs should be slightly higher than the suspect's. There should be no windows in the room and the suspect should sit with his back to the door.

Preparation

Interrogators should review all case reports, including interviews and interrogations. They should also request a criminal records check on the suspect and any associates in the crime and be familiar with the nature and quality of the evidence and lab reports.

The Interrogation Itself

In an in-custody interrogation the suspect should first be advised of his constitutional rights under the *Miranda* decision, explained earlier in this chapter. If the suspect does not waive these rights the interrogator should proceed no further. If the suspect asks for an attorney the interrogator should facilitate the attorney's attendance and make no effort to conduct the interview until the attorney has arrived and has had time to consult with the suspect. If at any time during the interrogation the suspect desires to discontinue it or wishes to have an attorney present the interrogator must discontinue all questioning.

The interrogation should proceed in a manner similar to an interview. The suspect should be allowed to tell all he knows about the crime and should not be interrupted until finished. Direct questions can then be asked to clarify facts or address inconsistencies.

The main difference in interview form is the intensity and aggressiveness of the questioning. Numerous questions may be asked, sometimes in rapid-fire order, to uncover or detect inconsistencies. Sometimes the same question is asked in many different ways in order to keep a suspect off-balance and uncover the truth. Interrogations can become confrontational, accusatory, adversarial. The investigator may use certain psychological techniques, such as changing the voice tone or reducing the physical distance between himself and the suspect. Although interrogations can become confrontational and aggressive, the investigator should never use or threaten to use violence against the suspect.

Special Agent David Vessel of the FBI writes that obtaining information that an individual does not want to provide is the sole purpose of an interrogation. He offers the following guidelines to ensure that an interrogation is successful:[72]

- *Preparing for the interrogation.* Preparation is the most important factor in conducting successful interrogations. Preparation includes considering proper setting and environment; knowing case facts; becoming familiar with the subject's background; and preparing to document the confession.

- *Distinguishing between interrogations and interviews.* There is a clear distinction between the processes of interview and interrogation. An interview should precede every interrogation. The interrogation with its special processes brings the investigation to a close, and the skills are different, such as confrontation rather than questioning.

- *Developing persuasive themes and arguments.* Themes and arguments include minimizing the crime, blaming the victim, decreasing the shamefulness of the act, increasing guilt feelings, and appealing to the subject's hope for a better outcome.

- *Establishing a plan.* Investigators should know how they are going to conduct the interrogation and follow that plan.

- *Building a good relationship.* Some ways to do this include focusing on empathizing with the subject's views of the world.

- *Allowing sufficient time.* Confessions or admissions involving a polygraph examination usually occur between the second and third hours of an interrogation. Generally, the chances of obtaining a confession increase 25 percent for every hour (up to four hours) of interrogation.

- *Acquiring adequate training.* Investigators should attend professional courses to improve their interrogation skills.

- *Knowing some interrogations will fail.* At least 10 percent of subjects will not confess regardless of the investigator's talent or hard work.

Michael R. Napier and Susan H. Adams, in an article in the *FBI Law Enforcement Bulletin*, report that certain words and phrases, such as *"accidents happen," "anyone in this situation could have . . .," "everybody makes mistakes," "I understand how you might . . ."* can give offenders a way to admit their involvement in a crime and provide investigators with a proven approach to obtaining confessions. They say that these magic words come from three commonly used defense mechanisms—rationalization, projection, and minimization. Investigators call these three defense mechanisms the *RPMs* of interrogation and use them to help suspects maintain their dignity, or save face, which often results in a confession.[73]

Special Tactics in Obtaining Confessions

Police have historically used special tactics, including lies, promises, and threats, to get suspects to confess to crimes. Louis DiPietro, in an article in the *FBI Law Enforcement Bulletin*, discusses the legality of these tactics. He states that in order to determine whether a suspect has given a confession freely and voluntarily, courts examine all the attendant circumstances on a case-by-case basis and generally rule that police interrogation tactics that suggest overreaching, intimidation, or coercion may combine to defeat the free and independent exercise of will. Thus the resulting confession is violative of due process.[74]

Even so, according to DiPietro, the use of lies, promises, and threats does not always render an otherwise voluntary confession inadmissible. But such tactics are important factors considered by courts in the totality-of-circumstances test to determine whether a confession is freely and voluntarily given. Although some deception may lawfully be used in interrogations, it may never be used to trick a suspect into waiving *Miranda* rights.

Lies Most courts view police trickery that simply inflates the strength of the evidence against a defendant as not significantly interfering with the defendant's "free and deliberate choice" to confess. The courts have ruled that the following use of lies that resulted in confessions did not render the confessions involuntary: a suspect was told that a witness had seen his vehicle near the scene of a rape;[75] a suspect was told that a witness had identified him;[76] a suspect was told that his fingerprints had been found at a crime scene.[77]

But the courts have ruled that the fabrication of tangible or documentary evidence by the police—unlike false verbal assertions—is a violation of defendants' rights. In *Florida v. Cayward* (1990), for example, the police fabricated two scientific reports that established that semen stains on a victim's underwear came from the defendant and showed the reports to the defendant, explaining their significance. The defendant confessed, but the confession was later ruled inadmissible.[78]

Promises Generally, the courts have held that a promise of leniency if a suspect confesses renders a confession involuntary when it is relied upon or prompts a defendant to confess.[79] The courts, however, have held that an officer's statements that simply suggest hope, without promising leniency, are generally considered insufficient inducement to render a confession inadmissible.[80]

The courts have also ruled that the following use of promises that resulted in confessions did not render the confessions involuntary:

- An investigator told an arrestee that he would make the arrestee's cooperation known to the U.S. Attorney's Office but gave no guarantee of a reduced sentence, although he did tell the arrestee that cooperating defendants usually "fared better time-wise."[81]
- Interrogators promised to release the suspect's girlfriend, who was being held in custody, if he confessed.[82]
- Investigators promised to release the suspect's brother if he confessed.[83]
- Investigators promised to release the defendant's son if the defendant gave a statement exculpating his son.[84]
- Investigators promised to see that the defendant received psychological help if he confessed.[85]
- Investigators promised that the defendant would receive rape counseling if he confessed.[86]
- Investigators promised that the suspect would receive treatment for drug addiction if he confessed.[87]
- Investigators promised that the suspect would receive treatment for alcoholism if he confessed.[88]

Threats Traditionally, the courts view an interrogating officer's use of threats as inherently coercive and a significant factor that weighs heavily against a finding of voluntariness. The use or threat of physical violence against a suspect obviously is sufficient to render a confession involuntary.

In a 1985 kidnapping case, a court of appeals held the defendant's confession to be involuntary because the officer's physical abuse of the co-arrestee created a coercive environment in which the defendant reasonably feared that he, too, was threatened with physical abuse.[89]

The courts have also held that police statements that threaten interference with normal family relationships are coercive and generally render a confession involuntary. The U.S. Supreme Court held a confession to be coerced when officers told an accused that if she did not cooperate her children would be deprived of state financial assistance and would be taken from her.[90] In another case, the Court ruled that threats made against a mother that she would not see her young child for a long time if she did not cooperate rendered that confession involuntary.[91]

Special Tactics Should Be Used with Care Investigators should review their state laws and appropriate appellate decisions before using threats, promises, lies, and other deceptions to induce confessions. They should also seek direction from their department's legal advisers before conducting critical interrogations.

DiPietro warns: "Criminal investigators preparing to interview a suspect should carefully assess and discuss with their legal advisers whether the use of a coercive interrogation technique involving either lies, promises, or threats will render confessions involuntary and thus unconstitutional."[92]

RECORDING THE INTERVIEW OR INTERROGATION

Interviews and interrogations should always be recorded to document the information received. Recorded interviews and interrogations can be used in court and for review in the investigation. Interviews and interrogations can be recorded as written statements or as audiotaped or videotaped records.

Written Statements and Confessions

A written statement should be taken after each interview of a victim or witness. The statement should begin with an introduction giving the place, time, date, and starting and ending times of the interview and the names of all persons conducting and present at the

EXHIBIT 7.5   Legal Definitions Relating to Interrogations

- *Admission*. A voluntary statement, contrary to a person's position on trial, that falls short of a confession.
- *Confession*. A direct acknowledgment of guilt.
- *Custodial interrogation*. The confinement of a person by law enforcement agents-officers. The person is not free to leave and is questioned about a crime.
- *Exculpatory*. Statements or evidence that tends to prove that a person was not the perpetrator of a criminal offense.
- *Incriminate*. To involve either one's self or another as responsible for criminal conduct.
- *Inculpatory*. Tending to involve one's self or another as responsible for criminal conduct.
- *Interrogation*. Questioning of a person to ascertain facts.

SOURCES: Irving J. Klein, *Constitutional Law for Criminal Justice Professionals*, 3d ed. (Miami: Coral Gables Publishing, 1992), pp. 691–699, and Irving J. Klein, *The Law of Arrest, Search, Seizure, and Liability Issues—Principles, Cases, and Comments* (Miami: Coral Gables Publishing, 1994). Reprinted by permission of publisher.

interview. The introduction is followed by the name, address, and age and date of birth of the subject. The statement contains the subject's account of the incident. The statement should be followed by a statement indicating that all information was given voluntarily, and the statement should be signed by the subject. Exhibit 7.6 on p. 195 presents a sample written statement.

Written statements may be prepared in several ways: in longhand by the subject; dictated to a secretary or investigator; tape-recorded for later word processing; prepared by the investigator based on the subject's statements and checked and signed by the subject.

All statements should be indexed on the case index sheet and included in the case folder. (The case folder and appropriate enclosures were discussed in chapter 3.) In very important cases, or cases that might wind up in court, consideration should be given to the preparation of audiotapes or videotapes. Nevertheless, written statements involving confessions too may be important in subsequent court proceedings. Caution should be used to ensure that suspects acknowledge they were advised of their constitutional rights and are making

their statement freely and voluntarily. The investigator and the suspect should initial each page of the confession, and both should sign the last page. The suspect should also initial any changes or additions or deletions he makes on the confession. This precludes the suspect's later statement, "I didn't read it and I didn't say that."

It is important to remember proper interviewing techniques before requesting a person to give a written statement, including allowing subjects to tell the complete account of the incident before asking specific questions and taking notes.

Videotaped Confessions

Perhaps the best way to illustrate that a confession was given freely and voluntarily is to videotape it.

William A. Geller, associate director of the Police Executive Research Forum, prepared a report for the National Institute of Justice on the use of video technology in criminal interrogations.[93] Geller's research revealed that, in 1990, approximately one-third of law enforcement agencies serving populations of fifty thousand or more were videotaping at least some of their interrogations. Videotaping suspects' statements and interrogations is most prevalent in felony cases—the more severe the felony, the more likely videotaping will be used. Homicide suspects' statements were taped by 89 percent of the agencies that used videotaping. Most of these agencies also made some use of video documentation of interrogations in other types of violent crime, such as rape, aggravated battery or assault, and armed robbery. Videotaping is also being used increasingly in drunk driving cases.

According to Geller, agencies that videotaped interrogations reported that they did so to refute defense attorney criticisms of police interrogation techniques and challenges to the completeness and accuracy of written confessions and audiotaped statements. Some agencies cited a desire to show clearly that suspects confessed voluntarily.

Agencies that didn't use videotaping reported that they believed that suspects are more afraid to talk freely in front of a camera, knowing that every detail could be seen and heard in court.

Only a few agencies in Geller's research reported that they used covert taping methods. Most either informed suspects that a tape was being made or simply left the camera or microphone in plain view.

YOU ARE THERE!

The Interview-Interrogation of Amy Fisher

On the afternoon of May 19, 1992, Mary Jo Buttafuoco, wife of Joey Buttafuoco, was found shot on the front porch of her home in Massapequa, Long Island. A short time later Detective Marty Alger of the Nassau County Police Department homicide squad arrested Amy Fisher and charged her with the attempted murder of Mrs. Buttafuoco. Fisher was then incarcerated in the Nassau County Jail and held on $2 million bail. The case became infamous as the "Lethal Lolita" case and was the subject of several books and movies. The following is an account by Richard Haeg, the private investigator hired by Amy Fisher's mother in the investigation.

Amy's attorney asked me to pick up the investigation for the defense, so on May 29, 1992, myself and retired New York City detective Richard Johnson, and the staff of Action Investigation, were thrust into an incredible investigation that, even though was settled, will probably never end. The first time I met Amy was the evening of May 29 in the visiting room of the Nassau County Jail. The first thing Amy told me was, "Get in touch with Joey. He'll get me out of here." I had to tell her, "Amy, Joey's the reason you're here. He gave the police your name."

Then I started my interview of her. At first, she was less than truthful with me. It was easy to tell when she was being less than truthful. She has a lazy eye and generally when she talks to you it is not very noticeable, but when she lies, the lazy eye doesn't move as fast as her other eye. She is the type of person that avoids eye contact when she is lying by looking all over the room and then the eye becomes very noticeable. That eye was like a veritable polygraph. I conducted numerous interviews with Amy, sometimes on a daily basis.

My interviews with Amy disclosed that she never actually shot Mrs. Buttafuoco, but rather, in a fit of anger, she hit her over the head with the gun and the gun accidentally discharged, injuring her. Although Amy's credibility was constantly in question, everything she told me proved to be the truth, which is not always the way things turn out in this business. Eventually, even though I think that Detective Alger and Fred Kline, the district attorney in charge of the case, realized that what Amy was saying had a ring of truth to it, Amy was allowed to plead to a lesser crime partly due to the fact that the Buttafuocos would be able to collect on an insurance policy that they would not have had access to if she was charged with the original crime.

As far as techniques in an interview, after being in this business for so long your techniques become more of an understanding of the person you are talking to rather than a style or approach you learn. I always try to listen more than talk in the beginning of any interview or interrogation. I consider an interrogation a more intense interview. I would have to say that an interrogation is sometimes thought of as being loud and a more "in your face" sort of process. This is not necessarily so. I have seen people crumble with silence or a look of knowing what they did or how they committed the crime and the interrogator never has to raise his or her voice. Of course, there are times that call for some "in your face." These techniques that everyone talks about are somewhat like a fishing expedition to see what or how the person being interviewed or interrogated will respond to you pushing his or her buttons. Having a daughter and stepdaughter living in my home who are almost the same age as Amy, I was able to understand her and just talk with her. I think that the more she knew I was there to help her, the more comfortable she was with telling the whole story.

SOURCE: John S. Dempsey, *An Introduction to Public and Private Investigations* (Minneapolis/St. Paul: West, 1996).

Geller reports that prosecutors said that videotaped interrogations and confessions helped them to assess the state's case, prepare for trial, and conduct plea negotiations. Defense attorneys, on the other hand, had mixed views. Some disliked the fact that videotaped statements are more difficult to attack than written transcripts or audiotapes, but others appreciated the details video recordings supply and the fact that they can also help clients to remember important details.

On a positive note, it is somewhat easier to secure admission of videotaped confessions into court as evidence than written confessions because with videotapes prosecutors can demonstrate the voluntary nature of the suspect's statement. As for the effect on

YOU ARE THERE!

Inconsistencies, Inconsistencies, Inconsistencies

Inconsistent statements by a subject often indicate that the subject is not telling the truth. A good investigator will attempt to discover inconsistencies when interviewing victims, witnesses, or suspects.

The following is a good example of an investigation that uncovered key inconsistencies.

The Crime

On February 17, 1994, a twenty-eight-year-old suburban homemaker called 911 and reported that as she was using a bank automatic teller machine (ATM) with her two-year-old daughter, a thief put a gun to her daughter's head, laughed, and ordered her to press the $200 button on the machine or he would kill the little girl. She said that after obtaining the money the thief fled in a silver Toyota occupied by three other men. On questioning, she stated that she had gone to the machine in order to withdraw $10 to take her daughter to breakfast and was just about to press the $10 button when the thief appeared. The woman then helped the police make a composite sketch of the suspect. The police verified that $200 had been removed from the machine at 7:52 A.M. with the woman's ATM card. The case received extensive local and national media attention.

Inconsistencies

- A check of the bank's ATM records revealed that a customer had made a withdrawal at 7:48 A.M.

- Detectives questioned the customer, who said he remained in the parking lot for several minutes after his transaction and saw no silver Toyota.

- The thief's description in the woman's composite sketch was inconsistent with her description of the thief in her 911 call.

- The woman told police that she would never use an ATM again but made another $200 withdrawal from the same ATM at 2 P.M. the same day.

- After her interview, the woman called detectives twice to report that television trucks were swarming around her house, but a check of the area and interviews with neighbors showed no signs of news crews.

- Investigators discovered it was impossible to take $10 from the ATM as the woman claimed she was doing when the thief approached; the lowest button on these machines is $20.

The Confession

Asked to come to the detectives' office the next day for additional questioning, the woman first stuck to her story. But when confronted with the inconsistencies, she admitted that she had fabricated the story. She stated that she didn't get enough attention from her husband and thought this was a good way to get it.

She was arrested for making a false report to the police.

---

convictions and sentences, police departments and prosecutors reported that videotaped interrogations helped them to negotiate more guilty pleas and longer sentences, and to secure more convictions. On the other hand, tapes sometimes worked for the defense by indicating that a confession was coerced or by leading a judge to impose a lesser sentence on a demonstrably contrite defendant.

Surreptitious Recording of Suspects' Conversations

Kimberly Crawford reports that the surreptitious recording of suspects' conversations is an effective investigative technique that, if done properly, can withstand both constitutional and statutory challenges.[94] She cites several cases in which the courts have ruled

EXHIBIT 7.6 **Sample Written Statement**

Anytown Police Department
Anytown, Texas

Case #: _____

Date and time of occurrence: _____

Location of occurrence: _____

I, _____ , am _____ years of age and reside at _____

_____

_____ . My telephone number is_____ .

At the time and place of occurrence:

_____

_____

_____

_____

_____

_____

_____

_____

_____

_____

I have read this statement consisting of ____ page(s) and I affirm to the truth and accuracy of the facts contained herein.

This statement was taken at (location) ____ on the ____ day of ____ at _____ (A.M./P.M.), 19____.

Officer taking statement: _____

Witness(es) to the statement: _____

_____

Signature of person giving the statement: _____

---

that the surreptitious recording of suspects' conversations did not violate the custodial interrogation rules decided in *Miranda*.

In *Stanley v. Wainwright* (1979), two robbery suspects were arrested and placed in the backseat of a police car. They were unaware that one of the arresting officers had turned on a tape recorder on the front seat of the car before leaving the suspects unattended for a short period of time. During that time, the suspects engaged in a conversation that later proved to be incriminating. On appeal, the defense argued that the recording violated the ruling in *Miranda* because the suspects were in custody at the time it was made, and placing of the suspects alone in the vehicle with the activated recorder was interrogation for purposes of

Miranda. The appeals court summarily dismissed this argument and found that the statements were spontaneously made and not the product of interrogation.[95]

In *Kuhlmann v. Wilson* (1986), the Supreme Court held that placing an informant in a cell with a formally charged suspect in an effort to gain incriminating statements did not amount to a violation of the defendant's constitutional rights, stating, "Since the Sixth Amendment is not violated whenever—by luck or happenstance—the State obtains incriminating statements from the accused after the right to counsel was attached, a defendant does not make out a violation of that right simply by showing that an informant, either through prior arrangement or voluntarily, reported his incriminating statements to the police. Rather, the defendant must demonstrate that the police and their informant took some action, beyond merely listening, that was designed deliberately to elicit incriminating remarks."[96]

In a 1989 case, *Ahmad A. v. Superior Court*, the California Court of Appeals confronted a Fourth Amendment challenge to the admissibility of a surreptitiously recorded conversation between the defendant and his mother.[97] The defendant, a juvenile arrested for murder, asked to speak with his mother when advised of his constitutional rights. The two were thereafter permitted to talk in an interrogation room with the door closed. During the surreptitiously recorded conversation that ensued, the defendant admitted his part in the murder. Reviewing the defendant's subsequent Fourth Amendment challenge, the California court noted that at the time the mother and her son were permitted to meet in the interrogation room, no representations or inquiries were made as to privacy or confidentiality. Finding the age-old truism "walls have ears" to be applicable, the court held that any subjective expectation that the defendant had about the privacy of his conversation was not objectively reasonable.

Crawford reports that these cases show that the mere placing of a recorder in a prison cell, interrogation room, or police vehicle does not constitute a violation of a suspect's rights. Instead, she says, in order to raise a successful Sixth Amendment challenge, the defense has to show that someone acting on behalf of the government went beyond the role of a mere passive listener (often referred to by the courts as a "listening post") and actively pursued incriminating statements from the suspect.

Crawford suggests that law enforcement officers contemplating the use of this technique comply with the following guidelines:

- To avoid a Sixth Amendment problem, this technique should not be used after formal charges have been filed or the initial appearance in court, unless the conversation does not involve a government actor, the conversation involves a government actor who has assumed the role of a "listening post," or the conversation pertains to a crime other than the one with which the suspect has been charged.

- To avoid conflicts with both Fourth Amendment and Title III of the Omnibus Crime Control and Safe Streets Act, suspects should not be given any specific assurances that their conversations are private.[98]

TRAINING FOR INTERVIEWING AND INTERROGATION

Most local, state, and federal law enforcement agencies provide extensive training to their officers in interviewing and interrogating techniques in their recruit training, in-service, and investigatory courses. Private security firms and other private firms also offer intensive courses in interview and interrogation techniques. For example, John E. Reid and Associates, Inc., a private company established in 1947, offers hundreds of training sessions in The Reid Technique of Interviewing and Interrogations, a three-day seminar program. More than 150,000 professionals in the law enforcement and security fields have attended this program. Participants come from both the private sector (retailing, finance, health care, manufacturing, and so on) and the public sector, including all levels of law enforcement and government from around the world. Sessions are held in cities around the nation; the company also offers onsite training programs.

 INVESTIGATIONS ON THE NET

John E. Reid and Associates
http://www.reid.com

For an up-to-date list of Web links, go to
http://info.wadsworth.com/dempsey

SUMMARY

Despite all the restrictions placed on law enforcement officers by the decisions of the U.S. Supreme Court, law officers are still effective in conducting interviews and interrogations and in successfully clearing serious crimes.

This chapter discussed the traits and skills necessary for an investigator to be an effective interviewer or interrogator. It described the interview, its purpose, and the types of interviews that can be conducted, the proper setting and preparation necessary for the interview, and the methods to be used in the actual interview.

It also discussed methods and techniques to be used when interviewing special populations, including children, victims of sexual abuse, and recalcitrant witnesses. It covered certain special aids that can be used in the interviewing-interrogation process, such as the cognitive interview, hypnosis, the polygraph, the psychological stress evaluator, narcoanalysis, and body language.

The chapter went on to examine the interrogation process, its purpose, and the setting and preparation necessary, as well as the methods that are used in the actual interrogation. It traced the development of current legal rules on interrogations through an analysis of U.S. Supreme Court cases from 1936 to the present. Finally, the chapter discussed methods of recording the interview or interrogation through written statements and videotaping.

LEARNING CHECK

1. Discuss the primary reason to conduct an interview or interrogation.

2. What should an investigator do before conducting an interview or interrogation?

3. Discuss the techniques that should be used in an interview, including the approach, the warm-up, the start, direct questioning, and ending the interview.

4. Name and briefly give the fact pattern of at least three cases leading to the noteworthy landmark U.S. Supreme Court case of *Miranda v. Arizona.*

5. List the warnings that must be given to a suspect in police custody prior to questioning by law enforcement personnel.

APPLICATION EXERCISE

You are a detective assigned to a major police department in a Midwest city. A leading contender for the U.S. figure skating team is assaulted by an unknown person while leaving the ice after a practice session. The man strikes her about both legs with a wooden stick. A few weeks later three men are arrested for the assault. One of the men is the husband of the skater's leading competitor; another is the competitor's bodyguard. The man charged with the assault states that he was hired by the husband and the bodyguard to put the figure skater "out of competition." The husband claims that his wife was aware of the assault and involved in its planning.

You realize that the competitor cannot be convicted of the assault merely on the uncorroborated testimony of co-conspirators. You have no evidence other than the husband's statements. Prepare a report for your supervisor indicating how you plan to interrogate the victim's competitor. Include your preparations for the interview and the strategy you will use.

WEB EXERCISE

Use the Internet to find the most recent Supreme Court cases regarding police interrogations issued after publication of this textbook. Prepare a report detailing how these recent cases have changed the constitutional rights of defendants accused of a crime and subjected to police interrogation.

KEY TERMS

anatomically correct dolls

body language

canvass

cognitive interview

forensic psychophysiology

hypnosis

informant

interrogation

interview

Miranda rules

narcoanalysis

polygraph

psychophysiological veracity

recalcitrant

SOURCES OF INFORMATION

8

CHAPTER GOALS

1. To show you the numerous people who can be used as sources of information for the investigator

2. To show you the numerous government and private records that an investigator can obtain to conduct his or her investigation

3. To alert you to certain techniques that will make it easier to obtain necessary information

4. To show you how the Internet has changed information gathering

5. To alert you to constitutional and legal limitations on sources of information

INTRODUCTION

Do you pay extra to your phone company to have an unlisted phone number and then find that you are subjected to the same annoying direct marketing calls as your friends? Did you ever fill out those coupons in a store or from a magazine to win a free trip to Hawaii? Do you know that most of the information about yourself that you consider private is out there in what is called **header information,** which is sold to and by information brokers to anyone with the money to buy it? That information you put on the coupon to win the free trip to Hawaii is header information. Information is tremendously important to the business world and also to investigators.

Obtaining information is the primary goal of the investigator. Information leads to the discovery of facts that may explain crimes and other occurrences in which the investigator is interested. Investigators obtain information from a multitude of sources. In today's society, from birth until death, people leave a plethora of facts about themselves and their activity through numerous sources, including other people and records.

Some have described the world we are living in as the Information Age. Much of the information that will be discussed in this chapter can be found in computer files and on the Internet, both of which can be accessed easily by the average person. Often investigators can obtain necessary information by making a telephone call or visiting the source of the information. Sometimes, however, they have to obtain a search warrant to acquire certain information or request the issuance of a subpoena if the case is going to be heard in court.

This chapter focuses on the numerous sources of information that are available to investigators, including both people and records. People can be classified as regular sources (victims and witnesses) and cultivated sources (informants and confidential informants). Records can originate with law enforcement sources; government sources at the federal, state, and local levels; and private sources, including business organizations, public utilities, and credit reporting agencies. This chapter also discusses the local public library as an excellent source of information and the Freedom of Information Act.

In addition, the chapter identifies numerous books and directories that are good sources of information, as well as the Internet. Finally, the chapter discusses constitutional and legal limitations on sources of information.

PEOPLE AS SOURCES OF INFORMATION

People are the primary source of information for the investigator. They may be classified as *regular sources* and *cultivated sources.*

Regular Sources

Regular sources are those people who come to the attention of the investigator because of their involvement or familiarity with a crime or incident. The type of people who are generally considered regular

People are often the best sources of information. Here, officers obtain information from a witness at a crime scene in Maryland.

© Tom Carter/Photo Edit

sources are *victims, witnesses,* and *suspects.* Victims and witnesses are discussed in this chapter; suspects are discussed more fully in chapter 7.

Victims Generally, the victims of a crime are the initial sources of information as to the when, where, who, what, how, and (sometimes) why of a crime. (Recall the discussion of NEOTWY in chapter 2.) The victim should be interviewed as soon as possible after the crime, using the techniques discussed in chapter 7. The investigator should also conduct follow-up interviews to ensure that any new information the victim recalls is obtained. Even if the victim cannot provide the identity of the perpetrator of the crime, he or she might be able to provide new leads for the investigator. However, investigators should be careful when using information from the victim to develop new leads, particularly in relation to the identity of a possible suspect. The victim may be emotionally affected by the crime and not entirely accurate in describing the suspect. Furthermore, eyewitness identification of suspects is notoriously inaccurate.

Witnesses Witnesses too should be interviewed as soon as possible after the crime and then reinterviewed at a later date. Victims and all witnesses should be separated from one another as soon as possible and interviewed separately with as much privacy as possible. If witnesses are juveniles, the investigator should make every attempt to contact their parents or guardians before questioning them.

At every major crime scene a canvass and a recanvass—the search of a neighborhood for possible witnesses—should be conducted, as described in chapter 7.

Cultivated Sources

Cultivated sources are those people who have special information on a particular crime or criminal or noncriminal activity. The primary cultivated sources are informants and **confidential informants.** The difference between informants and confidential informants is that the latter are generally paid by the investigator and should be registered with the investigator's agency. In addition, the confidential informant's identity is withheld from the public.

Informants There are numerous people who, in the course of their personal lives or occupations, are privy to certain ongoing events or conditions. Excellent sources of information on both people and events are people who do business in a particular area, including mail carriers, newspaper delivery people, building superintendents, maintenance workers, cab drivers, hotel and motel employees, public utility employees, and proprietors and employees of local businesses. They can be sought out and questioned about events they may have witnessed in the course of their daily routines or about people in their assigned areas. People who frequent a particular area, such as the homeless, street people, prostitutes, and drug dealers, are another excellent source of information. Other good sources of information about a person are bartenders and waiters at bars and restaurants that the person may frequent or the person's hairdresser or barber.

Confidential Informants As noted in chapter 7, the word *informant* connotes someone who has special knowledge of a crime, incident, or ongoing criminal enterprise. The confidential informant provides an investigator with confidential information about a past or future crime and does not wish to be known as the source. The investigator must take special precautions to protect the identity of confidential informants to prevent them from becoming targets for violence or revenge. People become confidential informants for several reasons. Some are civic-minded citizens who wish to rid a neighborhood of the scourge of drug dealing, for example. But most confidential informants are motivated by less humanitarian incentives, such as financial remuneration from law enforcement authorities, deals made with officials to avoid criminal prosecution or punishment themselves, or outright revenge or rivalry toward corrupt or illegal associates.

Investigators should be very careful in dealing with informants, realizing that their reasons for informing may be merely their own self-interest. Informants should not be allowed to commit crimes in order to assist in an investigation.

Ray K. Robbins offers the following advice on working with informants.

An informant, to be effective, must be treated properly. Proper treatment of informants should minimally

202 PART II / THE TOOLS OF INVESTIGATIONS

include fair treatment, maintaining reliability, and remaining in control of the informant.

Irrespective of the informant's character, background, or status, treat the subject fairly. Always be truthful, and fulfill all ethical promises made to the informant; distrust erodes an investigator-informant relationship. Never allow an informant to take charge of any phase of an investigation, and never tolerate an informant's breaking the law.

In dealing with criminals and other less respectable individuals, be fully familiar with your agency's policies concerning such matters, and seek agency approval before entering into an investigator-informant relationship. Always contact the district attorney in cases of doubt when making a deal with the informant. This action safeguards against allegations of misconduct or inappropriate behavior on your part.[1]

In an article on the use of informants in drug cases, special agent Gregory D. Lee, an instructor in the Office of Training, Drug Enforcement Administration, tells us: "Confidential informants may be the best assets law enforcement agencies have at their disposal. Whether acting out of a feeling of honor or a love of money, they can provide valuable information that often leads to successful prosecutions. Officers who learn to handle these informants effectively—whatever their motives—can help society win the war on drugs."[2]

Lee offers investigators seven steps to follow to increase the likelihood of managing informants successfully:

1. *Learn to identify and recognize potential informants.* Investigators develop this skill with experience.

2. *Recruit informants.* Establish a rapport and explain the department's policy on awards and rewards in order to recruit informants.

3. *Document all contacts.* Document and maintain informant files to give a true picture of performance. Update files whenever changes occur.

4. *Develop relationships.* Know the limitations of individual informants, but do not accept anything less than their maximum effort.

5. *Maintain relationships.* Keep informants active by exposing them to situations that enhance, not limit or restrict, their ability to perform at their maximum potential.

6. *Use informants to the fullest.* Continue to use informants to keep them from losing interest. Encourage other investigators to use these informants.

7. *Control informants.* Manage informants successfully by controlling them. Investigators cannot allow informants to run investigations, regardless of how insistent or argumentative they become. Investigators ultimately make the decisions during cases, and informants must realize this.[3]

Special agent James E. Hight in a 2000 *FBI Law Enforcement Bulletin* article warns investigators that improper officer-informant relationships can seriously damage the credibility of a law enforcement agency. Officers who operate informants must remain aware of potentially disastrous situations and their consequences. He advises that by maintaining a strictly professional relationship with informants, law enforcement can avoid damaging its reputation. He provides the following operational recommendations for working with informants:[4]

- *Keep promises.* Investigators who break promises will find it difficult to gain cooperation from future informers. Investigators should exercise great care when making any promises to an informant, whether they are about money, protection, relocation, or other benefits. In situations where the informant will testify, investigators should consult the prosecutor before discussing any promises or offers of assistance.

- *Tell the truth.* Once informants decide that they cannot trust an investigator, they may stop or slow the amount of significant information they give. However, not telling the truth may be appropriate if it becomes necessary to protect the integrity of a case or to safeguard the confidentiality of others involved.

- *Safeguard confidentiality.* This is extremely important for the safety of the informant, the investigator, and the operation.

- *Avoid relationship problems.* Investigators should never use the informant relationship for personal profit. They should never accept loans or gifts from the informant. They should avoid unprofessional comments and language that informants may perceive to be offensive.

- *Verify all information.* Investigators should make every effort to verify and substantiate through independent means all information that the informant provides.

RECORDS AS SOURCES OF INFORMATION

Records are documents that can be obtained and studied to obtain facts on incidents and people. The number of public and private records capable of providing information are as numerous as the individual investigator will permit them to be; they are limited only by the investigator's energy and initiative. Many records are public—that is, any member of the public may gain access to them. The primary public sources of records for the investigator are law enforcement sources; government sources, including federal, state, and local agencies (the Freedom of Information Act, discussed later in this chapter, makes the tasks of obtaining and reviewing these records easier for the investigator); and the local public library. Private sources include business organizations, public utilities, the Internet, and credit reporting agencies.

Often the investigator can obtain necessary information over the telephone or in person. When an official or unofficial request fails to yield results, the investigator might have to obtain a search warrant or request the issuance of a subpoena if the case is going to be heard in court.

The Paper Trail

When investigators begin the task of obtaining information on a subject, they are well on the way to establishing a **paper trail.** Records from the motor vehicle department, for example, yield information that will lead them to other sources. Each source, then, may lead to many more sources, which can add to the investigator's knowledge of the subject. Throughout their lives, people themselves leave a paper trail of information.

Keepers of Records

Enormous amounts of public and private records and documents exist that the investigator can access and study in order to conduct an investigation successfully. The key to finding possibly useful records is to establish contacts with record custodians, particularly those who can be called on with some degree of regularity. Osterburg and Ward describe some methods that can be used to simplify the acquisition of records:

> Because people are generally more responsive to people they know, it is important to form a good working relationship from the start. . . . Several methods of gaining cooperation are possible. One would exploit the notion many people entertain: that they can unravel a mystery or be a sleuth. A second method would stress the value of the contribution, suggesting that without it the case might not have been solved. Activating latent aspirations ensures future cooperation. Another would be to thank the custodian personally and send a letter to his or her superior praising the employee's contribution to public safety and how it reflects on the company. Still another means would be to inform the employee of the outcome of the case, particularly if the information he or she provided helped to apprehend or identify the offender. In summary, treating a potential source of information with respect could be the basis for establishing and maintaining a good working relationship between record custodian and investigator.[5]

Law Enforcement Sources

A tremendous number of sources of information exist in law enforcement agencies on the federal, state, and local levels as well as in private security and investigatory agencies. Investigators should first check their own agency for internal information before checking other sources. Many agencies cross-reference data on individuals and events and maintain a name file or subject file, making the task of searching records much easier.

In addition to searching their own agency for information, investigators may seek access to information maintained by state police, highway, and investigation agencies; sheriff's departments; local police departments; departments of public safety; and federal law enforcement agencies. Key federal law enforcement agencies that maintain potentially useful data are the Department of Justice (which has administrative control over the Federal Bureau of Investigation, the Drug Enforcement Administration, the U.S. Marshals Service, and the Immigration and

An Austin, Texas, police officer uses her laptop computer to complete a field report. The information she records may be important to an investigator researching a case.

Naturalization Service); the Treasury Department (which administers the Bureau of Alcohol, Tobacco and Firearms, Internal Revenue Service, Customs Service, and the Secret Service); the Department of the Interior (which administers the Fish and Wildlife Service and the National Park Service); the Department of Defense; the U.S. Postal Service; and the Department of Transportation (which administers the U.S. Coast Guard).

Of particular interest to investigators are the Bureau of Alcohol, Tobacco and Firearms and the National Crime Information Center (**NCIC**). The Bureau of Alcohol, Tobacco and Firearms is the primary source of information on records of firearms dealers and manufacturers as well as people who legally possess machine guns and other heavy weapons.

The NCIC, administered by the FBI, is a tremendous computerized database of criminal information. It collects and retrieves data about people wanted for crimes anywhere in the fifty states; stolen and lost property, including stolen automobiles, license plates, identifiable property, boats, and securities; fingerprint searches, mug shots, convicted sex offender registries; and other criminal justice information. The NCIC also contains criminal history files and information on the status (prison, jail, probation, or parole) of criminals. It contains millions of active records, which are completely automated by computers that process more

than 270,000 inquiries every twenty-four hours, seven days a week. It operates virtually uninterrupted day and night.

The NCIC is dedicated to serving and supporting criminal justice agencies—local, state, and federal—in their mission to uphold the law and protect the public. It also serves criminal justice agencies in the District of Columbia, the Commonwealth of Puerto Rico, the U.S. Virgin Islands, and Canada. Although the FBI administers NCIC, approximately 70 percent of its use is by local, state, and other federal agencies. In 2000, the NCIC was renamed NCIC 2000. The new system provides a major upgrade to the services already mentioned, and extends these services down to the patrol car and the mobile officer.[6]

In addition to the NCIC, the FBI maintains the National Instant Criminal Background Check System (NICS), which provides access to millions of criminal history records from all fifty states and the District of Columbia for matching subject information for background checks on individuals attempting to purchase a firearm.[7]

Besides law enforcement agencies, other criminal justice agencies—including courts, jails, prisons, and probation and parole offices—have enormous amounts of information that may aid the investigator.

The National Institute of Justice (NIJ), the research arm of the Department of Justice, through its National Criminal Justice Reference Service (**NCJRS**), offers a comprehensive source of information to criminal justice practitioners and academics. The NCJRS is one of the most extensive sources of information on criminal justice in the world. Created by the National Institute of Justice in 1972, it contains specialized information centers to provide publications and other information services to the constituencies of each of the five U.S. Department of Justice, Office of Justice Programs (OJP) bureaus, and to the Office of National Drug Control Policy. Each OJP agency has established specialized information centers, and each has its own 800 number and staff to answer questions about the agency's mission and initiatives.

On the NCJRS Web site, you can:

- Search the abstracts database, with summaries of more than 160,000 criminal justice publications, including federal, state, and local government reports, books, research reports, journal articles, and unpublished research.

- Search the collection of fifteen hundred full-text publications.
- Obtain information on criminal justice grants and funding.
- Obtain the calendar of events for significant criminal justice meetings.
- Order all print publications of the Department of Justice.
- Subscribe to the *Justice Information* electronic newsletter.
- Join the NCJRS mailing list.

The NCJRS maintains a monthly catalogue that provides timely and important information for students and practitioners in the criminal justice system. The catalogue also gives abstracts of the most recent research. You can subscribe to the catalogue and get on the NCJRS mailing list by writing to NCJRS, P.O. Box 6000, Rockville, Maryland 20849–6000 or through the Web site.

 INVESTIGATIONS ON THE NET

National Crime Information Center (NCIC)
http://www.fbi.gov/hq/cjisd/ncic.htm

National Criminal Justice Reference Service (NCJRS)
http://www.ncjrs.org

For an up-to-date list of Web links, go to
http://info.wadsworth.com/dempsey

Exhibit 8.1 lists specific law enforcement sources of information.

Several professional organizations are involved in the analysis of law enforcement information. One is the International Association of Law Enforcement Intelligence Analysts (IALEIA), which is a professional association dedicated to enhancing the general understanding of the role of intelligence analysis as well as developing international qualification and competence standards and curricula; furnishing advisory and

 YOU ARE THERE!

U.S. Department of Justice Program Bureaus

- *National Institute of Justice (NIJ):* The research, evaluation, and development bureau of the U.S. Department of Justice, whose mission is to develop knowledge that can help prevent and reduce crime and improve the criminal justice system

- *Office of Juvenile Justice and Delinquency:* Through a cycle of research, demonstration, replication, and training initiatives, provides leadership, coordination, and resources to prevent and respond to juvenile delinquency and child victimization

- *Office for Victims of Crime (OVC):* Committed to enhancing the nation's capacity to assist crime victims and to providing leadership in changing attitudes, policies, and practices to promote justice and healing for all victims of crime

- *Bureau of Justice Statistics (BJS):* The statistical arm of the U.S. Department of Justice, responsible for collecting, analyzing, and reporting data related to criminal victimization and the administration of justice

- *Bureau of Justice Assistance (BJA):* Provides funding, training, technical assistance, and information to states and communities in support of innovative programs to improve and strengthen the nation's criminal justice system

related services on intelligence analysis matters; conducting analytic-related research studies; and providing the ability to disseminate information about analytical techniques and methods. Another professional organization of interest to intelligence analysts is the International Association of Crime Analysts (IACA), which is dedicated to enhancing effectiveness and consistency in the fields of crime and intelligence analysis.

Government Sources

Enormous numbers of records exist at government offices throughout the United States in the form of

YOU ARE THERE!
Regional Information Sharing Systems

The Regional Information Sharing Systems (RISS) program consists of six multistate projects that facilitate regional criminal information exchange and support services such as intelligence analysis, buy money, equipment loans, training, communications, and technical assistance to federal, state, and local law enforcement agencies throughout all fifty states. The purpose of the RISS program is to enhance the ability of criminal justice agencies to identify, target, investigate, and prosecute multijurisdictional drug trafficking, organized crime, and white-collar crime.

The six RISS projects and the states that participate in them are these:

- *New England State Police Information Network (NESPIN).* Maine, New Hampshire, Vermont, Massachusetts, Connecticut, and Rhode Island.

- *Middle Atlantic-Great Lakes Organized Crime Law Enforcement Network (MAGLOCLEN).* Indiana, Michigan, Ohio, Pennsylvania, New York, New Jersey, Delaware, Maryland, and several Canadian departments.

- *Regional Organized Crime Information Center (ROCIC).* Texas, Oklahoma, Louisiana, Arkansas, Mississippi, Alabama, Tennessee, Kentucky, West Virginia, Virginia, North Carolina, South Carolina, Georgia, and Florida.

- *Mid-States Organized Crime Information Center (MOCIC).* North Dakota, Nebraska, Kansas, Minnesota, Iowa, Missouri, Wisconsin, and Illinois.

- *Rocky Mountain Information Network (RMIN).* Arizona, New Mexico, Colorado, Utah, Nevada, Idaho, Wyoming, and Montana.

- *Western States Information Network (WSIN).* California, Oregon, Washington, Alaska, and Hawaii.

SOURCE: Richard B. Abell, "Effective Systems for Regional Intelligence Sharing," *Police Chief*, Nov. 1988, p. 58.

YOU ARE THERE!
The EPIC Aids in the Drug War

The EPIC (El Paso [Texas] Intelligence Center), managed by the Drug Enforcement Administration (DEA), monitors narcotic activities worldwide and provides information to DEA agents and other law enforcement agencies. It records information about ongoing investigations being conducted by a number of agencies; gathers intelligence about narcotics and drugs being transported by vehicles, aircraft, and vessels both within the United States and worldwide; and maintains files on many drug traffickers. Access to the EPIC is through the National Law Enforcement Telecommunication System.

Other agencies that participate in EPIC are the Bureau of Alcohol, Tobacco and Firearms; the Border Patrol; the Coast Guard; the Customs Service; the Internal Revenue Service; and the Secret Service.

databases. These records relate to the public and private lives of U.S. citizens and exist at the federal, state, and local levels of government.

Federal Government The federal government, with its various departments, agencies, and commissions, maintains numerous general and detailed records. The *U.S. Government Manual* and the *Congressional Directory* are two excellent sources to help you find information in the federal bureaucracy. Most federal departments and agencies also publish their own directories, which include important phone numbers to call for information. Almost all telephone books publish the names, telephone numbers, and addresses of federal agencies with local offices. Exhibit 8.2 on p. 208 lists federal departments, agencies, and commissions that are information sources. Exhibit 8.3 on p. 209 shows some interesting facts about social security numbers.

The federal Freedom of Information Act (FOIA), which will be discussed later in this chapter, is an

YOU ARE THERE!

Interpol: Information Worldwide

Interpol (International Criminal Police Organization) is used to access information on crimes, criminals, and missing persons all around the world. U.S. membership in Interpol is through the U.S. National Center Bureau, which is administered by the Department of Justice and staffed by representatives from all federal law enforcement agencies. The bureau is responsible for processing information on international investigations between all U.S. law enforcement agencies, Interpol headquarters in France, and other member nations.

The mission of Interpol is to track and provide information that may help other law enforcement agencies apprehend criminal fugitives, thwart criminal schemes, exchange experience and technology, and analyze major trends of international criminal activity. It attempts to achieve its mission by serving as a clearinghouse and depository of intelligence information on wanted criminals.

Interpol's main function is informational; it is neither an investigative nor an enforcement agency. Police officials of any member country may initiate a request for assistance on a case that extends beyond their country's jurisdiction.

EXHIBIT 8.1 **Information Available from Law Enforcement Sources**

Arrest reports

Complaint and follow-up reports

Lost and stolen property lists and descriptions

Field interrogation reports

Fingerprint files

Identification photos

Warrant files

Traffic accidents and citations

Wanted notices

Have arrested notices

Gun permit applications and registrations

Pawnshop records

Towed and repossessed vehicles

Aided and injured reports

Special unit files (bunco, sex crimes, juveniles)

Jail files (including lists of visitors)

Modus operandi (MO) files

Criminal history files

Nickname files

---

color of eyes, a handwriting exemplar, and sometimes a social security number and photograph.

Records generally available from the motor vehicle department, for a fee, include driver's license, driving record, accident reports, and vehicle history (known as a body file). Many states provide this information to any requestor as long as he or she prepares a form or mails a letter and pays a specified fee to the

 INVESTIGATIONS ON THE NET

International Association of Law Enforcement Intelligence Analysts
http://www.ialeia.org

International Association of Crime Analysts
http://www.iaca.net

For an up-to-date list of Web links, go to
http://info.wadsworth.com/dempsey

----

excellent tool to use in obtaining information from all federal agencies.

State Government State governments are responsible for granting licenses and regulating businesses. In order to receive these licenses, applicants must fill out forms, which are then kept on file with the appropriate state agencies.

The following paragraphs describe some important state government offices that are excellent sources of information.

MOTOR VEHICLE DEPARTMENTS Driver's licenses, auto registrations, and other business transactions involving automobiles include much personal information, such as name, address, date of birth, gender, height, weight,

EXHIBIT 8.2 **Federal Sources of Information**

Department of Agriculture
Department of Commerce
    Bureau of the Census
    Commercial Intelligence Division
    Patent Office
Department of Defense
    Air Force
    Army
    Navy
Department of Education
Department of Health and Human Services
    Centers for Disease Control
    Food and Drug Administration
    The National Library of Medicine
    Social Security Administration
Department of Energy
    Office of Security Affairs
Department of Housing and Urban Development
Department of Interior
Department of Justice
    National Institute of Justice
        National Criminal Justice Reference Service
Department of Labor
Department of State
Treasury Department
    Bureau of Alcohol, Tobacco and Firearms
    Comptroller of the Currency
    Customs Service
    Internal Revenue Service
    Secret Service
Central Intelligence Agency
Civil Aeronautics Board
Coast Guard
Commodity Futures Trading Commission
Customer Product Safety Commission
Environmental Protection Agency
Equal Employment Opportunity Commission
Farm Credit Administration
Federal Communications Commission
Federal Deposit Insurance Corporation
Federal Election Commission
Federal Maritime Commission
General Services Administration
Postal Service
Securities and Exchange Commission

motor vehicle department. Many motor vehicle departments maintain a standardized form with all possible searches and fees for each search listed. Such forms ask the requestor to check the searches he or she desires and submit the appropriate fee. Private investigators often maintain a computerized account with many state motor vehicle departments and pay a monthly fee for each computerized transaction they request.

In 1994, Congress passed the Drivers Privacy Protection Act. The impetus for this law was the noteworthy 1989 murder of the actress Rebecca Schaeffer, who was killed at her home in California by a stalker. The stalker traced Schaeffer's address through the motor vehicles division. This law placed some restrictions on the states in making motor vehicle records on licensed drivers and car owners available to the public. Until then, states earned millions of dollars a year selling drivers' personal information to a variety of groups, including direct marketers, charities, political campaigns, civic groups, or businesses. States challenged the federal law in courts, but the US. Supreme Court upheld it in a unanimous 2000 decision. Some groups, including insurance companies are exempt.[8]

OTHER STATE DEPARTMENTS Some of the other good departmental sources are these:

- *Department of State or Department of Labor* is a good source of information on persons applying for licenses for certain occupations, professions, trades, or crafts. Exhibit 8.4 lists jobs that many states license.

- *Social Services Department* is useful in supplying information on applicants for and recipients of public assistance.

- *Hunting and Fishing Licenses* can supply information on persons requesting or holding fishing and hunting licenses.

LOCAL GOVERNMENT The records of local governments at the municipal, county, and town levels provide invaluable information for investigators. Such records can be searched at the local town hall or city hall. Some of these records provide information not only on the subject of the request but also on members of the subject's family, as well as other information that

EXHIBIT 8.3   **Social Security Number Index**

Social security numbers (SSN) consist of nine digits divided into three parts and are separated by hyphens, as follows: 000-00-0000. The first three digits, except in the 700 series, make up the area number, which identifies the state or area of issuance. (The 700 series indicates issuance to employees in the railroad industry through June 1963. At that time, new number issuance in this area was discontinued.) The next two digits in the SSN break the number within the area of issuance into convenient groups. The last four digits are a straight numerical series from 0001 to 9999 within each group.

Initial Numbers	State of Issuance
001–003	New Hampshire
004–007	Maine
008–009	Vermont
010–034	Massachusettes
035–039	Rhode Island
040–049	Connecticut
050–134	New York
135–158	New Jersey
159–211	Pennsylvania
212–220	Marlyand
221–222	Delaware
223–231	Virginia
232–236	West Virginia
237–246	North Carolina
247–251	South Carolina
252–260	Georgia
261–267	Florida
268–302	Ohio
303–317	Indiana
318–361	Illinois
362–386	Michigan
387–399	Wisconsin
400–407	Kentucky
408–415	Tennessee
416–424	Alabama
425–428	Mississippi
429–432	Arkansas
433–439	Louisiana
440–448	Oklahoma
449–467	Texas
468–477	Minnesota
478–485	Iowa
486–500	Missouri
501–502	North Dakota
503–504	South Dakota
505–508	Nebraska
509–515	Kansas
516–517	Montana
518–519	Idaho
520	Wyoming
521–524	Colorado
525	New Mexico
526–527	Arizona
528–529	Utah
530	Nevada
531–539	Washington
540–544	Oregon
545–573	California
574	Alaska
575–576	Hawaii
577–579	District of Columbia
580	Virgin Islands
581–58	Puerto Rico
586	Guam
700–729	Railroad Board

(586 Groups 20 to 28—American Samoa)
(586 Groups 60 to 78—Phillipine Islands)

Caution: Although the area number shows the state in which the social security number was issued, it does not necessarily always indicate where the individual lived, either when applying for the number or at any later time. A person may obtain an SSN from any social security office. Thus, a resident of one state may get a number from a nearby state or some state he or she is passing through. Once a person is assigned an SSN, that number is used wherever the person lives or works.

| EXHIBIT 8.4 | Jobs That Many States License |

Aircraft mechanics	Pest controllers
Aircraft pilots	Pet groomers
Alarm installers and contractors	Physicians
Auctioneers	Pharmacists
Auto inspectors	Police officers
Auto wreckers	Private investigators
Bankers	Private security guards
Brokers	Real estate agents and brokers
Barbers, hairdressers	Scrap dealers, junkyard dealers
Bill collectors	
Builders, carpenters	Security dealers, stock-brokers
Building contractors	Surveyors
Building wreckers	Talent agents
Certified public accountants	Teachers
Dentists	Therapists
Embalmers, undertakers	Travel agents
Notaries public	Veterinarians
Pawnbrokers, secondhand dealers	X-ray technicians

| EXHIBIT 8.5 | Information Available at the Local Level |

Birth certificates	Mortgages
Building permits	Occupational licenses
Death records	Pending litigation
Deeds	Pet licenses
Divorce records	Property appraisals
Judgments	School records
Library records	Small claims court records
Liens	Tax records
Marriage records	Voters' registration

may be of use. Exhibit 8.5 details specific information available from local sources.

The Freedom of Information Act (FOIA)

To counteract fears that false information was being filed against individuals or that U.S. citizens had no access to tax-supported record systems, Congress passed the **Freedom of Information Act (FOIA)** in 1966.[9] This act recognized the "public's right to know" by setting up a formal request procedure for public access to government records. Before the FOIA, a person had to prove a direct interest in the information requested. Under the law, the burden of proving a legitimate reason for denial rests with the government.

The Freedom of Information Act was amended in 1974 by the Privacy Act. Under these acts, a person has the right to review and amend incorrect information about himself or herself and to subject the report to judicial review if the agency refuses to amend the data. The **Privacy Act of 1974** also prescribes information-collection procedures designed to improve the accuracy of the data collected.

These two acts and their amendments prohibit the review and release of information that falls into the following categories:

- Matters related to national security
- Information relating to internal personnel rules and practices of a federal agency
- Information specifically exempted by dozens of other federal laws already on the books—the "catch-all exemption"
- Privileged trade-secret information and confidential commercial information
- Internal agency *Miranda* and policy discussions
- Personal privacy
- Law enforcement investigations
- Federally regulated banks
- Oil and gas wells[10]

Except for the catch-all exemption, these exemptions are not mandatory, meaning that the government is permitted, but not required, to withhold the information. Even if records fall within these categories, they still can be released at the government's discretion. This is particularly true if one can show that disclosure would be "in the public interest."

Furthermore, even though portions of a requested document may be covered by an exemption and therefore exempt from release, the FOIA requires the government agency to release the remainder of the document or file after the exempt material has been edited out. The law enforcement exemption does not apply to all law enforcement records but is primarily designed to protect the confidentiality of documents whose untimely disclosure would jeopardize criminal or civil investigations or cause harm to persons who help law enforcement officials.

The FOIA gives citizens access to all records of all federal agencies, unless those records fall within one of the categories listed here. A citizen may attempt to make an informal telephone request to an agency to obtain documents. However, agencies frequently require that requests be made in writing. Once a citizen has filed an FOIA request, the burden is on the government to release the documents promptly or show that they are covered by one of the act's exemptions.

At most agencies, a designated FOI officer is responsible for responding to FOIA requests. According to the statute, the agency must respond to a citizen's written FOIA request within ten working days, although the agency may ask for an extension if it has a backlog of requests to process. The agency must have a procedure for handling the backlog that ensures that responses will be made in a reasonable and timely fashion. An agency may also charge the citizen the reasonable costs of locating and copying documents.

If the agency refuses to disclose all or part of the information, or does not reply within ten working days to a written request, a citizen may appeal to the head of the agency or file a lawsuit in a federal court.

An excellent guide to the provisions of the FOIA and how to use this act to obtain information is *How to Use the Federal FOI Act*, a thirty-two-page guide prepared by the FOI Service Center, which is a project of The Reporters Committee for Freedom of the Press, located in Washington, D.C.[11] This guide clearly explains the law and its exemptions and also provides sample FOI request letters, appeal letters, major U.S. Supreme Court FOI cases, and a directory of agencies, with their addresses, that may contain FOI information. It is also helpful to research the Freedom of Information Act and its various reference guides and regulations on the Internet.[12]

 INVESTIGATIONS ON THE NET

Department of Justice, Freedom of Information Officer
http://www.usdoj.gov/04foia/04_1.html

Other federal agencies, Freedom of Information Officer
http://www.usdog.gov/04foia/other_age.htm

For an up-to-date list of Web links, go to http://info.wadsworth.com/dempsey

----

Written requests for information from federal records should be addressed to the Freedom of Information officer of the particular federal or local agency. See Exhibit 8.6 for a sample FOIA request letter.

The Local Public Library

Your local public library is a significant source for obtaining information. In addition to providing access to the books and records that each particular library maintains, many libraries can obtain a requested book through an interlibrary loan program.

Besides books (and hundreds of magazines, including back issues), libraries offer access to all kinds of encyclopedias, dictionaries, directories, and other information sources (see the following section, "Books and Directories as Sources of Information"). Books and other records are usually indexed in the library's card catalogue, many of which are computerized or maintained on microfiche. Public libraries catalogue their books using the Dewey Decimal System, whereas colleges and universities generally use the Library of Congress numbering system.

Libraries also have maps and atlases that may aid the investigator, in addition to telephone books, national and local newspapers, magazines, and journals, all of which can be viewed on computer, microfilm or microfiche. Many libraries also maintain sophisticated computerized information sources for newspapers, magazines, journals, and other references.

Certain libraries selected by the U.S. Superintendent of Documents participate in the U.S. Federal

EXHIBIT 8.6   **Sample FOIA Letter**

Your address
Daytime phone number

Date

Freedom of Information Office
Agency
Address

FOIA Request

Dear FOI Officer:

Pursuant to the federal Freedom of Informtion Act, 5 U.S.C. 552, I request access to and copies of [here, clearly describe what you want. Include identifying material, such as names, places, and the period of time about which you are inquiring. If you think they will help to explain what you are looking for, attach news clips, reports, and other documents describing the subject of your research].

I agree to pay reasonable duplication fees for the processing of this request in an amount not to exceed $____. However, please notify me prior to your in- curring expenses in excess of that amount.

If my request is denied in whole or part, I ask that you justify all deletions by reference to specific ex- emptions of the act. I will also expect you to release all segregable portions of otherwise exempt material. I, of course, reserve the right to appeal your decision to withhold any information.

I look forward to your reply within 10 business days, as the statute requires.

Thank you for your assistance.

Very truly yours,

Your name and signature

Depository Library Program. These libraries receive all federal government publications free of charge and make them available to library patrons.

Generally, U.S. federal depository libraries, as well as some other libraries, maintain a copy of the *Con- gressional Directory,* which contains the names, addresses, and telephone numbers of members of Congress and the names, addresses, and telephone numbers of every Freedom of Information officer in every agency of the federal government.

Your local librarians are also an important source of information. If they cannot answer a particular ques- tion, they will doubtlessly know where to send you to get it.

Private Sources

Numerous private sources of information are available to the investigator. Chief among these are business organizations, public utilities, and credit reporting agencies.

Business Organizations Resourceful investigators can obtain information from numerous businesses. A sample of some of these businesses and the kind of information that might be contained in their records follows:

- *Auto rental and leasing companies.* Identity of individuals leasing automobiles, their driver's license information, the make and model of the car used, and the mileage driven
- *School and college records.* Biographical data, handwriting samples and student signatures, educational achievements, and school directo- ries and yearbooks
- *Express and transportation companies.* Records of shipment of goods and quantities shipped, their value, destination, and consignee
- *Hospitals.* Information on patient illnesses or injuries, dates of admission and release
- *Taxi companies.* Records of trips made by drivers for each customer, listing time, date, location from, and destination
- *Travel agencies and airlines.* Records of names and addresses of passengers, dates of ticket purchases, travel dates, points of disembarking, hotel accommodations, and travel itineraries
- *Laundries and dry-cleaning businesses.* Records of names, addresses, and dates of service
- *Moving companies.* Records of people moving or storing furniture, destinations, dates, and addresses
- *Newspapers.* Files of back issues and lists of subscribers
- *Real estate companies.* Records of residents and former tenants of rental property, as well as records of buyers and sellers of property

- *Better Business Bureaus.* Identities of local businesses, reputations of businesses and firms, and information about rackets and confidence games
- *Bank and loan companies.* Records on bank accounts and deposits, loan information, and credit records
- *Hotel associations.* Records on persons presenting bad checks, gamblers, and employees of hotels and motels
- *Apartment houses and complexes and condominium and cooperative complexes.* Records of current and former tenants and possible forwarding addresses

Public Utilities Public utility companies, which include gas, electric, water and sewer, and telephone companies, are valuable sources of information on customers who may be the subject of an investigation. Many of them maintain their records according to the street addresses of their subscribers and thus are able to provide investigators with information on current subscribers as well as people who had used their services previously at the same address.

Telephone directories, both regular phone directories and **criss-cross** or **reverse directories,** are excellent sources of information. Investigative offices usually have numerous telephone directories from different areas in a region and for various years. The criss-cross or reverse directory is extremely helpful because it lists phone numbers by street address, enabling an investigator to determine who may reside at a certain address and who that person's neighbors are.

Unpublished phone listings are not available in regular and reverse or criss-cross directories, but the security department of most telephone companies will assist law enforcement officers in acquiring these numbers.

If investigators need a phone book from a distant area, they can usually find one at a local library or through a local telephone company. Libraries and phone companies may also have copies of phone directories from previous years.

Telephone directories offer much more than just phone listings and addresses of residences and businesses in an area. Many contain information on all federal, state, and local government offices in the area (generally these are called the *blue pages*), information about annoying or harassing phone calls, area codes, zip codes, time zones, local community and business associations, and emergency care guides. Some telephone directories include pages on seating arrangements at local ballparks and theaters.

The Internet also provides quick and easy access to phone numbers around the nation from regular and reverse or criss-cross directories.

Credit Reporting Agencies Credit reporting agencies serve as clearinghouses for businesses to check the creditworthiness of applicants. Consumer credit includes automobile financing, credit card purchases,

YOU ARE THERE!

The Criss-Cross or Reverse Directory

Criss-cross telephone directories are very similar to the regular telephone directory except that instead of looking up a person's name you can access the directory by telephone number or by address. The directory is divided into two sections:

- *Telephone number listings.* Start the search with the telephone number in the numerical listing. On the line next to the telephone number will be the name and address of the person with that telephone number.
- *Address listings.* Start the search with the subject's street address in the alpha or numerical listing. On the line next to the street address will be the name of the telephone subscriber and the telephone number. Information on neighbors will, of course, be in sequence.

These directories are very useful for businesses such as advertising, marketing, and real estate because a researcher can easily obtain the names, addresses, and telephone numbers of most people on a particular street or in a particular geographical area. People who request unpublished numbers from the phone company are not listed in a criss-cross telephone directory.

These directories are available for sale or rental by local phone companies. Often a local public library will have a copy of the local criss-cross directory on hand for use by patrons.

charge accounts, personal loans, and service credit. Because ours is a consumer credit–oriented society, almost every person with access to a credit card leaves a paper trail, which can help investigators trace a person's movements or whereabouts. In a dramatic example, investigators were able to link serial murderer Ted Bundy to several murders across the country because he used a credit card to purchase gasoline for his car.

See chapter 15 for a discussion of the myriad information available from credit reporting agencies and also the Fair Credit Reporting Act.

BOOKS AND DIRECTORIES AS SOURCES OF INFORMATION

As already mentioned, numerous books and directories are available at or through local public libraries that can assist investigators in obtaining information or sources of information. These directories often give the mailing address and phone number of persons or organizations in whom investigators are interested. Some even give home addresses and phone numbers. The following are among the most frequently used:

- *Who's Who in America.* This series of publications in numerous areas of notoriety and expertise (for example, theater, education, business, sports) offers bibliographical information on people involved in those fields. The most basic Who's Who is published by Marquis Who's Who of New Providence, New Jersey. It consists of three volumes and is revised and reissued every two years. It is indexed by profession and area of the country.

- *Where's What: Sources of Information for Federal Investigators.* This book emphasizes the existence rather than the availability of recorded information. It explains what documents are available for inspection and the information that may be disclosed.

- *Confidential Information Sources: Public and Private.* This book was written by an information scientist with experience in security. It discusses credit-reporting agencies, medical records, and

student records. It has an outstanding appendix that deals with the probability of finding a particular item of information in records.

- *Directories in Print.* This book, prepared annually by Gale Research of Detroit, Michigan, is designed to supply business and industry with lists of the many directories printed by business and reference book publishers, trade magazines, chambers of commerce, and federal, state, and city governmental agencies. This book, formerly known as the *Directories of Directories,* lists more than fourteen thousand directories worldwide. It includes descriptive listings in general business, specific industries, banking, finance, insurance, real estate, and other fields. The directories themselves include names, addresses, and phone numbers.

- *The Encyclopedia of Associations.* This is a basic guide to information on specific associations, including trade, business and commercial, religious, educational, cultural, and hobby organizations. Because many Americans are "joiners," this book can be an invaluable aid to investigators in tracking down individuals. This encyclopedia, which is updated periodically and thoroughly indexed, is broken down into seventeen categories of associations. Each entry lists the full name of the association, its address, the number of members, various committees, and the association's publications, which often include a directory of members.

- *General encyclopedias.* Most libraries contain numerous encyclopedias in their reference section that the investigator can use to research any number of topics. A recent computerized search of one local library's card catalogue disclosed 352 separate encyclopedias in its reference collection. These encyclopedias ranged alphabetically from encyclopedias of adoption, Afro-Americans, and agriculture to encyclopedias of vampires, vitamins, and zoology.

- *Business directories.* Many business organizations, such as Dun & Bradstreet, Standard and Poors, and Moody's, offer scores of directories of American businesses and business leaders, as well as financial, business, products, wholesale, and retail dealers. Some examples are *Dun & Bradstreet Ratings,* which contains records of businesses, including financial credit data, organizational data, stockbrokers, and wholesale and retail dealers; *Moody's Bank and Finance Manual,* which contains business and corporation information; and *MacRae's Blue Book,* which contains information on all manufacturers of industrial equipment, products, and materials, listing manufacturers alphabetically by company name, product classification, and trade name.

- *Legal directories.* There are numerous directories of lawyers prepared by state bar associations. One of the most distinguished of these is the *Martindale-Hubbell International Law Directories,* published by Martindale-Hubbell of New Providence, New Jersey. This series of directories contains information on all of the lawyers in the world and is revised yearly.

- *Medical directories.* Most state medical societies offer a state medical directory listing all doctors licensed in the state and their specialties, biographies, and addresses. The directories are generally updated yearly or every other year and also contain information on all hospitals in the state.

The number of individuals and the amount of information you can find in these directories is surprising. For example, this author is listed in the directories of several academic organizations or academies he belongs to, several professional organizations, as well as the alumni directories of three universities he attended.

INFORMATION BROKERS

Information brokers are private persons or corporations that provide detective databases to private investigators throughout the nation. Detective databases are specialized information resources designed to help detectives, attorneys, skip tracers, and other interested parties locate people, find assets, uncover motor vehicle records, and trace college transcripts, credit histories, phone numbers, forwarding addresses, references, and other related data. Private investigators

using their personal computer and a modem can contact any number of these databases online.

Information brokers obtain their information from numerous sources, including public records, news sources, corporate mailing lists, and marketing lists. They also access and catalogue header information— the information that people provide when they fill out forms for business purposes, such as obtaining a loan, opening an account, or almost any other purpose, such as name, address, phone number, date of birth, employment, and the like.

People interested in obtaining names and services provided by information brokers can access the Private Investigators Mall, a Web site maintained by the National Association of Investigative Specialists.

 INVESTIGATIONS ON THE NET

Information on information brokers
http://www.pimall.com/name/brokers.asp

For an up-to-date list of Web links, go to
http://info.wadsworth.com/dempsey

Some information brokers and investigators may use a form of trickery known as ***pretexting*** to get private information like bank accounts and phone numbers. They call a bank, phone company, or other business and claims to be the customer whose records they are seeking. This often works, because customer service representatives are trained to provide help to customers.

Another ruse to obtain information is the so-called Trojan check. The information broker sets up a dummy corporation and sends a check for a small amount of money to the target of his investigation, either as a supposed rebate or award. When the target deposits or cashes the check, information about the target's bank account is imprinted on the canceled check. The broker can then use the information to approach the bank.

Private investigator James J. Rapp is one notable example of how to use ruses to obtain personal information. Rapp, who claimed on his Web page that he could quickly get anyone's private telephone records or bank account balances for as little as $100, became the subject of a lawsuit by the Federal Trade Commission in 1999. In the lawsuit it was claimed that his employees would call banks, pretending to be doddering and confused customers, in order to obtain social security numbers and other information—like the maiden name of an account holder's mother.[13]

Rapp was also indicted by a Golden, Colorado, grand jury for providing confidential information to news organizations about the Jon Benet Ramsey murder investigation. He was also charged with giving the media private information about the victims of the Columbine High School shooting and using subterfuge to get everything from unlisted telephone numbers to bank records.[14]

Rapp has been accused of using deception to ferret out personal information to build a $1 million business. It has been reported that he obtained information on murder victim Ennis Cosby's credit card records; home addresses of organized crime detectives in Los Angeles; visits by television's *Ally McBeal* star, Calista Flockhart, to a Beverly Hills, California, doctor when the tabloids were filled with articles saying that she suffered from eating disorders; and the phone records of Kathleen E. Willey, the former White House volunteer who claimed that former president Bill Clinton made unwanted sexual advances toward her.

The case against Rapp is the biggest test of whether practices that on their face are deceptive are also illegal. Essentially, it is not illegal to lie about identity, except when impersonating a police officer or government official. The Colorado authorities hope to build a successful prosecution against Rapp because that state is one of the few that make it a crime to impersonate someone else for gain. Until this case, deceptions by private investigators and information brokers have not been prosecuted and no federal law specifically prohibits impersonating someone to get confidential information.

Another ruse used in the detective industry to obtain information is to employ former reporters not only for their investigative skills but for their willingness to trade on their past occupation to gain access to sources who would be unlikely to speak to a private investigator.

These days, much of the work done by private investigators involves business disputes. The demands of these corporate clients have helped to transform the world of private detectives from a slightly seedy business dominated by ex-cops into a more sophisticated, multibillion-dollar industry with access to the best surveillance equipment and computer databases. But this growth has collided with privacy concerns, particularly over deceptions used to obtain confidential information about individuals and businesses. In interviews, investigators around the country have said that despite publicly stated policies to the contrary, pretending to be a journalist is a common practice in the industry, one rarely discovered by subjects of investigations. Those who use the pretext often justify it as the only means of getting accurate information.

Pretending to be a journalist is not illegal, but according to Bill Kovach, curator of the Nieman Foundation for Journalism at Harvard University, it raises broader ethical questions about the use of ruses and pretexts by private detectives. He says that the practice of detectives posing as journalists also erodes public trust in the press and jeopardizes its independence: "The only reason people feel confident talking to journalists is that they believe they are talking to an independent source representing their interests and the interests of the truth, not to someone who is part of the police apparatus, whether public or private."[15]

THE INTERNET REVOLUTION AND SOURCES OF INFORMATION

The Internet provides quick and easy access to literally millions of organizations and people around the world, including persons, organizations, businesses, government, and education sources. All a user needs is a computer, a modem, Internet software, and a mouse. Millions of people today use the Internet as a form of communication, entertainment, and business. Also, most students today are very familiar with the Internet and use it for their personal business and research. Much of the information sources discussed in this chapter can be accessed through the Internet so that you don't have to take the time to travel to a library, call a corporation, or look for a book. The Internet not only has revolutionized society but has revolutionized investigations by enhancing the ability of investigators to access tremendous amounts of data at a moment's notice without even leaving their workplace. Knowing

INVESTIGATIONS ON THE NET

General research
http://www.refdesk.com/index.html

Investigations research
http://www.nalionline.org

Law enforcement and policing
http://www.officer.com

Criminal justice research
http://www.ncjrs.org

For an up-to-date list of Web links, go to
http://info.wadsworth.com/dempsey

DEMPSEY'S LAW
Working the Trash

Professor Dempsey, you have given us a tremendous amount of information about sources of information. Which source do you think is most fruitful?

One I haven't told you about yet: people's garbage.

Garbage?

Yes, garbage. Think about it. Think about the things you throw in the garbage can every day and then put into trash bags and place outside your house. By searching your garbage, I can get a pretty good profile of your lifestyle and also some very specific information about you.

I can find out what you eat and drink, if you smoke, what medicines or illegal drugs you use, what you read, and even your love life, if you happen to throw out those cards and letters you get from your significant other. If you throw out the mail after you read it I can find some very specific information, including your social security number. I can find out places and items of purchase if you throw out your bills or banking statements. If you throw out your phone bill, I can even document who you talked to on the phone and the times and dates you did.

Investigators often "work the trash."

how to surf the Net through search engines, checking business, media, educational, government Web sites and exploring links attached to many of them, is becoming essential for investigations. Students are urged to use the numerous Web sites highlighted throughout this text to improve their knowledge.

CONSTITUTIONAL AND LEGAL LIMITATIONS ON SOURCES OF INFORMATION

There are certain constitutional, legal, and traditional limitations on access to and use of information.

The Bill of Rights—the first ten amendments to the U.S. Constitution—guides law enforcement agencies in protecting the personal rights of all citizens. The Fourth, Fifth, Sixth, and Eighth Amendments, as well as the Fourteenth Amendment, limit what investigators may or may not do. State and local laws and regulations also limit access to certain information.

The Freedom of Information Act and the Privacy Act of 1974, discussed earlier, as well as their various amendments protect personal rights by providing certain safeguards against invasion of personal privacy by limiting access to records maintained by public or private agencies and permitting individuals to determine what records may be collected, maintained, used, or disseminated by agencies. They also permit an individual to gain access to records that may be collected and maintained. Records must be collected and maintained only for a necessary and lawful purpose.

References on legal and policy issues on the collection, processing, and storage of intelligence and investigative and juvenile records is available through the National Institute of Justice and the National Criminal Justice Reference Service.

YOU ARE THERE!

Does the Fourth Amendment Protect Your Garbage?

In 1984, the police in Laguna Beach, California, received information from an informant that Billy Greenwood was engaged in drug dealing from his house. They made observations of the house and found numerous cars stopping there at night. The drivers would leave their cars and enter the house for a short time and then leave. The police made arrangements with the local garbage collector to pick up Greenwood's trash, which he left in brown plastic bags in front of his house, and take it to the station house. The police searched the garbage and found evidence indicating a drug business, including razor blades, straws with cocaine residue, and discarded telephone bills with numerous calls to people who had police records for drug possession. Using this evidence, the police obtained a search warrant for Greenwood's house. When they executed the warrant, they found hashish and cocaine, and they arrested Greenwood.

Greenwood appealed his conviction, stating that the seizure of his garbage by the police without a warrant was a violation of his Fourth Amendment rights. Two California courts ruled that the search of Greenwood's garbage was indeed a violation of the Fourth Amendment. But on appeal, the U.S. Supreme Court ruled that searches of a person's discarded garbage were not violations of the Fourth Amendment.

Speaking for the Court, Justice Byron White stated: "It is common knowledge that garbage bags left on or at the side of a public street are readily accessible to animals, children, scavengers, snoops, and other members of the public. Requiring police to seek warrants before searching such refuse would therefore be inappropriate."

SOURCE: *California v. Greenwood*, 486 U.S. 35 (1988).

SUMMARY

Many people believe that the most important part of getting information is not knowing the information but knowing where to find it. If you can find it, you will know it. Being familiar with the sources of information is among the most important investigative skills. Obtaining information today is easier than it ever was because of the Internet. Investigators today who do not know how to use computers and the Internet are as illiterate as long-ago investigators who did not know how to read and write.

This chapter discussed the various sources of information available to investigators. It focused on people as sources of information, including regular sources and cultivated sources, and records as sources of information, including criminal justice agencies, government sources at the federal, state, and local levels, and private sources such as business organizations, public utilities, and credit reporting agencies. The chapter also identified numerous books and directories and the Internet as sources of information. Finally, the chapter reviewed constitutional and legal limitations on sources of information.

LEARNING CHECK

1. List certain individuals who could serve as excellent cultivated sources of information for an investigator.

2. Describe several types of information that may be available at a local law enforcement agency.

3. Name several books or directories that may be obtained at your local public library that could give you information about a person, business, or association.

4. Discuss the benefits of the Internet to investigators.

5. List several constitutional and legal limitations on obtaining information.

APPLICATION EXERCISE   Think of a large corporation that conducts business in your area—possibly K-Mart, J. C. Penney, McDonald's, or your local gas and electric company. Go to your local public library and research that corporation and then prepare a report based on your research. Information that might be of interest to you would be the location of the main corporate offices; the names of the firm's president, chief operating officer, and members of the board of directors; the corporation's gross and net profits last year; and its stock price. Include also any other information that you feel is important to your knowledge of the corporation.

WEB EXERCISE   Research the Internet and locate and find some information brokers who provide information over the Internet. Prepare a report listing three of these brokers, the types of information they provide, and the cost of using the broker.

KEY TERMS

confidential informant	NCIC
criss-cross directories	NCJRS
cultivated sources	paper trail
Freedom of Information Act (FOIA)	pretexting
header information	Privacy Act of 1974
information brokers	reverse directories

9

SURVEILLANCE AND UNDERCOVER INVESTIGATIONS

CHAPTER GOALS

1. To introduce you to the concept of surveillance and its importance in investigating

2. To explain the preparations and techniques necessary to conduct an effective surveillance

3. To show you how undercover investigations fit into the general role of public and private investigating

4. To acquaint you with the many purposes, techniques, and types of undercover investigations

5. To show you the many job opportunities available in undercover investigations

INTRODUCTION

Did you ever watch television detective shows or movies and envision yourself participating in those exciting and dramatic events, being like those fictional heroes and heroines? I hope you realize that most surveillances and undercover operations are not similar to their television and movie representations. Most surveillances and undercover actions are in fact quite boring, but can also be very dangerous.

Do you know someone who may be tempted to engage in criminal activities at her workplace, such as stealing or taking drugs? Did you realize that most of corporate America is constantly taking precautions against such events?

Surveillances and undercover operations are often critical parts of the investigating process. Surveillances may be quite costly in both personnel and equipment. If conducted improperly, they can tip off the subject to the fact that he is being watched. But sometimes surveillance is the only possible option available to the investigator for obtaining information in a case. Undercover work, or playing the role of another person to conduct an investigation, also has a vital role in police, government, and private investigating.

This chapter discusses the reasons and preparation for surveillance, as well as the surveillance itself, various types of surveillances, effective surveillance techniques, and methods used to record and debrief the surveillance. It discusses the laws on electronic surveillance as well.

The chapter also looks at the purposes and types of undercover investigations, the qualities needed to be an effective undercover investigator, the preparations necessary to carry out an undercover assignment, and tactics that can be used by the undercover agent. The chapter concludes with a look at the danger in undercover investigations, the problems inherent in participating in illegal activity by the investigator, and the legal issue of entrapment.

DEFINITION AND PURPOSES OF SURVEILLANCE

A **surveillance** is the covert observation of places, persons, and vehicles for the purpose of obtaining information about the identities or activities of sub-jects. The word *covert* means secret or hidden. The person conducting the surveillance is generally called a **surveillant.** The person being watched is generally called the **subject.** Surveillance is used extensively in both public and private investigations for a variety of reasons.

Public Investigations

Surveillance is also used extensively in public criminal investigations to gain information, to determine whether to continue or discontinue an investigation, to obtain an arrest or search warrant, and to secure information to obtain probable cause to make an arrest. Surveillance is often used in career criminal cases, drug cases, and organized crime cases.

Private Investigations

Surveillance is used extensively in private investigations. Although no longer the primary reason for surveillance, domestic cases remain a large part of private investigation surveillance. According to Sam Brown and Gini Graham Scott: "Sometimes the spouse just wants to know. He or she already suspects something, and really just seeks some confirmation. It can be hard to know the truth, but for many people, that's really better than being up in the air, guessing, suspecting, but never really knowing. They realize where they stand now and can deal with that."[1]

Besides domestic cases, some of the other reasons for surveillances today in private investigations are insurance fraud cases, corporate cases, and child custody cases.

In insurance fraud cases the investigator tries to observe and possibly take photographs of persons who have filed insurance claims for injuries. Often insurance companies have investigators on their staffs to conduct these surveillances or they may hire local private investigators to conduct them. The investigator attempts to obtain photographic evidence of the claimant performing certain physical activities that would be impossible to perform if he were actually suffering from the claimed injuries. For example, he might be mowing the lawn, dancing at a club, or walking without the cane that he now claim he needs.

In corporate cases the investigator may try to track the activities of company executives to observe whom

YOU ARE THERE!

The Gotti Surveillance at the Ravenite on Mulberry Street

The five-story tenement apartment building was almost directly across the street from the Ravenite [social club]. . . . [The police] wanted to rent one particular vacant apartment that faced Mulberry Street. The first month's rent and a security deposit were paid by a money order from an upstate corporation the landlord had never heard of.

Having achieved the first important penetration of Dellacroce's [Gotti's boss] security screen, Gurnee [the lead police investigator] now developed the rest of his plan. First, he decreed, detectives would arrive at the observation post at 5 A.M., before the neighborhood stirred, and would not leave the apartment—not even to go to the bathroom, he insisted firmly—until 10 P.M., when they could slip away under cover of darkness. Second, the apartment would be sealed tight, with the window facing the Ravenite open just far enough to admit the lenses of video and still cameras, and the curtains drawn to cover as much as possible. . . .

Gurnee prepared a photo montage of all the mafiosi he thought would appear at the Ravenite at some point or other, and taped it above the window as a guide for detectives trying to identify men who came into the line of vision. And with that, the newly revitalized Operation Acorn was under way in the early spring of 1979.

Almost immediately, they struck pay dirt. Completely unaware of the surveillance post only eight feet away, mafiosi lingered in front of the Ravenite in the warm spring sunshine and discussed business.

Just after 3 A.M. on a hot night in June, Gurnee, accompanied by two expert lock pickers from the intelligence division—men proud of their reputation as capable of picking any lock in the entire city of New York in only a matter of seconds—went to work on the Ravenite. They picked the locks in no time flat, but as Gurnee, carrying bugging equipment he hoped to install inside the club, entered the place, he immediately encountered the German shepherd watchdog. . . . The next day he made two requests. One was to his wife, a skilled cook: Could she make up a batch of her best meatballs? The second was to the police department's veterinarian: Could he provide some animal tranquilizer pills, sufficient to put a large guard dog to sleep?

. . . . [Gurnee] got into the Ravenite. He drilled a pinhole through the floor right under the table at which Dellacroce customarily sat, and concealed a tiny bug.

The bug was not productive, for Dellacroce, now convinced that the club was bugged, virtually stopped talking business inside. So did everybody else, but that provided the observation post with a bonus, for the police targets all began to stroll the street outside the club to discuss business—often right in range of the post's cameras and microphone.

Gurnee had a field day with his camera, and the pictures he took raised a number of interesting questions. Most intriguingly, there was the presence of [organized crime kingpin] John Gotti.

SOURCE: John Cummings and Ernest Volkman, *Goombata: The Improbable Rise and Fall of John Gotti and His Gang* (New York: Avon Books, 1990).

---

they meet and determine what they discuss. In today's highly competitive business world, a disloyal executive can make a fortune by trading or selling company secrets to a competitor. Generally the best method to use in corporate surveillance is to follow the executive from the company parking lot around lunchtime. Often, these secret meetings occur in a restaurant at lunchtime, just like other business meetings. It is best to obtain photographic and audio evidence if at all

possible. In some cases, criminal charges may be brought. However, in most cases, the presentation of evidence to the subject is sufficient for the person to admit guilt, resign, or make restitution.

Surveillance is also used in child custody cases to obtain evidence for use in a legal proceeding to show that a person is an "unfit parent" or to find a child who has been kidnapped by a noncustodial parent or who is not taken home after a visitation. Custody cases can

DEMPSEY'S LAW
A Child Custody Surveillance Case

Professor, do you have any stories about child custody cases?

Sure, Tom. This one involves a former night school student, a middle-aged woman who worked for a P.I. One night her assignment was to follow a woman— let's call her Irene—and attempt to make observations about her character. She was involved in a custody fight with her husband over their two children. The husband alleged she was an unfit mother who abused alcohol and drugs.

My student picked the subject up at her home and tailed her to a local bar that she went to every Friday evening. My student had researched the case and knew where the subject would take her, so she was dressed appropriately for the Friday night club scene. After a short time my student, who was standing at the bar close to the subject, turned to her and asked her, "Do you have a cigarette? I stopped smoking, but I'm having a hard time, particularly when I'm drinking." The subject gave her a cigarette and the two started to exchange small talk about how difficult it is to break bad habits. Eventually, the subject mentioned that she was trying to stop using cocaine, but it was impossible. She then asked the investigator if she would like to purchase some *blow*—cocaine—from her and use it in the ladies' room. At this time my student graciously turned her down and left the bar to write her observations and the dialogue in her notebook. What does this case prove once again?

People love to talk.

CAREER FOCUS
Investigator for Surveillances

Kroll's Associates, an industry-leading surveillance-investigative company, is seeking quality investigators to perform surveillance and investigations. Minimum requirements are that individuals be self-starters, detail-oriented, and possess the ability to write quality reports and obtain quality videotape. Applicants must have a valid driver's license and clear driving and criminal records.

SOURCE: Kroll's Associates; http://www.krollworldwide.com/employment/employment.cfm.

who teaches a forty-hour surveillance course, puts it this way:

> It's not like the movies. It's hours and hours of boredom, of tedious watching, and waiting. And then, all of a sudden, all hell can break loose. . . . You need people who can shift gears quickly if something goes sideways. . . . They need to be predictable in their responses, [and need to] know the plan, stick with it, and not try to improvise.[2]

Comparing the reality of surveillance to its television depiction, a licensed private investigator said, "For example, take Tom Selleck in *Magnum P.I.* He does his surveillance in a red Ferrari. Now, what private investigator would do that? The idea is to fade into the landscape, to be discreet, not stand out and announce yourself."[3]

Effective surveillance takes not only skill but also preparation. The preparation involves doing your homework, being prepared, having a cover story, checking equipment, having a temporary headquarters or a telephone base, notifying the local police, blending, and being aware of convoys.

Do Your Homework Investigators must know their NEOTWY (recall chapter 4), before conducting a surveillance. They must know the subject's habits, her daily routine, when she leaves for work, where she goes, whom she meets. They should have her photograph or complete description, know the car she uses and other cars available to her, know entrances and exits for buildings the subject may enter. They should

be difficult, especially if the subject takes the child a distance from the legal residence.

Preparation for the Surveillance

Surveillance is very demanding work. Los Angeles Police Department Sergeant Grady Dublin, an International Association of Chiefs of Police (IACP) instructor do a test run of the surveillance a day or two before it will occur. They should know the streets, the terrain, any detours, any hazards.

Lois Pilant writes that investigators conducting surveillances must:

- Show exceptional common sense and good judgment
- Be able to operate both independently and as a team member
- Show strong leadership qualities
- Demonstrate presence of mind and have a proven track record of dependability in times of high stress
- Be extremely patient
- Be street savvy and have the gift of gab[4]

Be Prepared A surveillance can go on for a long period of time, and it may be difficult to drop the surveillance to attend to personal needs. Before the surveillance the investigator should avail himself of food, drink, and a toilet. One of the benefits of using a van for surveillance is that a portable toilet can be installed in the rear for emergency use, curtained off to ensure privacy.

If the surveillance could involve following a person on foot in an urban area, the surveillant should have exact change or the token or fare card necessary to follow the subject onto a bus, subway, or other means of public transportation. It is important to have several different articles of clothing that can be changed rapidly to deter recognition by the subject. Most important, the surveillant should answer the following questions before beginning: *Do I have a map for the area or areas that will be involved in the surveillance? Do I have sufficient gas in the vehicle? Do I have extra gas and water in the event of a breakdown?*

Have a Cover Story The surveillant should have a **cover story** if challenged by the subject or an associate, and should have cover articles, such as a newspaper or paperback book that he could look at to appear as if he is not watching the subject.

Check Equipment Any equipment that is going to be used in the surveillance, including the vehicle that will be used, should be thoroughly inspected beforehand. The vehicle should be checked for mechanical problems. Recording equipment, including transmit-

ters, should be checked before leaving the office. Batteries should be tested to ensure that they are fully charged. Only virgin batteries and recording tapes should be used in most recordings and transmissions. If a case is important enough to spend resources on surveillance, why trust a used battery or tape? And never assume a virgin battery that has just been taken from the factory wrapping is fully charged—it too should be tested.

Have a Temporary Headquarters or Telephone Base The surveillance team should have a temporary headquarters in which to assemble for debriefing if the surveillance is terminated, if the subject appears to be staying put for a long time, or for any other reason. The team should also have a telephone base with a common number where they can call the base operator to leave a message for the other team members or to receive messages from them.

Notify the Local Police Both public and private investigators should notify the local police in the area they are conducting their surveillance of their presence. If the police respond to calls of suspicious persons, their activity may blow the investigators' cover.

Blend Surveillants must be able to **blend** in wherever they are assigned to conduct a surveillance: they should be of average size, build, and appearance and have no noticeable peculiarities in either appearance or mannerism. They should dress like those living or working in the area of the surveillance. For example, in a financial section of a city, the surveillant should be dressed in a business suit and carry a briefcase. In an industrial area, the surveillant should be dressed more casually.

Surveillants cannot appear to be just hanging out. They should be involved in some normal activity for the area, such as talking in a corner telephone booth or sitting on a park bench during lunch hour—eating a hot dog and reading the local paper.

Some surveillance involves locations, such as nightclubs, expensive restaurants, or dances or social events, where the surveillant will look more in place if accompanied by a date. Although it might save money for an investigator to bring along a friend as a partner, this is not recommended. One should avoid using amateurs for a professional's job. Investigators must also consider the issue of confidentiality. The friend might tell everyone he knows about the interesting evening he had and compromise the confidentiality of the investigation.

Be Aware of Convoys A *convoy* is a deliberate attempt to evade a surveillance and often involves prior knowledge that a surveillance will occur. People or vehicles similar in appearance to the people or vehicles believed to be the subject of the surveillance are sent out in the hopes that the surveillants will follow one of the convoys rather than the subject under investigation.

However, convoys can also be used effectively by criminal justice agencies in high-profile criminal trials when the jury is being sequestered at a hotel or motel. One such case was the 1992 trial of John Gotti. Knowing that the press had made preparations to follow the bus taking the jurors to their destination, court officials moved several similar looking buses out of the court parking garage, effectively confusing press representatives.

Another example of the use of a convoy was after the June 2001 execution of Timothy McVeigh, convicted of the 1995 Oklahoma City federal building bombing. A black hearse that the state police escorted from the federal prison in Terre Haute, Indiana, was a decoy used as a security measure. McVeigh's body was actually removed from the penitentiary in a van shortly after the execution. The body was taken to a funeral home and cremated, and the ashes were given to one of McVeigh's lawyers.[5]

THE SURVEILLANCE

There are two primary types of surveillance: the *stationary surveillance* and the *moving surveillance*. This section discusses both types as well as what a surveillant should do if a tail is made, common mistakes in maintaining surveillances, testing tails, and practicing surveillances.

The Stationary Surveillance

In a stationary surveillance the investigator generally watches a particular house or building and notices who comes in and out, possibly taking photographs or videos. If it is an important case, the surveillant might rent a house or apartment in the immediate vicinity. This way, there is a place to store equipment and a window from which to observe with binoculars, telescope, cameras, and night vision devices. In addition, the surveillant has access to necessities such as telephone, water, food, and bathroom.

In stationary surveillances it is extremely important that surveillants relieve each other properly at the end of shifts. They must also be very careful about blending to ensure that they look like the type of people who would live on such a block. The stationary surveillance was the technique used by the investigators who developed the evidence that led to John Gotti's conviction and sentence to life imprisonment after he had been found not guilty in three previous trials.

In most stationary surveillance cases it would not be cost-effective to rent a house or an apartment. Instead, they are conducted by sitting in private cars or unmarked police cars at a discreet distance from the location. The average criminal and sometimes the average citizen has an easy time "making" an unmarked police car. Instead of using a typical unmarked car, investigators should consider using a business-type vehicle (for example, phone company or utility company trucks), or if at all affordable, a surveillance van. Modern surveillance vans generally have windows to look out from and take photos and videos but into which people on the outside cannot see. Some of the best surveillance vans have periscopes that permit the investigator to watch and photograph areas in a 360-degree circumference from the van. (Recall the coverage of surveillance vans and other surveillance equipment in chapter 6.)

If costs preclude the use of high-tech surveillance vans, taxis or business vehicles are good alternatives. When using local business trucks investigators must know how many workers are usually assigned to the vehicles and the clothing or uniforms they wear. In any scenario, investigators must be aware of how they look to others. For example, a taxicab with two males in the front seat spells *police*. So do private autos carrying two white males in a black neighborhood or two black males in a white neighborhood. Always consider a gender mix when using an auto for a stationary surveillance. A young male and a young female, sitting together in the front seat of a car and looking as if they are having an argument or falling in love, will rarely seem suspicious.

Whether working alone or with a partner, the stationary surveillance can be a challenge. As one licensed private investigator put it:

You just can't leave your car or your post when you're on a surveillance, because that could be the very moment when the subject suddenly decides to leave himself. And then you've missed him, and you may not even know it. So you absolutely have to stay there and you have to stay awake, which sometimes can be hard to do. . . . And then there's the boredom and the loneliness. . . . Plus another problem can be just going to the bathroom or eating, because you can't get out, and you can't leave anything on the street. You have to bring any food into the car with you before the surveillance, and if you have to go to the bathroom, well, you have to improvise, say, by urinating into a milk carton. . . . When the subject suddenly appears or leaves, the investigator has to be ready to take off too, call of nature or not.[6]

The Moving Surveillance

There are three basic types of moving surveillances or *tails:* the **rough tail,** the **loose tail,** and the **close** or **tight tail.** The rough tail is used in cases where it is not of utmost importance to keep the subject from knowing about the tail. Organized crime individuals and other professional criminals know they are under constant surveillance. In the rough tail it is usually unnecessary to take extraordinary means to remain undetected. In contrast, in a loose tail it is of utmost importance to remain undetected and less important to keep the subject under constant surveillance. In the close or tight tail it is of extreme importance not to lose the subject but equally important not to be detected. One of the best examples of the close or tight tail is following suspects in a kidnapping case. Moving surveillances can be conducted by foot or by automobile.

Foot Surveillance A one-person tail, also known as a *shadow,* is the most undesirable way of following someone by foot. The risk is too great that the subject will detect the one-person tail. It is better to use, at a minimum, a two-person team of mixed gender.

A typical foot surveillance can be conducted by three persons, using the *ABC method.* The A surveillant is closest to the subject. The B person follows the A person, usually on the same side of the street. The C surveillant may be on the opposite side of the street or may be in front of the subject. All three surveillants can at prearranged intervals shift positions in many different manners. For example, A can move ahead of the subject, with C taking the position following the subject and B moving to the other side of the street. This constant moving will reduce the likelihood that the subject will "make" the tail.[7]

Prearranged signals should be used if any of the surveillants believes that the subject has made the tail. The signals should indicate if a surveillant is dropping out of the tail or if another surveillant should drop out.

Precautions should be taken when turning corners or entering buildings so that the closest surveillant does not appear to be following the subject. If the subject boards a public bus or train or goes into the subway, at least one of the surveillants should enter the public vehicle and sit behind the subject on the same side of the bus. The other surveillants may try to get ahead of the bus and board at a later stop. If the subject enters a taxicab and the surveillants have access to a vehicle, they should follow the taxi; if they have no access to a vehicle, at least one of the surveillants should attempt to hail another taxi and follow the subject's taxi. In all cases a member of the surveillance team should record the license plate and name of the taxi company, and the time and place at which the trip began so that they can check the records of the company for the final destination in the event the cab can't be followed.

Automobile Surveillance Maintaining a successful auto surveillance is extremely difficult considering highway conditions, traffic control devices, driving habits, and other problems associated with auto traffic in the United States.

It is always better to have more than one vehicle in the surveillance team. If there is only one vehicle, it makes the chances of detection or losing the subject vehicle that much greater. When several cars are used, surveillants can drop back and change positions, much as they do in foot surveillances. With autos this is actually easier to do because the surveillants can transmit directions and suggestions using portable radios. Radio transmissions are also crucial during an auto surveillance so that all members of the surveillance know the location of the subject. If two cars are used, it is best to have one serve as a lead car, driving in front of the subject, with the second car following. With two cars the surveillants can also leapfrog, changing positions to lessen the chance of the subject making the surveillance. If three or more surveillance vehicles are available, the third and fourth cars can maintain surveillance on parallel blocks and be ready to fall into the lead or follow the auto if the subject makes a turn from his route.

Although it is better to have several vehicles in a moving surveillance, it cannot always be done. Budgetary considerations often dictate that only one vehicle can be used.

The type of vehicle used by the surveillance team is also very important. If a nondescript blue Chevy has been behind you for a few miles and then turns off at a highway exit and then another nondescript blue Chevy appears behind you three exits later, it may not seem to matter. However, if a very distinctive car—a 2001 Ford Mustang GT, sky blue with red pinstriping, convertible with the top down—appears behind you again and again, you will probably notice it. The investigator conducting a surveillance that could last several days might consider using a rental car and changing it daily.

When following a car it is best to stay one or two car lengths back. If it is affordable, two surveillants should be in the surveillance car so that one can concentrate on driving and the other can make observations.

If the subject pulls into a parking spot on the street or in a parking lot, the surveillance team should park as far as possible from the subject and follow his movements through binoculars, resuming the surveillance when he returns to the car.

Nighttime surveillance is usually more difficult because with their headlights and taillights on, many cars look similar in the dark, and investigators may find themselves tailing the wrong car. The solution is to mark the subject car, if possible, beforehand—spray some fluorescent paint onto the license plate, rear fender, or taillight.

An effective method of making auto surveillance easier is to place a vehicle tracking system on the subject auto. The vehicle tracking system emits electronic beeps or signals to a receiver in the surveillance car. Unfortunately, vehicle tracking systems are expensive and difficult to retrieve, because the surveillant cannot just walk up to the subject auto to retrieve the system, particularly if the car is parked on private property. (Recall the discussion of vehicle tracking systems in chapter 6.)

Finally, investigators need to drive carefully and defensively to avoid a traffic accident. In the event of an accident, the surveillant could not only suffer injury but blow the operation.

What If the Tail Is Made?

If the surveillant has good reason to believe he has been "made," he should immediately discontinue the surveillance and make evasive moves designed to prevent the subject from turning the surveillance back onto the surveillant. The surveillant must ensure that the subject does not follow him to his home or office.

Common Mistakes in Maintaining Surveillances

Investigators can make many mistakes when maintaining surveillances. One of the biggest is to make any of the following assumptions:

- The subject has checked into a hotel or motel at 2300 hours (eleven o'clock at night). This means she is going to spend the night.

- The subject has entered a store in a mall. She will leave using the same entrance.

- The subject has returned to her home or apartment. She will probably stay for a long time or the night.

- The subject begins to run or to speed. This means she has made the tail.

Here are some other mistakes an investigator can make: staying parked in the same spot for too long; using a conspicuous car; having both surveillants in the front seat for an extended period of time; approaching the parking position furtively; parking in a prohibited zone, thereby attracting attention; failing to manage the changeover to a relieving team unobtrusively; telephoning repeatedly from the same store or other phone location.

Testing a Tail

Many subjects who anticipate a tail or who have had experience with surveillance will attempt to test a tail. On a public transit conveyance such as a bus, taxi, subway, or railroad, the subject may board and then wait until the moment when the doors begin to close to exit the conveyance. If in a car the subject may circle a certain block two or three times and then return to the place where he began. In a building, the subject may walk through the front door and then make an immediate U-turn and exit the building, looking to see if he will "bump into someone." The same technique can be used in a store in a mall. Investigators conducting a surveillance should be aware of these tricks in order to avoid detection.

Surveillances Require Practice

A surveillance is a complicated undertaking, particularly if there are a number of investigators involved. When investigators have the time, they should conduct mock foot and auto surveillances. These mock events should involve investigators who normally would work together; other investigators should evaluate their effectiveness.

RECORDING THE SURVEILLANCE

All surveillances should be recorded in writing and may also be recorded with videos.

Written Notes

Written notes are essential in a surveillance. What did the subject do? Where? When? With whom? How? Why? If possible, the notes should be taken as the event unfolds. If it is not possible to record the notes contemporaneously, the investigator should record them as soon as possible after the event.

Photographs

Surveillances may require taking photographs. When taking photos it is always best to take as many as possible and from as many different angles and distances as possible. Each photo should be backed up including the following information: date, time, location of photographer, and subject; camera, lens, lens setting, and frame number of the photo; identification of subject and any associates.

In addition, the investigator's written reports should include the brand, model, and serial number of the camera used and the brand, name, speed, and so on, of the film.

It has become standard for investigators to use the 35 millimeter camera for surveillance purposes. However, there is now a tremendous variety of automatic (point-and-shoot) cameras on the market that take very good photos and have attachments such as telephoto lenses available. These cameras require no training or sophisticated knowledge of photography.

Also available are a vast array of night vision devices that can be attached to cameras or scopes, enabling an investigator to see and take photographs in virtual darkness. Because these devices are quite expensive, investigators should get the best possible technical advice before purchasing them to ensure they get the best value for their money. (Recall the discussion of night vision devices in chapter 6.)

Often photographs serve as leverage in a case. When confronted with a photo depicting them at a particular time or event, subjects may feel compelled to stop evading and tell the truth.

Video

The use of video cameras to record pertinent moments can be very effective in a surveillance, particularly a stationary surveillance. In many cases, a video camera can be put in a hidden location and turned on, letting the investigator perform other duties. These types of hidden cameras are used extensively at banks and department stores. The investigator must practice using this equipment before taking it on a surveillance.

DEBRIEFING THE SURVEILLANCE

After every surveillance the members of the surveillance team should hold a meeting and debrief the surveillance. *What did we do right? What did we do wrong?* People learn by their mistakes, and if the mistakes are brought out and thought about, they might not occur again. Even if the surveillance was a success and no obvious mistakes were made, the team members should still hold the debriefing and brainstorm alternatives to some of the methods they used. There is never only one way to conduct a surveillance.

In unsuccessful surveillances, the debriefing will focus not only on mistakes but possibly on a new plan or new techniques.

THE LAW AND ELECTRONIC SURVEILLANCE

Listening in on other people's conversations through electronic means is covered both by case law and legislative law. Both have evolved significantly over the years.

Case Law History

In *Olmstead v. United States* (1928), one of the earliest U.S. Supreme Court cases involving electronic surveillance, the Court ruled that government agents did not require a search warrant to intercept conversations over the telephone because a telephone is not an extension of a person's home and therefore is not protected by the constitutional guarantees of the Fourth Amendment. In this case, bootleggers were using their personal telephones to conduct business. Federal agents tapped their lines and used the conversations they heard in the prosecution of the bootleggers. After

their conviction, the defendants appealed their case, arguing that a seizure of their conversation had occurred and that the government should have secured a warrant—therefore, the use of their conversations was a violation of their Fourth Amendment protection against illegal search and seizure.[8]

In *On Lee v. U.S.* (1952) and *Lopez v. U.S.* (1963), the U.S. Supreme Court ruled on the use of a concealed transmitter worn by an undercover agent. The Court ruled that the use of the concealed transmitter did not violate provisions of the Constitution.[9]

In 1967, in *Berger v. New York* the Court authorized the use of **bugs** and **wiretaps** in instances where states had legislation authorizing the use of such devices and where officers obtained a warrant based on probable cause.[10]

In the landmark case of *Katz v. U.S.* (1967), the Court ruled that when a person makes an effort to keep a telephone conversation private, even in a public place, a warrant based on probable cause must be obtained in order to intercept such conversation.[11]

In 2001, in *Kyllo v. United States,* the Court ruled that the use of new sophisticated modern electronic surveillance systems may require a search warrant if applied toward a private residence.[12]

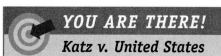

YOU ARE THERE!

Katz v. United States

Mr. Justice Stewart delivered the opinion of the court.

The petitioner was convicted in the district court of the Southern District of California under an eight-count indictment charging him with transmitting wagering information by telephone from Los Angeles to Miami and Boston, in violation of a federal statute. At trial the government was permitted, over the petitioner's objection, to introduce evidence of the petitioner's end of telephone conversations, overheard by FBI agents who had attached an electronic listening and recording device to the outside of the public telephone booth from which he had placed his calls. In affirming his conviction, the court of appeals rejected the contention that the recordings had been obtained in violation of the Fourth Amendment, because "there was no physical entrance into the area

occupied by the petitioner." We granted certiorari [accepted the case for consideration] in order to consider the constitutional questions. . . .

Wherever a man may be, he is entitled to know that he will remain free from unreasonable searches and seizures. The government agents here ignored "the procedure of antecedent justification". . . . [T]hat is central to the Fourth Amendment, a procedure that we hold to be a constitutional precondition of the kind of electronic surveillance involved in this case. Because the surveillance here failed to meet that condition, and because it led to the petitioner's conviction, the judgment must be reversed.

It is so ordered.

SOURCE: *Katz v. United Sates*, 389 U.S. 347 (1967).

YOU ARE THERE!
Kyllo v. U.S.

In June 2001, the U.S. Supreme Court made an important decision on the constitutional limits on new privacy-threatening technology by ruling that police use of a thermal imaging device to detect patterns of heat (suggesting an indoor marijuana-growing operation) coming from a private home is a search that requires a warrant.

The case, *Kyllo v. United States*, was a federal drug prosecution that began in 1992, when two federal agents trained a device called Agema Thermovision 210 on a home in Florence, Oregon, where, on the basis of tips and utility bills, they believed marijuana was being grown under high-intensity lamps. Although the imager cannot see through walls, it can detect hot spots, and in this case disclosed that part of the roof and a side wall were warmer than the rest of the building and the neighboring houses. The agents used that information to get a warrant to enter and search the home, where they found more than a hundred marijuana plants growing under halide lights. The resident, Danny Kyllo, entered a conditional guilty

plea while continuing to contest the validity of the search. He served one month in jail.

When Kyllo's Supreme Court appeal was argued, the government strongly defended use of thermal imagers on the ground that in detecting heat loss, the devices neither reveal private information nor violate the "reasonable expectation of privacy" that is the Supreme Court's test under the Fourth Amendment.

The Court ruled in this decision that the warrant requirement would apply not only to the device at issue in this case but also to more sophisticated systems in use or in development that let the police gain knowledge that in the past would have been impossible without a physical entry into the home.

The Court applied this rule only to homes and didn't address warrantless imaging of other locations.

SOURCE: Linda Greenhouse, "Justices Say Warrant Is Required in High-Tech Searches of Homes," *New York Times*, June 12, 2001, pp. A1, A29.

Legislative Law History

In 1968, in response to many complaints about illegal electronic surveillance by federal law enforcement agencies, Congress passed Title III of the Omnibus Crime Control and Safe Streets Act of 1968, 18 U.S.C. 2510–2520, which prohibits the interception of wire and oral communications by federal law enforcement officers except in one of the following circumstances: when one party consents; with a court order; and in emergency cases involving national security or organized crime, provided that judicial authorization is later received.[13]

The court order permitting the electronic interception of wire and oral communications is called an **ex parte order.** The order may not remain in effect longer than is necessary to achieve its objective, and in any event no longer than thirty days; however, there is no limitation on the number of extensions that may be granted. Ex parte orders contain a minimization

requirement with regard to electronic surveillance. *Minimizing* means that officers, through the use of body mikes, phone taps, and so on, must make every effort to monitor only those conversations that are specifically related to the criminal activity under investigation. As soon as it becomes apparent that the conversation is not of a criminal nature, they must cease their efforts to eavesdrop.

In 1986, Congress enacted the Electronics Communications Privacy Act, which regulates more recent forms of electronic surveillance. The law requires police to obtain prior court orders before using such devices. If a prior court order is not obtained, the evidence will not be admissible in court. This law also provides both criminal and civil penalties and extends Title III of the 1968 omnibus crime bill.[14]

In 1994, Congress enacted the Communications Assistance for Law Enforcement Act (CALEA), which requires telephone companies to modify their digital technology to enable law enforcement agencies to continue to engage in electronic surveillance of criminals and terrorists.[15]

The laws on the electronic surveillance of communications also apply to the use of the Internet and e-mail. (See chapter 14 for more on computer crime.)

Title III and the subsequent electronic surveillance legislation contain what is known as the *exhaustion provision*. This provision permits the government to establish the necessity for the electronic surveillance in three different ways, essentially saying that all standard investigatory methods have been exhausted: standard investigative techniques have been tried and failed; standard investigative techniques are reasonably likely to fail; and standard investigative techniques are too dangerous to try.

In a recent article on electronic surveillance Thomas D. Colbridge states:

> Electronic surveillance is a Fourth Amendment search when it is used by the government in a manner that infringes a reasonable expectation of privacy. Reasonableness is the standard that should motivate both the

investigator and the court. If investigators can reasonably explain the necessity for electronic surveillance, the court will use its reason and common sense to evaluate their judgment.[16]

Most of the federal legislation on electronic surveillance has preempted state legislation on the subject. Consequently, state laws governing this surveillance must meet at least the minimum requirements for authorization in the federal statute.

DEFINITION AND PURPOSES OF UNDERCOVER INVESTIGATION

An *undercover investigation* may be defined as a form of investigation in which an investigator assumes a different identity in order to obtain information or achieve another investigatory purpose. In other words, the undercover investigator plays the role of another person.

EXHIBIT 9.1   Bugging and Antibugging Devices

- *Bug*. An electronic device placed in a premise that transmits conversation to a receiver or recorder; it can be found taped under desks or in false ceilings, or behind a picture or in the plumbing or anywhere in a room.

- *Bug detector*. An electronic device placed in a room that produces a tone that can pick up any form of electronic transmission. When the bug detector indicates there is some sort of transmitter in a room, sweepers, using handheld equipment, can find exactly where it is.

- *Bugging*. A generic term for eavesdropping or listening in to conversations by electronic means.

- *Pen register*. A device that records all numbers dialed from a telephone.

- *Phone tap detection device*. A device that will indicate whether or not a tap is on a phone line.

- *Scrambler*. A device attached to the telephone that scrambles the speaker's voice to everyone except those who have a similar device set to a prearranged code.

- *Sweep*. An examination of a premise for the presence of any bugging devices.

- *Tap*. An electronic device placed on a telephone line that transmits conversation to a receiver or recorder.

- *Tap and trace*. A device that records numbers dialed to a telephone and provides the name of the subscriber of the phone from which the call is made.

- *Vehicle tracking system (also known as transponder, beacon, beeper, electronic tracking device)*. A battery-operated device that emits radio signals that permit it to be tracked by a directional finder-receiver; generally, it is attached to a car that is going to be followed.

- *Voice amplifier*. A device that will pick up sound from a distance away; has been called a *bionic ear*. Generally, it is a microwave dish.

- *White noise blocker (also known as a jammer)*. A device that blocks the recording of any conversation in a room. When a person plays back the recording, he hears only a whirring sound.

An undercover investigation is similar to a surveillance yet also quite different. In a surveillance, the investigator's primary purpose is to follow a subject or observe what is going on in a particular area or involving a particular person or persons. In an undercover investigation, the investigator may be merely observing. However, he may also be performing certain actions designed to get other people to do something, or react to, or interact with the investigator in a certain way. The primary function of the investigator in these cases is to play a role without anyone realizing that he is playing a role.

Most undercover investigations are complicated and can incur legal challenges that can create liabilities for law enforcement agencies, private investigating agencies, and even the investigator, if done improperly. In a three-part series on undercover investigations in *Security Management* magazine, Eugene F. Ferraro, a certified protection professional (CPP) and chairman of the American Society for Industrial Security (ASIS) Standing Committee on Workplace Substance Abuse and Illicit Drug Activity, describes the following stages of an undercover investigation:[17]

- *Planning phase.* In this phase of the investigation, the objective must be established and an investigative team selected. A cover story must be established for the undercover operative and that person must be covertly placed into the operation.
- *Case management.* In this phase, the case is managed and coordinated between the major players in the operation, including the undercover investigator, supervisors, managers, law enforcement agencies, and legal representatives.
- *Communication.* Effective communications must be developed between all of the members of the operation. Methods of communication include written reports, e-mail, telephone conversations, and case files.
- *The investigation.* This is the vehicle for achieving the objectives of the undercover operation.
- *Closure.* Eventually, the operation must be shut down when the objectives are met or when an emergency occurs that endangers the undercover.

An undercover investigation can serve numerous purposes, most of which are related to obtaining information: information for a client; information for an attorney in a legal proceeding; information for law enforcement purposes, such as that necessary to substantiate probable cause to make an arrest, obtain warrants, and continue investigations.

TYPES OF UNDERCOVER INVESTIGATIONS

Gary T. Marx identifies several general types of undercover investigations, including police undercover investigations, federal undercover investigations, and private security undercover investigations, all of which are discussed here.[18] Several very important types of undercover investigations are covered in great detail in other chapters in this text. (See chapter 10 for discussions of proactive decoy and blending, and repeat offender programs to address violent crimes; see chapter 11 for a discussion of sting programs to address property crimes; and see chapter 12 for a discussion of undercover drug operations, in particular conspiracy operation and the buy-and-bust.)

Police Undercover Investigations

Police undercover investigations generally include drug undercover investigations; stings, including fencing stings that involve the buying and selling of stolen goods and other contraband, and warrant stings; decoy operations targeted against the crimes of robbery, burglary, and assault; antiprostitution operations; and operations involving the infiltration of undercover officers into criminal settings and the subsequent arrest of people involved in organized crime, white-collar crime, and corruption.

Police undercover officers have a dangerous yet often rewarding, job. In a news article, some of the two hundred undercover officers of the New York City Police Department's Transit Bureau talked about their jobs.

> "Undercovers are a better breed—more gutsy," said Officer William Diaz, a thirty-four-year-old transit officer in an elite anti-crime unit in downtown Brooklyn. "We'll go anywhere. I like being on the road and I like being in action." To conceal his identity from the criminals who work the stations he patrols, he continually grows a beard, cuts it off, and grows it again.

YOU ARE THERE!

Covert or Overt Investigations in the Workplace?

Covert or undercover operations should be used only when there is no other way to resolve a case. Covert operations are useful in the following circumstances:

- There is consistent, reliable information suggesting employee misconduct or criminal activity, but not enough information to prevent the activity or identify those involved.

- Losses have occurred in a specific area, but there is no information on how the losses occurred or who is responsible.

- There is a strong suspicion of on-the-job alcohol or drug abuse or drug dealing in the workplace, but no definite evidence.

- It is necessary to determine whether employees are following company policies and procedures, but routine auditing is impossible.

The following are not good cases for covert operations:

- To determine the strength of a union's activity campaign by identifying workers sympathetic to the union; this is illegal and can hurt employee relations and morale.

- When the losses are too small to justify the expense of an undercover operation.

SOURCE: "Covert or Overt? That Is the Question," *Security Management*, July 2000.

Officer Diaz's thirty-three-year-old partner, Denise James, said her commitment to undercover work arose from seeing crime's toll on her own Brooklyn neighborhood, Bedford-Stuyvesant. She attended the College of Staten Island, and after graduation she became a medical laboratory technician at Hunter College. But she was looking for more of a challenge, and she said, "I got tired of people taking crack and robbing people in hallways. I wanted to make a small dent on crime in my neighborhood." . . . She added: "What I like is surprising people. You get the perpetrator. The victim is thankful. When you make the collar, the criminal says, 'You're a cop?' That's what I call satisfying."

Another Brooklyn undercover transit officer, Joseph Wagner, twenty-six, whose disheveled ponytail and muscular build make him look something like a construction worker who has hit hard times, said his desire to go undercover originated as a child "playing cops and robbers." He added, "I've always wanted to be right in the middle of it. Being undercover is about getting your man."[19]

Federal Undercover Investigations

Federal undercover investigations generally include efforts to detect and arrest people involved in political corruption, insurance fraud, labor racketeering, and other types of organized conspiracy crimes.

Perhaps the classic case of a successful federal undercover investigation was the work of FBI special agent Joseph D. Pistone, who assumed the cover identity of Donnie Brasco. Pistone began his infiltration of La Cosa Nostra (the American Mafia) in 1976 and continued it for six years. Pistone was so completely accepted by the Mafia that he was able to move freely among all the Mafia families and learn their secrets. He was so effective that he had to terminate his undercover operations in 1982 because he was about to be inducted into the Mafia as a "made man," and expected to kill another mafioso. As a result of Pistone's work more than one hundred federal criminal convictions were obtained, dealing a severe blow to Mafia operations throughout the United States. Pistone's exploits were detailed in a book and the movie *Donnie Brasco*.[20]

Some federal undercover investigations have led to ethical questions—for example, the Abscam operation. Abscam was an undercover operation conducted by FBI agents between 1978 and 1980. Posing as Arab sheikhs, the agents offered bribes to members of Congress in order to receive favors. The sting resulted in the conviction of seven members of Congress, along with other officials, as well as harsh criticism of the FBI for its undercover methods.[21]

Private Security Undercover Investigations

According to Marx, private security undercover investigations generally involve inventory losses, pilferage, willful neglect of machinery, unreported absenteeism, "general employee attitudes," and "delicate investigations."[22] Many other categories can be added to private security undercover investigations, including criminal, marital, civil, and child custody cases, to name only a few. This section covers four important private security undercover investigations: shopping services or mystery shoppers, silent witness programs, internal intelligence programs, and the store detective or loss prevention specialist. (See chapter 15 for a detailed description of the many methods and types of undercover investigations conducted by private security investigators.)

Shopping Services and Mystery Shoppers Private security firms offer prospective business clients **integrity shoppers** and other **shopping services** to test the integrity and efficiency of retail business personnel. These services are performed by "shoppers"— actually, undercover agents posing as customers—and are designed to deter inventory **shrinkage,** detect dishonest employees, and provide evidence for prosecuting employees caught stealing.

Stores contract shopping services, or mystery shopping services, to make discrete observations in their stores. For a fee, a **mystery shopper** will visit a store and observe the performance and operations of store personnel. The shopping service then prepares a report that is sent to the store manager and corporate managers.[23]

Almost every major U.S. retail company regularly uses mystery shoppers. As of 1998, there were five hundred mystery shopping companies nationwide, double the number of five years earlier. Banks are tested on how hard reps work to open new accounts, restaurants are timed to see how fast service is, and a mall greeter may be monitored for the consistency of her smile. The finding reported by mystery shoppers are used to train employees for customer satisfaction.

Mystery shoppers also observe and judge other attributes of employees: attitude, courtesy, approach, appearance, knowledge, and salesmanship. Undercover agents observe the actions of the employees and question them while posing as ordinary customers. They also

---

YOU ARE THERE!

To Catch Cheating Men

Former New York City Police Department detective Gerry Palace operates Check-A-Mate, a full-service private investigation agency, which uses real-life decoys to test a man's propensity to cheat on his spouse. Palace sends female undercover agents out into Manhattan nightspots to test subjects who are suspected of being unfaithful. The agents are told to engage in conversation with the subjects and then ask key questions, such as, "So, a good-looking guy like you has to be married, right?"

All of Palace's female agents work part-time and have other jobs in film, theater, or modeling. Furthermore, every woman he employs has been a victim herself—cheated on by a man.

The agents wear hidden tape recorders to record anything said by the subjects. These recordings can then be replayed for the clients.

SOURCE: Daniel Jeffreys, "Bait and Snitch Is His Game: Ex-NYPD Detective Uses Real-Life Decoys to Catch Cheating Wall Street Men," *New York Post*, Aug. 18, 1999, pp. 28–29.

YOU ARE THERE!

Meet Jim Jolly, the Mystery Shopper

"It's a sin in my book to be out of coffee," said Jim Jolly. Jolly is a mystery shopper—one of thousands of people who visit stores looking for things like empty shelves, misplaced goods, stale muffins, and dirty bathrooms. His employer is C & S Mystery Shoppers of North Brunswick, New Jersey, whose mission is to give store executives a view of what it is like for regular people to shop in their stores.

For a single store visit and copious notes on its condition, C & S charges about $35 and the cost of a bag of groceries, which the shopper gets to keep. Another company, Mystery Shoppers Inc. of Houston, videotapes its visits, using a hidden camera, and then plays the tapes for the store manager. A package of visits can cost as much as $1,000.

SOURCE: Jennifer Steinhauer, "The Undercover Shoppers: Posing as Customers, Paid Agents Rate the Stores," *New York Times*, Feb. 4, 1998, pp. D1, D23.

DEMPSEY'S LAW
Integrity Shoppers

Professor Dempsey, a friend of mine was just arrested and lost her job as a cashier at the Feel-Well drugstore in town. She said that she was the victim of integrity shoppers. What's that?

Many retail businesses employ integrity shoppers to test their employees' honesty and adherence to the rules and regulations established by the business. Let me give you the following scenario. It describes the operation of a specific team of integrity shoppers who were actually students of mine in a night class here at the college.

Mary, age forty, rushing through the busy aisles of a large pharmacy downtown, hurriedly selects an item of cosmetics costing $4.50. Clutching the item and a five-dollar bill she passes other customers waiting on the checkout line and addresses the cashier in an excited manner, "I have to get back to work or I'll be fired. Look, take the five, that'll cover the tax." She then quickly places the bill on the counter in front of the cashier. Without waiting for a reply, she turns and rushes out of the store.

At the same time, Mary's daughter, Linda, age twenty-one, who is also Mary's partner, waits by the hair dye at the front of the store looking as if she cannot decide which product to buy. In actuality, she is carefully watching the cashier her mother left the bill in front of to determine what the cashier will do

with it. If the cashier puts the money into her pocket instead of ringing it up on the cash register, Linda signals her mother, who is waiting outside. The two women then approach the store manager, identify themselves as company security, and report the transaction. The cashier is removed from her station and brought to the manager's office.

Mary and Linda generally try to get the employee to prepare a written statement describing her actions and any other previous illegal acts she has engaged in at the store. Because Mary and Linda are not police officers or government officials, they do not have to read the subject her *Miranda* rights prior to questioning. Often the employee will give the names of other employees who steal from the store.

After obtaining the written statement, Mary and Linda notify the police, who respond and arrest the employee based on the written complaint of the store manager.

Professor Dempsey, isn't that entrapment?

No! Providing someone with an opportunity to commit a crime is not entrapment. The cashier did not have to pocket the five. She should have followed proper company procedures, which, no doubt, involved ringing up the sale or notifying the store manager to account for any cash overage or shortage.

---

report on the following conditions at the business: appearance, lighting, displays, housekeeping, and the like.

Silent Witness Programs Private investigating firms also offer prospective corporate clients silent witness programs. These programs provide a method for honest, dedicated employees who are concerned about wrongdoing in the workplace to volunteer helpful information without compromising themselves. They use some techniques familiar to the Neighborhood Crime Watch and media TIPS programs, making a telephone number readily available to employees throughout a facility or company. Materials explain the program and

guarantee anonymity, and all calls are monitored by trained personnel in the private investigating firm's communications center.

Internal Intelligence Programs Another type of program offered is the internal intelligence program, in which private investigative firms plant undercover agents in the corporation's business operations to make observations and report back to the company.

These programs have been used successfully to combat theft of funds and merchandise, use of alcohol or drugs on the job, gambling, sabotage, or other illegal activity.

DEMPSEY'S LAW
Tom, the Store Detective

Professor Dempsey, I want to get into law enforcement, but I don't want to be a police officer. I want something more like a business or retail job. Can you tell me something about store detective work?

Sure, but why don't we ask Tom? He's a store detective—or more properly called a loss-prevention specialist—at that new clothing store in the area, Bob's. Tom, what do you do and how do you do it?

Well, professor, I've been working at Bob's since it opened last year. We have two store detectives working each shift. One works the cameras and one works the floor. Our job is to catch as many shoplifters as possible. After we catch them, we call the police, and they arrest them.

Tom, what you do mean "by working the cameras and working the floor?" Could you explain that better to your classmates?

Sure. We have video cameras all over the store. Some of them focus strictly on the cashiers so we can monitor their actions, and some of them focus on the entire store. We have video monitors in the security office that we continually monitor. One of the security people sits in the office watching the video monitors and looking

for people shoplifting. If he sees suspicious activity that indicates possible shoplifting activity he notifies his partner, who is working the floor by radio. The floor person then goes to that area and stands by as the camera person continues to monitor the video. If the person actually shoplifts, the camera person can press a button that provides an immediate photo of the activity and then notifies the floor person to move in to make an apprehension. The floor person is then assisted by the camera person and some other store personnel in making the apprehension.

Tom, is loss prevention always a two-person operation?

No. Some stores only use one person. That person walks around the store posing as a regular customer and makes discreet observations. That's not a good idea, however. It's always better to work with the cameras because they can give you direct evidence of the shoplifting. In this business there's no room for a bad stop—meaning apprehending someone who hasn't actually taken any property. If you make a bad stop, the store can be sued and you can be sued.

The Store Detective or Loss Prevention Specialist
One of the most common types of undercover private investigators is the **store detective,** or **loss prevention specialist.** Shoplifting is a very common crime in the United States and seriously affects companies' profits.

In a National Retail Security survey it was disclosed that the average shrinkage for surveyed department stores was 2.09 percent. Using this rate, a department store chain with merchandise sales of $1 billion would have shrinkage of almost $21 million. In the judgment of the survey's respondents, 38 percent of all shrinkage was caused by shoplifting. Retailers use the term *shrinkage* to describe the difference between inventory on hand at the beginning of the year and inventory on hand—minus sales—at year end.[24] *Loss prevention* refers to the use of methods to

reduce the amount of shrinkage in retail stores. In a study analyzing 166,000 shoplifting incidents submitted by 101 retail firms, it was discovered that CDs, over-the-counter medications, and health and beauty products are among the most frequently stolen items. According to the study, discount, department store, and supermarket retailers reported the highest apprehension rates, catching shoplifters in action more often.

According to the U.S. Department of Labor's Bureau of Labor Statistics, approximately twenty thousand persons worked as store detectives in department or clothing and accessories stores, in 1998.[25]

The goal of the store detective is to apprehend people stealing property from the store. After apprehending the shoplifter the store detective retrieves the stolen property. In many cases the police are called in and arrest the violator and process him through the criminal justice system. Some stores use sophisticated camera equipment to scan the store for people stealing merchandise, whereas other stores rely on the store detective "roaming" the store, appearing to look like an ordinary shopper.

Many college students work their way through college with jobs as store detectives or loss prevention specialists. Store detective is also a good entry-level job in private security from which employees can work their way up to security management.

The legal justification for the use of store detectives is the common law doctrine of the *shopkeeper's privilege.* Under this theory, a storekeeper or shopkeeper can reasonably detain and question a person if the shopkeeper has a justified suspicion that an illegal act, such as theft, has taken place on the shop's premises. This doctrine holds that even if it is later found that no crime took place, the detention is proper if based on the following conditions:

- *Detention.* Detention does not need to be physical restraint—it may arise out of words, conduct, gestures, or threats as long as the detainee believes that he or she is not free to leave the premises.

- *Probable cause.* The detention of the subject must be based on probable cause, significant facts that would cause a reasonable person to believe than an offense has occurred and that the subject committed it.

- *Reasonableness.* The detention of the subject must be reasonable considering the factors of physical surroundings, physical contact, and the type and level of any threats.

- *Consistency.* Retailers must have policies that are applied evenhandedly without regard to the subject's race or other personal factors.[26]

In a year 2000 survey of forty U.S. retail stores employing store detectives, most retailers reported that they currently assign their store agents to patrol for shoplifters, audit store asset protection initiatives, and create loss prevention awareness among all store staff. They select new store detectives primarily on ethical and decision-making criteria. The use of force is the highest-ranked training topic. Finally, more than 66 percent of the survey participants indicated that concerns about civil liability had caused them to change their training programs for store detectives.[27]

The National Retail Federation (NRF) is the world's largest retail trade association. Its membership includes the leading department, specialty, independent, discount, and mass merchandise stores in the United States and fifty other nations around the world. It runs a national Loss Prevention Conference and Exhibition in which industry leaders and loss prevention experts explore the latest industry trends, introduce the latest technology, and promote the best practices for combating retail loss.

 INVESTIGATIONS ON THE NET

National Retail Federation
http://www.nrf.com

For an up-to-date list of Web links, go to
http://info.wadsworth.com/dempsey

THE UNDERCOVER INVESTIGATION

The undercover investigation is perhaps the most sensitive and most dangerous type of investigation. If the undercover investigator is **burned**—that is, if his or her true identity is discovered or assumed identity found to be false—not only is the investigation compromised but the life of the investigator may be in peril. Selecting which person to do the job is probably the most important part of the investigation.

The Undercover Investigator

The undercover investigator should be an experienced investigator who knows all the skills and nuances of the trade. He or she should be an expert in blending techniques and have above-average communication skills. He or she must be an intelligent, calm person capable of concealing nervousness or discomfort in threatening situations and capable of adapting to changing conditions.

The undercover investigator must have a general understanding of the type of role he or she will be playing. When investigators are playing the role of a drug addict or criminal, they must be familiar with the roles

EXHIBIT 9.2   **Shoplifting Methods**

- Palming—grabbing the product in your hand—is the simplest and most common method used for shoplifting. Palming is often aided by the use of a package, handkerchief, or glove. An accomplice may stand to screen the shoplifter.

- Purses and pockets are common places to conceal shoplifted items. Also used are shopping bags and boxes from other stores, umbrellas, schoolbooks, knitting bags, strollers, baby carriages, sample cases, briefcases, overnight bags, and lunch boxes.

- A loose coat can conceal items.

- A full skirt can conceal items. A proficient professional can "crotch-carry" as much as a twenty-five-pound ham or eight cartons of cigarettes.

- Rubber bands can be snapped around bundles of ties, stockings, or socks.

- Hats, gloves, scarves, coats, sweaters, and purses can be worn out of the store.

- Coats or sweaters may be thrown down over merchandise desired, and then picked up with the merchandise concealed inside.

- Jewelry and other accessories can be dropped into clothing or inserted into the hair.

- In fitting rooms, tight or closely fitting garments can be put on under street clothes.

- Packages and purses can be rearranged to conceal the addition of a dress or blouse.

- Shoplifters may cause intentional confusion with merchandise: handling so much clothing or so many products that sales personnel lose track, or an accomplice or other party might distract sales personnel.

- Also common is price switching: taking a price from one product with a higher price and relabeling it with a lower price label.

- Shoplifters may step around the end of the counter, using the excuse of wanting to see something, in order to steal expensive articles from the unlocked side of a showcase.

- Shoplifters may distract sales personnel with persistent bell ringing while an accomplice steals merchandise.

- Also common is removing small items from a display case and hiding them in another part of the store for later retrieval by an accomplice.

- A customer may enter a market with an empty paper bag in her purse, fill the bag with merchandise, and then exit through an unmanned checkout lane. If questioned, she assures the clerk that she has already checked out.

- Boxed items that are easily opened and reclosed may have more valuable items inside them.

- Supermarket shoplifters have been known to open an expensive package of tea and pour the contents into a pocketbook, where it settles at the bottom.

- A customer may place an item in her purse and at the checkout counter ask for credit, explaining that another member of the family bought the item by mistake. If the clerk refuses the refund because the shoplifter doesn't have a receipt, the shoplifter wins. The shoplifter, of course, also wins if the store grants the refund.

SOURCE: *Investigations Department Training Manual* (Encino, CA: Pinkerton Security and Investigation Services, 1990), pp. 131–135. Reprinted with permission of Pinkerton Investigative Services.

and know how such a person would act in every possible situation. If they are assuming the role of a person in a certain occupation, they must be thoroughly versed in that occupation. They must fit into the environment of the investigation. Speech, conversation, mannerisms, behavior, knowledge, attitude, opinions, interests, and clothing—all must match those of the undercover milieu. The ability to observe, remember, and make sound judgments is essential.

The most important consideration in selecting an undercover investigator is if the individual's true identity will not be recognized. In a small police

YOU ARE THERE!

Shoplifting and Employee Theft Hurt Retail Profits

- According to research, almost 43 percent of retail shrinkage is attributable to employee theft.

- It has been estimated that shoplifting is the single largest crime affecting U.S. retailers, with annual losses totaling over $2 billion.

- In 2000, it was estimated that fifty-four hundred persons are arrested or detained for shoplifting every day and up to sixty-nine million acts of shoplifting occur per year in the United States, most going undetected.

- Experts report that the costs of employee theft are business failures, lost jobs, lower tax revenues, and higher prices passed on to consumers.

- Most retail theft is established by audits rather than witnessed, so it is not always clear whether the theft is perpetrated by customers, staff, or suppliers.

- It has been estimated that a 2 to 3 percent loss of sales to shoplifting can amount to approximately a 25 percent of loss in profit. For some smaller businesses or those on otherwise tight margins, retail theft can not only affect productivity and competitiveness but actually threaten economic survival. This crime affects not only the businesses but also other consumers, who subsidize store losses by paying elevated prices.

- Methods of controlling retail theft range from relatively simple display practices, such as putting fewer items on display or placing stickers on packages, to sophisticated electronic surveillance mechanisms. Technology constantly allows new ways of tagging stock to inhibit retail theft.

SOURCES: C. W. Osborn, "Restructuring to Reduce Losses," *Security Management*, Dec. 1998, pp. 63–68; Michael C. Budden, *Preventing Shoplifting Without Being Sued* (Westport, CT: Quorum Books, 1999); Charles A. Sennewald, *Shoplifters v. Retailers: The Rights of Both* (New York: New Century Press, 2000); Diana Nelson and Santina Perrone, *Understanding and Controlling Retail Theft* (Woden Act: Australian Institute of Criminology, 2000).

YOU ARE THERE!

Civil Recovery Programs and Shoplifting

Many businesses use civil recovery programs to deal with shoplifters. The company instigates civil court proceedings against thieves to recover monetary damages. In civil recovery remedies, the store is a direct party to the action (as opposed to its role in the criminal justice process, where the public prosecutor is not required to consult the store in any plea bargaining processes) and thus can gain some control of the process to recover lost revenues and deter future theft. Forty-nine states have some version of civil recovery law. Most of these proceedings are pursued at the same time criminal hearings are being held and involve three stages after an incident in which someone is taken into the store's custody: the inquiry, the letter or demand stage, and the lawsuit. Civil recovery generally entitles the merchant to recover the value of damaged or unrecovered merchandise; the time and money spent in pursuing the property, including employee, security, and investigative costs; and any related expenses.

SOURCE: Audrey J. Aronsohn, "Teaching Criminals the Cost of Crime," *Security Management*, May 1999, pp. 63–68.

YOU ARE THERE!
Controlling Employee Theft

Employee theft cannot be eliminated, but it can be controlled by good management techniques and judicious, intelligent application of acceptable security procedures. Here are four ways for retailers to do this:

1. Honest people, for the most part, stay honest; dishonest people tend to stay dishonest. Employers should conduct complete background investigations including previous employment records and should carry out in-depth applicant interviews.

2. Employees should be made to feel that they are part of the firm and that their contributions are important to its future. Disgruntled and disaffected employees represent the greatest threat for theft and vandalism. Employers should also pay well. The most important control against employee theft is a good salary or wage. It will not stop the confirmed thief, but there is little doubt that more stealing goes on where employees are underpaid than where they are overpaid.

3. An unequivocal company policy or code of ethics should be impressed on all employees at an initial orientation. The policy must clearly indicate the ethical standards expected of the employees, as well as the consequences of violating those standards. The penalties must not be applied selectively, and the company must itself operate according to a high ethical standard.

4. Adequate security measures must be taken. The security measures range from sophisticated computer security systems to undercover investigations.

SOURCE: Mark Lipman and W. R. McGraw, "Employee Theft: A $40 Billion Industry," *The Annals*, July 1988, pp. 51–59.

---

department, it is very difficult to use an officer who has considerable experience in patrol or detective duties as an undercover officer because it is likely that that person would be recognized by the subjects of the investigation. In private investigations, it is very difficult to use experienced investigators in the same general geographic area where they have performed ordinary investigative duties.

Because of the inherent difficulties in using experienced—and thus possibly easily recognized—personnel in an undercover capacity, there is always a temptation to use newly appointed police officers or recently hired investigators for undercover assignments. Yet this practice can be extremely dangerous. If the investigator does not have the experience and personal characteristics necessary for undercover assignments, he is likely to be uncovered.

Instead of using newly assigned officers or newly hired investigators, consideration should be given to a temporary exchange of experienced officers or investigators from other jurisdictions.

The Michigan Department of State Police recognized the problem of the lack of experienced undercover officers in particular locales. In response, it established twenty-three multijurisdictional undercover drug teams that work throughout the state. These teams are staffed through the rotation of officers to and from their home departments. Each department prescribes a period of time for its officers to work on the team—usually from eighteen to thirty-six months. However, for purposes of stability, the team commander positions are long-term assignments. The rotation benefits the teams by reducing the potential for burnout and corruption, and also ensures the availability of new faces for undercover assignments.[28]

The Michigan Department of State Police also provides a formal training program for its undercover officers. New officers attend a one-week basic narcotics school that covers such topics as drug identification, preparation for undercover assignments (with a strong emphasis on officer safety), informants, tactical planning, stress management, and the law. The subjects are taught through a combination of lectures, hands-on exercises, and videotaped role-playing exercises.

YOU ARE THERE!
Electronic Article Surveillance and Ink Tags

Electronic article surveillance and ink tags are two modern, effective methods of reducing shoplifting and other retail crime.

Electronic article surveillance (EAS) is the term used to describe anti-shoplifting protection systems for both apparel and packaged products. They involve an electronically detectable element (tag) pinned onto a garment or affixed by means of an adhesive to an item. Transmitters and receivers are placed at store exits to detect the presence of the tags as shoppers leave the stores. At the point of purchase, these tags are either removed or rendered inoperative, so that the purchaser may exit the premises without setting off an alarm.

EAS is an option for retailers to prevent shoplifting and employee theft; the technology— how and when it is applied and what it can do for retailers—continues to evolve. The three main current types of EAS technology are radio frequency, acousto-magnetic, and radio frequency identification (RFID). An important issue with EAS is when the tags are attached to a product and by whom—the store itself or the manufacturer. The latter, called *source tagging*, has steadily gained momentum in the industry in recent years. With source tagging, merchandise is floor-ready and doesn't sit in a warehouse waiting to have a tag applied.

Ink tags are attached to apparel in the same way as the more familiar EAS tags, but with these, if tampered with, ink vials break and stain the garment. A warning to this effect is printed directly on the tag. A garment with an ink stain can be neither worn nor sold, so shoplifters cannot gain any benefit from stealing it. The ink tags now available are compact (little more than one inch in diameter), reusable, and can be removed easily by shop assistants with a special tool at the point of sale.

Numerous studies have reported reductions in crime or shrinkage after implementation of EAS and ink tag systems in particular stores.

SOURCES: Robert L. DiLonardo, "Defining and Measuring the Economic Benefit of Electronic Article Surveillance," *Security Journal*, 7(1), 1996, pp. 3–9; Ann Longmore-Etheridge, "The Evolution of EAS," *Security Management*, Dec. 1998, pp. 44, 48–50; Robert L. DiLonardo and R. V. Clarke, "Reducing the Rewards of Shoplifting: An Evaluation of Ink Tags," *Security Journal*, 7(1), 1996, pp. 11–14.

Four months after the basic school, the undercover team members attend a one-week advanced narcotics course. This follow-up program refines their investigative skills through tactical planning and team building. A realistic scenario serves as the vehicle to develop problem-solving skills. The officers participate in a four-day role-playing scenario that begins with the briefing of an informant and includes undercover contacts with suspects, actual surveillance in the community, intelligence gathering, drafting of search warrants, and identification of forfeitable assets. During the scenario, students interact with role players and others. The scenario ends with a mock trial.

The International Association of Undercover Officers is a professional society for people interested in undercover operations. It was established for the purpose of promoting safety and professionalism among undercover officers.

 INVESTIGATIONS ON THE NET

International Association of Undercover Officers
http://www.undercovercops.org

For an up-to-date list of Web links, go to
http://info.wadsworth.com/dempsey

Preparation for the Undercover Investigation

Extensive and detailed preparations are necessary before conducting an undercover investigation to ensure both the success of the investigation and the safety of the undercover officer.

YOU ARE THERE!
The Future of Retail Security

A recent study by loss prevention specialists on the future of retail security efforts during the first twenty years of the twenty-first century revealed the following:

- *Retail crime.* The most probable and significant crimes retailers will face over the next twenty years will be criminal exploitation of the new technology formats, including the Internet, that retailers use to sell merchandise. The second most probable and significant problem will continue to be employee theft. Shoplifting too will continue to be a problem.

- *Personnel programs.* The most probable and significant loss prevention tool in the future will be better employee selection techniques. The most significant program will be preemployment integrity screening.

- *Loss prevention operatives,* such as store detectives, will continue to be used but increased use of uniformed guards and off-duty law enforcement officers was rated least likely and least significant.

- *Transaction exception reporting.* This is likely to be the most important technology for retailers in the future. Retailers are also likely to depend on enhanced electronic article-asset surveillance systems such as electronic tags, merchandise alarms, and CCTV. There will also probably be moderate use of benefit denial devices, such as ink tags, mechanical clamps, and internal electronic switches.

SOURCE: Read Hayes, "An Inventory of What's in Store," *Security Management,* Apr. 2000, pp. 72–76.

YOU ARE THERE!
Racial Profiling and Store Security

A woman working in a branch of a national chain of retail children's clothing stores in Cambridge, Massachusetts, was told by her supervisors that in order to prevent theft, she should follow black customers as they browsed. The woman, who is white, complained to the Massachusetts Commission Against Discrimination and the state attorney general.

The attorney general's office sent black and white undercover "testers" to the stores and became convinced that there was a pattern of conduct of targeting people based on skin color. The store chain, in the face of a lawsuit, agreed to a settlement that required them to bring in anti-discrimination training, to spend $100,000 for an independent consultant to examine the companies policies with an eye to rooting out discrimination, and to donate $50,000 to a Boston group that helps children.

Over the years, some civil rights advocates have said that black people encounter discrimination when they are shopping. They call this phenomenon *retail racism,* a consumer version of *racial profiling,* where police officers focus on people of color for spot checks. A sprinkling of lawsuits have been brought by shoppers contending they were suspected of being shoplifters and subjected to humiliating searches purely because they are black. A major national toy store has been hit with a federal civil rights suit for rejecting personal checks in predominantly black sections of the Washington, D.C., area.

SOURCE: Carey Goldberg, "Accused of Discrimination, Clothing Chain Settles Case: Massachusetts Found 'Racial Retailing,' " *New York Times,* Dec. 22, 2000, p. A16.

YOU ARE THERE!
Academic Studies Aid Loss Prevention Personnel

There have been numerous academic studies that provide loss prevention personnel with information to help them design security programs to reduce shop lifting. Some of these are as follows:

- Professional shoplifters—those who steal to derive all or part of their income—are the minority of shoplifters, but they tend to steal more items and take items of greater value than do amateurs. The best strategies against these professional thieves are CCTV systems, EAS devices, displaying high-priced items inside a locked showcase or securing them to shelves with merchandise cables, and deploying many sales representatives and undercover agents on the sales floor.

- The best strategies to deter amateur shoplifters are the use of very visible CCTV cameras or very obvious EAS devices; overt security, including signs warning of the penalties for shoplifting; and notification of parents of teenagers who shoplift.

- A shoplifting prevention experiment conducted in Great Britain indicated that store redesign and electronic tagging were effective short-term solutions to the problem of shoplifting.

- A study of shoplifters in Stockholm, Sweden, revealed that males stole more electronic items and females stole more clothing, perfume, and cosmetics. However, the value of the goods stolen was about the same. The most common times for being caught were Monday to Thursday, as well as late afternoons. Most of the shoplifters were unemployed.

- A study on the effectiveness of increasing the frequency with which articles at great risk of theft are inventoried revealed a 100 percent reduction in shrinkage of the target articles and an 85 percent reduction in nontarget item shrinkage. In this study, employees knew about the increased inventory counts but shoppers did not, thus leading the researcher to assume that the reduction in shrinkage was due to deterrence of employee theft.

SOURCES: Read Hayes, "Tailoring Security to Fit the Criminal," *Security Management*, July 1999, pp. 110–116; D. P. Farrington, "Measuring, Explaining and Preventing Shoplifting: A Review of British Research," *Security Journal*, 12(1), 1999, pp. 9–27; E. Sarasalo, B. Bergman, and J. Toth, "Repetitive Shoplifting in Stockholm, Sweden," *Criminal Behavior and Mental Health*, 8(4), 1998, pp. 256–265; Barry Masuda, "Displacement vs. Diffusion of Benefits and the Reduction of Inventory Losses in a Retail Environment," *Security Journal*, 3, 1992, pp. 131–136.

Identification Undercover investigators should always have personal papers to document the role they are playing. A driver's license and credit cards in the name of the person the investigator is supposed to be are essential. If investigators are assuming certain occupational or professional credentials, they should have documentation—a union card, or a wallet-size professional license or diploma, for example.

Background Records If an investigator is assuming a role and identity that could be checked through the examination of public or private records, then those records need to be created and placed at the location that might be the subject of an inquiry, such as the personnel office of a corporation, or a public agency. Undercover investigators should have a complete background history prepared for them, including name, current and past addresses, and past working experience.

Cover Story A fictitious personal history—a cover story—should be prepared for the undercover investigator. Investigators should have a thorough knowledge of the contents of their assumed history, and documentation should exist to prove this personal history.

Getting In Only one or two people in an organization should know that an undercover investigator is joining the organization. The security director and the head of personnel, if not subjects in the investigation, should be notified; but it must be emphasized in the

YOU ARE THERE!
Legal Cases and the Shopkeeper's Privilege

Carcone v. Senpike Mall Co. (1993)

Three twelve-year-old boys were hanging around a shopping center's fence at the rear of the property, a location prone to vandalism. While attempting to detain one of the youths, a mall employee placed his hands on him. All three boys were put into a security vehicle, taken to the security office, questioned, photographed, and then released to their parents. The parents sued the mall for false arrest and battery. The court ruled that there was no probable cause that the boys had committed a crime, making the detention improper. There were no posted signs in the area where the boys were lingering that made doing so illegal. The other actions of security were considered unreasonable. The court also found that touching the one boy was a battery.

Gortanez v. Smitty's Super Valu (1984)

Two youths were falsely accused of stealing a fifty-nine-cent air freshener after paying for other merchandise in the store. An off-duty police officer working as a security officer apprehended the youths at their car. He frisked and yelled at one of the subjects but never told him what merchandise he was suspected of taking. The other youth intervened and was placed in a choke hold by the officer, which eventually necessitated medical treatment. The court noted that the possible theft of a fifty-nine-cent item did not warrant such aggressive treatment by security.

Brown v. Wal-Mart (1998)

A man was detained by store security after an undercover security officer saw him put something in his pocket. After a brief investigation by management it was determined that the item the man had placed in his pocket was a ring he had purchased in the store and did have a receipt for. The detention lasted about ninety seconds and management apologized for the delay. However, during the detention, another customer made derisive remarks to him and accused him of being a thief. The man claimed that he had been humiliated and sued the store for false imprisonment and infliction of emotional distress. The court rejected the suit and ruled that the store's detention was conducted in a reasonable manner, over a reasonable time, and on reasonable grounds.

SOURCE: Alan Kaminsky, "An Arresting Policy," *Security Management*, May 1999, pp. 59–61.

---

strongest manner possible that this information has to remain confidential.

Knowledge of Investigation Subjects Undercover officers must be thoroughly briefed on the subjects involved in the investigation. They should know in particular of the existence of possible dangers they could experience and how to avoid them.

Knowledge of Geographic Area Undercover investigators must have detailed knowledge of the geographic area of the investigation to ensure that they move about expeditiously and safely there. Furthermore, there is no better indication that a person may be an imposter than lack of knowledge about key buildings, highways, or other locations with which those who live in or frequent the area are familiar.

Tactics for the Undercover Investigation

There are numerous procedures or tactics that undercover officers must follow to ensure the success of the investigation and not compromise their assumed identity.

Be Prepared for Questions Undercover investigators must be prepared for the eventuality that someone might ask them if they are undercover operatives. They need to know how to say *no* in a convincing manner, such as appearing to be shocked by the question, or just playing dumb. Hesitating or seeming embarrassed could be seen as an admission.

Blend In Undercover investigators must blend into the operation and act as naturally as any new worker

An undercover officer must be adept at playing a role. Here, Detective J. G. Smith of the Indianapolis Police Department works undercover in Muncie, Indiana, infiltrating motorcycle gangs.

Undercover officers must blend into their environment. Here, New York City Detective Mary Glatzle waits for a mugger to attack. Glatzle earned such a reputation for her decoy work that she was dubbed "Muggable Mary."

An undercover agent poses as a street person.

or person would in the particular environment. They should get to know co-workers slowly; do their job effectively, but no better or worse than others; and most important, follow the habits of co-workers. Undercover investigators should not be aggressive and should not ask questions. Their job is to observe and report.

Go Slow Care must be taken to conduct the undercover investigation as slowly as necessary. Frequently, employees engaging in illegal conduct may be nervous and may suspect any new employee, especially a new employee who seems too eager to make friends or ask questions.

Get Out Before It Goes Down Generally, it is best to take the undercover investigator out of the operation before the arrest or exposure of the subject so that it doesn't seem that he or she had anything to do with it. Generally, if the operation has been successful in obtaining information, the security department can obtain or develop evidence to arrest the subject or bring the subject's actions to light without involving the undercover investigator.

What Not to Do Authors Wayne W. Bennett and Karen M. Hess warn undercover investigators not to write any investigatory notes that the subject may discover and read, not to carry any identification other than the cover ID, not to communicate overtly with headquarters, and not to suggest, plan, initiate, or participate in criminal activity.[29] They offer the following checklist for the planning of an undercover assignment:

- Is there any alternative to undercover work?
- What information is needed from the assignment?
- Is adequate information about the subject available?
- Have you established a good cover?
- How will you communicate with headquarters?
- What will you do if you are arrested?
- Do you have an alternative plan if the initial plan fails?
- Do you have a plausible reason for leaving once the assignment is completed?

ADVICE FROM EXPERTS

FBI Special agent Joseph D. Pistone offers agents the following suggestions on tactics to use when operating in an undercover fashion:

First, keep your fabricated past simple and as close to the truth as possible. Construct a criminal past that allows you to work alone and without violence.

Second, do not indicate that you have a great deal of money; that leads people to believe that you are a cop or a person who can be conned out of his or her money.

Never keep notes or anything that could expose your identity. You can never know when you will be searched.

Try for acceptance in the target group without drawing attention. Do not be pushy. Use brief introductions, short conversations, appearances in one place or another, or hints that show you know your way around. Try to leave a trail of credibility, but build slowly. The quickest way to be identified as a law enforcement officer is to move too fast. You have to play by the rules of the street, to show that you have the time. Let the target check you out and come to you.

Continue to be your own person and keep your personality intact. Some undercover agents think they must drink heavily or take drugs to blend in or demonstrate their toughness, but that is a serious mistake. If you compromise your own standards and personality, smart criminals see right through the facade. An undercover agent must realize that at some point down the line he or she will have to testify in court about his or her activities. If the undercover officer took drugs or engaged in any serious wrongdoing, his or her credibility will be seriously questioned, and the effectiveness of the testimony greatly diminished.

Not every law enforcement officer has the capacity to work undercover. New police officers or criminal investigators are not generally hired with undercover work in mind. Instead, they are selected and trained to perform overt police duties. Undercover assignments require a strong, disciplined personality, capable of working alone without backup.

While you are pretending to be somebody else, you will encounter the same personality conflicts you would find anywhere. There will be people you will like and people you will not. You must override your natural inclinations for association and learn to cultivate whoever can help your investigation. You must learn to swallow your gripes and control your temper.

Finally, undercover agents must make difficult decisions on their own, often right on the spot. You must accept the consequences of being wrong and making mistakes, because you will have nobody to hide behind on the street. You must be street-smart, disciplined to work, and willing to take the initiative.[30]

Professor James J. Ness of Southern Illinois University, who worked as an undercover police officer in Cairo, Illinois, makes the following recommendations:[31]

- One officer is not enough. A person working alone is isolated, and the tendency for corruption is much greater.
- The primary factor in an undercover investigation is the safety of the individual conducting it.
- Undercover operations are not cost-effective. They require a great deal of time and money to begin and shouldn't be attempted on a part-time basis or without adequate support.
- Agents should never go into a situation cold. There should be goals set for any operation and a basis of sound, reliable information. Secrecy is a must.
- Training is essential.
- Operations should be closely monitored by superiors and mechanisms should be available to help agents deal with stress.
- It is important to know when to end an operation. When it is not producing the anticipated results, it should be terminated.

COMMUNICATING WITH SUPERVISORS

It is essential that undercover investigators have a **contact** they can immediately call or see at any hour of the day or night. Without this contact, investigators may find themselves out in the cold with no assistance.

Telephone conversations with the contact should take place far from the undercover operation to ensure that the call is not being recorded or otherwise overheard. Investigators should make no calls from their home, for the phone may be tapped.

It is best to make any telephone calls to the contact from pay telephones far away from the operation or site of the investigation or from cell phones. The investigator should continually change the location of the telephone from which the calls are made to avoid setting a pattern. Telephone calling cards should not

YOU ARE THERE!

An Ex-Cop, Now Professor, Goes Undercover

James J. Ness has been in policing for twenty-seven years, working in patrol, plainclothes, and investigations in several different police agencies. After completing his master's degree at Southern Illinois University-Carbondale, he remained at the university as director of the *Police Executive Study,* which was funded by the Law Enforcement Assistance Administration (LEAA). Later, he assumed the position of chief of police in a rural Illinois town. In 1983, he joined the faculty of Southern Illinois University-Carbondale. While a professor there, he also worked part-time as an officer in a small rural town. In 1984, he was hired by the director of the Southern Illinois Enforcement Group to conduct undercover investigative work for a local police agency. Ness discusses some crucial aspects of his work in undercover investigation.

- *Preparing the cover.* I had to establish an identity. With the help of police agencies, I was fitted with real IDs in the name of James Nolan—a real traffic citation, a real driver's license, prescriptions, and so on. When my wife, Ellyn, joined me in the operation, she too developed a bogus identity. I was given a set of Indiana license plates registered to a dummy address and a gas credit card issued to a dummy corporation.

- *Notes and records.* The paperwork associated with undercover assignments is demanding; it requires detailed information so that logical conclusions can be drawn. One of the hardest parts of undercover work is remembering the details of events. Agents can't carry notebooks with them or keep running out to their cars to jot down information. In addition, all money spent must be accounted for. All food and drink, gas, motel, and any other expenses require receipts. It can be very difficult to keep personal money and department money separated.

- *Personal toll.* At times throughout the experience, Ellyn and I wondered who we really were and what we were doing. We were befriending people we might be arresting someday. They had families, dreams, and needs just like the rest of us, but sometimes they crossed the line between right and wrong. Undercover work is not the glamorized and sensationalized experience it appears to be in TV series. In reality, the hours are long and at times very boring. One can only frequent so many bars in an evening with great enthusiasm. We were certainly always on the edge, worried that someone might find out who we were or that we might not be able to handle the situation, but the excitement was not of the TV type.

SOURCE: James J. Ness and Ellyn K. Ness, "Reflections on Undercover Street Experiences," in James N. Gilbert, ed., *Criminal Investigation: Essays and Cases* (Columbus, OH: Merrill Publishing, 1990), pp. 105–111. Adapted and reprinted with permission of the authors.

---

be used because they leave a paper trail that suspicious subjects can study.

In addition, undercover investigators must be very careful with written reports or communications. In a sensitive case there should be several **mail drops** to which they can send correspondence and from which they can receive correspondence.

Personal meetings between undercover investigators and their contact should also be considered extremely dangerous. Precautions must be taken to ensure that these meetings are not observed.

It is advisable for the undercover investigator to have an associate in the operation who can facilitate communications and secure help in the event of an emergency.

RECORDING THE UNDERCOVER INVESTIGATION

As in all types of investigating, record keeping and reporting are essential in undercover investigations. Collecting facts and detailed information is essential so that logical conclusions can be drawn. While assigned to the undercover investigation, investigators

GUEST LECTURE
Professor David Owens, Lieutenant, Retired, Syracuse, New York, Police Department

On Life as an Undercover

During the early 1970s, I could think of nothing more exciting than to be transferred from my uniform patrol assignment to the Organized Crime Division of the Syracuse Police Department (later renamed the Special Investigations Division). That was where a young police officer could leave the routine duties of investigating auto accidents, missing persons, domestic disputes, and minor thefts for the challenging work of apprehending bookmakers, pimps, prostitutes, porn merchants, and drug dealers.

At the time, Syracuse had an organized group of criminals running a variety of large-stakes gambling operations throughout the area. There was also nightly activity involving pimps and their prostitutes who worked the bars and street corners of the central business district. Heroin was very popular in the poor neighborhoods and the city high schools. As a college town, Syracuse was also a place where there was constant demand for marijuana, hallucinogens, and any other drug that would appeal to the Woodstock Generation.

In short, it was an exciting time to be involved in proactive plainclothes police work. So in 1972 I traded my blue uniform and large revolver for blue jeans, a leather jacket, a snub-nosed pistol, and a shoulder holster. Instead of a black-and-white squad car, I was given a desk and a typewriter and told to share a four-door sedan with about eight other investigators. I quickly learned that most of my fellow officers chose to drive their personal cars with the promise of twenty gallons of free gasoline each week. Those were the good old days.

Almost fifteen years later and after many different assignments, I returned to the Special Investigations Division as commanding officer. I had witnessed many changes in my job during those years. Although young investigators still wore blue jeans and leather jackets, they were now armed with high-powered semiautomatic pistols. And because of liability issues, they no longer drove their personal vehicles on the job. Instead, they were assigned well-equipped department-issued "concealed identity" cars and trucks.

During my twenty-year career with the Syracuse Police Department I rotated through Special Investigations twice as an investigator and, as I said, finally as its boss. When the public envisions the undercover officer they perceive the deep-cover, covert operative who leaves home and exists in the underworld totally cut off from family and friends. A good example of this is the legendary FBI agent Donnie Brasco. What the public and even a lot of police officers don't realize is that most undercover investigators have a variety of experiences. Mine, for example, consisted of many short-term undercover assignments where I would frequent neighborhood bars in search of the local bookmaker or prostitute. In the latter case, should I be solicited for sex for a fee, the suspect, usually a woman, would immediately be arrested. If lucky, I'd have the paperwork done soon enough to end my shift and be home in time for dinner. In the case of the former, if I was successful in placing wagers with the bookmaker, I'd string the case along for a few months while I continued to put other suspects down and try to work my way up the organized crime ladder in search of the boss who ran the operation. This strategy would frequently lead to the use of wiretaps and the eventual arrest of as many as fifty to a hundred defendants.

We did a lot of unglamorous work in the Special Investigations Division. Much of my time was spent on long and lonely surveillances. Good surveillance work is critical in proactive investigations, whether it means doing the tedious backup of a narcotics officer who is making a buy or the vice detective who is trying to build a case against a prostitute. However, one never knows when boredom will suddenly change to danger and violence. I've seen many officers seriously injured while investigating narcotics and prostitution cases. One time, while trying to handcuff a prostitute, I was clawed by the woman, who dug her long and dirty fingernails into my face. We had undercover officers beaten and seriously injured by suspects with weapons ranging from meat cleavers to hammers. In all of these incidents, help in the form of backup investigators was close at hand and arrests quickly made.

In vice and narcotics investigations, the real danger for the undercover officer comes from the fact that

On Life as an Undercover continued

if he or she is effective in a deception, the criminal may try to cause injury, not knowing that the agent is a law enforcement officer. At times the undercover operative may be required to flash large amounts of money, and no matter how close the backup is, the operative is at high risk of being robbed, injured, or even murdered. Yes, this can be a very dangerous assignment. You must think carefully about all aspects of working undercover before you commit yourself to this sort of life.

The good news is that most officers do not experience that level of violence. What most of us dealt with were the high levels of stress that comes with being a proactive agent. The officer needs to be aware of this point and make plans to cope with negative energy while playing the role. Whether or not you are in a deep-cover mode or engaged in surveillance work, your hours are never fixed. I missed holiday celebrations, birthdays, and a few school plays because of the unpredictable nature of the job. Another problem area is that you are almost constantly engaged in deceptive covert tactics. In other

words, you are living a lie! This can have serious negative impact on one's health, and family life. You will spend months making buys, meeting with informants, doing endless paperwork, and tedious surveillance in dirty and uncomfortable environments only to see your gambling or narcotics cases dismissed or settled with a small fine. These frequent disappointments can sometimes get you down.

In retrospect, I have asked myself many times if my undercover career was worth it. The answer is always a resounding *yes*. I learned more about the criminal element and human nature during those years than in any other assignment. It is important that the potential agent be the sort of person who is independent and can work with a minimum of supervision. However, you must also be able to maintain a strong sense of right from wrong. For, in the work of the undercover officer, it is easy to allow the underworld to rub off on you. Should you ever find yourself involved in an undercover assignment, it will be up to you not to let that happen. The consequences of such poor judgment could ruin your life.

cannot record notes or jot down information. They cannot continually run into a bathroom or other private area to write down facts, names, phone numbers, addresses, and so on. Instead, they must memorize certain data until they have the opportunity to write it down.

Also, business receipts must be obtained and there must be an accounting for all money spent. In some operations officers will be expected to spend their own money and then receive compensation from the employer or police agency. In other operations they are given a certain amount of funds to spend. In both cases, employers and supervisors expect them to account for any funds used or requested.

DANGER IN THE UNDERCOVER INVESTIGATION, AND ILLEGAL ACTIVITY

Obviously, undercover investigations can be very dangerous to investigators if their cover is blown. Careful attention to the details, including the suggestions

made in this chapter, will reduce the potential dangers. Furthermore, investigators should take no chances with their safety. If they have any doubt whatsoever about the integrity of their cover, they should immediately abort the mission and notify their contact from a safe location. No investigation is as important as the safety of the investigator.

Undercover investigators, even those directly involved in investigating illegal drug use, should never engage in illegal activity. Using drugs can affect their reasoning ability, conduct, and powers of observation. It can cause them to say things that they shouldn't and can compromise their testimony in court.

Of course, they must have a cover story in the event that they are offered drugs. Several good stories are these: "I'm on probation, dude. No way, they test me every week. Ain't going behind bars again for nothing." "I can't do substances, man. I'm in AA, it's my last shot. If I screw up this time, my wife is leaving me. Can't take the chance."

Undercover investigators must not only avoid engaging in illegal conduct but also avoid any conduct that might compromise their status. As one private investigator who hires undercover investigators says: "The problem with letting go, with getting drunk, is the operative is likely to make a mistake. This whole undercover business involves walking a line that is so thin between who you are, and who you are supposed to be, that the longer you walk it, the easier it is to fall off."[32]

ENTRAPMENT

Often people believe that undercover operations by the police amount to **entrapment.** What is entrapment? Entrapment is defined as inducing an individual to commit a crime that he or she did not contemplate for the sole purpose of instituting a criminal prosecution against the offender.[33] Entrapment is a defense to criminal responsibility that arises from improper acts committed against an accused by another, usually an undercover agent. *Inducement* is the key word; when police play on the weaknesses of innocent persons and beguile them into committing crimes they normally would not attempt, it can be deemed entrapment and the evidence barred under the exclusionary rule.

However, the police, by merely giving a person the opportunity to commit a crime, are not guilty of entrapment. For example, an undercover officer sitting on the

---

YOU ARE THERE!

Jacobson v. United States

In February 1984, a fifty-six-year-old Nebraska farmer (hereinafter "the defendant"), with no record or reputation for violating any law, lawfully ordered and received from an adult bookstore two magazines that contained photographs of nude teenage boys. Subsequent to this, Congress passed the Child Protection Act of 1984, which made it illegal to receive such material through the mail. Later that year, the U.S. Postal Service obtained the defendant's name from a mailing list seized at the adult bookstore, and in January 1985 began an undercover operation targeting him.

Over the next two and a half years, government investigators, through five fictitious organizations and a bogus pen pal, repeatedly contacted the defendant by mail, exploring his attitude toward child pornography. The communications also contained disparaging remarks about the legitimacy and constitutionality of efforts to restrict the availability of sexually explicit material, and finally, offered the defendant the opportunity to order illegal child pornography.

Twenty-six months after the mailings to the defendant commenced, government investigators sent him a brochure advertising photographs of young boys engaging in sex. At this time, the defendant placed an order that was never filled.

Meanwhile, the investigators attempted to further pique the defendant's interest through a fictitious letter decrying censorship and suggesting a method of getting material to him without the "prying eyes of U.S.

Customs." A catalogue was then sent him, and he ordered a magazine containing child pornography.

After a controlled delivery of a photocopy of the magazine, the defendant was arrested. A search of his home revealed only the material he received from the government and the two sexually oriented magazines he had lawfully acquired in 1984.

The defendant was charged with receiving child pornography through the mail in violation of 18 U.S.C. 2252(a)(2)(A). He defended himself by claiming that the government's conduct was outrageous, that the government needed reasonable suspicion before it could legally begin an investigation of him, and that he had been entrapped by the government's investigative techniques. The lower federal courts rejected these defenses, but in a five to four decision the Supreme Court reversed his conviction based solely on the entrapment claim.

In *Jacobson*, the Supreme Court held that law enforcement officers "may not originate a criminal design, implant in an innocent person's mind the disposition to commit a criminal act, and then induce commission of the crime so that the Government may prosecute."

SOURCES: *Jacobson v. United States*, 112 S.Ct. 1535 (1992), and Thomas V. Kukura, J.D., "Undercover Investigations and the Entrapment Defense: Recent Court Cases," *FBI Law Enforcement Bulletin*, Apr. 1993, pp. 27–32.

sidewalk, apparently drunk, with a $10 bill sticking out of his pocket is not forcing a person to take the money even though he is giving a person the opportunity to do so. If a person takes advantage of the apparent drunk and takes the money, he is committing a larceny. The entrapment defense is not applicable in this situation. However, when the police action is outrageous and forces an otherwise innocent person to commit a crime, the entrapment defense may apply.

In *Jacobson v. United States* (1992), the Supreme Court ruled that the government's action of repeatedly, for two and a half years, sending a man advertising material of a sexual nature that eventually resulted in his ordering an illegal pornographic magazine constituted entrapment. It ruled that law enforcement officers "may not originate a criminal design, implant in an innocent person's mind the disposition to commit a criminal act, and then induce commission of the crime so that the government may prosecute."[34]

Thomas V. Kukura, in an article about this case in the *FBI Law Enforcement Bulletin*, makes the following recommendations:

> To ensure that undercover investigations do not give rise to successful claims of entrapment or related

defenses, all law enforcement officers should consider the following three points before conducting undercover investigations. First, while reasonable suspicion is not legally necessary to initiate an undercover investigation, officers should nonetheless be prepared to articulate a legitimate law enforcement purpose for beginning such an investigation. Second, law enforcement officers should, to the extent possible, avoid using persistent or coercive techniques, and instead merely create an opportunity or provide the facilities for the target to commit a crime. Third, officers should document and be prepared to articulate the factors demonstrating a defendant was disposed to commit the criminal act prior to government contact.

Such factors include a prior arrest record, evidence of prior criminal activity, a defendant's familiarity with the terminology surrounding a particular criminal venture, and a defendant's eagerness to engage in the criminal activity. The most convincing evidence of predisposition will typically occur during the initial government contacts, which officers should carefully document to successfully defeat the entrapment defense.[35]

SUMMARY

This chapter covered the art and techniques of surveillance and undercover work in investigations. Surveillances and undercover operations are not the simple, exciting exploits portrayed in the movies and on television. Generally, they are boring and can be very dangerous. They also may cause serious emotional problems for those engaged in them.

Students are urged to read this chapter carefully, as well as the other chapters that refer to surveillance and undercover techniques, before actually embarking on a career in such areas. They should consult with relatives and friends who may be involved in these careers. Those who want the excitement and glamour of surveillance and undercover operations as depicted on television and in the movies, but without the possibility of physical and emotional danger, should focus their goals on acting careers instead—usually, no one really gets hurt in those shows.

LEARNING CHECK

1. What is the primary reason for investigators to conduct a surveillance?
2. What are some of the most important preparations a surveillant should make prior to a surveillance?
3. Describe the best techniques for a surveillant to use when conducting a surveillance of a moving vehicle.
4. Name and describe at least three types of undercover investigations.

5. During an undercover investigation, the investigator is approached by subjects of the investigation who offer him drugs. What should the investigator do? Why?

APPLICATION EXERCISES **1.** Test your ability to do a foot surveillance. Team up with a friend and plan the surveillance. Your friend will be the subject; you will be the surveillant. You may even form a surveillance team of three or four friends. The rules are simple: (a) The subject starts from a prearranged location at 1300 hours (that is, one o'clock in the afternoon), or another starting time. (b) The surveillant or surveillance team is free to follow the subject and use any techniques appropriate to conduct the surveillance. (c) If the subject spots the surveillant or member of the surveillance team at any time, that surveillant must drop out of the surveillance. When all members are spotted, the surveillance is over.

Members of the exercise team will reassemble at a prearranged location and debrief the operation.

2. As a narcotics investigator for the Problem County sheriff's office, you are assigned to conduct a monthlong undercover investigation of Problem County Community College, which has been experiencing drug sales and drug use on campus. You have been selected because of your youthful appearance. Your mission is to develop information on dealers and make undercover buys. At the completion of your investigation, arrest warrants will be obtained that will be executed by uniformed deputy sheriffs. Your contact at the college is the director of security, a former Problem County deputy sheriff.

Based on your reading of this chapter, discuss the preparations you will make to ensure the success of this operation and protect your undercover status.

WEB EXERCISE   Use the Internet to research the federal laws on electronic surveillance, as well as similar laws in your own state. Compare and contrast these laws and prepare a brief report to your professor on your research.

KEY TERMS

blend	mystery shoppers
bugs	rough tail
burned	shadow
close tail	shopping services
contact	shrinkage
cover story	store detective
entrapment	subject
ex parte order	surveillance
integrity shoppers	surveillant
loose tail	tight tail
loss prevention specialist	wiretaps
mail drop	

THE INVESTIGATION OF VIOLENT CRIMES

10

CHAPTER GOALS

1. To give you a sense of the violent crime situation in the United States, including murder, rape or sexual assault, robbery, aggravated assault, and kidnapping

2. To acquaint you with the methods police use to conduct murder, rape or sexual assault, robbery, aggravated assault, and kidnapping investigations

3. To introduce you to the methods used by medicolegal investigators to conduct death investigations

4. To familiarize you with the proactive techniques used by the police to deal with the crime of robbery

5. To discuss some special issues in violent crime, such as the use of DNA in solving murder, rape, or sexual assault cases; workplace violence; domestic violence; and criminal personality profiling

INTRODUCTION

In the year 2000, in Florida, a fourteen-year-old youth, angry at his teacher because he wouldn't let him talk to two girls, fired one bullet into the teacher's head, killing him. The police arrested the youth moments later.

That same year, two men walked into a Wendy's restaurant at closing time. They accosted the manager and forced him to take his six employees to a large freezer box in the store's basement. They then bound and gagged all seven employees with duct tape, blindfolded them, covered their heads with plastic bags, and shot them one by one. They left five dead and two others for dead. The motive for the murders was robbery. Police arrested the shooters several days later.

On the day after Christmas 2000, a man walked into the Internet consulting company in Wakefield, Massachusetts, where he worked, and murdered seven co-workers for no apparent reason other than that his pay had been garnished by the IRS to pay back taxes he owed. Police arrested the man a short time later.

In May 2001, two men walked into an apartment above the famed Carnegie Deli in Manhattan and shot five people, three of them fatally, in a robbery to steal marijuana. The police arrested one of the shooters the next day and the other one several months later based on a tip provided by a viewer to the television show *America's Most Wanted,* which had reported on the case the previous evening.

These acts of extreme violence seem very familiar to those of us who read the daily newspapers and watch the nightly news. They occur in large and small cities, as well as suburban areas and rural areas all over the United States. Law enforcement is able to identify and arrest most of the perpetrators of these crimes. In addition to these crimes of murder, police also confront myriad cases of rape or sexual assault, robbery, aggravated assault, and kidnapping.

What are the techniques that law enforcement uses to investigate and clear and solve these crimes? This chapter will discuss the investigation of violent crimes, including murder, rape or sexual assault, robbery, aggravated assault, and kidnapping. It will also discuss the identification procedures used by law enforcement to help victims identify suspects, including eyewitness identification, lineups, showups, and photo arrays. It will cover some special issues in the investigation of violent crimes, including the use of DNA in solving murder and rape or sexual assault cases, workplace violence, domestic violence, and criminal personality profiling.

In keeping with the intent of this book to provide more "what's it all about" information than "how to" information, much of the material on methods of investigation presented here is quite general. For more specific methods for each crime, I urge students to research the scholarly and professional sources noted here, paying special attention to information offered by the professional associations that have a presence on the Internet. Most importantly, I urge students to interact closely with those true experts, both academic and professional, who have done or are doing the real work of investigating and to listen to their advice and learn from their experience. A textbook can never replace the real lessons one can learn from these true experts.

VIOLENT CRIMES

According to the most recent *Uniform Crime Reports,* published by the FBI, there were 1,431,703 crimes of violence reported in the United States in the latest reporting year. There were 15,533 murders, 89,107 forcible rapes or sexual assaults, 409,670 robberies, and 916,383 aggravated assaults. The clearance rates for these crimes were 69 percent for murder, 49 percent for rape or sexual assault, 29 percent for robbery, and 59 percent for aggravated assault.[1]

The following sections will cover the techniques and procedures used by the police to investigate and clear these crimes.

HOMICIDE INVESTIGATIONS

Homicide is the killing of one human being by another. Unjustified, unexcused killings are *criminal homicides.* Generically, criminal homicide can be subdivided into three categories; **murder, manslaughter,** and *criminally negligent homicide.* Illegal killings are usually called murder when they are premeditated, deliberate, intentional, and malicious. Voluntary manslaughter is an intentional killing but without malice, such as in the heat of passion, and involuntary manslaughter is when a person causes the death of another unintentionally

YOU ARE THERE!
Massacre at Wendy's

On May 24, 2000, John B. Taylor, age twenty-six, a former employee, and Craig Godineaux, age thirty, entered the Wendy's restaurant on Main Street in Flushing, New York, at closing time. When they left, $2,000 in cash went with them, and seven employees had been shot. Five died; two others were left for dead.

Upon entry into the restaurant, Taylor accosted the manager and forced him to bring his six employees to a large freezer box in the store's basement. He and Godineaux then bound and gagged all seven employees with duct tape, blindfolded them, covered their heads with plastic bags, and shot them one by one.

The New York City police arrested Taylor and Godineaux forty-eight hours later. There were three witnesses, including one of the employees who had been shot and played dead. Upon his arrest, the murder weapon was found in Taylor's possession, as well as a videotape from a Wendy's surveillance camera showing the activities of Taylor and the employees before going down into the basement.

Taylor, out on parole, had tried to rob five other fast food restaurants in 1999 and was wanted on a warrant since November 1999 for jumping bail. He had worked at that particular restaurant a year earlier. Godineaux had served three prison terms in the 1990s for robbery and drug offenses and had worked as a security guard in a clothing store.

On May 28, four days after the crime, two men robbed an electronics store across the street from Wendy's. They went into the back room where two managers were counting money, bound them with duct tape, and took about $20,000.

Merchants, residents, and shoppers on Main Street were terrified.

SOURCES: Robert D. McFadden, "Two Charged in Wendy's Case as Confession Details Emerge," *New York Times*, May 29, 2000, p. B1; "Near Massacre Site, Another Robbery," *New York Times*, May 29, 2000, p. B3.

but recklessly by consciously taking a grave risk. Criminally negligent murder is similar to manslaughter but involves a lesser culpable state, criminal negligence.

Methods of Investigation

Several methods of investigation are used in murder cases, including response to the scene, crime scene processing, analysis, and reconstruction, interviews and interrogations, record checks, identification procedures, theory formation, apprehension of perpetrator, and preparation for trial with prosecutors.

Response to the Scene   Generally, the police respond to a homicide scene when a person calls 911 and reports finding a dead body or other suspicious activity that could indicate violence. When the police find a dead body they establish a crime scene and comply with the crime scene procedures discussed at length in chapter 3 of this text. They rope off the crime scene to prevent the entry of unauthorized persons and the destruction of physical evidence. Then police investiga-

tors respond and interview witnesses or interrogate possible suspects. They also conduct canvasses to seek and interview any possible witnesses to the crime.

Crime Scene Processing, Analysis, and Reconstruction   As indicated in chapter 3, the police take photos and make sketches of the crime scene, including the dead body. They collect the physical evidence that might be used to identify the victim and the perpetrator and determine the cause and method of death. In large police departments, the task of evidence collection usually falls to a specialized crime scene or forensic unit.

After the crime scene is processed, the body is removed to the local medical examiner's or forensic pathologist's morgue for the purpose of conducting a postmortem—an autopsy—to determine cause of death. In many police jurisdictions a homicide is only closed with the arrest of the perpetrator. The physical evidence from the crime scene is taken to the crime lab, where it undergoes sophisticated criminalistic examination.

YOU ARE THERE!

Murder Above the Carnegie Deli: *America's Most Wanted* Helps to Catch One of the Suspects

In May 2001, two men walked into a sixth floor apartment above the famed Carnegie Deli in New York City with the intent to rob Jennifer Stahl, thirty-nine, a former actress who used the apartment to deal high-grade marijuana. As one of the men confronted Stahl, the other began tying up four friends who were visiting her. Although they offered no resistance, Stahl and the four others were shot in the head execution-style, three of them fatally.

Shortly after the shootings, the police released a surveillance film from a security camera in the hallway of Stahl's building. Within days, acquaintances identified the two men as Joseph Sean Salley, age thirty-nine, and Andre S. Smith, age thirty-one.

Smith was arrested twelve days after the crime, after turning himself into police.

The second suspect, Salley, was arrested on July 15, 2001, after the authorities tracked him to a homeless shelter in Miami based on calls to the *America's Most Wanted* television program. Investigation revealed that after the May shooting, Salley traveled south through Virginia, Georgia, Louisiana, and finally Florida. While on the run he had money wired to him,

retrieving cash in New Orleans just steps ahead of detectives.

America's Most Wanted had broadcast two earlier segments about the case on May 19 and May 26. They yielded a few tips but nothing concrete. On July 14, a third segment was shown, and a woman called the telephone tip line to say she thought Salley was one of a group from the shelter doing work on her house. Also, a supervisor at the shelter called the tip line and reported Salley was a resident there.

Investigators believe Salley and Smith immediately fled to New Jersey after the crime, where they divided the cash stolen in the robbery: $1,000. They also divided up twelve quarter-ounce bags of marijuana stolen from Stahl's apartment. Police had previously sent detectives to Mississippi, Texas, Georgia, and Louisiana looking for Salley. NYPD cops who were in New Orleans drove to Miami just after the tip came in to pick him up.

SOURCE: Daniel J. Wakin and Richard Lezin Jones, "Suspect Held in Three Killings Above Deli: Recognized from TV, Man Is Caught in Florida," *New York Times*, July 16, 2001, pp. B1.

The investigators then engage in crime scene analysis and reconstruction, which includes the examination of physical evidence, photos, sketches, and statements and interviews of the responding officers, responding medical personnel, and witnesses. It also includes interrogations of suspects, examination of **medical examiner** or **coroner,** or other forensic specialists, reports, and any other available information in order to determine what actually occurred at the scene. Crime scene analysis and reconstruction is basically the use of all the available evidence to turn back time to try to reconstruct the occurrences prior to and during the crime. It is similar to going to the instant replay camera, but without the benefit of that device.

A key element of the crime scene analysis and reconstruction is the attempt to establish a **time line.**

This means trying to account for all the activities and whereabouts of the principals in the case during the time surrounding the murder, including the victim, suspects, witnesses, and other persons connected to the crime. A very important item in the time line is the time-of-death estimate. Interviews, interrogations, observations, medical testimony, and other information are used to help develop the time line. The time line can help establish one of the three elements the investigator looks at when trying to determine the identity of the perpetrator: opportunity. By creating the time line, the investigator can attempt to determine if the suspect could have committed the crime during the time frame in which it occurred. Recall that in the O. J. Simpson murder case (details were covered in chapter 5 of this text), the time line was an essential element in the trial. Could the suspect, Simpson, have gone to the

YOU ARE THERE!
Violence in the United States

Imagine that you are sitting on a plane headed to Las Vegas for a fun vacation. Just as you get buckled up to await takeoff, you hear screaming and yelling. People start rushing off the plane, and you see a little girl being trampled in the aisle during the rush. You try to retrieve some of your things from your seat, but someone yells to you, "Get off the plane! Your life is more important than your stuff!" As you exit the plane, you find out that a man armed with a handgun had run past security and onto your plane and entered the cockpit and took the pilot and copilot hostage, demanding to be taken to Antarctica, where he had to destroy an alien military base.

This is a true story. On July 27, 2000, a mentally disturbed man armed with a 10 millimeter automatic pistol ran past the metal detectors at Gate 33 at JFK International Airport, dashed onto an elevated jetway, and boarded a National Airlines Boeing 757 set to fly

to Las Vegas. He then took the pilot and copilot hostage. Police responded in approximately three minutes, and heavily armed officers from a special unit boarded the plane and helped the last of the 143 passengers to escape—many by sliding down an inflatable chute in the rear of the plane, which had been opened earlier by a quick-thinking flight attendant. For approximately three hours police engaged in hostage negotiations with the disturbed gunman, who first demanded that the pilot take him to Miami. He later changed his mind and demanded to be taken to Buenos Aires, and last, to Antarctica. Finally, the man surrendered to the police.

SOURCES: John Sullivan and Randy Kennedy, "Armed Intruder Exposes Limits of Air Security," *New York Times*, July 29, 2000, p. A1; and Michael Cooper, "Man Charged in Hostage-Taking on Plane," *New York Times*, July 29, 2000, p. B6.

---

crime scene and committed the murders during the time from when he was last seen before the murder and the time he was next seen after the murder? The prosecution insisted that Simpson fit into the time line. The defense insisted that he could not.

Traditional time line analysis can now be automated on computers, according to an article by Craig W. Meyer and Gary M. Morgan in the *FBI Law Enforcement Bulletin*. Time line analysis can help law enforcement investigators record and analyze large amounts of data, prepare for witness interviews, and write affidavits; it can also facilitate the assimilation of large volumes of information gathered from such investigative techniques as search warrants, record reviews, and wiretaps. Time lines can help during interrogations by providing investigators with succinct information that may aid in accusing subjects and help redirect protests made by subjects concerning their guilt. In addition, time lines give investigators a tool for presenting their case to others, including managers, prosecutors, and jurors. Various spreadsheet programs are available to help investigators construct, consolidate, and link time lines effectively.[2]

Interviews and Interrogations Interviews and often interrogations are extremely important in murder investigations. Recall that interviews and interrogations were covered at length in chapter 7 of this text.

The interviews start immediately at the crime scene when the investigator interviews the first responding officers, medical personnel, and any witnesses present, and begins the canvassing process. During the canvassing process, the investigator seeks to interview all people who could have possibly witnessed the crime or events leading to the crime or occurring after it. Canvasses are essential—investigators must canvass, recanvass, walk the streets, burn the shoe leather, interview again and again, and then go back and canvass and interview some more. This is where they will get the essential information.

Interviews must be conducted with all family members, relatives, friends, acquaintances, co-workers, and anyone else who may know or have known the victim. Anyone calling with information must be interviewed on the phone immediately and then interviewed in person. All of these persons should be interviewed again as circumstances warrant.

Homicide is the killing of one human being by another. Here, a deputy coroner's investigator carries the body of a small child, one of five members of a family who were victims of a murder/suicide. The husband, upset over the breakup of his marriage, shot his wife and three children in 1998 in the Los Angeles area.

Record Checks The police must make numerous record checks in a murder investigation. These include records of 911 calls or other calls to the police, telephone records, arrest records, DMV records, and the like. Recall that record checks were covered in chapter 8 of this text.

- *911 calls.* The investigator should access and study all calls made to 911 or other police units regarding the crime and should also access and study all calls to 911 or police units regarding the location of the crime in recent history.

- *Arrest and other police records.* The investigator should review arrest and other pertinent police records of all witnesses, subjects, and other persons involved in the investigation.

- *Phone records.* The investigator should access and review all phone calls made to or by the

victim around the time of the murder, as well as similar records of suspects and other key persons in the investigation. The investigator should also canvass all public phones in the area of the crime and access their records.

- *DMV, work, and other records.* Investigators should review all appropriate records, including the victim's and the subject's department of motor vehicle records. It is a good idea to review the work records of any suspects, including their time records for the time around the murder. It is also a good idea to canvass the crime scene area for any traffic tickets or citations issued on the day of the murder. We should note here that the key information that led to the capture of David Berkowitz for the notorious Son of Sam murders in 1977 and 1978 was a traffic ticket issued to his vehicle on the night of a murder.

It is also a good idea to assign investigators to copy down the plate numbers of any vehicles parked in the area of the crime scene and contact their owners to determine if they may have witnessed any incidents while in the area.

Identification Procedures Witnesses will be asked to help identify the perpetrator, to give a physical description, and possibly to help a police artist prepare a composite drawing of the perpetrator, which can be given to other investigators, police patrol units, and the press for publication. (Recall the discussion of composite sketches in chapter 6 of this text.)

Witnesses may be asked to view photos of previously arrested individuals who might bear some resemblance to the perpetrator. If the victim is able to identify the perpetrator from photos, the police will attempt to locate, and then arrest and interrogate the person, and place him or her in a lineup so that the victim can attempt to make a positive identification.

Investigators also use showups and photo arrays to show to any witnesses. Identification procedures such as showups, photo arrays, and lineups are discussed extensively later in this chapter.

Theory Formation A theory or hypothesis is an attempt to develop an idea about the crime, who may have done it, and why it happened. Theories are constructed based on facts developed from the analysis and reconstruction of the crime, evidence and information provided by witnesses, and other persons knowledgeable about the victim or possible subjects, such as family members, relatives, friends, co-workers, and acquaintances.

A key process in developing a theory is to address the three issues of *motive, means,* and *opportunity.* Who had a motive to kill the victim? Who had the means (access to particular type of murder weapon, strength to do the physical acts involved in the murder, and so on)? Who had the opportunity (could have been present at the murder scene)? Recall that some of the most damaging information in the O. J. Simpson murder case involved motive, means, and opportunity. *Possible motive:* One of the victims was his former wife, and they had had violent episodes in their marriage. *Means:* Simpson had the physical strength to engage in the acts that caused the murders; also, evidence was presented that he had purchased a knife similar to the type of knife that could have been used in the murders. *Opportunity:* Could Simpson be placed in the time line? These were all important factors in the police and prosecution theory of the crime. As you well know, however, the jury didn't believe the police and prosecution theories of the case.

It is important to remember that investigators should not blindly adhere to one theory alone. If they do not consider alternative theories they could seriously hurt their investigative efforts if it later turns out that their original theory was wrong.

When developing theories, investigators often make up lists of possible suspects and investigate each one as they attempt to eliminate him or her from suspicion.

Apprehension of the Perpetrator If a suspect is identified, the police must locate and apprehend that person. There are numerous ways to accomplish this, including issuing BOLO (*Be on the Lookout For*) alarms to their own officers and other agencies, cooperating with other agencies and the media, and contacting informants and others who may have contact with the suspect.

Preparation for Trial with Prosecutors Bringing a suspect before the courts to answer the charges against him is the job of the prosecutor, but the information used in this process comes from the investigators. It is essential that investigators maintain excellent case records during all phases of the investigation. Recall the information in chapter 4 of this text.

For those interested in homicide investigations, the International Homicide Investigators Association (IHIA) is an organization of homicide investigation professionals, forensic pathologists, medical examiners, crime laboratory directors, criminalists, criminal prosecutors, and forensic professionals from around the world.

Various states have their own homicide investigators' Web site to share resources and information with surrounding jurisdictions. One such organization is the Maryland Homicide Investigation Association.

 INVESTIGATIONS ON THE NET

- -

International Homicide Investigators Association
http://www.ihia.org

Maryland Homicide Investigation Association
http://members.aol.com/mdhia

For an up-to-date list of Web links, go to http://info.wadsworth.com/dempsey

- -

Forensic Death Investigations

The homicide investigation is one of the most important and complicated investigations that law enforcement conducts. Police investigators are charged with finding and arresting the person or persons responsible in criminal homicide cases. But the medical examiner or coroner is charged with the actual determination of the cause of death and the manner and time of death—that is, the forensic death or medicolegal examination. A medical examiner is generally a physician, sometimes a forensic pathologist, whereas a coroner is a public official; both, however, are responsible for determining cause and manner of death. There are numerous texts on the subject of **forensic death investigations.**[3]

Forensic pathology, which is the science of recognizing and interpreting diseases and injuries in the human body, is the basis of any medicolegal investigation. Often, careful attention to an apparent suicidal, accidental, or even natural death may reveal that a

YOU ARE THERE!

Failure to Conduct a Proper Death Scene Investigation: The Vincent Foster Case

During the early years of President Bill Clinton's administration, one of his closest aides and personal friends, Vincent Foster, was found dead of an apparent gunshot wound to the head in Fort Marcy Park in Arlington, Virginia. The initial investigation indicated that the wound was self-inflicted and the case was carried as a suicide. But continuing public debate over the conduct of the investigation led to a hearing by the U.S. Congress.

The failure of investigators to comply with proper crime scene photography procedures in the investigation led to considerable controversy over whether Foster's death was really a suicide or a murder. Investigators failed to take photographs of Foster before moving his body and failed to take photographs of his car and the relative positions of the body and the car. The mistakes made by the investigators shocked crime scene experts. Vernon Geberth, author of *Practical Homicide Investigation*, which has been called the authoritative text on death investigations, said,

> Crime scene photographs are permanent and comprehensive pieces of evidence. It's imperative. It's a basic requirement. It's extremely important in an investigation because it shows the body's position and other patterns which can never be re-created. I can't believe it. Who's to say this was a suicide? If this is true [proper photographs were not taken], this is the most sloppy death investigation I have ever heard of.

Robert Ressler, a former special agent with the FBI and author of several books and many articles on

homicide investigations, also seemed shocked by the failure of investigators to take proper photographs in the Foster case: "It's unspeakable. I can't imagine any competent investigator would not take crime scene photographs."

Failure to conduct a proper crime scene examination in death cases can make it impossible to solve and prosecute these cases. In this investigation, it was reported that the investigators also made these other mistakes:

- *They failed to test Foster's shoes for evidence.* A residue test would have shown whether Foster had walked in the park or if his body had been carried there after he died elsewhere.

- *They failed to make impressions of footprints around Foster's body.* The impressions would have indicated if Foster had been alone, or if others were with him or had carried him.

- *They failed to conduct fiber sweeps of Foster's clothes and his car.* The fiber sweeps would have revealed whether Foster's body had been carried, and if someone else had driven his car.

SOURCES: John S. Dempsey, *An Introduction to Public and Private Investigations* (Minneapolis/St. Paul: West, 1996); Christopher Ruddy, "Cops Made Photo Blunder at Foster Death Site," *New York Post*, Mar. 7, 1994, p. 4.

---

criminal homicide has occurred. In addition to forensic pathology, other scientific specialties can aid investigators.

Generally, deaths that fall into the following categories are within the realm of the medical examiner's or coroner's office: accidental deaths, suicides, homicides, suspicious, sudden, or unexpected deaths without an attending physician, and any others specified by state law. In these cases it is essential that the cause and manner of death be determined correctly. Together, the police and the medical examiner form a

team that will ultimately see a case through the criminal justice system, and it is hoped, result in a conviction of the person responsible.

The police begin the forensic death investigation by processing the death scene using the crime scene procedures discussed earlier in this chapter and in depth in chapter 3 of this text, including protecting, preserving, photographing, sketching, searching, recording, and analyzing the crime scene. The medical examiner or coroner responds to the crime scene to make a preliminary examination of the body before the official postmortem examination. Failure to conduct a proper crime scene examination in death cases can make it impossible to solve and prosecute these cases.

A good working relationship between police investigators and the medical examiner's office or coroner's office is essential if an effective death investigation is to be accomplished. Dr. William G. Eckert, forensic pathologist and the medical examiner for Panama City, Florida, emphasizes, "It is very important for police investigators to be present at autopsies. The information exchanged can be beneficial to both agencies."[4]

A postmortem examination may ultimately involve several other scientists in addition to a pathologist. But as soon as it has been determined that a crime was committed, it becomes a police function to determine who committed the offense. The medical examiner will assist the police effort by documenting the necessary medical evidence and preserving it for retrieval.

Helpful information investigators can collect for the medical examiner includes time and location where the deceased was found; weapons present at the scene; conditions at the scene; last contacts with the deceased; evidence of drug use, as well as any prescription medicine or drug paraphernalia found at the scene; evidence of sexual deviation; information on the victim's occupation; and drug and sexual habits.[5]

Investigators should be aware that prescription drugs, although legal, are the leading cause of drug-related deaths in the United States. All prescription medication containers found at a crime scene, both full and empty, should be confiscated. Medications should be inventoried by noting brand and generic names, the date of the prescription, the number of pills dispensed, and the number of pills remaining. The number of pills remaining, compared with the date they were purchased, may be relevant to an investigation. An empty bottle of one hundred Valium (diazepam) issued only days before the death with instructions to take four tablets a day has obvious implications.[6]

The postmortem assists homicide investigators by providing essential investigatory information and answering important questions such as time of death estimate; order of wounds; type of weapon; how it was used; if the injuries are consistent with the circumstances; if there was a struggle to death; if there is evidence of defensive wounds; if the deceased was under the influence of drugs or alcohol; and if there was a sexual assault before or after the death.[7]

Other medical experts can also be helpful in the death investigation. Recall the discussion of forensic specialties in chapter 6 of this text. For example, odontology (forensic dentistry) can be useful in determining the identity of a body. Thorough examination of the teeth, gums, and jawbones can provide information on the victim's age, race, habits, and even occupation, in some cases. Bite mark evidence is another area where odontology can be very important. Often, murderers bite their victims; thus, the bite mark evidence can be compared with the bite pattern of a possible suspect. Also, ballistics experts can determine the types of bullets used in a shooting case and other important ballistic details.

Other specialties useful to the medical examiner include forensic anthropology, which can involve archaeological excavation, with examination of hair, plant materials, and insects. A forensic anthropologist can use skeletal remains to determine the age, sex, race, height, and other characteristics of a body. Injuries and cause of death can often be determined by the forensic anthropologist. Forensic entomology is the science of insects. In murder cases, insects are often the first witnesses to the crime as they begin to gather around the dead body and enter and lay eggs in the body's orifices. If a body has not been discovered for several days, the forensic entomologist is generally the best person to determine time of death. Forensic toxicologists can determine the presence of poisons or other substances in a body.

There are more than three thousand jurisdictions and thousands of people who routinely perform death investigations in the United States, and there is no universal system to cover this. In some jurisdictions these duties rest with pathologists, in some with medical examiners, in some with coroners. In order to address this problem and to identify, delineate, and assemble a universal set of investigative tasks that should be performed at every death scene, the National Institute of Justice formed a medicolegal review panel of 144 professionals from across the country to create agreed-upon national standards. It published these standards as the *National Guidelines for Death Investigation*. Exhibit 10.1 provides a summary of these guidelines.

National Institute of Justice Medicolegal Death Investigation Guidelines

Section A: Investigative Tools and Equipment

Section B: Arriving at the Scene
1. Introduce and identify self and role.
2. Exercise scene safety.
3. Confirm or pronounce death.
4. Participate in scene briefing.
5. Conduct scene "walk-through."
6. Establish chain of custody.
7. Follow laws related to collection of evidence.

Section C: Documenting and Evaluating the Scene
1. Photograph scene.
2. Develop descriptive documentation of scene.
3. Establish probable location of injury or illness.
4. Collect, inventory, and safeguard property and evidence.
5. Interview witness(es) at the scene.

Section D: Documenting and Evaluating the Body
1. Photograph the body.
2. Conduct external body examination (superficial).
3. Preserve evidence on body.

4. Establish decedent identification.
5. Document postmortem changes.
6. Participate in scene debriefing.
7. Determine notification procedures for next of kin.
8. Ensure safety of remains.

Section E: Establishing and Recording Decedent Profile Information
1. Document the discovery history.
2. Determine terminal episode history.
3. Document decedent medical history.
4. Document decedent mental health history.
5. Document social history.

Section F: Completing the Scene Investigation
1. Maintain jurisdiction over the body.
2. Release jurisdiction of the body.
3. Perform exit procedures.
4. Assist the family.

SOURCE: National Institute of Justice, *National Guidelines for Death Investigation* (Washington, DC: National Institute of Justice, 1997), pp. 11–48.

The Cold Case Investigations Concept

During the very busy crime years of the 1960s, 1970s, and 1980s, when crime rates and murder rates grew at ever-increasing speed, the police were overwhelmed. When an unsolved murder case grew old and the trail grew cold, no new work was done on it and possible perpetrators went unapprehended and unpunished. New homicide cases were coming in every day. Homicide investigators did the best they could with each case and then went on to the next one. Although they still sought new information to pursue the cold cases, they did not have the time to actually pursue them. Clearance rates for homicides dropped significantly.

With the 1990s came a significant decrease in crime, including murders, on a nationwide level. Also at this time, widespread use of high-tech crime-solving

methods, such as national databases, DNA testing, and the Internet, became common. As a result of the new technology and the additional time available to investigators, the **cold case investigation** concept was developed to address the older underworked cases. Thus, the cold case investigation concept arose from several different phenomena: the decrease in homicide clearance rates; the decrease in homicides and other crimes in the 1990s; and the proliferation of new crime-solving technology.

The cold case concept is the use of particular investigative squads consisting of highly experienced and sophisticated homicide investigators to work exclusively on unsolved murders. Since the early 1990s, cold case squads have operated in many major cities and in local, state, and federal agencies. Many of these agencies have Web sites with photos of wanted suspects, escaped prisoners, and descriptive cold case reviews, asking the public for help. Cold case squads

GUEST LECTURE
Professor Patrick Ryan, Detective Sergeant, Retired, NYPD

The role of homicide liaison detective is unique. Most working detectives, as a routine part of their investigations, interface with the pathologists at autopsies of homicide victims, sharing information between the crime scene and the lab. In some of the larger police departments, the role is formalized with one or more detectives devoted full-time to the tasks.

The homicide liaison detective is a translator, putting detectivese into the language of medical professionals and vice versa. He or she has a foot in two camps: the police department and the medical examiner's office. It is important for field detectives to know whether or not a particular subdural hematoma was fatal, or the exact time of death, or even the exact cause of death when multiple injuries are present. Indeed, the detective would not know a blood vessel in the victim's skull showed damage unless the pathologist said so. Similarly, information from the crime scene—the relative positions of victim and perpetrator, witnesses' positioning of the weapon, the victim's position when found, and so on—are helpful and at times vital pieces of information in aid of the pathologist's examination. The homicide liaison detective facilitates the exchange of such information.

An actual case helps show how the process works. On a Wednesday in the Sunset Park section of Brooklyn, New York, firefighters found a thirty-seven year old female, DOA and badly burned, at the scene of a fire in a three-story walk-up. Detectives interviewed the victim's husband and eight-year-old daughter. Daddy was distraught, but to the detective, his statements and demeanor were not credible. The eight-year-old reported that her parents had argued loudly and violently the previous Sunday night. The child had not witnessed the tussle, but she did hear her parents screaming behind a closed bedroom door. The detective suspected that the husband had killed his wife on Sunday and then committed arson on Wednesday to cover up. When the husband checked himself into a hospital soon after the detective's interview became an interrogation, he became suspect number one.

The homicide liaison detective got involved. In this case, the time of death was critical. It was also very important to ascertain if the burns from the fire caused the death or if some other means were responsible. The liaison detective knew from experience that internal organs begin to decay before skin does. After explaining the field detective's assessment to the pathologist, it became an easy task for the doctor to examine the kidneys and determine beyond reasonable doubt that the victim had died three days before her skin was damaged by fire. Confronted with the scientific proof, the husband confessed and confirmed the field detective's suspicion.

That case can be multiplied many times. The homicide liaison detective, however, does more than coordinate investigations and autopsies. Being the closest police officer to the greatest number of homicides, the homicide liaison detective is positioned excellently to record the means, location, and severity of wounds for pattern analysis. In large jurisdictions, it is often difficult to compare the way people are killed, simply because individual investigators do not get the chance to compare notes. A particular gun or knife can point to a serial killer only if someone has looked at all the homicides. A good homicide liaison detective keeps wound charts on all victims, with multiple sorting criteria: sex, race, type of weapon, location of wound, and so on.

Often overlooked or unknown, the tasks of the homicide liaison detective are limited only by the inquisitiveness, intuitiveness, and imagination of the person holding the job.

often receive favorable media coverage for closing a case after a lengthy time period.

Cold case squad (CCS) members review case files, compare notes, compile new lead sheets, and follow leads. They are unencumbered by other cases, shift changes, and the normal flow of distractions and obstacles experienced by regular detectives. Many have liaisons with the local prosecutor's office.

One of the first cold case units was the result of a merger of the Washington, D.C., Metropolitan Police Department (MPD) and the FBI. The MPD and the FBI assigned experienced homicide and violent crime investigators to the squad. The squad was not assigned to shift rotations and did not respond to fresh homicide scenes or catch any new cases. All cases investigated were at least one year old and could not be addressed by the original homicide squad because of workload, time constraints, or lack of viable leads. The cold case squad (CCS) investigated all remaining viable leads, and in most situations, identified new leads and additional witnesses. They also used new technology such as AFIS and DNA. (AFIS and DNA are described in detail in chapter 6 of this text.) In five years, the CCS closed 157 previously unsolved homicide cases, leading to the prosecution of some of the most violent and notorious repeat offenders in the city.[8]

Florida's Metro-Dade Police Department also formed a cold case squad from some of the homicide section's most experienced detectives. It solved 110 homicides in its first ten years in operation. This squad handles local cases and helps out-of-town detectives who are conducting investigations of their own.[9]

In Texas, the San Antonio Police Department posts cold cases on the Internet and its Web site invites tips from the public via e-mail. This procedure contributed to solving the murders of two high school students more than one thousand days after the murders. In addition, the Texas attorney general's cold case unit is available to assist and coordinate with local authorities to establish multijurisdictional resources and to provide training on case investigation.[10]

RAPE OR SEXUAL ASSAULT INVESTIGATIONS

The common law definition of **rape** is an act of forced sexual intercourse by a man of a woman. Today, many states have changed their laws, and call rape and other forcible sexual crimes *sexual assault.* Sexual violence is a serious but often unreported problem in our society. For example, a 2001 study in the *Journal of the American Medical Association* reported that one in five adolescent girls endures physical or sexual violence at the hands of a dating partner. The abused girls, the study found, were more likely to report other problems, such as drug abuse, unhealthy weight control practices, risky sexual behavior, pregnancy, and suicide attempts, as more serious than sexual assault.[11]

Methods of Investigation

Several methods of investigation are used in rape or sexual assault cases, including response to the scene, crime scene processing, analysis and reconstruction, interviews and interrogations, identification procedures, record checks, theory formation, apprehension of perpetrator, and preparation for trial with prosecutors.

Sometimes, police may respond to a rape or a sexual assault as a result of a 911 call. Or the victim may contact the police quite a time after the incident or may actually come into the police facility to report the case. In all cases, however, the police should fully process the crime scene in an attempt to obtain evidence and identify the suspect. Of particular interest in a rape case are any items that might contain serological evidence, such as bedsheets, clothing, and the like.

A rape investigation generally begins when a victim reports the incident to the police. The victim is interviewed and asked to identify the perpetrator. In rape cases victims should be brought to a hospital as soon as possible to receive medical attention and also to safeguard any physical evidence. Doctors use what is called a *rape evidence kit* to collect any vaginal, oral, or anal semen evidence, as well as other evidence. This kit is then turned over to the police to be analyzed in the serology unit of the crime lab. The victim's clothing should also be taken to test for evidence of the crime.

If the victim cannot identify the perpetrator, she will be asked to give a physical description of him and possibly to help a police artist prepare a composite drawing, which can be given to other investigators, police patrol units, and the press for publication. (It is the practice of most police agencies not to give the name or address of a rape victim, or any victim of a sexual assault, to the press.)

The victim may be asked to view photos of previously arrested individuals who might bear some resemblance to the perpetrator. If the victim is able to identify the perpetrator from photos, the police will attempt to locate the perpetrator, arrest him, interrogate him, and place him in a lineup so that the victim can attempt to identify him. Police will also conduct canvasses in the area where the crime happened in order to find possible witnesses. During the investigation the police may interview people previously arrested or suspected of a similar crime. The investigators' knowledge of a particular community and their contacts or informants are very important in identifying and apprehending perpetrators.

Modus operandi (MO) information is very important in rape investigations, as well as in other investigations. An MO is the summary of the habits, techniques, and peculiarities of a person's behavior. Its usefulness is based on the probability that the same criminal will use a similar MO when committing different crimes. Investigators have traditionally maintained MO files based on gender and race. They can research these files by combining the description of the perpetrator given by the victim with the MO of the filed perpetrator and crime to find possible matches. Using this MO research procedure, investigators can retrieve photos of possible subjects and show them to the victim for possible identification. Many law enforcement agencies have computerized their MO files and are using them in computerized investigations. (See chapter 4 and chapter 6 of this text.)

Many police departments have created special investigatory units to deal specifically with victims of sexual abuse. They often use female investigators to ease the interview process with both adult and juvenile victims.

Many police departments use anatomically correct dolls in an effort to facilitate interviews with child victims of sexual abuse. The dolls can be useful in reducing stress, establishing rapport, determining competency, and learning the child's sexual vocabulary. However, experts warn that the improper use of dolls can block communication and cause severe case problems for prosecutors.[12] Recall that chapter 7 of this text discusses at length interviews with victims.

Many states and regions have sexual assault inves-

tigator associations designed to share information and resources with those in their jurisdictions. An example of one is the California Sexual Assault Investigators Association (CSAIA).

INVESTIGATIONS ON THE NET

California Sexual Assault Investigators Association
http://www.csaia.org

For an up-to-date list of Web links, go to
http://info.wadsworth.com/dempsey

ROBBERY INVESTIGATIONS

Robbery is taking or attempting to take anything of value from the care, custody, or control of a person or persons by force or threat of force or violence or by putting the victim in fear. Approximately half of the robberies reported are street robberies, sometimes referred to as muggings; the other half occur at commercial locations or at homes.

Home invasion robberies are increasing throughout the United States. These robberies, although similar to burglaries (discussed in Chapter 11 of this text) are actually quite different. In home invasion robberies, confrontation with the residents is generally the key element in the offense. Home invaders prefer to make direct entry into a targeted residence and they carry items that connote control and confrontation, such as firearms, handcuffs, and masks. Home invaders usually target the resident, not the residence, and they do not have to overcome residential alarm systems because most systems are not activated when the residence is occupied.[13]

Methods of Investigation

There are two primary investigative methods for robberies: *reactive measures* are used after a robbery is actually committed; *proactive methods* are used to prevent robberies from occurring.

Reactive Methods of Investigation The reactive methods of investigating robbery cases are very similar to those in other violent crimes, including response to the scene, crime scene processing, analysis and reconstruction, interviews and interrogations, identification procedures, record checks, theory formation, apprehension of perpetrator, and preparation for trial with prosecutors.

A robbery investigation generally begins when a victim reports the incident to the police or the police receive a 911 report of a robbery in progress. If the perpetrator has fled the crime scene, the police attempt to obtain the identity or a description of the perpetrator. The victim is interviewed and asked to identify the perpetrator. In serious robbery incidents, the police may follow the crime scene procedures discussed earlier and in more detail in chapter 3 of this text.

If the victim cannot identify the perpetrator, he or she will be asked to give a physical description and possibly help a police artist prepare a composite drawing of the perpetrator, which can be given to other investigators, police patrol units, and the press for publication.

The victim may be asked to view photos of previously arrested individuals who might bear some resemblance to the perpetrator. If the victim is able to identify the perpetrator from photos, the police will attempt to locate, and then arrest and interrogate the perpetrator and place him or her in a lineup so that the victim can attempt to make a positive identification. Police will also conduct canvasses in the area where the robbery happened in order to find possible witnesses. During the investigation, the police may interview persons previously arrested or suspected of similar crimes. The use of MO files is very important in the robbery investigations. As in all cases, investigators' knowledge of a particular community and their contacts or informants are critical in identifying and apprehending perpetrators.

Proactive Methods of Investigation There are several proactive methods of investigations to prevent crimes of robbery. Some of these are repeat offender programs; decoy programs, including blending and decoy operations; and stakeouts. These are used by public law enforcement agencies to apprehend robbers before they actually attack their victim. Other proactive measures involve security methods that are used by commercial locations to prevent crimes of robbery against their businesses, such as armed guards and CCTV cameras.

REPEAT OFFENDER PROGRAMS Borrowing from the noted criminologist Marvin Wolfgang's research that indicated that the same predatory street criminals (career criminals, or repeat offenders) are responsible for the majority of crimes in the United States, the police started to direct their investigative resources to the career criminal, using repeat offender programs (ROPS). There are two major ways to conduct a repeat offender, or ROP, program.

The first is to target certain people for investigation. Once criminals are identified, the police can use surveillance techniques, following them and waiting to either catch them in the act of committing a crime or immediately after a crime occurs.

The second way is through case enhancement. Case enhancement involves using extra efforts and resources to investigate cases involving suspects with extensive prior criminal records. Specialized career criminal detectives can be notified of the arrest of a robbery suspect by other officers and then determine from the suspect's conviction or arrest rate whether or not the arrest merits enhancement. If it is decided to enhance the case, an experienced detective assists the officer in preparing the case for court and debriefs the suspect to obtain further information. A major police tactic in case enhancement is to establish a liaison with the prosecutor's office. This way, the police can alert the prosecuting attorney to the importance of the case and the suspect's past record in order to ensure more zealous efforts by the prosecutor.

DECOY PROGRAMS One of the primary purposes of police patrol is to prevent crime through the creation of a sense of omnipresence, so that potential criminals are deterred from crime by the presence or potential presence of the police. Omnipresence may work, but it is not economically feasible to have the necessary saturation level to deter all crime. Furthermore, omnipresence does not work in areas where ordinary police patrols cannot see crime developing, such as the inside of a store or the hallway of a housing project. In addition, we have seen that reactive investigations of crimes, with the intent to identify and arrest perpetrators, often are not very effective.

During the past three decades, an innovative proactive approach to apprehending criminals in the course of committing a crime has developed: decoy programs. These programs take one of two forms: blending and decoy operations.

In **blending operations,** officers dress in civilian clothes to blend into an area and patrol it on foot or in unmarked police cars in an attempt to catch a criminal in the act of committing a crime. Officers may target areas where a significant amount of crime occurs, or they may follow particular people who appear to be potential victims or potential offenders. In order to blend, officers assume the roles and dress of ordinary citizens—construction workers, shoppers, joggers, bicyclists, physically disabled persons, and the like— so that without being observed as officers they can be close enough to intervene should a crime occur.

In **decoy operations,** officers dress as, and play the role of, potential victims—drunks, nurses, businesspeople, tourists, prostitutes, blind persons, isolated subway riders, or defenseless elderly persons—waiting to be the subject of a crime. Meanwhile, a team of backup officers stand by to apprehend the perpetrator in the act of committing the crime. Decoy operations are most effective in combating the crimes of robbery, purse snatching and other larcenies from the person, burglaries, and thefts of and from autos.

Descriptions of decoy operations in New York and other cities contain numerous successful applications.[14] The New York City Police Department's Street Crime Unit (SCU) has been extremely successful and has served as a model for numerous other police agencies. The SCU consists of experienced volunteer officers who are aggressive and "street smart." They receive extensive training in decoy techniques and are assigned to high-crime areas.[15] Each of New York's seventy-six patrol precincts has its own decoy unit, called anticrime units. Each unit is composed of officers who have made large numbers of arrests and who request the assignment.

Among the more effective decoy and blending operations was another NYPD unit, the Taxi-Truck Surveillance Unit, which was organized to combat the growing number of nighttime assaults on truck drivers and cabdrivers. For a period of five years, specially equipped officers from both patrol and detective units were selected to play the roles of cabbies and truckers; this undercover approach ultimately reduced assaults and robberies of cabbies and truckers by almost 50 percent.[16]

Another successful decoy operation was begun by the Miami Police Department with the establishment of an undercover decoy operation targeting tourist rob-beries. Known as STAR (Safeguarding Tourists Against Robberies), this twelve-officer unit had its members pose as tourists sitting in parked rental cars near busy areas. When robbers struck, a backup team moved in to assist in the arrest. STAR resulted in a 33 percent decrease in tourist robberies.[17]

Anticrime and decoy strategies focus on reducing serious and violent street crime, apprehending criminals in the act, making quality arrests, and maintaining a high conviction record. By using police as decoys to apprehend criminals, court cases are much more likely to be prosecuted successfully. Decoy operations overcome the problem police encounter when witnesses and victims are reluctant to cooperate with them and prosecutors because of fear, apathy, or interminable court delays.

A San Francisco police sergeant defined the goals and operations of a decoy program:

> The underlying theory . . . is that the type of criminal responsible for most violent street crime is an opportunist. The criminal walks the streets looking for a victim who is weaker than himself, looking for an opportunity to make a "score" without any danger to himself or any danger of apprehension. The decoy program is intended to respond to this type of criminal.[18]

There has been some criticism of decoy operations. A former police commander says, "Decoy operations are often seen as entrapment, even though they rarely come close to it."[19] Furthermore, decoy programs, in which officers dress and assume the role of a victim, can be very dangerous for the officers.

STAKEOUT OPERATIONS Many crimes occur indoors, out of view of passing patrol officers. A **stakeout** consists of a group of heavily armed officers who hide in an area of a store or building waiting for an impending holdup. If an armed robber enters the store and attempts a robbery, the officers yell *"Police!"* from their hidden areas; if the perpetrator fails to drop his weapon, the officers open fire. Stakeouts are effective in cases where the police receive a tip that a crime is going to occur in a commercial establishment, or when the police discover or come upon a pattern. A typical pattern would be that a group of liquor stores in a certain downtown commercial area have been robbed at gunpoint with a consistency that indicates that it might happen again. Stakeouts are extremely expensive in terms of police resources and also controversial, because they invariably involve death or serious injury to the perpetrator.

The Detroit Police Department, which once had a stakeout unit called STRESS (Stop the Robberies, Enjoy Safe Streets), disbanded it because of the many deaths of perpetrators and the public furor that attended a series of highly publicized killings of robbers.[20]

Some states and regions have professional associations of robbery investigators to share information and knowledge about their area. An example is the Colorado Association of Robbery Investigators (CARI). Another organization is the Eastern Armed Robbery Conference (EARC), which is dedicated to the exchange of intelligence information among local, state, and federal investigators across the eastern United

INVESTIGATIONS ON THE NET

Colorado Association of Robbery Investigators
http://www.co-asn-rob.org

Eastern Armed Robbery Conference
http://www.earc.org

For an up-to-date list of Web links, go to
http://info.wadsworth.com/dempsey

DEMPSEY'S LAW
Blending to Catch Robbers

As a supervisor in the Sixtieth Precinct in Brooklyn, I was assigned as the anticrime sergeant for several years. The anticrime unit worked in plainclothes to attempt to apprehend suspects attempting to commit robberies. One of the techniques we used in this unit was blending—dressing like everyone else in the area and going about normal street activities (that is, "doing our sidewalk act"). We used several methods in our blending operations. Sometimes we targeted possible locations where robberies took place, sometimes we targeted likely victims, and sometimes we targeted likely suspects.

While targeting possible victims we looked for indications that a person presented a target for a robbery attempt (for example, a tourist with a camera over his shoulder, a woman with a pocketbook, or an elderly person dragging a shopping cart behind her), and we would follow the subject from a discreet location, sometimes by foot and sometimes using a non-police-looking vehicle, and we would wait. If we saw activity that indicated a crime was about to go down, we would wait until we had probable cause and then move in to make the arrest.

In our area in Coney Island we worked primarily on the boardwalk, in the amusement area, and in the commercial areas of the precinct. We were good at blending and were proud that even our fellow officers who were patrolling on foot or in vehicles right in front of us didn't recognize us.

I loved that kind of work and I loved catching the bad guys. After we took down a suspect and cuffed him, he would invariably look at us in a shocked manner, as if he had no idea we were the police. It was really cool. Although I have been retired almost fifteen years now, whenever I am back in the city or in some commercial area I still find myself eyeballing the pocketbooks and shopping carts.

Sometimes, anticrime units would be assigned to large events, such as parades, rock concerts, and the like, to provide intelligence information on crowd movements and possible impending criminal incidents. For example, when we observed large roving bands of youths (the press used to call them *wolf packs*) that looked as if they were up to no good, we would radio the temporary headquarters' commander of their location and direction of travel. For example, after rock concerts at Madison Square Garden, hundreds of youths would come out of the Garden and the subway, at both the Seventh Avenue and Eighth Avenue exits, and start to band together and move uptown toward the theater district. We knew they were heading up there to snatch chains from the tourists and theatergoers.

States and Canada, including law enforcement officers, prosecutors, crime analysts, and corporate security specialists. The organization conducts quarterly conferences at various locations from Maine to Florida, which are hosted by member police departments.

Special Proactive Measures for Commercial Robberies Commercial institutions such as stores, businesses, banks, hotels, casinos, trucking and cargo firms, and similar institutions are very prone to robbery because they usually have significant cash and property on hand. These institutions engage in numerous proactive security measures to prevent robberies and investigate their occurrence. In this section we have included numerous boxes and Web sites to give students an idea of the diversity of the problems encountered by commercial institutions and the measures they take to counteract these threats.

Generally, banks have large proprietary security departments that provide myriad corporate security services, including investigations. Banks that use uniformed guards at their branches generally hire them from contract agencies. Banks also use armed guards and armored car services for money transfers.

According to FBI statistics, the number of bank robberies per year has declined since 1996, but recently robbers are getting away with larger amounts of money per incident and seem more prone to violence than ever before. Both the numbers of assaults reported during robberies and the number of incidents in which the robber brandishes a weapon or makes a threat have increased.

ATM machines in particular are often targets of robbers. There have been numerous incidents of assaults, robberies, rapes, abductions, and other crimes at these units located at banks, stores, malls, and other locations. Many localities have enacted laws requiring surveillance cameras at all ATM locations.

Trucking firms and trucking depots generally have a proprietary security force to deal with crimes against them and use contract security firms for other security services at fixed locations such as terminals. The main security problems for cargo companies and depots are cargo theft, hijacking, and employee theft.

Traditional security controls for the safety of truckers and their cargo are timed and specialized routes and driver call-ins to company dispatch centers. Modern electronic computerized tracking and communication systems have enhanced security's ability to geographically track and communicate with truckers immediately and accurately and ensure their safety and the safety of their cargo.

DEMPSEY'S LAW
Working as a Decoy to Catch Perps

When I was with the Sixtieth Precinct anticrime team in Brooklyn, I supervised a group of plainclothes officers whose job was to apprehend suspects—we called them *perps*—in the act of committing crimes.

In addition to the blending operations I described earlier, we used to engage in decoy operations. Our officers would dress as and assume the mannerisms of likely targets of robbery. Some of the roles our decoys would play were senior citizens out shopping, nurses leaving hospitals late at night, disabled persons, winos and homeless people, clergy people (priests, nuns, rabbis)—basically the type of targets these "hero" perps would go after. While the decoy officer did his or her sidewalk act, the rest of us would remain out of

sight just waiting for a perp to hit. Once the perp moved in, we moved in too. Our philosophy in decoy was always "Let the perp come after us instead of a real victim—we're tougher than the perp."

Personally, my favorite decoy operation was the senior citizen ruse. It particularly annoyed me that certain perps would target these elderly and sometimes disabled persons for robberies and then would beat them and steal their meager possessions. It really bothered me that the perps used to refer to robberies of senior citizens as candy robberies—as easy as taking candy from a baby. I really loved taking these perps down.

I often wish I were still doing this work.

The American Trucking Association (ATA) is a professional organization representing the trucking and cargo industry. Its Transportation Loss Prevention and Security Council offers prevention programs to combat cargo theft, and to give security advice, industry news, and other services to truckers and trucking and cargo companies across the nation. ATA operates the Cargo TIPS (Cargo Theft Information Processing System) system, a national cargo theft database, which provides information regarding cargo thefts.

INVESTIGATIONS ON THE NET

American Trucking Association
http://www.truckline.com

Cargo TIPS (Cargo Theft Information Processing System)
http://www.cargotips.org

For an up-to-date list of Web links, go to http://info.wadsworth.com/dempsey

----

Hotels and motels are often prone to robberies because they are open twenty-four hours a day, seven days a week. As some of the boxed features and Web sites in this section show, there are numerous security efforts directed at these locations. Various hotel and motel associations offer security assistance to its members. Many of these associations have a presence on the Web, including the American Hotel and Motel Association and its educational institute, and the International Hotel and Motel Association.

Among the myriad security concerns at casinos are the protection of both customers and the assets of the casino from robbery and theft. Casinos generally operate a proprietary security department and hire some contract security guards for certain duties. They use sophisticated access control and CCTV systems and make extensive use of armed security guards.

Gaming areas, which contain enormous amounts of cash, are usually monitored from the casino's control center, which is staffed by security personnel. A security booth is prominently situated next to the cage area where chips are cashed and other monetary transactions take place. Security controls all entrances to

INVESTIGATIONS ON THE NET

American Hotel and Motel Association
http://www.ahma.com

American Hotel and Motel Association Educational Institute
http://www.ei-ahma.org

International Hotel and Restaurant Association
http://www.ih-ra.com

For an up-to-date list of Web links, go to http://info.wadsworth.com/dempsey

----

the cage area. Also, security officers accompany personnel during movements of money anywhere on and off site and escort employees whenever necessary. They also will escort any patrons upon their request.

There are security checkpoints, CCTV cameras, and sophisticated access control systems to separate the public and the back-of-the-house areas, such as loading docks, money rooms, employee-only areas, and the like. Security officers are trained to look constantly for possible victims while patrolling the casino floors, such as people who leave a purse at a slot machine or display large amounts of money inappropriately. They try to take a quiet approach to moving in on drunks and other disorderly persons without raising the awareness of other patrons.

In Las Vegas, all casino and other private security departments exchange updates and get together to network at monthly meetings of the Las Vegas Security Chiefs Association, which includes representatives from all police units involved with tourist security and safety and the Las Vegas Metro Police.[21]

Most casinos in one area will engage in information sharing with other casinos, because the same criminals usually frequent all of them. For example, two casinos in Connecticut, the Mohegan Sun Casino and the Foxwoods Casino, share visual information about criminal activities on gaming floors by using digital image transmission systems, so the two security departments can quickly compare visual notes and step in and stop a crime in progress. When security at

YOU ARE THERE!
Robbery at Tiffany's: An Inside Job

New York's swank Fifth Avenue was the scene of a daring armed robbery on a Sunday night in early September 1994. Items worth more than $1.25 million were stolen from Tiffany's, the famous jewelry store. The police conducted an intense investigation, collected crucial tips, and engaged in a stakeout that led to the arrest of five men within a week. Two were Tiffany employees: a security supervisor (the mastermind) and a guard. It was eventually discovered that the two gunmen and the security supervisor were cousins.

Several weeks before the crime, two of the men involved concocted the plan during a picnic in Brooklyn's Prospect Park. At first, they were joking when they discussed their plans. But they soon became serious, and with the benefit of inside information on alarms, guard schedules, keys, videotaping systems, and other security secrets, they settled on a midnight robbery over Labor Day weekend. Another cousin, also a guard at Tiffany's, was chosen as a gunman. In addition, they found two men who agreed to sell the stolen property.

The security supervisor called in sick on the night of the robbery. He and the two gunmen bound their cousin the guard and three others with duct tape. They then fled with 464 pieces of jewelry and the surveillance tapes of their crime. No shots were fired, and the three made a clean escape.

An inside job was immediately suspected: only insiders would know about the operation of the store's security system, the location of keys and video cameras, and the existence of a covert backup system.

Confidential tips led the police to a man named Teddy and a building in Harlem. Three men were arrested as the result of a police stakeout. A search found a gun, duct tape, jewelry taken during the robbery, and security badges similar to those worn by Tiffany guards. The mastermind of the crime, Scott Jackson, thirty-one, had been Tiffany's loss prevention operations coordinator since September 1989.

The suspects' comical attempts to dispose of the stolen loot resulted in anonymous tips to the police. An attempt was made to sell a $6,000 diamond bracelet for $300 in Harlem, and expensive Tiffany pieces were displayed for sale like costume jewelry in Times Square. This led to the apprehension and arrest of these criminals.

---

either casino spots a suspicious individual on the floor, live digitized video can be transmitted immediately to the other casino.[22]

Convenience stores and gas stations that are open twenty-four hours a day, seven days a week offer tempting targets for robbers. Pay particular attention to the feature in this chapter on security efforts employed by 7-Eleven stores nationwide.

AGGRAVATED ASSAULT INVESTIGATIONS

An aggravated assault is an attack on a person in which the assailant inflicts serious harm or uses a deadly weapon. A simple assault is an attack that inflicts little or no physical harm on the victim.

Methods of Investigation

The methods of investigation used in aggravated assault cases are very similar to those used in other violent crimes, including response to the scene, crime scene processing, analysis and reconstruction, interviews and interrogations, identification procedures, record checks, theory formation, apprehension of perpetrator, and preparation for trial with prosecutors

An aggravated assault investigation generally begins when a victim reports the incident to the police or the police receive a 911 report of an assault in progress. If the perpetrator has fled the crime scene the police attempt to obtain the identity or a description of the perpetrator. The victim is interviewed and asked to identify the perpetrator. In many aggravated assault cases the victim knows the assailant, which greatly facilitates

YOU ARE THERE!
Three Types of Bank Robberies

Three types of bank robberies have been identified: the one-on-one robbery, the bank takeover, and the morning glory.

- *One-on-one robbery.* This is the most typical robbery. It occurs between the teller and robber; the robber either passes a note to the teller or makes a verbal demand for money. Approximately 80 percent of all bank robberies are one-on-ones. In these cases, because the robber only gains access to the cash drawer of one teller, monetary losses are low.
- *Bank takeover robbery.* This type of armed robbery occurs when one or more persons enter the branch, announce the robbery, and take control of the building. They usually brandish weapons and make verbal demands. Cash losses are

higher than with one-on-one robberies because the perpetrators get access to the cash drawers of more than one teller and possibly the vault.

- *Morning glory robbery.* This type of robbery is similar to the bank takeover, but it is committed in the morning, usually before the branch has opened for business. The perpetrators gain access to the bank by taking one or more hostages as employees arrive at work in the morning. This type leads to the most significant monetary loss because the robbers' goal is to get to the vault. They are usually armed, and the chances for violence are high.

SOURCE: Timothy H. Hannan, "Bank Robberies and Bank Security Precautions," *Journal of Legal Studies*, *11*, 1982, 83–92.

---

making an arrest. In serious aggravated assault cases the police may use the complete crime scene procedures discussed earlier in homicide cases, because such cases can turn into murder cases if the victim dies.

Assault is an attack in which the assailant inflicts harm on the victim. Here, police take a statement from a woman at a hospital emergency room.

KIDNAPPING INVESTIGATIONS

Kidnapping is the seizure and abduction of a person by force or threat of force and against the victim's will. There are several types of kidnapping incidents, including child abduction, illegal trafficking of people, and corporate kidnapping.

Although most of us think of child abduction as the act of a stranger, research indicates otherwise. Studies have found that abductions by family members represent the most prevalent type of child abduction. Children from birth to five years generally have a greater risk of victimization by parents or other trusted caregivers. In contrast, more independent school age children who experience lapses in supervision by caretakers are more accessible and more often victimized by acquaintances or strangers outside their homes.[23]

People traffickers generally lure their victims—many of whom suffer from poverty, unemployment, and gender discrimination in

YOU ARE THERE!
Ways Banks Try to Prevent Robberies

Banks traditionally use three security methods to prevent robberies: uniformed security officers, cash control procedures, and dye packs.

- *Security officers.* There is widespread debate in the banking industry over the effectiveness of uniformed security officers, both armed and unarmed. Although they may have some deterrent value in thwarting the amateur robber, there is little evidence that they deter the professional or experienced robber. Indeed, one-on-one robberies often occur without a security guard even being aware of them. However, there are advantages in having uniformed security officers: they offer a sense of security for customers and they are credible witnesses for the police.

- *Cash control.* Banks place strict limits on the amount of cash permitted in vault and safes and at individual teller stations. Once the cash level reaches its limit at individual teller stations, the teller must return the excess money to the vault.

- *Dye packs.* These are attached to a pack of money that is supposed to be given to the robber by the teller. After the robber leaves the bank, the packs explode and the money and person carrying it are covered in ink. The dye packs render the money useless and clearly identify the carrier. When they were first introduced, dye packs were a great deterrent to bank robbery. But as the news media began reporting their use and showing them on television, their effectiveness dwindled. Robbers began instructing tellers not to give them the "bomb" and threatened them if they did. Now, tellers are generally reluctant to give out the dye pack. Also, as a result of sloppy handling, some banks have seen detonations inside branch facilities. There are transmitters used to activate the dye packs and they must be properly positioned so that the packs do not detonate until after the robber has left.

Banks make extensive use of robbery analysis and risk assessment measures to design proper precautions against robbery. In robbery analysis, security managers study past robberies and use statistical analysis to identify trends and potential problem areas in need of improvement. They compare branch statistics with other banks that have reported to local law enforcement and the FBI. In risk assessment, security managers gather historical information for each branch and use the statistical data and information from studies to create a branch risk assessment form to survey and rate the bank's facilities. Developing a scoring system and a rating factor process allows them to assign a risk assessment score to each facility. This information is then used to determine how to reduce the rating to an acceptable level through methods such as additional equipment, increased training, and new procedural controls.

Banks use their risk analysis and robbery survey results to create proper training for employees in robbery deterrence. A significant correlation between training and robberies has been found; monetary losses and the number of robberies temporarily decrease after intensive employee training programs. The heightened alertness and vigilant adherence to procedure apparently has an impact. However, as time passes, robbery activity usually returns to, or near, previous levels

---

their home countries—to the United States with false promises of employment opportunities. Once these victims reach this country, however, traffickers force them to work as sweatshop laborers, domestic servants, agricultural workers, or prostitutes.[24]

Corporate kidnapping is a serious problem in the business world. Corporate kidnapping in the twenty-first century is all about money—large sums demanded by kidnappers who know what international corporations have been willing to pay to save their workers. The employers, in turn, take out large insurance polices to defray this cost of doing business in the developing world.[25] See chapter 13 of this text for some specific examples of this practice.

YOU ARE THERE!

Chicago PD and FBI Help Banks to Learn the Facts

The Chicago Police Department and the Chicago office of the Federal Bureau of Investigation conducted research called the Chicago Bank Robbery Initiative to determine the crucial factors that influence bank robbers' decisions, the security measures with the greatest deterrent effect on bank robberies, and the actions most effective in helping police apprehend suspects. The research revealed that the prime time for bank robberies is from 10:00 A.M. to 3:00 P.M. Also, Friday is the day of choice. The average offender is a male over age thirty who is not armed. Interviewed offenders had all graduated to bank robbery from other types of commercial robbery. Security inspections revealed that CCTV is the preferred surveillance device of area financial institutions, but images often had poor quality and cameras were often positioned too far away from the area being monitored.

SOURCE: P. Carroll and R. J. Loch, "Chicago Bank Robbery Initiative," *FBI Law Enforcement Bulletin*, Apr. 1997, pp. 9–18.

YOU ARE THERE!

Some Very Basic ATM Site Security Measures

- Persons inside ATM enclosure areas should have an unobstructed view of the surrounding area.
- Shrubbery and vegetation should not provide means of cover or concealment for possible criminals.
- Adequate lighting is essential at all times.
- There should be visible CCTV coverage.
- Emergency signal devices should be available.

SOURCE: Pamela A. Collins, Truett A. Ricks, and Clifford W. Van Meter, *Principles of Security and Crime Prevention*, 4th ed. (Cincinnati: Anderson, 2000).

YOU ARE THERE!

Security at Las Vegas's Venetian Casino and Hotel

The Venetian Casino in Las Vegas has more than four hundred security personnel. Most are patrol officers. There are usually about ninety officers on duty during a normal shift, with the number increasing on weekends and during special events. There is an investigations unit, which conducts background checks on all employees, due diligence probes, and other investigations. When hiring security personnel, the casino looks for candidates with casino security experience or experience in law enforcement, the military, or private security. All must pass drug testing and thorough background reviews. All Venetian officers are trained in casino operations; first aid, including the use of portable defibrillators, CPR, and water rescue; and other normal security functions and duties.

    The security department maintains a close liaison with the metropolitan police department and other security departments. The Venetian has more than twelve hundred CCTV cameras in place that are pan-tilt-zoom inside domes or track cameras, allowing for joystick manipulation. According to the director of security, the cameras monitoring the casino can zoom down and count the freckles on someone's hand. The Venetian has one central monitoring and dispatch area for the hotel and a second for the casino. Both operate around the clock, documenting occurrences inside the hotel and the casino. There are always at least two monitoring officers on duty at each station.

SOURCE: Ann Longmore-Etheridge, "Illusions of Grandeur: In Las Vegas, City of Illusions, the New Venetian Casino Has Created the Illusion of a City, But the Security Is No Chimera," *Security Management*, Sept. 1999, pp. 54–60.

YOU ARE THERE!
How Marriott Hotels Prevent Robberies

In the mid-1990s, security managers at Marriott Hotels noticed an increase in robberies at some of the line's hotels, including Residence Inn, Fairfield Inn, and Courtyard. Many of the criminals were armed, causing fears that hotel staff or guests could be injured. As a first step toward a solution, security management inspected police reports in the areas most affected by these crimes and found that crimes at local convenience stores in the same areas as the hotels had decreased at about the same rate that the hotel robberies had increased. They found that the convenience stores had recently added CCTV cameras and monitors to many of their stores in crime-ridden areas. The CCTV monitors were placed on the store counters where customers and passersby could see that they

were being recorded. Clearly, area criminals had found that the hotels had become easier targets than the convenience stores.

Marriott added a "lobby pack" security system for certain hotels in the areas where the robberies occurred. The lobby pack had a CCTV camera, a monitor, a VCR, and a lock box to secure the VCR. In the hotels where the lobby packs were installed, robberies decreased 43 percent in 1998 from the previous year. In 1999, robberies decreased an additional 33 percent.

SOURCE: Teresa Anderson, "No Room for Crime," *Security Management*, Dec. 1999, pp. 22–23.

DEMPSEY'S LAW
Hotel and Motel Traveler Safety Tips

- Don't answer the door in a hotel or motel room without verifying who it is. If a person claims to be an employee, call the front desk and ask if someone from the staff is supposed to have access to your room and for what purpose.

- When returning to your hotel or motel late in the evening, use the main entrance of the hotel. Be observant and look around before entering parking lots.

- Close the door securely whenever you are in your room and use the locking devices provided.

- Don't needlessly display guestroom keys in public or carelessly leave them on restaurant tables, at the swimming pool, or other places where they can be easily stolen.

- Do not draw attention to yourself by displaying large amounts of cash or expensive jewelry.

- Don't invite strangers to your room.

- Place all valuables in the hotel or motel's safe deposit box.

- Do not leave valuables in your vehicle.

- Check to see that any sliding glass doors or windows and any connecting room doors are locked.

- If you see any suspicious activity, report your observations to the management.

SOURCE: American Hotel and Motel Association.

YOU ARE THERE!

How 7-Eleven Protects Its Stores

The Southland Corporation of Dallas has twenty-one hundred company-owned and twenty-nine hundred franchised 7-Eleven stores across the United States. Their security operations are based on several studies conducted since the mid-1970s by Southland, the Western Behavioral Sciences Institute (WBSI), the National Institute of Justice (NIJ), the National Association of Convenience Stores, and the Athena Research Corporation. Based on this research, the company gained insight into how robbers think and what deters them from committing crime. It has led to the development of security strategies by 7-Eleven that have reduced robberies by 70 percent in the past twenty years. The average monetary loss to robberies at 7-Eleven is $37.00. This crime deterrence program, which has helped the company reduce robberies and made customers and employees feel safer, is based on several major components.

- *Cash control.* The smallest amount of cash possible is kept at the store. 7-Eleven uses a five-hundred-pound cash control unit that serves as a drop safe and can only be opened by authorized personnel (generally the manager) who must enter his or her PIN. There is a ten-minute time delay before the cash unit opens.

- *Visibility.* Stores are brightly lit inside and outside. The cash register and clerks are clearly visible from outside the store, as are all places inside the store.

- *Training.* Employees are trained to handle robberies as calmly and quickly as they would any other transaction. All new employees receive two-day training involving robbery deterrence, violence avoidance, loitering, physical assault, gang activity, and recommended general security procedures to be followed in the event of an emergency situation. The training stresses that the safety of store personnel and customers is far

more important than protecting the company's money or property during a robbery. Store techniques include cooperating with the robber by giving up the money, and never resisting, staring, talking unnecessarily, or arguing.

- *CCTVs and alarms.* There are video cameras and alarms in all stores nationwide. A fixed color CCTV is located near the front of each store with a clear view of the front door and cash register. VCRs maintain a record of all activity in the store. Each store also uses both fixed and remote activator alarm devices that transmit signals to a remote monitoring system. Store employees are encouraged to carry the remote alarm activators on their belts or in the pockets of their smocks.

- *Escape routes.* 7-Elevens are designed with only one entrance and exit. Fencing and landscaping with large bushes is used to thwart easy egress and block alleys or other escape routes that could be used by robbers.

- *Relationship with the local police.* 7-Eleven provides satellite offices for local police departments at which officers can make phone calls, complete paperwork, and meet with residents of the neighborhood they patrol. These Police Community Network Centers (PCNC) provide a dedicated telephone, drawers for storing forms and paperwork, and racks for displaying crime prevention literature. Studies have indicated that a strong police presence acts as a deterrent to robbery. Store employees and customers have consistently reported they feel safer with an increased police presence in their store and area.

SOURCE: Scott Lins and Rosemary J. Erickson, "Stores Learn to Inconvenience Robbers: 7-Eleven Shares Many of Its Robbery Deterrence Strategies," *Security Management*, Nov. 1998, pp. 49–53.

Methods of Investigation

The methods of investigation in kidnapping cases are similar to those involved in other violent crimes, including response to the scene, crime scene processing, analysis and reconstruction, interviews and interrogations, identification procedures, record checks, theory formation, apprehension of perpetrator, and preparation for trial with prosecutors. Nevertheless, each abduction case is unique and requires a thorough investigation that includes detailed victimology, intensive neighborhood and roadblock canvasses, timely witness interviews, detailed crime scene searches, media coordination, computer-aided case management systems, and geographic profiling services.

Police departments emphasize that the main concern in a kidnapping investigation is the victim's safety. Their primary objective is to effect the safe return of the kidnapped victim. Secondary objectives include the identification, apprehension, and prosecution of suspects and recovery of any ransom payments.

Kidnapping investigations are reactive and require investigators to make plans or modify existing plans on a moment's notice, based on the requirements of a situation. The personnel involved in a kidnapping case include missing person personnel, residence team, command post personnel, responding personnel, and crime scene unit. Many law enforcement agencies insist that decisions about ransom payments are the responsibility of the victim's family alone.[26]

Federal law enforcement agencies, particularly the FBI, may be called in to assist local and state agencies in kidnapping investigations (see the next section). The Task Force on Missing and Exploited Children as mandated by the Violent Crime Control and Law Enforcement Act of 1994 coordinates federal law enforcement resources to assist state and local authorities in investigating the most difficult cases of missing and exploited children.[27]

Congress passed the Victims of Trafficking and Violence Protection Act of 2000 to counter the growing problem of international trafficking of people faced by the United States and the world. It offers assistance to foreign and state and local law enforcement agencies in dealing with this problem.[28]

FBI Assistance in Kidnapping Cases

The FBI exercises jurisdiction and investigative responsibilities pursuant to federal statutes on kidnapping. Individual FBI field offices around the country serve as the primary points of contact for persons requesting FBI assistance.

The FBI's Child Abduction and Serial Murder Investigative Resources Center (CASMIRC) operates under its National Center for the Analysis of Violent Crime (NCAVC) to provide investigative support through the coordination and provision of federal law enforcement resources, training, and application of other multidisciplinary expertise, to assist federal, state, and local authorities in matters involving child abductions, mysterious disappearances of children, child homicide, and **serial murder** across the country. The NCAVC has a rapid response unit that applies the most current expertise available in such matters.

Upon being notified that a child has been abducted, FBI field offices and the NCAVC coordinate an immediate response. The National Child Search Assistance Act of 1990 states that law enforcement agencies may not observe a waiting period before accepting a missing child report and that each missing child that is reported to law enforcement must be entered immediately into the state law enforcement system and National Crime Information Center (NCIC).

Vital to the resolution of these cases, FBI special agents join local law enforcement in coordinating and conducting comprehensive investigations. FBI evidence response team personnel may conduct the forensic investigation of the abduction site, while a rapid start team may immediately be deployed to coordinate and track investigative leads, which often number in the thousands.

Like the local police, the FBI's primary objective in kidnapping investigations is to effect the safe return of the victim. Secondary objectives include the identification, apprehension, and prosecution of the subjects and the recovery of any ransom payments. Each field office establishes effective liaison to ensure that local law enforcement agencies are made aware of the FBI's resources, legal jurisdiction, and investigative policy on child abductions.

Field offices will respond to cases involving the mysterious disappearance of a child whenever and however they come to the attention of FBI personnel. All reports of circumstances that indicate a minor has or has possibly been abducted are afforded an immediate preliminary inquiry. In order for the FBI to initiate any investigation, it must have specific facts that indicate that a violation of federal law within the FBI's jurisdiction may have occurred. In the preliminary inquiry, the FBI will evaluate all evidence, circumstances, and information to determine if an investigation is warranted under the Federal Kidnapping Statute of Title 18

USC Section 1201. If such an investigation is warranted, the FBI will immediately enter the investigation in partnership with state and local authorities in an effort to fully determine the case status.

Research has indicated that subjects who abduct children usually are not first-time offenders, but are serial offenders who often travel during the commission of multiple sexual offenses against children. Interstate travel by the offender could predicate prosecution under Title 18 USC, which makes it a federal violation for a person to travel in interstate commerce for the purpose of engaging in any sexual act with a person under eighteen years of age.

National Center for Missing and Exploited Children

The National Center for Missing and Exploited Children (NCMEC) is a private, nonprofit organization established in 1984 that operates under a congressional mandate and works in cooperation with the U.S. Department of Justice's Office of Juvenile Justice and Delinquency. As the nation's resource center for child protection, the NCMEC spearheads national efforts to locate and recover missing children and raise public awareness about ways to prevent child abduction, molestation, sexual exploitation, and victimization. These goals are accomplished by coordinating the

INVESTIGATIONS ON THE NET

National Center for Missing and Exploited Children
http://www.missingkids.com

FBI Web Site on Missing Persons, Kidnappings, Parentally Abducted Children
http://www.fbi.gov/mostwant/kidnap

For an up-to-date list of Web links, go to http://info.wadsworth.com/dempsey

efforts of law enforcement, social service agencies, elected officials, judges, prosecutors, and educators in the public and private sectors to break the cycle of violence.

The NCMEC provides a wide range of free services to law enforcement, including technical case assistance, information analysis and dissemination, photograph and poster preparation and rapid dissemination of such, age enhancement of photographs, facial reconstruction and imaging services, database searches, educational materials and publications, and training.

The NCMEC also maintains a twenty-four-hour multilingual hotline (1–800-THE-LOST) and a Web site. These provide assistance to parents and law enforcement agencies about missing or sexually exploited children, a central location to receive reports of missing children sightings, information to parents on how to better safeguard their children, and reunification assistance to parents once their children are found.

Anyone interested in missing persons, kidnappings, and parentally abducted children should see the FBI Web site that offers photographs, fact patterns, and wanted information on many recent cases.

POLICE EYEWITNESS IDENTIFICATION PROCEDURES

Often law enforcement officers apprehend suspects based on descriptions given by vic-

Jill Perkins works in front of a wall of missing children posters at the National Center for Missing & Exploited Children/New York Branch, Mohawk Valley Office in New Hartford. She is the office manager and they work out of the Better Covenant Church

© Syracuse Newspapers/The Image Works

YOU ARE THERE!
The Etan Patz Kidnapping Case

The twenty-two-year search for Etan Patz officially ended on June 19, 2001 in a Manhattan courtroom, when a judge granted the father's wish and pronounced the child, who had disappeared when he was six, legally dead.

The exhaustive hunt for Etan, who vanished from a city street in May 1979, took investigators to the Middle East, Germany, Switzerland, and throughout the United States. Etan was last seen May 25, 1979, as he left his SoHo home to catch the bus for school. It was the first time he had been allowed to walk the two blocks alone.

For two decades, the boy seemed to be a symbol of the plight of missing children. A photograph of Etan, a blue-eyed child with sandy hair, appeared on milk cartons, posters, and in newspapers as far away as Israel. His disappearance came before the era when missing children's faces appeared regularly on milk cartons and made-for-TV movies explored a seeming epidemic of vanished children. To honor the boy, President Ronald Reagan declared May 5 as National Missing Children's Day. The National Center for Missing and Exploited Children was founded in 1984 to address cases like Etan.

At the court hearing in 2001, Stuart R. GraBois, a former U.S. prosecutor who had investigated Etan's

disappearance since 1985, told the judge, "We have information that Etan Patz is dead." The lawyers said they believed that a convicted pedophile, José A. Ramos, fifty-six, in jail in Pennsylvania for child molesting, had sexually assaulted and killed Etan. At the time, Ramos was living in a tenement less than a mile from the Patzes' Prince Street apartment. According to court papers, he acknowledged spending time with Etan on the day he disappeared.

Stanley K. Patz, Etan's father, pursued the declaration of death because the family planned to sue Ramos for wrongful death. Patz's lawyers said there was not enough evidence in the case to charge Ramos criminally.

According to the evidence compiled by investigators, Ramos told a cellmate that he had brought Etan to his apartment that day and sexually assaulted him. The cellmate allegedly quoted Ramos as saying, "Etan is dead, there is no body, and there will never be a body."

SOURCES: Katherine E. Finkelstein, "Court Declares Etan Patz, Missing for 22 Years, Dead," *New York Times*, June 20, 2001, p. B2; Dean E. Murphy, " Seeking an End and a New Start in the Case of Etan Patz," *New York Times*, June 17, 2001, p. 25.

---

tims of violent crimes. To ensure that the apprehended person is actually the perpetrator, the police must obtain assistance from the victim or employ other identification procedures. The following sections discuss procedures they use to identify suspects properly as the actual perpetrators of crimes.

Lineups, Showups, and Photo Arrays

Lineups, showups, and photo arrays are important parts of the police investigation process, as are procedures requiring suspects to give samples of their voice, blood, and handwriting to be used in identification-comparison procedures.

A lineup is the placing of a suspect with a group of other people of similar physical characteristics (such

as race, age, hair color, hair type, height, and weight) so that a witness or victim of a crime has the opportunity to identify the perpetrator of the crime. Lineups are usually used after an arrest.

A showup involves bringing a suspect back to the scene of the crime or another place (for example, a hospital where an injured victim is) where the suspect can be seen and possibly identified by a victim or witness. The showup must be conducted as soon as possible after the crime, and with no suggestion that the person is a suspect. A showup too is usually used after an arrest.

A photo array is similar to a lineup, except that photos of the suspect (who is not in custody) and others are shown to a witness or victim. Photo arrays are used prior to arrest.

Could these procedures be construed as violating a defendant's freedom against self-incrimination as provided by the Fifth Amendment to the U.S. Constitution? The following cases detail the key landmark decisions of the Supreme Court in lineup, showup, and photo array cases.

United States v. Wade In *United States v. Wade*, the Supreme Court in 1967 made two very important decisions about lineups.[29] It ruled that a person can be made to stand in a lineup and perform certain actions that were performed by the suspect during the crime, such as saying certain words or walking in a certain fashion. The Court also ruled that once a person is indicted, that person has a right to have an attorney present at the lineup.

Kirby v. Illinois In 1972, in *Kirby v. Illinois*, the Supreme Court ruled that the right to counsel at lineups applies only after the initiation of formal judicial criminal proceedings, such as an indictment, information, or arraignment—that is, when a person formally enters the court system.[30] An *information* is a formal charging document drafted by a prosecutor and presented to a judge. An *indictment* is a formal charging document returned by a grand jury based on evidence presented to it by a prosecutor. The indictment is then presented to a judge. Indictments generally cover felonies. An *arraignment* is a hearing before a court having jurisdiction in a criminal case, in which the identity of the defendant is established, the defendant is informed of the charge or charges and of her rights, and the defendant is required to enter a plea. In *Kirby*, the Court reasoned that because a lineup may free an innocent person, and the required presence of an attorney might delay the lineup, it is preferable to have the lineup as soon as possible, even without an attorney.

Thus in a postarrest, preindictment lineup, there is no right to have an attorney present. Many police departments, however, will permit an attorney to be present at a lineup and make reasonable suggestions, as long as there is no significant delay of the lineup.

Stoval v. Denno In *Stoval v. Denno* (1967), the Supreme Court ruled that showups are constitutional and do not require the presence of an attorney.[31] The Court addressed the issue as follows:

> The practice of showing suspects singly to persons for purpose of identification, and not a part of a lineup, has been unduly condemned. . . . However, a claimed violation of due process of law in the conduct of a confrontation depends on the totality of the circumstances surrounding it and the record in the present case reveals that the showing of Stoval to Mrs. Behrendt in an immediate hospital confrontation was imperative.

Subsequent to *Stoval v. Denno*, a federal appellate court established a set of guidelines phrased in the form of questions that could decide the constitutionality of a showup. A careful review of the questions reveals that the court clearly prefers lineups to showups but will permit showups if certain conditions are met:

- Was the defendant the only individual who could possibly be identified as the guilty party by the complaining witness, or were there others near him or her at the time of the showup so as to negate the assertion that he or she was shown alone to the witness?
- Where did the showup take place?
- Were there any compelling reasons for a prompt showup so as to deprive the police of the opportunity of securing other similar individuals for the purpose of holding a lineup?
- Was the witness aware of any observation by another or any other evidence indicating the guilt of the suspect at the time of the showup?
- Were any tangible objects related to the offense placed before the witness that would encourage identification?
- Was the witness identification based on only part of the suspect's total personality?
- Was the identification a product of mutual reinforcement of opinion among witnesses simultaneously viewing the defendant?
- Was the emotional state of the witness such as to preclude identification?[32]

United States v. Ash In *United States v. Ash* (1973), the Supreme Court ruled that the police could show victims or witnesses photographic displays containing a suspect's photograph (photo arrays) without the requirement that the suspect's lawyer be present.[33]

Other Identification Procedures

We know than any type of testimony is governed by the Fifth Amendment. However, in most cases coming before it, the Supreme Court declared that procedures that are not testimonial are not under the purview of the Fifth Amendment. (*Testimonial* refers to oral or written communication by a suspect, as opposed to the taking of blood or exemplars as indicated in this section). A sample of such cases follows.

Schmerber v. California In 1966, in *Schmerber v. California*, the Supreme Court ruled that the forced extraction of blood by a doctor from a man who was arrested for driving while intoxicated was not a violation of that man's constitutional rights.[34]

Winston v. Lee In *Winston v. Lee* (1985), the Supreme Court clarified its position on medical provisions regarding prisoners.[35] When the Court decided the Schmerber case, it warned, "That we today hold that the Constitution does not forbid the States' minor intrusions into an individual's body under stringently limited conditions in no way indicates that it permits more substantial intrusions, or intrusions under other conditions."[36] The Rudolph Lee case provided the test of how far police can go in attempting to retrieve evidence from a suspect's body.

Lee, a suspect in a robbery, was shot by the victim. The police endeavored to have a bullet removed from Lee's body in order to use it for a ballistics examination.

Justice William J. Brennan, speaking for the Court, wrote the following: "We conclude that the procedure sought here is an example of the 'more substantial intrusion' cautioned against in *Schmerber*, and hold that to permit the procedure would violate respondent's right to be secure in his person guaranteed by the Fourth Amendment."[37]

United States v. Dionisio In *United States v. Dionisio*, the Supreme Court in 1973 ruled that a suspect must provide voice exemplars (samples of his or her voice) that can be compared with the voice spoken at the time of the crime.[38]

United States v. Mara In 1973, in *United States v. Mara*, the Supreme Court ruled that it was not a violation of constitutional rights for the police to require a suspect to provide a handwriting exemplar (a sample of his or her handwriting) for comparison with handwriting involved in the crime.[39]

YOU ARE THERE!

United States v. Wade

On September 21, 1964, a man with a piece of tape on each side of his face forced a cashier and a bank official to put money into a pillowcase. The robber then left the bank and drove away with an accomplice, who was waiting outside in a car.

In March 1965, six months after the robbery, an indictment was returned against Wade and an accomplice for the robbery. Wade was arrested on April 2, 1965. Two weeks later, an FBI agent put Wade into a lineup to be observed by two bank employees. Wade had a lawyer, but the lawyer was not notified of the lineup. Each person in the lineup had strips of tape on his face, similar to those worn by the robber, and each was told to say words that had been spoken at the robbery. Both bank employees identified Wade as the robber. Wade was convicted based on the identification by the witnesses.

On appeal, the Supreme Court ruled that placing someone in a lineup and forcing that person to speak or perform other acts at the lineup did not violate the Fifth Amendment privilege against self-incrimination. The Court held, however, that because Wade had been indicted and was represented by counsel, the lawyer should have been allowed to be there.

SOURCE: *United States v. Wade*, 388 U.S. 218 (1967).

Eyewitness Identification Concerning eyewitness identification, in 2001 the National Institute of Justice produced a guide for law enforcement for the collection and preservation of eyewitness evidence that represented a combination of the best current, workable police practices and psychological research. It describes practices and procedures that, if consistently applied, will increase the overall accuracy and reliability of eyewitness evidence. Although not intended to state legal criteria for the admissibility of evidence, it sets out rigorous criteria for handling eyewitness evidence that are as demanding as those governing the handling of physical trace evidence. It outlines basic procedures that officers can use to obtain the most reliable and accurate information from eyewitnesses.[40]

On July 18, 1982, Ralph E. Warkinson was shot during a robbery attempt at his place of business. Warkinson fired at the shooter and believed he hit him in the side. The police brought Warkinson to a local hospital emergency room. Twenty minutes later, the police responded to a reported shooting and found Rudolph Lee suffering from a gunshot wound to the left chest area. Lee said he had been shot during a robbery attempt by two men. When Lee was taken to the hospital (the same one to which Warkinson had been taken), Warkinson identified Lee as the man who had shot him. After a police interrogation, Lee was arrested for the shooting.

In an effort to obtain ballistics evidence, the police attempted to have Lee undergo a surgical procedure under a general anesthetic for the removal of the bullet lodged in his chest. Lee appealed to the courts, which ruled in his favor and against the operation. The Commonwealth of Virginia appealed the case to the U.S. Supreme Court. The Court ruled that such surgical procedure, without Lee's permission, would be a violation of his Fourth Amendment rights.

SOURCE: *Winston v. Lee* (1985), 470 U.S. 753 (1985).

SPECIAL ISSUES IN VIOLENT CRIME

This section covers some special issues in violent crime procedures, including using DNA in solving murder and rape cases; workplace violence; domestic violence; and criminal personality profiling.

Use of DNA in Solving Murder and Rape Cases

As shown in chapter 6 of this text, DNA is extremely important in solving murder and rape cases. However, a significant problem is the current backlog in unprocessed DNA evidence. A 1999 study by the U.S. Justice Department found that about 180,000 rape kits nationwide were untested. According to police in California, their system is overwhelmed. As of 2001, the LAPD crime lab had about 1,400 rape kits waiting for DNA analysis for possible matching with California's computer DNA database, as well as potential DNA evidence in 1,200 murder cases that had not been tested. At the sheriff's crime lab, which services areas outside the city, another 1,200 rape kits and 1,200 homicide cases awaited analysis. These are cases where it is possible that the perpetrator may be someone in the state database but the information is not being processed for possible hits.[41]

DNA testing is so detailed that one analyst can complete work on only about two cases each month. The LAPD lab has just two criminalists qualified to conduct such testing. The sheriff's lab has only eight qualified technicians. Together, the two labs receive an average of more than nine cases daily where DNA testing might prove critical.

In 2000, the New York City Police Department lab had a backlog of sixteen thousand rape kits from older cases. The city spent $12 million to send them to private firms for analysis. In California, many police departments are sending their DNA cases to private labs despite the higher cost. For example, the Torrance Police Department, part of Los Angeles County, pays private labs an average of $6,000 per case,—four times what it would cost for the sheriff's lab. In Long Beach, also part of the county, police no longer send biological evidence to the sheriff's lab unless they have a suspect already in custody.

Workplace Violence

On June 18, 1990, a man with a violent past and a failing marriage who was angry over a repossessed car, entered a GMAC auto finance loan office in southern Florida, and in two minutes shot and killed eight workers and a customer and wounded four others with twenty-eight bullets from a .30 caliber carbine.[42]

In San Leandro, California, in June 2000, a sausage factory owner who had complained he was being harassed by the government over heath violations shot and killed three meat inspectors, one from the U.S. Department of Agriculture and one from the state, who had come to the plant to perform inspections.[43]

Workplace violence is one of the most serious problems facing American society.

Workplace violence was once defined as physical misbehavior, ranging from heated arguments to homicide, occurring between co-workers at their place of employment, but has been extended in recent years to include any criminal misbehavior committed against people in the workplace.[44] The National Institute for Occupational Safety and Health (NIOSH) and the Occupational Safety and Health Administration (OSHA) have studied workplace violence.

In addition to the crimes committed during workplace violence, there are other significant problems linked to this dilemma, including worker compensation claims, insurance costs, lost productivity, employee counseling, grievances, lawsuits, and the extra cost of security. Estimates of workplace violence vary dramatically in academic studies, but it is enormous. Approximately 24 percent of workplace violence incidents involve a weapon, nearly 74 percent of the incidents occur when someone else is present, and about 52 percent of the victimizations are not reported to the police.[45] Exhibit 10.2 highlights some recent cases.

Corporations across the nation are working on this problem and developing strategies and procedures for dealing with it. There have been numerous books, studies, and articles devoted to the issue.[46]

Domestic Violence

Domestic violence, including spousal abuse and lover abuse, is one of the most serious problems for the police, as well as for U.S. families and society in general. National surveys have led researchers to estimate that during any one year 1.7 million U.S. citizens face a spouse threatening them with a knife or gun. The studies also estimate that well over 2 million U.S. citizens have experienced a severe beating at the hands of a spouse and that 50 to 60 percent of all husbands assault their wives at least once during their marriage.[47] A Police Foundation study concluded that the majority of domestic homicides were preceded by previous police calls to the residence.[48] FBI crime statistics indicate that 30 percent of female homicide victims were killed by their husbands or boyfriends, and 4 percent of male homicide victims were killed by wives or girlfriends. Nine of every ten female homicide victims were killed by males.[49] In 1999, according to the Bureau of Justice Statistics, male intimates killed 1,218 women.[50]

A recent University of Michigan study found that violence between intimate couples of opposite gender may start very early. In a survey of suburban, middle-class high school students, about 36 percent of girls and 37 percent of boys said they had experienced physical abuse from a date. Half of the girls—and just 4 percent of the boys—said their worst abusive experience "hurt a lot." Among the other key findings were that 44 percent of the girls stayed with the boys after moderate violence, including slapping, and 36 percent stayed after severe abuse, including choking and punching.[51]

Traditional Police Response to Domestic Violence A reviewer of two books on family violence writes that "domestic violence has a long history in all cultures, but it is only during the last twenty years or so, and only in some advanced industrial nations, that this type of human conflict has gotten the attention and reactions of the criminal justice system."[52]

EXHIBIT 10.2   Some Fatal Cases of Workplace Violence

- December 26, 2000: Seven workers are killed at an Internet consulting company in Wakefield, Massachusetts, by a co-worker whose pay had been garnished by the IRS for back taxes.
- March 20, 2000: Five people are killed at a car wash in Irving, Texas, by a man who had been fired from his job there.
- December 30, 1999: Five workers are killed at a hotel in Tampa, Florida, by a co-worker.
- November 2, 1999: Seven people are killed at a Xerox office in Honolulu by a co-worker.
- July 29, 1999: Nine people are killed by a former day trader at a brokerage office in Atlanta. He then commits suicide.
- March 6, 1998: Four executives are killed by a former accountant in Newington, Connecticut. He then commits suicide.
- December 18, 1997: Four employees are killed by a fired employee at a maintenance yard in Orange, California. He is then killed by the police.
- September 15, 1997: Four workers are killed at a parts plant in Aiken, South Carolina, by a fired assembly-line worker.

SOURCE: "Other Fatal Shootings of Employees at Workplaces in the United States Since 1995," *New York Times*, Dec. 27, 2000, p. A15.

The police, the courts, and society in general have traditionally adopted a hands-off policy toward domestic violence, treating it as a private affair that should be dealt with in the family. The police have generally not made arrests in domestic violence cases, even in those involving assaults with injuries that constitute a felony. Two assumptions prevailed: the arrest would make life worse for the victim, because the abuser might retaliate, and the victim would refuse to press charges.

Most police departments had no formal policies on domestic violence, and officers used many different techniques to deal with the problem when called to the scene. Among the techniques used were attempting to calm down both parties, mediating the conflict, and referring the participants to social service agencies for assistance in dealing with their problems. Often officers would escort abusive spouses out of the residence and advise them not to return until the next day or until things calmed down. Some officers would place abusive spouses in the police car and drive them to a location where it would take them a lot of time to figure out where they were and find their way home. Other officers just ignored domestic violence cases.

Two important lawsuits brought forward by women's groups in New York City (*Bruno v. Codd*, 1978) and Oakland, California (*Scott v. Hart*, 1979) began to change the police response in domestic violence cases. The suits charged that the police departments had denied women equal protection of the law by failing to arrest people who had committed assaults against them. As a result of the lawsuits, both departments formulated official written policies mandating arrests in cases of felonious spousal assault.[53]

Minneapolis Domestic Violence Experiment Subsequent to these lawsuits, the Police Foundation conducted the Minneapolis Domestic Violence Experiment (1981 to 1982). This experiment was designed to examine the deterrent effect of various methods of dealing with domestic violence, including mandatory arrest. During this experiment, officers called to incidents of domestic violence were required to select at random one of a group of instructions to tell them how to deal with the incidents. The officers' forced choice required them to do one of the following: arrest the offender, mediate the dispute, or escort the of-

fender from the home. Repeat violence over the next six months was measured through follow-up interviews with victims and police department records of calls to the same address.[54]

The findings indicated that arrest prevented further domestic violence more effectively than did separation or mediation. Repeat violence occurred in 10 percent of the arrest cases, compared with 19 percent of the mediation incidents and 24 percent of the separation incidents. The actual sanction imposed by arrest involved little more than an evening in jail; only 3 of the 136 people arrested were ever convicted and sentenced.

The Minneapolis experiment has been replicated in a number of other localities. In a conflicting finding, a study in Omaha revealed that arrest by itself did not appear to deter subsequent domestic conflict any more than did mediation or separating the spouses in the dispute.[55]

Police Response to Domestic Violence Today Despite the lack of a clear consensus on the effectiveness of arrest in domestic violence cases, police departments nationwide began to establish new guidelines for these cases. Many police departments today have **proarrest policies**: an abusive spouse must be arrested if the assault is a felony, even if the victim refuses to prosecute. Several states have expanded the arrest power of police in domestic violence cases, giving officers the power to make arrests for misdemeanor assaults that did not occur in their presence, for violations of orders of protection, or both. Some states enacted laws mandating arrest in cases of felonious domestic assault.[56] Many police departments have followed the lead of the Seattle Police Department, which has listed a number of factors (for example, gunshot wounds, broken bones, and intentionally inflicted burns) that should always be considered to involve a felony and thus should always involve an arrest.[57]

Mandatory arrests for domestic violence, however, are still controversial. Eve Buzawa argues that a mandatory arrest policy may deter female victims from calling the police in the first place; many victims simply want the police to help with the immediate crisis but do not necessarily want an arrest.[58] Also, some women feel that arresting an abusive spouse might make him angrier and cause him to commit further violence against them.

Many localities, including Washington, D.C., and Detroit, are forming special police task forces to deal with enforcing domestic violence laws. The Detroit Police Department, in 1996, deployed a fifty-member homicide-reduction task force charged with investigating every domestic homicide reported to police.[59]

Criminal Personality Profiling

Criminal personality profiling, or psychological profiling, is an attempt to identify an individual's mental, emotional, and psychological characteristics. The profile is developed primarily for crimes of violence such as homicides, sadistic crimes, sex crimes, arson without apparent motive, and crimes of serial or ritual sequence. The profile attempts to provide investigators with corroborative information about a known suspect or with possible leads to an unknown subject. According to John Douglas and Alan Burgess, compiling the profile involves the following seven steps:

- Evaluating the criminal act itself
- Evaluating the specifics of the crime scene
- Analyzing the victim
- Evaluating the preliminary police reports
- Evaluating the medical examiner's autopsy protocol
- Developing the profile with critical offender characteristics
- Making investigative suggestions based on the profile[60]

The FBI has classified the serial murderer into two basic types based on evidence and the pathology present at the crime scene. Exhibit 10.3 describes the different profile characteristics of the organized and disorganized murderer, while Exhibit 10.4 describes the differences at crime scenes involving organized and disorganized murderers.

The FBI's National Center for the Analysis of Violent Crime, described earlier in the section on kidnapping, is organized into three divisions: Behavioral Analysis Unit (BAU), Child Abduction Serial Murder Investigative Resources Center (CASMIRC), and Violent Criminal Apprehension Program (VICAP).

The BAU provides behaviorally based investigative and operational support by applying case experience, research, and training to complex and time-sensitive crimes involving acts or threats of violence. BAU assistance is provided through "criminal investigative analysis"—a process of reviewing crimes from both a behavioral and investigative perspective. It involves reviewing and assessing the facts of a crime and interpreting offender behavior and interaction with the victim, as exhibited during the commission of the crime or as displayed in the crime scene.

The CASMIRC provides investigative support through the coordination and provision of federal law enforcement resources, training, and application of other multidisciplinary expertise to assist authorities in child abductions, mysterious disappearances of children, child homicide, and serial murder across the country.

The VICAP facilitates cooperation and communication between law enforcement agencies and supports their efforts to investigate, identify, track, apprehend, and prosecute violent serial offenders. VICAP is a nationwide data information center designed to collect, collate, and analyze crimes of violence, specifically murder. Cases examined by VICAP include solved or unsolved homicides or attempts—especially those that involve an abduction, are apparently random, motiveless, or sexually oriented, or are known or suspected to be part of a series; missing persons cases where the circumstances indicate a strong possibility of foul play and the victim is still missing; and unidentified dead bodies where the manner of death is known or suspected to be homicide.

Cases involving an arrested or identified offender can be submitted to the VICAP system by local law enforcement investigators for comparison and possible matching with unsolved cases. Once a case is entered into the VICAP database, it is compared continually

INVESTIGATIONS ON THE NET

National Center for the Analysis of Violent Crime
http://www.fbi.gov/hq/isd/cirg/ncavc.htm

For an up-to-date list of Web links, go to http://info.wadsworth.com/dempsey

----

YOU ARE THERE!
A Sample VICAP Alert

The O'Fallon, Illinois, Police Department submitted the following case to the FBI for the alert of the VICAP. The FBI published it and requested that any agency with a case exhibiting similar modus operandi contact O'Fallon, even if the case was not a homicide.

The Crime

At approximately 9 P.M. on Friday, December 31, 1999, the O'Fallon Police Department received a 911 call from a local clothing store. Upon entering the building, responding officers observed that the front of the business appeared undisturbed. But a blood trail led them to the women's restroom. Here, the officers found a white female dead from a close-range gunshot wound to the head. The victim was lying on her back, unclothed from the waist down. Her shirt and undergarments were disheveled, partially exposing her breasts. The victim's legs were posed in an open position, indicating a possible sexual assault. However, subsequent laboratory examination for sexual assault proved inconclusive. The victim had a small abrasion on the inner right thigh and a hand impression on the breast area, consistent with a person wearing thick gloves.

The death appeared to have occurred between 2:30 and 3:15 P.M. Investigators believe the victim, who was working alone, was standing in front of the cash register when she was shot. No money was missing from the register.

Crime Scene

The clothing store is a one-story brick structure positioned approximately two blocks from a major highway on a dead-end road. The rear of the building adjoins a railroad track and overlooks large farm fields. The front of the building faces the rear of a convenience store-gas station. The business district is located at the interchange of Interstate 64 and U.S. Highway 50 in O'Fallon. Investigators found no shoeprints at the scene. Also, they located no finger-prints on the victim's body that resulted in the development of a suspect.

Possible Suspect Information

A patron of the clothing store reported that he and his daughter had been shopping at about 2:10 P.M. on the day of the incident. They observed a suspicious male who appeared to be shopping alone. He was described as a white male in his forties or early fifties; five foot six to five foot eight in height; weighing between 170 and 175 pounds; unshaven but no beard; wearing a gray T-shirt, dark ski jacket, dark jeans, and white tennis shoes. He drove a maroon 1990s-model vehicle, possibly a Pontiac, with a blue license plate that had mountains in the background. The witnesses could remember only a partial number of "3V8."

An employee of a realty company, located near the crime scene, reported that at approximately 3 P.M. on the date of the incident, a suspicious male entered the establishment. In the course of their ensuing conversation, the man asked the employee if she was working alone. She pretended that other people were in the building. When she asked for his name, he left without answering. He was described as a white male, five foot six to five foot eight in height, weighing about 170 pounds, with light brown hair parted on the side, and wearing blue jeans and a short-sleeved, green plaid shirt.

Alert to Law Enforcement

Law enforcement agencies should bring this information to the attention of all crime analysis personnel and officers investigating homicides or crimes against persons, sex crimes, and robberies. Any agency with solved or unsolved crimes similar to this one should contact the O'Fallon, Illinois, Police Department or the FBI's Violent Criminal Apprehension Program.

SOURCE: "VICAP Alert: Attention: Homicide Sex Crimes, and Robbery Units," *FBI Law Enforcement Bulletin*, Apr. 2001, pp. 18–20.

EXHIBIT 10.3   **Profile Characteristics of Organized and Disorganized Murderers**

Organized Murderers	Disorganized Murderers
Average to above average intelligence	Below average intelligence
Socially competent	Socially inadequate
Skilled work preferred	Unskilled work
Sexually competent	Sexually incompetent
High birth order status	Low birth order status
Father's work stable	Father's work unstable
Inconsistent childhood discipline	Harsh discipline as child
Controlled mood during crime	Anxious mood during crime
Use of alcohol with crime	Minimal use of alcohol
Precipitating situational stress	Minimal situational stress
Living with partner	Living alone
Mobility with car in good condition	Lives/works near crime scene
Follows crime in news media	Minimal interest in news media
May change jobs or leave town	Significant behavior change (drug/alcohol abuse, religiosity, etc.)

SOURCE: Robert K. Ressler, Ann. W. Burgess, Roger L. Depue, et al., "Crime Scene and Profile Characteristics of Organized and Disorganized Murderers," *FBI Law Enforcement Bulletin*, Aug. 1985, pp. 3–7.

EXHIBIT 10.4   **Crime Scene Differences Between Organized and Disorganized Murderers**

Organized Murder Scenes	Disorganized Murder Scenes
Planned offense	Spontaneous offense
Victim a targeted stranger	Victim/location known
Personalizes victim	Depersonalizes victim
Controlled conversation	Minimal conversation
Crime scene reflects overall control	Crime scene random and sloppy
Demands submissive victim	Sudden violence to victim
Restraints used	Minimal use of restraints
Aggressive acts prior to death	Sexual acts after death
Body hidden	Body left in view
Weapon/evidence absence	Evidence/weapon often present
Transports victim or body	Body left at death scene

SOURCE: Robert K. Ressler, Ann W. Burgess, Roger L. Depue, et al., "Crime Scene and Profile Characteristics of Organized and Disorganized Murderers," *FBI Law Enforcement Bulletin*, Aug. 1985, pp. 3–7.

YOU ARE THERE!

Using Criminal Personality Profiling to Catch a Killer: Richard Trenton Chase, the Vampire Killer

On Monday night, January 23, 1978, David Wallin, twenty-four, returned to his suburban rented home just north of Sacramento, California, from work, and found his twenty-two-year-old wife, Terry, three months pregnant, dead in their bedroom. Her abdomen had been slashed. The first police officer who entered the home later said he had nightmares for months from viewing the carnage.

The major knife wound was a gaping one from chest to umbilicus; portions of the intestines had been left protruding from it, and several internal organs were missing. There were stab wounds to the victim's left breast, and inside those wounds the knife appeared to have been moved about somewhat. There was also evidence that some of the woman's blood had been collected in a yogurt container and drunk.

The following are FBI special agent Robert Ressler's first notes on the probable perpetrator of this terrible crime. These notes were used in the development of the criminal personality profile that eventually led to the capture of Richard Trenton Chase, the Vampire Killer:

> White male, age twenty-five to twenty-seven years; thin, undernourished appearance. Residence will be extremely slovenly and unkempt and evidence of the crime will be found at the residence. History of mental illness, and will have been involved in use of drugs. Will be a loner who does not associate with either males or females, and will probably spend a great deal of time in his own home, where he lives alone. Unemployed. Possibly receives some form of disability income. If residing with anyone, it would be with his parents; however, this is unlikely. No prior military record; high school or college dropout. Probably suffering from one or more forms of paranoid psychosis.

What led Ressler to prepare this profile as he did?

- This was a sexual killing even though there was no evidence of a sex act committed at the crime.

- Such crimes are usually perpetrated by males, and are usually intraracial: white against white, black against black.

- The greatest number of sexual killers are white males in their twenties and thirties. This simple fact allows elimination of whole segments of the population.

- From the appearance of the crime scene, it was obvious that we were dealing with a "disorganized" killer, a person who had a full-blown and serious mental illness.

- It takes eight to ten years to develop the depth of psychosis that would surface in this apparently senseless killing. Paranoid schizophrenia is usually first manifested in the teenage years. Adding ten years to an inception-of-illness age of about fifteen would put the slayer in his mid-twenties.

- The killer displayed introverted schizophrenia, which manifests itself in not eating well, disregarding one's appearance, not caring about cleanliness or neatness. No one would want to live with such a person, so the killer would have to be single.

- The killer would be too disordered to drive somewhere, thus he lived in the area near the victim.

Based on a citizen's tip once the profile was announced in the media, the police arrested Richard Trenton Chase. He matched Ressler's profile remarkably.

SOURCE: Robert K. Ressler and Tom Shachtman, *Whoever Fights Monsters: My Twenty Years Hunting Serial Killers for the FBI* (New York: St. Martin's Press, 1992).

against all other entries on the basis of certain aspects of the crime. The purpose of this is to detect signature aspects of homicide and similar patterns of MOs, which will, in turn, allow VICAP personnel to pinpoint those crimes that may have been committed by the same offender. If patterns are found, the law enforcement agencies involved are notified. This process becomes especially important when a suspect has traveled around the country.

VICAP staff prepare "VICAP Alert" notices for publication in the FBI's *Law Enforcement Bulletin*. These notices generally offer offender descriptive data, information on crimes committed, background, MO, maps showing travel and dates, photographs of the offender and vehicles, and name and telephone number of a contact person in the requesting agency.

SUMMARY

This chapter covered the numerous acts of extreme violence that seem to occur daily in the United States, including murder, rape or sexual assault, robbery, aggravated assault, and kidnapping. It covered many of the techniques law enforcement uses to investigate and solve these crimes. It discussed the procedures used by law enforcement to help victims identify suspects, including lineups, showups, photo arrays, and eyewitness identification. It also covered some special issues in the investigation of violent crimes, including the use of DNA in solving murder and rape or sexual assault cases and workplace violence, domestic violence, and criminal personality profiling.

This textbook went into production just one month after the worst case of mass murder in the history of the United States: the murder of thousands in the attacks on the World Trade Center and the Pentagon on September 11, 2001. Since that fatal day, the most massive murder investigation in U.S. history has taken place.

Recall for a few minutes the methods we noted in this text to investigate murders: response to the scene; crime scene processing, analysis, and reconstruction; interviews and interrogations; record checks; identification procedures; theory formation; apprehension of perpetrator; and preparation for trial with prosecutors. Using information developed during the first six methods after the September 11 attacks, we hope that investigators can proceed to the final two steps, clear this case, and bring those who committed this crime to justice.

LEARNING CHECK

1. Describe some of the methods the police use to solve crimes of murder.

2. Describe some of the methods the police use to solve rape or sexual assault cases.

3. Describe some proactive measures the police use to apprehend robbers.

4. Name and describe two measures used by the police to help a victim identify suspects after a violent crime.

5. Discuss some of the uses of VICAP in investigating murder cases.

APPLICATION EXERCISE

You have been selected to participate in a college work-study program with your local police department. Your professor and the chief of police collaborate and prepare an assignment for you. The police chief calls you in for an interview and tells you the following:

"Because of reduced crime rates and increases in our budget we are anticipating increasing the size of our detective division by two investigators. We would like them to work exclusively on old unsolved cases that did not receive sufficient attention due to previous staffing and workload problems.

"Your task is to research how we should do this. We are particularly interested in finding out how other departments around the country have addressed this problem.

"Prepare a detailed report for my review indicating your findings and recommendations. Also, I want you to include a list of all the resources you use in your project, including academic and professional resources, as well as Internet sources."

WEB EXERCISE

Your professor assigns the following topic for an extra credit exercise: Prepare an eight- to ten-page report on resources available from the federal government to help local law enforcement agencies solve violent crimes. Locate several such programs from Internet Web sites and summarize these programs. Properly document the Internet sources you use.

KEY TERMS

blending operations

cold case investigations

coroner

criminal personality profiling

decoy operations

domestic violence

forensic death investigations

kidnapping

manslaughter

medical examiner

modus operandi (MO)

murder

proarrest policies

rape

rape evidence kits

serial murder

sexual assault

stakeouts

time line

workplace violence

THE INVESTIGATION OF PROPERTY CRIMES

11

CHAPTER GOALS

1. To give you a sense of the property crime situation in the United States, including burglary, larceny or theft, motor vehicle theft, and arson

2. To acquaint you with the methods police use to conduct reactive investigations of burglary, larceny or theft, motor vehicle theft, and arson

3. To familiarize you with methods used by private security to investigate property crime

4. To introduce you to the many proactive measures that can be taken by businesses and the public to prevent property crimes

5. To discuss the role of the federal government in assisting in the investigation of arson crimes

INTRODUCTION

Property crime has a tremendous negative affect on persons, businesses, and U.S. society in general. According to *Uniform Crime Reports,* prepared by the FBI, the dollar loss to burglary victims in the latest reporting year was over $3 billion; larceny or theft victims, $4.7 billion; motor vehicle theft victims, $7 billion; and arson victims, $1 billion.[1]

The monetary losses involved in these property crimes are only the tip of the iceberg. There are also tremendous personal, business, and social costs involved. Some of the personal costs are the physical and emotional injuries victims suffer as a result of being a crime victim. Among the business costs of property crime are bankruptcies, business failures, the cost of increased insurance, loss of profit, reduced productivity, higher overhead, and much more. Among the social costs are the cost of investigating, prosecuting, and incarcerating offenders and the emotional effect of crime on our society.

Also, consider the enormous personal cost of crime to the victim. Imagine that you come home from a hard day at work or school and you discover there has been a burglary in your home—all of your property and belongings are gone. Or, you wake up in the morning and discover your car is stolen. These experiences seriously affect your life and sense of security.

This chapter will discuss the property crimes of burglary, larceny or theft, motor vehicle theft, and arson. It will give you a sense of how these crimes occur and methods the police and private security use to investigate them and to protect against them.

As was mentioned in chapter 10, in keeping with the intent of this book to provide more "what's it all about" than "how to" information, much of the material on methods of investigation presented here is quite general. For more specific methods of investigation information for each crime, students are urged to research the scholarly and professional sources noted here, paying special attention to information offered by the professional associations that have a presence on the Internet. Most importantly, students are urged to interact closely with those true experts, both academic and professional, who have done or are doing the real work of investigating and to listen to their advice and learn from their experience. A textbook can never replace the real lessons one can learn from these experts.

PROPERTY CRIME

The most recent *Uniform Crime Reports* published by the FBI indicated that there were 10,270,777 property crimes reported in the United States in the latest reporting year, including 2,099,739 burglaries, 6,957,412 larcenies, 1,147,305 motor vehicle thefts, and 66,321 arsons. The clearance rates for these crimes were 14 percent for burglary, 19 percent for larceny, 15 percent for motor vehicle theft, and 17 percent for arson.[2]

People have always been worried about crime and have taken measures to isolate or protect themselves against it. Peace and security in one's neighborhood and home is one of humankind's most treasured values. As Professor George L. Kelling has written, "Citizens have armed themselves, restricted their activities, rejected cities, built fortress houses and housing complexes both inside and outside the cities, and panicked about particular groups and classes of citizens."[3] The police as well as private security are constantly investigating and attempting to prevent property crime in our communities in order to maintain a sense of security and well-being in our lives.

The Police and Property Crime

In response to crime, the public police routinely patrol residential and commercial areas looking for suspicious persons and other conditions that may indicate that a crime is in progress. They also respond to calls of these crimes in progress, as well as calls about suspicious persons or circumstances. The police, by their routine patrol, attempt to provide a sense of omnipresence (they are always around, or at least, always seem to be around) in the hope of making citizens and businesspeople feel safe and secure in their neighborhoods. Most of the arrests that the police make are the result of their attempts to provide this sense of omnipresence and their attempts to respond to and investigate the calls made to them.

The following reported incident from the June 23, 2000, *Tampa Tribune* shows the value of the normal routine presence of the police in a neighborhood.

> A sheriff's deputy was getting coffee at McDonald's Thursday morning in Tampa when patrons suggested he check out two teens who had just run out of the store. The teens had reason to run. A quick check of the Honda Accord they had driven to the restaurant

and left in the parking lot showed the car was stolen. Inside the car, deputies found two more teens asleep in the backseat. They also found a stolen gun. The teens in the car were arrested. The deputies also arrested the two who ran, in a parking lot.[4]

This example, just one of millions of such occurrences every year in the United States, shows that the police, just by stopping for coffee, were able to apprehend four persons in possession of a stolen vehicle, recover a victim's stolen vehicle, take another illegal gun off the street, and possibly prevent a rash of more crime that these individuals could have committed.

In addition to their omnipresence and response to crime, the police also investigate past property crimes in an attempt to clear these crimes and bring those responsible for them to justice.

Private Security and Property Crime

Private security efforts are extremely important in investigating, preventing, and clearing property crime. Businesses and other private concerns make special concentrated efforts to detect and apprehend persons committing these crimes as indicated in this chapter and many other chapters of this text.

One particular, relatively recent, effort of the business community to prevent crime and to improve conditions in the communities in which they do business is the concept of Business Improvement Districts (BIDs). Business Improvement Districts are private organizations that oversee critical services, such as sanitation and security, for businesses in a defined geographical area or district. They collect assessments from each participating business in their area in return for providing supplemental services, including street lighting, security patrols, and garbage pickup.

Since the 1980s, numerous BIDs have been created in New York City, such as the Grand Central Partnership, the Bryant Park Restoration Corporation, and the 34th Street Business Improvement District.[5] As of 1999, forty public-private partnerships have sprung up in the city, some having revenues of $1 million or more. The city collects the assessment from the property owners and returns it to the BIDs to use for its services. The BIDs maintain proprietary security departments and also hire contract security firms to patrol on foot and in vehicles throughout the district and cooperate with the local police. These BIDs have received world-wide attention and acclaim as an example of a method to ensure security and other services.[6]

Also, residents have sought the assistance of private security to help the police protect their community. The following is a good example of the modern philosophy of involving citizens, private security, and the police in anticrime efforts:

> If a resident of a building on 77th Street between 2nd and 3rd Avenues in New York City senses suspicious activity on the block, the resident can press a button in the middle of a key chain transmitter that sends a radio frequency signal to a receiver. Immediately a device mounted on a building on the block receives the signal and a loud siren is triggered with an alert message that screams incessantly, "Intruder on the block, call the police." Also, a police siren and a series of strobe lights go off. The alarm company's central office identifies the caller based on the personal ID code embedded in the alarm signal and calls 911. This is an experimental system being used by the 77th Street Block Association designed to protect their block. If fifty residents on a block participate in the Safe-Block security technology program they can buy the alarm device for $70 with a $6 monthly fee.[7]

BURGLARY

Burglary can be defined as the unlawful entry of a structure in order to commit a crime therein. Burglaries may be residential or commercial.

A recent crime survey study of residential burglary reported that the following factors increased the risk of residential burglary: lack of security, low levels of occupancy, living in a detached house, and living in inner-city areas.[8] The same study reported that in most burglaries with entry, forcible means were used to gain entry and in 22 percent of the cases the offender entered through an open window or an unlocked door. In 25 percent of the burglaries, someone was at home and was aware of what was happening and in 11 percent of the burglaries, violent or threatening behavior was used. In this study, 48 percent of all households had security lights and 24 percent had burglar alarms. Security devices were very effective in reducing the risk of burglary victimization.

Another interesting recent study focused on the motives, background, and working methods (modus operandi) of commercial burglars. The study revealed that in many cases burglars planned their crimes by collecting information on a firm and the goods stored as well as information on the storage and transport of valuable goods, machinery, and other products.[9]

Methods of Investigation

There are several methods of investigation used in burglary cases, including response to the scene, crime scene processing, analysis, and reconstruction, interviews and interrogations, identification procedures, record checks, theory formation, apprehension of perpetrator, and preparation for trial with prosecutors.

Burglary investigations generally commence when a person discovers the burglary and notifies the police. In some cases the police will receive a 911 call about a possible break-in in progress, and sometimes the police will come upon a past burglary or a burglary in progress while on routine patrol.

At major burglaries, the police may institute crime scene procedures as indicated in chapter 3 of this text. Using crime scene processing, analysis, and reconstruction, investigators can seek to identify offenders using physical evidence. Police pay special attention to points of entrance or exit. Latent fingerprints that can be obtained from locations that might have been touched by the perpetrator can be processed by the police crime lab, which attempts to link those prints to known prints in its fingerprint files. The emergence of sophisticated computerized fingerprint comparison systems—Automated Fingerprint Identification Systems (AFIS)—has made this task easier. (See chapter 6 of this text for more on AFIS.)

Police can also process tool mark (burglars' tools) evidence (the impressions made by tools such as crowbars or pry bars) found at the point where the burglar entered the premises. The tool mark evidence can be compared to tool mark evidence already in police records from previous burglaries. Tools may bear unique microscopic characteristics because of manufacturing processes and previous use. These characteristics can be transferred to the surfaces that are contacted by the tools, such as the use of a crowbar or pry bar on a door or window. Evidence tool marks can be compared to recovered tools. In the absence of a questioned tool, examinations can determine which type of tool produced the mark and whether the mark

is of value for comparison. The lab will make a cast of the tool mark, if needed. If it is not possible to submit the tool-mark evidence, investigators submit a cast of the tool mark. Photographs can be used to locate tool marks but are of no value for identification purposes. Investigators obtain samples of any material deposited on the tools, and in order to avoid contamination of evidence, do not place the tool against the tool-mark evidence.[10]

In addition, insulation from broken or forced-open safes can adhere to persons, clothing, tools, and other substances and also transfer to vehicles used for taking stolen property from the scene. This evidence may be submitted to the crime laboratory for examiners to remove and analyze the debris.

Police also use the interview and interrogation process described in chapter 7 of this text in burglary investigations. They interview residents, witnesses, and any other persons who may have information on the crime. They also interrogate persons suspected of committing the crime.

Sometimes, if they have reason to believe that a person is making a false report of the burglary in order to cover business losses, make fraudulent insurance claims, or for any other reason, they investigate the person making the report.

In burglary cases, the police will examine all appropriate records, including reports of past crimes at the same location or similar crimes in the same area to determine if a pattern is present; then they work on the pattern. In cases in which the police suspect a false report they may look into business records of the complainant. Also, the police may ask witnesses to give descriptions or to participate in identification procedures such as showups, photo arrays, and lineups.

When attempting to develop a theory about the crime, the police pay special attention to MO information. They investigate persons using similar MOs in other crimes. They also consider pattern information on past crimes at the location or similar crimes in the area to identify particular suspects.

Proactive Measures Against Burglary

Homeowners and businesses can take numerous proactive security measures to prevent burglary, including alarm systems, security surveys, and private security and self-protection methods.

Alarm Systems The concept that "one's home is one's castle" is very important to Americans. People build perimeter protection such as fences, walls, and shrubbery around their homes to protect them and maintain their privacy. They also spend fortunes on outdoor security lighting, locks, and burglary and anti-intrusion alarm systems.

Modern alarm system electronic sensors positioned throughout the house detect things like broken glass, fluctuations in sound waves, changes in temperature, and the like. When a sensor indicates that someone may have broken into a house, the sensor transmits an identifying serial number to the main control unit, which sounds the alarm. Simultaneously, the control unit dials the monitoring station and sends electronic transmissions or messages that identify the house's location as well as the point of entry. The central station operator calls the residents to verify that a break-in has occurred. If a resident doesn't respond or does not provide the password, the monitoring station calls the local police department.[11]

Home alarms are getting more sophisticated. Security companies are adopting sophisticated wireless technology, allowing homeowners to manage the family computer, living room audio system, and alarm system at the same time. In the new so-called smart house, the usual keypad control mounted near the front door is replaced by a touch screen that can display a wide array of information and controls. If a homeowner is going away for a few days, for example, she can set the alarm and also program the audio system to play in the evenings so the house would seem occupied. It can even control the thermostat so a pet can remain warm.

Home Security Surveys Numerous police departments throughout the United States offer **home security surveys** and business security surveys free of charge. They also offer **Operation Identification** programs that involve engraving identifying numbers (usually Social Security numbers) onto property such as bicycles, televisions, and other personal electronic items with the goal of returning the property to owners if it is stolen and then recovered by the police. The program also involves displaying decals on windows announcing that a house is equipped with an alarm or has participated in an Operation Identification program.[12]

Private Security and Self-Protection Measures Many studies reveal reported declines in burglaries at residences where people engaged in theft deterrence programs such as property marking compared with control groups of nonparticipating residences.[13]

Many homes today are built in private, gated communities, which offer owners a sense of security because the entire community is enclosed in perimeter fencing or walls and have one means of entrance and exit to the community. At the entrance-exit, there is generally a conspicuous guard booth manned by a security guard who checks all persons entering the community. Some communities have installed electronic turnstiles at their entrances requiring residents to enter an identification card in order for the gates to rise to permit entry. People without identification cards are questioned by the security guard, who checks with the homeowners to see if the person should be admitted.

In multiple dwellings, such as apartment houses, security is often a major concern. Some dwellings employ security guards or doormen to regulate entry into the building and to patrol the building. Others have sophisticated access-controlled entrances that require visitors to be allowed into the building by a particular tenant.

Condominium and co-op complexes have similar security concerns and countermeasures. Some condominium and co-op complexes use security guards and CCTV technology. Multiple dwellings like these often put CCTV systems into laundry and recreation rooms, parking lots, equipment storage and maintenance rooms, hallways, and entrances.

In an example of condominium security, the Capri Gardens Condominium, a five-hundred-resident complex in North Miami, Florida, which has three four-story residential buildings and a one-story recreation center, has two uniformed security officers on duty between 8 P.M. and 8 A.M., seven days a week. Their duties include patrolling the grounds, calling police if an incident occurs, and acting as a witness for the police in the event of any crime or incident. By using an $18,000 CCTV surveillance system, vandalism has recently been curtailed and two residents involved in suspicious activity were caught and evicted. In addition, $4,000 in

YOU ARE THERE!
How Princeton University Protects Student Dorms

Since the early 1990s, Princeton University has been equipping all dormitories and other buildings with automatic locks and a system for unlocking the doors using a slim plastic card—called a proximity card—which is issued to each student. Students refer to it as a "prox card." Since 1998, all dormitories are locked all the time. The prox card, similar to a smart card, also serves as photo ID for the student, library card, charge card for all purchases on campus, and meal card. To get into a dormitory, a student flashes the card at a black plastic box near the dormitory entrance (thus the name *proximity card*). Inside the box, a transmitter sends all information on the student's entry to the school's main computer. This information is stored for three weeks.

But some students consider the stored entry information an invasion of their privacy. Other students claim that many students routinely use other students' cards, such as their roommate's. One student said, "If people's parents come, everyone says, 'Have someone prox you in and come up to my room.'" She said that students often let others enter the dormitories under the assumption that the people were friends or relatives of dormitory residents or simply residents who had forgotten their cards.

SOURCE: Peter Wayner, "Closed-Door Policy: Princeton's Electronic Security System, Designed to Protect Students, Makes Some Feel Safer and Others Uneasy," *New York Times*, Nov. 12, 1998, p. E1.

YOU ARE THERE!
The Value of Good Lighting, Fences, and Gates

Good lighting deters criminals and provides a sense of safety for users and the ability to observe the premises. Sodium lights are best because they provide ten times the light of an incandescent bulb with the same electrical wattage. Lights should always be on.

Fences, gates, and other perimeter barriers do not keep out all those who are determined to get in, but they do perform four important functions:

- They delineate the boundaries and define any unauthorized persons within as trespassers.
- They discourage wanderers and opportunistic thieves.
- They delay penetration for an amount of time sufficient for police or security to respond.
- They channel legitimate traffic to a limited number of entrances and exits that can be managed by security and access control equipment.

Fences can be secured with intrusion sensors that provide immediate electronic indication of people attempting to get over or under them.

SOURCES: Dan M. Bowers, "Assigning a Place for Parking Security," *Security Management*, Dec. 1999, pp. 63–67; Terry Pristin, "A Push for Security Gates That Invite Window Shopping," *New York Times*, Aug. 1, 2000, p. B8.

property damage has been documented and recovered from several residents who crashed their vehicles into the condo's entrance gate.[14]

LARCENY OR THEFT

Larceny or theft is the unlawful taking of property from the possession or constructive possession of another. It includes crimes such as shoplifting, pocket picking, purse snatching, fraud, embezzlement, theft from motor vehicles, theft of motor vehicle parts and acces-

sories, bicycle thefts, and the like, in which no use of force or violence occurs. When force or violence or threats of such use is involved, the larceny or theft is classified as a robbery. When it is accompanied by the illegal entrance into a structure, it is classified as a burglary; and when the object stolen is a motor vehicle it is classified as motor vehicle theft.

Several chapters of this text discuss in detail particular types of larceny or theft and the methods used for investigating such crimes:

Chapter 9, "Surveillance and Undercover Investigations," provides detailed information on retail larceny or theft, including shoplifting and employee theft. It discusses retail loss prevention and store detective programs aimed at shoplifters and internal thieves; silent witness programs, shopping services, and mystery shoppers; civil recovery programs; electronic article surveillance and ink tags; closed circuit television (CCTV); current legal cases on the shopkeeper's privilege; and academic studies on loss prevention.

Chapter 14, "The Investigation of Computer Crime," provides material on larceny or theft crime that involves the use of computers, including fraud, stock fraud, auction fraud, cybercrime, identity theft, and theft of computers. It also looks at methods of investigating these crimes.

Chapter 15, "Private Sector Investigations," includes detailed material on larceny or theft crimes and investigations that are handled by private security, including embezzlement, insurance fraud, theft of intellectual property rights, and industrial espionage. It gives many examples of specific investigations as well as proactive measures to prevent crimes conducted in these areas.

In addition to their discussions of these crimes and the methods of investigating them, these chapters provide numerous Web sites of professional investigative organizations and associations in these areas.

Methods of Investigation

Several methods of investigation are used in larceny or theft cases, including response to the scene, crime scene processing, analysis, and reconstruction, interviews and interrogations, identification procedures, record checks, theory formation, apprehension of perpetrator, and preparation for trial with prosecutors.

Generally, police become aware of crimes of larceny or theft when a person reports their occurrence. The public police patrol areas of stores on foot and in vehicle patrols and respond to incidents and requests for service when they are called. Because of the low probability of clearing many of these crimes, the police invest very little investigatory time on some of them. Recall the discussion of the research revolution in investigating in chapter 1 of this text, and the emphasis that investigators now put on the most solvable crimes using programs such as MCI (Managing Criminal Investigations).

Private security firms, however, concentrate on the large theft problem in our society, particularly as it relates to shoplifting and employee dishonesty. Loss prevention is one of the primary concerns of retail businesses in the United States. Shoplifting and employee theft are significant security problems for most of them. Most large retail businesses have a propriety security department that performs numerous duties in loss prevention, safety, and internal auditing. Smaller businesses and stores may have a proprietary security employee on duty, or may hire a security guard from a contract guard service.

Proactive Measures Against Larceny or Theft

The police conduct numerous decoy programs, including blending and decoy operations, and other proactive programs, such as stings, to investigate and prevent property crimes by arresting those who attempt to commit them. Recall the many types of such programs and many examples of each discussed in chapters 9 and 10 of this text.

As we noted earlier, private security is constantly involved in proactive measures for detecting and preventing thefts of corporate assets. See chapter 9, "Surveillance and Undercover Investigations," chapter 14, "The Investigation of Computer Crime," and chapter 15, "Private Sector Investigations" of this text for more on this.

MOTOR VEHICLE THEFT

Motor vehicle theft is defined as the theft or attempted theft of a motor vehicle, including the stealing of automobiles, trucks, buses, motorcycles, motor scooters, snowmobiles, and the like.

Vehicle theft is the number one property crime in the country, costing more than $7 billion each year. Approximately 1.1 million vehicles are stolen nationwide each year and more than 30 percent are never recovered. Many motor vehicles are stolen for their parts. The parts are then removed in automobile **chop shops** and later used to repair other damaged autos. (Chop shops are garages that strip a stolen car of usable parts for sale to auto repair businesses.) The National Insurance Crime Bureau (NICB) reports that many stolen vehicles are shipped overseas or driven across state and international borders for resale—approximately two hundred thousand vehicles are

YOU ARE THERE!

Auto Accident Fraud: Operation Twisted Metal

In a joint investigation and sting operation, the San Diego Police Department, California Department of Insurance, the National Insurance Crime Bureau (NICB), Immigration and Naturalization Service (INS), and the FBI successfully penetrated a large-scale staged auto accident ring operating out of San Diego.

Undercover agents worked closely with the subjects of the investigation, who planned and executed eleven staged accidents and two staged auto thefts. The subjects were tape-recorded describing the manner in which they staged the collisions, how the scheme was concocted with the participating attorneys and doctors, and how the participants divided the proceeds. During the course of the investigation, over five hundred undercover contacts were made in a twenty-two-month period. Over forty separate fraudulent claims were made to private insurance carriers based on the eleven staged collisions.

In May 1998, fourteen subjects were indicted in the Southern District of California, including "cappers," attorneys, administrators, chiropractors, and "stuffed passengers."

The following are some key terms used by those who stage auto accidents:

- *Cappers.* These individuals recruit stuffed passengers who will be used to submit fraudulent claims to the insurance companies. They are paid a percentage of the total receipts from the false claims.

- *Stuffed passengers.* These individuals are recruited to make false claims about their involvement in automobile accidents. They are typically coached on the details of the fictitious collisions and resulting fictitious injuries.

- *Nail car.* This is the victim vehicle involved in the staged accident that is hit by the hammer car. The vehicle is generally "stuffed" with passengers, who then file the false insurance claims with the assistance of legal professionals.

- *Hammer car.* This is the "at fault" vehicle in a staged accident that hits the nail car. This car is typically insured, and the insurer is often defrauded of an average of $6,000 per claimant per accident.

- *Kickback.* This is a term for fees paid to cappers by unethical attorneys and medical providers for the referral of accidents.

SOURCE: Federal Bureau of Investigation, *Major Investigation, Twisted Metal;* http://www.fbi.gov/contact/fo/sandiego/twisted/twisted.htm.

---

illegally exported each year. Newer models are more likely to be illegally shipped abroad, whereas older vehicles are mainly stolen for their parts. Sometimes cars are stolen for use in other crimes or for "joyriding."[15]

An interesting study of car thieves in Great Britain revealed that most of the offenders interviewed said they began to steal cars in their early to mid-teens, with the help of more experienced offenders. The influence of friends, the excitement of stealing cars, and boredom were the primary reasons given for first becoming involved in car theft. Over time, the opportunity to make money from car theft apparently became increasingly important, and over one-third progressed to "professional" car theft for financial gain. Over half

described themselves as "specialists"—stealing cars more or less to the exclusion of other crimes. Specialists were more likely to have had a youthful obsession with cars. Although accepting that car theft was morally wrong, most offenders did not consider it a serious crime. The excitement of car theft apparently overcame any appreciation of the threat of punishment. Nine out of every ten offenders said they were not deterred by the prospect of being caught. Most of those who said they had stopped stealing cars attributed this to increased responsibilities and maturity. The threat of penal sanctions seemed relatively unimportant in stopping them. Offenders said car alarms deterred them.[16]

YOU ARE THERE!
Shoplifting and Fencing: Operation American Dream

In the mid-1990s, a Pakistani criminal syndicate ran a large-scale shoplifting-fencing-repackaging business in the Atlanta metropolitan area. They targeted stores in and on the outskirts of the city, stealing over-the-counter medicines, pharmaceuticals, razors, health and beauty aids, computers, DVDs, stereos, TVs, clothing, shoes, and household goods from nationally recognized retail stores.

The Georgia Bureau of Investigation (GBI), after a six-month investigation, arrested the participants and closed down the operation. But within a few weeks, the gang simply regrouped and was back in operation. At this time, private security investigators for the Dayton Hudson Corporation (DHC), the owners of nationally known retail stores like Target, began to investigate the group. They discovered that its operation expanded far beyond Atlanta.

Operation American Dream was then established with the private security investigators, GBI, the Atlanta Police Department, the Immigration and Naturalization Service (INS), the Internal Revenue Service (IRS), and the FBI. The investigation disclosed that the principals in the Atlanta fencing operation were conspiring with other foreign nationals in Baltimore, New York, and Pakistan to fence and repackage millions of dollars of stolen merchandise. In addition to fencing stolen items, they had been involved in money laundering, illegal alien smuggling, auto theft, interstate transportation of stolen goods, and attempted murder.

The leaders of the operation, thirty predominantly illegal Pakistani nationals, who operated convenience stores that were receiving the stolen merchandise, recruited a group of over two hundred professional shoplifters and illegal Pakistani immigrants. The shoplifters, also called *boosters*, would steal from retail stores primarily in small towns where store security was minimal. They would operate in groups of four or five, often using distraction techniques to steal merchandise. The group leaders supported them with vehicles and legal help if they were arrested. The stolen merchandise would later be taken to a warehouse, where it was repackaged and shipped to co-conspirators in New York, Baltimore, and Pakistan. The merchandise would then be resold to retail stores.

In October 1999, a 214-count indictment resulted in the arrests of numerous subjects for multiple counts of conspiracy, money laundering, and interstate transportation of stolen property. Over $1.6 million in stolen retail merchandise and one-half million dollars in currency were seized.

SOURCE: Federal Bureau of Investigation, *Major Investigations, Operation American Dream;* http://www.fbi.gov/majcases/dream/dream.htm.

Carjacking is the use of force to steal cars from their drivers. Carjackers strike in major cities, suburban towns, and rural areas; they may rob and kill victims to possess their luxury vehicles, convert parts to cash, commit another crime, or just have transportation. Although many carjacking victims have been alone or isolated at the time of the carjacking, in numerous cases offenders have targeted parents with children. Many armed confrontations have occurred while victims were at red lights, stop signs, fast food drive-through lines, automatic teller machines, self-service gas stations, convenience stores, parking lots, shopping centers, pay telephones, and self-service car washes. Causal theories proposed for armed carjackings include the anti-theft device theory (circumvention of anti-theft devices); the economic theory (sale of vehicle and parts for cash), the desperation theory (desperation for immediate money), the availability theory (victims are easy prey), and the brazen theory (arrogance and thirst for confrontation).[17]

Methods of Investigation

Several methods of investigation are used in auto theft cases, including response to the scene, crime scene processing, analysis, and reconstruction, interviews

YOU ARE THERE!

How Museums, Libraries, and Archives Try to Prevent Property Crime

The primary security concerns at museums, libraries, and archives are the protection of valuables, access control, perimeter protection, vandalism, order maintenance, and crowd control. These institutions have valuable collections of art, artifacts, books, manuscripts, and other treasures that can never be replaced.

Although there are no reliable figures on the extent of art theft, Interpol estimates that it is exceeded in dollar value only by drug trafficking, money laundering, and arms dealing. Protecting collections without impeding the public's ability to enjoy them is a delicate balancing act.

Large museums, libraries, and archives generally have a proprietary security department and make extensive use of security guards at entrances and in exhibits. Guards also engage in order maintenance with unruly patrons. Also used are a variety of devices to prevent entry and prevent theft of art, such as motion detectors; infrared sensors that monitor a room's temperature and can see the shapes of warm bodies moving through it; ultrasonic sensors that trigger an alarm if their sound waves strike a foreign object; and microwave sensors hidden in the walls. Libraries have electronic markings on books and other valuables that trigger electronic sensors at exits to reduce thefts.

Formerly, museum display cases holding valuable art had metallic strips that sounded an alarm when the glass was broken, but it was felt that they took away from the attractiveness of the display. Now museums use acoustic sensors that can be as small as a quarter; they set off an alarm when they detect glass breaking or being cut.

A camera trained on a specific object can be programmed to sound an alarm at any shift in the object's outline. Some institutions are even considering a sort of LoJack system for artwork: little wireless transmitters that could track the location and movement of every object in their collections. Conservators, though, are often wary of affixing anything to old works of art.

To protect against insider thefts, these institutions check employee backgrounds carefully, issue card keys to restrict access in buildings, guard storage rooms that hold the bulk of most collections, enforce strict rules for signing objects in and out, and teach guards to watch their fellow employees as closely as they watch strangers. With today's tiny, high-resolution video cameras and Internet technology, museum and security officials can even view the galleries and their guards from a central control room or other remote location.

At museums, fire poses a greater threat than crime. Many art museums are reluctant to use sprinkler systems for fear than an accident could flood their paintings. Some use sprinklers whose pipes stay empty until the fire is detected; others use chemicals or gases to extinguish fires, although one of the popular gases was found to threaten the ozone layer. Many use quick-closing fire doors to isolate and contain fires. Some of the newest fire alarms can sample air for minute particles of combustion, and gauge smoke, heat, light, and air ionization.

One of the most frequent problems at museums are visitors who feel they must touch the art. Some museums use electric-eye-type sensors that beep or play recorded messages when people get too close. Others place works behind railings or glass. Some museums rely on psychology: a strip of brass along the floor, about a foot and a half from the wall, has been effective in keeping people from getting too close to displays. However, the most ubiquitous security concern may be the visitor for whom those "Do Not Touch" signs are a challenge rather than a warning.

SOURCES: Michael Cooper, "The Walls Have Ears, and Other High-Tech Crime Gadgets," *New York Times*, Apr. 19, 2000, p. 4; Cooper, "The Big Dangers: Fire and Fingers," *New York Times*, Apr. 19, 2000, p. 4; "Library Security," *Security Management*, Feb. 2000, p. 17.

DEMPSEY'S LAW
Using Decoy and Blending Operations to Apprehend Property Criminals

As I indicated when we discussed violent crime, the police use various blending and decoy operations to apprehend criminals in the act of committing a crime. In my experience as the anticrime supervisor in my precinct in Brooklyn we engaged in many of these operations and were quite successful. Let me give you some more examples of our blending and decoy operations.

While blending in commercial as well as residential areas, we would often come upon people in the act of committing crimes that they never would have attempted if a uniformed officer was around. I can remember numerous arrests we made of people snatching pocketbooks or other personal property from shoppers and from storekeepers. Sometimes we just came upon crimes as they were going down, and sometimes we would target potential offenders or vic-

tims and follow them. I recall several times when we actually caught a burglar in the act of going into someone's windows either from the street level or from a fire escape. It was always an adrenaline rush when we would follow them in and then take them down.

Sometimes we would use techniques similar to those decoy operations we used against robbers. We would park a car in a residential or commercial parking area that had experienced high incidences of thefts of and from autos and then wait for a thief to go into action. Sometimes, one of us would leave personal property such as a briefcase or suitcase on the sidewalk next to a pay phone and act as if he were making a call and not paying attention to the property. Of course, the backup team was always ready. I will never forget the shocked looks on the perps' faces when we took them down.

and interrogations, identification procedures, record checks, theory formation, apprehension of perpetrator, and preparation for trial with prosecutors.

Generally, the police become aware of automobile larcenies when people report their occurrence to the police or when the police stop a vehicle for a traffic violation in the course of their regular patrol duties or suspect that a vehicle is stolen. When police receive a report of a stolen car, they transmit a stolen car alarm, or alert, which is then broadcast to other police units on patrol and is stored in law enforcement and motor vehicle computers, including the National Criminal Information Center (NCIC) for subsequent checks. When police stop motorists for safety violations or traffic offenses they access information from these computers to determine whether or not the autos stopped are stolen.

Special police auto larceny units also check auto body shops and car salvage lots to determine if there are stolen autos or stolen auto parts there. Police also investigate the possibility of false auto theft reports where the auto is not stolen but in fact abandoned or

destroyed and then reported as stolen for insurance remuneration.

The introduction of mobile digital terminals in police vehicles enables the police to quickly check suspicious vehicles to determine whether or not they are stolen. Jerome H. Skolnick and David H. Bayley discuss computer terminals in Houston Police Department patrol cars:

> The terminals increase enormously the amount of relevant information patrol officers have. For example, they can determine before they step out of their cars if the vehicle they have just signaled to a stop is stolen, or if its owner, who may be the driver, is wanted in any connection. Officers cruising down the street often idly type in the license plate numbers of cars driving ahead or parked at sleazy motels or private clubs in the faint hope that something interesting will turn up, like hitting a jackpot in a slot machine. The public is generally unaware just how much Big Brother is watching through the new technology.[18]

A good example of the use of modern mobile communications systems is the experience of the

DEMPSEY'S LAW
"Professor, They Stole My Car": A Typical Auto Theft Ring Operation

Professor, my '89 Mustang was just stolen. I parked it outside my house like I always do and then when I went out in the morning it was gone. I called the police and an officer responded and took a report. Why did someone take it? Do you think the police will get it back for me?

Sorry about your car. The answer to your second question, I am sorry to say, is no. You will probably never get your car back. In answer to your first question, let's discuss the typical auto theft ring operation. As an example, let's use my favorite car, which similar to yours, was a 1989 Mustang GT, ragtop. It was sky blue.

It starts like this. Someone has an accident with his car and the left quarter panel is damaged. Now, of course, no one with a mint '89 Mustang GT ragtop will want to drive the car with a damaged quarter panel. When the owner takes it to a repair shop, the repair operator will attempt to replace the part with a similar part. In some cases like this, a disreputable repair operator will start to get the typical auto theft ring operation into action. The typical auto theft ring operation is made up of people on the fringes of organized crime, and often many of the operatives are wannabes. (A *wannabe* is a person who desires to make a name or reputation for himself in order to associate with organized crime people.) A call is made to a member of the ring, and the necessary part is placed on order from the ring.

The actual auto thieves, usually young males, search streets and parking lots for a vehicle identical to the one for which the part is needed. For example, if the damaged vehicle is an '89 Mustang GT, ragtop, sky blue, the thieves will search for that identical car. If they can't get a sky blue one, they will get any colored one and the part will later be painted. The thieves are generally local and know their neighborhoods of operation very well, as well as information on vehicles in the area. They start their search in the early morning hours when they know the fewest police officers are patrolling the streets. Or they sometimes operate in parking lots of shopping malls, transportation depots, or other areas during regular business hours. Generally, they ride three in a car. When they observe their target vehicle they strike quickly. Using keys or professional tools they get into the car in minutes, and then one of the three drives the stolen car away. The driver takes the car to a chop shop, where other members of the ring immediately remove or cut out the required part. The part is then delivered to the disreputable repair operator, who then repairs the damaged vehicle.

Sometimes the chop shop will cut up the rest of the auto and save some of the parts for future orders, but in most cases the employees crush the rest of the car to avoid identified car parts being discovered by the police on the premises.

Professor, if I had an alarm or a club on the car, would they have still stolen it?

Generally, experienced auto thieves will bypass vehicles with alarms or clubs. They could easily get past the alarms and the clubs, but it would take more time and they want to work as quickly as possible. They don't want the risk that a ringing alarm or unnecessary noise will awaken a nearby resident who will then call the police. They don't want to call attention to themselves and they don't want to do anything that would alert the police. However, if they cannot find their target vehicle, they will take the chance and steal the car with the alarm or the club.

Sometimes newer model cars are stolen for other reasons than parts. These cars are generally kept intact but the VIN and other possible identifying numbers and information are changed, and the cars are equipped with bogus paperwork and then sold as used or new automobiles. Often they are shipped overseas.

This takes us to the carjacker. Stealing a car by breaking into it usually involves causing some damage to it. In order to keep a new car from getting damaged, some thieves resort to carjacking by force to steal the car.

Organized auto theft is a big business in America.

YOU ARE THERE!
Leading Metropolitan Areas for Auto Theft

In 2001, the National Insurance Crime Bureau (NICB) reported that the Phoenix metropolitan area had the highest vehicle theft rate in the country, followed by the Miami and Detroit metropolitan areas.

The NICB's study analyzed vehicle theft rates of metropolitan statistical areas (MSAs) using vehicle theft data collected from the FBI. Of the top ten metro areas in the nation for vehicle theft, the NICB found that seven are ports or communities with easy access to the Mexican or Canadian borders. Port and border communities accounted for two-thirds of the top twenty-five vehicle theft areas in the nation.

The study found that the ten metropolitan areas with the highest vehicle theft rates were these:

1. Phoenix
2. Miami
3. Detroit
4. Jersey City (Hudson County, New Jersey)
5. Tacoma
6. Las Vegas
7. Fresno, California
8. Seattle
9. Jackson, Missouri
10. Flint, Michigan

SOURCE: National Insurance Crime Bureau, *Top Theft Areas;* http://www.nicb.org/services/hotspotsrelease.html.

YOU ARE THERE!
Most Commonly Stolen Vehicles

According to a National Insurance Crime Bureau (NICB) survey released in 2001 the most commonly stolen vehicles in the United States in 1999 were these:

1. Honda Accord
2. Toyota Camry
3. Oldsmobile Cutlass
4. Chevrolet full-size pickup
5. Honda Civic
6. Toyota Corolla
7. Jeep Cherokee
8. Chevrolet Caprice
9. Ford Taurus
10. Chevrolet Cavalier

The NICB list of the top fifty most frequently stolen vehicles included fifteen pickup trucks, minivans, and SUVs. It reported that the study confirmed the growing popularity of such vehicles on a national basis among thieves. Vehicle thieves follow market trends and target the most popular vehicles because they provide the best market for stolen vehicle parts and illegal export to other countries.

The NICB also reports that there are city-by-city differences in consumer vehicle preference that affect which vehicles are targeted by thieves there. For example, American cars are more attractive to thieves in Chicago, while pickups are more frequently stolen in Dallas. In the Los Angeles area, thieves target Japanese models.

SOURCE: National Insurance Crime Bureau, *List Vehicles Stolen for Parts or Illegal Export;* http://www.nicb.org/services/top_stolen_cars.html.

Union/Essex Counties Auto Theft Task Force. The New Jersey counties of Essex and Union experience some of the highest number of vehicle thefts in the nation. In an effort to reduce these thefts and to arrest auto thieves, twelve law enforcement agencies, including the Union and Essex County prosecutors' offices, the Essex County Sheriff, the New Jersey Port Authority, and municipal departments in Cranford, East Orange, Elizabeth, Hillside, Irvington, Linden, Newark, and Union, established the Union/Essex Counties Auto Theft Task Force. Its officers are equipped with portable mobile data terminals (**MDTs**). In its first five months of existence the task force recovered 160 vehi-

cles worth $1.5 million and arrested 60 adult auto theft suspects and 101 juvenile suspects.[19]

The MDTs used by the Union/Essex Counties Auto Theft Task Force are "menu-driven," so an officer need only fill in the blanks on a computer screen when accessing a database or completing an arrest or incident report. Each MDT is linked directly to the NCIC and New Jersey's State Criminal Information Center.

Each MDT has an emergency "hot key" that, when pressed, summons all vehicles with MDTs to back up an officer in distress. Task force records indicate that officers get an answer in just twenty to twenty-two seconds when they use the MDT to run a check on an out-of-state driver's license, vehicle identification number, or license plate. An answer to an inquiry on a New Jersey driver or vehicle comes even faster.

Proactive Measures Against Motor Vehicle Theft

Law enforcement agencies conduct extensive proactive sting operations designed to combat auto theft. One example involving stolen cars was an FBI sting in New Jersey, in which agents posed as fences who bought 170 stolen trucks and luxury cars worth $9 million over a two-year period. The investigation led to the dismantlement of the stolen car ring and numerous arrests.[20] Another example was Operation Road Spill, in which agents established a bogus company, Southern Leasing Systems of South Kearny, New Jersey. The agents posed as shady businesspeople who were willing to pay cash for stolen BMWs, Acura Legends, and other luxury cars. During the investigation they bought 120 stolen cars for a fraction of their value.[21]

Also, police are aided in their efforts to find stolen cars by **tracking devices** that are installed in vehicles and connected to the police computers. For example, the LoJack Company markets a vehicle recovery system that is becoming increasingly popular as police agencies across the country try to reduce the incidence of car theft and carjackings. The company first markets the police tracking unit to area law enforcement agencies, then appeals to car owners who install the unit in the hopes their car could be recovered if stolen. For an additional fee, car owners can also install a starter-disabler device. The system includes a lighted compass-type device that shows the area in which the stolen vehicle is traveling, a digital printout for information, and a description of the vehicle. The police tracking computer provides the police officer, via the dispatcher, all pertinent information about the stolen vehicle. The monitor installed in the patrol cars has a strength indicator that tells officers if they are within one mile of the stolen vehicle, giving them time to call for backup help.[22]

The marking of **vehicle identification numbers,** or VINs—numbers assigned to each vehicle as it is manufactured; VINs are similar to a birth certificate for each vehicle—and other numbers in anti-theft programs known as Automobile Component Parts Anti-Theft Marking programs are also helping the police.

According to a nationwide research survey involving auto theft investigators from forty-seven law enforcement agencies in the United States, automobile component parts anti-theft marking was effective in inhibiting chop shop operations and deterring motor vehicle thefts. Findings suggested that these anti-theft labels assisted most big city and state auto theft investigators in arresting and prosecuting auto and auto parts thieves. This research also suggested that parts marking might be more effective if auto theft investigators and patrol officers were given more training in how to investigate label removal and tampering, and if they were given more access to ultraviolet lights or other detection equipment.[23]

Federal law enforcement agencies also assist state and local agencies in the investigation of auto theft. The Interstate Property Crimes Squad of the FBI, among other duties, investigates interstate property crimes such as commercialized auto thefts and chop shops, thefts of cargo from interstate shipments, and transportation of stolen property from one state to another.

Also assisting in the effort to apprehend motor vehicle thieves and prevent motor vehicle theft is the National Insurance Crime Bureau (NICB), a not-for-profit organization that receives support from approximately one thousand property and casualty insurance companies. The NICB partners with insurers and law enforcement agencies to facilitate the identification, detection, and prosecution of insurance criminals. It seeks and enters into collaborative relationships with the police and others to detect, prevent, and deter fraud and theft.

Another professional association for motor vehicle theft investigators is the International Association of Auto Theft Investigators (IAATI), which is an organization of over three thousand members representing over thirty-five countries. IAATI includes representatives of law enforcement agencies as well as many others with a legitimate interest in auto theft investigation, prevention, and education. Membership also includes the insurance industry, automobile manufacturers, car rental companies, the National Insurance Crime Bureau and its sister agencies in Canada and Europe. IAATI promotes cooperation in investigations of auto theft by providing its members

INVESTIGATIONS ON THE NET

National Insurance Crime Bureau
http://www.nicb.org

International Association of Auto Theft Investigators
http://www.iaati.org

For an up-to-date list of Web links, go to
http://info.wadsworth.com/dempsey

with an array of experience, training, and resources in areas such as technical developments, trends, intelligence information, and investigative assistance.

ARSON

Arson is defined as the willful or malicious burning or attempt to burn buildings, vehicles, or property. Arson is classified by the FBI's *Uniform Crime Reports* as a property crime, but we must remember that the crime of arson can lead to murder and serious injury and thus can also be considered a violent crime. Recall the

Arson is the willful destruction of a building by fire or explosion. Here, Detroit police block off the street near a burning abandoned building. Detroit experiences many arsons on Halloween night, sometimes called Devil's Night.

worst case of arson in U.S. history: the September 11, 2001 attack on the Twin Towers of the World Trade Center in New York City, as well as the attack on the U.S. Pentagon. Recall also the bombing of the Alfred P. Murrah Federal Building in Oklahoma City in 1995, which killed 168 people and injured 675 others. These cases are covered in detail in chapter 13, "The Investigation of Terrorist Activities," of this text.

Crimes involving arson and explosives are among the most devastating crimes confronting our society. They destroy property, disrupt human lives, and place an ever-increasing economic burden on our nation's citizens.

Arson is investigated by many agencies with joint jurisdiction, such as local and state fire marshals, state police, county sheriffs, and local police and fire departments. In addition, many private insurance companies assist law enforcement agencies in the investigation of arson. Many insurance companies have full-time fire loss investigators.

Methods of Investigation

Several methods of investigation are used in arson cases, including response to the scene, crime scene processing, analysis, and reconstruction, interviews and interrogations, identification procedures, record checks, theory formation, apprehension of perpetrator, and preparation for trial with prosecutors.

The crime scene process and procedures discussed in chapter 3 of this text are extremely important in arson investigations. Careful preservation and collection of evidence at the scene can help investigators determine the presence of **accelerants** (materials that speed the progress of the fire) introduced to a fire scene. Examinations of debris recovered from scenes can identify gasoline, fuel oils, and specialty solvents. Investigators should search for the following at questioned arson scenes: candles, cigarettes, matchbooks, Molotov cocktails, or any electronic or mechanical devices that may have been used to start the fire. In addition, they should search for cloth or paper burn trails, burn trails on carpeted or hardwood floors, and the removal of personal property or commercial inventory.

A serious crime scene problem with arson crimes is that when firefighters and emergency medical personnel respond to the fire, they must take many actions—such as moving debris—that might destroy evidence in order to perform necessary life-saving and fire-fighting functions.

At the crime scene, arson investigators first begin to look for the **point of origin**—the area in which the fire actually started—which often is the most heavily damaged area in the fire. They try to determine the point of origin by reconstructing furniture, walls, windows, and doors. They look for the direction of heat flow by checking for deep charring, indicating the highest temperature and duration of heat. Two or more points of origin may indicate a definite arson, ruling out other causes of fire.

Investigators then try to determine how the fire started and to rule out accidental or natural causes that could involve the electrical system and electrical appliances, gas sources, heating units, and match and smoking accidents.

They try to discover **incendiary material**—the fire-starting mechanisms used by the fire-setter. Incendiary material includes *ignition devices,* such as matches, candles, chemicals, gas and electrical wiring systems, and the like; *plants,* which are the materials placed around the ignition device to feed the flame, such as newspapers, rags, clothing, and similar articles; *accelerants,* which are the materials that speed the progress of the fire, such as kerosene, gasoline, alcohol, lighter fluid, paint thinners, and other solvents; and *trailers,* which are the materials used to spread the fire. The trailer is ignited by the blaze from the plant and carries the fire to other parts of a room or building. Trailers can be rope, toilet paper soaked in alcohol or similar fluid, rags, newspapers, and other similar articles.

After the crime scene response and processing, investigators submit physical evidence to the crime laboratory, which conducts the analyses that may aid in the reconstruction and investigation of the case.

In addition to crime scene analysis, investigators attempt to determine if arson was involved by looking for possible reasons for the suspected arson. For example:

- The owner may seek to profit: economic gain, insurance, cutting his losses.

- A business may seek to eliminate competition by burning down a competitor.

- There may be extortion by organized criminals.

- There may be labor-management problems.

- Fire was set because of vandalism, excitement.

- The arson is used in an attempt to hide evidence of another crime (the body of a murder victim, for example).

- Pyromaniac fire-setters were involved.

- Vanity hero fires were involved; there have been many cases where voluntary firefighters and others start a fire in order to respond to them and perform heroic efforts.

One writer offers the following items of circumstantial evidence that might be important in proving that a fire was indeed arson:

- *Evidence of planning and preknowledge*—for example, taking out or increasing insurance coverage, removing items, making off-hand remarks, making unusual changes

- *Evidence of participation*—for example, disabling or turning off alarms or sprinkler systems, bringing materials to be used in the arson onto the premises, leaving doors open, rearranging combustibles to provide better fire load.

- *Evidence of exclusive access*—that is, owner had the only keys

- *Fire behavior*—accidental or natural causes are eliminated

- *Evidence of motive*

© Bettmann/CORBIS

Sometimes arson is more than just a property crime. Here, police investigate the Happy Land Social Club fire in the Bronx, New York. Eighty-seven people were killed after a jealous boyfriend set the fire.

- *False exculpatory statements* made by "innocent victim"[24]

Federal Assistance in Arson Investigations

The Bureau of Alcohol, Tobacco and Firearms (ATF) of the U.S. Treasury Department has numerous programs and resources to assist federal, state, and local investigators with cases of arson and explosion. ATF derives its statutory authority under Title XI of the Organized Crime Control Act of 1970. Some of these programs and resources are the following:

- *National Response Team (NRT)*. ATF has a national response capability to assist federal, state, and local investigators at scenes of significant arson and explosive incidents. Four geographically based teams cover the United States and each can respond within twenty-four hours to provide service on-site. These teams can assist in suspicious commercial fires, criminal bombings, explosions at explosives and ammunition manufacturing plants, legal fireworks factories, and illegal explosive device manufacturing operations. The teams are each composed of veteran special agents having postblast and fire origin-and-cause expertise; forensic chemists; explosives enforcement officers; fire protection engineers; **accelerant detection canines; explosives detection canines;** and intelligence and audit support. They help reconstruct the scene, identify the seat of the blast or origin of the fire, conduct interviews, and sift through debris to obtain evidence related to the bombing or arson.

  - *International Response Team (IRT)*. This unit responds to arson and explosive incidents on U.S. property abroad and assists foreign governments in such cases at their request. The IRT has supervisory special agents, a cadre of fire origin-and-cause specialists, explosive specialists having postblast expertise, explosives technology experts, and forensic chemists.

- *Arson task forces.* The ATF has arson task forces in numerous major cities in the United States; 33 percent of its arson criminal cases are initiated by these task forces. Each task force is uniquely configured, reflecting such varying factors as environment, manpower, and management techniques. A valued member of the task force is the ATF auditor. ATF has forty-five auditors available nationwide to assist the task forces in substantiating profit-motivated schemes, to which 92 percent of the auditors' time is dedicated.

- *Criminal investigative analysis.* This is a joint program with the FBI at the Arson and Bombing Investigative Services Subunit (ABIS) of the National Center for the Analysis of Violent Crime (NCAVC). This unit's primary mission is to construct profiles of unidentified offenders through a detailed analysis of violent crimes and aberrant behavior. The ABIS is responsible for assisting in investigations of arson fires, bombings, terrorism, computer intrusions, and related violent crimes submitted to the NCAVC by federal, state, local, and foreign law enforcement agencies. The ABIS is called upon to provide consultations relating to criminal investigative analysis of arson and bombing offenses. These consultations involve on-site crime scene assessments, interview and investigative technique strategies, personality assessments, training programs, and research interviews.

- *Explosives technology support.* Explosives technology personnel in ATF offer technical expertise in the explosives and bomb disposal fields. They construct facsimiles of explosive and incendiary devices, prepare destructive device determinations for court purposes, provide expert analyses of explosive-incendiary devices, and provide on-site investigative technical assistance at bombing or arson scenes. They also provide technical advice on federal explosives storage and regulations and provide training in all aspects of explosives handling and destruction.

- *Certified Fire Investigator program.* A large number of ATF special agents have been trained as certified fire investigators (CFIs). CFIs use modern, sophisticated investigative and analysis techniques beyond those normally used by a discipline that formerly was based solely on

experience. These techniques involve scientific and engineering technology such as computer fire modeling and mathematical equations that describe the chemical and physical behavior of fire.

- *Dipole Might.* This is a joint research project involving ATF, the U.S. Army Corps of Engineers, and the Defense Nuclear Agency. Dipole Might is a computerized database and investigative protocol for the investigation of large-scale vehicle bombs.

- *National Explosives Tracing Center.* This center traces explosives from the manufacturer to the purchaser or possessor for the purpose of aiding law enforcement officials in identifying suspects involved in criminal violations, and in establishing stolen or ownership status.

- *Explosives detection canines.* These dogs have been conditioned to detect explosives, explosives residue, and postblast evidence. Because of their conditioning to smokeless powder and other explosive fillers, these canines can also detect firearms and ammunition hidden in containers and vehicles, on persons, or buried underground.

- *Accelerant detection canines.* These specially trained dogs can detect a variety of ignitable liquids that could be used to initiate a fire.

- *Explosives interdiction.* ATF targets the illicit manufacturers and distributors of explosive devices that present considerable hazards.

- *Forensic laboratory support.* The ATF's multidisciplined laboratories support its explosives and

 INVESTIGATIONS ON THE NET

International Association of Arson Investigators
http://www.firearson.com

International Association of Bomb Technicians and Investigators
http://www.iabt.org

For an up-to-date list of Web links, go to http://info.wadsworth.com/dempsey
----

arson programs. They routinely examine arson debris to detect accelerants, as well as explosive devices and explosives debris to identify device components and the explosives used.

- *Training programs.* The ATF offers training programs in arson and explosives for state and local investigators and prosecutors. It also educates the public through television, radio, newspapers, videotapes, news releases, and training programs to increase awareness of the dangers of and federal penalties for the illegal possession, manufacture, and distribution of explosive devices. Some of these training programs are the following: Advanced Cause and Origin; Advanced Explosives Destruction; Advanced Explosives Investigative Techniques; Arson for Prosecutors; Complex Arson Investigative Techniques; Seminar on Terrorism and Explosives; Underwater Explosives Recovery Specialist.

A professional organization for those interested in arson investigations is the International

Arson is often related to hate crimes. Here, a man surveys damage to a synagogue door in Paris, France, in October 2000, following an overnight firebomb attack.

Association of Arson Investigators (IAAI). Another professional organization of interest to arson and bombing investigators is the International Association of Bomb Technicians and Investigators (IABTI).

YOU ARE THERE!

Arson Prevention for America's Churches and Synagogues

In the aftermath of numerous suspicious fires at churches and synagogues, the International Association of Arson Investigators offers the following advice to proprietors of churches and synagogues:

External Security

Arsonists, like burglars, fear light.

- Illuminate the exterior and entrances.
- Use motion-activated lighting near doors and windows.
- Keep shrubbery and trees trimmed so buildings can be observed by passing patrols.
- If in a rural setting, ensure crops are far enough away to allow proper illumination of the area.

- Do not allow church signs to block the view of the building.
- Many churches have basement entries that are hidden from view; these should be secured with locking ground-level doors when church is not in use.
- Ladders, external stairways, and fire escapes allowing access to the roof should be secured.
- Painting the building white or constructing it with light-colored brick makes a human figure more readily seen at night.
- Consider fencing the areas or sides that are not readily visible to patrols or neighbors.

You Are There! continued

Internal Security

- Use properly installed deadbolt locks on all exterior doors.

- Windows that can be opened should have adequate locks on them.

- Consider decorative or wrought iron protection for windows. (Windows used as emergency exits must still be able to be opened in an emergency.) Doors should have similar protection.

- Consider installing a combination burglar and fire alarm with a phone dialer.

- If there is a private security firm in your area, consider a contract with them because they will check the building at unscheduled intervals.

- Keep a current list of all individuals who have access to church keys, and change locks periodically.

Community Awareness and Cooperation

- Keep church leaders informed of problems.

- Be aware of individuals who may be disgruntled or likely to cause damage to church property through arson or vandalism.

- Be aware that vandalism may precede arson!

- Open avenues of communication with fire and law enforcement officials about the arson problem churches are facing.

- Appoint a person from the church to be a liaison with law and fire officials.

- Promote neighborhood watches and educate the neighbors with the lighting arrangements (motion lights, and so on).

- Initiate an arson hotline.

- Educate neighbors on recognizing unusual activities.

- Encourage neighbors to make note of strangers spending time in the neighborhood, either on foot or in vehicles. Write down the license plate numbers of suspicious vehicles and inform the proper authorities.

- Have all guests register, and remove register from church each night.

- Raise public awareness through the news media that the problem exists.

- Be aware that individuals may pose as service technicians to get into the church.

- Arsonists may carry a liquid accelerant in an inconspicuous container, such as a beverage container.

- Do not advertise on church signs or bulletins when church will not be in use.

- Involve your insurance agent.

SOURCE: International Association of Arson Investigators.

SUMMARY

Property crime—including burglary, larceny or theft, motor vehicle theft, and arson—is generally not investigated as intently by the police as are crimes of violence such as murder, rape, robbery, felonious assault, and kidnapping. Crimes of arson that result in very serious property losses or serious injuries or death are an exception to this, however. These types of arsons are treated as violent crimes.

Nevertheless, property crimes have a tremendous negative effect on persons, businesses, and U.S. society in general. They result in enormous monetary loss and have tremendous personal and social costs. The basic methods of investigation for property crimes are similar to those for violent crimes, including response to the scene, crime scene processing, analysis, and reconstruction, interviews and interrogations, identification procedures, record checks, theory formation, apprehension of perpetrator, and preparation for trial with prosecutors. The private sector has attempted to assist public law enforcement in dealing with many forms of property crime by using private security programs and techniques, both reactive and proactive.

This chapter discussed property crime in the United States and police and private security efforts to investigate and prevent these crimes. The specific crimes discussed were burglary, larceny or theft, motor vehicle theft, and arson. The section on arson included the many programs offered by the federal government to assist federal, state, and local authorities investigate the crime of arson.

LEARNING CHECK

1. Describe two criminalistic techniques that may be used in a burglary investigation.
2. Name and discuss two proactive measures that may be used to prevent burglaries.
3. Discuss the major reasons for the theft of motor vehicles.
4. Describe some of the major crime scene evidence that may be present in an arson investigation.
5. Name and discuss several federal programs to assist state and local officers in the investigation of arson incidents.

APPLICATION EXERCISE

You have been hired as a special assistant to the police chief of a small local police department that has approximately fifty sworn officers, five of whom are investigators. The town has experienced a rash of suspicious fires of commercial buildings on Main Street, the town's primary thoroughfare. The local fire chief has told the police chief that he has reason to believe the fires were intentionally set but doesn't have the personnel or expertise in his department to conduct a proper arson investigation. The police chief tells you that the police department also has no trained arson investigators and no crime lab. She asks you to explore the possibility of asking for federal assistance in these cases.

Prepare a memo to the chief listing the resources that are available at the federal level that might assist the department.

WEB EXERCISE

As a private investigator and security consultant, you have been hired by the Age with Dignity Leisure Village, a retirement community located twenty miles west of a busy urban area. The director of the community has told you that there has been a rise in property crimes in the community, including burglaries of residences and thefts from autos in the parking lots.

The local sheriff's office and the state police are very busy dealing with the drug-related crime and violence in the urban area and do not have the resources to assist the retirement community other than with occasional patrols through the community and rapid response to emergencies, crimes in progress, investigation of past crimes, and response to service calls.

The community director asks you to provide him with self-help advice to try to prevent the property crime from occurring. Access the Internet and research Web sites that offer this type of advice. Recall some of the Web sites covered earlier in the text involving private security.

KEY TERMS

accelerant

accelerant detection canines

arson

burglary

chop shops

explosives detection canines

home security surveys

incendiary material

MDTs

Operation Identification

plants

point of origin

tracking devices

trailers

vehicle identification numbers

THE INVESTIGATION OF CONTROLLED SUBSTANCES AND DRUG OFFENSES

CHAPTER GOALS

1. To introduce you to the problems that controlled substances cause in our society

2. To acquaint you with the major illegal drugs of abuse, including narcotics, depressants, stimulants, hallucinogens, cannabis, and anabolic steroids

3. To make you aware of the laws on controlled substances

4. To acquaint you with the many agencies involved in the enforcement of the controlled substance laws

5. To acquaint you with the many methods used by law enforcement to investigate and arrest drug traffickers

INTRODUCTION

Illegal use of controlled substances and other drugs causes death. It causes death to those who use these substances by destroying their minds and bodies, as well as children, born and unborn. It causes death to those who illegally manufacture, distribute, and sell them as they kill each other to reap more profits. It causes death to those committed and brave enforcers of the law who are killed trying to enforce that law. It even causes death to the uninvolved who just are doing their jobs. For example, in August 2001 two pilots who were approaching a huge 270-acre brush fire in California's Mendocino County to drop eight hundred gallons of fire retardant onto the blaze were killed as their planes collided in the smoke above it. A man operating a clandestine drug laboratory as part of a ring involving the Hell's Angels motorcycle gang was subsequently arrested on two counts of murder for causing the death of both pilots, one count of manufacturing drugs, and one count of causing the fire that the pilots were fighting.[1]

The toll of death caused by illegal drugs never seems to stop. In July 2001, a former Ivy League medical resident who put cocaine in a four-month-old boy's bottle to quiet him was sentenced to five to ten years in prison for the child's 1997 death in Philadelphia. The man and the child's mother were on a two-day drug binge when the child died.[2]

This chapter will discuss the U.S. drug problem and provide information about the main drugs of abuse in our nation. It will discuss the laws we have and use to fight this scourge and will list and discuss the mission and operations of the various federal, state, and local agencies involved in enforcing these laws.

It will discuss the primary methods of enforcing drug laws, including source control, interdiction, disrupting domestic distribution, disrupting wholesaling, and disrupting street sales, and the tools available to law enforcement to perform these duties. It will also discuss proactive, covert investigative techniques for drug investigations, including infiltration, stakeouts, and undercover buy-and-busts.

THE U.S. DRUG PROBLEM

Before discussing the drug problem, we must first ask, "What is a drug?" A drug can be good or bad; it can save a life when it is used properly, and it can destroy a life when used improperly. According to Howard Abadinsky, the term *drug* derives from the fourteenth-century French word *drogue*, meaning a dry substance; most pharmaceuticals at that time were prepared from dried herbs.[3]

In our current culture the word has two connotations. One is extremely positive, referring to the medicines that cure illnesses and improve people's health. The other is extremely negative and reflects the abusive nature of certain drugs and their psychoactive or psychotropic effects—that is, their ability to cause alterations in mood and behavior. This chapter will deal with the second connotation: drugs that are used or abused primarily to change mood and behavior.

Many substances, including caffeine, nicotine, and alcohol, fall into this definition. But caffeine, nicotine, and alcohol are not illegal drugs. We will limit our discussion of drugs to those that are considered controlled substances under the Comprehensive Drug Abuse Prevention and Control Act of 1970 (The Controlled Substance Act [CSA]).

Is the use of illegal drugs common in the United States? Are illegal drugs a serious problem for U.S. society? According to the **U.S. Drug Enforcement Administration (DEA):**[4]

- The latest statistics for illegal drug use in the United States reveal that 87.7 million Americans had tried an illegal drug, and that 14.8 million Americans had used drugs in the past month. In the latest reporting year, 55 percent of high school seniors reported they had used an illegal drug, and 28.3 percent of thirteen and fourteen-year-olds reported using an illegal drug.

- The strength of drugs has increased. THC, the psychoactive ingredient of marijuana, now averages 7.6 percent as compared to 1.5 percent in the 1970s; the national average purity of heroin is 35 percent; and South American heroin, which is readily available in many East Coast cities, ranges from 70 to 80 percent pure.

- Seventy-five percent of the male adults arrested in New York City for committing a violent crime tested positive for drug use. In cities such as Albuquerque, New Mexico, and Fort Lauderdale, Florida, these figures ranged as high as 64 percent.

- According to surveys, employees who test positive for drug use make more than twice as many workers' compensation claims, use almost twice the medical benefits, and take one-third more leave time than nonusers. They are also 60 percent more likely to be responsible for accidents. The Office of National Drug Control Policy (ONDCP) estimates that the monetary cost of illegal drug use to U.S. society is $110 billion a year.

- One-quarter to one-half of all incidents of domestic violence are drug-related.

- Substance abuse is identified as one of the key problems exhibited by 81 percent of the families reported for child maltreatment, and 3.2 percent of pregnant women—nearly eighty thousand mothers—use drugs regularly.

The National Household Survey on Drug Abuse, an annual survey conducted by the Substance Abuse and Mental Health Services Administration (SAMHSA), estimates the prevalence of illicit drug use in the United States and monitors the trends in use over time. It is based on a representative sample of persons from the U.S. population ages twelve and older. The following are some important statistics from the latest available study:[5]

- An estimated 14.8 million Americans are current users of illicit drugs.

- More than one of every ten American youths ages twelve to seventeen are current users of illicit drugs.

- More than 17 percent of young adults ages eighteen to twenty-five are current users of illicit drugs.

- An estimated 208,000 Americans are current users of heroin. The average age of the heroin abuser is 21.3 years old.

- There were an estimated 991,000 new inhalant users in the latest reporting year, with 62 percent of them between the ages of twelve and seventeen.

- Heroin-related deaths are rising as a result of the increasing purity and decreasing price of that drug.

The Drug Abuse Warning Network (DAWN) estimated that for the latest reporting year there were an esti-

mated 601,776 drug-related emergency department visits in the continental United States, with over one million mentions of a particular drug (on average, 1.8 drugs were involved per visit—meaning that the majority of people being treated attributed their emergency to using more than one drug). Besides alcohol, cocaine was the most frequently mentioned drug, followed by heroin or morphine and marijuana. DAWN is a nationally representative survey of hospitals with emergency departments conducted annually by SAMHSA. The survey is designed to capture information about emergency department visits that are induced by or related to the use of an illegal drug or the nonmedical use of a legal drug.[6]

Drug use often has fatal consequences. For example, in Houston, Texas, in August 2001, at least eighteen persons died in less than a week from suspected overdoses (ODs), possibly caused by fatal cocktails of cocaine and heroin known as *speedballs*. Most were men in the same neighborhood; one was a sixteen-year-old girl. ODs are rising across the country; sometimes

---

YOU ARE THERE!

Some Quick Facts on American Drug Abuse

- Babies born to drug-abusing mothers cost taxpayers $20 billion a year.

- Illegal drug-related deaths are estimated at twenty thousand annually.

- Drug-using teens are three times more likely to commit suicide than their nonusing peers are.

- Drug abusers collecting Social Security disability payments cost taxpayers over $1.7 billion a year.

- Three-quarters of illegal drug users are employed—15 percent of them admit to working while under the influence of drugs.

- Workers who use drugs are responsible for 40 percent of industrial fatalities.

- Health care costs directly attributable to illegal drug use exceeds $30 billion a year.

SOURCE: National Drug Enforcement Officers Association; http://www.ndeoa.org/facts.html.

they result from drugs that are too pure or are laced with a toxic substance.[7]

The drug use problem is not limited to the United States. In August 2001, Iran admitted it has a serious drug problem with 1.3 million addicts in a population of 63 million, and at least 1 million more casual users. However, some say there may be more than 3 million addicts—as much as 5 percent of the population. By comparison, Britain, with a similar population, has a reported 200,000 addicts. Drugs are readily available in Iran because it is the major land route for much of the heroin and opium smuggled to Western Europe from Afghanistan and Pakistan.[8]

MAJOR DRUGS OF ABUSE

The Drug Enforcement Administration (DEA) categorizes illegal drugs into six basic categories: narcotics, depressants, stimulants, cannabis, hallucinogens, and anabolic steroids.[9] This section will discuss each of these six categories. Accompanying boxed features will focus on one particular drug in each category.

Narcotics

The term *narcotic* derives from the Greek word for stupor and originally referred to a variety of substances that induced sleep. In a legal context, narcotic refers to opium, opium derivatives, and their synthetic substitutes.

Narcotics can be administered orally, transdermally (through skin patches), or injected. They are also available in suppositories. As drugs of abuse, they are often smoked, sniffed, or self-administered by subcutaneous ("skin popping") and intravenous ("mainlining") injection. Aside from their clinical effects in the treatment of pain, cough suppression, and acute diarrhea, narcotics produce a general sense of well-being by reducing tension, anxiety, and aggression. These effects are helpful in a therapeutic setting but contribute to their abuse.

Narcotics use can bring drowsiness, inability to concentrate, apathy, lessened physical activity, constriction of the pupils, dilation of the subcutaneous blood vessels causing flushing in the face and neck, constipation, nausea and vomiting, and most significantly, respiratory depression.

EXHIBIT 12.1   Categories of Controlled Substances

- *Narcotics* include: heroin, morphine, codeine, hydrocodone, hydromorphone, oxycodone, methadone and LAAM, fentanyl and analogs, other narcotics

- *Depressants* include chloral hydrate, barbiturates, benzodiazepines, glutethimide, other depressants

- *Stimulants* include cocaine, amphetamine-methamphetamine, methylphenidate, other stimulants

- *Cannabis* includes marijuana, tetrahydrocannabinol, hashish and hashish oil

- *Hallucinogens* include LSD, mescaline and peyote, amphetamine variants, phencyclidine and analogs, other hallucinogens

- *Anabolic steroids* include testosterone (cypionate, enanthate), nandrolone (decanoate, phenproprionate), oxymetholone

SOURCE: Drug Enforcement Administration, *Controlled Substances Uses and Effects;* www.dea.gov/concern/abuse/charts/chart4/contents.htm.

Among the main hazards of the illicit use of narcotics are the risks of infection, disease, and overdose. Also, many medical complications ensue from the adulterants found in street drugs and in the nonsterile practice of injecting. Because there is no simple way to determine the purity of a drug that is sold on the street, the effects of illegal drug use are unpredictable and can be fatal.

Repeated use of narcotics produces tolerance and physical and psychological dependence. **Tolerance** means that continuing use of the drug produces a shortened duration and decreased intensity of its effects, and thus the user needs to administer progressively larger and larger doses to attain the desired effect. **Physical dependence** means the alteration of normal body functions, necessitating the continued presence of the drug in order to prevent the withdrawal or abstinence syndrome. **Psychological dependence** means that the addict, even after the physical need for the drug has passed, continues to be consumed by the psychological need for it.

YOU ARE THERE!
Focus on a Narcotic: Heroin

Heroin was first synthesized from morphine in 1874. The morphine is extracted as opium from the seedpod of certain varieties of poppy plants. Heroin was not extensively used in medicine until the beginning of the twentieth century. It received widespread acceptance from the medical profession until its potential for addiction was discovered. The first comprehensive control of heroin in the United States was established with the Harrison Narcotic Act of 1914.

Pure heroin is a white powder with a bitter taste. Most illicit heroin is a powder that may vary in color from white to dark brown because of impurities left from the manufacturing process or the presence of additives. A *bag*, slang for a single dosage unit of heroin, may contain 100 mg of powder, only a portion of which is heroin; the remainder could be sugars, starch, powdered milk, or quinine. The street term for mixing the heroin with the other substances is *cutting*. Traditionally, the purity of heroin in a bag has ranged from 1 to 10 percent; more recently heroin purity has ranged from 1 to 98 percent, with a national average of 35 percent.

Until recently, heroin in the United States was almost exclusively injected either intravenously or subcutaneously. Injection is the most practical and efficient way to administer low-purity heroin. The availability of higher-purity heroin has meant that users now can snort or smoke the drug. Snorting and smoking may appeal to new users because it eliminates the fear of acquiring syringe-borne diseases, such as HIV/AIDS and hepatitis, and the historical stigma attached to intravenous heroin use.

According to the National Household Survey on Drug Abuse, about 2.4 million people had used heroin at some time in their lives, and nearly 130,000 had used it in the month preceding the survey.

SOURCES: Drug Enforcement Administration, *Heroin,* http://www.dea.gov/concern/abuse/chap2/narcotic/heroin.htm; U.S. Department of Health and Human Services, National Institute on Drug Abuse, *Heroin Abuse and Addiction* (Washington, DC: National Institute on Drug Abuse, 2000).

YOU ARE THERE!
Osama bin Ladin, the Taliban, Afghanistan, and Opium and Heroin

In July 2000, the Taliban—the protectors of the terrorist Osama bin Laden—won international acclaim when their leaders banned the growing of opium poppies. Many of Afghanistan's impoverished farmers had counted on the harvest to feed their families, and the Taliban had used tax proceeds from it to buy arms. Before declaring the end of poppy cultivation, Afghanistan had produced some 75 percent of the world's supply of opium. However, in the weeks following the terrorist attacks on the World Trade Center and the U.S. Pentagon on September 11, 2001, it was reported that the Taliban government had actually earned tens of millions of dollars from the export of heroin and other narcotics since proclaiming that it was ending opium poppy cultivation. It was also reported that the Taliban had stockpiled huge amounts of opium and heroin.

The Taliban relied on revenues from the drug trade for years, using the proceeds to buy weapons to fight the Northern Alliance, the rebel group estimated to control the 5 to 15 percent of Afghanistan not controlled by the Taliban. It is estimated that the Taliban earned $15 to $27 million annually from taxes levied on opium production, and together with revenue from trading the drug, their total annual revenue from the drug trade was $40 to $50 million.

Reports say that bin Laden does not actually traffic in drugs but makes money off the heroin trade by hiring out his fighters to guard laboratories and escort drug convoys moving through Iran to Turkey, where the opium base is processed into heroin.

SOURCE: Michael R. Gordon and Eric Schmitt, "Afghanistan Remains a Major Drug Trader Despite Taliban Ban on Poppy Growing," *New York Times,* Sept. 26, 2001, p. B4.

Depressants

Historically, people have used chemical agents to induce sleep, relieve stress, and allay anxiety. Although alcohol is one of the oldest and most universal agents used for these purposes, it is not a controlled substance and will not be discussed further in this chapter. Hundreds of other substances have been developed that produce central nervous system (CNS) depression. These drugs have been referred to as "downers," sedatives, hypnotics, minor tranquilizers, anxiolytics, and antianxiety medications. Unlike most other drugs of abuse, most depressants, except for methaqualone, are produced by pharmaceutical companies but then diverted to the illicit market.

Two groups of depressants have dominated the legal and illegal market for almost a century: first barbiturates, and now benzodiazepines. Barbiturates were very popular in the first half of this century. In moderate amounts, these drugs produce a state of intoxication that is very similar to alcohol intoxication. Symptoms include slurred speech, loss of motor coordination, and impaired judgment. Depending on the dose, and frequency and duration of use, a person can rapidly develop tolerance, physical dependence, and psychological dependence on barbiturates. Because of concern over the addiction potential of barbiturates and the ever-increasing numbers of fatalities associated with them, alternative medications have been developed. Today, only about 20 percent of all depressant prescriptions in the United States are for barbiturates.

Benzodiazepines, a substitute for barbiturates, were first marketed in the 1960s and were found to be safer and less addictive than barbiturates. Today they account for about 30 percent of all prescriptions for controlled substances. However, they share many of the undesirable side effects of barbiturates, including addiction. Abuse of these drugs usually occurs as part

---

YOU ARE THERE!

Focus on a Depressant: Benzodiazepines

The benzodiazepine family of depressants are used therapeutically to produce sedation, induce sleep, relieve anxiety and muscle spasms, and prevent seizures. Fifteen different benzodiazepines are presently marketed in the United States and an additional twenty are marketed in other countries.

Benzodiazepines differ from one another in how fast they take effect and how long the effects last. Shorter-acting benzodiazepines, used to manage insomnia, include estazolam (ProSom), flurazepam (Dalmane), quazepam (Doral), temazepam (Restoril), and triazolam (Halcion). (The names in parentheses are trade names.)

Benzodiazepines with longer durations of action include alprazolam (Xanax), chlordiazepoxide (Librium), clorazepate (Tranxene), diazepam (Valium), halazepam (Paxipam), lorazepam (Ativan), oxazepam (Serax), and prazepam (Centrax). These longer-acting drugs are primarily used for the treatment of general anxiety. Midazolam (Versed) is available in the United States only in an injectable form for an adjunct to anesthesia. Clonazepam (Klonopin) is recommended for use in the treatment of seizure disorders.

Flunitrazepam (Rohypnol), which produces diazepam-like effects, is becoming increasingly popular among young people as a drug of abuse. The drug is not marketed legally in the United States, but is smuggled in by traffickers.

Individuals who abuse benzodiazepines often maintain their drug supply by getting prescriptions from several doctors, forging prescriptions, or buying diverted pharmaceutical products on the illicit market. Abuse is frequently associated with adolescents and young adults who take benzodiazepines to obtain a high. This intoxicated state results in reduced inhibition and impaired judgment. Concurrent use of alcohol or other depressants can be life-threatening. Abuse of benzodiazepines is particularly high among heroin and cocaine abusers. Approximately 50 percent of people entering treatment for narcotic or cocaine addiction also report abusing benzodiazepines.

SOURCE: Drug Enforcement Administration, *Benzodiazepines;* http://www.dea.gov/concern/abuse/chap3/depress/benzo.htm.

of a pattern of multiple drug abuse. For example, heroin or cocaine abusers will use benzodiazepines and other depressants to augment their high or alter the side effects of overstimulation or withdrawal of narcotics.

Stimulants

Stimulants are sometimes referred to as "uppers" and reverse the effects of fatigue on both mental and physical tasks. Two commonly used stimulants are nicotine, found in tobacco products, and caffeine, an active ingredient in coffee, tea, some soft drinks, and many nonprescription medicines. However, because these two substances are not considered controlled substances they will not be discussed further in this chapter.

Some stimulants are considered controlled substances and are available by prescription for legitimate medical use in the treatment of obesity, narcolepsy, and attention deficit hyperactivity disorders. As drugs of abuse, stimulants are frequently taken to produce a sense of exhilaration, enhance self-esteem, improve mental and physical performance, increase activity, reduce appetite, produce prolonged wakefulness, and to get high.

Stimulants are both diverted from legitimate channels and clandestinely manufactured exclusively for the illicit market. They are taken orally, sniffed, smoked, and injected. Smoking, snorting, or injecting stimulants produces a sudden sensation known as a *rush* or a *flash*. Abuse is often associated with a pattern of binge use—that is, consuming large doses sporadically. Heavy users may continue their abuse until they reach delirium, psychosis, and physical exhaustion. Tolerance can develop rapidly, and both physical and psychological dependence can occur. Abrupt cessation is commonly followed by depressions, anxiety, drug craving, and extreme fatigue (*crashing*). Physical side effects can include dizziness, tremor, palpitations, and excessive sweating. Psychological effects include agitation, hostility, panic, aggression, and suicidal or homicidal tendencies. Paranoia, sometimes accompanied by both auditory and visual hallucinations, may also occur. Overdoses may produce death.

Cannabis

Cannabis sativa, or the hemp plant, grows wild throughout most of the tropic and temperate regions of the world. Before the development of synthetic fibers, the cannabis plant was cultivated for the tough fiber of the stem. Cannabis contains chemicals called *cannabinoids*. One of these, delta-9-tetrahydrocannabinol (THC) is believed to be responsible for most of the characteristic psychoactive effects of the drug.

Cannabis products are usually smoked. Their effects are felt within minutes, reach their peak in ten to thirty minutes, and may linger for two or three hours. Low doses tend to induce a sense of well-being and a dreamy state of relaxation, which may be accompanied by a more vivid sense of sight, smell, taste, and hearing as well as by subtle alterations in thought formation and expression. Use can cause driving, occupational, or household accidents that result from a distortion of time and space relationships and impaired coordination. Stronger doses intensify reactions, such as shifting sensory imagery, rapidly fluctuating emotions, a flight of fragmentary thoughts with disturbed association, and a dulling of sensation. Very high doses may result in image distortion, a loss of personal identity, and fantasies and hallucinations.

Three drugs that come from cannabis— marijuana, hashish, and hashish oil—are currently distributed on the U.S. illicit market. Having no currently accepted medical use in treatment in the United States, they remain under Schedule 1 of the CSA. Today, cannabis

© Steve Starr/CORBIS

Weapons are often involved in drug sales. Here, police seize crack cocaine, a revolver, and money from a raid on a crack house.

YOU ARE THERE!

Focus on a Stimulant: Cocaine

Cocaine, the most potent stimulant of natural origin, is extracted from the leaves of the coca plant (Erythroxylon coca), which is indigenous to the Andean highlands of South America.

Illicit cocaine is usually distributed as a white crystalline powder or an off-white chunky material. Cocaine base is converted into the powder form, which is called cocaine hydrochloride, by diluting it with other substances. The substances most commonly used in this process are sugars such as lactose, inositol, and mannitol, and local anesthetics, such as lidocaine. The adulteration of cocaine increases its volume and thus multiplies profits. The main methods for taking cocaine are snorting, injecting, and smoking (including freebase and crack cocaine). *Snorting* is inhaling cocaine powder through the nose, where it is absorbed into the bloodstream through the nasal tissues. *Injecting* is using a needle to release the drug directly into the bloodstream. *Smoking* involves inhaling cocaine vapor or smoke into the lungs, where it is absorbed into the bloodstream as quickly as when it is injected.

Crack is the street name given to cocaine that has been processed from cocaine hydrochloride to a ready-to-use freebase for smoking. Rather than requiring the more volatile method of processing freebase cocaine using ether, crack cocaine is processed with ammonia or sodium bicarbonate (baking soda) and water, and heated to remove the hydrochloride, thus producing a form of cocaine that can be smoked. The term *crack* refers to the crackling sound heard when the mixture is heated, presumably from the sodium bicarbonate.

On the illicit market, crack, or *rock,* is sold in small, inexpensive dosage units. Smoking this form of the drug delivers large quantities of cocaine to the lungs, producing effects comparable to intravenous injection. These effects are felt almost immediately, are very intense, and do not last long.

Excessive doses of cocaine may lead to seizures and death from respiratory failure, stroke, cerebral hemorrhage, or heart failure. Evidence suggests that users who smoke or inject cocaine may be at even greater risk than those who snort it.

Colombia is the world's leading producer of cocaine. Three-quarters of the world's annual yield of cocaine is produced there, both from cocaine base imported from Peru and Bolivia and from locally grown coca. Cocaine production is very important to some regions of Columbia. For example, the Caguan River valley, an area of jungle towns and coca fields in southern Columbia, is a major cocaine-producing area. It has no organized government presence and is controlled by rebels fighting the federal government. The economy is built on coca production, and coca paste has become the main currency. The rebels regulate and tax the thriving trade in coca leaves and coca paste. Traffickers buy the paste, process it into cocaine, and ship it by the ton to quench the United State's insatiable appetite for the drug. People are paid for their work in coca. They, in turn, pay for necessities with the paste, which is soft and powdery, like flour.

Cocaine shipments from South America transported through Mexico or Central America generally move overland or by air to staging sites in northern Mexico. The cocaine is then broken down into smaller loads for smuggling across the U.S.–Mexico border. The primary cocaine importation points in the United States are in Arizona, southern California, southern Florida, and Texas. Typically, the drugs are transported in land vehicles driven across the Southwest border. Cocaine is also carried in small, concealed, kilogram quantities across the border by couriers, known as *mules,* who enter the United States either legally through ports of entry or illegally through points along the border.

Cocaine traffickers from Colombia have also established a labyrinth of smuggling routes throughout the Caribbean, the Bahaman Island chain, and south Florida. They often hire traffickers from Mexico or the Dominican Republic to transport the drug. The traffickers use a variety of smuggling techniques to transfer the drug to U.S. markets. These include airdrops of five hundred to seven hundred kilograms in the Bahama Islands or off the coast of Puerto Rico, mid-ocean boat-to-boat transfers of five hundred to two thousand kilograms, and the commercial shipment of multitons of cocaine through the port of Miami. Bulk

You Are There! continued

cargo ships are also used to smuggle cocaine to staging sites in the western Caribbean–Gulf of Mexico area. These vessels are typically 150- to 250-foot coastal freighters that carry an average cocaine load of approximately 2.5 metric tons. Commercial fishing vessels are also used for smuggling operations. In areas with a high volume of recreational traffic, smugglers use the same types of vessels as those used by the local population.

SOURCES: Drug Enforcement Administration, *Cocaine,* http://www.dea.gov/concern/cocaine.htm; Juan Forero, "Where a Little Coca Is as Good as Gold," *New York Times,* July 8, 2001, p. WR12.

YOU ARE THERE!

Focus on a Cannabis Substance: Marijuana

Marijuana is the most commonly used illicit drug in America. The term *marijuana,* as commonly used, refers to the leaves and flowering tops of the cannabis plant. It is a tobacco-like substance produced by drying these parts of the plant. It varies significantly in its potency, depending on the source and selection of plant materials used. Marijuana is usually smoked in the form of loosely rolled cigarettes called *joints* or hollowed out commercial cigars called *blunts.* Joints and blunts may be laced with a number of adulterants including phencyclidine (PCP), substantially altering the effects and toxicity of these products. Street names for marijuana include pot, grass, weed, Mary Jane, and reefer. Although marijuana grown in the United States was once considered inferior because of a low concentration of THC, the psychoactive element of marijuana, advancements in plant selection and cultivation have resulted in highly potent domestic marijuana.

The latest in marijuana growing is indoor underground farms equipped with diesel-powered lights and ventilation systems. They also use hydroponics technology: growing plants in water in which nutrients have been added.

SOURCE: Drug Enforcement Administration, *Marijuana;* http://www.dea.gov/concern/marijuana.html.

is carefully cultivated illicitly, both indoors and outdoors, to maximize its THC content, thereby producing the greatest possible psychoactive effect.

Hallucinogens

Hallucinogens are among the oldest known group of drugs that have been used for their ability to alter human perception and mood. For centuries, many of the naturally occurring hallucinogens found in plants and fungi have been used for medical, social, and religious practices. In more recent years, a number of synthetic hallucinogens have been produced, some of which are much more potent than their naturally occurring counterparts.

The biochemical, pharmacological, and physiological bases for hallucinogenic activity are not well understood. However, we do know that, taken in nontoxic dosages, these substances produce changes in perception, thought, and mood. Physiological effects include elevated heart rate, increased blood pressure, and dilated pupils. Sensory effects include perceptual distortions that vary with dose, setting, and mood. Psychological effects include disorders of thought associated with time and space. Time may appear to stand still, and forms and colors seem to change and take on new significance. This experience may be pleasurable or extremely frightening. Hallucinogens are unpredictable, each time they are used.

Weeks or even months after some hallucinogens have been taken, users may experience *flashbacks,* reoccurrences of certain aspects of the drug experience without actually taking the drug. The occurrence of flashbacks is unpredictable but is more likely during times of stress.

The abuse of hallucinogens in the United States reached a peak in the late 1960s, but there was a resurgence in their use in the 1990s, particularly at the junior high school level. One of the most common dangers of

YOU ARE THERE!
Focus on a Hallucinogen: LSD

Lysergic acid diethylamide (LSD) is the most potent and highly studied hallucinogen known. It was originally synthesized in 1938. Because of its structural similarity to a chemical present in the brain and its similarity in effects to certain aspects of psychosis, LSD was used as a research tool to study mental illness. Although there was a decline in its illicit use from its initial popularity in the 1960s, LSD made a comeback in the 1990s. The average effective oral dose is from 20 to 80 micrograms with the effects of higher doses lasting for ten to twelve hours. LSD is usually sold in the form of impregnated paper *(blotted acid)*, tablets *(microdots)*, or thin squares of gelatin *(windowpanes)*.

During the first hour after ingestion, users may experience visual changes with extreme changes in mood. In the hallucinatory state, they may suffer impaired depth and time perception, accompanied by distorted perception of the size and shape of objects, movements, color, sound, touch, and their own body image. During the period, their ability to perceive objects through the senses is distorted. They may describe "hearing colors" and "seeing sounds." The ability to make sensible judgments and see common dangers is impaired, making users susceptible to personal injury. They may also injure others by attempting to drive a car or by operating machinery.

After an LSD "trip," the user may suffer acute anxiety or depression for a variable period of time; flashbacks have been reported days or months after taking a dose.

SOURCE: Drug Enforcement Administration, *LSD;* http://www.dea.gov/concern/abuse/chap5/lsd.htm.

YOU ARE THERE!
Focus on Anabolic Steroids

Steroids encountered on the illicit market include boldenone (Equipoise), ethlestrenol (Maxibolin), fluxoymesterone (Halotestin), methandriol, methandrostenolone (Dianabol), methyltestosterone, nandrolone (Durabolin, Deca-Durabolin), oxandrolone (Anavar), oxymetholone (Anadrol), stanozolol (Winstrol), testosterone, and trenbolone (Finajet). In addition, a number of bogus or counterfeit products are sold as anabolic steroids.

When used in combination with exercise training and a high protein diet, anabolic steroids can promote increased size and strength of muscles, improve endurance, and decrease recovery time between workouts. These steroids are usually taken orally or by intramuscular injection. Users concerned about drug tolerance often take steroids on a schedule called a *cycle*. A cycle is a period of between six and fourteen weeks of steroid use, followed by a period of abstinence or reduction in use. Users also tend to "stack" the drugs, using multiple drugs concurrently. Although the benefits of these practices are unsubstantiated, most users feel that cycling and stacking enhance the efficiency of the drugs and limit their side effects.

Some users engage in "pyramiding," in which they slowly escalate steroid use (increasing the number of drugs used at one time or the dose and frequency of one or more steroids), reach a peak amount at midcycle, and then gradually taper the dose toward the end of the cycle. The escalation of steroid use can vary with different types of training. Bodybuilders and weight lifters tend to escalate their dose to a much higher level than long-distance runners or swimmers.

SOURCE: Drug Enforcement Administration, *Steroids;* http://www.dea.gov/concern/abuse/chap7/steroids.htm.

hallucinogen use is impaired judgment that often leads to rash decisions and accidents.

Anabolic Steroids

Anabolic steroid abuse has become a national concern. Anabolic steroids have been used illicitly by weight lifters, bodybuilders, long-distance runners, and other athletes who claim that these drugs give

them a competitive advantage or improve their physical fitness.

Recent reports estimate that 5 percent to 12 percent of male high school students and 1 percent of female students have used anabolic steroids by the time they are seniors. Concerns over a growing illicit market and prevalence of abuse, combined with the possibility of harmful long-term effects of steroid use,

(text continues on p. 328)

YOU ARE THERE!
Focus on Club Drugs

The term *club drug* is a general term used for certain illicit substances, primarily synthetic, that are usually found at nightclubs, bars, and raves (all-night dance parties). Substances that are often used as club drugs include, but are not limited to MDMA (Ecstasy), GHB (gamma hydroxybutyrate), Rohypnol, Ketamine, and methamphetamine.

To some, club drugs seem harmless. In reality, however, these substances can cause serious physical and psychological problems and even death. Often, the raves where these drugs are used are promoted as alcohol-free events and give parents a false sense of security that their children will be safe attending such parties. These parents are not aware that raves may actually be havens for the illicit sale and abuse of club drugs.

There are numerous dangers associated with the use of club drugs.

- MDMA can cause a user's blood pressure and heart rate to increase to dangerous levels, and can lead to heart or kidney failure. It can cause severe hypothermia from the combination of the drug's stimulant effect with the often hot, crowded atmosphere of a rave.

- MDMA users may also suffer from long-term brain injury. Research has shown that MDMA can cause damage to the parts of the brain that are critical to thought and memory.

- GHB and Rohypnol are central nervous system depressants that are often connected with drug-facilitated sexual assault, rape, and robbery. These drugs cause muscle relaxation, loss of consciousness, and an inability to remember what happened during the hours after ingesting the drug.

- Ketamine is an animal anesthetic that, when used by humans, can cause impaired motor function, high blood pressure, amnesia, seizures, and respiratory depression.

- Methamphetamine, or meth, is a powerfully addictive stimulant that dramatically affects the central nervous system. Increased energy and alertness, decreased appetite, convulsions, high body temperature, shaking, stroke, and cardiac arrhythmia are all symptomatic of meth abuse.

The latest *Pulse Check Trends* report by the Office of National Drug Control Policy reveals this information about club drugs:

- Availability of club drugs has increased dramatically across the nation, especially for Ecstasy, which has increased in nearly every city.

- Ketamine availability is increasing in most cities, whereas GHB and Rohypnol are concentrated in the South and West, where availability trends are mixed.

- Club drug users and sellers tend to be young, white, middle-class males and females who use or sell the drugs in combination with other drugs, such as hallucinogens, cocaine, heroin, marijuana, methamphetamine, and prescription drugs.

- Club drug activity generally occurs in suburban areas, although Ecstasy is very popular in urban areas as well.

- Ecstasy user and seller groups are also expanding to include more blacks and Hispanics, and use and sales settings continue to expand from exclusively nightclubs and raves to high schools, private parties, and on the streets.

- As the Ecstasy supply increases, the use of adulterants, especially other stimulants, is also increasing.

MDMA (Ecstasy)

MDMA, known as Ecstasy, or E, is a Schedule 1 synthetic, psychoactive drug possessing stimulant and hallucinogenic properties. It combines the chemical variations of the stimulant amphetamine or methamphetamine and a hallucinogen, most often mescaline. It was first synthesized in 1912 to be used as an appetite suppressant. Chemically it is an analogue of MDA, a drug that was popular in the 1960s. In the late 1970s, MDMA was used to facilitate psychotherapy by a small group of therapists in the United States. Illicit use of the drug became popular in the late 1980s and

You Are There! continued

early 1990s. It is frequently used in combination with other drugs. However, it is rarely consumed with alcohol because alcohol is believed to diminish its effects.

Ecstasy is taken orally, usually in tablet or capsule form, and its effects last approximately four to six hours. Users say it produces profoundly positive feelings, empathy for others, elimination of anxiety, and extreme relaxation. It is said to suppress the need to eat, drink, or sleep. Often its use results in severe dehydration or exhaustion. Some other adverse effects include nausea, hallucinations, chills, sweating, increases in body temperature, tremors, involuntary teeth clenching, muscle cramping, and blurred vision. Its users also report aftereffects such as anxiety, paranoia, and depression. An Ecstasy overdose is characterized by high blood pressure, faintness, panic attacks, and in the most severe cases, loss of consciousness, seizures, and a drastic rise in body temperature. Ecstasy overdoses can be fatal because they may result in heart failure or extreme heat stroke.

Clandestine laboratories operating throughout Western Europe, primarily the Netherlands and Belgium, manufacture significant quantities of the drug in tablet, capsule, or powder form. Some Ecstasy labs operate in the United States. Israeli organized crime syndicates, some composed of Russian émigrés associated with Russian organized crime syndicates, are the primary source of U.S. distribution. The drug is smuggled in shipments of ten thousand or more tablets via express mail services, couriers aboard commercial airline flights, or through air freight shipments from European cities to U.S. cities. It is sold wholesale in bulk quantity. The retail price in clubs is about $20 to $30 per dosage unit. Traffickers use brand names and logos as marketing tools and to distinguish their product from that of competitors. The logos are produced to coincide with holidays or special events. Some of the most popular logos are butterflies, lightning bolts, and four-leaf clovers.

Persons involved in the wholesale distribution of Ecstasy are often different from the image of the typical drug distributor. For example, Sean Erez, a thirty-one-year-old Israeli, used very unexpected couriers. Erez pleaded guilty in July 2001 to using young Hasidic men and women, most ages eighteen to twenty, to carry Ecstasy into the United States. The *Hasidim* are a number of Jewish sects that originated in Eastern Europe in the eighteenth century; the men

wear the distinctive garb of that era, including formal hats and long black coats, and tend to have side curls and beards.

Erez's couriers were recruited from Hasidic neighborhoods in New York State and were usually told they would be smuggling diamonds, although prosecutors said that some knew they were carrying drugs. Most were paid $1,500 on delivery of up to forty-five thousand pills.

Erez fled to Amsterdam in 1998 but was extradited to Brooklyn in 2001. He is alleged to have learned his trade from an Amsterdam-based dealer, Oded Tuito, who also used a creative collection of couriers: senior citizens, strippers, and in one case, a mentally retarded teenager.

Also unlike some other drugs that tend to be concentrated in ghetto and other low-income areas, Ecstasy is seen in all income areas. For example, in July 2001, New York City narcotics detectives raided a studio apartment in Manhattan's financial district and seized more than a million Ecstasy tablets and nearly $200,000 in cash. The two subjects arrested were Israeli citizens and major wholesale drug dealers.

In 2001, New York City succeeded in its efforts to close down a notorious nightclub, Twilo, which had a history of concealing rampant Ecstasy use. Twilo was one of some Manhattan clubs that hired a private ambulance service to wait outside their doors to take overdose victims to hospitals to avoid the response of city police and ambulances.

Among some of the problems at Twilo were these: a medical student died of an overdose after collapsing at the club; a city ambulance crew responding to a 911 call was blocked by club security from entering the club, and when they finally made their way in, three clubgoers, two unconscious and one semiconscious, were found and treated for drug overdoses. Clubgoers have sued the club, saying that security tried to hide them from ambulance crews when they suffered overdoses.

Lately, Ecstasy seems to be moving from the clubs to common use throughout society. Three months after closing Twilo and some other clubs that facilitated its use, nearby emergency room doctors reported that they were still treating a large number of young people for Ecstasy-related overdoses. Law enforcement officials attribute these overdoses to other area nightclubs that continue to allow drug use,

You Are There! continued

but they admit that in a recent trend it has evolved from a club drug to something commonly used among friends and at small parties.

Ketamine

Ketamine hydrochloride, known as Special K and K, is a general anesthetic for human and veterinary use. Ketamine produces effects similar to PCP with the visual effects of LSD. Users say its "trips" are better that those of PCP or LSD because its overt hallucinatory effects are short-acting, lasting an hour or less. The drug, however, can affect the senses, judgment, and coordination for eighteen to twenty-four hours. Ketamine sold on the streets comes from diverted legitimate supplies, primarily veterinary clinics. Its appearance is similar to that of pharmaceutical grade cocaine, and it is snorted, placed in alcoholic beverages, or smoked in combination with marijuana. Ketamine was placed in Schedule III of the CSA in August 1999.

Rohypnol

Flunitrazepam, marketed under the brand name Rohypnol, belongs to the benzodiazepines class of drugs. It has never been approved for medical use in the United States so doctors cannot prescribe it and pharmacists cannot sell it. However, it is legally prescribed in over fifty other countries and is widely available in Mexico, Colombia, and Europe, where it is used for the treatment of insomnia and as a pre-anesthetic. It is in Schedule IV of the CSA. Like other benzodiazepines (such as Valium, Librium, Xanax, and Halcion), flunitrazepam's pharmacological effects include sedation, muscle relaxation, reduced anxiety, and prevention of convulsions. However, its sedative effects are approximately seven to ten times more potent than Valium's. Its effects appear approximately fifteen to twenty minutes after administration and last approximately four to six hours.

It causes partial amnesia; individuals are unable to remember certain events that they experienced while under the influence of the drug. This is particularly dangerous when the drug is used to aid sexual assault; victims may not be able to clearly recall the assault, the assailant, or the events surrounding the assault.

Flunitrazepam has become widely known as a *date-rape drug.* It is also abused for other reasons, often to produce profound intoxication or to boost the high of heroin and modulate the effects of cocaine. It

is usually consumed orally, often combined with alcohol, and taken by crushing tablets and snorting the powder. The use of this drug in combination with alcohol is particularly serious because the two substances increase each other's toxicity.

GHB

Gamma hydroxybutyrate (GHB), known as liquid x, Georgia home boy, Goop, gamma-oh, and grievous bodily harm, is a central nervous system depressant abused for its ability to produce euphoric and hallucinatory states and its alleged ability to release a growth hormone and stimulate muscle growth. Although GHB was originally considered a safe and "natural" food supplement and was sold in health food stores, the medical community soon became aware that it caused overdoses and other health problems.

GHB can produce drowsiness, dizziness, nausea, unconsciousness, seizures, severe respiratory depression, and coma. It can be found in liquid form or as a white powdered material. It is taken orally, frequently combined with alcohol. Abusers include high school and college students and rave party attendees who use it for its intoxicating effects. Some bodybuilders also abuse GHB for its alleged anabolic effects.

Several cases have documented the use of GHB to incapacitate women for the commission of sexual assault. In 1990, the Food and Drug Administration (FDA) issued an advisory declaring GHB unsafe and illegal except under FDA-approved, physician-supervised protocols. In 2000, GHB was placed in Schedule I of the Controlled Substances Act.

SOURCES: Drug Enforcement Administration, *MDMA (Ecstasy),* http://www.dea.gov/concern/mdma/mdma.htm; Michele Spiess, *MDMA (Ecstasy)* (Washington: DC: Office of National Drug Control Policy, 2001); Edward Wong, "Unlikely Suspects," *New York Times,* July 15, 2001, p. WK2; William K. Rashbaum, "Two Men Arrested As Police Seize One Million Ecstasy Tablets," *New York Times,* July 19, 2001, p. B3; David Rohde, "Ecstasy Overdoses Continue Despite Nightclub's Closing," *New York Times,* Sept. 4, 2001, p. B3; Drug Enforcement Administration, *Ketamine,* http://www.dea.gov/concern/ketamine.htm; Drug Enforcement Administration, *Flunitrazepam,* http://www.dea.gov/concern/rohypnol.htm; Office of National Drug Control Policy, *Pulse Check Trends in Drug Abuse,* http://www.whitehousedrugpolicy.gov/publications/drugfact/pulsechk/midyear2000/highlights.html; National Criminal Justice Reference Service, *Club Drugs,* http://www.ncjrs.org/club_drugs/club_drugs.html; Drug Enforcement Administration, *Gamma Hydroxybutyrate,* http://www.dea.gov/concern/ghb.htm.

YOU ARE THERE!

Focus on Other Drugs: OxyContin, Fry or Wet, and Inhalants

OxyContin

OxyContin abuse started in remote communities in Appalachia and rural Maine around 1999 and started to affect cities and suburbs in the eastern United States soon thereafter. It has since spread throughout the country. OxyContin is the trade name for the narcotic oxycodone, which is a synthetic opiate developed in Germany in 1916. It is a narcotic painkiller prescribed to millions for chronic pain. OxyContin is designed to release its active ingredient, oxycodone, over twelve hours, but abusers can get an immediate high by crushing the pills and snorting or injecting the powder. The drug gives abusers a heroin-like high without the needles or the stigma. Users call the high achieved from OxyContin an *oxybuzz*. The illicit street price of OxyContin is $12 a milligram or $40 for a forty-milligram pill. It is commonly called hillbilly heroin.

In 2001, a rash of robberies of pharmacies occurred in numerous states, including Maine, Vermont, Pennsylvania, Ohio, West Virginia, Kentucky, Florida, and California. In these robberies, the robbers did not demand or take cash; they demanded oxyContin. The surge in OxyContin robberies seems to reflect the high price the drug now commands on the street and its powerfully addictive high.

In August 2001, Purdue Pharma, the maker of OxyContin, reported it was working to develop a painkiller like OxyContin that would also contain a compound, a narcotic antagonist, to combat abuse. This will not affect the drug if it is taken normally. But if an abuser crushes a drug tablet and injects or snorts the powder the antagonist will block its opiate effect and reduce its appeal.

Fry or Wet

A 2001 study reported that cigarettes soaked in embalming fluid—the kind used to preserve dead bodies—are fast becoming the drug of choice for those looking for a new kind of high. Users, mostly teenagers and people in their twenties, are buying tobacco and marijuana cigarettes, soaking them in embalming fluid, drying them off, and then smoking them. "The idea of embalming fluid appeals to peo-

ple's morbid curiosity about death," said Dr. Julie Holland, a professor at New York University School of Medicine. The cigarettes, often called *fry* or *wet,* are dipped in embalming fluid, a compound of formaldehyde, methanol, and ethanol—solvents easily found in school science labs.

Inhalants

Inhalants are a chemically diverse group of psychoactive substances composed of organic solvents and volatile substances commonly found in adhesives, lighter fluids, cleaning fluids, and pain products. Their easy accessibility, low cost, and ease of concealment make inhalants, for many, one of the first substances abused. There are more than a thousand different household and commercial products that can be used as inhalants. Although not regulated under the CSA, a few states place restrictions on the sale of these products to minors. Studies have indicated that between 5 percent and 15 percent of young people in the United States have tried inhalants, although most do not become chronic abusers.

Inhalants may be sniffed directly from an open container or *huffed* (inhaled through the mouth) from a rag soaked in the substance and held to the face. Alternatively, the open container or soaked rag can be placed in a bag where the vapors can concentrate before being inhaled. Although inhalant abusers may prefer one particular substance because of odor or taste, a variety of substances may be used because of their similar effects, availability, and cost. The lungs allow rapid absorption of the substance and blood levels peak quickly. Entry into the brain is so fast that the effects of inhalation can resemble the intensity of effects produced by intravenous injection of other psychoactive drugs.

Inhalant intoxication resembles alcohol inebriation, with stimulation and loss of inhibition followed by depression at high doses. Abusers report distortion in perceptions of time and space. Many users experience headache, nausea or vomiting, slurred speech, loss of motor coordination, and wheezing. A characteristic "glue sniffer's rash" around the nose and mouth may be seen. An odor of paint or solvents on clothes, skin, and breath is sometimes a sign of inhalant abuse.

You Are There! continued

The chronic use of inhalants has been associated with a number of serious health problems, such as kidney abnormalities and liver toxicity. Also it can result in memory impairment, attention deficit, and diminished nonverbal intelligence. Deaths resulting from heart failure, asphyxiation, and aspiration have occurred.

SOURCES: Fox Butterfield, "Theft of Painkiller Reflects Its Popularity on the Street," *New York Times*, July 7, 2001, p. A6; Paul Tough, "The Alchemy of Oxy-Contin," *New York Times Magazine*, July 29, 2001, p. 33; Barry Meier, "Maker Chose Not to Use a Drug Abuse Safeguard," *New York Times*, Aug. 13, 2001, p. A11; Clemente Lisi, "Kids Smoke 'Embalmed' Cigarettes," *New York Post*, July 29, 2001, p. 21; Drug Enforcement Administration, *Inhalants*, http://www.dea.gov/concern/abuse/chap8/inhal.htm; Michele Spiess, *Inhalants* (Washington, DC: Office of National Drug Control Policy, 2001).

YOU ARE THERE!
Clandestine Labs

Drugs of abuse in the United States come from a variety of sources, including the diversion of legitimate pharmaceuticals to the illicit market. Continuing efforts on the part of state and federal governments to reduce the amount of dangerous and illicit drugs available for abuse, combined with the demand for psychoactive substances, have contributed to the proliferation of clandestine laboratories.

Clandestine laboratories are illicit operations consisting of chemicals and equipment necessary to manufacture controlled substances. The types and numbers of laboratories seized, to a large degree, reflect regional and national trends in the types and amounts of illicit substances that are being manufactured, trafficked, and used. Clandestine labs have been found in remote locations like mountain cabins and rural farms, but they are also operated in single and multifamily residences in urban and suburban neighborhoods, where their toxic and explosive fumes can pose a significant threat to the health and safety of residents.

The production of some substances, such as methamphetamine, PCP, MDMA, and methcathinone, requires little sophisticated equipment or knowledge of chemistry. The synthesis of other drugs, such as fentanyl and LSD, requires much higher levels of expertise and equipment. Some clandestine lab operators have little or no training in chemistry and follow underground recipes; others employ chemistry students or professionals as "cooks."

The clandestine production of all drugs depends on the availability of essential raw materials. The distribution, sale, import, and export of certain chemicals that are important to the manufacture of common illicitly produced substances have been regulated since the enactment of the Chemical Diversion and Trafficking Act of 1988.

Law enforcement officers entering clandestine labs may be exposed to chemical concentrations well above recommended safety levels, which puts them at risk for serious, debilitating, and even life-threatening illnesses. Officers entering these labs should use full face-piece respirators or self-contained breathing apparatus to provide protection to their lungs. Also, they must protect their hands and other parts of the body from contact with chemicals because of the possibility of burns.

SOURCES: Drug Enforcement Administration, *Clandestine Labs*, http://www.dea.gov/concern/abuse/chap8/clan.htm; Robb Pilkington, "Clandestine Drug Labs and Chemical Exposure," *Law Enforcement Technology*, 28(7), July 2001, pp. 96–98.

YOU ARE THERE!

They Even Sell Viagra on the Street

Three workers for Pfizer Pharmaceuticals were charged in August 2001 with the theft of Viagra pills, a popular drug for erectile dysfunction, from their manufacturing plant in Brooklyn. They were charged with selling them in bulk—by the thousands—for a dollar a pill, according to a federal indictment.

Others have been charged with being middlemen in the scam and reselling the stolen pills for $3 a dose. Samuel "Fat Sam" Rooz, forty-nine, who was indicted on charges of conspiring to sell more than eight thousand pills, boasted that he had inside guys getting him his product. The indicted men also dealt in the diabetes pill Glucotrol, the infection drugs Dynacin and Levaquin, the acid reflux drug Aciphex, and the antipsychotic Risperdol.

They were fingered when a co-worker, who was busted earlier in the scam, agreed to turn FBI informant.

SOURCE: Laura Italiano and William J. Gorta, "Pfizer Trio Pilfered Viagra: Feds," *New York Post*, Aug. 11, 2001, p. 3.

led Congress in 1991 to place anabolic steroids into Schedule III of the CSA.

The CSA defines anabolic steroids as any drug or hormonal substance chemically and pharmacologically related to testosterone (other than estrogens, progestins, and corticosteroids) that promotes muscle growth. Most illicit anabolic steroids are sold at gyms, competitions, and through the mail. For the most part, these substance are smuggled into the United States. In addition, a number of bogus or counterfeit products are sold as anabolic steroids.

A limited number of anabolic steroids have been approved for medical and veterinary use. The primary legitimate use of these drugs in humans is for the replacement of inadequate levels of testosterone resulting from a reduction or absence of functioning testes. In veterinary practice, anabolic steroids are used to promote feed efficiency and to improve weight gain, vigor, and hair coat. They are also used by veteri-

narians to treat anemia and counteract tissue breakdown during illness and trauma.

The adverse effects of large doses of multiple anabolic steroids are not well established. However, there is increasing evidence of serious health problems associated with the abuse of these agents, including cardiovascular damage, liver damage, and damage to reproductive organs.

Physical side effects include elevated blood pressure and cholesterol levels, severe acne, premature balding, reduced sexual function, and testicular atrophy. In males, abnormal breast development can occur. In females, anabolic steroids have a masculinizing effect, resulting in more body hair, a deeper voice, smaller breasts, and fewer menstrual cycles. Several of these results are irreversible.

A complete description of each of these drugs—including name of drug, classification, Controlled Substance Act (CSA) schedule, trade or other names, medical uses, physical dependence level, psychological dependence level, tolerance, duration of effect, usual method of use, possible effect, effects of overdose, and withdrawal syndrome—can be found at http://www.usdoj.gov:80/dea/concern/concern.htm.

THE CONTROLLED SUBSTANCES AND DRUG LAWS

There are numerous federal and state laws that define and regulate controlled substances and other illegal drugs.

Federal Laws

The Controlled Substances Act (CSA), Title II of the Comprehensive Drug Abuse Prevention and Control Act of 1970, is the basic drug regulation law of the United States, the legal foundation of the government's fight against abuse of drugs and other substances. It is a consolidation of numerous laws regulating the manufacture and distribution of narcotics, stimulants, depressants, hallucinogens, anabolic steroids, and chemicals used in the illicit production of controlled substances. It places substances in the act under the regulation of the Drug Enforcement Administration (DEA) and the Food and Drug Administration (FDA). People who want to handle one of these controlled substances, such as importers, manufacturers, wholesalers, hospitals, pharmacies, physicians, and researchers, must register with the DEA, receive an identifying number, and maintain records of their transactions.[10]

The CSA places all substances that are in some manner regulated under existing federal law into one of five schedules, based on the substance's medical use, potential for abuse, and safety or dependence liability. The act also provides a mechanism for substances to be controlled, or added to a schedule; decontrolled, or removed from control; and rescheduled or transferred from one schedule to another. The procedure is found in Section 201 of the act (21 U.S.C. 811).

The threshold issue of whether or not a substance is controlled is whether it has potential for abuse. If a drug does not have a potential for abuse, it cannot be controlled. Although the term *potential for abuse* is not defined in CSA, there is much discussion of the term in the legislative history of the act. The following indicate that a drug or other substance has a potential for abuse:

- There is evidence that persons are taking the drug or other substance in amounts sufficient to create a hazard to their health or to the safety of other individuals or to the community.

- There is significant diversion of the drug or other substance from legitimate drug channels.

- Persons are taking the drug or other substance on their own initiative rather than on the basis of medical advice from a practitioner licensed by law to administer such drugs.

- The drug is a new drug so related in its action to a drug or other substance already listed as having a potential for abuse to make it likely that the drug will have the same potential for abuse, thus making it reasonable to assume that there may be significant diversions from legitimate channels, significant use contrary to or without medical advice, or that it has substantial capability of creating hazards to the health of the user or to the safety of the community. Of course, evidence of actual abuse of a substance is indicative that a drug has a potential for abuse.

The five schedules of the CSA and their descriptions are as follows:

- *Schedule I.* The drug or other substance has a high potential for abuse; the drug or other substance has no currently accepted medical use in treatment in the United States; there is a lack of accepted safety use of the drug or other substance under medical supervision. Some examples of Schedule I substances are heroin, LSD, marijuana and methaqualone.

- *Schedule II.* The drug or other substance has a high potential for abuse; the drug or other substance has a currently accepted medical use in treatment in the United States or a currently accepted medical use with severe restrictions; abuse of the drug or other substance may lead to severe psychological or physical dependence. Some examples of Schedule II substances are morphine, PCP, cocaine, methadone, and methamphetamine.

- *Schedule III.* The drug or other substance has a potential for abuse less than the drugs or substances in Schedules I and II; the drug or other substance has a currently accepted medical use in treatment in the United States; abuse of the drug or other substance may lead to moderate or low physical dependence or high psychological dependence. Some examples of Schedule III substances are anabolic steroids, codeine and hydrocodone with aspirin or Tylenol, and some barbiturates.

- *Schedule IV.* The drug or other substance has a low potential for abuse relative to the drugs or other substances in Schedule III; the drug or other substance has a currently accepted medical use in treatment in the United States; abuse of the drug or other substance may lead to limited physical dependence or psychological dependence relative to the drugs or other substances in Schedule III. Some examples of Schedule IV substances are Darvon, Talwin, Equanil, Valium, and Xanax.

- *Schedule V.* The drug or other substance has a low potential for abuse relative to the drugs or other substances in Schedule IV; the drug or other substance has a currently accepted medical use in treatment in the United States; abuse of the drug or other substance may lead to limited physical dependence or psychological dependence relative to the drugs or other substances in Schedule IV. Some examples of

Schedule V substances are over-the-counter cough medicines with codeine.

Schedule I drugs are forbidden to be dispensed and can only be used by researchers. Schedule II, III, and IV and some Schedule V drugs require a prescription when dispensed by a pharmacy.

The CSA was amended by the Comprehensive Crime Control Act of 1984. This act included a provision that allows the administrator of DEA to place a substance, on a temporary basis, into Schedule I when necessary to avoid an imminent hazard to the public safety.

The Anti-Drug Abuse Act of 1986 created a new class of substances called *controlled substance analogues*. These are substances that are not controlled but may be found in the illicit traffic. They are structurally or pharmacologically similar to Schedule I or II controlled substances and have no legitimate medical use. These substances are treated under the CSA as if they were controlled substances in Schedule I.

State Laws

Before the creation of the federal drug laws, many states regulated illegal drugs through their criminal laws. Since the CSA was established in 1970, states rewrote their drug laws to reflect the federal laws and regulations.

DRUG ENFORCEMENT AGENCIES

There are numerous drug law enforcement agencies and drug policy-making agencies throughout the United States under the authority and control of federal, local, and state agencies. This section will list the main ones and give you a sense of their mission and operations.

Federal Agencies

The federal agencies involved in drug enforcement and drug policy include the Office of National Drug Control Policy, the U.S. Department of State Bureau for International Narcotics and Law Enforcement, the Drug Enforcement Administration, the Internal Revenue Service, U.S. Customs, the Coast Guard, the United States Department of Defense, and many other federal agencies.

The Office of National Drug Control Policy The U.S. government's drug policies are under the control of the Office of National Drug Control Policy (ONDCP). The principal purpose of ONDCP is to establish policies, priorities, and objectives for the nation's drug control program, the goals of which are to reduce illicit drug use, manufacturing, and trafficking; drug-related crime and violence; and drug-related health consequences. To achieve these goals, the director of ONDCP is charged with producing the national drug control strategy, which directs the nation's antidrug efforts and establishes a program, a budget, and guidelines for cooperation among federal, state, and local agencies. The director of ONDCP evaluates, coordinates, and oversees both the international and domestic antidrug efforts of U.S. executive branch agencies and ensures that such efforts sustain and complement state and local antidrug activities. The director advises the President of the United States on changes in the organization, management, budgeting, and personnel of federal agencies that could affect the nation's antidrug efforts, and on federal agency compliance with their obligations under the strategy.

The year 2000 national drug control strategy had the following strategic goals and objectives: educate and enable America's youth to reject illegal drugs as

Federal law enforcement agents play a major role in investigating big smuggling cases. Here, federal agents escort one of the nearly sixty airline employees and foodservice workers arrested at Miami airport during "Operation Ramp Rats," which focused on employees smuggling drugs, explosives, and weapons into the United States.

© Reuters/Getty News Images

EXHIBIT 12.2   **Federal Law Enforcement Agencies Involved in Drug Law Enforcement**

Department of Justice

Drug Enforcement Administration

Federal Bureau of Investigation

Immigration and Naturalization Service

Marshals Service

Department of the Treasury

Bureau of Alcohol, Tobacco and Firearms

Customs Service

Internal Revenue Service

Department of Transportation

Coast Guard

Department of Defense

Air Force

Army

Navy

Postal Service

Postal Inspection Service

SOURCE: Howard Abadinsky, *Drugs: An Introduction* (Belmont, CA: Wadsworth, 2001).

well as alcohol and tobacco; increase the safety of America's citizens by substantially reducing drug-related crime and violence; reduce health and social costs to the public of illegal drug use; shield America's air, land, and sea frontiers from the drug threat; break foreign and domestic drug sources of supply.[11]

The Office of National Drug Control Policy describes its enforcement policy as follows:

> Even the best prevention programs will fail without strong, effective law enforcement efforts, including strong sanctions against drug offenders. Few efforts are as important as law enforcement in controlling drug use and related crime. Key priorities for domestic law enforcement are the disruption and dismantling of drug-trafficking organizations, including seizure of their assets, and the investigation, arrest, and prosecution and imprisonment of drug offenders. Domestic law enforcement initiatives emphasize attacking drug trafficking organizations at every level—from drug

kingpin to street-corner dealer—through a careful coordination of federal, state, and local law enforcement efforts.

> The international strategy maintains interdiction as an important component and emphasizes the United States' pursuit of cooperative efforts with other nations that possess the political will to defeat international drug syndicates in building their institutions, attacking drug production facilities, interdicting drug shipments in both source and transit countries, and dismantling drug trafficking organizations.[12]

The ONDCP offers a tremendous amount of research material for those interested in drugs, drug enforcement, and drug treatment.

 INVESTIGATIONS ON THE NET

Office of National Drug Control Policy
http://www.whitehousedrugpolicy.gov

For an up-to-date list of Web links, go to
http://info.wadsworth.com/dempsey

U.S. Department of State Bureau for International Narcotics and Law Enforcement The U.S. Department of State's Bureau for International Narcotics and Law Enforcement Affairs advises the President, Secretary of State, other bureaus in the Department of State, and other departments and agencies in the U.S. government on the development of policies and programs to combat international narcotics and crime. The bureau's International Narcotics Crime Program has three primary goals: to combat the growing threat to our national security posed by international organized crime; to help emerging democracies strengthen their national law enforcement institutions; and to strengthen efforts by the United Nations and other international organizations to assist member states in combating international criminal activity.

Drug Enforcement Administration The Drug Enforcement Administration (DEA) of the U.S. Department of Justice serves as the lead federal agency in the enforcement of the controlled substances laws of the United States. Its mission is to enforce controlled substances laws and regulations and bring to the justice

INVESTIGATIONS ON THE NET

U.S. Department of State Bureau for International Narcotics and Law Enforcement
http://www.state.gov/g/inl/

For an up-to-date list of Web links, go to http://info.wadsworth.com/dempsey

----

system those organizations and principal members of organizations involved in the growing, manufacture, or distribution of controlled substances appearing in or destined for illicit traffic in the United States.

Its primary responsibilities include

- Investigation and preparation for the prosecution of major violators of controlled substance laws operating at interstate and international levels

- Investigation and preparation for prosecution of criminals and drug gangs who perpetrate violence and terrorize citizens through fear and intimidation

- Management of a national drug intelligence program in cooperation with federal, state, local, and foreign officials to collect, analyze, and disseminate strategic and operational drug intelligence information

- Seizure and forfeiture of assets derived from, traceable to, or intended to be used for illicit drug trafficking

- Enforcement of the provisions of the Controlled Substances Act as they pertain to the manufacture, distribution, and dispensing of legally produced controlled substances

- Coordination and cooperation with federal, state, and local law enforcement officials on mutual drug enforcement efforts and enhancement of such efforts through exploitation of potential interstate and international investigations beyond local or limited federal jurisdictions and resources

- Coordination and cooperation with federal, state, and local agencies, and with foreign governments, in programs designed to reduce the availability of illicit abuse-type drugs on the U.S. market through nonenforcement methods such as crop eradication, crop substitution, and training of foreign officials

- Responsibility, under the policy guidance of the Secretary of State and U.S. ambassadors, for all programs associated with drug law enforcement counterparts in foreign countries

- Liaison with the United Nations, Interpol, and other organizations on matters relating to international drug control programs

The following are some of the major programs implemented by the DEA:

- *Foreign cooperative investigations.* DEA special agents assist their foreign counterparts by developing sources of information and interviewing witnesses. Agents work **undercover** and assist in surveillance efforts on cases that involve drug traffic affecting the United States. They provide information about drug traffickers to their counterparts and pursue investigative leads by checking hotel, airport, shipping, and passport records.

- *Office of Diversion Control.* Of all the major drugs of abuse, only marijuana is available as a natural, harvested product. The others, whether illicit drugs such as cocaine, heroin, methamphetamine, or legitimately produced pharmaceuticals, must be produced or manufactured. Many of the problems associated with drug abuse are the result of legitimately manufactured controlled substances being diverted from their lawful purpose into the illicit drug traffic. The DEA attacks this problem from two fronts. First, it continually monitors the movement of substances manufactured for legitimate medical use across the U.S. borders and investigates diversion programs directed at physicians who sell prescriptions to drug dealers or abusers; pharmacists who falsify records and subsequently sell the drugs; and employees who steal from inventory. Second, it uses diversion investigators, special agents, chemists, pharmacologists, and others to regulate and monitor products of illicit processing or synthesis involving the use of large quantities of industrial chemicals. The chemical control program attempts to disrupt the illicit production of controlled substances by preventing diversion of chemicals used to make these drugs.

- *State and Local Drug Task Force Program.* The DEA State and Local Drug Task Force Program consists of state and local task forces staffed by DEA special agents and state and local police officers. Participating officers are deputized to perform the same functions as DEA special agents. Combining federal leverage and the specialists available to the DEA with state and local officers' investigative talents and detailed knowledge of their jurisdiction leads to highly effective drug law enforcement investigations.

- *Organized crime drug enforcement task forces.* These task forces combine federal, state, and local law enforcement efforts in a comprehensive attack against organized crime and drug traffickers. These units have been effective by fostering collaboration among many different law enforcement agencies and using prosecuting attorneys at the early stages of investigations.

- *High Intensity Drug Trafficking Areas (HIDTAs).* This program addresses drug trafficking in the thirty-one areas of the country that are the major centers of illegal drug production, manufacturing, importation, or distribution.

- *Southwest Border Initiative (SWBI).* This operation is a cooperative effort by federal law enforcement agencies to combat the substantial threat posed by Mexico-based trafficking groups operating along the U.S. Southwest border. They target groups that are transporting multiton shipments of heroin, methamphetamine, and marijuana, as well as trafficking groups from Colombia that transport equally huge amounts of cocaine. The SWBI attacks organizations by targeting the communication systems of their command and control centers. Working in concert, the DEA, the FBI, U.S. Customs, and U.S. Attorney offices around the country conduct wiretaps that ultimately identify all levels of the Mexico- or Colombia-based organizations. The strategy allows the DEA to track the seamless continuum of drug traffic as it gradually flows from Colombia or Mexico to the U.S. streets where it is distributed. The rationale behind this operation is that the best way to attack any organized crime syndicate is to build strong cases against its leadership and their command and control functions.

- *Operation Pipeline.* This is a nationwide highway interdiction program that focuses on private motor vehicles. It is one of the DEA's most effective operations. The rationale for this program is that the nation's highways have become major arteries for drug transportation, including tons of drugs flowing north and east from Florida and the nation's Southwest border, while millions of dollars of drug profits return South and West, as if traveling through a pipeline. The DEA provides training, real-time communication, and analytic support to state and local agencies in this operation.

- *Operation Convoy.* This sister operation to Operation Pipeline targets drug transportation organizations that use commercial vehicles to traffic drugs. It is involved in long-term surveillance undercover operations and other enforcement activities aimed at transportation organizations.

- *Demand reduction.* This program seeks to reduce demand for illegal drugs by raising public awareness education for communities and businesses.

- *Marijuana eradication.* Under its Domestic Cannabis Eradication and Suppression Program, the DEA attempts to curb the cultivation and availability of both outdoor and indoor supplies of marijuana.

- *Mobile Enforcement Teams (MET) Program.* This program deploys entire DEA teams to local areas to attack violent drug organizations in their neighborhoods and restore a safer environment for the residents of these communities.

- *Asset forfeiture.* This program seizes profits from drug-related crimes, as well as property used to facilitate these crimes.

 INVESTIGATIONS ON THE NET

Drug Enforcement Administration
http://www.dea.gov

DEA Diversion Control Program
http://www.deadiversion.usdoj.gov

For an up-to-date list of Web links, go to
http://info.wadsworth.com/dempsey

YOU ARE THERE!

The Drug Enforcement Administration Museum

The Drug Enforcement Administration Museum is open to the public with regular hours, but admission is by appointment only. Located in Arlington, Virginia, the museum is operated by the DEA's Office of Public Affairs. It also conducts programs and tours for schools and other community groups.

Inside the museum a variety of exhibits outline the DEA's mission, history, and some of its more notable feats in enforcing U.S. controlled substance laws. One featured exhibit is "Illegal Drugs in America: A Modern History." This exhibit traces drug use in America from the opium dens of the 1800s to the international crime organizations that run the "narcobusiness" today. The exhibit traces the impact drugs have had on American society and the counternarcotics efforts used to combat the problem. It also traces the DEA's evolution from part of the Treasury Department to the force it is today.

SOURCES: Sheila Burnette, "Police Museums Worldwide," *Law and Order*, Aug. 2001, pp. 71–74; Drug Enforcement Administration, http://www.usdoj./gov/dea/museum.

- *Money laundering.* Money laundering is the process used by drug traffickers to convert bulk amounts of drug profits into legitimate money. Tracking and intercepting this illegal flow of drug money is an important tool in identifying and dismantling international drug trafficking organizations.
- *Aviation.* The DEA uses aircraft for its domestic and international undercover operations, collection of intelligence, and group aerial reconnaissance.
- *Training.* The DEA provides training programs for its agents and other federal personnel as well as state, local, and international law enforcement counterparts.
- *Intelligence.* The DEA is the major intelligence-gathering agency directed toward drug enforcement. It helps initiate new investigations of major drug organizations and strengthens ongoing

ones. It develops information that leads to seizures and arrests, and provides policy makers with drug trend information on which programmatic decisions can be based.

U.S. Customs Another federal agency heavily involved in drug enforcement is U.S. Customs. The most important drug law enforcement programs of U.S. Customs are these:

- *Anti-drug initiative seizures.* During their routine border inspections, U.S. Customs seizes an enormous amount of drugs at the various U.S. borders. In the latest reporting year, it seized almost 1.3 million pounds of marijuana, 150,000 pounds of cocaine, and 2,500 pounds of heroin.[13]
- *Air and Marine Interdiction Program.* The Air and Marine Interdiction Division of U.S. Customs is the premier integrated air and marine law enforcement interdiction agency in the United States. The air and marine branches of U.S. Customs are strategically located along the southern border of the country and in Puerto Rico and the Virgin Islands, focusing on detecting and intercepting air and marine smugglers. They use sophisticated radar and interception boats, planes, and helicopters and operate closely with the U.S. Coast Guard and other military units to apprehend suspects. They also cooperate with and support foreign law enforcement and military agencies in support of their counternarcotic programs.
- *Canine Enforcement Program.* The U.S. Customs Canine Enforcement Program is a major part of their narcotic interdiction effort. It has 533 canine teams stationed at seventy-three ports of entry across the continental United States, and in Hawaii and Puerto Rico, including airports,

INVESTIGATIONS ON THE NET

U.S. Customs
http://www.customs.treas.gov

U.S. Customs Canine Enforcement Program
http://www.customs.treas.gov/enforcem/k9.htm

For an up-to-date list of Web links, go to http://info.wadsworth.com/dempsey

CAREER FOCUS

Positions with the DEA

Special Agent

DEA special agents are a select group of men and women from diverse backgrounds whose experience and commitment unify during training to make them the best federal drug law enforcement agents in the world. They play a vital and unique role in combating the serious problem of drug trafficking and are offered many opportunities for multifaceted experiences in the United States and overseas.

Duties

- Conduct surveillance
- Infiltrate drug trafficking organizations
- Arrest violators
- Confiscate illegal drugs
- Conduct money laundering investigations
- Collect and prepare evidence
- Testify in criminal court cases

Qualifications

- U.S. citizens, between twenty-one and thirty-six years of age.
- Excellent physical condition.
- College degree with GPA of 2.95 or better. Additional consideration will be given to those who have degrees in special skill areas: criminal justice/police science or related disciplines, finance, accounting, economics, foreign language (with fluency verified) in Spanish, Russian, Hebrew, Arabic, Nigerian, Chinese or Japanese, computer science and information systems, and telecommunications, electrical, or mechanical engineering.

- Substantive professional or administrative or certain law enforcement experience may be qualifying. Other special skills or experience (military officer, foreign language fluency, pilot-maritime experience, technical-mechanical skills, or accounting-auditing experience) may also be qualifying.
- Full disclosure of past drug use; successful completion of a polygraph examination, psychological suitability assessment, and an exhaustive background investigation.

Forensic Chemist

Candidates must fulfill several requirements.
- U.S. citizen.
- Able to meet physical requirements.
- Able to pass a complete background investigation.
- A four-year degree from an accredited college or university with a major in one of the physical sciences, life sciences, or engineering. Such course of study must have included thirty semester hours of chemistry, six semester hours of physics, and mathematics through differential and integral calculus; or possess a combination of education and experience with coursework equivalent to a major mentioned above, to include at least thirty semester hours in chemistry, plus appropriate experience or additional education.

SOURCES: Drug Enforcement Administration; http://www. dea.gov/job/agent/page-05.htm, and http://www.dea.gov/job/chemist/qualifications.htm.

marine terminals, and borders. In the latest reporting year it recorded over eleven thousand narcotic and currency seizures resulting in the confiscation of hundreds of tons of narcotics with a street value exceeding several billion dollars.[14]

- *Training programs.* The U.S. Customs Service provides comprehensive training for federal, state, and local and foreign narcotics control enforcement agencies.

Internal Revenue Service The Internal Revenue Service assists in the enforcement of the drug laws by using its Criminal Investigation Division to lend its financial investigative expertise to narcotics and money

INVESTIGATIONS ON THE NET

Internal Revenue Service, Criminal Investigation
http://www.treas.gov/irs/ci/ci_structure/index.htm

For an up-to-date list of Web links, go to http://info.wadsworth.com/dempsey

----

INVESTIGATIONS ON THE NET

U.S. Coast Guard
http://www.uscg.mil

For an up-to-date list of Web links, go to http://info.wadsworth.com/dempsey

----

laundering investigations conducted in conjunction with other law enforcement agencies at the local, state, and federal levels.

U.S. Coast Guard The U.S. Coast Guard is the lead federal agency for maritime drug interdiction and shares responsibility for air interdiction with the U.S. Customs Service. The Coast Guard's mission is to reduce the supply of drugs from the source by denying smugglers the use of air and marine routes in the transit zone, a six-million-square-mile area including the Caribbean, Gulf of Mexico, and eastern Pacific. The Coast Guard coordinates closely with other federal agencies and countries in the region to disrupt and deter the flow of illegal drugs. In addiction to deterrence, Coast Guard drug interdiction accounts for nearly 56 percent of all U.S. government seizures of cocaine each year. For the latest reporting year, the Coast Guard seized cocaine with an estimated import value of approximately $4.4 billion.[15] The basic element of the Coast Guard's operational law enforcement effort is the boarding team, which is made up of members of a station's or cutter's crew who are specially trained and qualified to conduct boarding of vessels at sea. Coast Guard boarding teams are armed, uniformed federal law enforcement officers.

United States Department of Defense The United States Department of Defense (DoD) through the U.S. Air Force, Army, and Navy is actively involved in narcotics enforcement interdiction as well as our nation's other drug enforcement programs.

DoD active duty military and reserve components, through Joint Task Force-Six (JTF6), provide transportation, equipment, intelligence, training, and other services to drug law enforcement agencies when they request domestic, operational, and logistical support

to assist them in their efforts to reduce drug-related crime.

DoD serves as the lead agency of the federal government for the detection and monitoring of aerial and maritime transit of illegal drugs to this country. Accordingly, it maintains a robust air and maritime surveillance system in the key drug transit zone using airborne and ground-based radar, ships and patrol craft, and command and control systems. Extensive intelligence collection and analysis support operations. DoD also maintains air surveillance along the Southwest border. In addition, it provides direct support to drug enforcement agencies along that border. It provides military-to-military cooperation with the Mexican Army and Navy to counter drug elements.

DoD supports air, ground, and marine operations by source nation forces and supports extensive foreign intelligence collection and analysis programs that aid operations in the cocaine-source nations, transit zone interagency operations, and international efforts to interdict cocaine and arrest drug kingpins and dismantle their organizations. It provides training by special operations forces and infrastructure development to partner nations. It maintains an air surveillance capability in the source zone using the hemispheric radar system (HRS) and Relocatable Over-the-Horizon Radar (ROTHR), as well as surveillance platforms operating from forward operating locations. This kind of support is critical to ensuring effective counterdrug operations throughout the hemisphere.

DoD provides extensive demand-reduction, drug testing, and education and awareness programs. It also has implemented drug-free workplace programs in all of its agencies.

DoD assists community groups by providing drug prevention information and education through the Young Marines Program and outreach programs funded in the National Guard state plans. These activities

INVESTIGATIONS ON THE NET

U.S. Department of Defense
http://www.defenselink.mil

For an up-to-date list of Web links, go to
http://info.wadsworth.com/dempsey

----

provide positive role models and drug awareness education for at-risk youth. In addition, military personnel volunteer in drug abuse prevention programs through various community-based programs.

Other Federal Agencies Other federal agencies are involved in the enforcement of our controlled substances laws. Among them are the Federal Bureau of Investigation, Immigration and Naturalization Service, Marshals Service, Bureau of Alcohol, Tobacco and Firearms, and Postal Inspection Service.

State and Local Agencies

Although this chapter has just spent considerable time discussing the federal drug enforcement agencies, it must be emphasized that state and local law enforcement officers make the majority of drug arrests in our nation and provide the majority of the personnel

assigned to our drug law enforcement efforts. Furthermore, most of the street-level personnel assigned to the various DEA state and local drug task forces and their organized crime task forces around the nation are local police officers, deputy sheriffs, and state troopers. These officers are vital to the mission of the task forces because they provide the local knowledge and contacts—the street smarts—necessary to infiltrate and affect local drug trafficking organizations. The personnel assigned to two of the DEA's most successful programs, Operation Pipeline and Operation Convoy, are state and local officers working our nation's highways.

Each of the forty-nine state law enforcement agencies, the nearly seventeen thousand local law enforcement agencies around the nation, and the nearly eight hundred thousand persons working for these agencies are involved in the enforcement of the controlled substances and drug laws on a twenty-four-hour-a-day, seven-day-a-week basis. Besides the uniformed officers making summary arrests of persons observed selling or possessing drugs, many of these agencies have specific units directed solely at the enforcement of the controlled substances laws, some addressing high-level cases aimed at infiltrating and dismantling organized distribution networks and some addressing street-level problems.

As an example of a local police department's activity in drug law enforcement, the New York City Police Department uses its Organized Crime Control Bureau (OCCB) to affect high- and midlevel drug-dealing organizations and uses its patrol force to make arrests of low-level, street drug dealers. The NYPD's OCCB is the central office for all investigations and enforcement operations on organized criminal activities, including narcotics, vice, auto crime, and traditional and nontraditional organized crime. The OCCB's mission is to improve the quality of life in New York City by combating all aspects of organized crime while maintaining high standards of safety and integrity.[16]

The mission of the Narcotics Division, OCCB's largest division, is to identify, arrest, and eliminate drug gangs and individuals who control drug operations. The division is also responsible for the timely investigation of citizen complaints of narcotic conditions. The personnel assigned to the Narcotics Division

© Andrew Lichtenstein/The Image Works

Local police officers make most of the controlled substances arrests in the United States. Here, officers in Bridgeport, Connecticut, search a suspected crack dealer in a raid on a crack house.

constitutes over 88 percent of the total personnel assigned to OCCB.

The Narcotics Division is organized into eight geographical boroughs; each borough has approximately ten precinct narcotics squads. Some boroughs have "Initiatives," which further focus narcotics enforcement through a command center that coordinates narcotics, uniform, and detective components.

The Narcotics Division also contains a number of specialty squads and task forces designed to provide both operational and investigative support to overall enforcement efforts. For example, the Drug Enforcement Task Force is a joint task force that consists of federal, state, and OCCB investigations working together to target middle- and upper-level drug trafficking and importers. The Kennedy Airport Narcotics Smuggling Unit (KANSU) is a joint effort between Narcotics Borough Queens and the United States Customs Service. KANSU was designed to interdict illegal narcotics from gaining entry into the country through Kennedy Airport. The Narcotics Investigation and Tracking of Recidivist Offenders (NITRO) unit coordinates, develops, maintains, and disseminates narcotics intelligence through debriefings and computer databases. This unit is designed to prioritize enforcement efforts against career felony offenders and New York City firearms violators identified by the NYPD.

As an example of state drug law enforcement, we will focus on the Texas Department of Public Safety (DPS). The Texas Department of Public Safety includes five divisions: Administration, Driver's License, Traffic Law Enforcement, Criminal Law Enforcement, and Texas Rangers.[17]

The Criminal Law Enforcement Division (CLE) focuses on narcotics trafficking, organized crime, and motor vehicle theft. The Narcotics Service of the CLE directs the state's enforcement efforts against illegal drug trafficking, supervises controlled substances registration, administers official prescription forms for Schedule II controlled substances, and supervises permits for reporting of precursor chemical activities. The Narcotics Service also assists state, federal, county, and local agencies in drug law enforcement. The ultimate goal is to eliminate illegal trafficking of controlled substances and deterring drug abuse in Texas.

The Narcotics Service's investigative priorities include cross-border smuggling, air and marine smuggling, clandestine drug laboratories, pharmaceutical

drug diversion, domestic marijuana eradication, financial investigations, assistance to federal, state, and local law enforcement agencies, and highway drug interdiction. Commissioned officers use overt and undercover investigative techniques to probe suspected drug rings.

The Narcotics Service provides personnel and assistance to the Texas Narcotics Control Program task forces throughout the state and the High Intensity Drug Trafficking Area drug squads in the state.

It also operates the Texas Narcotics Information System (TNIS), an automated drug intelligence and information system for local, state, and federal law enforcement agencies.

The Texas Highway Patrol, with over seventeen hundred officers, in addition to patrolling the Texas highways and carrying out other duties, concentrates on drug interdiction. For a ten-year period, DPS troopers led the nation in the seizure of several controlled substances with the seizure of over 10,800 pounds of cocaine, almost 336,000 pounds of marijuana, and over $41 million in currency.

International Cooperation

Many foreign nations, with the financial and organizational support of the United States, are actively engaged in narcotics law enforcement directed at organized growing, manufacturing and distribution networks. Many nations, also with the financial and organizational support of the United States, are involved in the eradication of drug field harvests. In one example, American pilots working as mercenaries under a U.S. State Department contract in Colombia

 INVESTIGATIONS ON THE NET

**Texas Department of Public Safety:
Criminal Law Enforcement Division,
Narcotics Service**
http://www.txdps.state.tx.us/criminal_law_
enforcement/narcotics/index.htm

**Texas Department of Public Safety: Traffic
Law Enforcement Division**
http://www.txdps.state.tx.us/tle/

For an up-to-date list of Web links, go to
http://info.wadsworth.com/dempsey

YOU ARE THERE!

Captain Robbie Bishop

Captain Robbie Bishop of the Villa Rica Police Department in Georgia was more than just your average officer. Bishop headed the Villa Rica ICE Team and was well-known throughout the interdiction community in U.S. law enforcement.

On Wednesday, January 20, 1999, Captain Bishop was shot and killed during a traffic stop on Interstate 20 at the eighteen mile marker, leaving behind his wife and two children. The funeral was held in Villa Rica, and was attended by almost four thousand officers, citizens, friends, and family. The funeral motorcade left Villa Rica and moved seventy-five miles north on I-75 to Dalton, Georgia. With patrol cars from across the country bumper-to-bumper, the procession was over seven miles in length.

SOURCE: Narcotic Drug Interdiction Association; http://members.aol.com/_ht_aK9resq/NDIAindex.html.

spray herbicides on fields of coca and heroin poppies that are often guarded by leftist rebels.[18]

Interpol Interpol (the International Criminal Police Organization) is a worldwide organization established to develop cooperation among nations on common police problems. It maintains a Drugs Sub-Directorate in its Criminal Intelligence Directorate, which is the central repository of professional and technical expertise in drug control in the Interpol framework. It acts as a clearinghouse for the collection, collation, analysis, and dissemination of drug-related information. It also monitors the drug situation on a global basis, coordinates international investigation, and maintains liaison with the United Nations, its specialized agencies, and other international and regional organizations involved in drug control activities. One of its important functions is to serve as a main source of professional and technical advice on narcotics matters to Interpol bodies such as the General Assembly, Executive Committee, and National Central Bureaus.[19]

The mission of the Drugs Sub-Directorate is to enhance cooperation among member countries and stimulate exchange of information between all national and international enforcement bodies concerned with countering the illicit production, traffic, and use of narcotic drugs and psychotropic substances. Drawing on the wide investigative and analytical experience of its multinational staff, the unit serves member states in information collection; responding to international drug investigation inquiries; collection and analysis of data obtained from member states for strategic and tactical intelligence reports, and the dissemination of these reports to concerned member states; identification of international drug trafficking organizations; coordination of international drug investigations where at least two member states are involved; holding of working meetings involving two or more states where the unit has identified common links in cases being investigated in those member countries in order to exchange information and establish future strategy; and organizing either regional or worldwide meetings on specific drug topics.

Interpol allows links to be made between drug cases being conducted by national administrations that would otherwise seem unrelated. When it is clearly established that there is good potential for developing a substantial case, it is given an operational name. As the case is developed, a working meeting of the concerned countries can be organized to bring together all of the officers to discuss all aspects of the case and devise future strategy. The case officers bring with them information such as fingerprints, photographs, identity documents, telephone numbers, addresses, criminal histories, and any other information related to the case.

METHODS OF DRUG ENFORCEMENT

According to Mark A. R. Kleiman, who has written extensively on drug enforcement, there are five levels of drug-law enforcement: *source control, interdiction, domestic distribution, wholesaling,* and *street sales.*[20]

This section will discuss each of these levels of enforcement and give concrete examples of each from the earlier section of the chapter that discussed drug enforcement agencies. It will also discuss the various legal tools available to enforce the drug laws.

Source Control

Source control involves actions aimed at limiting the cultivation and production of the sources of controlled substances including the poppy, coca, and cannabis or marijuana plants. The U.S. Department of State and the DEA are actively involved in source control efforts both in foreign nations and in the United States. Nonenforcement source control efforts include such methods as crop eradication and crop substitution.

There are major problems with attempting to eradicate coca, poppy, and marijuana plants. First, attempts to do so by cutting or burning result in healthier and more bountiful growth, while uprooting coca plants causes the soil to become unproductive for as long as eight to ten years. Also, successful attempts at eradication with the use of aerial herbicides that are either sprayed or dropped as pellets and melt into the soil when it rains, kill many other species of plants and remain in the soil and affect future plantings. Second, the growing of opium and coca in source countries is a major part of the economy for some, and foreign governments risk alienating a large portion of their population if they try to take away this source of income.

Interdiction

Interdiction involves the interception and seizure of drugs being smuggled into the United States. As was discussed earlier in this chapter, U.S. law enforcement agencies, primarily the DEA and U.S. Customs, as well as the Coast Guard and the military, are involved in interdiction activities. Most of these activities occur at the U.S. borders, particularly the Southwest border, and in the air and sea routes surrounding the Caribbean and the Gulf of Mexico.

Disrupting Domestic Distribution

This involves the disruption of high-level trafficking and the dismantling of high-level drug organizations at the interstate and international levels. The DEA serves as the lead U.S. law enforcement agency in disrupting domestic distribution, assisted by numerous other federal, state, and local law enforcement agencies through its various state and local drug task forces and organized crime drug enforcement task forces. Also, key elements in disrupting domestic distribution are the various state and local law enforcement agencies involved in operations like Operation Pipeline and Operation Convoy, which target transporters of illegal drugs on the nation's highways.

Disrupting Wholesaling

This involves focusing on midlevel drug dealing at the local level by federal, state, and local authorities. The DEA's High Intensity Drug Trafficking Area (HIDTA) enforcement activities, described earlier, play a big role in disrupting midlevel drug wholesaling operations. The DEA's state and local drug task forces, and the organized crime and narcotics units of various state and local police departments are also involved in these activities.

Disrupting Street Sales

This involves the arrests of low-level drug dealers and the disruption and dismantling of low-level drug selling gangs and individuals at the local level. Members of all state and local law enforcement agencies throughout the United States, including uniformed officers on patrol and plainclothes officers on special narcotics assignments, are directly involved. In addition to making arrests for actually selling illegal drugs, these local officers are responsible for making arrests for crimes related to drug dealing, including violent crimes such as murder, robbery, and aggravated assault, and property crimes such as burglaries and larcenies.

Tools for Drug Enforcement

Law enforcement has numerous tools to assist it in its efforts to enforce the drug laws, including federal and state criminal laws, tax laws, conspiracy laws, money laundering laws, and criminal and civil forfeiture laws.

Federal and State Criminal Laws The major federal law regarding controlled substances is Title II of the Comprehensive Drug Abuse Prevention and Control Act of 1970 (the Controlled Substances Act), which was discussed earlier in this chapter. States also have their own criminal laws on controlled substances.

Tax Laws The government can pursue drug offenders by using the tax laws to charge people with failing to report their entire income for tax purposes.

Conspiracy Laws The criminal charge of conspiracy refers to an agreement between two or more persons to commit a criminal act and the commission of at least one overt act in the furtherance of the conspiracy. Therefore, using conspiracy laws, law enforcement officers can charge someone with conspiracy before a crime actually takes place.

The RICO statute (Racketeer Influenced and Corrupt Organizations) of the Organized Crime Control Act of 1970 is a good example of a federal conspiracy law. The RICO statute makes it a crime to conspire to violate drug laws as part of an agreement to participate in an enterprise by engaging in a pattern of racketeering activity. Members of the conspiracy do not need to know each other or even be aware of each other's criminal activities. All that needs to be shown is each member's agreement to participate in the enterprise or organization by committing two or more racketeering acts, such as gambling or drug violations, within a ten-year period.

Another good example of a conspiracy law is the Continuing Criminal Enterprise (CCE) statute. This statute is similar in purpose to RICO but targets only illegal drug activity. It makes it a crime to commit or conspire to commit a continuing series of felony violations (the courts have ruled that "series" means three or more violations) of the Comprehensive Drug Abuse Prevention and Control Act of 1970 when the violations are undertaken in concert with five or more persons.

Money Laundering Laws The Money Laundering Control Act of 1986 (Title 18 U.S.C. Sections 1956 and 1957) specifies that a person is guilty of money laundering if he or she, knowing that the property involved represents the proceeds of an illegal activity, attempts to conceal or disguise the nature, location, source, ownership, or control of the proceeds or attempts to avoid a transaction-reporting requirement, with the intent to promote an unlawful activity or with the knowledge that the monetary instrument or funds represent the proceeds of an unlawful activity.

For a conviction, the prosecutor must prove that the defendant engaged in a monetary transaction in excess of $10,000, the defendant knew the money was the fruit of criminal activity, and the money was in fact the fruit of a specified unlawful activity.[21]

Criminal and Civil Forfeiture Laws There are state and federal laws, including the 1984 Comprehensive Forfeiture Act, that provide for the forfeiture of property used in criminal activity or obtained with the fruits of criminal activity. Four types of property are subject to forfeiture:

- *Contraband* includes property that is illegal to possess—for example, controlled substances.
- *Derivative contraband* includes vehicles or vessels used to transport contraband, including planes, boats, and motor vehicles.
- *Direct proceeds* includes cash.
- *Derivative proceeds* includes real estate and stock.

Criminal forfeiture is applicable only as part of a successful criminal prosecution, whereas civil forfeiture can be used even without criminal action and requires less evidence and fewer due process guarantees than criminal forfeiture proceedings. In civil forfeiture the legal actions are directed against property involved in a crime rather than a person.

PROACTIVE, COVERT, UNDERCOVER INVESTIGATIVE METHODS FOR DRUG INVESTIGATIONS

At least three general methods can be used in conducting proactive, covert, undercover drug investigations.

Infiltration

Infiltration involves gaining entry into criminal organizations that sell large amounts of drugs. The intent of this kind of undercover operation is to buy larger and larger amounts of drugs in order to reach as high as possible into the organizational hierarchy. This approach is based on the awareness that lower members of the criminal hierarchy have access only to a fixed quantity of drugs. To obtain larger amounts they have to introduce the investigator to their source or connection, generally someone in the upper echelon of the organization or a member of a more sophisticated organization. Infiltration operations require sophisticated electronic surveillance measures and large sums of money. Furthermore, they can be very lengthy and dangerous to undercover investigators.

Stakeouts

Another method used to go after drug syndicates or drug locations is the *stakeout*. A stakeout involves a fixed surveillance of a particular location; the surveillant makes detailed observations of the conditions that indicate drug sales, such as the quick arrival and departure of numerous autos and persons at a particular location. It is best if these observations are recorded on video to establish probable cause for obtaining a search warrant. If a judge agrees, she can issue a search warrant, which can then be executed against a particular person, automobile, or premise. Stakeouts can be very lengthy and involve sophisticated electronic surveillance.

Undercover Buy-and-Busts

Another type of covert method of drug investigation is the undercover **buy-and-bust.** In this operation, an undercover police officer purchases a quantity of drugs from a subject and then leaves the scene, contacts the backup team, and identifies the seller. The backup team, in or out of uniform, responds to the location of the sale and arrests the seller, based on the description given by the undercover officer. The legal basis of the arrest is probable cause to believe that a crime was committed and that the subject is the perpetrator of the crime. Based on the legal arrest, the backup team can search the subject and seize any illegal drugs. If the arrest occurs inside a premise, the backup team can seize any illegal substances that are in plain view. The undercover officer then goes to the police facility where the subject was taken and makes a positive identification of the subject from a hidden location, generally through a one-way mirror or window. By viewing the suspect through the one-way mirror or window, the undercover officer cannot be seen and can be used again in the same role.

The buy-and-bust is generally used in low-level drug operations brought to police attention by complaints from the community. The purpose is to take the person into custody as quickly as possible to eliminate that particular criminal and quality-of-life problem in the neighborhood.

Having a sufficient number of officers is extremely important in these operations. The basic players in the game are the undercover officer (U/C); the ghost officer (an officer who closely shadows or follows the U/C as he or she travels in an area and approaches the dealer); the backup team, consisting of at least five officers, if possible, who can watch from a discreet loca-

YOU ARE THERE!

The Legality of Undercover Drug Investigations: *Gordon v. Warren Consolidated Board of Education*

Law enforcement and high school officials had placed an undercover officer into regular classes to investigate student drug use. After the investigation, several students were arrested and convicted of participating in the drug trade. They appealed their convictions, claiming that the actions of the school officials violated their rights under the First Amendment of the United States Constitution. Their appeal was dismissed by appellate courts, ruling that the presence of the police officer working undercover did not constitute any more than a "chilling" effect on the students' First Amendment rights, because it did not disrupt classroom activities or education and it did not have any tangible effect on inhibiting expression of particular views in the classroom.

SOURCE: *Gordon v. Warren Consolidated Board of Education,* 706 F.2d 778 6th Cir. (1983).

tion to ensure the safety of the U/C and ghost officer, and who can move in when ready to arrest the dealer; and the supervisor, who is perhaps the most critical member of the team. He or she plans and directs the operation and makes all key decisions.

The arrest in the buy-and-bust operation may be delayed until the officers obtain an arrest warrant.

There are several professional organizations for those interested in narcotics investigation and interdiction. One example is the International Narcotics Interdiction Association (INIA) which is a nonprofit, educational, corporation dedicated to providing high quality interdiction training for narcotics professionals. There are currently over one thousand local, state, federal, and foreign members registered with INIA. Its Web site has the latest information and trends in targeting narcotics traffickers. Other associations are the National Narcotic Officers' Associations Coalition (NNOAC), which is made up of individual state narcotics associations representing more than fifty thousand law enforcement officers. NNOAC actively researches, monitors, and supports legislative initiatives

DEMPSEY'S LAW
SNAPping in the Seventy-Ninth Precinct

In the late 1980s, I was assigned as a captain in the New York City Police Department's Seventy-Ninth Precinct, which covers a large part of Bedford Stuyvesant, Brooklyn. The NYPD had a drug enforcement program called SNAP—Street Narcotics Abatement Program. The program was designed to close down crack houses and smoke shops at the local precinct level by using a team of experienced aggressive uniformed officers. I was the leader of the Seventy-Ninth Precinct SNAP.

Several times a week we would go out "snapping." There were ten people assigned to the unit in addition to myself. We had a lieutenant, two sergeants, and six police officers. We also were able to borrow two undercovers from the Brooklyn North Narcotics District to assist us in each operation we conducted. We had the use of three vehicles, two unmarked, nondescript autos and a marked RMP.

Before hitting the streets, we would have a meeting in my office and discuss the locations we were going to hit and plan our operations. We made sure we all understood the conditions at these locations and what was expected of each member of the team. We would then leave the station house in three vehicles and arrive at three different prearranged locations in the area of the intended buy operation. The undercover would go off to the target crack house or smoke shop and make a buy. After the buy went down, the

U/C would radio us and tell us that the buy had gone down and describe the seller (JD) if possible. ("JD"—John or Jane Doe—meant the unknown dealer. A description might be JD, male, black, Yankee hat, or JD, female, white, orange blouse, red hair, and so on.)

We would then simultaneously drive to the location in the three vehicles and force entry into the location. We had several battering rams and sledgehammers. Generally these tools were sufficient to allow us immediate entry into the premises, but it was more difficult with the heavily fortified locations (many used multiple layers of Plexiglas). It took us longer to get into those locations. We would always have several officers waiting in the rear or side entrances of the locations to watch for persons fleeing the location.

Once we gained entrance, we would immediately secure all the persons present and then conduct a search of the persons and the area. Of course, our legal rationale for the search was that we were making an arrest and the searches were incident to the arrest. The undercover buy was the legal rationale for entry into the premise.

Once the premise was secured and all persons were searched we would remove them to the station house under arrest. Sometimes we only had one collar, sometimes ten to twenty.

INVESTIGATIONS ON THE NET

International Narcotics Interdiction Association
http://www.inia.org

National Narcotic Officers' Associations Coalition
http://www.natlnarc.org

National Drug Interdiction Association
http://members.aol.com/_ht_a/K9resq/NDIAindex.html

For an up-to-date list of Web links, go to http://info.wadsworth.com/dempsey
----

INVESTIGATIONS ON THE NET

Arizona Narcotic Officers Association
http://www.aznarcoticofficer.org

Texas Narcotic Officers Association
http://www.tnoa.org

California Narcotic Officers Association
http://www.cnoa.org

For an up-to-date list of Web links, go to http://info.wadsworth.com/dempsey
----

DEMPSEY'S LAW
Undercovers, Tracks, Drinking Water Out of Toilet Bowls

I was never an undercover. I guess because most people always thought I looked too much like a cop. However, I supervised and commanded many undercovers and undercover operations. Also, I have many friends who were undercovers.

Undercovers are a rare breed. Generally, they don't look like cops and don't act like cops—if they did they wouldn't be effective U/Cs. They try to blend into any situation they find themselves in. (Recall our discussion of undercover officers and undercover operations in chapter 9 of this text.)

In the NYPD, we referred to undercovers by several names. The names "uncle" and "U/C" were synonymous with undercover officer.

Here are just a couple of real stories told by undercovers:

I was in this club looking to buy some E. While surveying the club before I made my buy, I went into the women's rest room. Here were three girls drinking water out of a toilet bowl. I couldn't believe it. I went over to the sink to make believe that I was going to wash my hands and then I realized that there was no water coming out of the faucets. I went to a drinking fountain I had seen outside the rest room, but there was no water coming out of that either. Imagine drinking water from a toilet. Why?

I left the women's room and went to the bar. I asked the bartender for a glass of water and he told me, "Forget it, we only sell bottled water." I said, "How much?" He said, "Six bucks." A few minutes later, I made my buy, went outside and notified the sergeant and identified the JD. The backup team went into the club and made the collar.

Later on I told the sergeant how weird it was to see people drinking water out of a toilet bowl, and he told me the reason. It seems that E makes a user extremely thirsty. The owners of the club are involved in the drug-selling operation and also are making a lot of dough by selling water to the kids who are extremely thirsty. They shut off all the water fountains and sinks so that kids are either forced to spend $6 for a little bottle of water, or else drink out of the toilet.

I was assigned to buy smack out of this basement in Alphabet City, a neighborhood in downtown Manhattan. It was like a bazaar. I had spent an hour at the office getting ready to look the part of the type of *skell* who uses heroin. I painted tracks on my arms, blackened out my front teeth with licorice, and of course, was wearing old clothing that looked and smelled as if I had lived in them for a year. I went out to the set.

Steerers were all over the street. One walked me over to this tenement and escorted me through a back alley that led to a door. Fortunately, I knew my ghost was doing his street act on the street and backing me up. Also, a couple of other U/Cs were with me. Inside looked like a busy checkout counter at a supermarket. At least ten people were lined up to buy drugs. A guy was walking up and down the line asking us to pull up our sleeves and show him our tracks. Fortunately, I had good tracks. Sometimes, if they see someone without tracks, they'll do them some damage and then throw them right out onto the street. I made my buy and then went outside and gave the sergeant the JD's script.

designed to increase the effectiveness of narcotics law enforcement and law enforcement in general. The mission of the National Drug Interdiction Association (NDIA) is to provide law enforcement personnel with a resource for information and training in areas of highway criminal enforcement.

Many states have their own professional organizations for narcotics investigations. For example, the Arizona Narcotic Officers Association (ANOA) has a mission to educate the membership, the public, and other law enforcement officers, in the state of Arizona, on the dangers of drug and narcotics abuse. It also provides training for law enforcement officers by the use of various training media, seminars, conference, and printed publications. Texas has the Texas Narcotic Officers Association (TNOA), and California has the California Narcotic Officers Association (CNOA).

DEMPSEY'S LAW

Beat Drugs: An Undercover's Nightmare

Among the numerous problems undercovers face are *beat drugs*. Beat drugs are substances that a drug dealer will sell to a buyer instead of the actual drug. Common ways of selling beat drugs are substituting oregano for marijuana, talcum powder for heroin, or an Excedrin tablet or other tablet for Ecstasy.

The biggest problem the undercover faces with beat drugs is when he or she returns to the same dealer or group of dealers to make another purchase of the drug. If the undercover doesn't mention the fact that the previously purchased drug was in fact beat, the dealer will know that the undercover actually didn't use it.

All drugs purchased by undercovers are tested as soon as possible in the police chemistry or controlled substances lab. They are given a "Q&Q"—an analysis of the quantity and quality (amount and purity) of each purchased drug. If a purchased drug contains only a beat substance and not an actual controlled substance, the testing chemist makes an immediate notification to the undercover.

YOU ARE THERE!

Efforts Against Money Laundering: Sting Charges Three with Laundering $8 Million in Drug Money

A brokerage house in the former World Trade Center in New York City had earned a reputation for handling illicit transactions in a very businesslike manner. It would wire money to businesses and banks around the world, without generating receipts or filing transaction reports as required by law. The money laundering operation was staffed by undercover officers working for Manhattan prosecutors and the NYPD with help from the Internal Revenue Service, the Securities and Exchange Commission, and other agencies. The busy, sophisticated, and seemingly well-connected brokerage house was staffed entirely by law enforcement officers since May 1999. Word spread quickly on the street that the brokers there would take cash from illicit transactions and wire it around the world without generating a paper trail.

In August 2001, a mother and her two sons were indicted for laundering $8 million in drug money through the phony brokerage house. Undercover law enforcement agents watched as the family picked up forty different bundles of cash from people at subway stations, cars, and other sites throughout Manhattan and the other boroughs and brought them to the brokerage office. They carried the money in packets, duffel bags, and shopping bags from upscale stores, in amounts ranging from $30,000 to $400,000.

SOURCE: Katherine E. Finkelstein, "Three Caught in a Sting Are Charged with Laundering $8 Million in Drug Money," *New York Times*, Aug. 17, 2001, p. B5.

SUMMARY

The introduction to this chapter began this way: "Illegal use of controlled substances and other drugs causes death. It causes death to those who use these substances by destroying their minds and bodies, as well as children, born and unborn. It causes death to those who illegally manufacture, distribute, and sell them as they kill each other to reap more profits. It causes death to those committed and brave enforcers of the law who are killed trying to enforce that law. It even causes death to the uninvolved who just are doing their jobs."

Let us concentrate on the last sentence. On September 11, 2001, nearly three thousand people were murdered and America's way of life was changed forever when terrorists flew planes into both towers of New York City's World Trade Center and the U.S. Pentagon. Most of these people were not involved in the use or sale of drugs and were, in fact, just doing their jobs. Investigation revealed that the person responsible for this attack was the terrorist Osama bin Laden. The Taliban sect of Afghanistan, the world's largest producer of opium and heroin and the protector of bin Laden, had annual earnings of up to $50 million from the drug trade. Bin Laden made money off the heroin trade by hiring out his fighters to guard drug laboratories and escort drug convoys. Surely, drugs do cause death.

In the aftermath of the September 11 attacks, security was tightened along the Mexico–U.S. border. Two weeks later it was disclosed that during the two preceding weeks drug seizures had fallen almost by half and the amount of drugs seized had taken a precipitous drop along the entire border with Mexico, compared with the same period a year earlier. From September 11 to September 23, 2001, 8,707 pounds of drugs were seized by U.S. Customs agents in 123 incidents. In the same period in 2000, there were 44,160 pounds of drugs seized in 227 incidents. Did the increased security at the U.S. borders actually deter the shipment of illegal drugs? Or could it have caused the drug dealers to get smarter? According to a spokesman for the U.S. Customs Service, "The drug dealers are not stupid. They watch us very closely, and they know we are on maximum alert now, so they just decided not to move their product for a while, or to look for another route." He also warned, "It's a business, and they've got too much product and people owe other people too much money not to start trying to move it."[22]

This chapter discussed the U.S. drug problem and provided information about the main drugs of abuse in our nation. It discussed the laws we have and use in the nation to fight this scourge and it listed and discussed the mission and operations of the various federal, state, and local agencies involved in enforcing the relevant laws.

It also discussed the primary methods of enforcing the drug laws, including source control, interdiction, disrupting domestic distribution, disrupting wholesaling, and disrupting street sales. Finally, it discussed the tools that law enforcement uses to enforce the drug laws and several proactive, covert investigative techniques to conduct drug investigations.

LEARNING CHECK

1. Name three programs the Drug Enforcement Administration (DEA) uses to make an impact on illegal controlled substances distribution.
2. Name three of the six categories of controlled substances and identify and discuss one drug in each category.
3. Name three other federal agencies, in addition to the Drug Enforcement Administration, that are involved in the investigation of controlled substances and discuss them.
4. Discuss the role of state and local law enforcement in the enforcement of the controlled substance laws.
5. Discuss the buy-and-bust operation.

APPLICATION EXERCISE   Select one substance or drug in each of the five schedules of the Controlled Substances Act of the Comprehensive Drug Abuse Prevention and Control Act of 1970 and prepare a report on each one using all of the following headings: Name of Drug, Classification, CSA Schedule, Trade or Other Names, Medical Uses, Physical Dependence Level, Psychological Dependence Level, Tolerance, Duration of Effect, Usual Method of Use, Possible Effect, Effects of Overdose, Withdrawal Syndrome.

WEB EXERCISE   Access the Web sites of three federal law enforcement agencies, find a successful drug arrest or seizure made by each, and discuss the details of each of those seizures.

KEY TERMS

buy-and-bust
Drug Enforcement Administration (DEA)
infiltration
interdiction
physical dependence

psychological dependence
source control
tolerance
undercover

13

THE INVESTIGATION OF TERRORIST ACTIVITIES

CHAPTER GOALS

1. To introduce you to the concept of international and domestic terrorism and its disastrous results

2. To acquaint you with the many sophisticated efforts to prevent and deal with terrorism by national, state, local, and private security agencies

3. To show you the methods used to investigate acts of terrorism

4. To explore the awful potential of weapons of mass destruction (WMD) and how our society can work to prevent the catastrophes their use can bring

5. To make you aware of the procedures used by the U.S. government to warn travelers about particular problems when traveling abroad

INTRODUCTION

As work on this book began in September 2001, our world changed.

On September 11, 2001, a series of unthinkable and incomprehensible events led to ultimate disasters in New York City, Washington D.C., and a grassy field in Pennsylvania. Those events shocked the world and changed world history.

In the minutes before and after 0800 on that date, four large commercial passenger jets lifted off at major airports in Boston, Newark, and just outside of Washington, D.C., en route to California. In several panicked calls from cell phones, passengers and airline crews told their families and loved ones about hijackers armed with knives attacking crew members and seizing control of the airliners.

At approximately 0848 hours, American Airlines Flight 11, a Boeing 767 scheduled to fly from Logan Airport in Boston to Los Angeles, with ninety-two people aboard, crashed into the 110-story north tower of the World Trade Center (WTC) in New York City's financial district (Building 1, 1 World Trade Center). The plane had departed Boston at 0745. At approximately 0903, United Airlines Flight 175, also a Boeing 767 and also headed for Los Angeles from Logan with sixty-three persons aboard, struck the south tower of the World Trade Center (Building 2, 2 World Trade Center). That flight had left Boston at 0758.

Witnesses reported seeing the planes crash into the towers, with flames and smoke pouring out of the buildings, and bodies falling or jumping from the highest floors. Within an hour, the two towers, symbols of America's strength, giant structures that had dominated and symbolized the Manhattan skyline since they first opened in 1976, disappeared: imploding, crashing to the ground, reduced to ash and gigantic heaps of rubble. Smoke permeated the skies of the entire New York City metropolitan area; crushed vehicles, body parts, clothing, and building material was strewn about the streets. The thick gray ash spread throughout the area. Thousands of people ran screaming through the streets, crowded onto the bridges leading from Manhattan, and wandered the streets in a state of shock.

A massive emergency response including the New York City Police Department, the New York City Fire Department, the police and rescue operations of the Port Authority of New York–New Jersey and the city's emergency medical service was immediate. These people entered the buildings in an attempt to rescue others. Many of them were lost forever, including much of the high command of the fire and Port Authority departments. Medical and emergency response personnel from around the world responded. Triage centers went into operation and ordinary residents passed out bottled water to the responding emergency personnel. By the evening of September 11, Buildings 5 and 7 of the World Trade Center had also collapsed and many buildings began to tremble and show signs of imminent collapse. The fires, smoke, and eerie ash continued blowing through the streets.

At approximately 0939 hours, American Airlines Flight 77, a Boeing 757 carrying fifty-eight passengers and six crew members on a scheduled flight from Dulles International Airport in Virginia, just west of Washington, D.C., also bound for Los Angeles, slammed into one of the five-sided, five-story concrete-walled structures of the U.S. Pentagon in northern Virginia—the headquarters and command center of the military forces of the United States of America. That plane had left Dulles at 0810.

At approximately 1010 hours, United Airlines Flight 93, a Boeing 757, which had departed from Newark, New Jersey, bound for San Francisco, with thirty-eight passengers, two pilots and five flight attendants onboard, crashed into a grassy field in Stony Creek Township, Pennsylvania, about eighty miles southeast of Pittsburgh. The plane, which left Newark at 0801 hours, had nearly reached Cleveland when it made a sharp left turn and headed back toward Pennsylvania just before the crash. It was later revealed that the plane's target was Washington, D.C.

Immediately, all airports in the United States were shut down, and all air travel was terminated. U.S. military personnel from around the world were placed on Force Protection Condition Delta (DefCon Delta), the highest military alert possible. Aircraft carriers, warships, and jet fighters were dispatched into New York City harbor and other major harbors and areas across the nation. The U.S. borders were closed. High-rise buildings like the Sears Tower in Chicago, the Renaissance Center in Detroit, the Peachtree Center in Atlanta, the Gateway Arch in St. Louis, the Space Needle in Seattle, the Trans-America Pyramid in San Francisco, and the CNN Center in Atlanta, were evacuated and closed to the public. Walt Disney World and Sea

World in Orlando, as well as hundreds of shopping malls, including the huge Mall of America in Bloomington, Minnesota, were evacuated and closed. Government buildings and monuments were shut down. America's financial markets shut down as well.

The swiftness, scale, and sophisticated coordinated operation, coupled with the extraordinary planning required, made most people realize that terrorism and mass murder had hit New York City, the United States, and indeed, the world. These attacks shocked us, even though there had been similar events, although not as massive, before. Terrorism was not new to the United States.

On July 17, 1996, TWA Flight 800 with 230 people aboard, left New York's Kennedy Airport on the way to France. Several minutes later, several miles off the coast of Long Island, the plane crashed into the ocean. Immediately, terrorism was suspected.

For years before the crash of Flight 800, most Americans had believed that terrorist attacks only occurred in foreign nations, but events in the few years prior to the crash had changed Americans' perceptions. Why?

In 1993, there was the first terrorist attack on New York City's World Trade Center, killing 6 and wounding 1,000. In 1995, there was the bombing of the Alfred P. Murrah Federal Building in Oklahoma City, killing 168 persons and injuring 675 others. Then there was the 1996 bombing at the Olympic Games in Atlanta, Georgia, which killed 1 person and wounded 111 others. During these years there were also terrorist acts committed against family planning clinics that provide abortions and churches, and many other depraved, senseless incidents. These events awakened Americans to the fact that terrorism had actually come ashore.

A sixteen-month investigation of the Flight 800 plane crash, involving the retrieval and forensic examination of approximately one million pieces of the aircraft, seven thousand interviews, and analysis by the best terrorism experts in the world revealed that no criminal activity had been involved in the explosion. However, is it any wonder that many Americans first believed it might be terrorism?

This chapter will discuss terrorism directed against Americans and American interests abroad, including foreign terrorism and domestic terrorism. It will describe federal, state, local, and private security efforts against terrorism, and methods of investigating terrorism, including proactive and reactive methods and the federal-local Joint Terrorism Task Force concept. It will discuss catastrophic disasters and weapons of mass destruction (WMD), as well as methods of assessing and preventing risks to American citizens traveling abroad.

TERRORISM

Terrorism has a long tradition in world history. Terrorist tactics have been used frequently by radical and criminal groups to influence public opinion and to attempt to force authorities to do their will. Terrorists have criminal, political, and other nefarious motives. Many may remember the terrorist activities that occurred during the 1972 Olympic Games in Munich, Germany, when terrorists attacked and took hostage the Israeli Olympic team and killed all of them; the 1988 explosion of Flight 103 in the air over Lockerbie, Scotland, killing all 270 persons aboard; the Oklahoma City federal building bombing; the first World Trade Center bombing in New York City; and the actions of the Unabomber.

Most major U.S. firms have been targeted by terrorists in some way. Political extremists and terrorists use the violence and suspense of terrorist acts such as bombing, kidnapping, and hostage situations to put pressure on those in authority to comply with their demands and

Terrorism hits New York City. Here, both towers of the World Trade Center are aflame before collapsing on September 11, 2001, after terrorists flew two airplanes into them.

© Allan Tannenbaum/The Image Works

cause the authorities and public to recognize their power. They use their activities to obtain money for their causes, to alter business or government policies, or to change public opinion. Attacks against executives are common in Latin America, the Middle East, and Europe, and they have spread to the United States. Successful terrorist techniques employed in one country spread to others. Governments and corporations have had to develop extensive plans to deal with terrorism.

According to Louis J. Freeh, former director of the FBI:

> Terrorists are among the most ruthless of criminals, but their motivation rarely stems from personal need or a desire for material gain. Unlike the majority of violent criminals, terrorists do not know their victims; in fact, one of the hallmarks of terrorism is its indiscriminate victimization. Also, unlike most serious criminal activity, terrorism invites—and even depends upon—media attention to ensure a maximum yield of terror.[1]

From 1968 to 2000, an average of 26 Americans per year have been killed as a result of terrorism. In 1998, the year of the Columbine tragedy, 28 students died in American schools. In 1999, of the 184 Americans abroad who were killed or injured by terrorists, 133 were businesspeople. U.S. interests remain the favored target of terrorists abroad.[2]

Another significant recent concern that falls into the terrorist camp is **cyberterrorism,** defined by the FBI as terrorism that initiates, or threatens to initiate, the exploitation of or attack on information systems. (Chapter 14, "The Investigation of Computer Crime," will discuss the issue of cybercrime in greater detail.)

The Terrorism Research Center, which is dedicated to informing the public of the phenomena of terrorism and information warfare, offers an interesting Web site. It features essays and thought pieces on current issues as well as links to other terrorism documents, research, and resources.

International Terrorism

According to John F. Lewis, Jr., retired assistant director of the FBI's National Security Division, the FBI divides the current international threat to the United States into three categories:

First, there are threats from foreign sponsors of **international terrorism.** The U.S. Department of State has designated seven countries as state sponsors

INVESTIGATIONS ON THE NET

Terrorism Research Center
http://www.terrorism.com

For an up-to-date list of Web links, go to
http://info.wadsworth.com/dempsey

----

of terrorism: Iran, Iraq, Syria, Sudan, Libya, Cuba, and North Korea. These sponsors view terrorism as a tool of foreign policy. Their activities have changed over time. Past activities included direct terrorist support and operations by official state agents. Now these sponsors generally seek to conceal their support of terrorism by relying on surrogates to conduct operations. State sponsors remain involved in terrorist activities by funding, organizing, networking, and providing other support and instruction to formal terrorist groups and loosely affiliated extremists.

Second, there are threats from formalized terrorist groups, such as the Lebanese Hizballah, Egyptian Al-Gama's Al-Islamiyya, and Palestinian Hamas. These autonomous organizations have their own infrastructures, personnel, financial arrangements, and training facilities. They can plan and mount terrorist campaigns overseas as well as support terrorist operations inside the United States. Some groups use supporters in the United States to plan and coordinate acts of terrorism. In the past these formalized terrorist groups engaged in such criminal activities in the United States as illegally acquiring weapons, violating U.S. immigration laws, and providing safe havens to fugitives.

Third, there are threats from loosely affiliated international radical extremists, such as those who attacked the World Trade Center. These extremists do not represent a particular nation. Loosely affiliated extremists may pose the most urgent threat to the United States at this time because they remain relatively unknown to law enforcement. They can travel freely, obtain a variety of identities, and recruit like-minded sympathizers from various countries.

Many cases of international terrorism have involved this country primarily by targeting U.S. citizens and interests abroad. Some memorable attacks in addition to the ones mentioned earlier in this chapter include the abduction of hostages in Lebanon in the mid-1980s; the 1996 detonation of an explosive device

YOU ARE THERE!

A Profile of Osama bin Laden, the Murderer

FBI TEN MOST WANTED FUGITIVE

MURDER OF U.S. NATIONALS OUTSIDE THE UNITED STATES; CONSPIRACY TO MURDER U.S. NATIONALS OUTSIDE THE UNITED STATES; ATTACK ON A FEDERAL FACILITY RESULTING IN DEATH

USAMA BIN LADEN

Date of Photograph Unknown

Aliases: Usama Bin Muhammad Bin Ladin, Shaykh Usama Bin Ladin, the Prince, the Emir, Abu Abdallah, Mujahid Shaykh, Hajj, the Director

The FBI "Wanted" poster for Osama bin Laden, the man responsible for the terrorist attacks on the World Trade Center and the Pentagon on September 11, 2001.

The following is a brief profile of Osama bin Laden, the man responsible for numerous truly heinous terrorist incidents, including the 2001 destruction of the World Trade Center.

Osama bin Laden was born in 1955 or 1957 in the city of Riyadh, the capital of Saudi Arabia. He was raised in a wealthy family, one of more than fifty children born to a Yemeni father. The family made its fortune from Saudi Arabia's oil and construction riches. Osama bin Laden himself is believed to be worth $300 million. It is alleged that he uses his fortune to finance activities that involve anywhere from several hundred to several thousand terrorists.

In the 1980s, bin Laden became a leader in the Afghani insurgency against invading Soviet troops and earned a reputation as a fierce warrior on the battlefield. It has been said that during this ten-year struggle, bin Laden received money from the CIA, which covertly financed the Afghani insurgents.

In 1989, he returned home to Saudi Arabia and in 1990 began a confrontation with the Saudi monarchy over its decision to invite U.S. troops into the country;

this led to his arrest by Saudi officials for criticism of the monarchy. He has been involved in attempts to overthrow the secular regimes in Egypt, Jordan, Syria, and the Palestinian territories and replace them with Islamic states.

In 1992, bin Laden moved to the Sudan and began to organize his al Qaeda (in Arabic this means *the Base*) terrorist organization, a worldwide network of radical Islamics. Investigators have uncovered a network of terrorist cells in Europe and Canada that mainly include Algerians, Tunisians, Libyans, and Moroccans affiliated with bin Laden. In 1996, Sudan, under intense pressure from the United States, forced bin Laden from that country. He resettled in Afghanistan with 180 followers and his three wives. There, sheltered by the ruling Taliban government, he trained terrorists at his training camps.

Bin Laden has been suspected of involvement in the following major terrorist incidents:

- The February 26, 1993, bombing of the World Trade Center, which killed six and injured a thousand.
- The November 13, 1995, car bombing in Saudi Arabia that killed five American servicepeople.
- The June 25, 1996, car bombing in Saudi Arabia that devastated an apartment complex housing U.S. servicepeople. At least nineteen were killed and four hundred wounded.
- The August 7, 1998 bombings at the U.S. embassies in Kenya and Tanzania that killed 224 persons and injured thousands.
- The December 1999 plot to attack U.S. installations during the year 2000 millenium celebrations.
- The October 12, 2000, suicide bombing of the *U.S.S. Cole* off the coast of Yemen that killed seventeen and injured thirty-nine others.
- The September 11, 2001, attack on the World Trade Center in New York City that killed almost three thousand people.
- The September 11, 2001, attack on the United States Pentagon that killed approximately two hundred people.

YOU ARE THERE!

Details of Some Major International Terrorism Cases

Bombing of Pan Am Flight 103

In 1988, 270 persons were killed when the jumbo jet was blown out of the sky over Lockerbie, Scotland. A crime scene search of 845 square miles of debris led investigators to the conclusion that the disaster was the result of a bombing. Two fingernail-size plastic fragments allowed them to trace the crash to a bomb inside a radio-cassette player.

In 2001, Abdel Basset al-Megrahi was convicted of the mass murder by a Scottish court convened in the Netherlands. Megrahi was one of two Libyan intelligence agents brought to trial. Evidence in the trial, largely collected by the FBI, linked him to the placement of a boombox in a suitcase in Malta that eventually found its way onto the doomed London-to-New York flight.

First World Trade Center Attack

Six persons were killed and more than one thousand others were injured in the blast on February 26, 1993, in New York City. In 1994, four men were convicted of bombing the World Trade Center. Abdel Rahman, also known as Omar Ahmad Ali Abdel Rahman, a blind Egyptian religious leader, was charged with being one of the planners of the bombing conspiracy and leading a terrorist organization that sprang up in the United States in 1989. Investigators also say he participated in conversations involving the planned bombing of the United Nations building and the assassination of Egyptian President Hosni Mubarak. Rahman and eleven others were convicted in federal court on charges of trying to assassinate political leaders and bomb major New York City landmarks. In 1995 another man, Ramzi Ahmed Yousef, was arrested as the main plotter behind the World Trade Center bombing.

U.S. Embassy Bombings

On August 7, 1998, simultaneous bombings occurred in the U.S. embassies in Dar es Salaam, Tanzania, and Nairobi, Kenya. These attacks killed over two hundred persons, including twenty Americans. As of June 2002, Osama bin Laden—who also uses the aliases of Usama bin Muhammad bin Ladin, Shaykh Usama bin Ladin, the Prince, the Emir, Abu Abdallah, Mujahid

Shaykh, Hajj, and the Director—was still wanted by the FBI in connection with these bombings.

Millenium Bomb Plot

On December 14, 1999, as the world was preparing to celebrate the year 2000 millenium, an Algerian terrorist attempted to enter the United States from Canada with the intention of setting off a bomb at the Los Angeles International Airport during the celebrations. The would-be bomber, Ahmed Ressam, was arrested at the border near Seattle with a trunk full of explosives. The FBI started a sweeping search for other suspects and information about the plot. Investigators developed information that the plot was linked to a worldwide network of terrorists orchestrated by Osama bin Laden. Ressam was convicted and sentenced to prison in May 2000.

In July 2001, an Algerian-born shopkeeper, Mokhtar Haouari, age thirty-two, who ran a gift shop in Montreal and as a sideline dealt in false identification documents, as well as check and credit card scams, was also convicted in the conspiracy. A third suspect, Abdel Ghani Meskini, offered testimony against the other plotters in exchange for a reduced sentence. The suspects said they were trained in guerilla camps in Afghanistan run by bin Laden.

Bombing of the *U.S.S. Cole*

On October 12, 2000, two Arabic-speaking suicide bombers attacked the U.S. destroyer *Cole* in the waters off Aden, killing seventeen American sailors. The FBI linked the bombing once again to Osama bin Laden, the fugitive Saudi, who had declared a worldwide "holy war" against the United States. Six men were arrested soon after the bombing. Bin Laden remains at large.

Sources: John F. Burns, "FBI's Inquiry in *Cole* Attack Nearing a Halt," *New York Times*, Aug. 21, 2001, p. A1; Niles Lathem, "Pan Am Bomber Hires Dershowitz for Appeal," *New York Post*, Aug. 9, 2001, p. 14; Laura Mansnerus, "Man Is Guilty in Bomb Plot at Millenium," *New York Times*, July 14, 2001, p. B1; Richard Bernstein, "Despite Terror-Thriller Plot, Bomb Trial Opens as a Dry Documentary," *New York Times*, Jan. 15, 1995, p. A31; Bernstein, "Behind Arrest of Bomb Fugitive, Informer's Tip, Then Fast Action," *New York Times*, Feb. 10, 1995, p. A31; *FBI Ten Most Wanted Fugitives: Usama bin Laden*, http://www.fbi.gov/most-want/topten/fugitives/laden.htm.

outside the Khobar Towers in Dhahran, Saudi Arabia, in which ten U.S. military personnel were killed; the August 7, 1998, bombings of the U.S. embassies in Nairobi, Kenya, and Dar es Salaam, Tanzania, which resulted in the deaths of twelve Americans and two hundred others; the terrorist attack on the *U.S.S. Cole* in the waters of Aden, which killed nineteen U.S. sailors; and the abduction and subsequent murder of *Wall Street Journal* journalist Daniel Pearl in February 2002. Prior to the September 11 attack, the most recent case of international terrorism occurring on our shores was on February 26, 1993, when foreign terrorists bombed the World Trade Center.[3]

Domestic Terrorism

According to John F. Lewis, Jr., **domestic terrorism** involves groups or individuals who operate without foreign direction entirely within the United States and target elements of the U.S. government or citizens.

He states that the 1995 federal building explosion in Oklahoma City and the pipe bomb explosion in Centennial Olympic Park during the 1996 Summer Olympic Games underscore the ever-present threat that exists from individuals determined to use violence to advance their agendas.

Lewis states that domestic terrorist groups today represent extreme right-wing, extreme left-wing, and special interest beliefs. The main themes espoused today by extremist right-wing groups are conspiracies having to do with the New World Order, gun control laws, and white supremacy. Many of these extremist groups also advocate antigovernment, antitaxation, or antiabortion sentiments and engage in survivalist training, with their goal to ensure the perpetuation of the United States as a white, Christian nation.

One particularly troubling element of right-wing extremism is the militia, or patriot, movement. Militia members want to remove federal involvement from various issues. They generally are law-abiding citizens who have become intolerant of what they perceive as violations of their constitutional rights. Membership in a militia organization is not entirely illegal in the United States, but certain states have legislated limits on militias, including on the types of training (for example, paramilitary training) that they can offer. The FBI bases its interest in the militia movement on the risk of violence or the potential for violence and criminal activity.

Experts have traced the growth of the militia movement in part to the effective use of modern communication mediums. Videotapes and computer bulletin boards and networks, such as on the Internet, have been used with great effectiveness by militia sympathizers. Promilitia facsimile networks disseminate material from well-known hate group figures and conspiracy theorists. Organizers can promote their ideologies at militia meetings, patriot rallies, and gatherings of various other groups espousing antigovernment sentiments.

Left-wing extremist groups generally profess a revolutionary socialist doctrine and view themselves as protectors of the American people against capitalism and imperialism. They aim to change the nation through revolutionary means rather than by participating in the regular political and social process.

During the 1970s, leftist-oriented extremist groups posed the predominant domestic terrorist threat in the United States. Beginning in the 1980s, however, the FBI dismantled many of these groups by arresting key members for their criminal activities. The transformation of the former Soviet Union also deprived many leftist groups of a coherent ideology or spiritual patron. As a result, membership and support for these groups has declined.

Special-interest terrorist groups differ from both extreme left-wing and right-wing terrorist groups because their members seek to resolve specific interests rather than pursue widespread political change. Members of such groups include animal rights advocates, supporters of environmental issues, and antiabortion advocates. Although some consider the causes that these groups represent understandable or even noteworthy, they remain separated from traditional law-abiding special interest groups because of their criminal activity. Through their violent actions, these terrorist groups attempt to force various segments of society, including the general public, to change their attitudes about issues they consider important.

FEDERAL EFFORTS AGAINST TERRORISM

The federal response to terrorism changed significantly after September 11, 2001.

YOU ARE THERE!

Details of Some Major Domestic Terrorism Cases

Oklahoma City Federal Building

At 9:05 A.M. on April 19, 1995, an explosion occurred at the Alfred P. Murrah Federal Building in Oklahoma City. The bombing destroyed the structure, killed 168 people, and injured 675. Later that day, an Oklahoma state trooper arrested Timothy McVeigh on Interstate 35 for driving without license plates. Several days later McVeigh was charged with the bombing. He was alleged to have links to white supremacist and patriot groups. McVeigh was convicted for his crimes in 1997 and executed in 2001.

Atlanta Olympic Games

On July 27, 1996 a bombing occurred in Centennial Olympic Park at the Atlanta Olympic Games; a women was killed and 111 other people were injured. In June 1997, the FBI linked the Olympic bombing to the January 16, 1997, bombing at the Sandy Springs Professional Building, which housed the Atlanta Northside Family Planning Services clinic (a clinic that provided abor-

tions) and the February 2, 1997, bombing of an Atlanta lesbian nightclub. The FBI claimed that letters mailed to the press by a militant religious cell known as the Army of God connected the group to the bombings.

Eric Robert Rudolph is still wanted by the FBI in connection with the bombing at Centennial Olympic Park in Atlanta; the bombing of a health clinic in Birmingham, Georgia, in which a police officer was killed and a nurse critically wounded; and the double bombings at the Sandy Springs building and at the Otherside Lounge in Atlanta. These bomb blasts injured more than 150 people. Rudolf is known to own firearms and to have targeted law enforcement. He is considered armed and extremely dangerous.

SOURCES: Kevin Sack, "Officials Link Atlanta Bombings and Ask for Help," *New York Times*, June 10, 1997, p. A1; Jo Thomas, "McVeigh Guilty on All Counts in the Oklahoma City Bombing," *New York Times*, June 3, 1997, p. A1; *FBI Ten Most Wanted Fugitives: Eric Robert Rudolph*, http://www.fbi.gov/mostwant/topten/fugitives/rudolph.htm.

Recent Reorganizations

Immediately following the tragic events of September 11, President Bush created the Office of Homeland Security under the direction of the former governor of Pennsylvania, Tom Ridge. The office's mission is to develop and coordinate the implementation of a comprehensive national strategy to secure the United States from threats and attacks. it coordinates the executive branch's efforts to detect, prepare for, prevent, protect against, respond to, and recover from terrorist attacks within this country. The President also established a Homeland Security Council that is responsible for advising and assisting him with all aspects of security. The council consists of the President and Vice President, the Secretary of the Treasury, the Secretary of Defense, the Attorney General, the Secretary of Health and Human Services, the Secretary of Transportation, the director of the Federal Emergency Management Agency (FEMA), the director of the FBI, the director of

the Central Intelligence Agency, and the assistant to the President for Homeland Security.[4]

Later, in June 2002, the President proposed creating a new cabinet-level agency, the Homeland Security Department, to replace the Office of Homeland Security. With the new cabinet agency, duties formerly belonging to other government agencies would be merged: border and transportation security, emergency preparedness and response, chemical, biological, radiological, and nuclear countermeasures, and information analysis and infrastructure protection.[5] As this book goes to print, legislation on this issue is still before Congress.

In November 2001, the President signed into law the Aviation and Transportation Security Act, which among other things established a new Transportation Security Administration (TSA) within the Department of Transportation to protect the nation's transportation systems and ensure freedom of movement for people and commerce. This new agency assumed the duties

YOU ARE THERE!

A Domestic Terrorist: The Unabomber

Thomas J. Mosser, an executive with the Young & Rubicam advertising firm in Manhattan, was killed by a mail bomb on December 10, 1994. The parcel had been mailed to his home.

The explosion and Mosser's murder were attributed to the work of a serial bomber known as the Unabomber, who was believed to be responsible for fourteen other bombings or attempted bombings beginning in 1978. The FBI reports that two people died and twenty-three others were injured in these explosions, which occurred over some sixteen years, as this deranged man terrorized his fellow American citizens.

The sequence of events related to the Unabomber is as follows:

- A bomb in an unmailed package exploded at Northwestern University in Illinois, May 25, 1978; a security guard was injured.

- A second person at Northwestern was injured on May 9, 1979, when a bomb exploded in the technical building.

- On American Airline Flight 444 (Chicago to Boston), twelve persons suffered smoke inhalation injuries on November 15, 1979. This bomb was traced to a mailbag aboard the airliner.

- The president of United Airlines, Percy Wood, was injured by a bomb on June 10, 1980. Again, the bomb was in a package mailed to his home.

- A bomb in a business classroom at the University of Utah exploded on October 8, 1981.

- At Vanderbilt University in Nashville a secretary was injured on May 5, 1982, when a bomb mailed to the head of the computer science department exploded.

- Two people were injured, one seriously, at the University of California, Berkeley, as a result of bombings: an electrical engineering professor on July 2, 1982 and a student on May 15, 1985.

- Alert employees of the Boeing Company in Washington State had a bomb safely dismantled on May 18, 1985 when they realized a mailed package contained an explosive device.

- On November 15, 1985, the research assistant to a psychology professor at the University of Michigan at Ann Arbor was injured when a bomb received at the professor's home exploded.

- On December 11, 1985, Hugh Campbell, the owner of a computer rental store in Sacramento, California, was killed by a bomb left at his store.

- In Salt Lake City, another employee in the computer industry was maimed by a bomb placed in a bag in the company parking lot on February 20, 1987.

- A geneticist at the University of California at San Francisco sustained injuries when he opened a package received in the mail at his home on June 22, 1993.

- A computer scientist at Yale University opened a package mailed to his office and was injured by a bomb on June 24, 1993.

The FBI was certain that these bombings were related and attributable to one suspect, the Unabomber. The bombs were all built from similar materials and had a comparable, sophisticated design.

In 1996, based on a tip provided by his brother, Theodore Kaczynski was arrested and charged with all the Unabomber attacks. At trial he was found guilty and sentenced to life imprisonment.

SOURCE: John S. Dempsey, *An Introduction to Public and Private Investigations* (Minneapolis/St.Paul: West, 1996).

---

formerly provided by the FAA. The newly established TSA recruited thousands of security personnel to perform screening duties at commercial airports and significantly expanded the federal air marshals program. It also created the positions of federal security directors to be directly responsible for security at airports, developed new passenger boarding procedures, trained pilots and flight crews in hijacking scenarios, and required all airport personnel to undergo background checks.[6]

YOU ARE THERE!

Catching the Oklahoma City Bomber, Timothy McVeigh: Feds Took the Credit, But Charley Caught Him

Police officer Charles J. Hanger of the Oklahoma Highway Patrol was on patrol on Interstate 35 in Oklahoma, sixty miles north of Oklahoma City, on April 19, 1995, when he observed a yellow 1977 Mercury Marquis in the opposite lane of traffic with no license plates. Hanger pursued the auto and stopped it, something he had done thousands of times in his police career.

When the driver reached for his license at the trooper's request, Hanger saw a bulge under his jacket. The bulge reminded Hanger of one of the dangers of his job: the armed felon. He ordered the driver out of the automobile and retrieved a loaded Glock semiautomatic pistol, two clips of ammunition, and a knife from under his jacket. The pistol had a live round in the chamber—a black talon bullet. The driver was arrested for driving without license plates, having no insurance, and carrying a concealed weapon. The time of the arrest was approximately ninety minutes after the infamous bombing of the Alfred P. Murrah Federal Building, which killed and injured hundreds of people. Trooper Hanger testified at the driver's trial on April 29, 1997.

The driver, of course, was Timothy J. McVeigh.

We all know how the government cracked the case and charged McVeigh with the worst terrorist attack against the United States of America until that date. But would he have been apprehended if Hanger had not made that routine traffic stop on I-35?

SOURCES: Jo Thomas, "Officer Describes His Arrest of a Suspect in the Oklahoma Bombing," *New York Times*, Apr. 28, 1997, p. A13; Peter Annin and Evan Thomas, "Judgment Day," *Newsweek*, Mar. 24, 1997, p. 41.

EXHIBIT 13.1   **Possible Terrorism Targets in the United States**

Terrorism targets generally fall into five broad categories, some overlapping, depending on the motives of those planning the attack.

- *Symbolic or public message targets* may include prominent landmarks, electrical utilities, pipelines, state and local government buildings, universities, certain federal government buildings, and businesses and industries involved in such areas as chemical production, animal research, forest or wood products, and refineries.

- *Government-owned or -operated facilities* consist of tunnels, computer facilities, airports, state capitals, bridges and overpasses, maritime facilities (for example, locks and harbors), law enforcement buildings, and support structures.

- *Military targets* include military bases, museums, and testing facilities. Although they are generally more secure than other potential targets, they offer an opportunity to greatly embarrass the military and the U.S. government.

- *Cybertargets* include the networks and control systems of utilities, air traffic control centers, financial networks, utility distribution networks, emergency 911 centers, and other vital services that rely on computers.

- *Individual victims* are the targets of kidnapping, extortion, assassination, and other attacks to accomplish terrorist objectives. Individuals most likely to be targeted include elected government officials, law enforcement personnel, tax collectors, court clerks, members of the judiciary and prosecution systems, and families in each of these categories. Threat assessment in this area requires not only evaluation of the individual or group making the threat but also an assessment of the vulnerability of the potential victim.

SOURCES: Stephen Bowman, *When the Eagle Screams: America's Vulnerability to Terrorism* (New York: Birch Lane Press, 1994); D. Douglas Bodrero, "Confronting Terrorism on the State and Local Level," *FBI Law Enforcement Bulletin*, Mar. 1999, p. 11.

YOU ARE THERE!
Training for the Unspeakable

Members of special weapons and tactical (SWAT) teams in the Tampa Bay, Florida, area participated in a five-day training program taught by Israelis to learn how to counter terrorism aimed at civilians using mass transportation.

Participants practiced response, entry, safety sweeps, searches for weapons and booby traps, protecting children and adults, and escorting civilians to safety. The training program covered operations such as mob control, hand-to-hand fighting, firearms and knives, behavior under stress, live fire drills and escalation, stealth fighting, live roadblock drills, terrorist booby traps, officer kidnapping situations, movement through crowds, car hijackings, and negotiations. The

final focus of the training program was on bus intervention, including snipers, security, and penetration. In reenactments using a real school bus, participants learned techniques for approaching the bus, carrying out entry strikes, securing the bus perimeter, securing movement inside the bus, braking the bus in gear, and dealing with booby traps.

In one exercise, the complete response time from actual strike commencement to securing the terrorists and hostages was reduced to 7.5 minutes.

SOURCE: Bruce Cameron, "School Bus Crisis: Preparing for the Unspeakable," *Law and Order*, May 2000, pp. 92–96.

Terrorism hits the heartland. Here, two federal law enforcement agents look at the rubble of the Alfred P. Murrah Federal Building on April 20, 1995, one day after a fuel-and-fertilizer truck bomb, left by Timothy McVeigh, exploded in front of the building.

In the six months following September 11, a total of $10.6 billion was spent on creating new mechanisms for homeland security, responding to and investigating terrorist threats, and providing security for likely terrorist targets.[7]

Earlier Efforts

Realizing that both international and domestic terrorism are serious national concerns, the federal government took several law enforcement measures to deal with terrorism even before September 11.[8]

The FBI was designated as the lead federal agency in the U.S. government response to terrorism. Its counterterrorism mission is to prevent acts of terrorism before they occur or to react to them after they happen by bringing the offenders to justice. The major objectives of the FBI domestic and international terrorism programs are to identify and prevent terrorist acts and to pursue the arrest and prosecution of responsible individuals. As part of the prevention effort, the FBI collects foreign intelligence information on groups and individuals whose activities threaten the security of the United States. The FBI's efforts are handled in several ways.

The FBI Counterterrorism Center combats terrorism three ways: it deals with international terrorism operations inside the United States and supports extraterritorial investigations; it deals with domestic

YOU ARE THERE!
They Stopped the Terrorists Before They Could Attack: They Saved the City

The police officers who patrol New York City, the NYPD, are called New York's Finest—an accolade they deserve every day. The finest of the Finest has to be NYPD's elite Emergency Service Unit. These are the men and women who risk life and limb to climb to the tops of the city's myriad bridges and skyscrapers to rescue potential "jumpers" from themselves, enter blazing buildings, and breathe life back into cardiac victims and others who are near death. The NYPD's ESU is also the city's SWAT team. They are the Marine Corps of the city, called in daily with their automatic weapons to combat armed terrorists and maniacs. Their action on July 31, 1997, was just one of the heroic things cops in New York did that day, but it saved the city from certain disaster.

The events began unfolding with the frantic waving of a man along a darkened Brooklyn street. A Long Island Railroad police officer, on patrol in his radio car, observed the man acting irrationally at 10:45 P.M. July 30, 1997. He was repeatedly screaming in Arabic, "Bomba" and cupping his hands and moving them apart to mimic an explosion. The officer took the man to the Eighty-Eighth Precinct station house in Fort Greene, Brooklyn, where an interpreter determined that bombs and plans to blow up New York City subways were at a house at 248 Fourth Avenue in the Park Slope neighborhood.

Just before dawn on July 31, the police closed off scores of blocks in Park Slope and called on the ESU to enter the building. The officers entered the cramped apartment, led by hero cops Joseph Dolan, age thirty-four, and David Martinez, age thirty-eight, shouting, *"Police! Don't move!"* whereupon one man reached for one of the officers' weapons, and another reached for one of four toggle switches on a pipe

bomb. Officers Dolan and Martinez shot both suspects before any actions against them could be taken. A nine-inch pipe packed with gunpowder and nails and a device in which four pipes had been wrapped together and equipped with toggle-switch detonators were among the explosives removed by the police. Further investigation revealed that the men were Middle-Eastern terrorists who had planned to carry out a suicide bombing of the New York City subways on that very day.

The police action came a day after a suicide bombing in a Jerusalem market had killed and injured scores. The lives of over a million New York City commuters and residents were disrupted by the police action and investigation, but no injuries or deaths ensued. Says Officer Martinez, "I felt a little sick when I woke up the next day. I started to realize I almost wasn't here. I started to think of the magnitude of what these people were going to do. They would have killed hundreds of people, little children, mothers, people they don't even know. It's a great feeling to know in some way you helped alter the future."

Mayor Rudolph Giuliani said, "They prevented a major terrorist attack from taking place."

SOURCES: "They Saved the City: New York Would Be Counting Its Dead If These Hero Cops Had Not Acted," *New York Post*, Aug. 3, 1997, p. 1; Rocco Parascandola, "Hail Storm for City's Finest of Heroes," *New York Post*, Aug. 3, 1997, p. 1; "Heroes of Bomb Scare: Courageous Cops of Emergency Unit Honored," *Daily News,* Aug. 3, 1997, p. 3; William K. Rashbaum and Patrice O'Shaughnessy, "Raiders Knew Lethal Risk: With Seconds to Spare, Cops Nearly 'Naked' vs. Bomb," *Daily News*, Aug. 3, 1997, p. 2; Dan Barry, "Police Break Up Suspected Bomb Plot in Brooklyn," *New York Times*, Aug. 1, 1997, p. A1.

---

terrorism operations; and it takes countermeasures relating to both international and domestic terrorism. Representatives from twenty federal agencies maintain a regular presence in the center and participate in its daily activities.

Federal-local Joint Terrorism Task Forces (JTTFs) in sixteen communities across the nation combine the resources of the FBI and other federal agencies with

the street-level expertise of local and state law enforcement officers. These teams have been highly successful in several critical operations around the country. JTTFs are discussed more fully later in this chapter.

Thirty-six legal attaché, or LEGAT, offices abroad work with host governments to prevent crimes against U.S. interests and to investigate those that occur. Among the many benefits of establishing legal attachés

INVESTIGATIONS ON THE NET

Transportation Security Administration
http://www.tsa.gov

Office of Homeland Security
http://www.whitehouse.gov/homeland

For an up-to-date list of Web links, go to
http://info.wadsworth.com/dempsey

----

are the close working relationships they form with the local law enforcement agencies, which have practical and operational familiarity with terrorist organizations that may pose a threat to Americans. These relationships enhance the FBI's ability to maintain a proactive, rather than reactive, posture in addressing threats. If a terrorist attack targeting U.S. citizens or interests does occur, the attachés can provide the FBI with an on-the-scene presence in the first critical hours of an investigation. Through this program, the U.S. government has successfully returned terrorists from other countries to stand trial for acts or planned acts of terrorism against U.S. citizens. Since the beginning of this program there have been approximately 350 extraterritorial jurisdiction cases.

The National Infrastructure Protection Center (NIPC) draws together personnel from federal law enforcement and intelligence agencies and state and local agencies, as well as experts from critical industries, to safeguard the interlocking computer, mass transport, and public utilities systems that power our society.

The Terrorist Threat Warning System transmits information and intelligence to other members of the law enforcement community. The system attempts to ensure the accurate, timely, and orderly dissemination of new information to those responsible for countering terrorist threats against individuals, property, and facilities in the United States. All federal government agencies and departments are reached through the warning system. If the threat information requires nationwide unclassified dissemination to all federal, state, and local law enforcement agencies, the FBI can transmit such messages over the National Law Enforcement Telecommunications System, or NLETS. In 1998 alone the FBI's Terrorist Threat Warning System disseminated

four separate warnings related to threats received against computer systems in the United States.

The Awareness of National Security Issues and Response (ANSIR) Program is designed to provide unclassified national security threat and warning information to as many as forty thousand U.S. corporate security directors and executives, law enforcement personnel, and other government agencies. ANSIR represents the first initiative by the U.S. government to provide this type of information to individual corporations that have critical technologies or sensitive economic information that could be targeted by foreign governments or organizations. Each FBI ANSIR coordinator meets regularly with industry leaders and security directors for updates on current national security issues.

The National Domestic Preparedness Program coordinates the efforts of a wide range of federal, state, and local agencies to enhance the abilities of communities around the country to respond to threats of **weapons of mass destruction** (**WMD**). The National Domestic Preparedness Office (NDPO) coordinates efforts with other U.S. government agencies to train federal, state, and local emergency response personnel to deal with such events. Over the past several years they have helped train emergency responders in approximately 120 cities, which are selected according to population density, upcoming large-scale events, critical infrastructure, and geographic orientation. Workshops, seminars, and a one-week training curriculum are offered.

The Strategic Information and Operations Center (SIOC) at the FBI headquarters is a round-the-clock operations facility that serves as a national command center during large-scale investigations or at times when risks to U.S. interests are heightened. This command center is staffed by personnel from several agencies depending on the nature of the incident or threat.

In addition to these FBI resources, other federal agencies are involved with crisis activities involving terrorism. The Bureau of Alcohol, Tobacco and Firearms (ATF), the law enforcement agency under the jurisdiction of the U.S. Department of the Treasury, has special responsibilities in cases of arson and explosives. Some of its programs that have an impact on the U.S. efforts to prevent and investigate acts of terrorism are its accelerant and explosives detecting canines, arson and explosives training, arson task forces, criminal investigative analysis, dipole might, explosives interdiction, explosives technology support, explosives tracing, forensic laboratory support, international response team, and national response team.[9] See chapter 11 for a full description of these ATF programs.

In May 2002, in the wake of massive criticism that the FBI had failed to properly handle information that could have led to the prevention of the September 11 attacks, Director Robert S. Mueller issued a press release outlining its complete reorganization and creating a new strategic focus for it. The FBI's new focus placed the following as its three priorities: protecting the United States from terrorist attack, protecting the United States against foreign intelligence operations and espionage, and protecting the Untied States against cyber-based attacks and high-technology crimes. The main organizational improvements Mueller proposed were a complete restructuring of the counterterrorism activities of the Bureau and a shift from a reactive to a proactive orientation; the development of special squads to coordinate national and international investigations; a reemphasis on the Joint Terrorism Task Forces; enhanced analytical capabilities with personnel and technological improvements; a permanent shift of additional resources to counterterrorism; the creation of a more mobile, agile, and flexible national terrorism response; and targeted recruitment to acquire agents, analysts, translators, and others with specialized skills and backgrounds.[10]

STATE AND LOCAL EFFORTS AGAINST TERRORISM

Even after the 1993 World Trade Center bombing, most state and local law enforcement administrators continued to view terrorism primarily as an international threat. Many administrators believed that metropolitan centers such as New York, Miami, and Chicago remained the most likely targets. A 1995 National Institute of Justice (NIJ) study confirmed that state and local law enforcement agencies viewed the threat of terrorism as real, but their response varied widely according to the size and resources of the agency and the nature of the threat in its community. Major cities developed prevention and preparation programs, often in cooperation with the FBI and its Joint Terrorism Task Forces (discussed later in this chapter); in contrast, smaller cities and counties usually operated on their own. Antiterrorism resources varied based on the existing threat potential. Some smaller jurisdictions developed regional alliances to address specific extremist groups and organizations operating locally.[11]

But these perceptions changed after the 1995 Oklahoma City explosion. D. Douglas Bodrero, former commissioner of public safety for the state of Utah and a senior research associate with the Institute for Intergovernmental Research, wrote in an article in the *FBI Law Enforcement Bulletin* that most jurisdictions have more recently realized the threat presented by extremist individuals and groups and now assess the threat that such groups pose to their respective communities and to related operational planning and readiness issues.[12]

He reports that the key elements of the state and local response to the terrorism threat include planning, assessment, target identification, intelligence, and training. Many larger localities and agencies offer training for dealing with terrorist problems, but smaller ones offer little other than civil disturbance and special weapons and tactical training. The Federal Emergency Management Agency (FEMA) provides limited funding to state emergency management agencies. The FEMA training focuses mainly on the roles and duties of various responding agencies, stressing the need for emergency agencies to work together for a unified response.

Although the FBI assumes the lead federal role in the investigation and prevention of domestic terrorism, every terrorist act is essentially local. Local law enforcement officers will respond first to a terrorist threat or incident and are the closest to sense the discontent among terrorist movements; they monitor the activity of extremist causes, respond to hate crimes, and serve as the foundation for an effective assessment of threatening activities in their own communities.

INVESTIGATIONS ON THE NET

Federal Bureau of Investigation
http://www.fbi.gov

Bureau of Alcohol, Tobacco and Firearms
http://www.atf.treas.gov

For an up-to-date list of Web links, go to
http://info.wadsworth.com/dempsey

PRIVATE SECURITY EFFORTS AGAINST TERRORISM

Members of corporate executive protection departments and others concerned with personal protection pay constant attention to terrorist possibilities and develop plans to deal with these eventualities in this country and abroad.[13] Most multinational corporations have detailed executive protection plans, crisis management teams, and threat assessment strategies. Sources of information about such security include the Bureau of Justice Statistics; *Security Management*, the magazine of the American Society for Industrial Security (ASIS); and the Office of Consular Affairs of the United States Department of State.[14]

Companies without security departments or those with smaller security departments often hire big contract security companies, such as the Wackenhut Corporation, Burns International, and Pinkerton Security and Investigation Services, to provide corporate and executive security services. These companies emphasize strategic prevention and conduct a threat assessment before establishing a prevention plan.

Often, executives without corporate security or executive protection specialists and celebrities hire private investigators to advise them on matters of personal safety. These executives and celebrities also often hire their own personal bodyguards, sometimes referred to as *chauffeurs*, to accompany them through their travels and in their business and social activities. Private investigator licenses are generally not required for such employment. However, many of the people hired in these roles are former law enforcement officers because they have easier access to obtaining licenses to carry firearms in localities that require such licenses. Also, in localities that allow full-time police officers to "moonlight" (work in another capacity while off-duty), many officers supplement their income this way.

INVESTIGATIONS ON THE NET

International Association of Professional Protection Specialists
http://www.iapps.org

For an up-to-date list of Web links, go to http://info.wadsworth.com/dempsey

----

The International Association of Professional Protection Specialists (IAPPS) is an organization for bodyguards and security personnel involved in protecting executives, dignitaries, celebrities, and others, as well as for couriers and other professional protectors. The IAPPS provides services and products to assist professional protection specialists to perform their duties.

CATASTROPHIC DISASTERS AND WEAPONS OF MASS DESTRUCTION (WMD)

According to an article by Joel Carlson, former FBI special agent and a member of the technical staff working on counterterrorism and the criminal use of nuclear materials at Sandia National Laboratories in New Mexico, catastrophic events, including terrorist attacks, that have plagued the United States for the past several years may become more frequent and deadly as criminals and terrorist groups exploit the availability of chemical substances, biological agents, and nuclear materials to construct weapons of mass destruction (WMD).[15]

Carlson writes that this material is available for several reasons, including the increased volume and types of substances produced, the failure of security systems to protect these materials, the transfer of prohibited weapons to irresponsible governments, and the proliferation of these materials in countries that

Emergency workers wearing biohazard suits deal with an anthrax investigation in Boca Raton, Florida, in October 2001.

previously did not perceive a need for sophisticated weaponry.

According to Carlson, the criminal use of chemical, biological, or nuclear materials could result in a disaster unparalleled in U.S. history and test the government's ability to avoid panic, disorientation, and loss of confidence in ensuring the public's safety. He writes that local and state public safety and emergency personnel may exhaust their experience, training, and capability attempting to protect the public from such potentially catastrophic and devastating consequences.

Because criminal misuse or the threat of misuse of chemical, biological, or nuclear materials on a domestic target poses the ultimate management challenge for public safety agencies and government leaders, the following federal responders will complement or supplement the resources of cities, counties, and states:

- The FBI serves as the lead federal agency for resolving a crisis perpetrated by a malevolent element in a WMD incident occurring inside the United States and its territories. (See the earlier list of FBI programs to deal with terrorism.)
- The Federal Emergency Management Agency (FEMA) supports the FBI by coordinating consequence management (evacuation planning or search-and-rescue efforts) of a WMD incident. FEMA also provides extensive training to local and state officials in preparation for mass disasters, including terrorist attacks. A *mass disaster* is defined as any catastrophic incident, criminal or otherwise, for which the local responsible government lacks the resources to fully investigate and restore order. FEMA provides assistance to local and state governments on request.
- The U.S. Department of State is the lead agency in coordinating U.S. resources in response to a WMD incident in a foreign country, should that government request such assistance.
- The U.S. Department of Defense provides specialized technical resources to assist in the mitigation of WMD devices or the consequences of their misuse, to supply logistical support to other federal responders, and to furnish additional assistance as defined by the situation and directed by the President.
- The U.S. Department of Energy provides technical and scientific assistance to locate hidden

nuclear material; to diagnose a suspected, improvised nuclear device; to plan the disablement of a nuclear yield or radiological dispersal device; and to advise local authorities on the hazards and effects of this eventuality.
- The Public Health Service and the Centers for Disease Control and Prevention respond with technical and scientific personnel and equipment to assist in the mitigation of the health concerns that arise from various aspects of WMD misuse.
- Other federal agencies respond with personnel and resources if the threat or attack requires their unique resources or jurisdictional authority.

METHODS OF INVESTIGATING TERRORISM

As with many types of investigations, there are two primary methods of investigating acts of terrorism: proactive and reactive. In addition, there is the federal-local **Joint Terrorism Task Force concept.** These three methods together can help prevent and detect acts of terrorism before they occur, and when that is not possible, investigate their occurrences, determine who was involved in their commission, and bring the

INVESTIGATIONS ON THE NET
- -
Federal Emergency Management Agency
http://www.fema.gov

U.S. Department of State
http://www.state.gov

U.S. Department of Defense
http://www.defenselink.mil

U.S. Public Health Service
http://www.hhs.gov/phs/

Centers for Disease Control and Prevention
http://www.cdc.gov

For an up-to-date list of Web links, go to
http://info.wadsworth.com/dempsey
- -

offenders to justice. (For more information on the methods of investigating arson and bombing incidents, see chapter 11.)

Proactive Methods

Much of the early part of this chapter discussed proactive techniques that are in use constantly to prevent acts of terrorism before they occur. These methods include ongoing and coordinated planning, intelligence gathering, and investigating activity by various agencies.

Reactive Methods

Numerous reactive investigative methods can be used to investigate acts of terrorism after they occur, including response to the incident, crime scene processing and analysis, following up on leads and tips, use of informants, surveillance, and other normal investigative activities.

Response to the Incident The local law enforcement agency is usually the first responder to scenes of terrorist crimes—just as it is on any crime scene. These officers must follow the normal first-responder duties of rendering aid to the injured, arresting suspects, questioning witnesses, and other issues discussed in chapter 3 of this text. It is essential that they safeguard the scene and preserve the evidence for processing by laboratory personnel and arson and terrorist specialists. As with the crime of arson, discussed in chapter 11, much of the evidence is present in the debris that follows a terrorist explosion.

Crime Scene Processing and Analysis Crime scene specialists and trained personnel from the various federal, state, and local investigating units described earlier in the chapter use their special skills to seek the means used to commit the crime and any evidence that might connect the crime to the persons responsible for it. It must be remembered, as already mentioned, that two small pieces of evidence were the keys to determining the cause of the Pan Am explosion over Lockerbie, Scotland. Investigators had painstakingly searched a crime scene of over 845 square miles of debris to find this evidence.

How extensive are terrorist crime scenes? Consider the World Trade Center attack. When the jumbo jets crashed into the buildings, several things occurred. First, the explosive force of a plane entering the building destroyed much of the immediate internal structure and the victims within. The planes, just refueled for their flights, contained thousands of pounds of fuel. The ensuing fireball, reaching incredibly high temperatures, incinerated all in its path. The fuel then worked its way down to lower floors, continuing its destruction. Shortly after the initial explosion the weakened building, with some of its steel infrastructure actually melting in the intense heat, collapsed under the weight of the crumbling upper floors. The end result: millions of pounds of crime scene material and evidence.

The crime scene investigation has been extensive. The first concern of this investigation was to account for and identify as many victims as possible. But before any identifications could be made, the remains had to be recovered. This required the detailed sifting of all the debris and material collected from the crime scene. Sifting was also conducted during the examination of the Oklahoma City bombing incident.

After suspected human remains are recovered from the debris of such catastrophes, determinations need to be made about their origin and identity. Efforts to identify recovered remains include such forensic disciplines as pathology, odontology, biology, and anthropology. For the most part, DNA is used to establish the identity of the deceased. Personal items found at the crime scene—such as jewelry and clothing—are also used for identification, but are considered presumptive in nature, because many of these items are not unique. Still, personal items provide investigators with information on the identity of the missing.

Following Up on Leads and Tips Here again are the canvasses and recanvasses, the interviews and reinterviews. Anyone with any information at all must be interviewed immediately. All leads must be followed through to their logical conclusions. Tip lines must be established and all tips must be followed up. Recall the information on this subject that is repeated throughout this textbook.

Use of Informants Informants can be very important in the investigation of terrorist incidents. A good example of the value of an informant's information was the February 1995 arrest of Ramzi Ahmed Yousef, ranked at the time as number one on the FBI's Most

Wanted List and believed to be the main plotter behind the 1993 World Trade Center bombing in New York City. Yousef was the target of an international manhunt spanning several countries and thousands of miles. He was located and arrested based on information provided by an unexpected informer who simply walked into the American Embassy in Islamabad, Pakistan. Authorities believed the informer was seeking to collect the $2 million reward that the U.S. State Department was offering for information resulting in Yousef's arrest. After receiving the informant's information, a team of Pakistani police and American law enforcement officials was assembled and sent to the hotel room where Yousef was believed to be; the team broke down the door and rushed into the room and found Yousef lying on his bed, a suitcase of explosives nearby.[16]

Surveillance Surveillance is used in terrorist investigations to follow suspects identified as involved in the crime. Recall the information on surveillance and undercover operations in chapter 9. Other methods of surveillance or information gathering techniques can also be used for intelligence purposes. Flight recorders in aircraft cockpits provide investigators with a multitude of details about a hijacking. Security cameras in public locations provide details on a terrorist's actions. Timothy McVeigh's truck was recorded on a security camera; terrorists involved in the September 11 attack were recorded on airport security systems. These types of surveillance systems are invaluable for the investigation of terrorist activities.

The Joint Terrorism Task Force Concept

Possibly the most important unit in investigating terrorism in the United States is the FBI–local Joint Terrorist Task Force. There are sixteen such units across the United States. Before the establishment of these task forces, ad hoc task forces of local and federal authorities would be established to investigate each new terrorist case as it occurred and then disbanded after the investigation. The new concept ensures that the unit remains in place, becoming a close-knit, cohesive group capable of addressing the complex problems inherent in terrorism investigation. Because federal, state, and local law enforcement resources

have been combined in these task forces, there is effective maximization of resources, provision of sophisticated investigative and technological resources, and linkage to all federal government resources in the United States and worldwide.[17]

The objectives of these task forces are twofold: to respond to and investigate terrorist incidents or terrorist-related criminal activity (reactive measures), and to investigate domestic and foreign terrorist groups and individuals targeting or operating in the area for the purpose of detecting, preventing, and prosecuting their criminal activity (proactive measures).

The key to the success of the JTTF task forces is the melding of personnel and talent from various law enforcement agencies in a single, focused unit. The local police members bring the insights that come from years of living and working with the people in their area. They have usually advanced through their careers from uniformed precinct patrol to various detective duties before being assigned to the task force. Each of the participating agencies similarly contributes its own resources and areas of expertise to the team. The integration of the many agencies, each bringing its own unique skills and investigative specialties to the task force, makes these units formidable in combating terrorism.

For example, the FBI-NYPD Joint Terrorism Task Force includes more than 140 members representing numerous federal and local agencies, such as the FBI, NYPD, U.S. Marshals Service, U.S. Department of State Diplomatic Security Service, the ATF, the Immigration and Naturalization Service, the New York State Police, the New York–New Jersey Port Authority Police Department, and the U.S. Secret Service. In an excellent article in the *FBI Law Enforcement Bulletin*, Robert A. Martin, former deputy inspector for the NYPD and former member of the FBI-NYPD JTTF, describes the operation of the task force:

> The FBI special agents bring vast investigative experience from assignments all over the world. The FBI legal attachés, assigned to U.S. embassies throughout the world, provide initial law enforcement information on international terrorism cases. Since many terrorist events are committed by suspects from other countries, it is necessary to gain the cooperation of law enforcement agencies from the countries of origin. Interagency cooperation is essential when investigating crimes committed internationally. The FBI will

YOU ARE THERE!

The FBI-NYPD Joint Terrorism Task Force: From the Empire State Building to Sarin Gas

The following are a few of the successful investigations undertaken by the FBI-NYPD Joint Terrorism Task Force.

On February 23, 1997, a seventy-year-old Palestinian visited the observation deck of the Empire State Building and opened fire with a handgun that he had legally purchased just one month after arriving in the United States, killing one person and wounding seven others before killing himself. A search of his clothing revealed a long rambling letter that expressed anti-United States and anti-Israel sentiments, along with a Florida nondriver's license identification card and a receipt for the weapon.

Members of the FBI-NYPD Joint Terrorism Task Force immediately responded to the scene to assist local investigators. The task force command center was opened and personnel from the numerous agencies involved in the task force began working to ascertain the shooter's identity, his origin, and whether he had any ties to organized terrorist groups. Within hours, the JTTF had answers to these questions. The FBI dispatched its legal attaché in Israel to the Gaza Strip to interview the subject's family. The FBI and local police in Florida interviewed several people who could help track the subject's movements while he lived there. The task force concluded that the shooter seemed mentally unstable, expressed hatred of Israel and the United States, had no connection to any organized international terrorist groups, and had operated alone.

On February 26, 1993, a massive explosion occurred in the public parking garage of the World Trade Center in New York City. Six persons were killed, more than one thousand were injured, and property damage exceeded a half-billion dollars. The site of the blast became one of the largest crime scenes in NYPD history. In the city, panic ensued. But within a month, the JTTF apprehended four individuals responsible for the attack. After a six-month trial, the presentation of 204 witnesses and more than a thousand pieces of evidence, the four were convicted on all thirty-eight counts against them. They were each sentenced to 240 years in prison. About 8 months later the prime fugitive wanted in connection with the bombing was apprehended in Pakistan and returned to the United

States. He was also found guilty and sentenced to 240 years in prison.

In June 1993, JTTF uncovered another deadly plot: a threat by a radical Islamic group who were making explosive devices and intended to use them on such targets as the United Nations building and the Lincoln and Holland Tunnels. Upon raiding the group's safe house JTTF agents found its members making the bombs they planned to use during simultaneous attacks on four targets. As a result of this investigation, the JTTF made fifteen arrests.

On July 17, 1996, TWA Flight 800 crashed off the coast of Long Island, New York, killing all 230 people aboard the plane. Initial speculation centered on terrorism as the cause of the crash. The JTTF spearheaded the investigation, working in tandem with the National Transportation Safety Board. During a sixteen-month investigation, the JTTF conducted more than seven thousand interviews and collected about one million pieces of aircraft (about 96 percent of the plane), which bomb technicians and laboratory personnel visually inspected. All 230 victims were recovered and subsequently identified. In the end, no evidence indicated that a criminal act had caused the incident.

In March 1997, the suspect of a mail-order fraud case invited the investigating detectives into his residence. The cluttered house contained a large cache of chemicals, gasoline, and fuel additives. The suspect told investigators that he used these products to make "super fuel" for the model airplanes that he raced. However, he offered no explanation for the far more ominous canister clearly marked "Sarin Gas" that the detectives also found in the house. They immediately exited the house and called for hazardous materials support personnel.

Sarin gas is a highly toxic chemical nerve agent that was used in a 1995 terrorist attack on three Tokyo subway lines in which twelve people were killed and fifty-five hundred required medical treatment. Fearing a potential weapon of mass destruction, the JTTF responded and worked with the NYPD's elite hazardous materials team. The Sarin gas canister was safely contained. With the cooperation of the U.S. Army, it was flown to facilities at Aberdeen, Maryland,

You Are There! continued

to be tested. Tests revealed that the canister was empty. The suspect later told the investigators that he had labeled the canister Sarin gas as a joke. He was arrested on numerous charges.

SOURCE: Robert A. Martin, "The Joint Terrorism Task Force: A Concept That Works," *FBI Law Enforcement Bulletin*, Mar. 1999, p. 23–27.

work in tandem with other agencies to develop investigative leads.[18]

ASSESSING TRAVEL RISK FOR U.S. CITIZENS ABROAD

The U.S. Department of State pays particular attention to the safety of Americans traveling abroad for both business and pleasure. It studies the risks of traveling to every country in the world, and issues **travel-warning** "Don't Go" lists for countries that it considers too dangerous for travel.[19] On its Web site it provides access to its travel information and services section, which offers **travel advisories** and consular information sheets. Users can click on any country of their choice and obtain the following information about travel safety there: description of the country, entry requirements for U.S. citizens, customs regulations, safety and security, crime information, criminal penalties, medical facilities, medical insurance, other health information, traffic safety and road conditions, aviation safety oversight, registration/embassy and consulate locations, consular access, rules on firearms and penalties, currency regulations, and photography restrictions.[20]

A list of the countries that the State Department recommends Americans avoid visiting is also available. The list remains current and changes over time.

Private corporations are also involved in assessing travel risk. For example, Real World Rescue is a leading company in teaching travel safety to government and humanitarian agency workers, business travelers, and increasingly, leisure travelers. Many leisure travelers enjoy roaming the Third World, and sometimes they run into trouble—such as kidnappings, which aren't ordinarily covered in travel guides. According to the chief consultant for the company, tourists over the last

---

EXHIBIT 13.2   **Some Travel Incidents Involving Tourists**

The following are some of the worst travel incidents and assaults against tourists during the years 1990 to 2000:

- April 2000: On Sipadan Island in Malaysia, twenty-one people, including ten foreigners, were kidnapped from a luxury diving resort. Islamic rebels from the nearby southern Philippines claimed responsibility for the abductions.

- March 2000: Two nineteen-year-old American women were murdered in a beach resort in Costa Rica where, five months earlier, two elderly Americans had been killed in a robbery.

- March 1999: In Uganda, eight tourists were hacked and beaten to death in a national park by a group of Hutu rebel soldiers.

- January 1998: In Santa Lucia, Guatemala, a bus carrying sixteen students and teachers from Maryland was forced to the side of a highway by armed men. The passengers were robbed and five women were raped.

- November 1997: In Luxor, Egypt, fifty-eight tourists were killed and twenty-five wounded in a volley of gunfire directed against tour buses in the Valley of the Kings.

- July 1995: In Srinigar, Kashmir, a separatist group took five tourists hostage in the Himalayas, demanding the release of fifteen political prisoners. One person was beheaded six weeks later when the conditions were not met. The four remaining tourists were never found and are believed dead.

- April 1993: In Miami, a German tourist in a rental car was robbed, beaten, and murdered. Her murder culminated a five-month period during which five other foreign tourists had been killed.

INVESTIGATIONS ON THE NET

U.S.State Department Travel Warnings
http://travel.state.gov/travel_warnings.html

For an up-to-date list of Web links, go to
http://info.wadsworth.com/dempsey

few years have become prime targets for crime. This has happened in part because special interest travel—such as adventure travel, ecotourism, and journeys to exotic locales—has become one of the fastest-growing segments of the estimated $519 billion U.S. travel market. As a result, like top businesspeople, some leisure travelers now make their trips accompanied by travel escorts (that is, bodyguards).[21]

SUMMARY

Sergeant Rob Hill of the Oklahoma City Police Department was among the first officers to arrive at the scene of the explosion at the Alfred P. Murrah Federal Building on April 19, 1995. Sergeant Hill was trying to rescue survivors when firefighters warned of the possibility of another explosion. He was about to follow their advice and leave with other rescuers when he saw two women on the seventh floor. "Don't leave us!" they pleaded. Hill decided to return to try to rescue the women. . . . He reached the seventh floor, crawled through a blown-out window, and came upon a fifteen-foot-wide pit. He could hear one of the two women trying to persuade her friend to jump from the window. Before either could jump, Hill yelled out that he was there. "I'll get you out!" he shouted. He pulled himself up onto a window frame, then moved carefully over two blown-out windows to get closer to the women. He hoisted one onto a window frame as Sergeant Robert Campbell, age thirty-nine, and Officer Jim Ramsey, age twenty-seven, both also of the Oklahoma City Police Department, threw a piece of metal over a narrow strip of floor to give the women an extra foothold. Using the metal plate to regain his own footing, Campbell grabbed one woman from the window frame and pulled her across as Hill and Ramsey returned to rescue the other.[22]

Sergeant Hill and two of his colleagues were able to rescue the two women and bring them to safety. They were among the scores of heroes in Oklahoma City that morning. Imagine if you were one of the women trapped on the seventh floor. Imagine if you were Sergeant Hill or one of his colleagues faced with the responsibility to rescue these women despite the extreme danger to yourself. Such is the terror associated with terrorism.

There were thousands of heroes like Sergeant Hill and his colleagues at the disasters in New York City and at the Pentagon on September 11, 2001, but many of them went down in the rubble that those buildings became.

Now that you have read this chapter, I hope you are more aware of the tremendous threat that international and domestic terrorism poses to U.S. citizens at home and abroad. I also hope that you realize how many professional, dedicated experts and investigators are on continual alert to prevent such terrorism and to investigate any occurrences and bring to justice those who commit them. Also, you should now realize that there are numerous investigating and specialized job opportunities for persons interested in the investigation of terrorism.

The lessons of September 11, 2001 will bring new techniques of investigation and new methods of protecting ourselves from the evils of terrorism. Terrorism is now a reality to all of us, and it is a reality that we will continue to fight to prevent.

LEARNING CHECK

1. Define terrorism.
2. List and describe three federal programs to deal with the threat of international and domestic terrorism.
3. Discuss some aspects of state and local efforts to deal with the threat of terrorism.
4. What problems arise for private corporations when their executives are traveling abroad and how do they address these problems?
5. Name and discuss three methods used to investigate acts of terrorism.

APPLICATION EXERCISE

You have been hired as a summer intern by a dot.com corporation in your area. The corporation has grown significantly in the past decade and is preparing to extend its operations to several foreign countries in Europe, South America, and Asia. Your manager, knowing that you are a student interested in and studying investigations, asks you to prepare a report for her discussing the major problems that company executives may face when traveling overseas and the measures the corporation can take to ensure their safety.

WEB EXERCISE

In order to celebrate your graduation from college, your parents have offered to take you on a week's vacation to any country of your choice in the world. However, they are very concerned about travel safety and ask you to research whatever country you wish to travel to and provide them with the following information: description of the country, entry requirements for U.S. citizens, customs regulations, safety and security, crime information, criminal penalties, medical facilities, medical insurance, other health information, traffic safety and road conditions, aviation safety oversight, registration/embassy and consulate locations, consular access, rules on firearms and penalties, currency regulations, and photography restrictions. Use the knowledge you have gained from this chapter to find this information for them.

KEY TERMS

cyberterrorism	terrorism
domestic terrorism	travel advisories
international terrorism	travel warnings
Joint Terrorism Task Force concept	weapons of mass destruction (WMD)

14

THE INVESTIGATION OF COMPUTER CRIME

CHAPTER GOALS

1. To introduce you to the many problems associated with the use of computers in business and at home

2. To alert you to the many forms of cybercrime, including fraud, identity theft, Web attacks, hacking, cyberstalking, computer use by pedophiles, computer theft, and other crimes

3. To familiarize you with the many types of computer viruses and other computer assaults and show you how you can protect yourself from them

4. To show you how public and private investigators investigate computer crime

5. To introduce you to methods that can be used to maintain the security and integrity of computer use

INTRODUCTION

Computer technology has facilitated the speed and ease of business transactions, personal communications, and information sharing and lowered the costs, but it has also enabled sophisticated criminals to tap into these legitimate uses and victimize computer users and society itself.[1] Consider these recent incidents:

As the summer school holiday of 2001 approached, schools across the nation were forced to close due to a proliferation of threats of Columbine-type attacks transmitted by e-mail.

A man who described himself as a day trader posted false press releases on the Internet reporting that a major telecommunications and Internet-related company would not meet its quarterly earnings estimates. The false reports drove down the company's stock price 3.6 percent and reduced its market value by more than $7 billion. The report was false. The trader walked away with a profit.[2]

A computer financial news service advised investors that a California manufacturer of fiberoptic communications equipment planned to restate its earnings for the last two years and that its chief operating officer had resigned. Investors rushed to sell their shares and the stock plunged from $103 to $45 in fifteen minutes. The drop stripped more than $2 billion from the company's market valuation before the NASDAQ stock market halted trading in the stock at about 10:30 A.M. The free fall dragged down stocks of several companies in similar businesses and the NASDAQ as well. The report was false.[3]

A fifteen-year-old New Jersey schoolboy racked up almost $273,000 in illegal gains by buying penny stocks and then hyping them up in a barrage of false e-mail messages to various Web bulletin boards that made the stocks seem hot. He sold the stocks as soon as the price rose.[4]

In August 2000, a forty-five-year-old Louisiana woman was charged by the St. Tammany's Parish Sheriff's Office with trying to turn her eleven-year-old daughter into an Internet porn star—doping the child and training her to perform sex shows for cyberpedophiles. Among the evidence were e-mails in which the woman boasted how she fed the girl Valium and White Russians to relax her inhibitions in front of the camera.[5]

In September 2000, the principal of a Catholic elementary school in New York City was arrested on charges that he distributed child pornography over the Internet.[6]

In 2000, the Love Bug virus struck and quickly spread around the world, causing billions of dollars in damage mostly to big corporations that were forced to shut down their internal communications to stamp it out. It came as an e-mail titled "ILOVEYOU" with an attachment that, if opened, infected the computer and e-mailed itself to everyone in the user's Microsoft Outlook address book. Later that year, the "Pokey" virus hit. The cartoon character mutated on the Web and spread itself via e-mails, wrecking PCs it got into by wiping out their system files. Kids were the targets of this virus. It appeared as an e-mail with the title "Pikachu Pokemon" and the message "Pikachu is your friend."[7]

A hacker stole more than fifty-five thousand credit card numbers from a major online retailer and then posted some of the information on the Net after the company ignored a demand for a $100,000 ransom for the numbers.[8]

After reading about these incidents, you may think that criminals have taken over the Internet and we are all facing doom. The good news, though, is that computer crime can be investigated, the persons who commit these crimes can be prosecuted, and with proper knowledge and precautions we can protect ourselves from computer crime.

This chapter will introduce you to the many problems associated with the use of computers in business and at home and to the methods used to maintain the security and integrity of computer use. It will cover the many forms of cybercrime, including fraud, identity theft, Web attacks, hacking, cyberstalking, computer use by pedophiles, computer thefts, and other crimes. It will familiarize you with the many types of computer viruses and other computer assaults and show how people and businesses can protect themselves from such attacks. The chapter will also cover the methods used by public and private investigators to investigate computer crime.

THE COMPUTER CRIME PROBLEM IN BUSINESS AND SOCIETY

Growing criminal use of the computer has caused significant harm to U.S. businesses, as the following surveys show.

- In a 2000 survey of two hundred companies carried out by *Security Management* magazine, more than 25 percent reported that they had suffered data loss from a **computer virus** in 1999. More than 70 percent indicated that they currently used virus detection systems. In addition, 15 percent reported hacking attempts, 10 percent system intrusion, 7 percent data alteration or defacing, and 4 percent data theft.[9]

- A 2000 survey of Fortune 500 companies by the Justice Department and the Computer Security Institute estimated that financial losses from computer crime between 1997 and 1999 exceeded $360 million. With the volume of e-commerce predicted to rise from more than $100 billion in 1999 to $1 trillion in 2003, computer crime was expected to continue to grow.[10]

- In a recent poll, visitors to the Web site of the American Society for Industrial Security (ASIS) were asked about threats to Internet business security. Of the respondents, 49 percent said that disgruntled employees posed the most dangerous threat to Internet business security, 21 percent said that the greatest threat was from independent hackers, 12 percent said it was from foreign governments, 9 percent cited foreign corporations, and 5 percent of respondents saw U.S. corporations as the main threat.[11]

- A national survey of six hundred corporate security directors revealed that 98.5 percent of responding businesses reported they had been victimized by computer crime. The most common target was intellectual property, such as new product information, product plans, pricing information, and customer prospects.[12]

- A computer crime and security survey by the Computer Security Institute and the FBI revealed that 75 percent of participants reported financial losses due to various breaches of computer security. The breaches ranged from financial fraud, theft of proprietary information, and sabotage on the high end to computer viruses and theft of laptop computers on the low end.[13]

Computer crime problems also plague the U.S. government. In August 2000, the General Accounting Office (GAO), the investigative arm of Congress, reported that the computer systems at the Environmental Protection Administration (EPA) were "riddled with security weaknesses." During their inquiry, investigators gained access to the EPA's computer network, guessed or decoded many passwords, and obtained high-level computer privileges.[14] In September 2000, more than a quarter of the government's major agencies failed a computer security review, showing significant problems in allowing unauthorized access to sensitive information. The auditors were successful in almost every test in readily gaining unauthorized access that would allow intruders to read, modify, or delete data for whatever purpose they had in mind.[15]

The GAO has identified computer security weaknesses at such government agencies as the Department of Defense, NASA, the Department of State, and the Environmental Protection Agency. The most serious problem found was overly broad access privileges afforded to large groups of users, many of whom share accounts and passwords.[16]

In addition to causing problems for business and government, computer crime affects the fabric of life in the United States. Almost every day, in almost every newspaper in the country, there are stories of children being propositioned by pedophiles on the Net, people being stalked by predators on the Net, and other such problems.

These days, computer technology overtakes itself with a new generation about once every three years. Meanwhile, increasingly sophisticated and computer-literate criminals employ new technologies virtually as soon as they appear. Working in partnership with federal, state, local, and international law enforcement agencies, the U.S. Department of Justice has developed the National Cybercrime Training Partnership (NCTP). The NCTP works with all levels of law enforcement to develop and promote a long-range strategy for high-tech police work in the twenty-first century, to improve public and political understanding of technology problems and solutions, and to ensure that technology solutions are fully implemented.[17]

CYBERCRIME

The dollar cost of electronic crime has been estimated to be as high as $10 billion a year. However, that is only the tip of the iceberg. We must consider the emotional cost of computer crime to its victims.[18] There are many definitions of computer crime or **cybercrime.** L. E. Quarantiello defines computer crime as "any illegal act in which knowledge of computer technology is used to commit the offense."[19] Martin L. Forst defines cybercrime as "all illegal activities that are committed by or with the aid of computers or information technology or in which computers are the target of the criminal enterprise."[20]

In an address to the U.S. Congress in March 2000, former FBI director Louis J. Freeh called cybercrime "one of the fastest evolving areas of criminal behavior and a significant threat to our national and economic security."[21]

This section will discuss some of the most common crimes on the Internet, including fraud, identity theft, Web attacks, hacking, cyberstalking, computer use by pedophiles, computer theft, and other crimes, and some of the methods being used by law enforcement and businesses to deal with these problems.

Fraud

The Internet presents many opportunities for various types of fraud, notably securities fraud. Because of its amorphous nature, companies are more susceptible to insider trading, and dissemination of misinformation can undermine an orderly market. Some specific examples of such fraud were given in the introduction to this chapter.

According to an article in the *Journal of Financial Crime*, problems already exist for companies because of the Internet and further complications are likely to follow.[22] In an attempt to deal with these problems, accounting firms are increasingly hiring former law enforcement people to investigate computer crime and establishing forensic—that is, scientific examination of evidence—and investigative services units. At the major accounting firm Ernst & Young, the forensic investigations section has more than tripled in two years, going from thirty to one hundred employees, most of them with law enforcement and other investigative backgrounds.[23]

In 2000, the FBI teamed up with the Department of Justice and the National White Collar Crime Center to establish the Internet Fraud Complaint Center (IFCC), which addresses fraud committed over the Internet. IFCC provides victims a convenient and easy-to-use

reporting mechanism that alerts authorities to a suspected criminal or civil violation. IFCC also offers law enforcement and regulatory agencies a central repository for complaints about Internet fraud, works to quantify fraud patterns, and provides timely statistical data of current fraud trends. This site lets those who have been bilked online to register a complaint with law enforcement. Analysts reviewing the complaints determine the jurisdiction of the complaint, conduct necessary investigative work, and distribute the information to the appropriate law enforcement agencies. Through such online reporting the IFCC expects to track trends and new fraud schemes.[24]

The U.S. Department of Justice also has a very informative Web site that explains the main types of Internet fraud, describes the methods being used by the federal government to go after it, and gives advice on how to deal with this problem.[25]

In June 2000 the FBI launched a major investigation of the Internet auction site eBay after a Sacramento lawyer tried to bid up the cost of a painting he had offered for sale by using at least five different Internet names to make bids. *Self-bidding,* also known as *shill bidding,* is forbidden by eBay rules and is illegal in the traditional auction world. Participation in a shill-bidding ring is a violation of federal laws prohibiting mail fraud and wire fraud.[26] It was estimated that more than $6.4 billion of merchandise was sold through online auctions in 2000. The Federal Trade Commission received 10,700 complaints about e-commerce crimes, ranging from credit card fraud to merchandise that was paid for but not delivered to delivery of damaged goods.[27]

Identity Theft

Law enforcement officials report that they are becoming increasingly worried about a sudden, sharp rise in

 INVESTIGATIONS ON THE NET

Internet Fraud Complaint Center (IFCC)
http://www.ifccfbi.gov

U.S. Department of Justice, Internet Fraud
http://www.Internetfraud.usdoj.gov

For an up-to-date list of Web links, go to
http://info.wadsworth.com/dempsey

YOU ARE THERE!

Some Types of Internet Auction Fraud

- *Failure to deliver.* A buyer pays for an item but never receives it from the seller. About 80 to 90 percent of the complaints the Federal Trade Commission receives pertain to this kind of fraud.

- *Misrepresentation.* A buyer receives an item that is less valuable than what was described.

- *Shill bidding.* A seller or an associate, posing as a buyer, places a fake bid intended to drive up prices.

SOURCE: Deborah Kong, "Internet Auction Fraud Increases," *USA Today*, June 23, 2000, p. 3B.

identity theft. Although identity theft is not new—criminals have been doing it for ages—the Internet is making it one of the signature crimes of the digital era. Web sites sell all sorts of personal information, and by using that information criminals can acquire credit and make purchases. The Social Security Administration received more than thirty thousand complaints about the misuse of Social Security numbers in 1999, most having to do with identity theft.[28] Similarly, one of the three major credit bureaus reported receiving over a half-million inquiries, with two-thirds of them related to identity theft.[29]

Identity theft may be defined as the criminal act of assuming another person's name, address, social security number, and date of birth in order to commit fraud. The Identity Theft and Assumption Deterrence Act of 1998 made identity theft a federal crime and enabled law enforcement agencies to investigate identity theft crimes and the associated fraud that often results.

According to the U.S. Secret Service, which has jurisdiction over credit card fraud and false documents, losses to victims and institutions in its identity fraud investigations totaled approximately $750 million in 1998. The U.S. Public Interest Research Group, a private consumer advocacy group, estimates that

forty thousand people each year are victims of identity theft.

The targets of identity thieves are often affluent credit-worthy consumers whose financial status may be assumed from the specific neighborhoods in which they live. The stolen identities can then be used to apply for driver's licenses, telephone numbers, car loans, and charge cards. They can also be used to steal benefits, such as pensions and Social Security payments.[30]

Identity thieves use a variety of tactics to obtain personal information. Besides the simple act of stealing a wallet or purse, they scavenge garbage, steal mail, and read credit reports and personnel records by using the Internet to access computerized personal information.[31]

- **Dumpster diving.** Identity thieves scavenge through garbage to retrieve discarded material of value. They obtain account numbers, addresses, and dates of birth from financial, medical, and personal records, all of which can be used to assume an identity. They especially like the social security numbers and prepared credit cards that can be obtained in garbage. With this information, an identity thief can set up fraudulent rented mailboxes.

- *Mail theft.* Identity thieves check mailboxes looking not only for new mail but also for paid bills or credit card payments that people leave in their mailboxes for the postal carrier to collect. They use information from these items to obtain credit or purchase products and services in the victim's name. Also, by working with cooperative postal employees, they can steal mail from mail processing areas. Identity thieves can also attempt to complete a change-of-address card in order to divert a victim's mail to a rented mailbox.

- *Internal access.* Identity thieves can obtain personal information illegally from a computer connected to a credit reporting bureau or from an employee accessing a company's database that contains personal identification information.

Several Web sites noted here can give you a good idea of identity theft. It is also a good idea to contact the three major national credit reporting agencies to learn more about the subject.

According to the director of the Privacy Rights Clearinghouse, a nonprofit group, a good percentage of identity theft is caused when people don't destroy unused credit applications or when these are stolen out of the mail.[32] In 2000, two insurance companies—the Chubb Group and Travelers Property Casualty Corporation—started offering financial protection against the expense of getting your name and your life back from identity theft. For a fee, customers can add a rider to their homeowner's or renter's insurance policy reimbursing them for lost wages or unpaid leaves, long-distance phone calls, notary fees, and certified mail to clean up the mess of identity fraud.

A 2000 survey of sixty-six identity theft victims conducted by the California Public Interest Research Group (CALPIRG) and the Privacy Rights Clearinghouse explored the problems that the victims face.[33] According to the survey:

- The average victim learned about the identity theft fourteen months after it occurred.

- More than half the victims considered their cases to be unsolved at the time of the survey, with their cases having been open an average of forty-four months.

 INVESTIGATIONS ON THE NET

Identity Theft: Prevention and Survival
http://www.identitytheft.org

Privacy Rights Clearinghouse
http://www.privacyrights.org

Future Crime Prevention Association
http://www.futurecrime.com

Equifax Credit Reporting Agency
http://www.equifax.com

Experian (formerly TRW)
http://www.experian.com

Transunion Corporation
http://www.tuc.com

For an up-to-date list of Web links, go to http://info.wadsworth.com/dempsey
----

- Victims spent an average of 175 hours actively trying to clear their names.

- The average total fraudulent charges made on new and existing accounts of survey respondents was $18,000.

- Respondents found out about the identity theft in one of two ways: they were denied credit or a loan because of a negative credit report created by fraudulent accounts, or a creditor or debt collection agency contacted them about lack of payment.

- Most of the respondents were victimized by "true name" fraud, in which the thief uses identifying information to open new accounts in the victim's name, or "account takeover," in which the thief makes fraudulent charges to a legitimate existing account.

- Most victims expressed dissatisfaction with police and credit bureau assistance.

 YOU ARE THERE!

These Are Identity Thieves

In June 2000, two people were arrested in Queens, New York, for using mail they had stolen from thousands of homes in Queens and Long Island neighborhoods to help them steal more than $1.5 million from banks and credit card companies. For eighteen months, starting in 1998, the two combed through hundreds of thousands of pieces of mail to retrieve credit card applications, checks, and personal information like Social Security numbers and driver's license numbers. They set up a computer database of all the information they collected and applied for credit cards and cashed stolen checks. A list of two thousand names were found in the computer database.

Identity theft crimes involving the postal system have been increasing rapidly. In 1999, postal investigators made more than five hundred arrests. The number has been doubling each year since 1996, when only fifty-three arrests were made.

SOURCE: Edward Wong, "Two Charged in $1.5 Million Mail Theft Scheme," *New York Times*, June 8, 2000, p. B8

Web Attacks

Web attacks have been a serious problem on the Internet. For example, over three days in February 2000, hackers or *cybervandals* brought Web giant Yahoo to its knees, then buy.com, then eBay; then CNN, then amazon.com, and finally, e*trade. Users could not connect to these sites or else suffered extremely long delays. The attackers used a variation of a so-called Smurf assault that resulted in a denial of service. A denial-of-service attack is a deliberate attempt to shut down a network operation by overloading it. The attack was launched through at least fifty locations. Attackers directed thousands of calls at the computer sites in a very short time, overloading them.[34]

Computer Hacking

Computer **hacking** is the willful and malicious penetration of a computer system to achieve some purpose. Once a hacker breaks into the system, he can use application programs in the system to retrieve information, change data, obtain access to accounts, disable internal computer systems, and damage the reputation of companies and agencies.

Research has revealed that typical computer hackers are white males between fifteen and thirty-four years of age; they begin using the computer for illegal purposes between the ages of ten and twenty-five. Hacking tools and methods are readily available on the Internet, and many require little technical expertise.[35]

Some of the reasons for hacking are financial motivation, a quest for status among other hackers, or just for the challenge and fun of it. Today, hackers often boast of their exploits, and they leverage the knowledge accumulated by other, earlier hackers to break into various computer systems for malicious purposes. Because hackers are able to alter critical files and use application programs without authorization, companies continue to implement and improve various security measures, such as passwords, to restrict unlawful access and protect system integrity.[36]

Another type of hacker is known as a "***hacktivist***"; these people commit denial-of-service attacks, disseminate spam, and deface Web sites believing they are carrying out acts of civil disobedience. They attempt to call attention to an issue by their crimes. In one example, a group recently defaced the official Web site of the Ku Klux Klan, replacing it with content from the Web site of Hate Watch, a civil rights group. Some consider hacktivists to be similar to freedom fighters and see their actions as a form of protest. But others say that they commit criminal acts of vandalism. Denying service to a computer is a federal crime.[37]

Although U.S. authorities occasionally charge a student or other hacker with hacking or infecting a public or private computer system with a virus, police officials and private security professionals concur that few of these cases ever result in prosecution. The chances of being prosecuted for hacking in the United States are one in ten thousand; the likelihood of going to prison is even lower.[38]

After an infamous incident involving a Cornell University graduate student, security professionals recognized a need for quick response to security incidents on the Internet. At that time the Computer Emergency Response Team (CERT) at Carnegie Mellon University was instituted as a central clearinghouse of computer security information and as a technical adviser on incident response for companies and government agencies. Today, many companies and institutions have established their own computer incident response team (CIRT) to deal with hacking problems on their networks. These teams evaluate computer security programs, establish policy, and respond to and correct the damage caused by hacking incidents. For example, when hackers recently broke into Stanford University's system, stealing more than forty-five hundred passwords, the university's CIRT responded by patching the system and getting passwords changed. The team also counseled students and faculty about good password selection and protection behavior.[39]

A recent report by an information technology consulting firm reported that Web sites that provide instructions on how to crack computer systems and commit technology-related frauds have cost businesses more than an estimated $1 trillion in 1999 in preventive maintenance, recovery, theft, and unrealized revenue. The report focused on the free or low-cost software tools provided by these Web sites that allow people with little technical knowledge (so-called **script kiddies**) to become instant system crackers, to defeat filtering software, to steal credit card numbers, and to cheat telephone companies. Tools offered on these Web sites include a disk containing four thousand viruses and guides to software bootlegging.[40]

Cyberstalking

While the Internet has transformed communication on a global level, it has also created a medium for stalking. Experts report that the typical cyberstalker is an emotionally disturbed loner for whom **cyberstalking** provides anonymity and the opportunity to conceal gender and identity. Although activities in cyberspace are protected by the First Amendment, computer users must abide by state and federal legislation. But the absence of geographic borders makes the application of territorial legal doctrine difficult. The free speech issues resulting from the use of cyberspace include anonymity, accountability, defamation, discrimination, harassment, obscenity, and the liability of online services and Internet service providers. Numerous states have enacted laws against electronic harassment, and law enforcement is constantly detecting and arresting offenders. In addition, organizations such as Women Halting Online Abuse and the CyberAngels have formed to educate the community about online harassment and to protect individuals from these crimes.[41]

Pedophiles

Internet-related crimes involving children include obscene material, child pornography, **pedophile** networking, and hate propaganda.[42]

A recent National Institute of Justice research survey on Internet victimization of youth indicated that as many as one in five children fell victim to Internet crime during the one-year study period, and concluded that Internet crime is increasing and that children are particularly vulnerable to online advances. The study focused on four types of online victimization: sexual solicitation and approaches, aggressive sexual solicitation, unwanted exposure to sexual materials, and harassment.[43]

Numerous law enforcement agencies are dealing with this problem by creating proactive units investigating such crimes. For example, Marty Kolakowski, an investigator for the Wayne County Sheriff's Department in Detroit, went online with the screen name Melissa83 in 1999 as a bait for pedophiles who prey on naïve, rebellious kids from broken homes. Kolakowski is not alone. He is one of thousands of cops from local, state, and federal law enforcement agencies nationwide who pose as potential victims of pedophilia, eventually meet the seducer, and arrest and bring him to prosecution.[44]

The FBI has published a pamphlet to help parents understand the complexities of online child exploitation, the signs that their child might be at risk online, the actions they can take if they suspect that their child is communicating with a sexual predator online, and actions to take to minimize the chances than an online exploiter will victimize their child.[45]

The guide was prepared by the FBI from actual investigations involving child victims as well as investigations in which police officers posed as children online. It indicates that some of the signs that a child may be at risk include his or her spending large amounts of time online, the parents' finding pornography on the child's computer, and the child's receiving phone calls from men the parent does not know or making phone calls to numbers the parent does not

---

YOU ARE THERE!

Problems on the Net

Every few days, it seems, television newscasts and newspapers carry reports of unspeakable acts conducted over the Internet. Pedophiles and sometimes even prisoners trade pornography and tips on kidnapping while trying to seduce children in electronic chat rooms. Right-wing lunatics post recipes for explosives and rouse the ire of chat room members with paranoid visions of immense conspiracies that only they can overthrow. Some examples:

- A California man was convicted of luring a thirteen-year-old girl from Kentucky through a computer network to engage in unlawful sexual activity.

- A Long Island, New York, man was charged with using the Internet to conspire with an accomplice in North Carolina to take turns raping, torturing, and sodomizing a fourteen-year-old-girl.

- A Minnesota prison inmate was indicted by a federal grand jury for conspiracy to traffic in child pornography over the Internet.

SOURCE: John S. Dempsey, *An Introduction to Policing*, 2nd ed. (Belmont, CA: Wadsworth/West, 1999), p. 119.

recognize. If they suspect that their child is being victimized, the FBI recommends that parents take the following actions: openly discuss their suspicions with the child, review what is on the child's computer, use the caller ID service to determine who is calling the child, and purchase a device that shows telephone numbers dialed from the home phone. To prevent online exploitation, parents should talk with their children about sexual victimization and potential online danger, keep the computer in a common room in the house, use blocking software or other parental controls, and maintain access to the child's online account.

The FBI conducts numerous sting operations targeted at online sexual predators. Here's one example.

> Georges Debeir befriended adolescent females he met in Internet chat rooms over a two-year period. He often promised gifts and money in exchange for sex-

ual favors. Eventually, he asked someone named Kathy to meet him. However, Kathy was an undercover FBI agent working for Innocent Images, a computer crimes unit that targets sexual predators and child pornographers on the Internet. Innocent Images is a $10-million-per-year program that has experienced a caseload increase of more than 550 percent in the last two years.[46]

The FBI reports that cyberpredators are mostly white males age twenty-five to forty-five years. Few have criminal records; many have advanced degrees and come from high socioeconomic backgrounds. Predators like Debeir generally receive very lenient sentences from judges, many of whom consider their actions to be victimless crimes. Defense attorneys say that the low sentences may reflect judges' discomfort with the nature of the FBI sting operations.

YOU ARE THERE!

Freedom on the Net: Anything Goes

Reno v. American Civil Liberties Union

In June 1997 the U.S. Supreme Court in *Reno v. American Civil Liberties Union*, No. 96–511, in a sweeping endorsement of free speech on the Internet, declared unconstitutional a federal law making it a crime to send or display indecent material online in a way available to minors.

The seven-to-two decision was the Court's first effort to extend the principles of the First Amendment into cyberspace. The Court's decision, written by Justice John Paul Stevens, struck down the 1996 Communications Decency Act, ruling that the Internet is entitled to the highest level of First Amendment protection, similar to the protection given to books and newspapers. The Court has continuously held that more limited First Amendment rights apply to speech on broadcast and cable television, where it has tolerated a wide array of government regulation. The Court's action upheld a 1996 decision by a three-judge federal district court in Philadelphia that had struck down the decency law in 1996 shortly after its passage.

The decision made it unlikely that any government-imposed restriction on Internet content would be upheld as long as the material has some intrinsic

constitutional value. The Court held that the indecent material at issue in the case was not precisely defined by the 1996 law but was merely referred to in one section of the statute as "patently offensive" descriptions of "sexual or excretory activities."

Here is an excerpt from Justice Stevens's decision:

> It is true that we have repeatedly recognized the government interest in protecting children from harmful materials. But that interest does not justify an unnecessarily broad suppression of speech addressed to adults. . . . [T]he government may not reduce the adult population to only what is fit for children.
>
> [In a previous case], we remarked that the speech restriction at issue there amounted to "burning the house to roast the pig." The [law] casting a far darker shadow over free speech, threatens to torch a large segment of the Internet community.
>
> As a matter of constitutional tradition, in the absence of evidence to the contrary, we presume that governmental regulation of the content of speech is more likely to interfere with the free exchange of ideas than to encourage it.

SOURCES: *Reno v. American Civil Liberties Union*, No. 96–511; John S. Dempsey, *An Introduction to Policing*, 2nd ed. (Belmont, CA: Wadsworth/West, 1999), p. 258.

YOU ARE THERE!

No More Ex-Cons on the Net

In 1997, the United States Parole Commission, alarmed by some of the information they had seen on the Net from parolees and aimed at parolees, added a new item to the things that federal parolees can be kept from doing, such as owning firearms, drinking to excess, and consorting with criminals. Now, using a computer to access the Internet was also on the list.

SOURCE: George Johnson, "Old View of Internet: Nerds. New View: Nuts," *New York Times*, Mar. 30, 1997, Section 4, p. 1.

YOU ARE THERE!

Cybermom on Patrol

Joanne Fazel is a cybermom. As a paid surfer for Microsystems Software, a Framingham, Massachusetts, based company that produces screening software, she spends her days hunting for material that she feels is inappropriate for children on the Web. The company she patrols for markets a product called Cyber Patrol, and it has enormous distribution. Eighty-five percent of people online have free access to the software through commercial providers. Its approved or not-approved list is huge. Cyber Patrol automatically blocks distasteful Web sites (Cyber-NOTs) and points to decent Web sites (Cyber-YESs) that the staff deems suitable.

To maintain this vigilant patrol, Microsystems employs seven women and five men who roam cyberspace day and night looking for pornography, violence, and cult ravings.

SOURCE: "Mom-and-Pop Web Cops," *New York Times Sunday Magazine*, May 11, 1997, p. 15.

Computer Theft

Theft of computers is another serious crime. A study conducted in England in the late 1990s revealed that recorded losses due to computer theft have increased

YOU ARE THERE!

Angels Help Patrol the Net But Are Under Attack by Darkspace

Angels have arrived on the Net. The CyberAngels—a branch of the Guardian Angels, the anticrime volunteers originally formed by Curtis Sliwa to prevent crime in the New York City subways—have begun patrolling the Net looking for pedophiles who may try to lure children.

The CyberAngels were formed in 1995 when Sliwa mentioned his e-mail address on his radio show and received more than three hundred messages from concerned parents. The group went global in 1995 when it was offered a Web site by an organization that helps parents monitor their children's Internet surfing.

The CyberAngels, who claim they have discovered gangs and death threats on the Net, have come under fire from other groups who use the Net and are wary of policing efforts. One such group, calling itself Darkspace, launched a campaign against them, nearly shutting down their system at one point by sending them over thirteen thousand e-mail messages.

SOURCE: "Patrolling Cyberspace, Looking for Clues and Crimes," *Law Enforcement News*, Feb. 29, 1996, p. 7.

as thieves have concentrated their efforts on high-value computer graphics machines. Repeat victimization appeared to be common; 25 percent of all computer thefts from business premises were repeat crimes. Repeat victimization was likely to occur within thirty days of a previous computer theft. A large proportion of computer thefts occurred early in the evening, between 7 and 9 P.M., and offenders rarely remained on the premises for more than a few minutes. External, physical prevention measures were not an effective deterrent to teams of professional computer thieves. Generally, thieves compiled "shopping lists" of the most popular hardware items and researched the market before committing thefts. Two main categories of offenders specializing in the theft of computers from businesses were professional teams and thieves working for trade journals and magazines that advertised secondhand computers.[47]

YOU ARE THERE!

Libraries Have to Watch Out for Guys Like This

A man was accused of using the Lakewood, Ohio, town library's computer to access an Internet site with pictures of nude boys. He would then load the images onto a floppy disk. He was arrested on a charge of illegally using a minor in nudity-related material.

Workers at the library told police that the man had been coming into the library for the last three weekends to log onto the World Wide Web.

SOURCE: *Newsday*, July 6, 1997, p. A43.

YOU ARE THERE!

Nabbing Pedophiles on the Net

Detective Daryl Rowland of the Huntington Beach, California, Police Department is one of the police investigators in the nation nabbing pedophiles who use the Internet.

Rowland spends his days cruising chat rooms, using a variety of alter egos he's developed to attract sex offenders. In one case, he's a twenty-four-year-old man looking for pictures of underage girls. In another, he poses as a father who molests his own son and offers him to other men. Then, he's a thirteen-year-old boy excited by the possibilities offered by the chat rooms.

Rowland arrested a thirty-nine-year-old Pennsylvania man who tried to arrange oral sex with a twelve-year-old boy. Rowland met and arrested the man in a Huntington Beach hotel. He also arrested a prominent California businessman on suspicion of distributing child pornography. The suspect had more than one hundred computer files with images of children engaged in sexual activity.

SOURCE: "Net Proceeds," *Law Enforcement News*, Jan. 31, 1997, p. 4.

Safeware Inc., the largest insurer of laptops and other computers, said that its clients reported 319,000 laptop computers stolen in 1999. Many are being stolen at airports, sometimes by organized rings of thieves. The teams operate this way:

> A two-person team waits by a busy security checkpoint for someone carrying a laptop (the *mark*). They then fall into place in front of the mark. One of the thieves passes through the metal detector gate without incident. The other waits until the mark has placed the laptop onto the conveyor belt, and then walks in front of the mark and through the gate in a way that deliberately causes a backup. The guy has all kinds of metal on him to set off the alarm. The security manager asks him to step back, empty his pockets, go through the device again. In the meantime, the targeted computer has already emerged on the other side, where the first thief simply walks off with it while its owner waits to get through the gate and get his laptop from the belt. By then, both thief and laptop are gone.[48]

Computer Viruses

Computer viruses wreak havoc in direct damage and disruption and in confusion and misinformation. Viruses are also known as *malware* (short for malicious software). A

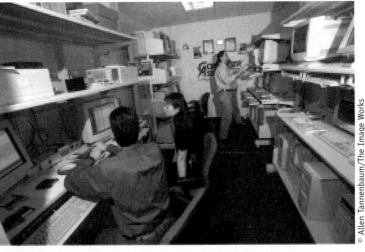

Computer viruses wreack havoc in terms of direct damage, disruption, confusion, and misinformation. Here, computer virus security researchers operate at a lab in Carlisle, Pennsylvania.

© Allen Tannenbaum/The Image Works

YOU ARE THERE!
He's a Cybercop

Special agent Jeffrey Herig of the Florida State Police is a cybercop, one of the law enforcement officers nationwide with the knowledge and sophistication to deal with the computer criminals and the computer crime that is proliferating in the Information Age.

When regular cops "hit the field," everyone knows they are going out onto the street. Cybercops don't go into the field; they go into "meet space"—cybertalk for what other cops call the field. Agent Herig spends most of his time cruising hard-drive scenes for evidence. Generally, he does so without ever leaving the Tallahassee lab he founded.

Here are some of his cases:

- One Medicaid swindler uploaded hundreds of phony claims, pocketing more than $200,000 in five months.

- Criminals sent bogus faxes, with official government seals and signatures, to county jails, authorizing the release of prisoners.

- Counterfeiters created fake driver's licenses, school transcripts, and price stickers.

- An electronic pocket organizer belonging to a murdered drug-gang member revealed names and phone numbers that helped convict four men in a federal drug-conspiracy trial.

Herig knows methods to recover deleted files from a hard drive. Is that legal? The courts haven't had a case on it yet, but you can be sure there will be a Mapp- or *Miranda*-type decision in this field in the near future as this science moves forward. To avoid possible future constitutional and legal problems, Herig and his colleagues have developed their own standards for seizing data: they don't scan a seized hard drive itself but rather a "mirror" copy of it, to avoid suspicion of tampering and to prohibit untrained personnel from destroying or corrupting data.

SOURCE: Peter Katel, "Cybercrooks, Beware: Here Come the Cybercops," *Newsweek*, June 9, 1997, p. 86.

---

virus can be defined as a program that can "infect" other programs by modifying them to include a—possibly evolved—copy of itself. *Infect* means that the program inserts itself into the chain of command so that attempting to execute a legitimate program results in the execution of the virus as well or instead.

Viruses rely on users unwittingly spreading them from one computer to another, but some viruses, usually using the Internet, find their own way to spread. There are various types of viruses and other malicious programs, including *boot sector infectors, file infectors, macro viruses, worms, Trojan horses*, and *memetic* (or meme) *viruses*.[49]

- Boot sector infectors (BSIs) infect the master boot record or DOS boot record, which contains the programs used to start up the computer. They may be spread by the exchange of diskettes.

- File infectors infect executable files and spread quickly through file systems and on networks.

They may be spread by the exchange of diskettes.

- Macro viruses infect macro programming environments. (A macro is an automated program that helps users avoid repetitive tasks.) These spread rapidly and account for the majority of virus incidents.

- **Worms** copy themselves across systems and networks without attaching to a host program. They usually use the Internet and find their own way to spread.

- **Trojan horses** replicate themselves and claim to do something desirable but instead do something the victim doesn't expect or doesn't want to happen. Trojans are often subdivided into two classes: password stealers and programs that do direct damage to files and file systems.

- **Memetic viruses** includes virus hoaxes (sometimes called metaviruses) and other types of

COMPUTER SECURITY TIPS

Top Ten Security Tips for Computer Users

10. Never give out your Social Security number, online or off. This information in the wrong hands is a license to steal.

9. Use a paper shredder. Don't just throw out unsolicited credit card applications. Shred them.

8. Don't use the same password over and over. Make new variations.

7. Watch your laptop at the airport. Be especially careful at X-ray security machines, which is where most laptop thefts occur.

6. Keep your antivirus software up to date. Hackers never rest. Every e-mail attachment can contain a possible virus, so scan it before you open it.

5. Use the latest versions and software patches for your e-mail and your browser. New security loopholes are constantly being discovered.

4. Don't accept cookies. If you have to, delete them when you are finished surfing.

3. Use a password to log onto your computer. Most operating systems let you set a password. It's a good idea to establish such a password and to change it regularly.

2. Turn off your computer when you are not using it. It's the only sure way to keep hackers out.

1. Never send an e-mail that you wouldn't want your spouse, or your boss, to read.

SOURCE: John R. Quain, "Top Ten Security Tips," *Newsday*, Aug. 16, 2000, pp. C16–17.

chain letters, erroneous security alerts, accurate but not very useful alerts, and vendor hype alerts.

One dangerous virus, called the Love Bug, was sent around the world on May 4, 2000. This rogue software program, borne by an e-mail message proclaiming "ILOVEYOU," jammed and crashed e-mail systems, destroying data on hundreds of thousands of computers. To defend themselves, thousands of corporations unhooked their computer systems from the Internet and began the laborious process of purging the program internally. The virus also attacked government agencies, including the White House, the Pentagon, Congress, and the British House of Commons. The Love Bug virus, like the earlier 1999 Melissa virus, was activated when a user clicked on an e-mail attachment and it was propagated automatically to all the e-mail addresses found on the user's computer.[50]

The best way to avoid infection is not to open e-mail attachments from unknown sources and to keep antivirus software up to date. Once a computer is infected, special software may be needed to repair any damaged files.

Other Crimes

Other forms of computer and Internet crime include illegal gambling, copyright violations, the spreading of hate mail and threats, and online scams.[51] In addition, organized criminals use the computer to launder money from criminal enterprises internationally.[52]

In his address to Congress on computer crime, former FBI director Freeh identified the use of the Internet by terrorists, foreign intelligence services, and organized criminals as national security threats.[53]

INVESTIGATING COMPUTER CRIME

Law enforcement and private industry are involved in numerous programs to prevent and investigate computer crime. Many were discussed earlier in this chapter. This section will focus on three particular areas of computer crime investigation: specialized technical techniques, proactive investigative techniques, and electronic surveillance and interception.

Specialized Technical Techniques

Key to solving computer crimes are traditional investigative skills and techniques, including establishing evidence of a crime, determining how the crime occurred, identifying likely suspects, developing the case for prosecution, proving damages, and assessing perpetrators as targets for litigation. Also important are knowledge of information security and fraud on the Internet, how to preserve evidence from attacks on computer hardware, and environmental support systems and computer hardware.[54] However, there is a difference between handling traditional, tangible evidence and computer evidence, and that difference is the fragility of computer evidence. It can be altered, damaged, or destroyed simply by turning a computer on or off at the wrong time. This means that the field of computer forensics requires special training and skills.

The FBI's Computer Analysis Response Team programs take a two-pronged approach to computer forensic examinations. First, field examiners, including more than one hundred individuals, help FBI agents with investigations and support state and local law enforcement agencies. Second, highly trained personnel at FBI headquarters conduct laboratory examinations of digital evidence that field agents are not trained to do.[55]

Sophisticated, highly technical procedures are involved in the investigation of computer crime. The International Association of Computer Investigative Specialists (IACIS) is made up of law enforcement professionals who are dedicated to education in the field of forensic computer science. Its members include federal, state, local, and international law enforcement professionals who are trained in seizing and processing computer systems. Their training incorporates forensic methods for searching seized computers with the rules of evidence and the laws of search and seizure. Investigators look for evidence that has been hidden, concealed, encrypted, protected with passwords, software time bombs, Trojan horses, and other devices that could destroy the evidence, the physical computer, or both. The association also offers expert advice to members on forensic examination procedures involving hard disk and floppy disk examination.

The IACIS also offers certification programs: Certified Electronic Evidence Collection Specialist (CEECS) and Certified Forensic Computer Examiner CFCE. It provides an opportunity to network with other law enforcement officers who are trained in computer forensics. The IACIS has published a set of forensic examination procedures to deal with the special problem of computer evidence. Exhibit 14.1 provides a description of these procedures.

Another organization providing networking for computer investigators is the High Technology Crime Investigation Association (HTCIA), which consists of peace officers, investigators, and prosecuting attorneys who investigate criminal activity involving computers

CAREER FOCUS

Computer Forensics Investigators

Positions with the New Jersey Attorney General's Office

The New Jersey Attorney General's Office, a state law enforcement agency that has a dedicated Computer Crimes Unit and is in the process of expanding its capabilities, is looking to hire computer forensics investigators.

Successful candidates will investigate computer crimes (both traditional and nontraditional offenses), execute search warrants, perform forensic examinations on seized computers and related items or media, and testify in Superior Court.

Candidates must possess moderate to high-level computer skills. Prospective candidates should have a law enforcement background, strong desire to become a law officer, or a keen interest to work on behalf of law enforcement as a civilian analyst. Prior experience with computer forensics and/or a B.S. in computer science or a related discipline is a definite advantage. Successful candidates for the law enforcement position must attend and complete an eighteen-week basic training course at a police academy.

SOURCE: High Technology Crime Investigation Association; http://www.htcia.org/classified_ads.htm.

INVESTIGATIONS ON THE NET

High Technology Crime Investigation Association (HTCIA)
http://www.htcia.org

International Association of Computer Investigative Specialists (IACIS)
http://www.cops.org

For an up-to-date list of Web links, go to http://info.wadsworth.com/dempsey

----

EXHIBIT 14.1   **Forensic Examination Procedures for Computers**

The International Association of Computer Investigative Specialists (IACIS) has developed the following investigative and technological procedures to ensure that competent, professional computer forensic examinations are conducted by IACIS members.

Forensic Examination Procedures

It is acknowledged that almost all forensic examinations of computer media are different and that each cannot be conducted in the exact same manner for numerous reasons; however, there are three essential requirements of a competent forensic examination. These are:

- Forensically sterile examination media must be used.
- The examination must maintain the integrity of the original media.
- Printouts, copies of data, and exhibits resulting from the examination must be properly marked, controlled, and transmitted.

Hard Disk Examination

The following are the IACIS recommended procedures for conducting a complete examination of computer hard disk drive (HDD) media:

1. Forensically sterile conditions are established. All media utilized during the examination process are freshly prepared, completely wiped of nonessential data, scanned for viruses, and verified before use.

2. All forensic software utilized is licensed to, or authorized for use by, the examiner and/or agency/company.

3. The original computer is physically examined. A specific description of the hardware is made and noted. Comments are made indicating anything unusual found during the physical examination of the computer.

4. Hardware/software or other precautions are taken during any copying or access to the original media to prevent the transference of viruses, destructive programs, or other inadvertent writes to/from the original media. We recognize that because of hardware and operating system limitations and other circumstances, this may not always be possible.

5. The contents of the CMOS as well as the internal clock are checked and the correctness of the date and time is noted. The time and date of the internal clock is frequently very important in establishing file creation or modification dates and times.

6. The original media is not normally used for the examination. A bitstream copy or other image of the original media is made. The bitstream copy or other image is used for the actual examination. A detailed description of the bitstream copy or image process and identification of the hardware, software, and media is noted.

7. The copy or image of the original HDD is logically examined and a description of what was found is noted.

8. The boot record data, and user defined system configuration and operation command files, such as the CONFIG.SYS file and the AUTOEXEC.BAT file, are examined and findings are noted.

9. All recoverable deleted files are restored. When practical or possible, the first character of restored files are changed from a HEX E5 to "_" or other unique character, for identification purposes.

10. A listing of all the files contained on the examined media, whether they contain potential evidence or not, is normally made.

11. If appropriate, the unallocated space is examined for lost or hidden data.

12. If appropriate, the "slack" area of each file is examined for lost or hidden data.

13. The contents of each user data file in the root directory and each subdirectory (if present) are examined.

14. Password protected files are unlocked and examined.

15. A printout or copy is made of all apparent evidentiary data. The file or location where any apparent evidentiary data was obtained is noted on each printout. All exhibits are marked, sequentially numbered, and properly secured and transmitted.

16. Executable programs of specific interest should be examined. User data files that could not be

Exhibit 14.1 continued

accessed by other means are examined at this time using the native application.

17. Comments and findings are properly documented.

Floppy Disk Examination

1. Forensically sterile conditions are established. All media utilized during the examination process are freshly prepared, completely wiped of nonessential data, scanned for viruses, and verified before use.

2. All forensic software utilized is licensed to, or authorized for use by, the examiner and/or agency/company.

3. The media are physically examined. A specific description of the media are made and noted. The media are marked for identification.

4. Hardware/software precautions are taken during any copying process or access to the original media and examination to prevent the transference of viruses, destructive programs, or other inadvertent writes to/from the original FD or to/from the examination equipment.

5. The write-protect capability of the floppy disk drive (FDD) on the examining machine is tested.

6. A duplicate image of the original write-protected FD is made to another FD. The duplicate image is used for the actual examination. A detailed description of the process is noted.

7. The copy of the examined FD is logically examined and a description of what was found is indicated. Anything unusual is noted.

8. The boot record data, and user defined system configuration and operation command file (if present) are examined and findings are noted.

9. All recoverable deleted files are restored. When practical or possible, the first character of restored files are changed from a HEX E5 to "_", or other unique character, for identification purposes.

10. The unallocated space is examined for lost or hidden data.

11. The "slack" area of each file is examined for lost or hidden data.

12. The contents of each user data file in the root directory and each subdirectory (if present) are examined.

13. Password protected files are unlocked and examined.

14. If the FD holds apparent evidentiary data that is to be utilized, a listing of all the files contained on the FD, whether they contain apparent evidentiary data or not, is made. The listing will indicate which files were printed, copied, or otherwise recovered.

15. A printout or copy is made of all apparent evidentiary data. The file or location where any apparent evidentiary data was obtained is noted on each printout. All exhibits are marked, sequentially numbered, and properly secured and transmitted.

16. Executable programs of specific interest should be examined. User data files that could not be accessed by other means are examined at this time using the native applications.

17. Comments and files are properly documented.

Limited Examinations

In many instances a complete examination of all of the data or media may not be authorized, possible, necessary, or conducted for various reasons. In these instances, the examiner should document the reason for not conducting a complete examination. Some examples of limited examinations would be:

- The scope of examination is *limited* by the search warrant or the courts.

- The equipment *must* be examined on premises. (This may require the examination of the original media. Extreme caution must be used during this type of examination.)

- The *media size* is so vast that a complete examination is not possible.

- The *weight of the evidence* already found is so overwhelming that a further search is not necessary.

- It is just *not possible* to conduct a complete examination because of hardware, operating systems, or other conditions beyond the examiner's control.

SOURCE: International Association of Computer Investigative Specialists, "Forensic Procedures"; http://www.cops.org/forensic_examination_procedures.htm.

as well as private-sector security professions involved in similar work.

Proactive Investigative Techniques

Most proactive law enforcement investigative techniques online focus on cybercrime. Online investigations of cybersex offenders usually focus on the distribution of child pornography and online solicitation of children for sex, as well as meetings with children for the purposes of sex. As mentioned earlier in this chapter, law enforcement uses proactive law techniques in this area. Investigators present themselves as children with appropriate victim profiles.[56]

Former Attorney General Janet Reno, while addressing the General Assembly of the International Association of Chiefs of Police, stated that the most cost-effective way for law enforcement to investigate cybercrime, including cybersex offenses, is to organize law enforcement resources on a national and regional basis so that not every jurisdiction has to purchase the expensive equipment required to detect and investigate it.[57] In an example of such a regional task force, Sergeant Sergio Kopelev supervises Operation Blue Ridge Thunder in Virginia, one of ten Internet task forces funded by the Office of Juvenile Justice and Delinquency Prevention. Training for law enforcement agencies and the public is available from the National Center for Missing and Exploited Children.[58]

Electronic Surveillance and Interception

In order to identify and track the source and direction of hacker communications, law enforcement uses sophisticated electronic devices. They obtain court orders and serve them on service providers in a communications chain.

The nation's communications networks are routinely used to commit serious criminal activities, including espionage. Organized crime groups and drug trafficking organizations rely heavily on telecommunications to plan and execute their criminal activities. Law enforcement agencies' ability to conduct lawful electronic surveillance of the communications of its criminal subjects is most important in acquiring evidence of crime. Such electronic surveillance requires legal court orders called *interception orders*

issued by high-level courts. Interception orders are limited to certain specified felony offenses. In recent years, the FBI has encountered an increasing number of criminal investigations in which the criminal subjects use the Internet to communicate with each other or with their victims. Because many Internet service providers (ISPs) lack the ability to discriminate communications to identify a particular subject's messages to the exclusion of all others, the FBI designed and developed a sophisticated electronic surveillance and monitoring device called ***Carnivore.*** This device provides the FBI with a "surgical" ability to intercept and collect communications that are the subject of the lawful court order while ignoring those which they are not authorized to intercept.

This type of tool is necessary to meet the stringent requirements of the federal wiretapping statutes.[59] If a court order provides for the lawful interception of one type of communication (for example, e-mail) but excludes all other communications (for example, online shopping) Carnivore can be configured to intercept only those e-mails being transmitted either to or from the named suspect.

In effect, Carnivore limits the messages viewable by human eyes to those included in the court order. Nevertheless, ISP knowledge and assistance is legally required to install the device.

The FBI's use of the Carnivore system is subject to intense oversight from internal FBI controls, the U.S. Department of Justice, and the courts. There are significant judicial penalties for misuse of the tool, including exclusion of evidence, as well as criminal and civil penalties. The system is not susceptible to abuse because it requires expertise to install and operate, and such operations are conducted, as required in the court orders, with close cooperation with the ISPs. The FBI shares information about Carnivore with industry to assist companies in their efforts to develop open standards for complying with wiretap requirements.

COMPUTER SECURITY METHODS

Several methods help maintain the integrity and security of computers, including *system control, encryption, computer use monitoring,* and *biometrics for computer access.* The information in this section is provided to help you understand the importance of computer security methods and to give you insights into how computer security can be violated.

System Control

According to a recent article on protecting computer networks, corporate security managers protect their computer networks without diminishing the level of efficiency by asking and answering the same type of questions that they ask about physical security: *What needs protection? Who might attack? How will they do it? How can risk be managed?*[60]

What Needs Protection? All aspects of the corporate computer environment need protection, including Web servers, mail servers, fire walls, and individual workstations.

Who Might Attack? There are several primary types of attackers: hackers, business rivals, foreign intelligence gatherers, and insiders.

- *Hackers.* These are a very diverse group ranging from programming geniuses who study the inherent weaknesses and vulnerabilities in software and networks to script kiddies, as described earlier in this chapter.

- *Business rivals.* Competitors may try to obtain information illicitly through virtual back doors.

- *Foreign intelligence.* Some countries are known to have active industrial espionage efforts against U.S. corporations.

- *Insiders.* Outsiders—people without any legitimate access—account for fewer than half the reported information security incidents in the United States. Most incidents of hacking are committed by people with some degree of legitimate access, ranging from employees to former employees, customers, and contractors. Insiders may be doing it for their own enjoyment or they may be working for rivals or foreign intelligence agencies. Former insiders also may take advantage of their knowledge of the system to retain access to the network. Sometimes, they continue to use access privileges that the company failed to terminate at the end of their employment.

How Will They Do It? Attackers try to enter the network by probing for information and locating IP addresses, services, and sources of more information.

- *Finding holes.* Once a target has been identified, attackers can employ freely available tool kits (programs) that find and exploit a wide range of problems in the computer system. They may also begin their search for network vulnerabilities in the physical world, by looking in dumpsters for documents that contain company phone lists with e-mail addresses that are also user names. Hackers use deception to get user names and passwords by convincing unaware employees to divulge their password or other security-related information.

- *Covering tracks.* Once attackers have a preliminary foothold into the system, their next step is to cover their tracks by using programs that cloak their activities and open a back door to the system so they can return. Now the attacker can probe the system for information or use it as a platform to attack other systems.

- *Attacking from within.* As already noted, insiders account for most security incidents. Generally they attack in the same way described here.

How Can Risk Be Managed? Once systems managers understand their company's exposure and level of threat, they have a good idea of the specific risks that must be managed and mitigated against. They must find ways to balance the need for security with usability through policy and tools.

The purpose of an information system security policy is to communicate that information security is a priority and that all employees are responsible and accountable for maintaining it. Such a policy also involves controlling privileges. Policies should be complemented by a layered defense designed to prevent those with limited privileges from easily gaining access to restricted parts of the network. The system administrator should regulate each user's rights and permissions with regard to file access, taking the appropriate security measures, such as additional log-in requirements at particularly sensitive areas.

Regular use of security tools can help system administrators do their jobs more efficiently and improve the overall security of the network. These tools include fire walls, VPNs, hacker tools, intrusion detection, and people.

- *Fire walls:* **Fire walls** are the basic building blocks of restricting network traffic, such as between the Internet and the internal systems. A fire wall lets a system administrator separate functional groups while still permitting required traffic in the area. It also provides an audit trail of authorized and blocked traffic, which may allow staff to spot probe attempts or other unauthorized activity.

- *VPNs,* or virtual private networks, provide transmission security-protection from passive observation of a data stream and from insertion attacks, where the attacker injects information into an established data stream.

- *Hacker tools.* Software such as security scanners or vulnerability assessment tools help system administrators view their networks from an attacker's perspective so that they can take corrective action.

- *Intrusion detection.* Intrusion detection systems (IDSs) detect malicious activity either by listening to the network wire or by monitoring logs. They compare the activity flagged to an internal database of attack signatures.

- *People.* Computer security is not just a technical problem. People are the most important part of the security system—from the system and network administrators who have day-to-day operational responsibility of the system to all the people involved in the security loop.

Encryption

Another method of ensuring computer security is **encryption**—that is, using algorithms to scramble the information on a computer so that it is not usable unless the changes are reversed. The growing use of computers and networks requires businesses, most notably those in financial services, to secure their computerized transactions and proprietary information. In response to these needs, widely available and sophisticated encryption technologies have been developed. The trend is to integrate robust digital encryption technologies into commercial desktop applications and networks. These are generally easy to use and unbreakable.[61]

The RSA encryption algorithm was widely used for more than a decade to protect the privacy of digital commerce and communication. It was originally awarded a U.S. patent in 1983. This technology, also known as *public key cryptography,* makes it possible for two people who have never met to exchange information securely. The RSA encryption algorithm was placed into the public domain in September 2000, permitting programmers to incorporate the technology into their products.[62]

Computer Use Monitoring

Another way to ensure computer integrity is to monitor computer use. In 2000, according to an American Management Association survey, 74 percent of companies monitored their employees' Internet and e-mail use and their phone calls.[63] More companies are tracking Internet use than any other office activity. Some 85 percent of the companies told employees about the monitoring.

For example, at Ritvik Toys, near Montreal, a systems manager monitors every Web site that his employees browse and every e-mail message they send or receive. This company is one of hundreds of companies that are looking at workers' correspondence on a routine basis. Reasons companies give for monitoring their employees' computer use is that such use overloads networks, slows computers, and could crash the system.[64]

Here is a good example of the positive results of successful computer monitoring. In 1999, managers at a New York City import-export company suspected it was being victimized by two employees. The company installed a software program called Investigator, which retails for about $99 a copy. It furtively logs every single stroke entered onto a computer. Investigation revealed that the two employees were deleting orders from the corporate books after they were processed, pocketing the revenues, and building their own company from within. The program picked up on their plan to return

to the office late one night to swipe a large shipment of electronics. As the suspects gained entry into the office, they were arrested by police hiding in the rafters of the firm's warehouse. They were charged with embezzling $3 million over two and a half years.[65]

In offices around the United States, managers are installing software that monitors their employee's computer activity, both online and offline, every message sent, every Web site visited, every file formatted, and every key stroked—even if the activity was not saved or was deleted. According to the American Bar Association, employers are free to monitor an employee's use of their networks as long as they don't violate labor and antidiscrimination laws by targeting union organizers, for example, or minorities.

In 1999, 28 percent of companies surveyed said they had dismissed employees for misuse or personal use of telecommunications equipment. Xerox fired forty employees for inappropriate use of the Internet, and the *New York Times* fired twenty-three workers for sending obscene e-mails on company computers.[66]

In a recent survey conducted by a market research and public opinion polling firm, 73 percent of employees with online access at work agreed that their employers have the right to monitor their e-mails and Internet usage at the office.[67]

EXHIBIT 14.2 **Company Monitoring of Employees**

Activity	Percent Monitoring
Internet use	54.1
Telephone use	44.0
E-mail messages	38.1
Computer files	30.8
Computer use	19.4
Job performance (using video cameras)	14.6
Telephone conversations	11.5
Voicemail messages	6.8

Disciplinary Action	Percent Taking
Telephone use	58.5
E-mail messages	44.8
Internet use	41.9

SOURCE: American Management Association.

YOU ARE THERE!
Freedom on the Net in China?

The owner of an Internet café in southern China was arrested in August 2000 and charged with subversion for posting articles critical of the Communist Party on the Internet. Jiang Shihua, the owner of the café in the city of Nanchong in Sichuan Province, is the third person in recent months known to be facing serious charges for political statements on the Internet.

China's leaders have embraced the Internet as a key to development but they also fear it, and special Web police units have been formed to search for illegal activities, including fraud and pornography as well as outlawed political debate. In August 2000, Chinese authorities also shut down New Culture Forum, a Web site in Shandong Province that sponsored lively debate.

SOURCE: Erik Eckholm, "China Arrests Owner of Internet Café," *New York Times*, Aug. 24, 2000, p. A4.

Biometrics for Computer Access

Another way to make computer systems more secure is to use **biometrics** for computer access. Recently, the U.S. Army announced that it is about to begin using biometric security systems to replace the password-based systems that now control access to everything from battlefield weapons to officers' clubs. The biometric security system will store digital images of soldiers' fingerprints, earlobes, and other characteristics. How does it work? First, computer scans identify a person's unique characteristics, such as eyeball patterns, fingerprints, and hand shapes. Then, the scans are stored digitally. Finally, a computer uses video cameras and sensors to match those templates with the patterns of would-be system users. The computer will still recognize a password, but the biometrics will validate identity. The system can lock in on a person as well as a user ID. The Army's plan relies heavily on fingerprints, already collected from all recruits and stored digitally. Fingerprints can be verified in two seconds or less by a device rigged to a personal computer's keyboard.[68]

Already, sperm banks, child care centers, and San Francisco International Airport have used security systems that recognize hand geometry. Canada's public health system uses thumb scans to block unauthorized access.

SUMMARY

Despite all the horror stories about the misuse of the Internet, it may be reassuring to read about the follow-up on this case:

Anthony Correnti, age twenty-six, of West Islip, New York, a schoolteacher who had taught in a private Manhattan high school and in a Long Island public school district, had prowled the Internet for years. He began stalking one of his victims online when she was only eleven years old. He pursued her even after she changed her screen name. He sent e-mail messages of "Let's get together" and "You're so hot, I want to go out with you" to this child. Later, he sent her nude photographs of himself.[69]

When the girl's mother discovered what was transpiring, she immediately contacted local police. The Suffolk County Police Department's Computer Crime Section traced e-mail sent to the minor to Correnti's computer. Upon examining Correnti's computer, authorities discovered that he had one of the most extensive pornography collections ever found, including pictures of adult men having sex with girls as young as four years old. Some of the photographs in his collection included nude students right in his own classroom.

Correnti was arrested. In addition to the computer crime charges, he was charged with sexually abusing five girls thirteen to sixteen years old.

In July 2001, Correnti pleaded guilty to using a child in a sexual performance, possessing a sexual performance by a child, and providing indecent material to a minor, and to counts of third-degree rape and third-degree sodomy. In September 2001, he was sentenced to ten to thirty years in prison.

Although this case is shocking, it is good to know that the mother and the police were successful in breaking this sexual predator's anonymity on the Internet and bringing him into the criminal justice system and that the district attorney and the judge were successful in carrying out justice. It is incumbent on all of us to know the evil and illegal uses of the Internet and how to address them.

This chapter introduced readers to the many problems associated with the use of computers in business and at home and to the methods used to maintain the security and integrity of computer use. It covered the many forms of cybercrime, including fraud, identity theft, Web attacks, hacking, cyberstalking, computer use by pedophiles, computer theft, and other crimes. It also familiarized readers with the many types of computer viruses and other computer assaults and showed how users can protect themselves from such attacks. Finally, the chapter covered the methods used by public and private investigators to investigate computer crime.

LEARNING CHECK

1. What is identity theft? Describe and discuss three ways identity thieves acquire victims' information.

2. What is a computer virus? Describe and discuss three types of viruses.

3. Discuss Carnivore.

4. Discuss three of the problems that computer crimes present to businesses and give two examples of each.

5. Discuss several methods used by the police to investigate computer crime.

APPLICATION EXERCISE

The principal of the local high school contacts you and hires you to assist in a problem occurring at her school. The school has a large computer lab and provides access to the Internet to all students. In addition, each student is assigned an e-mail account that can be accessed at school or at home. Several students have contacted the principal and informed her that they have received offensive and stalking-type e-mail messages. The principal wants you to investigate and determine who is sending the inappropriate e-mail. Prepare a brief report to the principal describing how you will investigate this case.

WEB EXERCISE

Contact your local server and e-mail provider and determine if it provides security advice to its users. If so, obtain the advice and prepare a report to your professor detailing this advice. Also, ask the server to provide you with the precautions it uses to maintain security and integrity of data on its systems.

KEY TERMS

biometrics

Carnivore

computer virus

cybercrime

cyberstalking

dumpster diving

encryption

fire walls

hacking

hacktivist

identity theft

memetic viruses

pedophiles

script kiddies

Trojan horses

Web attacks

worms

PRIVATE SECTOR INVESTIGATIONS

15

CHAPTER GOALS

1. To introduce you to the three major forms of private sector investigations, including proprietary security investigations, contract security investigations, and independent private investigations

2. To provide you with knowledge of the activities engaged in by proprietary security investigators, contract security service investigators, and independent private investigators

3. To provide you with an overview of the major types of investigations conducted by private sector investigators

4. To introduce you to the myriad noncriminal investigations and services conducted by the private sector including preemployment background investigations, drug testing, financial investigations, product liability, finding missing persons, sexual harassment, personal injury, wrongful death, medical malpractice, domestic-marital, and miscellaneous services

5. To acquaint you with the myriad criminal investigations conducted by private sector investigators, including violent and property crimes, theft and fraud, insurance fraud, and industrial espionage

INTRODUCTION

Consider the following scenario:

You are a hospital patient and see a doctor approaching your bed. You observe him inject something into your intravenous tube. You awake several days later, find out that you had suffered a seizure, had been critically ill, and are lucky to be alive. You tell hospital officials your story about the doctor, but they don't believe you. Thirteen years later, you read in the newspapers that the doctor you suspected of harming you has been accused of being a serial killer who used his medical knowledge and job opportunities to kill numerous patients in the United States and around the world.

This is a true story. In 1984, Dr. Michael Swango, while a medical student, was nicknamed Double-O Swango by his fellow students, who joked that he had a license to kill because of the large number of his cases that ended in death. During his tenure as a hospital intern, besides the incident involving the near-fatal attack on you, a nineteen-year-old woman mysteriously died after a fatal injection caused her heart to stop. Several years later, he was convicted of attempting to kill some co-workers by lacing their doughnuts and coffee with an arsenic-based pesticide. He served two years in prison.

Then, in 1993, he obtained a job as a doctor in a Veterans' Affairs Hospital. During his three months there, three of his patients died after being administered lethal injections. Subsequently he practiced medicine in Zimbabwe, where it was charged he poisoned seven patients, five of them fatally. At the time of his arrest, he was on his way to Saudi Arabia to be a doctor in another hospital.

Why was Dr. Swango allowed to continue his reign of serial murder for thirteen years? Why did he land job after job despite his history? Perhaps the answer lies in the fact that no one at any of his jobs conducted an effective preemployment background investigation to determine his work experience and background before they hired him. They just took him at his word. Preemployment background investigations are among the most important investigations performed by private sector investigators. Failure to conduct a proper preemployment background investigation can subject a corporation or business to enormous financial liability judgments. It can also, as in Dr. Swango's case, result in deaths.

This chapter will discuss private sector investigations, including proprietary security investigations, contract security investigations, and independent private investigations.

Among the main noncriminal investigations and services performed by private sector investigators and discussed in this chapter are preemployment background investigations, drug testing, financial investigations, product liability investigations, missing persons, sexual harassment, personal injury, wrongful death, medical malpractice, domestic-marital, and other miscellaneous investigations and services.

Among the many criminal investigations performed by these private sector investigators and discussed in this chapter are violent and property crimes, theft and fraud, insurance fraud, and industrial espionage.

MAJOR FORMS OF PRIVATE SECTOR INVESTIGATIONS

Investigatory services in the private sector are provided by proprietary security departments in corporations and businesses, large contract security service companies, and independent private investigators.

Leading private security expert Robert D. McCrie, associate professor for security management at John Jay College of Criminal Justice, City University of New York, provides this commentary on the current role of private investigators:

> Organizations use the services of outside investigators for many reasons: Preemployment screening (vetting), internal investigations, executive protection, and the testing of controls are the principal reasons. Many organizations today have their own internal investigative departments. But the need for external investigators—the term "detective" is dated—always exists. The use of outside investigators has increased considerably in recent years, in part because the need for in-house investigations has grown due to legal and insurance requirements. Further, in-house departments have sometimes been downsized.
>
> Investigators generally provide excellent value to their clients. In some instances, the use of investigative expertise would have saved much time and money for organizations. But finding a competent investigator is not easy. One has to evaluate the individual for his or her ability, appropriateness, and efficiency for a given assignment. The care and feeding of those uncommon

superior investigators involves keeping in touch and giving regular assignments or paying a modest retainer.[1]

This section will include a description of each of the forms of private sector investigators and give some examples of the investigations and services provided by each one.

Proprietary Security Investigations

Most large corporations and businesses have their own **proprietary** (in-house) **security** departments that provide a wide range of security services, including **investigations.** Sometimes some of these large corporations and businesses may also use major contract (outside) security service companies to conduct all or some of their investigating services.

Some corporations use a combination of in-house and outside investigators. For example, Pacific Gas and Electric Company handles many of its investigations in-house but also hires outside investigators to help work on cases at distant affiliate locations; it considers it advantageous to hire an agency familiar with the local police and business community. Other important factors when considering using inside or outside investigators include turnaround time, cost, flexibility, expertise, and confidentiality. Due diligence investigations are heavily weighted toward in-house investigations, but other investigations are about evenly divided between outsource and in-house.[2]

Most investigations conducted by proprietary security personnel concentrate on such matters as pre-employment background checks for new employees, internal crime and loss prevention, insurance cases, credit applications, and civil litigation cases.

In an example of corporate preemployment background investigations, the National Football League (NFL) and its teams use intensive preemployment background examinations of graduating college players entering the pro football draft every year. They check criminal records, interview law enforcement officials at the players' colleges, and speak to coaches, friends, and the players themselves. In 2000, 68 of the 323 draft-eligible players had "reportable information," meaning there was some aspect of the player's background that raised eyebrows on the league's security staff, ranging from speeding tickets to drug possession,

fights, and violations of National Collegiate College Association (NCAA) rules. An increasing number of individual teams are combining their security personnel with the league's resources to ensure that nothing is missed.[3]

Contract Security Investigations

Many large corporations and businesses, as well as many smaller ones, use the services of **contract security** companies, which provide numerous security services and **investigations.** Also, many private individuals use the services of these companies. One of the largest contract security companies is Pinkerton, which is a leading provider of global security services, including uniformed security officers, investigations, consulting, business intelligence, security systems integration, and employee selection services. Pinkerton protects the employees and total assets of thousands of businesses worldwide, including more than 80 percent of the Fortune 1000. This centuries-old company is today a subsidiary of Securitas AB, based in Stockholm, Sweden, which is the largest security company in the world, with annual revenues of $4 billion and 114,000 employees in more than thirty-two countries throughout North and South America, Europe, and Asia. Securitas AB also owns Burns International Services, American Protective Services, and First Security Services.[4]

Pinkerton offers the following specialized investigating services:

- *Background investigations.* These services include applicant checks, comprehensive backgrounds, and technical backgrounds. Applicant checks are intended for entry-level positions and positions in which no money is handled. They include driving records, civil and criminal court records, social security number verification, credit reports, and past employment verification. Comprehensive backgrounds are intended for higher-level positions, or jobs that involve handling money or sensitive information. These backgrounds include the basic checks and can also include verification of identity, education and professional credentials, contact and interviews of listed references, and exploration of resumes. Technical backgrounds are very comprehensive investigations for government and government contractor positions in the nuclear industry.

- *Fraud investigations.* These involve the investigations of questionable insurance claims; they unearth the facts of the claim and present them in a manner that is comprehensive, documented, and understandable. They include workers' compensation, disability, property, casualty, or product liability claims.

- *Undercover investigations.* These involve confidential **undercover operations** and inquiries that can detect and develop evidence of theft, embezzlement, bribery, kickbacks, harassment, conflicts of interest, sabotage, and substance abuse. These investigations may attempt to prevent illegal acts by employees, business associates, or outside individuals.

- *Claims investigation-surveillance.* These services help insurance companies and the self-insured fight fraudulent claims by detecting fraud and providing detailed, reliable reports and admissible evidence. The methods used include activity checks, surveillance, claimant and witness interviews, reviews of medical and autopsy reports, skip tracing, and records searches. The records searched include Department of Motor Vehicle (DMV), previous employment, education, professional credentials, neighborhood checks, and the like. Claims investigated include property and casualty claims, workers' compensation, liability, malpractice, theft or burglary, contestable death, accidental death, and dismemberment and disability.

- *Executive protection.* These include programs for the prevention of terrorism, kidnapping, extortion, and bodily harm to individual executives and businesses.

- *Due diligence–asset searches.* These include verification of deeds and titles, litigation, liens, assets, or personal or corporate reputations to minimize the risks involved in lending or underwriting.

- *Intellectual property protection.* This involves searching and protecting trademarks, patents, and copyrights to prevent and recover losses due to counterfeit products.

Another major contract security service company is the Wackenhut Corporation, a leading provider of security-related and diversified human resource services to business, industry, and government agencies on a worldwide basis, including the United States and over fifty other countries on six continents.

The Investigations Division of Wackenhut reports that it tackles business crime of every kind, at every level, across the country and overseas.

> We utilize the latest approaches to tell you if you have employees who are stealing, using drugs, not doing their jobs, abusing authority, engaging in discrimination or sexual harassment, committing fraud—and who they are. We can also provide you with a timely and proactive approach and tell you how vulnerable you are to criminals on the outside—and protect you.[5]

Wackenhut advertises the following specialized investigative services:

- *Background investigations.* Preemployment screening and thorough background investigations. Wackenhut uses its National Research Center, a twenty-four-hour-a-day, seven-day-a-week operation that handles preemployment screening and public record investigations.

- *Shopping services.* Professional shoppers conduct integrity, efficiency, and facility analyses, which help identify losses, curt or abrasive behavior of some employees, and poor conditions leading to customer dissatisfaction.

- *Hotline programs.* These include various hotline reporting programs that are staffed by trained investigators around the clock, every day of the year. These hotlines encourage the reporting of criminal activity, drug dealing, drug use, gambling, misconduct, sexual harassment, discrimination, weapons possession, safety violations, fraud, or ethics and compliance violations.

Wackenhut is also a world leader in private prison construction and management. It operates prisons across the United States, as well as in Britain, Australia, New Zealand, South Africa, and the Caribbean.[6]

Another large contract security service provider, and one of the largest financial investigating firms in the United States, is Equifax Employment Services of Atlanta, Georgia, which has branch offices in numerous U.S. cities. With annual corporate revenues of $1.1

billion, Equifax is the nation's largest consumer and commercial credit reporting firm. The company offers a variety of risk management and financial services. It can collect information quickly, accurately, and inexpensively. It can also provide a variety of basic information in preemployment screening.

Another leading financial investigating firm in the United States is Kroll's Associates, which is headquartered in New York City. During the merger mania of the 1980s, Kroll's was Wall Street's major "private eye," specializing in digging up dirt in heated takeover battles. When the merger mania of that decade cooled, Kroll kept its grip on the top rung of financial investigating by continuing to do financial investigations for the U.S. government, foreign governments, and large corporations. Clients pay an average of $1,500 a day for the services of a Kroll agent, and the company's employees are well paid by industry standards. Senior managers earn $100,000 to $300,000 a year, and top executives make as much as $500,000 a year. Kroll recruits former federal and state prosecutors, former agents from the FBI, CIA, and IRS, and former diplomats and Congressional aides to be agents.[7]

Independent Private Investigations

Independent private investigators are generally self-employed persons or members of small one- or two-person firms. Many smaller companies and businesses

INVESTIGATIONS ON THE NET

Pinkerton Security and Investigation Services
http://www.pinkertons.com

Wackenhut Corporation
http://www.wackenhut.com

Equifax Employment Services
http://www.equifax.com

Kroll's Associates
http://www.krollworldwide.com

For an up-to-date list of Web links, go to http://info.wadsworth.com/dempsey
----

hire independent private investigators to conduct investigations. Private individuals requiring investigatory services also use private investigators. Independent private investigators generally charge from $35 to over $100 per hour.

In most states private investigators are required to be licensed by the state. Licensing requirements generally include state residency, U.S. citizenship, training or work experience as a police officer or investigator, or apprenticeship under a licensed private investigator. Many also require a clean arrest record, passing a background investigation, and passing an oral or written examination. Some states have no regulations.[8]

OVERVIEW OF PRIVATE SECTOR INVESTIGATIONS

There are several ways we can categorize the investigations and services provided by private sector investigators. For example, authors Pamela A. Collins, Truett A. Ricks, and Clifford W. Van Meter categorize these investigations and services as follows:[9]

- *Legal investigations.* These investigations involve the courts, including both criminal and civil litigation. In these cases, the investigator locates witnesses, conducts interviews, gathers and reviews testimonial, documentary, and physical evidence, takes photographs, and testifies in court.

- *Corporate investigations.* These involve investigating criminal or other misconduct in the workplace. They might involve the investigation of theft of company assets, drug abuse in the workplace, and myriad other conditions. Some of these investigations may involve undercover operations.

- *Financial investigations.* These involve accounting and finance skills and tend to focus on uncovering and developing cases against employees or clients who are suspected of embezzlement or fraud. They generally involve developing confidential financial profiles of persons or companies who may be parties to large financial transactions and often involve working with investment bankers and accountants to determine the how's and who's of thefts. Often these investigators have the Certified Fraud Examiner (CFE) designation described later in this chapter.

YOU ARE THERE!
Private Investigators, Politicians, and Famous Names

Terry Lenzner, president of Investigative Group International (IGI), a graduate of Harvard Law School, and a former attorney with the U.S. Justice Department, has had many high-profile political clients, including President Bill Clinton and his wife. He investigated the lives of Monica Lewinsky and Paula Jones in Clinton's impeachment trial.

Some of Lenzner's other clients have included the former heavyweight boxing champion Mike Tyson, the Democratic Party, and Larry Ellison, the CEO of Oracle. It is alleged that Lenzner worked for Ellison in digging up information against Bill Gates, and Microsoft. Jon S. Corzine, a candidate for the Democratic nomination for U.S. senator from New Jersey in 2000, admitted that he paid at least $200,000 to a lawyer who hired private investigators to conduct an inquiry into Jim Florio, his opponent in the primary, and members of Florio's campaign staff. Florio complained that the investigators had intended to dig up salacious details about his personal life in an effort to smear his reputation. According to the *New York Times*, although it is a common and accepted practice for political candidates to assign staff members to research their rivals, the use of private investigators is controversial because such investigators are not directly supervised by campaign staff members and often pride themselves on using intimidation or deception to gain information.

Nevertheless, political candidates and their surrogates have turned to private investigators, from President Clinton and Senator Edward M. Kennedy to scores of local officials. Many government watchdog groups say it is a practice best avoided, because private investigators are often difficult to control and the public regards many of them as unscrupulous.

SOURCES: Judy Bachrach, "The President's Private Eye," *Vanity Fair*, Sept. 1998, pp. 192–216; Brad Stonje, "Diving into Bill's Trash," *Newsweek*, July 10, 2000, p. 49; Adam Cohen, "Peeping Larry," *Newsweek*, July 10, 2000, p. 49; Kate Kelly, "The Corporate Spy: Lenzner," *Time*, July 10, 2000; and David Kocieniewski, "Corzine Admits Paying Lawyer Who Had Private Investigators Check Out Florio," *New York Times*, May 31, 2000, p. B5.

- *Loss prevention investigations.* These are generally conducted for retail organizations and include investigations of both internal and external theft of assets. These investigators are responsible for finding and apprehending employees and customers who steal merchandise or cash, or destroy property. They also may audit stock and other company possessions.

- *Insurance fraud investigations.* These investigations generally involve fraud against insurance carriers, such as automobile, workers' compensation, disability, health care, life, homeowners, and others.

- *Computer fraud investigations.* These investigations involve developing evidence to prove computer or cybercriminal activities; sometimes this type of investigation is called computer forensics.

- *Core investigations.* These investigations involve the entire panoply of investigative services for businesses or individuals, including crimes or wrongs committed or threatened; background investigations of people and businesses; preemployment background checks of job applicants; conduct and honesty of employees, agents, contractors, and subcontractors; incidents and illicit or illegal activities by persons against companies or company property; retail shoplifting; internal theft by employees or other employee crime; the truth or falsity of statements or representations; the whereabouts of missing persons; the location or recovery of lost or stolen property; the causes, origin of, or responsibility for fires, libel or slander, losses, accidents, injuries, or damages to property; the credibility of informants, witnesses, or other persons; and the security of evidence to be used before investigating committees, boards of award or arbitration, or in the trial of civil or criminal cases and the preparation thereof.

Exhibit 15.1 provides a comprehensive list of duties that may be performed by private investigators.

YOU ARE THERE!

"The Best Surveillance People I've Ever Had Were Females"

"The best surveillance people I've ever had were females who did not have a law enforcement background," said Richard "Bo" Dietl, head of Bo Dietl and Associates Security and Investigations. He said that at least 40 percent of the investigators in his agency are women. "They're great on surveillance. No one suspects a woman is following them. They're also great on eavesdropping for the same reasons."

According to the managing director of Kroll's Associates, "We need people with legal expertise, computer expertise, forensics experts. Those people come in all genders, shapes, and sizes."

Among the women profiled in a *New York Post* special on "Breaking Through Gender Barriers" are these:

- A twenty-five-year-old Brown graduate who spends her workdays hunting down information behind multimillion-dollar business deals. She is a former book publisher.
- A twenty-eight-year-old former junior-high teacher.

- A twenty-eight-year-old former employee of an art firm.
- A twenty-five-year-old who graduated from Harvard and studied Romance poetry at Oxford. Her biggest case was an investigation into art stolen from Holocaust survivors during World War II. The probe led to major New York art galleries and former members of the Office of Strategic Services, the forerunner of the CIA.
- A Columbia Law School graduate and former assistant U.S. attorney, who worked for several years at the prestigious law firm of Cravath, Swaine and Moore. Last year, while providing services to Madison Square Garden, she helped bust a major ticket-scalping ring, resulting in the firing of seven employees.

SOURCE: Todd Venezia, "These Tough Gals Are Private Eye-Openers: Charlie's Angels Have Nothing on New Breed of Supersleuths," *New York Post*, July 19, 2000, pp. 20–21.

EXHIBIT 15.1   **Things Private Investigators Do**

Assist attorneys in case preparation.

Reconstruct accidents for insurance companies and attorneys.

Review police reports for attorneys (many private investigators are former members of police departments and thus can offer attorneys an "inside look" at police terminology and jargon).

Do surveillance and observations for insurance companies and attorneys.

Do background investigations of possible spouses.

Do background investigations of possible employees.

Do criminal investigations of cases that police do not because of a lack of resources.

Run credit checks.

Do financial resources checks.

Investigate missing people cases the police can't put enough resources into.

Investigate missing people cases that are not police cases (no crime involved).

Check into conduct of spouses or lovers.

Investigate suicides.

Offer personal protection.

Offer executive protection.

Offer premise or meeting protection.

Create travel itineraries.

Do honesty or "shopper" testing.

Investigate insurance or workers' compensation frauds.

Reconstruct auto accidents.

Work undercover for private firms to uncover: criminal activity, drug use, work rule violations.

Investigate product liability claims.

Serve subpoenas.

MAJOR TYPES OF PRIVATE SECTOR NONCRIMINAL INVESTIGATIONS

Numerous types of private sector noncriminal investigations not only provide important services for society but also provide job opportunities for persons interested in investigations. This section will discuss the following noncriminal investigations conducted by private sector investigators, including preemployment background investigations, drug testing, financial investigations, product liability, finding missing persons, sexual harassment, personal injury, wrongful death, medical malpractice, domestic-marital, and miscellaneous services.

Preemployment Background Screening

Recall the Dr. Michael Swango case from the introduction to this chapter. Swango was a serial murderer who went from one medical job to another, killing patients as he went along. Yet he continued to be hired, and no employer conducted an examination of his background before hiring him. **Preemployment background screening** are among the most important types of investigations conducted in the private investigations sector.

Businesses are increasingly being held liable for injuries that their employees inflict on third parties. Many states hold companies liable for negligent hiring and negligent retention, holding that they have a duty to investigate employees' backgrounds properly to determine if they have harmful character traits.[10]

With increasing regularity, courts are holding employers liable for acts committed by employees on the job, and sometimes while off-duty. *Negligent hiring* means that an employer has hired someone without properly confirming that the information on his or her application is accurate and factual. Preemployment screening should include, at a minimum, criminal history, verification of prior employment, education claims, and social security number. The applicant's driving record, credit report, and professional licenses should also be reviewed.[11]

Lawsuits for negligent hiring or retention can be based on negligently conducting a preemployment investigation, failing to conduct an investigation, or hiring with knowledge of a dangerous propensity. If no facts were available before hiring an employee but became known during the course of employment, a case for negligent retention can be made. Companies who serve the public have an added responsibility to exercise due caution in their hiring practices.

The U.S. Department of Commerce reports that 30 percent of all business failures are the result of poor hiring practices. Embezzlement costs industry $4 billion a year. Other employee crime, both blue and white collar, costs another $45 to $50 billion annually. Statistics also indicate that most people who steal, cheat, defraud, or embezzle are never detected by their former employers and that 25 percent of applicants stretch the truth or lie on their preemployment applications.[12]

As a result, many corporations today conduct extensive preemployment-background investigations before they hire in order to screen out dishonest or disreputable people. These background investigations may be conducted by in-house personnel, contract investigating firms, or independent private investigators.

A survey of *Security Management* readers shows that of all preemployment selection tools, criminal records checks are most common, with 93.6 percent of respondents routinely checking them. Other preemployment screening methods mentioned included employment history, 91.1 percent; education records, 75.2 percent; drug screens, 71.5 percent; and integrity tests, 14.5 percent.[13]

Traditionally, many corporations used polygraph (lie detector) examinations in preemployment screening and internal investigations. However, the 1988 Employee Polygraph Protection Act (EPPA) prohibited the use of preemployment polygraph examinations in the private sector except for government employers, law enforcement agencies, and certain industries. Many of the corporations involved in these areas, as well as many law enforcement agencies, still use polygraph examinations and polygraphists in their preemployment background examinations. (For more on polygraphs, see chapter 7.)

The American Polygraph Association (APA) is the leading polygraph professional association in the United States. It consists of two thousand members dedicated to the establishment of the highest standards of moral, ethical, and professional conduct in the polygraph field. It offers its members advanced training in techniques and instrumentation and provides members research and information in the field.

YOU ARE THERE!

He Was a Serial Killer But Continued Getting Jobs as a Doctor: The Michael Swango Case

When Michael J. Swango was a medical student at Southern Illinois University, classmates called him Double-O Swango, joking that he had a license to kill because of the large number of his cases that ended in deaths.

In 1984, when he was a medical resident at Ohio State University Hospital, Swango was accused of causing a patient to have a seizure after injecting something into her intravenous tube. The patient survived and told hospital officials about the attack, but they did not believe her. An investigation by the hospital cleared him.

Still, Swango was not allowed to continue his residency there for a second year. He returned to his native Illinois and worked as an emergency medical technician with the Adams County Ambulance Service. While there, he was convicted of lacing his co-workers' doughnuts and coffee with an arsenic-based ant killer. Five people became ill, but no one died. He was sentenced to five years in prison, but served only two.

When he was released from prison, Swango used false names and documents to try to get a number of medical positions. He was hired by a Veterans Hospital in South Dakota, but fired when his past became known.

In 1993, Swango was hired as a medical resident by the Stony Brook Health Sciences Center, in Stony Brook, New York, after lying to the admissions office and saying that his previous conviction for poisoning stemmed from a "barroom brawl." As a Stony Brook intern, he was assigned to the Veterans Affairs Medical Center in Northport, New York. During his tenure there, three of his patients died after being administered lethal injections. Another of his patients fell into a coma after being given an injection of a paralyzing medication; the man subsequently died.

After he had worked there for three months, Stony Brook officials learned about his criminal past, which had been featured in newspapers and on national television, and fired him. However, officials at the time said they had determined that no harm had come to the 147 patients he treated there.

After being dismissed by Stony Brook in 1993, Swango went to practice medicine in Zimbabwe. Subsequently, authorities there issued a warrant for his arrest on charges that he poisoned seven patients, five of them fatally.

He was arrested in 1997, while stopping over in Chicago en route to a new job as a doctor in Dhahran, Saudi Arabia, charged with making a false statement to Stony Brook officials, and began serving a three-and-a-half-year prison sentence.

Finally, in July 2000, after exhuming the bodies of the three patients found dead in the Northport Veterans Affairs Hospital, and finding the poisons in their bodies, federal investigators charged Swango with the 1993 murders. He was charged with the 1984 murder of a nineteen-year-old patient at the Ohio State University Hospital by giving her a potassium injection that caused her heart to stop.

As of 2000, the FBI, the Department of Veterans Affairs, and prosecutors around the world were investigating and building other cases against him. In September 2000 Swango pled guilty to the three murders at the Northport Veterans Hospital and was sentenced to three life sentences.

SOURCES: Michael Cooper, "Former Doctor Charged in Death of Three Patients," *New York Times*, July 12, 2000, p. B1; James B. Stewart, *Blind Eye: The Terrifying Story of a Doctor Who Got Away with Murder* (New York: Simon & Schuster, 1999); Charlie LeDuff, "Prosecutors Say Doctor Killed to Feel a Thrill," *New York Times*, Sept. 7, 2000, p. B1.

Because the polygraph can no longer be used in some preemployment screenings, many corporations have turned to paper-and-pencil screening tests for potential employees. Experts have reported that these screening aids are efficient, inexpensive, and reliable and that job applicants often are astonishingly revealing in providing information on questionnaires. These tests are designed to measure six aspects of an applicant's behavior: freedom from disruptive alcohol and substance use, absence of maladaptive personality

YOU ARE THERE!
Preemployment Background Investigations for Law Enforcement Candidates

Generally, law enforcement agencies conduct very extensive preemployment-background investigations of candidates for positions in their agencies.

In a comprehensive article in the *FBI Bulletin*, Thomas A. Wright offered the following basics for a thorough background investigation for law enforcement applicants:

- *Preliminary interview.* In this interview the investigating officer should advise the applicant of the details of the background investigation process and facts about employment in the department, including salary, benefits, and responsibilities.

- *Background investigation booklet.* This booklet should contain questions for the applicant to answer about important aspects of his or her past, including residences, schools, jobs, military service, arrests and summonses, and any other information the department wishes to investigate. This booklet becomes the basic document for the background investigation.

- *Photos and prints.* The photos will be used to show to neighbors and former employers, in case they do not recognize the applicant by name. The prints are sent to the FBI and the local state criminal identification agency to determine any previous police record.

- *Education.* The applicant's school experience should be investigated to determine his or her attendance and disciplinary history.

- *Employment.* The applicant's employment experience should be investigated to determine his or her honesty, self-initiative, attitudes, job performance, absenteeism, tardiness, and use of sick leave.

- *Credit check.* The applicant's credit history should be examined to clarify his or her previous history in fulfilling obligations.

- *Criminal history.* Every police agency covering areas where the applicant might have lived or attended school should be contacted to see if there is any information on his or her conduct while living there.

- *Driving record.* The applicant's record of traffic accidents and traffic summonses and citations should be investigated.

- *Military history.* The applicant's military record should be investigated to determine any disciplinary actions or medical problems that may affect his or her police employment.

SOURCE: Thomas H. Wright, "Preemployment Background Investigations," *FBI Law Enforcement Bulletin*, Nov. 1991, pp. 16–21.

---

traits, likelihood of being fired, trustworthiness, likelihood of quitting, and likelihood of having an on-the-job accident.[14] Companies can also check on the validity of information provided in job applications, such as academic credentials, professional references, criminal convictions, workers' compensation claims, credit history, certifications and licenses, and motor vehicle records.

Many scam operations provide false preemployment background information to prospective employers. Sometimes friends pose as corporate executives or other professional references but other scams can be more elaborate. Some sham corporations have been established that receive information from a dishonest job seeker and then supply that information in response to a basic employment verification call. Also, some individuals sell illegitimate college degrees to job seekers and establish fake offices that investigators call to verify the information.[15]

Considering the growing proliferation of scam operations, preemployment investigators must go beyond the normal methods of checking applicants' backgrounds. Generally, most employers verify a job applicant's previous five-year work history by relying on the names and telephone numbers of references supplied by the applicant. The investigator must ensure that these references are legitimate by verifying them through the particular company's human resource department. In addition, the investigator must verify the legitimacy of the company itself by checking the local

YOU ARE THERE!
The Polygraph Protection Act of 1988 (EPPA)

Formerly, the polygraph was used extensively in private industry for screening job applicants and preventing employee theft. Its use in preemployment screening was severely limited by the Employee Polygraph Protection Act (EPPA), signed into law in June 1988. In addition to limiting the use of the polygraph, this law, which is enforced by the U.S. Department of Labor under the authority of the Secretary of Labor, banned the use of any other lie detector tests in the workplace, except for the polygraph. Such lie detector machines are psychological stress evaluators, deceptographs, and voice stress analyzers.

The EPPA prohibited random polygraph testing by private sector employers and the use of the polygraph for preemployment screening. The law provides that an employer cannot ask or tell job applicants to take a polygraph as part of the job interviewing process and that an employee under investigation may not be fired for refusing to take a polygraph examination nor solely on the basis of the test results. The law exempts the United States government or any state or local government from its provisions and restrictions.

The EPPA allows the use of the polygraph for preemployment screening for employers whose primary

business is the provision of certain types of security services, companies that manufacture or dispense controlled substances, and in businesses doing sensitive work under contract to the federal government, such as nuclear plants, power facilities, water companies, and the like. The law also provides that other private industries can still request employees to take a polygraph test as part of an internal criminal investigation but that the firm must justify a reasonable suspicion that the employee was involved in the alleged offense. The suspected employee must be notified in writing forty-eight hours in advance of the test and may have a lawyer present during the testing.

SOURCES: F. Lee Bailey, Roger E. Zuckerman, and Kenneth R. Pierce, *The Employee Polygraph Protection Act: A Manual for Polygraph Examiners and Employers* (Severna Park, MD: American Polygraph Association, 1989). See also James J. Kouri, "Federal Polygraph Law: A Blow to Private Security," *The NarcOfficer*, May 1989, pp. 37–39; Hugh E. Jones, "The Employee Polygraph Protection Act: What Are the Consequences?" *The NarcOfficer*, May 1989, pp. 41–42; and Norman Ansley, "A Compendium on Polygraph Validity," *The NarcOfficer*, May 1989, pp. 43–48.

INVESTIGATIONS ON THE NET

American Polygraph Association (APA)
http://www.polygraph.org

For an up-to-date list of Web links, go to
http://info.wadsworth.com/dempsey

chamber of commerce, business reference books, and the state government's corporate business department. If the applicant claims that a business he or she has worked for has closed, the investigator can verify this through state corporate records, old business directories, or phone books. The applicant should provide tax documentation (W-2s) as proof of employment.

A problem for background investigators is that they cannot expect to get much help from an appli-

cant's former employer. Many previous employers will not divulge information about past employees.

The following paragraphs discuss some of the most important areas covered in preemployment background investigations.

- *Military records.* Applicants should be asked for a copy of their DD-214, which is the standard document given to all U.S. military personnel on discharge. This form provides dates of entry and separation from the service and all locations where the serviceperson was assigned, in addition to other information. Investigators should also request a military record search from the military records facility of the National Personnel Records Center in St. Louis, Missouri.

- *Educational records.* Often a deceptive applicant with computer and printer technology skills can create realistic-looking diplomas. The investigator should personally check the colleges or schools applicants claim to have attended and request that they have the school mail a copy of their official transcript to the investigator. If a school has closed down, its records are generally sent to the state's department of education and the investigator can check there. Legitimate degrees from distance learning educational institutions can be checked through the Distance Education and Training Council (DETC), which evaluates and gives accreditation to such college training. (The DETC's Web site is www.detc.org.)

- *Criminal history.* This is generally checked through an examination of a jurisdiction's public court records. Some industries require a state police or FBI check.

- *Credit history.* Corporations must be very careful when using preemployment credit checks to make a hire or no-hire decision. Various court cases, federal law, and Federal Trade Commission (FTC) opinions have established a series of precedents that govern when a credit report can and cannot be used to deny someone employment. Many companies have been sued by rejected applicants for making erroneous hiring decisions based on credit reports.[16]

Three companies—Trans Union, Experian, and Equifax—maintain credit reports on anyone who has ever used a credit card, held a mortgage, taken out a car loan, bought insurance, or used credit in any other way. Each agency offers two types of credit reports. The first is used by banks and other lenders to determine whether a person has strong enough credit to obtain a loan. The second is used by potential employers to check an applicant's credit history. The employee credit report usually contains the following types of credit activity: trade lines (a record of all the credit accounts the person has ever had), credit balances, the highest amount ever owed, and payment history. It also contains some civil records and judgments, including bankruptcies and liens. Generally, the credit reporting agencies charge $10 for each report.

Whenever a company plans to use a credit report in a hiring decision, it must follow the requirements of the Fair Credit Reporting Act (FCRA), which is enforced by the Federal Trade Commission. The FCRA is a law designed to protect the privacy of consumer report information and guarantee that the information supplied by consumer reporting agencies is as accurate as possible. Under FCRA rules, an employer is required to notify the job candidate if a consumer report will be requested. Also, if the company decides to take an "adverse action" against the candidate (that is, not offer the person the job) because of the information in the credit report, it must notify the applicant in advance, give the applicant a copy of the report, and provide a written explanation of his rights under the FCRA. The applicant is then allowed to dispute any inaccurate information in the report.

Experts recommend that if a report indicates that a job applicant has bad credit, it should not be taken at face value. The company should investigate any mitigating factors, such as catastrophic family illnesses, that might explain the bad credit history.

In 2000, the U.S. General Accounting Office (GAO) reported that an analysis of 530 background investigations of employees of the U.S. Department of Defense (DoD) were woefully inadequate. All 530 of these people received top secret clearance even though investigators had not always verified such basic information as residency, citizenship, or employment. The agency responsible for conducting DoD investigations currently faces a backlog of more than six hundred thousand cases. The backlog is due to failed management reforms and inadequate oversight, which could take several years and millions of dollars to fix.[17]

Furthermore, compounding these problems at DoD, another survey of fifteen hundred cases found that employees of defense contractors received security clearances by the Defense Department's Office of Hearings and Appeals (the Pentagon agency in charge of clearances for contractors' employees) despite sometimes extensive histories of drug use, alcoholism, sexual misconduct, financial problems, or criminal activity.[18]

Some corporations are turning to personnel service companies to recruit, screen, and hire new employees. In addition to identifying potential job candidates, these services conduct extensive background investigations that include everything from criminal records checks to drug tests.[19]

Background Investigations for Law Enforcement Candidates Because of the trust and discretion given to law enforcement officers, it is essential that the men and women attempting to obtain law enforcement positions in our society receive thorough background investigations and interviews.

In an effective law enforcement applicant background investigation, a candidate's past life—his or her past employment, school records, medical records, relationships with neighbors and others, and military record—is placed under the microscope. The investigator looks for evidence of incidents that might point to unfavorable traits or habits that might affect the individual's ability to be a good police officer. Such factors include poor work habits, dishonesty, use of alcohol or drugs, and a tendency to violence.

In addition to background investigations, law enforcement candidates are also subject to psychological investigations. These can include, in addition to regular psychological instruments, oral hearings consisting of an interview with a psychologist or a department official or series of departmental officials. Often these are "stress interviews" in which the examiners attempt to see how a candidate will perform under stress.

Drug Testing

Numerous reports over the past decade by organizations such as the Substance Abuse and Mental Health Services Administration (SAMHSA), the National Institute on Drug Abuse (NIDA), the U.S. Department of Labor, and numerous others indicate that substance abuse is a serious problem in the workplace. Substance-abusing workers have been found to be less productive and have higher absenteeism rates, higher workers' compensation claims, higher turnover rates, and higher accident rates than those who do not abuse drugs. Other costs of drug abuse in the workplace are diverted supervisory and managerial time, friction among workers, damage to equipment, poor decisions, and damage to the company's public image.[20]

A review of the trends in employee drug testing reveals that prior to 1987, it was very uncommon, and by 1996, it was very common. In 1988, the Federal Drug-Free Workplace Act was passed, requiring companies doing certain types of work or having certain types of contracts with the federal government to test for drugs. In 1990, the U.S. Department of Transportation (DoT) passed regulations that mandated **drug testing** in safety-sensitive positions, and in 1994 it ex-

panded the number of employees subject to random or periodic testing. Some 90 percent of human resource managers polled felt that drug testing is effective in dealing with drug abuse in the workplace.[21] Today, the DoT mandates drug testing for the approximately 8.34 million workers who operate ships, aircraft, trucks, buses, and trains.[22]

Workplace studies that have measured accident rates show that drug testing reduces accidents. For example, a study involving the Southern Pacific Railroad showed that after implementation of drug testing, accidents dropped from over two thousand the year before testing began to about three hundred during the first six months of the program's fourth year.[23]

Employers cite four primary reasons for employee drug testing:[24]

- Concern over the economic costs of drug abuse, including increased health care costs, absenteeism, and on-the-job accidents
- Fear of liability for injuries caused by employee drug use
- Belief that drug use increases the amount of employee theft
- Desire to control conduct of employees

The New York Academy of Medicine reports that the large majority of workers who are not drug users seem to support the prospect of eliminating the drug culture from their workplaces and seem willing to sacrifice a certain degree of personal privacy to achieve this goal.[25] A 2000 survey of companies using preemployment selection tools revealed that 71.5 percent of them use drug screens.[26]

Information from the National Household Survey on Drug Abuse (NHSDA) revealed that 35 percent of full-time workers said their employers tested for drug use at the time of hiring; 20 percent reported random drug testing programs; 28 percent reported drug testing programs based on reasonable suspicion by a supervisor; and 23 percent reported the use of drug testing in conjunction with work-related accidents.[27]

Drug testing programs can include testing of job applicants, testing for cause, and random testing. To ensure accuracy and reliability, the U.S. Department of Health and Human Services has issued technical and scientific guidelines for employee drug testing. Standard procedures involve an initial screening assay followed by a confirmation assay. The National Institute on Drug Abuse offers a laboratory certification program.

Traditionally, drug testing has been done by urine analysis; as of 1995, for example, urine testing was the most common form of employee drug testing, and the average cost per person tested was $35. However, drug testing by hair analysis is gaining popularity. Much of the research on hair testing is being conducted by the National Institute of Justice, in collaboration with the National Institute on Drug Abuse. Because hair analysis and urine testing address different time periods of illicit drug use, hair testing should not be expected to replace urinalysis. However, it offers promise as a supplementary technique. Because it detects exposure over prolonged periods of use, it can also be done less often than urinalysis and could potentially reduce testing costs. In several court rulings, the results of hair testing have been found reliable and acceptable as corroborative evidence of drug use.[28]

Some personnel service companies recruit, screen, and hire new employees for corporations. These companies conduct extensive background investigations that include everything from criminal record checks to drug tests. Many that screen job applicants for marijuana, cocaine, and other narcotics take urine samples and send them to regional laboratories where test results are usually available within a few days. Some companies have saved a significant amount of money by changing to in-house screening and send only samples that test positive for drugs to a lab.[29]

Hallcrest Systems, Inc., in a report for the U.S. Department of Justice, issued a series of guidelines for private businesses and law enforcement agencies to take when workplace drug crimes are discovered or suspected and offered tips to help employers determine whether drug crimes are taking place on their premises. The guidelines are based on the establishment of a relationship between businesses and law enforcement agencies to increase the chances for successful investigations and prosecutions and to improve the odds of saving the company's money and reducing liability. The report recommended that businesses take such internal steps to eradicate drug abuse in the workplace as reviewing their current policy, assessing the workplace drug problem, obtaining legal advice, contacting appropriate law enforcement agencies if necessary, and publicizing successful drug investigations and prosecutions to deter would-be offenders. It also recommended that

law enforcement agencies establish relationships with the business community by using outreach and drug education and training programs, assigning officers as liaisons with businesses, and developing a written policy concerning the handling of requests for workplace drug crime investigations.[30]

The American Hospital Association (AHA) has a policy recommending that hospitals perform preemployment, for-cause, and postaccident testing. Also, according to its policy, unannounced screening (random testing) should occur for workers who have tested positive and are participating in a return-to-work agreement. According to a consultant, however, only about 30 to 40 percent of hospitals actually perform preemployment screening, many claiming they can't afford it. Virtually all perform for-cause testing, but none do random not-for-cause testing.[31]

Seriously affecting the validity of drug testing is the proliferation of numerous cottage industries supporting efforts to foil detection in drug tests, including using others' urine (clean urine) as a substitute for one's own and using urine adulterants to fool the test.

The American Civil Liberties Union believes that workplace drug tests are often inaccurate, do not prevent drug use, and violate workers' right to privacy.[32]

Although illegal drugs or controlled substances, particularly opiates, cocaine, marijuana, amphetamines, and others, receive much attention, alcohol is, by far, the biggest substance abuse problem in society. A report by the Bureau of National Affairs estimates that one in twelve American workers abuses alcohol, more than double the abuse rates of marijuana, cocaine, and amphetamines combined. Financial estimates of alcohol-related losses sustained by U.S. employers range from $9 billion to as much as $150 billion annually. The U.S. Department of Health and Human Services has reported that alcohol is the leading cause of accidental death through motor vehicle crashes, falls, and fires. Alcohol abuse also leads to absenteeism, tardiness, higher health care costs, increased accidents and injuries at work, and reduced productivity. Some companies do screen prospective employees for intoxication.[33]

Financial Investigations

Financial investigations are conducted by proprietary investigating departments, contract investigative services, and private investigators. Many involve financial crimes and fraud and are covered later in the chapter. Others involve credit applications. Here are three examples of these investigations:

- *Due diligence investigations.* These investigations involve giving due diligence advice to companies contemplating entering into a business contract with another company or individual. (*Due diligence* means careful attention to details so that a company cannot be held liable for negligence.) These cases may involve a venture capitalist giving a loan to a prospective business, a franchisor lending money to a franchise, or a firm considering merging with another firm. The investigator checks out the subject's financial background, bill-paying history, and other financial dealings. In order to find this information, the investigator normally uses credit reporting agencies and national computerized databases.

- *Postjudgment collection.* These cases attempt to locate financial assets such as bank accounts, real estate, securities, and motor vehicles that the client can attach to settle a legal judgment prior to obtaining a writ of execution from the court to start a collection process.

- *Prejudgment investigation.* This occurs when an attorney is evaluating whether or not to take a case based on the possible damages that may be recovered. The investigator attempts to find the assets owned by the person the attorney's client wants to sue.

Product Liability

Corporations and private investigators investigate **product liability** cases—that is, lawsuits in which a client claims to have been injured by a certain product. A good recent example of product liability is the large number of lawsuits against Ford Motor Company and the Bridgestone-Firestone Tire Company that resulted in the recall of 6.5 million tires in August 2000. Investigators believe that three specific brands of Firestone tires caused accidents that left forty-six people dead and more than eighty injured. The tires were original equipment on two million Ford Explorer sport utility vehicles built since 1991. Investigators discovered

Product liability lawsuits involve clients who claim to have been injured by a certain product. Here, a woman in a lawsuit against the Bridgestone/Firestone Tire Company appears at an October 2000 press conference, showing the blown-out tire from her 2000 Ford Pickup.

that these tires were produced at Firestone's Decatur, Illinois, factory by replacement workers during a union work dispute.[34]

The investigator's job is to determine whether the product was up to current safety standards and if anyone involved with the product was negligent. Whether the product was defective depends on the current state of the art, and negligence depends on whether those involved in the product—from the manufacturer, to the distributor, to the retailer—did something they should not have done or didn't do something they should have done.

The investigator reviews the facts of the case to determine what happened and why it happened. The investigator also seeks to discover whether the product was involved in product liability complaints in the past. Because the product liability field can be quite technical and specialized, investigators often bring in experts or specialists in these cases. In addition, some investigators with previous experience in specialized fields, such as aviation or engineering, specialize in these cases.

Finding People—Missing Persons

Often investigators are hired to find people who are missing, have dropped out of sight, or are trying to hide. The police do not have the resources to fully investigate all missing person cases and generally concentrate their efforts on cases that are suspicious or indicate foul play, and on cases involving missing children and senile or disabled persons.

A private investigator may also be hired by a parent to locate a child taken in a custody dispute by the ex-spouse and removed to another jurisdiction outside of the court that is supervising the custody agreement. In these cases, the investigator may obtain a custody order from the court and proceed to attempt to locate the child, then travel to that location and execute the court order.

In a typical missing persons case, one of the first steps the investigator might take is to simply use the white pages of the telephone directory to see if there is a listing in the area where the person might be or might have fled to. Investigators also do name searches through public records to attempt to locate addresses and sometimes names of relatives, personal contacts, and business associates who might provide leads to the person's whereabouts. Some of these records may be marriage, divorce, voter registration, lawsuit, and real property records that

are accessible to all members of the general public, including investigators. Many investigators also access this information through national computerized databases from their personal computers.

Sexual Harassment

The U.S. Supreme Court has decided several cases on **sexual harassment** in the past decade. The general rule the Court has established is that employers could be held liable for both actual harassment and **hostile environment sexual harassment.** The Court affirmed this policy in 1998 in three cases when it ruled that employers may be held liable for a hostile environment created by a supervisor. The Court also declared that sexual harassment does not differentiate between genders and that males could be held liable for sexual harassment of males, and women for women. Some courts have applied the decisions to other unlawful forms of harassment, such as racial, religious, ethnic, and disability harassment.[35]

In 1999, the Equal Employment Opportunity Commission (EEOC) issued a series of guidelines for busi-

---

YOU ARE THERE!
Finding Someone on the Net: People-Finders

Since the great expansion of Internet use, there are myriad stories of people who have found lost relatives, friends, and others by using the search engines that serve as giant phone books and locating devices on their personal computer. People-finders exist on search engine sites and other Web sites and often can lead to someone's phone number, fax number, and e-mail address. Many of these sites even provide a map to the subject's house and listings of nearby neighbors, hotels, restaurants, and post offices.

This is all fine if you are the looker, but what if you do not want to be found? Most people-finder sites obtain their data from phone books that the search site obtains and either scans or retypes into its database. If you have an unlisted phone number it will not appear in these databases, but if the number was ever listed it may appear if an old phone book was used as

part of the database. Also, many public and corporate records are now being used by these sites to build their databases. Try one of these sites to find someone.

- Switchboard: http://www.switchboard.com
- Infospace: http://www.infospace.com
- Lycos: http://www.lycos.com
- Anywho: http://www.anywho.com
- Knowx: http://www.knowx.com
- Locateme: http://www.locateme.com
- 1–800-U.S. Search: http://www.1800ussearch.com
- People Finder: http://www.people-finder.com

SOURCE: Tina Kelley, "You Can Search, But Can You Hide?" *New York Times*, Nov. 26, 1998, p. G1.

YOU ARE THERE!

You, Too, Can Find Anybody

Private investigator Joseph Culligan, author of *You, Too, Can Find Anybody*, and an investigator for TV personality Montel Williams, gave a course in January 1999 in Nashville, Tennessee, to 160 private eyes, police officers, and skip tracers (they track folks who skip their debts) on the latest methods to find missing people. The course cost $225. Among the trade secrets Culligan shared was how to access alarm-system registrations, which are invariably public information and include the owner's name, phone numbers (listed or not), and next of kin. He also discussed searching dog licenses, other esoteric public records, and Internet searches.

SOURCE: "Hide and Seek: Gone Today, Here Tomorrow," *New York Times*, Jan. 17, 1999, p. WK13.

nesses to clarify what employers need to do to comply with the 1998 Supreme Court decisions. These guidelines mandate the following:

- Establish a sexual harassment policy.
- Post the policy.
- Investigate all cases promptly.
- Offer remedies to injured parties.
- Train employees to avoid harassing others.
- Create safeguards to prevent incidents of sexual harassment.

The EEOC stipulates that the investigation of all sexual harassment complaints should start within twenty-four hours after a complaint is received and should be completed as quickly as possible. At a minimum, the investigative process should include interviews with the victim, the alleged harasser, and all witnesses identified by either party. It also requires that copious notes documenting the investigative procedures and all results should be made and kept in an investigation file separate from employee personnel files. The company must report the results of the investigation in a timely manner to the employee who made the complaint.

Personal Injury

In personal injury cases the percentage of liability is determined by a jury or an expert, and evidence related to the extent of damages is presented using medical records and expert and victim testimony. The job of actually determining who was at fault often belongs to the private sector investigator hired by the attorney or insurance company.

In these cases investigators search for and interview witnesses, take photographs, and seek out additional information related to the incident. For example, in an auto accident the investigator looks for evidence of faulty road conditions, such as faulty paving, traffic signs blocked by overgrown trees, snow or ice conditions, improper lane markings, and the like. In cases involving injury while operating certain equipment or machinery the investigator attempts to identify the owner of the equipment and its manufacturer and any defects present. The investigator looks for facts that might have been missing from the police report and for witnesses that the police may have missed.

In vehicle accident cases, investigators engage in *accident reconstruction* analysis in an attempt to duplicate the events leading to the accident. The task of accident reconstruction has been simplified and enhanced in recent years with the help of computer simulations, which can be presented in a court hearing.

Wrongful Death

Often, people who don't believe a police or coroner's official report that someone's death was from natural causes or an accident or suicide will hire a private sector investigator to reopen the case. In these cases, the investigator will attempt to find new witnesses and sources, reinterview persons involved in the case, and do a much larger investigation than the public agency had time to do. The investigator may also hire a private forensic pathologist to reexamine the official reports. In cases involving accidental deaths in or by motor vehicles and other vehicles or those involving the operation of equipment, the investigator might solicit the assistance of a specialist to determine if there was product liability involving the vehicle or machinery for which the manufacturer, distributor, or retailer might be accountable.

Medical Malpractice

Private investigators may be hired by attorneys handling medical malpractice cases for a patient, doctor, or hospital. The investigator attempts to discover who is at fault for the malpractice. Could it be the doctor, hospital staff, paramedics? Could it be the result of an existing condition of the person? Could it be the result of an improper diagnosis by the doctor? In order to answer these questions the investigator interviews all persons involved in the case and reviews all the official documents and the past histories and records of the persons involved. The investigator might also hire medical experts to determine if the care given to a person was consistent with the current standard of medical care required to be given to people with that particular medical condition.

Domestic-Marital

Often people who believe that their spouses may be having an affair or cheating on them with another person hire private investigators to confirm these beliefs or to obtain evidence for a legal action. Generally, private investigators conduct a surveillance of the subject and attempt to obtain photographic evidence of the activities of the person and anyone with whom he or she is in contact.

Many investigators do not like to become involved in domestic or marital investigations because they can become very emotional and also involve an inordinate amount of time in surveillances and stakeouts. Furthermore, participating in such investigations can be a little like stepping into the middle of a soap opera.

Miscellaneous Services

Private investigators often become involved in numerous varied types of services for their clients, including executive and personal protection, security advice and crisis management, guard and patrol services, and service of subpoenas.

Executive and Personal Protection Often executives and celebrities hire private investigators to advise them on matters of personal security. They may also hire persons as personal bodyguards, sometimes referred to as chauffeurs, to accompany them through the course of their business and social activities. Private investigator licenses are generally not required for such employment; however, people hired in these roles tend to be former law enforcement officers because it is easier for them to obtain licenses to carry firearms in localities that have restrictive firearms regulations. Also, in localities that allow full-time police officers to work while off duty, many officers supplement their income in these roles.

Executive and personal protection has fueled the demand for bullet-resistant garments, defensive driving schools, bomb control, personal alert safety systems, personal protection devices, protection training, risk assessment services, and vehicle and travel security.

Security Advice and Crisis Management Very often private sector investigators, because of their experience and expertise, are hired as consultants by firms or individuals seeking advice in implementing security and contingency plans in the event of emergencies or crises. Consultants are problem solvers who generally bring a great deal of experience and competence to an assignment. Their contacts, resources, and independence contribute to their usefulness to clients.

Guard and Patrol Services Many private sector investigators combine their investigative services with guard and patrol services. The guard and patrol service is the largest component of the security industry in terms of revenues and number of persons employed. More people are employed as contractual security guards on a full-time basis than are employed by the public law enforcement sector. The security guard and patrol services market has grown steadily in the past two decades. Current growth comes from companies switching from proprietary security officers to those provided by an outside contractor. In recent years, the decline of law enforcement services relative to demand and high levels of reported crime has encouraged further growth of this industry. Many of these firms also offer investigative services and alarm and armored car services.

Service of Subpoenas Often courts or other government offices will hire a local private investigative firm to serve subpoenas to individuals requiring them to

CAREER FOCUS

Executive Protection

Entry-Level Position at Gavin de Becker

The private security firm of Gavin de Becker offers an entry-level executive protection position providing coverage to clients at their home or office, during travel, award shows, premiers, and so on. All candidates must have professional demeanor, excellent communication skills, excellent physical condition, and be trainable.

Benefits include paid medical, dental, vision, and a 401K retirement plan. The forty-eight-hour work-week is usually four twelve-hour days. We work twenty-four/seven. While we travel with clients all over the world, the majority of the work is here in Los Angeles. Employees must live in the L.A. area. There are annual performance reviews and salary increases.

The screening process includes a written test, a very difficult physical fitness test, videotaped oral interview, oral board, and so on.

SOURCE: LawEnforcementJobs.com; http://www.lawenforcementjobs.com/Job-apply.cfm?JobID=8145&lejsHeader=TRUE.

---

appear in court or at another government hearing. The local private investigator's knowledge of the community greatly assists him or her in locating and serving these subpoenas. Generally, the investigator is paid a fee for each subpoena served.

MAJOR TYPES OF PRIVATE SECTOR CRIMINAL INVESTIGATIONS

Although crimes and criminal investigations generally fall under the jurisdiction of the public police, private sector investigators often conduct criminal investigations for their corporations, businesses, or clients, corporate or private. In this section we will briefly discuss private sector investigations in the following criminal areas: violent and property crime, theft and fraud, insurance fraud, and industrial espionage.

It has been estimated that crimes against businesses total an estimated $90 billion, most of it due to employee theft and other forms of misconduct. As a result, corporations have established prevention and self-help strategies, as well as enforcement strategies to combat crime in the workplace.[36] Corporate crimes include those committed against corporations by officers, directors and employees (fraud, theft, embezzlement, corruption), crimes committed against corporations by external forces (robbery, burglary, larceny, piracy), and crimes committed for corporations by internal forces (regulatory noncompliance, tax evasion, bribery, and false financial statements).[37]

Violent and Property Crimes

The public police are generally called in to investigate serious violent and property crimes in the workplace. In addition, corporate investigation departments, contract security service companies, and private independent investigators may also investigate these crimes to apprehend the violator and to prevent a reoccurrence. Recall the discussions in chapter 10, "The Investigation of Violent Crimes" and chapter 11, "The Investigation of Property Crimes," of numerous programs to combat robberies and other crimes at banks, convenience stores and other business facilities.

In addition, contract investigative services and independent private investigators are often hired by clients to investigate crimes. These investigators only supplement the investigations done by police investigators and do not replace them.

Theft and Fraud

Theft of corporate assets can be devastating to businesses. It can include theft by outsiders or insiders. Employee theft can have a more devastating effect on retail businesses than victimization by burglars, robbers, and shoplifters. Specific measures to prevent employee theft are a drug-free workplace, preemployment screening, crime prevention and loss awareness, and employer-employee communications. Other crime prevention measures are inventory and money controls, target hardening (use of security devices, such as locks, gates, alarms, and the like), and use of professional consultants and vendors to enhance physical security. Companies also use aggressive undercover operations and proactive measures such as those described later in this chapter to deal with crime. Efforts to combat employee theft in retail businesses are covered at length in chapter 9, "Surveillance and Undercover Investigations." The tremendous amount of computer crime in business and industry and efforts to deal with this problem is discussed at length in chapter 14, "The Investigation of Computer Crime."[38]

Fraud is an enormous problem for U.S. businesses. In 1999, the American Institute of Certified Public Accountants issued a new auditing standard, titled SAS No. 82, to detail the auditor's responsibility to detect and report material misstatement in financial statements due to fraud. The two relevant types of misstatements are misstatements arising from fraudulent financial reporting and misappropriation of assets. Other considerations in preventing and detecting corporate fraud include managerial controls, employee screening, forensic accounting, and others.[39]

Private businesses use financial controls, preventative methods, and internal investigative teams to combat all types of fraud. Private security professionals can offer substantial assistance to public law enforcement officials by providing comprehensive and accurate investigative reports of incidents, and public law enforcement officials can also help businesses by providing suggestions on how to conduct investigations.[40]

A survey of five thousand businesses, government agencies, and nonprofit agencies revealed the following average loss for each respondent as a result of employee fraud.

- Check fraud by employees, including forgeries and mail room theft, resulted in an average loss of $624,000, nearly twice the figure in a 1994 poll.

- Theft of company bank accounts by employees using ATM cards resulted in an average loss of $300,000, nearly double that of 1994.

- Theft and misuse of company credit cards resulted in an average loss of $1.1 million, triple that of 1994.

- Loss from employee expense account abuse resulted in an average loss of $141,000, nearly seven times more than in 1994.[41]

As an example of internal fraud and theft, recently a mail room clerk at a nonprofit foundation stole $650,000 in checks over three months, pawning them off to an intermediary for pennies on the dollar. The foundation did not know anything was wrong until students who had been awarded research grants started calling from schools around the world, asking when the money would arrive. The mail room clerk took the checks to a teller at a bank, who deposited them into false accounts.[42]

Banks use fraud investigators to look into merchant fraud and businesses hire fraud investigators to look into fraud by customers. For example, the First Data Corporation of Atlanta, which processes credit and debit card transactions as well as information related to financial transaction over the Internet, by check, and via wire transfer, aggressively investigates fraud with its own proprietary investigating department. In addition to their security investigations for First Data, these security investigators conduct field investigations for retailers and merchant fraud investigations for banks on a contract basis.[43]

Internal stealing generally starts in the mail room; but workplace theft is costliest when committed by high-ranking employees who tend to have access to large amounts of funds. The median loss from crimes by managers is $250,000, four times that of crimes by lesser employees. The median loss from owners and executives is $1 million, sixteen times that of their employees.[44]

Security professionals report that, in some ways, workplace thieves have become easier to catch through technology such as video cameras, decoys, and other tools. But computers, modems, and the Internet also offer employees new ways of tampering with financial records, transferring funds, and covering their tracks. Security professionals also report that there are several reasons why fraud is increasing. In the 1990s, for example, as labor shortages threatened growth, some companies eliminated preemployment screening to speed up hiring. Another reason is that with pressure to post record earnings quarter after quarter, many businesses have cut back on departments like accounting and security that help detect theft but do not generate revenue. Management looks at internal controls as cost centers, not profit centers.

Fraud examiners also attribute much of the recent wave of office criminality to the stock market boom that created hordes of overnight millionaires and some employees' resultant impatience with their occasional pay raise. Also, there is a widening gap between executive and worker compensation. Corporate chief executives earn an average four hundred times what their regular employees do. The disparity in pay has fueled discontent and eroded loyalty to such a degree that stealing on the job is often seen as acceptable behavior.

The Association of Certified Fraud Examiners (ACFE) reports that companies usually lose 6 percent of their annual revenues to employee theft. One consequence of the growth in employee theft has been a large gain in the number of fraud investigators. Membership in the ACFE, the principal professional group for fraud examiners, has increased to about twenty-five thousand in 2000, up from about eight thousand in 1992.

ACFE is dedicated to fighting fraud and white collar crime. With offices in North America and Europe and chapters around the globe, ACFE responds to the needs of antifraud professionals. It certifies qualified individuals as **Certified Fraud Examiners (CFEs),** who are trained in the highly-specialized aspects of detecting, investigating, and deterring fraud and white collar crime. Each member of the association designated as a CFE has earned certification after an extensive application process and after passing the uniform CFE examination.

These examiners come from various professions, including auditors, accountants, fraud investigators, loss prevention specialists, attorneys, educators, and criminologists. They gather evidence, take statements, write reports, and assist in investigating fraud in its varied forms. They are employed by most major corporations and government agencies and also provide consulting and investigative services. CFEs have investigated more than one million suspected cases of civil and criminal fraud. Another type of business fraud is the theft of **intellectual property rights** or counterfeiting. The manufacture and sale of counterfeit (**knock-off or copycat**) **goods** creates health and safety problems for consumers, economic losses for trademark owners, and criminal problems for society. Counterfeit products are estimated to constitute 3 to 6 percent of world trade. In some countries that do not have adequate protection against counterfeiting and piracy, the level of piracy in music and video recording is at 100 percent, and in other industries (books, computer programs) it has reached 95 percent.[45]

In order to protect consumers, to safeguard the intellectual property rights of trademark owners, and to ensure product integrity, companies and industry

representatives maintain alliances with law enforcement officials around the world in addition to other efforts they make to combat this problem. For example, the Calvin Klein Cosmetics Company uses aggressive countermeasure programs, including lobbying, to gain enforcement support. The company distributes product identification information to the worldwide law enforcement community to facilitate identification of suspected counterfeit products related to its registered trademarks. Organizations such as the World Customs Organization, the World Trade Organization, the World Intellectual Property Organization, and others assist in seeking effective legislative and enforcement protection for intellectual property rights worldwide.[46] In one example of the seriousness of piracy, the U.S. compact disk industry claims it lost $287 million in CD sales to piracy in 2000 in just one country alone: Malaysia.[47]

Medical fraud is also an extremely serious problem. Billions of dollars are lost each year in frauds against Medicare, Medicaid, and insurance and health maintenance organizations. As an example, in August 2000 Dr. Niels H. Lauersen, a well-known fertility specialist with a busy, celebrity-studded practice, had his medical license suspended by the New York State Department of Health, which declared him "an imminent danger to public health." Lauersen was charged with numerous counts of negligence, incompetence, fraudulent practices, and moral unfitness. He has also been prosecuted by the federal government for a fraud scheme in which he billed insurance companies for gynecological cases that actually involved fertility procedures.[48]

The International Association of Financial Crimes Investigators (IAFC) is a professional organization of

INVESTIGATIONS ON THE NET

- -

Association of Certified Fraud Examiners (ACFE)
http://www.cfenet.org

International Association of Financial Crimes Investigators
http://iafci.org

For an up-to-date list of Web links, go to http://info.wadsworth.com/dempsey

- -

law enforcement officers and special agents of the credit card industry that provides services and an environment within which information about financial fraud, fraud investigation, and fraud prevention methods can be collected and exchanged.

Insurance Fraud

Insurance investigations are a major part of the private sector investigating industry. Insurance company investigators and private investigators hired by insurance companies conduct surveillances on persons who may be engaged in **insurance fraud.** For example, a person may claim an injury from a work-related action and go on disability or workers' compensation or sue an employer. The investigator may follow the subject or conduct a clandestine stakeout in an attempt to gain evidence that the subject is not suffering from any work-related or accident-related injuries. Often investigators are able to photograph a subject performing some action, like mowing a lawn or dancing at a club, that would not be possible if the individual were actually suffering from the results of the alleged injuries.

Workers' compensation fraud is an ongoing problem that can cost businesses enormous sums of money if not handled properly. Management must act quickly after detecting the first signs that an employee may be

Insurance fraud is a serious problem in the U.S. Here, New York State Attorney General Eliot Spitzer shows a photograph of a car that was part of an insurance fraud scheme in New York State that cost state insurance companies $1 billion a year.

lying about a workplace injury to collect benefits. Waiting even a month or two can make it impossible to gather enough evidence. If the investigation is delayed, critical time-sensitive evidence of fraud through proper video surveillance will be missed. In addition, witnesses will no longer have fresh memories of the incident. Key elements of the investigation are the interview of witnesses, documentation of all injuries and conditions at the site of the injury, and document analysis. All reports prepared by the complainant, including medical and government reports, should be analyzed to determine if any inconsistencies exist.[49]

An excellent source for insurance fraud investigations is the National Insurance Crime Bureau (NICB). The NICB provides investigative services for insurers and law enforcement agencies in the investigation and prosecution of organized rings and persons or companies perpetrating insurance fraud.

The National Society of Professional Insurance Investigators (NSPII) is an organization established for the purpose of providing recognition, encouragement, and support to individuals involved in conducting insurance investigations. The NSPII sponsors seminars and workshops offering in-depth case management concepts and principles for fraud detection and prevention. It keeps its members aware of relevant legislative issues and actions and recent court decisions. It also serves as a resource center providing technical and legal information to the industry as it becomes available. Members include independent investigators, insurance company personnel, and attorneys.

Industrial Espionage

Espionage is the practice of spying to acquire information. The term *industrial espionage* refers to the practice of obtaining business or technological information through surreptitious means. This practice has long existed and is a growing concern today, especially in the defense, aerospace, manufacturing, microelectronics, and computer industries.

Corporations can obtain information about each other's business, operations, and technology legally through the Freedom of Information Act; by reading technical or business publications; or by attending trade shows and business conventions. They can obtain information semi-legally through employees who change jobs, and illegally through bribery or blackmail. Although the practice of industrial espionage is most commonly ascribed to industry, theft of scientific ideas and technological advances has been a problem among governments as well.

Industrial espionage is generally easy to carry out. Agents can install wiretaps or bugs; steal, buy, or transcribe documents; steal equipment; or simply observe with their own eyes. (As noted in an earlier chapter, a wiretap is a device put on a telephone system to intercept telephone conversations. A bug is a microphone that can intercept conversations in a room or other location.) Sometimes the agent is a *plant*—a person who is positioned in a target organization for an extended period of time—or an *insider*—a member of the targeted organization who has shifted loyalties and who produces information on a regular basis.

Many firms employ disreputable people to surreptitiously and illegally record or intercept phone calls or conversations in corporate meetings.

The other side of espionage is *counterespionage,* which is the prevention and thwarting of hostile espionage. Counterespionage uses some of the same methods as espionage itself. One method of disabling an adversary's espionage program is by planting one's own agent (a *mole*) into the adversary's espionage organization. Another method of thwarting espionage is sweeping any locations where important meetings and discussions are held, which includes using electronic means to locate and remove any wiretaps or bugs that might be present and using electronic devices to prevent the surreptitious recording of conversations. Sweeping operations have opened a whole

new field of employment for private security investigators with electronic or technical expertise. Also, counterespionage needs have developed a whole new industry providing space-age products in such areas as audio and video surveillance.

In an example of industrial espionage, in August 2000 a jury decided that the Walt Disney Company stole ideas for its Wide World of Sports complex at Walt Disney World from two businessmen and had to pay $240 million in damages to them. The jury found Disney guilty of fraud, theft of trade secrets, breaking an implied contract, and breaching a confidential relationship.[50]

Another significant example of possible industrial espionage was the celebrated case of former General Motors executive Jose Ignacio Lopez de Arriortua, who was accused of committing industrial espionage when he jumped to rival Volkswagen A.G. Lopez's actions sparked a bitter dispute between the automotive giants over trade secrets.[51]

A 1999 article shows the ease with which sensitive proprietary technical and personnel information can be obtained as a result of a company's insufficient access control and security procedures. The article's author, while doing research on a series of novels he intended to write on high-technology espionage, conducted an experiment in which he personally visited twelve high-tech companies of various sizes in a certain area in a northwestern state. In eleven of the twelve companies, he was able to penetrate the facilities and had numerous opportunities to steal sensitive proprietary information. He was able to roam the hallways and offices of the companies and freely chatted and received important proprietary information from employees and security guards. He was able to view important documents on workers' computers and on their desks. In only one company was he challenged by an alert receptionist who denied him entrance to the workplace. The author concluded that small companies need to take security more seriously.

> Throughout this project, I could have been stopped by a skeptical receptionist who need only have asked probing questions about the nature of my business and who I was there to see. A visitor sign-in program and a requirement that all visitors be escorted by the person with whom they have an appointment would also have deterred me. In addition, I would have been thwarted by an electronic access control system in which doors to various suites were locked.[52]

SUMMARY

Investigations are big business in the United States and the source of many jobs for students interested in such employment in the public and private sector. Students are urged to access the numerous corporate Web sites presented in chapter 1, this chapter, and other chapters to research the many job opportunities and the qualifications for obtaining them.

Public law enforcement is extremely busy providing traditional police and emergency services to our communities and cannot give sufficient attention to the many problems discussed in this chapter; furthermore, many of these issues are beyond the scope of public law enforcement.

Think about some of the critical public sector investigations we have discussed and consider some of the problems that would not be addressed if they were not conducted. Would you feel comfortable running a business if there were no professionals to investigate potential employees' backgrounds? Should we allow people using illegal drugs to work in our nation's industries? Who would investigate the critical issues such as personal injury, product liability, malpractice, industrial espionage, and insurance fraud that are beyond the legal scope of public law enforcement?

Reflect back on the case of Dr. Michael Swango. Don't you think we should investigate the backgrounds of people we are trusting with our lives?

LEARNING CHECK

1. Describe some of the major duties of a proprietary corporate security department's investigating unit.
2. Identify three types of investigative services or activities performed by a typical contract security services provider and give a brief description of each.
3. Identify and discuss the basic information that is verified in a preemployment background investigation.
4. Describe the steps you would take to investigate an allegation of sexual harassment at your business.
5. Discuss the extent of drug screening in industry.

APPLICATION EXERCISE

You are the regional manager of preemployment background investigations for a major contract security services company. Your company is under consideration to be hired by a large hospital in your area to conduct background investigations of all personnel they intend to hire. The hospital administrator tells you that the hospital has suffered significant liability damages in the past for misconduct and unprofessional conduct committed by employees. Several employees last year were arrested by the local police on charges of drug sales, drug possession, driving while intoxicated, and larceny. In addition, the hospital is suffering significant losses in its cafeteria and gift shop operations.

The hospital administrator asks you to prepare a brief report to her detailing the type of preemployment background investigations you are going to perform.

WEB EXERCISE

Search the Web and find the Web site of a major national contract investigating service provider. Use the Web site to find possible job opportunities for college graduates at their firm.

KEY TERMS

Certified Fraud Examiner (CFE)

contract security investigations

drug testing

hostile environment sexual harassment

industrial espionage

insurance fraud

intellectual property rights

knock-off or copycat goods

preemployment background screening

product liability

proprietary security investigations

sexual harassment

undercover (covert) operations

NOTES

Chapter 1

1. This history of investigating relies primarily on the following works: William G. Bailey, ed., *Encyclopedia of Police Science* (New York: Garland, 1989); Augustine Costello, *Our Police Protectors* (Montclair, NJ: Patterson Smith, 1972 [1885]); Arthur Griffiths, *Mysteries of Police and Crime*, Vol. 1 (New York: Putnam, 1899); Arthur L. Hayward, ed., *Lives of the Most Remarkable Criminals*, 2d ed. (New York: Dodd, Mead, 1927 [1735]); James D. Horan, *The Pinkertons: The Detective Dynasty That Made History* (New York: Crown, 1967); Sanford H. Kadish, *Encyclopedia of Crime and Justice* (New York: Free Press, 1983); Roger Lane, *Policing the City: Boston 1822–1885* (New York: Atheneum, 1971); Emanual H. Levine, *The Third Degree: A Detailed and Appalling Exposé of Police Brutality* (New York: Vanguard Press, 1930); Peter Laurie, *Scotland Yard* (New York: Holt, Rinehart, 1970); Jay Robert Nash, *Encyclopedia of World Crime* (Wilmette, IL: Crime Books, 1990); Patrick Pringle, *Hue and Cry: The Story of Henry and John Fielding and Their Bow Street Runners* (London: Morrow, 1965); Sir Leon Radiznowciz, *A History of English Criminal Law and Its Administration from 1750* (London: Stevens & Sons, 1948); Thomas Repetto, *The Blue Parade* (New York: Free Press, 1978); Quentin Reynolds, *Headquarters* (New York: HarperCollins, 1955); James F. Richardson, *The New York Police: Colonial Times to 1901* (New York: Oxford University Press, 1970); Jerome H. Skolnick and James J. Fyfe, *Above the Law: Police and the Excessive Use of Force* (New York: Free Press, 1993); Howard O. Sprogle, *The Philadelphia Police* (New York: AMS Press, 1974 [1887]); Philip J. Stead, *Vidocq: Picaroon of Crime* (London: Staples, 1953); George W. Walling, *Recollections of a New York Chief of Police* (New York: Caxton, 1887); Mark D. Warren, "The Early Years of the Detective Bureau," *Spring 3100* (Jan.-Feb. 1992).

2. Pringle, *Hue and Cry,* p. 81.

3. Repetto, *The Blue Parade*, p. 28.

4. Nash, *Encyclopedia of World Crime*, p. 3047.

5. Repetto, *The Blue Parade*, p. 29.

6. Mark H. Haller, "Chicago Cops, 1890–1925," in Carl B. Klockars, ed., *Thinking About Police: Contemporary Readings* (New York: McGraw-Hill, 1983), pp. 90–91.

7. Haller, "Chicago Cops," p. 98.

8. Haller, "Chicago Cops," p. 91.

9. Haller, "Chicago Cops."

10. Mark D. Warren, "Specialty Squads," *Spring 3100* (Nov.-Dec. 1992), p. 9.

11. Warren, "Specialty Squads," p. 9.

12. Warren, "Specialty Squads," p. 9.

13. Lawrence W. Sherman, "Police in the Laboratory of Criminal Justice," in Roger G. Dunham and Geoffrey P. Alpert, eds., *Critical Issues in Policing: Contemporary Issues in Policing*, 2d ed. (Prospect Heights, IL: Waveland Press, 1993), p. 78.

14. Peter Greenwood and Joan Petersilia, *The Criminal Investigation Process Vol. I: Summary and Policy Implications* (Santa Monica, CA: Rand Corporation, 1975).

15. Federal Bureau of Investigation, *Crime in the United States: Uniform Crime Reports, 1993* (Washington, DC: Federal Bureau of Investigation, 1994).

16. Bureau of Justice Statistics, *Reporting Crimes to the Police* (Washington, DC: National Institute of Justice, 1985).

17. Albert Reiss, *The Police and the Public* (New Haven, CT: Yale University Press, 1971).

18. Greenwood and Petersilia, *Criminal Investigation Process*.

19. Greenwood and Petersilia, *Criminal Investigation Process*.

20. Greenwood and Petersilia, *Criminal Investigation Process*, pp. vi–vii.

21. W. Spellman and D. K. Brown, *Calling the Police: Citizen Reporting of Serious Crime* (Washington, DC: Police Executive Research Forum, 1981).

22. Mark Willman and John Snortum, "Detective Work: The Criminal Investigation Process in a Medium-Size Police Department," *Criminal Justice Review, 9,* 1984, pp. 33–39.

23. National Advisory Commission on Criminal Justice Standards and Goals, *Police* (Washington, DC: U.S. Government Printing Office, 1983).

24. Donald F. Cawley et al., *Managing Criminal Investigations: Manual* (Washington, DC: U.S. Government Printing Office, 1977).

25. Ilene Greenberg and Robert Wasserman, *Managing Criminal Investigations* (Washington, DC: U.S. Government Printing Office, 1975); and Cawley, *Managing Criminal Investigations*.

26. Greenberg and Wasserman, *Managing Criminal Investigations*.

27. Greenberg and Wasserman, *Managing Criminal Investigations*.

28. William Morris and Mary Morris, *Morris Dictionary of Word and Phrase Origins* (New York: HarperCollins, 1988), p. 343.

29. Skolnick and Fyfe, *Above the Law*, p. 43.

30. Skolnick and Fyfe, *Above the Law*, p. 43.

31. Levine, *Third Degree*, p. 96.

32. National Commission on Law Observance and Enforcement, *Lawlessness in Law Enforcement* (Vol. 2 of the Wickersham Report). (Washington, DC: U.S. Government Printing Office, 1931.

33. *Brown v. Mississippi*, 297 U.S. 278 (1936).

34. *Miranda v. Arizona*, 384 U.S. 436 (1966).

35. Marcia Chaiken and Jan Chaiken, *Public Policing—Privately Provided* (Washington, DC: U.S. Government Printing Office, 1987);

William C. Cunningham and Todd H. Taylor, *The Hallcrest Report: Private Security and Police in America* (Portland, OR: Chancellor Press, 1985).

36. William C. Cunningham, John J. Strauchs, and Clifford W. Van Meter, *Private Security: Patterns and Trends* (Washington, DC: U.S. Government Printing Office, 1984), p. 1.

37. William C. Cunningham, John J. Strauchs, and Clifford Van Meter, *The Hallcrest Report II: Private Security Trends: 1970 to 2000* (Boston: Butterworth-Heinemann, 1990).

38. Sandy Granville Sheehy, "The Adventures of Harold Smith, Art Supersleuth," *Town and Country Monthly*, Oct. 1992, p. 118.

39. Dick Adler, "Brian Jenkin's Excellent Adventures," *Inc.*, Oct. 1991, p. 47.

40. Thomas Bancroft, "Growth Business," *Forbes*, Sept. 1992, p. 516.

41. Pamela Marin and Warren Kalbacker, "Love Dicks," *Playboy*, Jan. 1991, p. 102; Steven Edwards, "The Rush to Private Eyes: Wary Lovers Check Up on Partners," *Macleans'*, Mar. 1990, p. 49; Bill Colligan, "Just Dial 1-900-CHEATER," *Newsweek*, July 29, 1991, p. 58.

42. Peter Wilkinson, "The Big Sleazy," *Gentlemen's Quarterly*, Jan. 1992, p. 112.

43. L. J. Davis, "International Gumshoe," *New York Times Magazine*, Aug. 30, 1992, p. 46.

44. "Checking Out Prospective Mates: Check-a-Mate, a Private Detective Service," *USA Today Magazine*, Dec. 1990, p. 4.

45. Tom Dunkel, "Holy Sleuth Frees Innocent Souls," *Insight*, Feb. 4, 1991, p. 52.

46. Scott Shuger, "Public Eye," *New York Times Magazine*, Sept. 13, 1992, p. 56.

47. Mark Ivey, "Philip Marlowe? No. Successful? Yes," *Business Week*, Oct. 21, 1991, p. 60.

48. Amanda Gardner, "Corporate Eyes," *Inc.*, Nov. 1991, p. 61.

49. "Doggone? Bloodhound Ron Dufault Runs Around in Circles to Help Pet Owners Find Their Missing Pooches," *People Weekly*, Sept. 10, 1990, p. 151.

50. Ronnie Virgets, "Secret Services," *New Orleans Magazine*, Mar. 1992, p. 36.

51. U.S. Department of Labor, Bureau of Labor Statistics, *Occupational Outlook Handbook: Private Detectives and Investigators*; http://www.bls.gov/oco/ocos157.htm.

52. U.S. Department of Labor, *Occupational Outlook Handbook*.

53. Sam Brown and Gini Graham Scott, *Private Eyes: The Role of the Private Investigator in American Marriage, Business, and Industry* (New York: Citadel Press, 1991), p. i.

Chapter 2

1. John N. Ferdico, *Criminal Law and Justice Dictionary* (Minneapolis/St. Paul: West, 1992), p. 236.

2. John Ayto, *Dictionary of Word Origins: The Histories of More Than 8,000 English-Language Words* (New York: Little, Brown, 1990), p. 304.

3. James McCord, *The Litigation Paralegal* (Minneapolis/St. Paul: West, 1988).

4. Association of Trial Lawyers of America, *Anatomy of a Personal Injury Lawsuit: A Handbook of Basic Trial Advocacy*, 2d ed. (Washington, DC: Association of Trial Lawyers of America, 1981).

5. Peter R. DeForest, F. E. Gaenssien, and Henry C. Lee, *Forensic Science: An Introduction to Criminalistics* (New York: McGraw-Hill, 1983).

6. Lois Pilant, "Outfitting Your Detective Unit," *Police Chief*, Mar. 1992, p. 34.

7. Pilant, "Outfitting Your Detective Unit," p. 34.

8. Glenn A. Walp and Malcolm L. Murphy, "Criminal Investigation Assessment Unit," *FBI Law Enforcement Bulletin*, Dec. 1994, p. 8.

9. Wackenhut Corporation, *Wackenhut Annual Report* (Coral Gables: Wackenhut Corporation, 1994).

10. Irving J. Klein, *Constitutional Law for Criminal Justice Professionals* (Miami: Coral Gables Publishing, 1986).

11. Jack Kuykendall, "The Municipal Police Detective: An Historical Analysis," in Dennis Jay Kenney, ed., *Police and Policing: Contemporary Issues* (New York: Praeger, 1989), pp. 88–91.

12. See Maury Terry, *The Ultimate Evil: An Investigation into a Dangerous Satanic Cult* (New York: Doubleday, 1987).

13. Rick Bragg, "After a Far-Flung, Weeklong Search, the Bodies of Two Children Are Found Inside Her Car," *New York Times*, Nov. 4, 1994, pp. A1, A30.

14. James N. Gilbert, "Investigative Ethics," in Michael J. Palmiotto, ed., *Critical Issues in Criminal Investigation*, 2d ed. (Cincinnati: Anderson, 1988), pp. 7–14.

15. See, for example: Thomas Barker and David L. Carter, *Police Deviance* (Cincinnati: Anderson, 1986); S. Bok, *Lying: Moral Choice in Public and Private Life* (New York: Pantheon, 1978); Frederick A. Ellison and Michael Feldberg, eds., *Moral Issues in Police Work* (Totowa, NJ: Rowman and Allanheld, 1985); Joycelyn M. Pollock, *Ethics in Crime and Justice: Dilemmas and Decisions*, 3rd ed. (Belmont, CA: West/Wadsworth, 1998); W. Heffernan and T. Stroup, eds., *Police Ethics: Hard Choices in Law Enforcement* (New York: John Jay Press, 1985); Carl B. Klockars, "The Dirty Harry Problem," *Annals of the American Association of Political and Social Science*, Nov. 1980, pp. 33–37.

16. Gilbert, "Investigative Ethics," p. 14.

Chapter 3

1. Rebecca Kanable, "Earth's Clues: Outside Experts and Geophysical Techniques Help Locate Clandestine Grave Sites," *Law Enforcement Technology*, 27(4), Apr. 2000, pp. 40–44.

2. *Katz v. United States*, 88 S.Ct. 507 (1967).

3. *Mincey v. Arizona*, 98 S.Ct. 2408 (1978).

4. Kimberly A. Crawford, "Crime Scene Searches: The Need for Fourth Amendment Compliance," *FBI Law Enforcement Bulletin*, Jan. 1999, pp. 26–31.

5. *Illinois v. Rodriguez*, 110 S.Ct. 2793 (1990).

6. Crawford, "Crime Scene Searches."

7. Andrew W. Donofrio, "First Responder Duties: Responsibilities of the First Officer at a Crime Scene," *Law and Order*, Apr. 2000, pp. 117–122.

8. J. Peterson, S. Mihajlovic, and M. Gilliland, *Forensic Evidence and the Police: Effects of Scientific Evidence on Criminal Investigations* (Washington, DC: National Institute of Justice, 1984).

9. W. Bodziak, *Footwear Impression Evidence* (New York: Elsevier, 1990).

10. D. H. Garrison, Jr., "Protecting the Crime Scene," *FBI Law Enforcement Bulletin*, Sept. 1994, pp. 18–20.

11. L. Eliopulos, *Death Investigator's Handbook: A Field Guide to Crime Scene Processing, Forensic Evaluations, and Investigative Techniques* (Boulder, CO: Paladin, 1993).

12. Garrison, "Protecting the Crime Scene."

13. William D. Gifford, "A Crime Scene Vehicle for the 21st Century," *FBI Law Enforcement Bulletin*, Nov. 1994, pp. 6–7.

14. National Institute of Justice, *Crime Scene Search and Physical Evidence Handbook* (Washington, DC: National Institute of Justice, 1973), p. 15.

15. Robert H. Lloyd, "Crime Scene Documentation and Reconstruction," *Law and Order,* Nov. 1994, pp. 35–36.

16. Lloyd, "Crime Scene Documentation and Reconstruction."

17. National Institute of Justice, *Crime Scene Search and Physical Evidence Handbook.*

18. Samuel R. Rod, "Close-Range Photogrammetry," *Law Enforcement Technology*, 28(2), Feb. 2001, pp. 98–100.

19. Vernon Geberth, *Practical Homicide Investigation: Tactics, Procedures, and Forensic Techniques*, 2d ed. (Boca Raton, FL: CRC Press, 1992).

20. Christopher Ruddy, "Cops Made Photo Blunder at Foster Death Site," *New York Post*, Mar. 7, 1994, p. 16.

21. Ruddy, "Cops Made Photo Blunder at Foster Death Site," p. 16.

22. Lloyd, "Crime Scene Documentation and Reconstruction."

23. Lloyd, "Crime Scene Documentation and Reconstruction," p. 36.

24. Ronnie L. Paynter, "Painting a Picture: Two- and Three-Dimensional Diagrams and Animations Can Help Illustrate What Happened in a Crime or Accident," *Law Enforcement Technology*, 28(2), Feb. 2001, pp. 32–34, 36.

25. Association for Crime Scene Reconstruction, "Crime Scene Reconstruction"; http://www.acsr.com.

26. Tom Bevel, "Applying the Scientific Method to Crime Scene Reconstruction," *Journal of Forensic Identification*, 51(2), Mar.–Apr. 2001, pp. 150–162.

27. American Society for Industrial Security, *Basic Guidelines for Security Investigations* (Alexandria, VA: American Society for Industrial Security, 1986), p. 28.

28. Richard H. Fox and Carl L. Cunningham, *Crime Scene Search and Physical Evidence Handbook* (Washington, DC: National Institute of Justice, 1985).

29. Donna Rogers, "Chain of Custody Evidence Tracking," *Law Enforcement Technology* 27(4), Apr. 2000, pp. 32–38.

30. Monte Clark, "Gizmos and Gadgets for the Crime Scene," *Law Enforcement Technology* 27(3), Sept. 2000, pp. 82–85.

31. Mary C. Nolte, "The Role of the Photon in Modern Forensics," *Law and Order*, Nov. 1994, pp. 51–54.

32. International Association of Bloodstain Pattern Analysts, "What Is Bloodstain Pattern Analysis?"; http://www.iabpa.org.

33. Richard Saferstein, *Criminalistics: An Introduction to Forensic Science* (Englewood Cliffs, NJ: Prentice-Hall, 2001).

34. Herbert L. MacDonell, *Bloodstain Patterns*, rev. ed. (Elmira Heights, NY: Golas Printing, 1997). See also MacDonell, *Flight Characteristics and Stain Patterns of Human Blood* (Washington, DC: U.S. Government Printing Office, 1971).

35. Nolte, "Role of the Photon in Modern Forensics."

36. Bruce Wayne Hall, "The Forensic Utility of Soil," *FBI Law Enforcement Bulletin*, Sept. 1993, pp. 16–18.

37. Robert Hunt, "The Benefits of Scent Evidence," *FBI Law Enforcement Bulletin*, Nov. 1999, pp. 15–18.

38. Rebecca Kanable, "Matching Shoeprints a Feat for Software," *Law Enforcement Technology* 27(7), July 2000, pp. 124–128.

39. "Inside O. J. Simpson Inc.," *Newsweek,* Oct. 17, 1994, p. 39.

Chapter 4

1. *Brady v. Maryland*, 373 U.S. 83 (1963).

2. New York City Police Department, *Detective Guide* (New York: NYPD, 1993), procedure 204–11.

3. John N. Ferdico, *Federico's Criminal Law and Justice Dictionary* (St. Paul, MN: West, 1992), p. 375.

4. George E. Rush, *The Dictionary of Criminal Justice*, 3d ed. (Connecticut: Dushkin Publishing Group, 1991), p. 264.

5. For examples, see Clarice R. Cox and J. G. Brown, *Report Writing for Criminal Justice Professions* (Cincinnati: Anderson, 1992); John C. Hazelet, *Police Report Writing* (Springfield, IL: Charles C. Thomas, 1960); Robert C. Lewis and Lou E. Ballard, *Writing Effective Reports on Police Investigations* (Boston: Holbrook Press, 1978); John B. Wilson and Sean P. Hayes, *A Competence-Based Approach to Police Report Writing* (Englewood Cliffs, NJ: Prentice-Hall, 1984).

6. Wesley Blanchard, "Digital Dictation a Boon for Warwick," *Police Chief*, Mar. 1990, p. 53.

7. Dennis George, "Computer-Assisted Report Entry: Toward a Paperless Police Department," *Police Chief*, Mar. 1990, pp. 112–114.

8. Sharon Hollis Sutter, "Holmes . . . Still Aiding Complex Investigations," *Law and Order*, Nov. 1991, pp. 50–52.

9. Sutter, "Holmes," p. 52.

10. Lois Pilant, "Spotlight on Computerized Criminal Investigations," *Police Chief*, Jan. 1993, pp. 39–41.

Chapter 5

1. *Gideon v. Wainwright*, 372 U.S. 335 (1963); *Argersinger v. Hamlin*, 407 U.S. 25 (1972).

2. *Williams v. Florida*, 399 U.S. 78 (1970).

3. *Apodaca v. Oregon*, 406 U.S. 404 (1972).

4. *Weeks v. United States*, 232 U.S. 383 (1914).

5. *Mapp v. Ohio*, 367 U.S. 643 (1961).

6. Christopher Vail, "Presenting Winning Testimony in Court," *Law and Order*, June 1992, pp. 96–99.

7. Robert L. Donigan, Edward C. Fisher, et al., *The Evidence Handbook*, 4th ed. (Evanston, IL: Traffic Institute, Northwestern University, 1980), pp. 208–214.

Chapter 6

1. Marc H. Caplan and Joe Holt Anderson, *Forensic: When Science Bears Witness* (Washington, DC: National Institute of Justice, 1984).

2. Peter R. DeForest, N. Petraco, and L. Koblinsky, "Chemistry and the Challenge of Crime," in S. Gerber, ed., *Chemistry and Crime* (Washington, DC: American Chemical Society, 1983), p. 45.

3. Joseph L. Peterson, *Use of Forensic Evidence by the Police and Courts* (Washington, DC: National Institute of Justice, 1987).

4. Peterson, *Use of Forensic Evidence by the Police and Courts*.

5. Peterson, *Use of Forensic Evidence by the Police and Courts*.

6. David Johnston, "Report Criticizes Scientific Testing at FBI Lab: Serious Problems Cited," *New York Times*, Apr. 16, 1997, pp. A1, D23; Mireya Navarro, "Doubts About FBI Lab Raise Hopes for Convict: On Death Row, but Seeking a New Trial," *New York Times*, Apr. 22, 1997, p. A8.

7. "What's Wrong at the FBI? The Fiasco at the Crime Lab," *Time*, Apr. 28, 1997, pp. 28–35.

8. Belinda Luscombe, "When the Evidence Lies: Joyce Gilchrist Helped Send Dozens to Death Row," *Time*, May 21, 2001, pp. 37–40.

9. This history relies primarily on the following: Caplan and Anderson, *Forensic*; Frederick R. Cherrill, *The Finger Print System of Scotland Yard* (London: Her Majesty's Stationery Office, 1954); Peter R. DeForest, R. E. Gaensslen, and Henry C. Lee, *Forensic Science: An Introduction to Criminalistics* (New York: McGraw-Hill, 1983); Carroll Hormachea, *Sourcebook in Criminalistics* (Reston, VA: Reston Publishing, 1967); James W. Osterberg, *The Crime Laboratory* (Bloomington: Indiana University Press, 1968); Henry T. F. Rhodes, *Alphonse Bertillon* (New York: Greenwood Press, 1968 [1956]); Harry Soderman and John J. O'Connell, *Modern Criminal Investigation* (New York: Funk and Wagnalls, 1945); Jurgen Thorwald, *Century of the Detective* (New York: Harcourt, Brace, Jovanovitch, 1965); Thorwald, *Marks of Cain* (London: Thames and Hudson, 1965); Thorwald, *Crime and Science* (New York: Harcourt, Brace, Jovanovitch, 1967); Joseph Wambaugh, *The Blooding* (New York: William Morrow, 1989).

10. Peterson, *Use of Forensic Evidence by the Police and Courts*, p. 5.

11. This section relies primarily on information from F. Cunliffe and P. B. Piazza, *Criminalistics and Scientific Investigation* (Englewood Cliffs, NJ: Prentice-Hall, 1980); DeForest, Gaensslen, and Lee, *Forensic Science*; Lois Pilant, "Equipping a Forensics Lab," *Police Chief*, Sept. 1992, pp. 37–47; Richard Saferstein, *Criminalistics: An Introduction to Forensic Science*, 7th ed. (Englewood Cliffs, NJ: Prentice-Hall, 2001); Saferstein, *Forensic Science Handbook* (Englewood Cliffs, NJ: Prentice-Hall, 1993); Charles C. Wilber, *Ballistic Science for the Law Enforcement Officer* (Springfield, IL: Charles C. Thomas, 1977).

12. "Hey Buddy, Got a Match? New System Does for Bullets What AFIS Did for Prints," *Law Enforcement News*, Apr. 30, 1994, p. 1.

13. Terry L. Knowles, "Meeting the Challenges of the 21st Century," *Police Chief*, June 1997, pp. 39–43.

14. "ATF Tightens Screws on Illicit Gun Sales with Gun- and Bullet-Tracing Databases," *Law Enforcement News*, Feb. 14, 2000, pp. 1, 6.

15. Carl E. King, "Make Drug Testing a Positive Experience," *Security Management*, Nov. 1993, p. 25.

16. Robert D. McCrie, ed., *Security Letter Source Book* (New York: Security Letter, 1992), p. 62.

17. Richard A. Dusak, "Automated Handwriting Technology a Boon to Police," *Police Chief*, Jan. 1997, pp. 39–41.

18. Saferstein, *Criminalistics*.

19. Judith Martin, "The Power of DNA," *Law and Order*, May 2001, pp. 31–35.

20. Peter J. Neufeld and Neville Colman, "When Science Takes the Witness Stand," *Scientific American*, May 1990, p. 46.

21. Warren E. Leary, "Genetic Record to Be Kept on Members of Military," *New York Times*, Jan. 12, 1992, p. A15.

22. C. Thomas Caskey and Holly A. Hammond, *Automated DNA Typing: Method of the Future?* (Washington, DC: National Institute of Justice, 1997).

23. Federal Bureau of Investigation, *DNA Analysis;* http://www.fbi.gov/hq/lab/org/dnau.htm.

24. Knowles, "Meeting the Challenges of the 21st Century."

25. Federal Bureau of Investigation, *Combined DNA Index System (CODIS);* http://www.fbi.gov/hq/lab/org/systems.htm.

26. National Commission on the Future of DNA Testing, *Future of Forensic DNA Testing: Predictions of the Research and Development Working Group* (Washington, DC: National Institute of Justice, 2000).

27. Martin, "The Power of DNA."

28. Janet C. Hoeffel, "The Dark Side of DNA Profiling: Unreliable Scientific Evidence Meets the Criminal Defendant," *Stanford Law Review*, 42, 1990, p. 466.

29. *Frye v. United States*, 293 F. 1013 (D.C. Cir.) 1923.

30. "DNA Fingerprinting ID Method May Streamline Investigations," *Current Reports: BNA Criminal Practice Manual*, 1(19), 1987, p. 1.

31. Ronald Sullivan, "Appeals Court Eases Rules on Genetic Evidence," *New York Times*, Jan. 11, 1992, p. 8.

32. "Supreme Court Clarifies Ruling on Admitting Scientific Evidence," *Criminal Justice Newsletter*, Dec. 1, 1997, p. 1.

33. "DNA Typing Endorsed by National Academy of Sciences," *CJ Update*, Fall 1992, p. 1.

34. National Commission on the Future of DNA Evidence, *Future of Forensic DNA Testing*.

35. National Commission on the Future of DNA Evidence, *Future of Forensic DNA Testing*, p. 1.

36. National Commission on the Future of DNA Evidence, *Future of Forensic DNA Testing*, p. 3.

37. "The Truth Is in Your Genes," *Law Enforcement News*, Dec. 15, 2000, p. 7.

38. Rebecca S. Peterson, "DNA Databases: When Fear Goes Too Far," *American Criminal Law Review*, 37(3), Summer 2000, pp. 1219–1237.

39. National Commission on the Future of DNA Evidence, *What Every Law Enforcement Officer Should Know About DNA Evidence* (Washington, DC: National Institute of Justice, 2000).

40. National Institute of Justice, *Understanding DNA Evidence: A Guide for Victim Service Providers* (Washington, DC: National Institute of Justice, 2001).

41. Tod W. Burke and Jason M. Rexrode, "DNA Warrants," *Law and Order*, July 2000, pp. 121–124.

42. Michael H. West and Robert E. Barsley, "Ultraviolet Forensic Imaging," *FBI Law Enforcement Bulletin*, May 1992, p. 14; see also J. Michael Aaron, "Reflective Ultraviolet Photography Sheds New Light on Pattern Injury," *Law and Order*, Nov. 1991, p. 34.

43. Colleen Wade, "Forensic Science Information Resource System," *FBI Law Enforcement Bulletin, 57*, 1988, pp. 14–15.

44. Lois Pilant, "Crime Laboratory Developments," *Police Chief*, June 1997, p. 31.

45. FBI, "Fingerprint Identification: An Overview"; http://www.fbi.gov/hq/cjisd/ident.htm.

46. Curtis C. Frame, "Lifting Latent Prints in Dust," *Law and Order*, June 2000, p. 75; see also Frame, "Picking Up Latent Prints in Dust," *Police Chief*, Apr. 2000, p. 180.

47. "High-Tech Crime Hunters," *Popular Mechanics*, Dec. 1991, p. 30.

48. T. F. Wilson and P. L. Woodard, *Automated Fingerprint Identification Systems—Technology and Policy Issues* (Washington, DC: U.S. Department of Justice, 1987), p. 5.

49. Harold J. Grasman, "New Fingerprint Technology Boosts Odds in Fight Against Terrorism," *Police Chief*, Jan. 1997, pp. 23–28.

50. U.S. Congress, Office of Technology Assessment, *Criminal Justice: New Technologies and the Constitution: A Special Report* (Washington DC: U.S. Government Printing Office, 1988).

51. William Folsom, "Automated Fingerprint Identification Systems," *Law and Order*, July 1986, pp. 27–28.

52. Los Angeles Police Department, *Annual Report, 1985,* 1986, p. 26.

53. William Stover, "Automated Fingerprint Identification— Regional Application of Technology," *FBI Law Enforcement Bulletin, 53,* 1984, pp. 1–4.

54. Judith Blair Schmitt, "Computerized ID Systems," *Police Chief*, Feb. 1992, p. 35.

55. John Ryan, "AFIS Pays Big Dividends for a Small City," *Law and Order*, June 2000, pp. 70–72.

56. "Something for Everyone in High-Tech," *Law Enforcement News*, Dec. 15, 1998, p. 17.

57. "Mobile Identification Technology," *Law and Order*, June 2000, pp. 76–78; Stephen Coleman, "Biometrics: Solving Cases of Mistaken Identity and More," *FBI Law Enforcement Bulletin*, June 2000, pp. 9–16; Rebecca Kanable, "Grip on Identification Information," *Law Enforcement Technology*, 27(6), June 2000, pp. 122–126.

58. Tony Lesce, "Verafind AFIS System: Flexible and Software Based," *Law and Order,* Dec. 1994, pp. 53–54.

59. Rebecca Kanable, "Live-Scan Is Making Its Print," *Law Enforcement Technology*, 26(4), Apr. 1999, pp. 77–81.

60. FBI, *Integrated Automated Fingerprint Identification System (IAFIS)*; http://www.fbi.gov/hq/lab/org/systems. htm.

61. FBI, *Latent Print Unit*; http://www.fbi.gov/hq/lab/org/lpu.htm.

62. "INS, FBI Plan a $200M Wedding—of Their Fingerprint Databases," *Law Enforcement News*, Mar. 31, 2000, p. 7.

63. Dominic Andrae, "New Zealand Fingerprint Technology," *Law and Order*, Nov. 1993, pp. 37–38.

64. "NAFIS Launched in South Wales," *Law and Order*, June 2000, p. 74.

65. Tony Doonan, "Palmprint Technology Comes of Age," *Law and Order*, Nov. 2000, pp. 63–65.

66. Stephen Coleman, "Biometrics: Solving Cases of Mistaken Identity and More," *FBI Law Enforcement Bulletin*, June 2000, pp. 9–16.

67. J. A. West, *Facial Identification Technology and Law Enforcement* (Sacramento: California Commission on Peace Officer Standards and Training, 1996).

68. Visionics Corporation, *Adaptive Surveillance: A Novel Approach to Facial Surveillance for CCTV Systems, Final Progress Report* (Jersey City, NJ: Visionics Corporation, 2001).

69. Coleman, "Biometrics," p. 13.

70. Associated Press, "High-Tech Security on Tampa Streets," http://www.washingtonpost.com; Dana Canedy, "Tampa Scans the Faces in Its Crowds for Criminals," *New York Times,* July 4, 2001, p. A1.

71. John J. Pavlis, "Mug-Shot Imaging Systems," *FBI Law Enforcement Bulletin*, Aug. 1992, pp. 20–22.

72. Pavlis, "Mug-Shot Imaging Systems," p. 22.

73. Darrel L. Sanders, "The Critical Role of Technology," *Police Chief*, July 1997, p. 6.

74. "Picture This: Digital Photos Beam from Texas to Virginia via High-Tech Patrol Cars," *Law Enforcement News*, June 15, 1997, p. 1.

75. Coleman, "Biometrics."

76. "High-Tech Crime Hunters," p. 31; see also O'Donnell, "Forensic Imaging Comes of Age," *FBI Law Enforcement Bulletin*, Jan. 1994, pp. 5–10.

77. "High-Tech Crime Hunters"; see also O'Donnell, "Forensic Imaging Comes of Age..

78. "No More Pencils, No More Books?," *Law Enforcement News*, Jan. 31, 1998, p. 5.

79. "The Face Is Familiar—and Computer-Generated," *Law Enforcement News*, Oct. 31, 1999, p. 7.

80. For a comprehensive article on advanced surveillance devices, see Lois Pilant, "Achieving State-of-the-Art Surveillance," *Police Chief*, June 1993, pp. 25–34.

81. Pilant, "Achieving State-of-the-Art Surveillance."

82. Tom Yates, "Surveillance Vans," *Law and Order*, Dec. 1991, p. 52.

83. Yates, "Surveillance Vans," p. 53.

84. Bill Siuru, "Seeing in the Dark and Much More: Thermal Imaging," *Law and Order*, Nov. 1993, pp. 18–20.

85. Siuru, "Seeing in the Dark and Much More."

86. Tom Yates, "'Eyes' in the Night," *Law and Order*, Nov. 1993, pp. 19–24.

87. Donna Rogers, "Contraband Cops: U.S. Customs and Border Patrol Agents Stem the Tide of Smuggling with High-Tech Tools," *Law Enforcement Technology*, 27(4), Apr. 2000, pp. 68–72.

88. Ronnie L. Paynter, "Images in the Night: Law Enforcement Sheds Light on Applications for Night Vision Technologies," *Law Enforcement Technology*, 26(5), May 1999, pp. 22–26.

89. National Sheriffs' Association, "Law Enforcement Aircraft: A Vital Force Multiplier," *Sheriff*, 52(1), Jan.-Feb. 2000, pp. 32–60.

90. Donna Rogers, "GPS: Getting the Proper Positioning," *Law Enforcement Technology*, 27(9), Sept. 2000, pp. 44–50; see also, National Institute of Justice, *GPS Applications in Law Enforcement: The SkyTracker Surveillance System, Final Report* (Washington, DC: National Institute of Justice, 1998).

91. Keith Harries, *Mapping Crime: Principle and Practice* (Washington, DC: National Institute of Justice, 1999); Ron Mercer, Murray Brooks, and Paula T. Bryant, "Global Positioning Satellite System: Tracking Offenders in Real Time," *Corrections Today*, 62(4), July 2000, pp. 76–80; Bill Siuru, "Tracking 'Down': Space-Age GPS Technology Is Here," *Corrections Technology and Management*, 3(5), Sept.-Oct. 1999), pp. 1–14.

92. U.S. Congress, Office of Technology Assessment, *Criminal Justice: New Technologies and the Constitution*, 1988.

93. "High-Tech Crime Hunters," p. 31.

94. *California v. Ciraolo*, 476 U.S. 207 (1986).

95. Alan M. Dershowitz, *Taking Liberties: A Decade of Hard Cases, Bad Laws, and Bum Raps* (Chicago: Contemporary Books, 1988), p. 209.

96. "Police Chemist Is Rebutted After Man's Execution," *New York Times*, August 30, 2001, p. A12.

Chapter 7

1. *Brown v. Mississippi*, 297 U.S. 278 (1936).

2. Richard D. Morrison, "Interviews, Critical Component of Investigation: Know What to Ask, When to Ask It, and How to Ask It," *Law and Order*, Aug. 1993, p. 73.

3. Morrison, "Interviews, Critical Component of Investigation."

4. Diane M. Munson, "The Child Victim As a Witness," *Juvenile Justice Bulletin* (Washington, DC: National Institute of Justice, 1989), p. 1.

5. David Gullo, "Child Abuse: Interviewing Possible Victims," *FBI Law Enforcement Bulletin*, Jan. 1994, pp. 19–22. The author cites as references for his article *Interviewing Child Victims of Sexual Exploitation* (Arlington, VA: National Center for Missing and Exploited Children, 1987); Loraine Stern, M.D., "Your Child's Health, Children and Sex," *Woman's Day*, Aug. 1990; Ann Wolbert Burgess, R.N., D.N.Sc., *Sexual Assault of Children and Adolescents* (Lexington, MA: Heath, 1978); Kathleen Coulborn Faller, M.S., Ph.D., *Child Sexual Abuse: An Interdisciplinary Manual for the Diagnosis, Case Management, and Treatment* (New York: Columbia University Press, 1988).

6. Gullo, "Child Abuse: Interviewing Possible Victims," p. 19.

7. Kenneth R. Freeman and Terry Estrada-Mullaney, *Using Dolls to Interview Child Victims: Legal Concerns and Interview Procedures* (Washington, DC: National Institute of Justice, Jan.-Feb. 1988).

8. Joseph J. Gillen and Clifford E. Thermer, "DNA-Based Exonerations Warrant a Reexamination of the Witness Interview Process," *Police Chief*, Dec. 2000, pp. 52–57; see also, "Cognitive Approach Aids Interviewers," *Law Enforcement News*, Feb. 14, 1990, pp. 1, 6; Laura Olsen, "Cognitive Interviewing and the Victim/Witness in Crisis," *Police Chief*, Feb. 1991, pp. 28–32; "Interview Style Pays Off," *Law Enforcement News*, Feb. 14, 1990), pp. 1, 6; R. Edward Geiselman,

"Enhancement of Eyewitness Memory: An Empirical Evaluation of the Cognitive Interview," *Journal of Police Science and Administration*, 12(1), 1984; R. Edward Geiselman, "Eyewitness Memory Enhancement in the Police Interview: Cognitive Retrieval Mnemonics Versus Hypnosis," *Journal of Applied Psychology*, 70(2), 1985, pp. 401–412; R. E. Geiselman and R. P. Fisher, "The Cognitive Interview: An Innovative Technique for Questioning Witnesses of Crime," *Journal of Police and Criminal Psychology*, 4(2), Oct. 1988.

9. R. Edward Geiselman and Ronald P. Fisher, *Interviewing Victims and Witnesses of Crime* (Washington, DC: National Institute of Justice, 1985), p. 3.

10. Geiselman and Fisher, *Interviewing Victims and Witnesses of Crime*.

11. Gillen and Thermer, "DNA-Based Exonerations Warrant a Reexamination of the Witness Interview Process."

12. Martin Reiser, "Hypnosis as a Tool in Criminal Investigation," *Police Chief*, Nov. 1976, pp. 36–40.

13. James N. Gilbert, *Criminal Investigation*, 3d ed. (New York: Macmillan, 1993).

14. Anne Cohen, "Hypnosis Under Attack," *Police Magazine*, July 1983, p. 38.

15. *Harding v. State*, 5 Md.App. 230, 246 A.2d 302 (1968).

16. *State v. Mack*, 292 N.W.2d 764 (1968).

17. *State v. Collins*, 296 Md. 670 (1983).

18. Alan W. Scheflin, "Hypnosis and the Courts: A Study in Judicial Error," *Journal of Forensic Psychology Practice*, 1(1), 2001, pp. 101–111.

19. E. K. Yager, "Hypnosis as an Investigative Tool," *Law Enforcement Quarterly*, Feb.-Apr. 1997, pp. 9–10.

20. E. G. Hall, "Watch Carefully Now: Solving Crime in the 21st Century," *Police*, June 1999, pp. 42–45.

21. Steven J. Lynn, Jeffrey Neuschatz, Rachael Fife, and Irving Kirsch, "Hypnosis in the Forensic Arena," *Journal of Forensic Psychology Practice*, 1(1), 2001, pp. 113–122; Scheflin, "Hypnosis and the Courts."

22. R. L. Ault, "Hypnosis: The FBI's Team Approach," *FBI Law Enforcement Bulletin*, Jan. 1980, pp. 5–8.

23. See T. M. Dees, "Polygraph Technology," *Law Enforcement Technology*, 22(7), July 1995, pp. 52–54; W. D. Holmes, "Interrogation," *Polygraph*, 24(4), 1995, pp. 237–258; J. A. Matte, *Forensic Psychophysiology: Using the Polygraph: Scientific Truth Verification: Lie Detection* (Williamsville, NY: J.A.M. Publications, 1996); Forensic Research, "Validity and Reliability of Polygraph Testing," *Polygraph*, 26(4), 1997, pp. 215–239.

24. Wayne W. Bennett and Karen M. Hess, *Criminal Investigation*, 4th ed. (Minneapolis/St. Paul: West, 1994) p. 248.

25. *Frye v. United States*, 54 App.D.C. 46, 293 F. 1013 (1923).

26. *State v. Bohner*, 210 Wis. 651, 246 N.W. 314 (1933).

27. *People v. Forts*, 18 N.C. (2d) 31 (1933).

28. Thomas E. Zehnle, "Polygraph Admissibility in the Post-Daubert Era," *Criminal Justice*, 12(2), Sept. 1997, pp. 11–13.

29. A. W. Whitworth, "Polygraph or CVSA: What's the Truth About Deception Analysis?" *Law and Order*, Nov. 1993, pp. 29–31.

30. Ronnie L. Paynter, "Detecting Deception: Polygraphists Give Tips on Getting at the Whole Truth," *Law Enforcement Technology*, 26(10),

Oct. 1999, pp. 86–88, 90, 92–94; Jonathan Marin, "He Said/She Said: Polygraph Evidence in Court," *Polygraph*, *29*(4), 2000, pp. 299–304; Robert J. Drdak, "Polygraph and Investigation, Perfect Partners: A Case Study," *Polygraph*, *29*(4), 2000, pp. 326–329.

31. F. Lee Bailey, Roger E. Zuckerman, and Kenneth R. Pierce, *The Employee Polygraph Protection Act: A Manual for Polygraph Examiners and Employers* (Severna Park, MD: American Polygraph Association, 1989); see also, James J. Kouri, "Federal Polygraph Law: A Blow to Private Security," *NarcOfficer*, May 1989, pp. 37–39; Hugh E. Jones, "Employee Polygraph Protection Act: What Are the Consequences?" *NarcOfficer*, May 1989, pp. 41–42; Norman Ansley, "A Compendium on Polygraph Validity," *NarcOfficer*, May 1989, pp. 43–48.

32. Whitworth, "Polygraph or CVSA."

33. Harold E. Russell and Allan Beigel, *Understanding Human Behavior for Effective Police Work* (New York: Basic Books, 1976).

34. Daniel Goleman, "Can You Tell When Someone Is Lying to You?" *Psychology Today*, Aug. 1982, p. 17, as cited in Charles G. Brougham, "Nonverbal Communications: Can What They Don't Say Give Them Away?" *FBI Law Enforcement Bulletin*, July 1992, p. 15.

35. Brougham, "Nonverbal Communications."

36. James W. Osterburg and Richard H. Ward, *Criminal Investigation: A Method for Reconstructing the Past* (Cincinnati: Anderson Publishing, 1992).

37. Colin Woods, "Making Confession Evidence Credible," *Crime Prevention Technology*, Apr. 1986, p. 1.

38. Louis DiPietro, "Lies, Promises, or Threats: The Voluntariness of Confessions," *FBI Law Enforcement Bulletin*, July 1993, pp. 27–32.

39. *McNabb v. United States*, 318 U.S. 332 (1943); *Mallory v. United States*, 354 U.S. 449 (1957).

40. *Escobedo v. Illinois*, 378 U.S. 478 (1964).

41. James A. Inciardi, *Criminal Justice*, 3d ed. (Orlando, FL: Harcourt Brace Jovanovich, 1990), pp. 280–281.

42. *Miranda v. Arizona*, 384 U.S. 436 (1966).

43. *Miranda v. Arizona*, 384 U.S. 436 (1966).

44. Alan M. Dershowitz, *Taking Liberties: A Decade of Hard Cases, Bad Laws, and Bum Raps* (Chicago: Contemporary Books, 1988), p. 10.

45. Dershowitz, *Taking Liberties*, p. 12.

46. *Harris v. New York*, 401 U.S. 222 (1971).

47. *Michigan v. Mosley*, 423 U.S. 96 (1975).

48. *Brewer v. Williams*, 430 U.S. 387 (1977).

49. *Nix v. Williams*, 467 U.S. 431 (1984).

50. *Rhode Island v. Innis*, 446 U.S. 291 (1980).

51. *New York v. Quarles*, 104 S.Ct. 2626 (1984).

52. *Moran v. Burbine*, 475 U.S. 412 (1986).

53. *Illinois v. Perkins*, 110 S.Ct. 2394 (1990).

54. *Pennsylvania v. Muniz*, 496 U.S. 582 (1990).

55. *Arizona v. Fulminante*, 111 S.Ct. 1246 (1991).

56. *Minnick v. Mississippi*, 111 S.Ct. 486 (1991).

57. *McNeil v. Wisconsin*, 111 S.Ct. 2204 (1991).

58. *Withrow v. Williams*, 112 S.Ct. 1745 (1993).

59. *Davis v. United States*, 114 S.Ct. 2350 (1994).

60. *Stansbury v. California*, 114 S.Ct. 1526 (1994); *Oregon v. Mathiason*, 429 U.S. 492 (1977).

61. *Dickerson v. United States* 20 S.Ct. 2326 (2000).

62. Sophia Y. Kil, "Supreme Court Cases: 1999–2000 Term," *FBI Law Enforcement Bulletin*, Nov. 2000, pp. 28–32.

63. Samuel C. Rickless, "Miranda, Dickerson, and the Problem of Actual Innocence," *Criminal Justice Ethics*, *19*(2), Summer-Fall 2000, pp. 2–55.

64. *Texas v. Cobb*, 121 S.Ct. 1335 (2001); see also Kimberly A. Crawford, "The Sixth Amendment Right to Counsel: Application and Limitations," *FBI Law Enforcement Bulletin*, July 2001, pp. 27–32.

65. Robert J. Fisher and Gion Green, *Introduction to Security*, 5th ed. (Boston: Butterworth-Heinemann, 1992), p. 134.

66. *State of West Virginia v. William H. Muegge*, 360 S.E. 216 (1987).

67. Kimberly A. Crawford, "Compelled Interviews of Public Employees," *FBI Law Enforcement Bulletin*, May 1993, p. 26.

68. *Garrity v. New Jersey*, 385 U.S. 493 (1967).

69. Crawford, "Compelled Interviews of Public Employees," p. 31.

70. *LaChance v. Erickson*, 118 S.Ct. 753 (1998).

71. Lisa A. Regini, "Supreme Court Cases: 1997–1998 Term," *FBI Law Enforcement Bulletin*, Oct. 1999, pp. 25–32; D. L. Schofield, "Ensuring Officer Integrity and Accountability," *FBI Law Enforcement Bulletin*, Aug. 1998, pp. 28–32.

72. David Vessel, "Conducting Successful Interrogations," *FBI Law Enforcement Bulletin*, Oct. 1998, pp. 1–6.

73. Michael R. Napier and Susan H. Adams, "Magic Words to Obtain Confessions," *FBI Law Enforcement Bulletin*, Oct. 1998, pp. 11–15.

74. DiPietro, "Lies, Promises, or Threats."

75. *Holland v. McGinnis*, 763 F.2d 1044, 1051 (7th Cir. 1992).

76. *Shedelbower v. Estelle*, 859 F.2d 727 (9th Cir. 1988).

77. *State v. Haywood*, 439 N.W.2d 511 (Nev. 1989).

78. *Florida v. Cayward*, 562 So.2d 347 (Fla. 1990).

79. *People v. Conte*, 365 N.W.2d 648 (Mich. 1985); *State v. Porter*, 455 N.W.2d 787 (Neb. 1990).

80. *Neil v. State*, 522 N.E.2d 912 (Ind. 1988).

81. *United States v. Nash*, 910 F.2d 749 (11th Cir. 1990).

82. *United States v. Scarpelli*, 713 F.Supp. 1144 (N.D. Ill. 1989.)

83. *State v. Holloman*, 731 P.2d 294 (Kan. 1987).

84. *Bruno v. State*, 574 So.2d 76 (Fla. 1991).

85. *Coates v. States*, 534 N.E.2d 1087 (Ind. 1989).

86. *Free v. State*, 732 S.W.2d 452 (Ark. 1987).

87. *McCarthy v. Bronson*, 683 F.Supp. 880 (D.Conn. 1988).

88. *Quandrini v. Clusen*, 864 F.2d 577 (7th Cir. 1989).

89. *Cooper v. Scroggy*, 845 F.2d 1385 (6th Cir. 1985).

90. *Lynumn v. Illinois*, 372 U.S. 528 (1963).

91. *U.S. v. Tingle*, 658 F.2d 1332 (9th Cir. 1981).

92. DiPietro, "Lies, Promises, or Threats," p. 31.

93. William A. Geller, *Police Videotaping of Suspect Interrogations and Confessions: A Preliminary Examination of Issues and Practices*

(Washington, DC: Police Executive Research Forum, 1993). This report is also the subject of William A. Geller, "Research Forum: Videotaping Interrogations and Confessions," *FBI Law Enforcement Bulletin*, Jan. 1994, pp. 24–27.

94. Kimberly A. Crawford, "Surreptitious Recording of Suspects' Conversations," *FBI Law Enforcement Bulletin*, Sept. 1993, pp. 26–32.

95. *Stanley v. Wainwright*, 604 F.2d 379 (5th Cir. 1979).

96. *Kuhlmann v. Wilson*, 106 S.Ct. 2616 (1986).

97. 263 Cal.Rptr. 747 (Cal.App. 2 Dist. 1989), 11 S.Ct. 102 (1991).

98. Crawford, "Surreptitious Recording of Suspects' Conversations."

Chapter 8

1. Ray K. Robbins, *Criminal Investigation Procedures* (Berkeley, CA: McCutchan Publishing, 1993), p. 96.

2. Gregory D. Lee, "Drug Informants: Motives, Methods, and Management," *FBI Law Enforcement Bulletin*, Sept. 1993, p. 15.

3. Lee, "Drug Informants," p. 14.

4. James E. Hight, "Working with Informants: Operational Recommendations," *FBI Law Enforcement Bulletin*, May 2000, pp. 6–9; see also Hight, "Avoiding the Informant Trap: A Blueprint for Control," *FBI Law Enforcement Bulletin*, Nov. 1998, p. 1.

5. James W. Osterburg and Richard H. Ward, *Criminal Investigation: A Method of Reconstructing the Past* (Cincinnati: Anderson, 1992), p. 297.

6. Federal Bureau of Investigation, *NCIC: National Crime Information Center;* http://www.fbi.gov/hq/cjisd/ncic.htm.

7. Federal Bureau of Investigation, *NICS: National Instant Criminal Background Check System;* http://www.fbi.gov/hq/cjisd/nics.htm.

8. John W. Fountain, "License Revoked for Small-Town Nosy Parkers: Car-Plate Books Fall Victim to Law," *New York Times*, Jan. 13, 2001.

9. The Freedom of Information Act appears in the U.S. Code at 5 U.S.C. 552. The law was amended in 1986 with the Freedom of Information Reform Act of 1986, Pub. L. No. 99–570, Section 1801–1804, 100 Stat. 3248 (1986).

10. Rebecca Daugherty, ed., *How to Use the Federal FOI Act*, 6th ed. (Washington, DC: FOI Service Center, 1987), p. 9.

11. Daugherty, *How to Use the Federal FOI Act.*

12. U.S. Department of Justice, *Making a FOIA Request;* http://www.usdoj.gov/04foia/04_.1.html, and http://www.usdoj.gov/04foia/index.html.

13. Stephen Labaton, "Data 'Brokers' Battle Critics of Deceptive Practices," *New York Times*, June 14, 1999, pp. 1, 6.

14. "Detective Couple Indicted Over Information Leaks," *New York Times*, June 27, 1999, p. 18.

15. Douglas Frantz, "Journalists or Detectives? Depends on Who's Asking," *New York Times*, July 28, 1999, p. A14.

Chapter 9

1. Sam Brown and Gini Graham Scott, *Private Eyes: The Role of the Private Investigator in American Marriage, Business, and Industry* (New York: Carol Publishing Group, 1991), p. 162.

2. Lois Pilant, "Achieving State-of-the-Art Surveillance," *Police Chief*, June 1993, p. 25.

3. Brown and Scott, *Private Eyes*, p. 144.

4. Pilant, "Achieving State-of-the-Art Surveillance," p. 25.

5. "Indiana: Decoy Hearse Used After Execution," *New York Times*, June 13, 2001, p. A31.

6. Brown and Scott, *Private Eyes*, p. 168.

7. Charles E. O'Hara and Gregory L. O'Hara, *Fundamentals of Criminal Investigation*, 6th ed. (Springfield, IL: Charles C. Thomas, 1994).

8. *Olmstead v. United States*, 277 U.S. 438 (1928).

9. *On Lee v. United States*, 343 U.S. 747 (1952); *Lopez v. United States*, 373 U.S. 427 (1963).

10. *Berger v. New York*, 388 U.S. 41 (1967).

11. *Katz v. United States*, 389 U.S. 347 (1967).

12. *Kyllo v. United States*, No. 99–8508 (2001).

13. S. Rep. No. 1097, 90th Cong., 2d Session; 18 U.S.C. 2510–2520.

14. S. Rep. No. 541, 99th Cong., 2d Session.

15. S. Rep. No. 402, 103d Cong., 2d Session; "No Tele-Phony Baloney: FBI Gets Its Wiretap Bill," *Law Enforcement News*, Nov. 15, 1994, pp. 1, 8.

16. Thomas D. Colbridge, "Electronic Surveillance: A Matter of Necessity," *FBI Law Enforcement Bulletin*, Feb. 2000, p. 25–31.

17. Eugene F. Ferraro, "How to Go Undercover," *Security Management*, June 2000, pp. 90–94; Ferraro, "Ordinary People," *Security Management*, June 2000, pp. 48–50, 99–101.

18. Gary T. Marx, "The New Police Undercover Work," *Urban Life*, Jan. 1980, pp. 399–446.

19. Clifford Krauss, "Undercover Police Ride Wide Range of Emotion: Boredom and the Adrenaline Rush," *New York Times*, Aug. 29, 1994, p. B3.

20. See James N. Gilbert, "Case Study: Donnie Brasco Infiltrates the Mob," in James N. Gilbert, ed., *Criminal Investigation: Essays and Cases* (Columbus, OH: Merrill, 1990), pp. 114–115.

21. John S. Dempsey, *Policing: An Introduction to Law Enforcement* (Minneapolis/St. Paul: West, 1994).

22. Marx, "The New Police Undercover Work."

23. Jennifer Steinhauer, "The Undercover Shoppers: Posing as Customers, Paid Agents Rate the Stores," *New York Times*, Feb. 4, 1998, pp. D1, D23.

24. John McNamara, "Helping Merchants Mind the Store," *Police Chief*, Oct. 1993, pp. 90–92.

25. U.S. Department of Labor, Bureau of Labor Statistics, *Occupational Outlook Handbook, 2000–2001;* http://www.bls.gov/oco/ocos157.htm.

26. Alan Kaminsky, "An Arresting Policy," *Security Management*, May 1999, pp. 59–61.

27. Read Hayes, "U.S. Retail Store Detectives: An Analysis of Their Focus, Selection, and Training," *Security Journal*, *13*(1), pp. 7–20.

28. James P. Tuttle, "A Training 'System' for Undercover Teams," *FBI Law Enforcement Bulletin*, May 1993, pp. 8–10.

29. Wayne W. Bennett and Karen M. Hess, *Criminal Investigation*, 3d ed. (St. Paul, MN: West, 1991).

30. James N. Gilbert, "Case Study: Donnie Brasco Infiltrates the Mob," in Gilbert, ed., *Criminal Investigation*, pp. 114–115.

31. James J. Ness and Ellyn K. Ness, "Reflections on Undercover Street Experiences," in Gilbert, ed., *Criminal Investigation*, pp. 110–111.

32. Brown and Scott, *Private Eyes*, p. 181.

33. George E. Rush, *The Dictionary of Criminal Justice*, 4th ed. (Guilford, CT: Dushkin Publishing Group, 1994).

34. *Jacobson v. United States*, 112 S.Ct. 1535 (1992).

35. Thomas V. Kukura, "Undercover Investigations and the Entrapment Defense: Recent Court Cases," *FBI Law Enforcement Bulletin*, Apr. 1993, p. 32.

Chapter 10

1. Federal Bureau of Investigation, *Uniform Crime Reports for the United States, 1999* (Washington, DC: Federal Bureau of Investigation, 2000).

2. Craig W. Meyer and Gary M. Morgan, "Investigative Uses of Computers: Analytic Time Lines," *FBI Law Enforcement Bulletin*, Aug. 2000, pp. 1–5.

3. Among the best books on death investigations are these (all published by CRC Press, Boca Raton, FL, 1992): Vernon J. Geberth, *Practical Homicide Investigation: Tactics, Procedures and Forensic Techniques*, 2d ed.; Dominick J. Di Maio and Vincent J. M. Di Maio, *Forensic Pathology;* Bal K. Jerath and Rajinder Jerath, *Homicide: A Bibliography*, 2d ed.

4. Richard D. Morrison, "Solving Homicide Cases: The Medical Examiner Can Provide Some Answers," *Law and Order*, Apr. 1994, p. 56.

5. Morrison, "Solving Homicide Cases."

6. Steven M. Houghlan, "Conducting Drug-Related Death Investigations," *Law and Order*, Apr. 1994, pp. 57–60.

7. Morrison, "Solving Homicide Cases."

8. C. L. Regini, "Cold Case Concept," *FBI Law Enforcement Bulletin*, Aug. 1997, pp. 1–6.

9. Ramesh Nyberg, "Investigations: Cold Case Squads Re-Activate Old Investigations," *Law and Order*, Oct. 1999, pp. 127–130.

10. Dru S. Fuller, "New Crime-Solving Technologies Help Close 'Cold Cases,'" *Criminal Law Update*, 7(4), 1999, pp. 4–7.

11. "Dark Side of Dating," *New York Times*, Aug. 5, 2001, p. WK2.

12. Kenneth R. Freeman and Terry Estrada-Mullaney, *Using Dolls to Interview Child Victims: Legal Concerns and Interview Procedures* (Washington, DC: National Institute of Justice, Jan.-Feb. 1988).

13. J. T. Hurley, "Violent Crime Hits Home: Home Invasion Robbery," *FBI Law Enforcement Bulletin*, June 1995, pp. 9–13.

14. ABT Associates, *New York City Anti-Crime Patrol: Exemplary Project Validation Report* (Washington, DC: U.S. Government Printing Office, 1974); and G. T. Marx, "The New Police Undercover Work," in C. B. Klockars, ed., *Thinking About Police: Contemporary Readings* (New York: McGraw-Hill, 1983), pp. 201–202.

15. Andrew Halper and Richard Ku, *New York City Police Department Street Crime Unit* (Washington, DC: U.S. Government Printing Office, n.d.).

16. Patrick J. McGovern and Charles P. Connolly, "Decoys, Disguises, Danger—New York City's Nonuniform Street Patrol," *FBI Law Enforcement Bulletin*, Oct. 1976, pp. 16–26.

17. "Miami Seeks to Aid Tourist-Crime Targets," *Law Enforcement News*, Oct. 31, 1991, p. 4.

18. Bernard Edelman, "Blending," *Police Magazine*, Sept. 1979, p. 53.

19. Anthony V. Bouza, *The Police Mystique: An Insider's Look at Cops, Crime, and the Criminal Justice System* (New York: Plenum Press, 1990), p. 93.

20. Bouza, *The Police Mystique.*

21. Ann Longmore-Etheridge, "Illusions of Grandeur: In Las Vegas, City of Illusions, the New Venetian Casino Has Created the Illusion of a City, But the Security Is No Chimera," *Security Management*, Sept. 1999, pp. 54–60.

22. Ann Longmore-Etheridge, "Digital Detecting," *Security Management*, Nov. 1999, pp. 24–25.

23. For information on this subject, see Monique C. Boudreaux, Wayne D. Lard, and Stephen E. Etter, "Child Abduction: An Overview of Current and Historical Perspectives," *Child Maltreatment*, 5(1), Feb. 2000, pp. 63–71; Wayne D. Lord, Monique C. Boudreaux, and Kenneth V. Lanning, "Investigating Potential Child Abduction Cases: A Developmental Perspective," *FBI Law Enforcement Bulletin*, Apr. 2001, pp. 1–10; Linda K. Girdner and Patricia M. Hoff, eds., *Obstacles to the Recovery and Return of Parentally Abducted Children* (Washington, DC: U.S. Department of Justice, 1994); S. E. Steidel, ed., *Missing and Abducted Children: A Law Enforcement Guide to Case Investigation and Program Management* (Arlington, VA: National Center for Missing and Exploited Children, 1994).

24. Ronnie L. Paynter, "Web of Deceit," *Law Enforcement Technology*, 27(7), July 2000, pp. 92–96.

25. Joseph B. Treaster, "Kidnapping with Money as the Only Object," *New York Times*, June 30, 2000, pp. A1, A6.

26. *Special Investigation Division Kidnapping Guidelines* (New York: New York City Police Department, 1991).

27. Federal Bureau of Investigation, *Child Abduction and Serial Killer Unit: Morgan P. Hardiman Task Force on Missing and Exploited Children* (Washington, DC: Federal Bureau of Investigation, n.d., NCJ # 167969).

28. Sabrina Feve and Cristina Finzel, "Trafficking of People," *Harvard Journal on Legislation*, 38(1), Winter 2001, pp. 279–290.

29. *United States v. Wade*, 388 U.S. 218 (1967).

30. *Kirby v. Illinois*, 406 U.S. 682 (1972).

31. *Stoval v. Denno*, 388 U.S. 293 (1967).

32. *United States v. O'Connor*, 282 F.Supp. 963 (D.D.C. 1968).

33. *United States v. Ash*, 413 U.S. 300 (1973).

34. *Schmerber v. California*, 384 U.S. 757 (1966).

35. *Winston v. Lee*, 470 U.S. 753 (1985).

36. *Schmerber v. California*, 384 U.S. 757 (1966).

37. *Winston v. Lee*, 470 U.S. 753 (1985).

38. *United States v. Dionisio*, 410 U.S. 1 (1973).

39. *United States v. Mara*, 410 U.S. 19 (1973).

40. "Eyewitness Evidence," *FBI Law Enforcement Bulletin*, July 2001, p. 15.

41. Thomas D. Elias, "LA's Crime Lab Shortage Delays DNA Testing: Thousands of Murders, Rapes Remain Unsolved in Backlog," *Newsday*, July 30, 2001, p. A16.

42. "A Decade Later, GMAC Shooting Still Resonates," *St. Petersburg Times*, June 18, 2000, p. 3B.

43. "Three Inspectors Killed at Sausage Factory," *St. Petersburg Times*, June 23, 2000, p. 4A.

44. Andrew G. Podolak, "Is Workplace Violence in Need of Refocusing?" *Security Management*, June 2000, pp. 151–152.

45. Bonnie S. Fisher, E. Lynn Jenkins, and Nicholas Williams, "Extent and Nature of Homicide and Non-Fatal Workplace Violence in the United States: Implications for Prevention and Security," in *Crime at Work: Increasing the Risk for Offenders*, Vol. II (Leicester, England: Perpetuity Press, 1998), pp. 65–82.

46. See, for example, Joseph A. Kinney, *Essentials of Managing Workplace Violence* (Charlotte, NC: National Safe Workplace Institute, 1995); D. W. Myers, "Workplace Violence Prevention Planning Model," *Journal of Security Administration*, *19*(2), 1996; and B. S. Michelman, P. Robb, and L. M. Coviello, "A Comprehensive Approach to Workplace Violence," *Security Management*, July 1998, pp. 28, 30–35.

47. Murray A. Straus, Richard J. Gelles, and Suzanne Steinmetz, *Behind Closed Doors: Violence in the American Family* (Garden City, NY: Anchor Press, 1980).

48. *Domestic Violence and the Police: Studies in Detroit and Kansas City* (Washington, DC: Police Foundation, 1977).

49. Federal Bureau of Investigation, *Uniform Crime Reports, 1990: Crime in the United States*.

50. Neil Websdale, Heather Moss, and Byron Johnson, "Domestic Violence Fatality Reviews: Implications for Law Enforcement," *Police Chief*, July 2001, pp. 65–74.

51. "Where New York's Anti-Crime Miracle Ends: Crime-Reduction Strategies Aren't Having as Much Impact on Domestic Homicide," *Law Enforcement News*, Apr. 30, 1997, p. 7.

52. T. S. Duncan, "Changing Perception of Domestic Violence," *Law Enforcement News*, Oct. 31, 1991, p. 13. The two books reviewed are Michael Steinman, ed., *Woman Battering: Policy Responses* (Cincinnati: Anderson, 1991), and Douglas J. Besharov, ed., *Family Violence: Research and Public Policy Issues* (Washington, DC: University Press of America, 1990).

53. Nancy Loving, *Responding to Spouse Abuse and Wife Beating: A Guide for Police* (Washington, DC: Police Executive Research Forum, 1980).

54. Lawrence W. Sherman and Richard A. Berk, *The Minneapolis Domestic Violence Experiment* (Washington, DC: Police Foundation, 1984).

55. Franklyn W. Dunford, David Huizinga, and Delbert S. Elliott, "The Role of Arrest in Domestic Violence Cases," *Criminology, 28*, 1990, p. 204.

56. Ellen G. Cohn and Lawrence W. Sherman, *Police Policy on Domestic Violence, 1986: A National Survey* (Washington, DC: National Institute of Justice, 1986).

57. National Institute of Justice, *Confronting Domestic Violence: A Guide for Criminal Justice Agencies* (Washington, DC: National Institute of Justice, 1986).

58. Eve Buzawa, "Police Officer Response to Domestic Violence Legislation in Michigan," *Journal of Police Science and Administration, 10*, 1982, 415–424.

59. "On the Other Side of the Law? Not Necessarily," *Law Enforcement News*, Dec. 31, 1996, p. 19.

60. John N. Douglas and Alan Burgess, "Criminal Profiling," *FBI Law Enforcement Bulletin*, Dec. 1986, pp. 9–23.

Chapter 11

1. Federal Bureau of Investigation, *Uniform Crime Reports for the United States, 1999* (Washington, DC: Federal Bureau of Investigation, 2000).

2. Federal Bureau of Investigation, *Uniform Crime Reports for the United States, 1999*.

3. George L. Kelling, "On the Accomplishments of the Police," in Maurice Punch, ed., *Control of the Police Organization* (Cambridge, MA: MIT Press, 1983), p. 164.

4. "Teens Face Array of Charges," *Tampa Tribune*, June 23, 2000, p. Metro 2.

5. Charles V. Bagli, "Business Group Fails to Mollify Giuliani: Grand Central District Shuffles Leaders, but Future Is Still Unclear," *New York Times*, Sept. 24, 1998, p. B5.

6. Terry Pristin, "Improvements on a Small Scale: Brooklyn BID Makes Strides Despite Its Modest Budget," *New York Times*, Feb. 20, 1999, pp. B1, B4.

7. Blaine Harden, "City Block Puts Its Thumbs to Work as Crime Busters," *New York Times*, Sept. 13, 2000, pp. A1, B3.

8. T. Budd, *Burglary of Domestic Dwellings: Findings from the British Crime Survey* (London: Great Britain Home Office, 1999).

9. M. Kruissink, "Commercial Burglary: The Offender's Perspective," *Security Journal*, *7*(3), Oct. 1996, pp. 197–203.

10. Federal Bureau of Investigation, "Toolmark Examinations," *Handbook of Forensic Services;* http://www.fbi.gov/hq/lab/handbook/examtool.htm.

11. David Kushner, "Stop, Thief! You've Got Mail: Alarm Systems Are Poised to Be the Command Centers of the Wired Home," *New York Times*, Mar. 9, 2000, p. G1; see also, Ellen Mitchell, "Getting Wired," *Newsday*, June 30, 2000, pp. C6, C7.

12. John S. Dempsey, *An Introduction to Policing*, 2d ed. (Belmont, CA: Wadsworth, 1999).

13. Gloria Laycock, *Property Marking: A Deterrent to Domestic Burglary? Crime Prevention Unit Paper No. 3* (London: Home Office, 1985); and Laycock, "Operation Identification, or the Power of Publicity," *Security Journal, 2*, 1991, pp. 67–72.

14. John Gochenouer, "Condo Can Do," *Security Management*, Jan. 2000, pp. 69–70, 115–119.

15. National Insurance Crime Bureau; http://www.nicb.org/services/hotspotsrelease.html.

16. C. Nee, *Car Theft: The Offender's Perspective* (London: Great Britain Home Office, 1993).

17. T. W. Burke and C. E. O'Rear, "Armed Carjacking: A Violent Problem in Need of a Solution," *Police Chief*, Jan. 1993, pp. 18–19, 21, 23–24.

18. Jerome H. Skolnick and David H. Bayley, *The New Blue Line: Police Innovation in Six American Cities* (New York: Free Press, 1986), pp. 100–101.

19. Andrew K. Ruotolo, Jr., "MDTs Aid Auto Theft Task Force," *Police Chief*, Sept. 1992, pp. 29–34.

20. "Car Sting Ring," *USA Today*, July 13, 1988, p. 3.

21. Robert D. McFadden, "FBI Sting: Hot Cars, Great Deals, Thirty Suspects," *New York Times*, Sept. 9, 1994, p. B1.

22. W. Oliver, "Tracking Stolen Cars with LoJack," *Law Enforcement Technology*, *22*(2), Feb. 1995, pp. 50–52.

23. P. Finn, L. Truitt, and L. Buron, *Opinions of 47 Auto Theft Investigators Regarding Automobile Component Parts Anti-Theft Labels* (Washington, DC: National Institute of Justice, 1996).

24. Frank Hart, "The Arson Equation: Arson + Circumstantial Evidence = Conviction," *Police Chief*, Dec. 1990, pp. 34–37.

Chapter 12

1. "Californian Arraigned in Death of Pilots," *New York Times*, Aug. 30, 2001, p. A14.

2. "Philadelphia Man Gets Prison Sentence for Feeding Cocaine to Baby," *APBnews.com;* http://www.APBnews.com.

3. Howard Abadinsky, *Drugs: An Introduction*, 4th ed. (Belmont, CA: Wadsworth, 2001).

4. Drug Enforcement Administration, *Drug Use in the United States;* http://www.dea.gov/concern/use.htm. The DEA cites the following as sources of its report: National Household Survey on Drug Abuse, National Center on Addiction and Substance Abuse Survey, Partnership for a Drug-Free America Survey, Substance Abuse and Mental Health Services Administration Survey, Arrestee Drug Abuse Monitoring Program, and the Office of National Drug Control Policy.

5. Substance Abuse and Mental Health Services Administration, National Household Survey on Drug Abuse (Washington, DC: Substance Abuse and Mental Health Services Administration, 2000); Drug Enforcement Administration, *Overview of Drug Use in the United States;* http://www.dea.gov/stats/overview.htm.

6. Office of National Drug Control Policy, *Factsheet: Key Findings from the 2000 DAWN Report;* http://www. whitehousedrugpolicygov. news/dawn2000_factsheet.html.

7. Jim Yardley, "Up to 18 May Have Died of Overdoses in Houston," *New York Times*, Aug. 15, 2001, p. A14.

8. Neil MacFarquhar, "Iran Shifts War Against Drugs, Admitting It Has Huge Problem," *New York Times*, Aug. 18, 2001, p. A1.

9. Drug Enforcement Administration, *Controlled Substances Uses and Effects;* http://www.dea.gov/concern/abuse/charts/chart4/contents.htm.

10. Drug Enforcement Administration, *Drugs of Abuse*; http://www.dea.gov/concern/abuse.

11. Office of National Drug Control Policy, *Strategic Goals and Objectives of the 2000 National Drug Control Strategy;* http://www.whitehousedrugpolicy.gov/publications/policy/99ndcs/goals.html.

12. Office of National Drug Control Policy, *Enforcement;* http://www.whitehousedrugpolicy.gov/enforce/enforce.html.

13. U.S. Customs, *Seizure Data: Fiscal Year 2000;* http://www.customs.treas.gov/enforcement/hardline/int00s.htm.

14. U.S. Customs, *Canine Enforcement Program;* http://www.customs.treas.gov/enforcem/k9.htm.

15. U.S. Coast Guard, *Drug Interdiction;* http://www.uscg.mil/hq/g-o/g-opl/mle/drugs.htm.

16. New York City Police Department, *Organized Crime Control Bureau: Narcotics Division;* http://www.ci.nyc.ny.us/html/nypd/html/occb/narco2.html.

17. Texas Department of Public Safety; http://www.txcdps.state.tx.us.

18. Juan Forero, "U.S. Pilots Fight Coca in Colombia: But Risky Role for Civilians Causes Unease Among Politicians," *New York Times*, Aug. 17, 2001, p. A8.

19. Interpol, *The Role of the Drugs Sub-Directorate;* http://www.interpol.com/public/drugs/default.asp.

20. Mark A. R. Kleiman, "Drug Enforcement and Organized Crime," *The Politics and Economics of Organized Crime* (Lexington, MA: Heath, 1985), pp. 67–87.

21. Abadinsky, *Drugs: An Introduction.*

22. Fox Butterfield, "Officials Say Increased Security Has Slowed Drug Smuggling," *New York Times*, Sept. 28, 2001, p. A16.

Chapter 13

1. Louis J. Freeh, "Responding to Terrorism," *FBI Law Enforcement Bulletin*, Mar. 1999, pp. 1–2.

2. "Terrorism," *Security Management*, July 2001, pp. 20–21.

3. John F. Lewis, Jr., "Fighting Terrorism in the 21st Century," *FBI Law Enforcement Bulletin*, Mar. 1999, pp. 3–10.

4. Office of Homeland Security, http://www.whitehouse.gov/response/faq-homeland.html; http://www.whitehouse.gov/news/releases/2001/10/20011008.html.

5. Office of Homeland Security; http://www.whitehouse.gov/deptofhomeland/.

6. Transportation Security Administration, http://www.tsa.gov/Agency/mission.htm; Office of Homeland Security, http://www.whitehouse.gov/homeland/six_month_update.html.

7. Office of Homeland Security, http://www.whitehouse.gov/homeland/six_month_update.html.

8. Lewis, "Fighting Terrorism"; Freeh, "Responding to Terrorism."

9. Bureau of Alcohol, Tobacco and Firearms, *ATF Online: Arson and Explosives: Programs;* http://www.atf.treas.gov/explarson/index.htm.

10. Federal Bureau of Investigation, www.fbi.gov/pressrel/speeches/speech052902.htm; http://www.fbi.gov/ page2/52902.htm.

11. Kevin Riley and Bruce Hoffman, *Domestic Terrorism: A National Assessment of State and Local Law Enforcement Preparedness* (Santa Monica: Rand Corporation, National Institute of Justice, 1995).

12. D. Douglas Bodrero, "Confronting Terrorism on the State and Local Level," *FBI Law Enforcement Bulletin*, Mar. 1999, pp. 11–18.

13. E. Meyr, "Tactical Response to Terrorism: The Concept and Its Application," *Law and Order*, Mar. 1999, pp. 44–47.

14. C. Roda, *Executive Safety* (Washington, DC: National Criminal Justice Reference Service, 1997).

15. Joel Carlson, "Critical Incident Management in the Ultimate Crisis," *FBI Law Enforcement Bulletin*, Mar. 1999, pp. 19–22.

16. Richard Bernstein, "Behind Arrest of Bomb Fugitive, Informer's Tip, Then Fast Action," *New York Times*, Feb. 10, 1995, p. 1.

17. Robert A. Martin, "The Joint Terrorism Task Force: A Concept That Works," *FBI Law Enforcement Bulletin*, Mar. 1999, pp. 23–27.

18. Martin, "The Joint Terrorism Task Force," p. 27.

19. Donald G. McNeil Jr., "The Dicey Game of Travel Risk: Anticipating the Unpredictable," *New York Times,* Mar. 7, 1999, Sec. 4, pp. 1, 4.

20. U.S. State Department, http://www.state.gov/; U.S. State Department, http://www.travelstage.gov/travel_warnings.html.

21. Joe Sharkey, "Tourists Stumble into the Line of Fire," *New York Times*, Apr. 30, 2000, p. WK 5.

22. "Finding Heroes Among the Wreckage: Five Are Hailed for Actions in Oklahoma City Bombing Aftermath," *Law Enforcement News*, Dec. 15, 1996, p. 7.

Chapter 14

1. K. W. Strandberg, "Cyber Crime Today," *Law Enforcement Technology*, 26(4), Apr. 1999, pp. 24–29.

2. "Internet Fraud"; http://www.Internetfraud.usdoj.gov., How Should I Deal With Internet Fraud?

3. Alex Berenson, "On Hair-Trigger Wall Street, a Stock Plunges on Fake News," *New York Times*, Aug. 26, 2000, pp. A1, C4; Berenson, "Suspect Is Arrested in Fake News Case," *New York Times*, Sept. 1, 2000, pp. B1, B5.

4. Neil MacFaraquhar, "Named a Market Swindler at Fifteen," *New York Times*, Sept. 22, 2000, pp. B1, B5.

5. Tracy Connor, "Cops: Mom Forced Kid into Cyberporn," *New York Post*, Aug. 25, 2000, p. 7.

6. David W. Chen, "Bronx Principal Arrested in Child Pornography Investigation," *New York Times*, Sept. 9, 2000, p. B2.

7. "'Pokey' Virus Infecting PCs," *Newsday*, Aug. 25, 2000, p. A65.

8. "A Hacker May Have Entered Egghead Site," *New York Times*, Dec. 23, 2000, p. C3.

9. Dequendre Neeley, "Protection Progress Report," *Security Management*, May 2000, p. 34.

10. Ron Stodghill, "Sipowicz Goes Cyber: As Internet Crime Proliferates, Local Cops—Most of Them Young—Pioneer a New Beat on the Web," *Time*, Apr. 10, 2000, p. 50.

11. "Online Poll," *ASIS Dynamics*, Nov.-Dec. 1999, p. 7.

12. D. L. Carter and A. J. Katz, "Computer Crime and Security: The Perceptions and Experiences of Corporate Security Directors," *Security Journal*, 7(2), July 1996, pp. 101–108.

13. R. Power, "CSI/FBI Computer Crime and Security Survey, 1997," *Computer Security Issues and Trends*, 3(2), Spring 1997.

14. "Computer Vulnerability Found at Federal Agency," *New York Times*, Aug. 13, 2000, p. 18.

15. "U.S. Agencies Get Failing Marks for Computer Security Systems," *New York Times*, Sept. 12, 2000, p. A21.

16. "Systems All Fouled Up," *Security Management*, June 2000, p. 14.

17. W. P. Williams, "National Cybercrime Training Partnership," *Police Chief*, Feb. 1999, pp. 17–27.

18. Williams, "National Cybercrime Training Partnership."

19. L. E. Quarantiello, *Cyber Crime: How to Protect Yourself from Computer Criminals* (Lake Geneva, WI: LimeLight Books, 1997).

20. Martin L. Forst, *Cybercrime: Appellate Court Interpretations* (San Francisco: Montclair Enterprises, 1999).

21. Federal Bureau of Investigation, "Congressional Statement on Cybercrime"; http://www.fbi.gov/congress/ congress00/ cyber032800.htm.

22. J. Drinkhall, "Internal Fraud," *Journal of Financial Crime*, 4(3), Jan. 1997, pp. 242–244.

23. Laura Pedersen-Pietersen, "The Hunt for Cybercrime," *New York Times*, Dec. 26, 1999, p. BU 8.

24. "Online Fraud," *Security Management*, Aug. 2000, p. 20; Internet Fraud Complaint Center; http://www.ifcc.fbi.gov.

25. U.S. Department of Justice, "Internet Fraud"; http:// www. Internetfraud.usdoj.gov.

26. Judith H. Dobrzynski, "FBI Opens Investigation of eBay Bids," *New York Times*, June 7, 2000, pp. C1, C22.

27. Deborah Kong, "Internet Auction Fraud Increases," *USA Today*, June 23, 2000, p. 3B.

28. Timothy L. O'Brien, "Officials Worried Over a Sharp Rise in Identity Theft: Internet's Role Is Cited," *New York Times*, Apr. 3, 2000, pp. A1, A19.

29. Matthew L. Lease and Tod W. Burke, "Identity Theft: A Fast-Growing Crime," *FBI Bulletin*, Aug. 2000, pp. 8–13.

30. S. Wexler, "Recovering Stolen Identities," *Law Enforcement Technology*, 26(4), Apr. 1999, pp. 36–39.

31. Lease and Burke, "Identity Theft."

32. "Insuring Against Identity Theft," *St. Petersburg Times*, June 18, 2000, p. 2H.

33. "Victims Describe Identity Theft," *Security Management*, Aug. 2000, p. 16.

34. Steven Levy and Brad Stone, "Hunting the Hackers," *Time*, Feb. 21, 2000, pp. 38–49.

35. M. A. Joyce and S. Barrett, "Evolution of the Computer Hacker's Motives," *Police Chief*, Feb. 1999, pp. 28–35.

36. Joyce and Barrett, "Evolution of the Computer Hacker's Motives."

37. Dequendre Neeley, "Hacktivism or Vandalism?" *Security Management*, Feb. 2000, p. 30.

38. A. Bequai, "Cyber Crime: The U.S. Experience," *European Journal on Criminal Policy and Research*, 4(4), 1996, pp. 119–122.

39. Dequendre Neeley, "You've Been Hacked. Now What?" *Security Management*, Feb. 2000, pp. 65–68.

40. Dequendre Neeley, "Underground Web Sites," *Security Management*, Jan. 2000, p. 34.

41. John M. Deirmenjiian, M.D., "Stalking in Cyberspace," *Journal of the American Academy of Psychiatry and the Law*, 27(3), 1999, pp. 407–413.

42. Marni Feather, *Internet and Child Victimization* (Woden Act, Australia: Australian Institute of Criminology, 1999).

43. National Institute of Justice, *Internet Crimes Against Children* (Washington, DC: National Institute of Justice, 2001).

44. Stodghill, "Sipowicz Goes Cyber."

45. Federal Bureau of Investigation, *Parent's Guide to Internet Safety* (Washington, DC: FBI, 1999); http://www.fbi.gov.

46. Debra Baker, "When Cyber Stalkers Walk," *ABA Journal*, *85*, Dec. 1999, pp. 51–54.

47. Paula Whitehead and Paul Gray, *Pulling the Plug on Computer Theft* (London: Great Britain Home Office, 1998).

48. Joe Sharkey, "A Rising Number of Laptop Computers Are Being Stolen at Airports by Organized Rings of Thieves," *New York Times*, Mar. 29, 2000, p. C10.

49. David Harley, "Living with Viruses: A Look at the Latest Virus Threats and Solutions," *Security Management*, Aug. 2000, pp. 88–94.

50. John Markoff, "A Disruptive Virus Invades Computers Around the World," *New York Times*, May 5, 2000, pp. Al, C9; see also, Brad Stone, "Bitten by Love: How the 'Love Bug' Went on a Worldwide Tear," *Newsweek*, May 15, 2000.

51. J. K. Hawkins, "Computer and Internet Crimes: Virtual Misdeeds That Cause Real Problems," *Sheriff*, Nov.-Dec. 1998, pp. 8–16.

52. James R. Richards, *Transnational Criminal Organizations, Cybercrime, and Money Laundering: Handbook for Law Enforcement Officers, Auditors, and Financial Investigators* (Boca Raton, FL: CRC Press, 1999).

53. Federal Bureau of Investigation, "Congressional Statement on Cybercrime"; http://www.fbi.gov/congress/ congress00/ cyber032800.htm.

54. R. L. Mendell, *Investigating Computer Crime: A Primer for Security Managers* (Springfield, IL: Charles C. Thomas, 1998).

55. Lois Pilant, "Electronic Evidence Recovery," *Police Chief*, Feb. 1999, pp. 37–48.

56. Sergio D. Kopelev, "Cyber Sex Offenders," *Law Enforcement Technology*, *26*(11), Nov. 1999, pp. 46–50.

57. Janet Reno, "Partners Against Crime," *Law Enforcement Technology*, *26*(12), Dec. 1999, pp. 62–66.

58. Ronnie L. Paynter, "Riding the Cyber Wave," *Law Enforcement Technology*, *26*(11), Nov. 1999, pp. 52–55.

59. Federal Bureau of Information, "Carnivore Diagnostic Tool"; http://www.fbi.gov/hq/lab/carnivore/carnivore. htm.

60. Scott Blake, "Protecting the Network Neighborhood," *Security Management*, Apr. 2000, pp. 65–71.

61. R. Godson, W. J. Olson, and L. Shelley, "Encryption, Computers, and Law Enforcement," *Trends in Organized Crime*, *3*(1), Fall 1997, pp. 82–83.

62. John Markoff, "Web Encryption Patent into Public Domain," *New York Times*, Sept. 7, 2000, p. C8.

63. Kathleen O'Brien, "Maybe They Should Just Send in a Camera Crew," *New York Times*, May 3, 2000, p. G1.

64. Lisa Guernsey, "You've Got Inappropriate Mail: Monitoring of Office E-Mail is Increasing," *New York Times*, Apr. 5, 2000, pp. C1, C10.

65. Charlotte Faltermayer, "Cyberveillance: Managers Are Increasingly Monitoring Employees' Computer Activity," *Time*, Aug. 14, 2000, pp. B22–B25

66. Faltermayer, "Cyberveillance."

67. "Did You Know That?" *Security Management*, Aug. 2000, p. 16.

68. Richard Willing, "Army's New Password: 'Biometrics': To Fight Hacks, Pentagon Turns to Body-Based ID Systems That Can't Be Faked," *New York Times*, June 22, 2000, p. 3A.

69. Laura Stiles, "Teacher Used Internet to Prey on Children," *Suffolk Life*, Oct. 3, 2001, pp. 23, 24.

Chapter 15

1. Robert D. McCrie, *Security Letter Source Book* (New York: Security Letter, 1994), p. 6.

2. E. R. Harris, "Planning an Investigative Strategy," *Security Management*, Nov. 1997, pp. 69–71.

3. Mike Freeman, "NFL Casts a Suspicious Gaze Over Prospects," *New York Times*, Apr. 11, 2000, pp. D1, D3.

4. "Securitas to Acquire Burns for $457 Million," *New York Times*, Aug. 4, 2000, p. C3.

5. Wackenhut Corporation; www.wackenhut.com/investig.html.

6. Henri E. Cauvin, "Wackenhut Set to Build New Prison in South Africa," *New York Times*, Aug. 12, 2000, p. C2.

7. Joseph B. Treaster, "Gumshoes with White Collars: Deal Spotlights New Shrewdness in Detective Business," *New York Times*, Aug. 29, 1997, p. D1, D4.

8. Karen M. Hess and Henry M. Wrobleski, *Introduction to Private Security* (Minneapolis/St. Paul: West, 1992).

9. Pamela A. Collins, Truett A. Ricks, and Clifford W. Van Meter, *Principles of Security and Crime Prevention*, 4th ed. (Cincinnati: Anderson, 2000).

10. M. B. Rosen, "Prescreen to Avoid Getting Burned," *Security Management*, Apr. 1993, pp. 38–40.

11. Patricia S. Jacobs, "Who's Minding the Guards?"; http://www. protect-mgmt.com/library/gards.html.

12. Jacobs, "Who's Minding the Guards?"

13. "Did You Know That?" *Security Management*, July 2000, p. 16.

14. McCrie, *Security Letter Source Book*.

15. John P. Beaudette, "The Truth Is Out There: Preemployment Screening," *Security Management*, Sept. 1999, pp. 135–140.

16. Frederick G. Giles, "Checking Credit When It's Due: Applicants Who Feel Discriminated Against Because of Their Credit History Can Bring a Lawsuit Against a Company," *Security Management*, June 2000, pp. 107–111.

17. "Background Checks," *Security Management*, May 2000, p. 21.

18. *Security Management*, Mar. 2000, p. 12.

19. John F. Kirch, "Screening for Drugs In-House," *Security Management*, June 2000, p. 22.

20. U.S. Department of Labor, *Employer's Guide to Dealing With Substance Abuse* (Washington, DC: U.S. Department of Labor, 1990); Eugene F. Ferraro, "Is Drug Testing Good Policy?" *Security Management*, Jan. 2000, p. 166.

21. *American Management Association Survey on Workplace Drug Testing and Drug Abuse Policies, 1996* (New York: American Management Association, 1996).

22. "DoT Proposes Drug Testing Changes," *Security Management*, Mar. 2000, p. 14.

23. Ferraro, "Is Drug Testing Good Policy?"

24. C. J. Dangelo, "Individual Worker and Drug Test: Tort Actions for Defamation, Emotional Distress and Invasion of Privacy," *Duquesne Law Review*, *28*, 1990, pp. 545–559.

25. J. M. Walsh, "Drug Testing in the Private and Public Sectors," *Bulletin of the New York Academy of Medicine*, *65*(2), Feb. 1989, pp. 166–172.

26. "Did You Know That?"

27. J. P. Hoffmann, C. Larison, and A. Sanderson, *Analysis of Worker Drug Use and Workplace Policies and Programs* (Washington, DC: National Institute of Justice, 1997).

28. B. A. Gropper, Jr., and J. A. Reardon Jr., *Developing Drug Testing by Hair Analysis* (Washington, DC: National Institute of Justice, 1993).

29. Kirch, "Screening for Drugs In-House."

30. Hallcrest Systems, Inc., *Combating Workplace Drug Crimes* (Washington, DC: National Institute of Justice, 1993).

31. Michael A. Gips, "Of Doctors and Drug Tests," *Security Management*, July 2000, pp. 15–16.

32. American Civil Liberties Union, *Workplace Drug Testing Is Ineffective and Unfair: Random Drug Tests Do Not Ensure a Drug-Free Workplace* (New York: American Civil Liberties Union, 1998).

33. Gary Winn and Thomas McDowell, "Waiting to Exhale: Security Must Understand How Breath Alcohol Detection Technologies Work and Their Relative Advantages and Drawbacks," *Security Management*, Nov. 1999, pp. 129–133.

34. Keith Naughton, "Throwing the Brakes on Tires That Peel Out: Firestone Issues a Recall as Accidents Pile Up," *Newsweek*, Aug. 21, 2000, p. 60; John Greenwald, "Firestone's Tire Crisis: Company Recalls 6.5 Million of Its Most Widely Used Tires," *Time*, Aug. 21, 2000, pp. 64–65.

35. Timothy S. Bland, "Get a Handle on Harassment," *Security Management*, Jan. 2000, pp. 62–67.

36. S. H. Traub, "Battling Employee Crime: A Review of Corporate Strategies and Programs," *Crime and Delinquency*, *42*(2), Apr. 1996, pp. 244–256.

37. J. Bologna and P. Shaw, *Corporate Crime Investigation* (Woburn, MA: Butterworth-Heinemann, 1997).

38. W. L. Cotton, P. H. Cogan, and M. K. Dueppen, *Total Asset Protection: A Business Owner's Guide to Preventing Internal Theft* (Washington, DC: National Institute of Justice, 1994).

39. Barbara R. Farrell and Joseph R. Franco, "Role of the Auditor in the Prevention and Detection of Business Fraud: SAS No. 82," *Western Criminology Review*, *2*(1), 1999, pp. 1–11.

40. C. A. Bradford and C. E. Simonsen, "Need for Cooperative Efforts Between Private Security and Public Law Enforcement in the Prevention, Investigation, and Prosecution of Fraud-Related Criminal Activity," *Security Journal*, *10*(3), Sept. 1998, pp. 161–168.

41. Greg Winter, "Taking at the Office Reaches New Heights: Employee Larceny Is Bigger and Bolder," *New York Times*, July 12, 2000, pp. C1, C8.

42. Winter, "Taking at the Office."

43. Bob Degen, "Security Profit Potential," *Security Management*, Nov. 1999, p. 28.

44. Winter, "Taking at the Office."

45. Thomas Blumer, *Counterfeit (Copycat) Goods Under International Law and the Laws of Selected Foreign Nations* (Washington, DC: U.S. Library of Congress, 1996).

46. Alfred T. Checkett, "Can We Do More to Fight Counterfeiting?" *Security Management*, Feb. 1999, pp. 129–130. For an informative article on understanding copyright risks and the "fair use defense," see Pamela R. O'Brien, "Understanding Copyright Risks," *Security Management*, Apr. 1999, pp. 68–73.

47. Eric Ellis, "Digital Underground: Malaysia's Attempts to Fashion Itself into the Silicon Valley of Asia Are Threatened by a Booming Piracy Industry," *Time*, Aug. 14, 2000, p. B26.

48. Jennifer Steinhauer, "Fertility Doctor Loses License During Review," *New York Times*, Aug. 12, 2000, pp. B1, B6.

49. David Howard, "Painful Fall or Profitable Fraud?" *Security Management*, Feb. 2000, pp. 76–82.

50. "Jury Rules Disney Stole Sports Complex Idea," *New York Times*, Aug. 12, 2000, p. C3.

51. Ferdinand Protzman, "FBI Seeks German Help on Lopez," *New York Times*, June 28, 1994, p. D2.

52. E. G. Ross, "Corporate Espionage Can't Be This Easy: Industrial Espionage," *Security Management*, Sept. 1999, pp. 75–81.

GLOSSARY

accelerant detection canines   Dogs that can detect accelerants by scent.

accelerants   Materials that speed the progress of a fire.

adversarial system   The defense and the prosecution present their respective sides as vigorously as possible.

age-progression photos   Photographs that are "aged" through the use of computer software.

anatomically correct dolls   Dolls with all anatomical features, including sexual organs, used to interview children.

anthropometry   The use of body measurements to record the identity of arrested criminals.

arson   The willful and malicious burning or attempt to burn structures, vehicles, or property.

automated fingerprint identification systems (AFIS)   Computer-based fingerprint identification systems.

automated information systems   Database systems capable of storing and allowing for retrieval of information in any manner desired.

ballistics   The study of the motion of projectiles in flight.

Bertillon measurements   Measurements of parts of the body in eleven key locations to identify a person.

biometric identification   The use of physical characteristics to identify people.

biometrics   Capture of physical characteristics and conversion into data for storage.

blend   To become part of a surrounding environment or culture.

blending operations   Blending officers into their surroundings in an attempt to catch a criminal in the act of committing a crime.

bloodstain pattern analysis   The study of the origin, trajectory, and patterns of bloodstains.

body language   The display of certain body movements; may express deception or truthfulness.

Brady material   See discovery.

bugs   Concealed electronic devices placed in a premise to transmit conversations.

burglary   Unlawful entry into a structure to commit a crime.

burned   When an officer is discovered by the person under surveillance.

buy-and-bust   The apprehension of a drug seller upon the purchase of drugs.

canvass   Interviewing a large number of potential witnesses.

Carnivore   A device used by the FBI to intercept information through the Internet while ignoring what it is not authorized to collect.

case folder   A file used for the collection and organization of all investigation documents and records.

case management   The procedure for collecting, recording, organizing, and preserving investigative information.

certified fraud examiner (CFE)   Investigators who are certified to conduct fraud investigations.

chain of custody   The written record of the possession and control of evidence from the time it is collected to its final disposition. Stresses the accountability of all who handle the evidence and the receipting of all its movements.

chop shops   Garages that strip stolen cars of usable parts to repair damaged vehicles.

circumstantial evidence   Evidence that establishes a fact or circumstance from which the court may infer another fact at issue.

close, or tight tail   A person is under constant surveillance and the surveillant remains undetected.

CODIS   Combined DNA Index System.

cognitive interview   An interview technique used to enhance the accuracy of a witness's reports.

cold case investigations   The investigation of old, unsolved crimes.

common law   Unwritten legal precedents created through everyday practice and supported by court decisions.

competency   Competent evidence that is admissible, in contrast with that which is not.

computer viruses   Malicious software programs written to damage or harass other computer systems.

computer-aided investigation   Computer programs used to analyze criminal information and prepare investigative plans.

computerized case management   Computer software used to collect, record, and organize investigative information.

computerized report writing   Digital dictation systems for creation of written reports.

confidential informant   An informant who provides an investigator with confidential information about a past or future crime and does not wish to be known as the source.

contact   An investigator who maintains contact with the undercover officer.

contaminated   Destruction of pristine evidence.

contract security investigations   Contracted external companies that provide investigative and security services.

cover story   A fictitious explanation for one's presence or activities.

covert (undercover) operations   Undercover investigations.

crime scene   The geographic location where a crime has been committed; may be extensive.

crime scene reconstruction   Use of scientific methods, evidence, and reasoning to gain explicit knowledge of the series of events that surround the commission of a crime.

crime scene sketch   A crime scene sketch depicts the overall area, allowing coordination of photographs with location of the evidence.

crime scene unit   A unit of investigators trained to secure, analyze, and process crime scenes.

crime scene vehicle   A vehicle used by investigators; holds crime scene processing supplies.

criminal and noncriminal investigations   Investigations of criminal and noncriminal matters.

criminal personality profiling   Psychological profiling.

criminalist   A forensic scientist who examines physical evidence.

criminalistics   Scientific discipline directed to the recognition, identification, and evaluation of evidence.

criss-cross, or reverse directories   Directories that list phone numbers by street address.

cultivated sources   People who have special information about a crime.

cybercrime   An illegal act committed through use of computer technology.

cyberstalking   The harassment of others by computer.

cyberterrorism   Terrorism that initiates, or threatens to initiate, the exploitation of or attack on information systems.

decoy operations   The use of police officers as "victims," a proactive attempt to detect criminal activity.

direct evidence   Directly establishes the main facts at issue in a case.

discovery   Also commonly known in U.S. criminal procedure as "Brady material," in reference to the landmark U.S. Supreme Court case, *Brady v. Maryland* (1963) in which the Court ruled that a defendant is entitled to know certain evidence that the prosecutor has against him or her.

DNA profiling, or genetic fingerprinting   The matching of a suspect, victim, evidence, or location through DNA.

documentary evidence   Tangible writings, pictures, and audible sounds.

domestic terrorism   Terrorism committed by citizens of the United States.

domestic violence   Violence in the family or between husband and wife or partners.

drug testing   Drug screening of employees.

due process revolution   Due process guaranteed to suspects pursuant to Supreme Court decisions.

dumpster diving   Scavenging through garbage to retrieve personal identification material.

encryption   A method of encoding information to prevent illegal use.

entrapment   Inducing an individual to commit a crime he or she did not contemplate.

ethics   The practical, normative study of the rightness and wrongness of human conduct.

evidence   All the means by which an alleged fact is established or disproved.

ex parte order   A court order permitting electronic interception of communications.

explosives detection canines   Dogs that can detect explosives residues by scent.

fire walls   A software program that prevents entry into computer networks.

first responding patrol officer   The first police officer responding to a crime scene.

follow-up investigation   All aspects of the investigative process; see *latent investigation*.

follow-up report   Reports on each investigatory action performed in the follow-up investigation of the incident.

forensic death investigation   Actual determination of the cause of death and the manner and time of death.

forensic photogrammetry   Three-dimensional measurements of the real world made directly from photographs for use in court.

forensic psychophysiology   The belief that a person is under stress when telling a lie.

forensic science   The examination, evaluation, and explanation of physical evidence related to crime.

Freedom of Information Act (FOIA)   An act recognizing the public's right to know; it sets up a formal request procedure for access to government records.

French method of detective work   Clandestine methods against political and criminal suspects by use of informers.

global positioning system   A satellite system used to locate any position on the map.

hacking   The willful and malicious penetration of another computer system.

hacktivists   People who commit denial-of-service attacks, disseminate spam, and deface Web sites believing they are carrying out acts of civil disobedience.

header information   Personal information that is sold to marketers.

hearsay   Rumor, or secondhand information.

home security surveys   A survey to determine the security features of a home.

hostile environment sexual harassment A workplace that promotes or tolerates sexual harassment.

hypnosis A state between wakefulness and light sleep, allowing for complete relaxation and intense concentration.

IAFIS Integrated Automated Fingerprint Identification System

incendiary material Items used to produce fire, such as matches, candles, chemicals, and gases.

incident report The first official report prepared in a criminal investigation.

identify theft The criminal act of assuming another person's identity.

industrial espionage Covert collection of industrial secrets or processes.

infiltration Gaining entry into criminal organizations.

informant Someone who has special knowledge of a crime or incident or an ongoing criminal enterprise.

information brokers Private persons or corporations that provide detective databases to private investigators throughout the nation.

insurance fraud investigations Investigations involving health care, insurance, workers' compensation, and related areas of fraud.

integrity shoppers Undercover agents who test the integrity of retail personnel.

intellectual property rights Protective trademarks or copyrights of intellectual property.

interdiction The interception and seizure of drugs.

international terrorism Terrorism on an international level.

interrogation The interview of a suspect.

interview An interview of someone who may have knowledge helpful in solving a crime.

investigare Latin for "to search into."

investigation The systematic and thorough examination and inquiry into something or someone.

joint terrorism task force concept Use of single focused units that meld personnel and talent from various law enforcement agencies.

judicial notice Facts that do not need to be proven; facts accepted by the court.

kidnapping The detention and taking of people against their will.

knock-off, or copycat goods Counterfeited products.

latent investigation All aspects of the investigative process; also called *follow-up investigation*.

leads Clues or pieces of information that aid in the progress of an investigation.

loose tail The person being followed is not under constant surveillance, but the surveillant remains undetected.

loss prevention specialist Store detective.

mail drop A method used by undercover agents to leave information for other investigators.

manslaughter Voluntary manslaughter is an intentional killing but without malice; involuntary manslaughter is when a person causes a death unintentionally but recklessly.

materiality The significance and importance of evidence to the outcome of the case.

MCI (managing criminal investigations) A series of guidelines for patrol officers and investigators.

MDTs Mobile digital terminals

medical examiner, or coroner Person charged with the forensic death or medicolegal examination.

memetic viruses Hoaxes, chain letters, erroneous alerts.

Miranda **rules** Warnings that police must read to a person in custody prior to any interrogation.

modus operandi (MO) The method by which criminals commit their crimes.

MtDNA Mitochondrial DNA.

mug shot Standard method of photographing arrested suspects.

murder Illegal killings are usually called murder when they are premeditated, deliberate, intentional, and malicious.

mystery shoppers Agents who visit a store and observe the performance and operations of store personnel.

narcoanalysis The use of truth serum.

NCIC National Crime Information Center.

NCJRS National Criminal Justice Reference Service.

NEOTWY An acronym formed by using the last letter of when, where, who, what, how and why.

night vision devices High-tech devices used to aid vision in the dark.

official written reports Narrative reports prepared by investigators using a typewriter or word processor.

operation identification A proactive effort to identify personal property before theft.

opinion evidence Evidence that generally is inadmissible in court, with exceptions.

overt or covert investigations Overt investigations are conducted openly; covert investigations are conducted in secret.

paper trail A series of documents through which a person's actions can be followed.

patterns Similarities that may link particular cases or indicate that the same person is committing a series of crimes.

PCR Polymerase chain reaction

pedophiles Sexual offenders who receive gratification from sexual contact with children.

photographic log A log kept of all photographs taken of a crime scene.

physical dependence The physical need to continue using drugs.

plants Materials placed around an ignition device to feed the flame.

point of origin The location where a fire starts.

polygraph A mechanical device used to measure respiration, circulation, and galvanic skin response to aid in detecting deception in suspects.

portrait parlé Literally, speaking picture; a method of describing the human head in a very detailed manner.

preemployment background screening Screening of potential employees.

preformatted reports Reports prepared on forms made available by the investigator's agency.

preliminary investigation The initial inquiry into a reported crime.

presumptions Deductions in law that may be made from certain sets of facts.

pretexting Pretending to be someone else to obtain information.

prima facie evidence Evidence, standing alone, that is sufficient to establish a given fact.

primary, case, or lead investigator The criminal investigator responsible for the proper investigation of the crime scene.

pristine Original condition.

private investigators Private detectives who serve organizational and individual interests.

proactive investigation The use of proactive investigative techniques to detect offenders before they offend.

proarrest policies Policies governing the mandatory arrest of violent domestic offenders.

product liability Lawsuits in which a client claims to have been injured by a certain product.

proprietary security investigations In-house corporation or business security department investigations.

psychological dependence Mental dependency on a drug usage.

psychophysiological veracity The belief that a person is under stress when telling a lie; same as *forensic psychophysiology.*

public investigator An investigator working for local, state, or federal government agencies.

questors Investigative unit created in fifth-century Rome.

rape Traditionally, forced sexual intercourse by a man of a woman.

rape evidence kits A kit used to collect sexual assault evidence.

reactive investigation Investigation instigated on the basis of a complaint registered by a victim or client.

real evidence Tangible objects introduced at trial.

recalcitrant Reluctant, uncooperative.

relevance Evidence that tends to prove or disprove a fact in dispute; evidence with bearing on a case.

repeat offender programs (ROPs) Law enforcement efforts directed specifically at career criminals.

research revolution Research into the workings of the criminal justice system, particularly police organizations and policing, beginning in the 1960s.

RFLP Restricted fragment length polymorphism.

rough tail Surveillant is following someone, but it is not important if discovered by the subject.

rules of evidence A set of regulations that act as guidelines for judges, attorneys, and law enforcement personnel who are involved in the trials.

script kiddies Hackers with little technical knowledge; they follow directions prepared by someone else.

serial murder A series of murders committed by the same offender.

sexual assault Rape and other forcible sexual crimes.

sexual harassment Unwanted and uninvited sexual contact.

shadow A one-person surveillance

shopping services Services performed by undercover agents posing as customers to test the integrity and efficiency of retail business personnel.

shrinkage The reduction in inventory due to theft or diversion.

source control The controlling of drug production before its distribution.

stakeouts A method of watching a location or person.

store detective A private detective who investigates pilferage and theft.

STR Short tandem repeat.

subject The person being watched.

surveillance The covert observation of places, persons, and vehicles for the purpose of obtaining information about the identities or activities of subjects.

surveillant The person conducting the surveillance.

temporary headquarters A temporary location used to provide support and command direction to investigators.

terrorism The use of terrorist actions; one of the hallmarks of terrorism is indiscriminate victimization.

testimony The information provided to the court by a witness.

theories Beliefs about a case based on evidence, patterns, leads, and tips.

thief-takers Individuals who served as a form of private police in sixteenth-, seventeenth-, and eighteenth-century France and England.

third degree The use of torture to obtain confessions.

time line   An attempt to account for all the activities and whereabouts of the principals in a case during the time surrounding a murder.

tips   Leads provided by citizens that aid in the progress of an investigation.

tolerance   Ability to tolerate higher doses of drugs.

tracking devices   Devices used to locate and track vehicles.

trailers   Materials used to spread a fire.

travel advisories   An advisory by the government of countries not to visit.

travel warnings   A warning by the government about dangerous situations affecting travelers.

Trojan horses   Type of computer virus.

ultraviolet forensic imaging   The use of ultraviolet lights to enhance details in photographs.

undercover   Covert investigation of criminal activity.

vehicle identification numbers   Unique numbers assigned to a vehicle by the manufacturer.

vestigare   Latin for "to track or to trace."

weapons of mass destruction   Chemical substances, biological agents, and nuclear materials that can be used for unparalleled destruction.

Web attacks   Large amount of hostile activity targeted at one particular company.

Will West case   The identification case that placed fingerprint technology above that of anthropometrics.

wiretaps   A method to allow listening in on phone conversations.

workplace violence   Criminal misbehavior committed against people in the workplace.

worms   Computer viruses.

BIBLIOGRAPHY

Books

Abadinsky, Howard. *Drugs: An Introduction.* 4th ed. Belmont, CA: Wadsworth, 2001.

American Civil Liberties Union. *Workplace Drug Testing Is Ineffective and Unfair: Random Drug Tests Do Not Ensure a Drug-Free Workplace.* New York: American Civil Liberties Union, 1998.

American Management Association. *American Management Association Survey on Workplace Drug Testing and Drug Abuse Policies, 1996.* New York: American Management Association, 1996.

American Society for Industrial Security. *Basic Guidelines for Security Investigations.* Arlington, VA: American Society for Industrial Security, 1986.

Association of Trial Lawyers of America. *The Anatomy of a Personal Injury Lawsuit: A Handbook of Basic Trial Advocacy.* 2d ed. New York: The Association of Trial Lawyers of America, 1981.

Ayto, John. *Dictionary of Word Origins.* New York: Arcade, 1990.

Bailey, F. Lee, Roger E. Zuckerman, and Kenneth R. Pierce. *The Employee Polygraph Protection Act: A Manual for Polygraph Examiners and Employers.* Severna Park, MD: American Polygraph Association, 1989.

Bailey, William G., ed. *The Encyclopedia of Police Science.* New York: Garland, 1989.

Barker, Thomas, and David L. Carter. *Police Deviance.* Cincinnati, OH: Anderson, 1988.

Barnhart, Edward R., ed. *Physicians' Desk Reference: PDR.* Oradell, NJ: Medical Economic Co., 1994.

Bayley, David H. *Forces of Order: Police Behavior in Japan and the United States.* Berkeley: University of California Press, 1976.

Bennett, Wayne W., and Karen W. Hess. *Criminal Investigation.* 3d ed. St. Paul, MN: West, 1991.

———. *Criminal Investigation.* 4th ed. Minneapolis/ St.Paul: West, 1994.

Bodziak, W. *Footwear Impression Evidence.* New York: Elsevier, 1990.

Bok, S. *Lying: Moral Choice in Public and Private Life.* New York: Pantheon, 1978.

Bologna, J., and P. Shaw. *Corporate Crime Investigation.* Woburn, MA: Butterworth-Heinemann, 1997.

Bouza, Anthony V. *The Police Mystique: An Insider's Look at Cops, Crime, and the Criminal Justice System.* New York: Plenum Press, 1990.

Budden, Michael C. *Preventing Shoplifting Without Being Sued: Practical Advice for Retail Executives.* Westport, CT: Quorum Books, 1999.

Brown, Sam, and Gini Graham Scott. *Private Eyes: The Role of the Private Investigator in American Marriage, Business and Industry.* New York: Citadel Press, 1991.

Burek, Deborah M., et al., eds. *Encyclopedia of Associations.* 25th ed. Detroit, MI: Gale Research, 1991.

Burgess, Ann Wolbert. *Sexual Assault of Children and Adolescents.* Lexington, MA: D. C. Heath, 1978.

Calvi, James V., and Susan Coleman. *American Law and Legal Systems.* Englewood Cliffs, NJ: Prentice-Hall, 1989.

Carroll, John M. *Confidential Information Sources: Public and Private.* 2d ed. Boston: Butterworth-Heinemann, 1991.

Cherrill, Frederick R. *The Finger Print System of Scotland Yard.* London: Her Majesty's Stationery Office, 1954.

Clarke, Ronald V., ed. *Crime Prevention Studies.* Mains, NY: Criminal Justice Press, 1993.

Cohn, Ellen G., and Lawrence W. Sherman. *Police Policy on Domestic Violence, 1986: A National Survey.* Washington, DC: National Institute of Justice, 1986.

Collins, Pamela A., Truett A. Ricks, and Clifford W. Van Meter. *Principles of Security and Crime Prevention.* 4th ed. Cincinnati: Anderson, 2000.

Costello, Augustine. *Our Police Protectors.* Montclair, NJ: Patterson Smith, 1972 (orig. 1885).

Cox, Clarice R., and J. G. Brown. *Report Writing for Criminal Justice Professionals.* Cincinnati, OH: Anderson, 1992.

Cummings, John, and Ernest Volkman. *Goombata: The Improbable Rise and Fall of John Gotti and His Gang.* New York: Avon Books, 1990.

Cunliffe, F., and P. B. Piazza. *Criminalistics and Scientific Investigation.* Englewood Cliffs, NJ: Prentice-Hall, 1980.

Cunningham, William C., John J. Strauchs, and Clifford W. Van Meter. *The Hallcrest Report II: Private Security Trends: 1970 to 2000.* Boston: Butterworth-Heinemann, 1990.

Cunningham, William C., and Todd H. Taylor. *The Hallcrest Report: Private Security and Police in America.* Portland, OR: Chancellor Press, 1985.

Daugherty, Rebecca, ed. *How to Use the Federal FOI Act.* 6th ed. Washington, DC: The FOI Service Center, 1987.

DeForest, Peter R., F. E. Gaenssien, and Henry C. Lee. *Forensic Science: An Introduction to Criminalistics.* New York: McGraw-Hill, 1983.

Dempsey, John S. *Policing: An Introduction to Law Enforcement.* Minneapolis/St. Paul: West, 1994.

———. *An Introduction to Public and Private Investigations.* Minneapolis/St. Paul: West, 1996.

———. *An Introduction to Policing*. 2d ed. Belmont, CA: Wadsworth/West, 1999.

Dershowitz, Alan M. *Taking Liberties: A Decade of Hard Cases, Bad Laws and Bum Raps*. Chicago: Contemporary Books, 1988.

Di Maio, Dominick J., and Vincent J. M. Di Maio. *Forensic Pathology*. Boca Raton, FL: CRC Press, 1992.

Donigan, Robert L., et al. *The Evidence Handbook*. 4th ed. Evanston, IL: Traffic Institute, Northwestern University, 1990.

Dunham, Roger G., and Geoffrey P. Alpert, eds. *Critical Issues in Policing: Contemporary Issues in Policing*. 2d ed. Prospect Heights, IL: Waveland Press, 1993.

Eck, John E. *Managing Case Assignments: The Burglary Investigation Decision Model Replication*. Washington, DC: Police Executive Research Forum, 1979.

Eliopulos, L. *Death Investigator's Handbook: A Field Guide to Crime Scene Processing, Forensic Evaluations, and Investigative Techniques*. Boulder, CO: Paladin, 1993.

Elliston, Frederick A., and Michael Feldberg, eds. *Moral Issues in Police Work*. Totowa, NJ: Rowman and Allanheld, 1985.

Faller, Kathleen Coulborn. *Child Sexual Abuse: An Interdisciplinary Manual for the Diagnosis, Case Management and Treatment*. New York: Columbia University Press, 1988.

Feather, Marni. *Internet and Child Victimization*. Woden Act, Australia: Australian Institute of Criminology, 1999.

Ferdico, John N. *Criminal Law and Justice Dictionary*. St. Paul, MN: West, 1992.

Fischer, Robert J., and Gion Green. *Introduction to Security*. 5th ed. Boston: Butterworth-Heinemann, 1992.

Fishel, Edwin C. *The Secret War for the Union: The Untold Story of Military Intelligence in the Civil War*. New York: Houghton Mifflin, 1996.

Forensic Sciences Foundation, Inc. *Death Investigation and Examination: Medicolegal Guidelines and Checklists*. Colorado Springs, CO: Forensic Sciences Foundation, 1986.

Forst, Michael L. *Cybercrime: Appellate Court Interpretations*. San Francisco: Montclair Enterprises, 1999.

Foss, Donald J., and David T. Hakes. *Psycholinguistics*. Englewood Cliffs, NJ: Prentice-Hall, 1978.

Geberth, Vernon. *Practical Homicide Investigation: Tactics, Procedures and Forensic Techniques*. 2d ed. Boca Raton, FL: CRC Press, 1992.

Gerber, S., ed. *Chemistry and Crime*. Washington, DC: American Chemical Society, 1983.

Gilbert, James N. *Criminal Investigation*. 3d ed. New York: Macmillan, 1993.

———. *Criminal Investigation: Essays and Cases*. Columbus, OH: Merrill, 1990.

Gill, Martin, ed. *Crime at Work: Studies in Security and Crime Prevention*. Leicester: Perpetuity Press, 1994.

Goldstein, Herman. *Policing a Free Society*. Cambridge, MA: Ballinger Press, 1977.

Greenwood, Peter, and Joan Petersilia. *The Criminal Investigation Process: Summary and Policy Implications*. Santa Monica, CA: Rand Corporation, 1975.

Griffiths, Arthur. *Mysteries of Police and Crime*, Vol. 1. New York: G P. Putnam's Sons, 1899.

Hanley, Julian R., W. W. Schmidt, and Ray K. Robbins. *Introduction to Evidence and Court Procedures*. 2d ed. Berkeley, CA: McCutchan, 1991.

Hayward, Arthur L., ed. *Lives of the Most Remarkable Criminals*. 2d ed. New York: Dodd, Mead & Company, 1927 (orig. 1735).

Hazelet, John C. *Police Report Writing*. Springfield, IL: Charles C. Thomas, 1960.

Heffernan, W., and T. Stroup, eds. *Police Ethics: Hard Choices in Law Enforcement*. New York: John Jay Press, 1985.

Hess, Karen M., and Henry M. Wrobleski. *Introduction to Private Security*. St. Paul, MN: West, 1992.

Horan, James D. *The Pinkerton Story*. New York: Putnam, 1951.

Horan, James D., and Howard Swiggett. *The Pinkertons: The Detective Dynasty That Made History*. New York: Crown, 1967.

Hormachea, Carroll. *Sourcebook in Criminalistics*. Reston, VA: Reston Publishing, 1967.

Inciardi, James A. *Criminal Justice*. 3d ed. Orlando, FL: Harcourt Brace Jovanovich, 1990.

Jakobovits, L., and Murray S. Miron, eds. *Readings in the Psychology of Language*. Englewood Cliffs, NJ: Prentice-Hall, 1967.

Jerath, Bal K., and Rajinder Jerath. *Homicide: A Bibilography*. 2d ed. Boca Raton, FL: CRC Press, 1993.

Jonosik, Robert J., ed. *Encyclopedia of the American Judicial System*. New York: Scribner's, 1987.

Joseph, A., and H. Allison. *Handbook of Crime Scene Investigation*. Boston: Allyn & Bacon, 1989.

Kadish, Sanford H. *Encyclopedia of Crime and Justice*. New York: Free Press, 1983.

Kenney, Dennis Jay, ed. *Police and Policing: Contemporary Issues*. New York: Praeger, 1989.

Kinney, Joseph A. *Essentials of Managing Workplace Violence*. Charlotte, NC: National Safe Workplace Institute, 1995.

Klein, Irving J. *Constitutional Law for Criminal Justice Professionals*. 3d ed. Miami, FL: Coral Gables Publishing, 1992.

———. *Law of Arrest, Search, Seizure and Liability Issues: Principles, Cases and Comments*. Miami, Fl: Coral Gables Publishing Co., 1994.

Klockars, Carl B., ed. *Thinking About Police: Contemporary Readings*. New York: McGraw-Hill, 1983.

Klotter, John C. *Criminal Evidence*. 5th ed. Cincinnati, OH: Anderson, 1992.

Lane, Roger. *Policing the City: Boston 1822–1885*. New York: Atheneum, 1971.

Lapin, Lee. *How to Get Anything on Anybody: Book II*. San Mateo, CA: ISECO, Inc., 1991.

Laurie, Peter. *Scotland Yard*. New York: Holt, Rinehart and Winston, 1970.

Levine, Emanual H. *The Third Degree: A Detailed and Appalling Expose of Police Brutality*. New York: Vanguard Press, 1930.

Lewis, Robert C., and Lou E. Ballard. *Writing Effective Reports on Police Investigations*. Boston: Holbrook Press, 1978.

Loving, Nancy. *Responding to Spouse Abuse and Wife Beating: A Guide for Police.* Washington, DC: Police Executive Research Forum, 1980.

Lukas, J. Anthony. *Big Trouble: A Murder in a Small Western Town Sets Off a Struggle for the Soul of America.* New York: Simon & Schuster, 1997.

MacDonell, Herbert L. *Bloodstain Patterns.* rev. ed. Elmira Heights, NY: Golas Printing, 1997.

Marquis, Albert Nelson. *Who's Who in America, 1994.* Providence, NJ: Marquis Who's Who, 1993.

Martindale-Hubbell International Law Directory, 1994. Providence, NJ: Martindale-Hubbell, 1993.

Marwich, Christine M. *Your Right to Government Information.* New York: Bantam Books, 1985.

Matte, J. A. *Forensic Psychophysiology: Using the Polygraph: Scientific Truth Verification: Lie Detection.* Williamsville, NY: J.A.M. Publications, 1996.

McCord, J. *The Litigation Paralegal.* St. Paul, MN: West, 1988.

McCrie, Robert D. *Security Letter Source Book.* 5th ed. New York: Security Letter, 1994.

Medical Society of the State of New York. *Medical Directory of New York State 1993–1994.* Lake Success, NY: 1993.

Miron, Murray S., and A. P. Goldstein. *Hostage.* New York: Pergamon Press, 1979.

Montney, Charles B., Pamela Dundas, and Jolen Marya Gedridge, eds. *Directories in Print 1994.* Detroit, MI: Gale Research, 1993.

Morris, William, and Mary Morris. *The Morris Dictionary of Word and Phrase Origins.* New York: Harper, 1988.

Murphy, Harry J. *Where's What: Sources of Information for Federal Investigators.* New York: Quadrangle/New York Times, 1976.

Nash, Robert. *Encyclopedia of World Crime.* Wilmette, IL: Crime Books, 1970.

Nelson, Diana, and Santina Perrone. *Understanding and Controlling Retail Theft.* Woden Act, Australia: Australian Institute of Criminology, 2000.

Nieto, Marcus. *Public Video Surveillance: Is It an Effective Crime Prevention Tool?* Sacramento: California Research Bureau, 1997.

O'Hara, Charles E., and Gregory L. O'Hara, *Fundamentals of Criminal Investigation.* 6th ed. Springfield, IL: Charles C. Thomas, 1994.

Osterburg, James W. *The Crime Laboratory.* Bloomington: Indiana University Press, 1968.

Osterburg, James W., and Richard H. Ward. *Criminal Investigation: A Method for Reconstructing the Past.* Cincinnati, OH: Anderson, 1992.

Palmiotto, Michael J., ed. *Critical Issues in Criminal Investigations.* 2d ed. Cincinnati, OH: Anderson, 1988.

Pinkerton Investigative Services. *Investigation Department Training Manual.* Encino, CA: Pinkerton Security and Investigation Services.

Police Foundation. *Domestic Violence and the Police: Studies in Detroit and Kansas City.* Washington, DC: Police Foundation, 1977.

Pollock, Joycelyn. *Ethics in Crime and Justice: Dilemmas and Decisions.* 3d ed. Belmont, CA: West/Wadsworth, 1998.

Pringle, Patrick. *Highwaymen.* New York: Roy, 1963.

———. *Hue and Cry: The Story of Henry and John Fielding and Their Bow Street Runners.* London: Morrow, 1965.

———. *The Thief Takers.* London: Museum Press, 1958.

Punch, Maurice, ed. *Control of the Police Organization.* Cambridge, MA: MIT Press, 1983.

Quarantello, L. E. *Cyber Crime: How to Protect Yourself from Computer Criminals.* Lake Geneva, WI: LimeLight Books, 1997.

Radiznowciz, Sir Leon. *A History of the English Criminal Law and Its Administration from 1750.* (4 vols.). London: Stevens and Sons, 1948–1968.

Ragle, Larry. *Crime Scene.* New York: Avon, 1995.

Reiss, Albert. *The Police and the Public.* New Haven, CT: Yale University Press, 1971.

Repetto, Thomas. *The Blue Parade.* New York: The Free Press, 1978.

Ressler, Robert K., Ann W. Burgess, and John E. Douglas. *Sexual Homicide: Patterns and Motives.* Lexington, MA: D. C. Heath & Co., 1988.

Ressler, Robert K., and Tom Shachtman. *Whoever Fights Monsters: My Twenty Years Hunting Serial Killers for the FBI.* New York: St. Martin's Press, 1992.

Reynolds, Quentin. *Headquarters.* New York: Harper & Brothers, 1955.

Rhodes, Henry T. F. *Alphonse Bertillon.* New York: Greenwood Press, 1968 (orig. 1956).

Richards, James R. *Transnational Criminal Organizations, Cybercrime, and Money Laundering: Handbook for Law Enforcement Officers, Auditors, and Financial Investigators.* Boca Raton, FL: CRC Press, 1999.

Richardson, James F. *The New York Police: Colonial Times to 1901.* New York: Oxford University Press, 1970.

Robbins, Ray K. *Criminal Investigation Procedures.* Berkeley, CA: McCutchan Publishing, 1993.

Rush, George E. *The Dictionary of Criminal Justice.* 4th ed. Guilford, CT: Dushkin Publishing Group, 1994.

Russell, Harold E., and Allan Beigel. *Understanding Human Behavior for Effective Police Work.* New York: Basic Books, 1976.

Rutledge, Devallis. *Courtroom Survival: The Officer's Guide to Better Testimony.* Sacramento, CA: Custom Publishing Co., 1987.

Saferstein, R. *Criminalistics: An Introduction to Forensic Science.* 2d ed. Englewood Cliffs, NJ: Prentice-Hall, 1981.

———. *Forensic Science Handbook.* Englewood Cliffs, NJ: Prentice-Hall, 1988.

———. *Criminalistics: An Introduction to Forensic Science.* 5th ed. Upper Saddle River, NJ: Prentice-Hall, 1993

———. *Criminalistics: An Introduction to Forensic Science.* 7th ed. Upper Saddle River, NJ: Prentice-Hall, 2001.

Senna, Joseph J., and Larry J. Siegel. *Introduction to Criminal Justice.* 5th ed. St. Paul, MN: West, 1991.

Sennewald, Charles A. *Shoplifters v. Retailers: The Rights of Both.* New York: New Century Press, 2000.

Shaffer, Ron, Kevin Klose, and Alfred E. Lewis. *Surprise! Surprise!* New York: Viking, 1979.

Shearing, Clifford D., and Philip C. Stenning, eds. *Private Policing.* Newbury Park, CA: Sage, 1987.

Sherman, Lawrence W., and Richard A. Berk. *The Minneapolis Domestic Violence Experiment.* Washington, DC: Police Foundation, 1984.

Skolnick, Jerome H., and David H. Bayley. *The New Blue Line: Police Innovation in Six American Cities.* New York: Free Press, 1986.

Skolnick, Jerome H., and James J. Fyfe. *Above the Law: Police and the Excessive Use of Force.* New York: Free Press, 1993.

Soderman, Harry, and John J. O'Connell. *Modern Criminal Investigation.* New York: Funk and Wagnalls, 1945.

Spellman, W., and D. K. Brown. *Calling the Police: Citizen Reporting of Serious Crime.* Washington, DC: Police Executive Research Forum, 1981.

Sprogle, Howard O. *The Philadelphia Police.* New York: AMS Press, 1974 (orig. 1887).

Stead, Philip J. *Vidocq: Picaroon of Crime.* London: Staples, 1953.

Steidel, S. E., ed. *Missing and Abducted Children: A Law Enforcement Guide to Case Investigation and Program Management.* Arlington, VA: National Center for Missing and Exploited Children, 1994.

Steinman, Michael, ed. *Woman Battering: Policy Responses.* Cincinnati: Anderson, 1991.

Stewart, James B. *Blind Eye: The Terrifying Story of a Doctor Who Got Away with Murder.* New York: Simon & Schuster, 1999.

Straus, Murray A., Richard J. Gelles, and Suzanne Steinmetz. *Behind Closed Doors: Violence in the American Family.* Garden City, NY: Anchor Press, 1980.

Stuckey, Gilbert B. *Evidence for the Law Enforcement Officer.* 3d ed. New York: McGraw-Hill, 1979.

Swanson, Charles R., Leonard Territo, and Robert W. Taylor. *Police Administration: Structures, Processes and Behavior.* New York: Macmillan, 1988.

Terry, Maury. *The Ultimate Evil: An Investigation Into a Dangerous Satanic Cult.* New York: Doubleday, 1987.

Thorwald, Jurgen. *The Century of the Detective.* New York: Harcourt, Brace and World, 1965.

———. *Crime and Science.* New York: Harcourt, Brace and World, 1967.

———. *The Marks of Cain.* London: Thames and Hudson, 1965.

Visionics Corporation. *Adaptive Surveillance: A Novel Approach to Facial Surveillance for CCTV Systems, Final Progress Report.* Jersey City, NJ: Visionics Corporation, 2001.

Walker, Samuel. *The Police in America: An Introduction.* 2d ed. New York: McGraw-Hill, 1992.

Walling, George W. *Recollections of a New York Chief of Police.* New York: Caxton Book Concern, 1887.

Waltz, Jon R. *Introduction to Criminal Evidence.* 3d ed. Chicago: Nelson-Hall, 1991.

Wambaugh, Joseph. *The Blooding.* New York: William Morrow, 1989.

Whitehead, Paula, and Paul Gray. *Pulling the Plug on Computer Theft.* London: Great Britain Home Office, 1998.

Wilber, Charles C. *Ballistic Science for the Law Enforcement Officer.* Springfield, IL: Charles C. Thomas, 1977.

Wilson, John B., and Sean P. Hayes. *A Competence-Based Approach to Police Report Writing.* Englewood Cliffs, NJ: Prentice-Hall, 1984.

Zalman, Marvin, and Larry Siegel. *Criminal Procedure: Constitution and Society.* St. Paul, MN: West, 1991.

Government Reports

ABT Associates. *New York City Anti-Crime Patrol: Exemplary Project Validation Report.* Washington, DC: U.S. Government Printing Office, 1974.

Blumer, Thomas. *Counterfeit (Copycat) Goods Under International Law and the Laws of Selected Foreign Nations.* Washington, DC: U.S. Library of Congress, 1996.

Budd, T. *Burglary of Domestic Dwellings: Findings from the British Crime Survey.* London: Great Britain Home Office, 1999.

Bureau of Justice Statistics. *Census of State and Local Law Enforcement Agencies, 1992.* Washington, DC: National Institute of Justice, Bureau of Justice Statistics, 1993.

———. *Report to the Nation on Crime and Justice.* 2d ed. Washington, DC: National Institute of Justice, Bureau of Justice Statistics, 1988.

———. *Special Report, Reporting Crime to the Police.* Washington, DC: National Institute of Justice, Bureau of Justice Statistics, 1985.

Caplan, Marc H., and Joe Holt Anderson. *Forensics: When Science Bears Witness.* Washington, DC: National Institute of Justice, 1984.

Caskey, C. Thomas, and Holloy A. Hammond. *Automated DNA Typing: Method of the Future?* Washington, DC: National Institute of Justice, 1997.

Cawley, Donald F., et al. *Managing Criminal Investigations: Manual.* Washington, DC: U.S. Government Printing Office, 1973.

Chaiken, Marcia, and Jan Chaiken. *Public Policing—Privately Provided.* Washington, DC: U.S. Government Printing Office, 1987.

Cotton, W. L., P. H. Cogan, and M. K. Dueppen. *Total Asset Protection: A Business Owner's Guide to Preventing Internal Theft.* Washington, DC: National Institute of Justice, 1994.

Cunningham, William C., and Todd H. Taylor. *The Growing Role of Private Security.* Washington, DC: U.S. Government Printing Office, 1988.

———. *The Growth of Private Security.* Washington, DC: U.S. Government Printing Office, 1984.

Federal Bureau of Investigation. *Crime in the United States: Uniform Crime Reports, 1993.* Washington, DC: Federal Bureau of Investigation, 1994.

———. *Crime in the United States: Uniform Crime Reports, 1990.* Washington, DC: Federal Bureau of Investigation, 1991.

———. *Crime in the United States: Uniform Crime Reports, 1999.* Washington, DC: Federal Bureau of Investigation, 2000

———. *Child Abduction and Serial Killer Unit: Morgan P. Hardiman Task Force on Missing and Exploited Children.* Washington, DC: Federal Bureau of Investigation, n.d.

———. *Handbook of Forensic Sciences.* Washington, DC: Federal Bureau of Investigation, 2001.

Finn, P., L. Truitt, and L. Buron. *Opinions of 47 Auto Theft Investigators Regarding Automobile Component Parts Anti-Theft Labels.* Washington, DC : National Institute of Justice, 1996.

Fox, Richard H., and Carl L. Cunningham. *Crime Scene Search and Physical Evidence Handbook.* Washington, DC: National Institute of Justice, 1985.

Freeman, Kenneth R., and Terry Estrada-Mullaney. *Using Dolls to Interview Child Victims: Legal Concerns and Interview Procedures.* Washington, DC: National Institute of Justice, 1988.

Geiselman, R. Edward, and Ronald P. Fisher. *Interviewing Victims and Witnesses of Crime.* Washington, DC: National Institute of Justice, 1985.

Girdner, Linda K., and Patricia M. Hoff, eds. *Obstacles to the Recovery and Return of Parentally Abducted Children.* Washington, DC: U.S. Department of Justice, 1994.

Greenberg, Ilene, and Robert Wasserman. *Managing Criminal Investigations.* Washington, DC: U.S. Government Printing Office, 1975.

Gropper, B. A., Jr., and J. A. Reardon, Jr., *Developing Drug Testing by Hair Analysis.* Washington, DC: National Institute of Justice, 1993.

Hallcrest Systems, Inc. *Combating Workplace Drug Crimes.* Washington, DC: National Institute of Justice, 1993.

Halper, Andrew, and Richard Ku. *New York City Police Department Street Crime Unit.* Washington, DC: U.S. Government Printing Office, n.d.

Harries, Keith. *Mapping Crime: Principle and Practice.* Washington, DC: National Institute of Justice, 1999.

Hoffman, J.P., C. Larison, and A. Sanderson, *Analysis of Worker Drug Use and Workplace Policies and Programs.* Washington, DC: National Institute of Justice, 1997.

Kakalik, James F., and Sorrel Wildhorn. *Private Police in the United States.* Washington, DC: National Institute of Justice, 1971.

Laycock, Gloria. *Property Marking: A Deterrent to Domestic Burglary: Crime Prevention Unit Paper No. 3.* London: Home Office, 1985.

MacDonnell, Herbert L. *Flight Characteristics and Stain Patterns of Human Blood.* Washington, DC: U.S. Government Printing Office, 1971.

Maguire, Kathleen, and Ann L. Pastore, eds. *Sourcebook of Criminal Justice Statistics, 1993.* Washington, DC: National Institute of Justice: Bureau of Justice Statistics, 1994.

Munson, Diane M. *The Child Victim As a Witness.* Washington, DC: National Institute of Justice, 1989.

National Advisory Commission on Criminal Justice Standards and Goals. *Police.* Washington, DC: U.S. Government Printing Office, 1973.

National Commission on Law Observance and Enforcement. *Lawlessness in Law Enforcement.* Washington, DC: U.S. Government Printing Office, 1931.

National Commission on the Future of DNA Testing. *The Future of Forensic DNA Testing: Predictions of the Research and Development Working Group.* Washington, DC: National Institute of Justice, 2000.

———. *What Every Law Enforcement Officer Should Know About DNA Evidence.* Washington, DC: National Institute of Justice, 2000.

National Institute of Justice. *Confronting Domestic Violence: A Guide for Criminal Justice Agencies.* Washington, DC: National Institute of Justice, 1986.

———. *Crime Scene Search and Physical Evidence Handbook.* Washington, DC: National Institute of Justice, 1973.

———. *Criminal Justice "Hot" Files.* Washington, DC: National Institute of Justice, 1986.

———. *Data Quality of Criminal History Records.* Washington, DC: National Institute of Justice, 1985.

———. *Directory of Criminal Justice Information Sources.* 8th ed. Washington, DC: National Institute of Justice, 1992.

———. *Intelligence and Investigative Records.* Washington, DC: National Institute of Justice, 1985.

———. *GPS Applications in Law Enforcement: The SkyTracker Surveillance System, Final Report.* Washington, DC: National Institute of Justice, 1998.

———. *Internet Crimes Against Children.* Washington, DC: National Institute of Justice, 2001.

———. *National Guidelines for Death Investigation.* Washington, DC: National Institute of Justice, 2001.

———. *Original Records of Entry.* Washington, DC: National Institute of Justice, 1990.

———. *Privacy and Juvenile Justice Records.* Washington, DC: National Institute of Justice, 1982.

———. *Privacy and the Media.* Washington, DC: National Institute of Justice, 1979.

———. *Privacy and the Private Employer.* Washington, DC: National Institute of Justice, 1979.

———. *Understanding DNA Evidence: A Guide for Victim Service Providers.* Washington, DC: National Institute of Justice, 2001.

———. *User Guide to NCJRS Products and Services.* Washington, DC: National Institute of Justice, n.d.

Nee, C. *Car Theft: The Offender's Perspective.* London: Great Britain Home Office, 1993.

New York City Police Department. *Special Investigation Division Kidnapping Guidelines.* New York: New York City Police Department, 1991.

———. *Detective Guide.* New York: New York City Police Department, 1993.

Peterson, J., S. Mihajlovic, and M. Gilliland. *Forensic Evidence and the Police: The Effects of Scientific Evidence on Criminal Investigations.* Washington, DC: National Institute of Justice, 1984.

Peterson, Joseph L. *Use of Forensic Evidence by the Police and Courts.* Washington, DC: National Institute of Justice, 1987.

Reeves, Brian. *Federal Law Enforcement Officers, 1993*. Washington, DC: National Institute of Justice, Bureau of Justice Statistics, 1994.

Riley, Kevin, and Bruce Hoffman. *Domestic Terrorism: A National Assessment of State and Local Law Enforcement Preparedness*. Santa Monica: Rand Corporation, National Institute of Justice, 1995.

Roda, C. *Executive Safety*. Washington, DC: National Criminal Justice Reference Service, 1997.

Spiess, Michele. *Inhalants*. Washington, DC: Office of National Drug Control Policy, 2001.

Substance Abuse and Mental Health Services Administration. *National Household Survey on Drug Abuse*. Washington, DC: Substance Abuse and Mental Health Services Administration, 2000.

U.S. Congress, Office of Technology Assessment. *Criminal Justice: New Technologies and the Constitution: A Special Report*. Washington, DC: U.S. Government Printing Office, 1988.

U.S. Department of Health and Human Services, National Institute on Drug Abuse. *Heroin Abuse and Addiction*. Washington, DC: National Institute on Drug Abuse, 2000.

U.S. Department of Labor. *Employer's Guide to Dealing with Substance Abuse*. Washington, DC: U.S. Department of Labor, 1990.

———. *Occupational Outlook Handbook, 2000–2001*. Washington, DC: U.S. Department of Labor, 2001.

West, J. A. *Facial Identification Technology and Law Enforcement*. Sacramento: California Commission on Peace Officer Standards and Training, 1996.

Wilson, T. F., and P. L. Woodard. *Automated Fingerprint Identification Systems—Technology and Policy Issues*. Washington, DC: National Institute of Justice, 1987.

COURT CASES

INDEX

PHOTO CREDITS